From Adult Education Society

From Adult Education to the Learning Society provides a valuable route map to the development of thinking in adult education and lifelong learning. It includes over 25 seminal articles from 21 years of the *International Journal of Lifelong Education* written by many of the leading authors in the field, from the UK, the USA, Australia and Europe.

Compiled to show the development of the field, the book is divided into four sections:

- From adult education...
- ...to lifelong education
- ...and lifelong learning
- ...to the learning society and beyond

The specially written Introduction by the editor contextualises the selection and introduces readers to the main issues and current thinking in the field.

This authoritative reference book provides – in one, easy-to-access place – a collection of articles that have led the field. It should find a place in every library and on every departmental bookshelf.

Peter Jarvis is Professor of Education at the University of Surrey. He is Editor of the *International Journal of Lifelong Education*, published by Taylor & Francis. He is author of many books in the field of adult education and lifelong learning, many of which are published by Routledge.

Education heritage series

From Adult Education to the Learning Society
21 years from the *International Journal of Lifelong Education*
Peter Jarvis

A Feminist Critique of Education
Christine Skelton and Becky Francis

From Adult Education to the Learning Society

21 years from the *International Journal of Lifelong Education*

Peter Jarvis

Routledge
Taylor & Francis Group

LONDON AND NEW YORK

First published 2006
by Routledge
2 Park Square, Milton Park, Abingdon, Oxon OX4 4RN

Simultaneously published in the USA and Canada
by Routledge
711 Third Avenue, New York, NY 10017

Routledge is an imprint of the Taylor & Francis Group

First issued in paperback 2011

© 2006 Routledge

Typeset in Baskerville by Wearset Ltd, Boldon, Tyne and Wear

British Library Cataloguing in Publication Data
A catalogue record for this book is available from the British Library

Library of Congress Cataloging in Publication Data
A catalog record for this book has been requested

ISBN13: 978-0-415-36494-2 (hbk)
ISBN13: 978-0-415-50945-9 (pbk)

Contents

Preface

Preparing this volume has been an exhilarating, challenging, frustrating and problematic process. However, it has been an immeasurably rewarding one. When I started the *International Journal*, with the help of Michael Stephens and with Teddy Thomas as my first co-editor, I had a hope of creating an academic library-based journal that would provide a forum for scholars around the world to examine lifelong education for that is what I was sure adult education would become. This has happened although not necessarily in the ways that I anticipated nor in ways with which I necessarily approve. Certainly the neo-liberal focus of a great deal of what is now called lifelong learning leaves a lot to be desired if one believes, as I do, that lifelong learning is a humanistic process – of which work is necessarily a part but not the only rationale for learning. Reworking through many of the papers that we have published in the *International Journal of Lifelong Education* I have found an exciting level of critical analysis coming from a range of academic disciplines, although the social sciences have necessarily predominated. To select the papers for this volume has led to all the emotions described above.

Clearly certain criteria had to be set to guide me and these were that:

- I had to finish with a comprehensive volume;
- the papers had to be of the highest academic standard and general relevance;
- no research report was to be included, neither were country-specific papers;
- no country would predominate, although it was recognised that Europe and the USA would occur most frequently;
- no author would be included more than once, although this was originally twice;
- the papers had to reflect the general ethos of the International Journal;
- at least one paper would come from the very first issue of the journal – that of Ettore Gelpi.

I initially reduced the selection to sixty-eight papers and then to thirty-three. At that time I asked the publishers if they would accept a selection of this size but was told that really they would like it to be even smaller and so I reduced it to the twenty-five that are included here. In this process of reduction many papers of really excellent quality had to be rejected. Indeed, there were sufficient papers to fill three volumes with ease, but the selection here fulfils the criteria I had set myself at the outset and I hope that the collection is something that remains useful to scholars in the field.

I have divided the volume into four sections in order to try to capture something of both the complexity of the field(s) of study included here but also the way in which it has (they have) changed over the twenty-one years included here. When the journal was first established adult education was the dominant term for most education that was carried out after initial (formal and institutional) education was completed, but by 1981 I had ceased to use the term, since I preferred to use 'education of adults' which implied the lifelong education which I was convinced was about to emerge. Hence, the first section of the volume is called 'From adult education'. However, it must be noted that terminology in different countries varies and 'adult education' is still widely used in many parts of the world. At the same time, in UK and some other parts of Europe, we saw the move to lifelong education but through the use of two terms – continuing education and recurrent education. These terms had differing emphases and ideological bases, with continuing education being the more conservative and, consequently, the one which was the more widely accepted. Hence, the second part of this volume is entitled 'to lifelong education'. But even this term has connotations that were not to be found acceptable to policy makers and politicians since it implied that the onus of responsibility is on the potential providers to ensure that there is sufficient provision whereas the contemporary neo-liberal global society wished to place the responsibility on the learners, amongst other reasons, and so lifelong learning replaced lifelong education – and hence the third section of this volume. But it was still widely recognised that learning is a social phenomenon and so such concepts as 'the learning organisation', 'the learning city' and 'the learning society' began to enter the educational vocabulary. Consequently, the final section of this volume reflects this. But time does not stand still! Hence, the question of what lies beyond it is raised. One or two new emphases are reflected in this final section. 'What lies beyond the learning society' constitutes the theme for our special issues for the twenty-fifth anniversary in 2007.

However, I do not wish to comment on individual papers in this introduction, suffice to note that I have tried to include papers that reflect the lifelong element of learning, although there are many areas that are missing. With the growth of the learning society, every branch of society is developing its own learning agenda, which is contributing to the decline in adult education as a separate field of study. Now increasing numbers of adults are being educated but the expertise of adult educators is often having to be re-discovered by those practitioners in the new sub-fields of study and practice – but there is a major place for a journal that spans all of them and offers both an international and a comparative forum. Perhaps the time has come for a greater integration of theory in order to prevent the wheel being re-invented with the development of every new sub-field. These then are major rationales for the *International Journal of Lifelong Education* in the future.

Many people have helped to make this journal a success since its foundation; first and foremost must be Teddy Thomas who acted as co-editor for many years and John Davies who served as book review editor over a very similar period. Since then Stella Parker and John Holford have built on this. However, our editorial correspondents who review all the papers have a great responsibility for insuring the standard of the work, some of whom have served for the whole of the journal's life. Amongst the correspondents, Ettore Gelpi's contribution to the very first issue is included here and Colin Griffin, who has been a reviewer since the journal began, is another who has a paper included here. Unfortunately some of the other correspondents had papers in the original sixty-eight papers which had to be omitted from the final selection. Clearly everybody who has ever sent us a paper for consideration for publication has contributed to the success of the journal and I am grateful to all of these. As was noted above, the majority of papers have come from Europe, North America and from Australasia, although we have been pleased to receive an increasing number from Africa and Asia. We hope that by the time the next selection of papers is published as a volume there will be an even broader spread.

Finally, my thanks must go to the many people who have worked at Falmer, Routledge and, now, Taylor and Francis who have worked behind the scenes to make this journal possible.

Peter Jarvis
Thatcham
Berks
July, 2004

Part 1

From Adult Education...

1 Deontological liberalism

The political philosophy of liberal adult education

Kenneth Lawson

A philosophy of individualism runs through liberal adult education. It can be seen in such educational goals as personal development and the idea of developing 'autonomous man'. It is implicit in the vocabulary of 'educational rights' and in claims for 'equality of educational opportunity'.

For some, this philosophy represents a strength while for others such as Colin Griffin (1983) and Nell Keddie (1980) the 'ideology of individualism' is a matter for reproach and criticism. Such criticism must be taken seriously as a challenge at the theoretical level and one which is as important as the more practical challenges to liberal adult education such as the withdrawal of public funds and the growing emphasis upon vocational education.

In the older traditions of adult education there was a strong 'utilitarian' element in the ideal of social purpose, the furtherance of social progress and the enhancement of the public good. More recently, however, there have been signs of a significant shift away from utilitarian forms of liberalism and liberalism in the Greek tradition based on the idea of the pursuit of 'the good'. There has instead been a movement towards a 'deontological' type of liberalism which is highly individualistic in character and which is based upon the ideas of 'rights' and 'justice'. It is a philosophy which denies that there can be a general, as distinct from a private, idea of 'the good'.

Deontological liberalism can now be seen as the dominant political and ethical philosophy underpinning liberal adult education and which provides much of its theoretical base. This paper is an attempt to explore the connections between adult education and its underlying philosophy.

The deontological tradition is not new. It goes back at least to John Locke in the 17th century but it has been very influentially restated by John Rawls (1972) and by Richard Nozick (1974) and it is the ideas of these writers that form the main subject for discussion.

The 'individual' in adult education

In a direct and obvious sense, it is individuals who are educated and this is likely to be denied only by those who believe that in some sense it is the 'community' or 'social classes' which are the subject of education.

'Education' according to Paterson (1979: 15) 'directly touches us in our personal being, tending our identity at its roots and ministering directly to our condition as conscious selves aspiring in all our undertakings to a greater fullness and completeness of being'.

For Wiltshire (1976: 139) 'individuation' is the goal of adult education in the sense of 'self-discovery and self-development voluntarily undertaken'.

Such views, to which many in adult education respond, might seem to be statements of fact but they are really prescriptions about the way in which individuals should be viewed and treated in education. 'Individuality' and 'self-identity' are not simply empirical facts. They represent implicit claims for a certain kind of status and they are ethical concepts. How are such claims justified and how are they related to the idea of 'rights' and to education as a process of 'individuation'?

The idea of a freely choosing 'autonomous self' is at the centre of much of our thinking. The integrity of a unique self and a concern for its preservation, literally a concern for 'self-interest', are important values. But there are other ways of seeing things, and in cultures such as in China it is the commonality rather than individuality which is the major concern.

Nevertheless, in adult education, theories and practices have emerged which are allegedly based on 'the way that we are'. These include the idea of 'student centredness' and the rights of adults to education and the right to choose their own educational goals.

Such ideas have led us toward a more subjective personal view of knowledge and away from the idea of publicly shared and tested knowledge as an epistemological paradigm. How we have arrived at this position may be a political as much as a philosophical question and it is to the boundaries of philosophy and socio-political theory that we must turn our attention.

Some basic tenets of deontological liberalism

Deontological liberalism, which is highly consistent with theories in adult education, is based upon the idea of justice and rights rather than upon a conception of a good society. The traditional virtues of tolerance, open-mindedness and a rejection of dogma are carried to their extreme in a refusal to define what is good for society. It is argued that no man can define what is good for another person and that no one has a right to impose anything upon others for their own good. Freedom of choice and the right to determine one's own future are deemed to be of a morally higher order than any imposed goals which are intended to serve the greatest good of the greatest number.

As Sandel (1982: 1) neatly expresses it, 'the core thesis' of deontological liberalism assumes that 'society, being composed of a plurality of persons, each with his own views, interests and conceptions of the good, is best arranged when it is governed by principles that do not themselves presuppose any conception of the good'. Therefore, instead of seeking general criteria for 'the good' such as the maximization of 'welfare' or 'utility' as the basis of social policy, some independent criterion has to be sought. Such a criterion is the moral and legal category of 'rights' and 'right' is prior to 'the good'.

Of all rights, the 'right to choose' is the most important, a view derived from Kant which assumes that our moral capacity resides in our ability to choose. Being free to choose is a minimum necessary requirement for being a moral agent.

Although autonomy is fundamental to deontological liberalism, it does not exclude the possibility of people agreeing on a particular policy. This happens when they combine for the purpose of defence or to provide common welfare services, but what they choose is irrelevant except insofar as it is an expression of free choice and conducive to the self-interest of each member of the group. Having chosen, the central concern is for the maintenance of their individual rights. Fairness as a regulating principle for the regulation of conduct and transactions between individuals or between individuals and the State is what really matters from the deontological point of view. This means that, in the last resort, whatever policy has been agreed upon by members of a group must be sacrificed if any individual is treated unjustly in order to maintain the policy.

Such a view is by no means as unrealistic as it might appear and it is exemplified in the argument that public expenditure should not be financed out of higher taxes on individuals even if some vital service such as education has to be cut as a consequence. In many respects, the deontological principle is operative in Britain under the present government. The case against taxation is presented in terms of its disincentive effects on effort or on investment but the claim in effect is that of Nozick who argues that it is a violation of a person's rights if he is forced to do certain things. In his view 'the State may not use its coercive apparatus for the purpose of getting some citizens to aid others'. For Nozick (1974: 169), 'Taxation of earnings from labour is on a par with forced labour' and it is by no means clear that claims to welfare rights over-ride rights to property. Conflicting claims have to be reconciled in the light of justice and not with reference to the worthwhileness of what is being claimed as a right.

Such a philosophy is essentially a defence of self-interest against State interests and as such it was an important piece of intellectual equipment in the 17th century. It continues to be important, but it conflicts with other points of view on both the left and the right which emphasize society and the State as being of greater importance than the individuals who comprise them.

John Locke's contribution

In order to understand more recent deontological theory, it might help if we consider some of its origins and John Locke is an obvious starting point.

Locke's thought is set within a framework of 'natural law' which is unfamiliar to most present-day readers, but the problems with which he deals are familiar ones.

In establishing a defence against an absolute monarchy, Locke tries to establish the supremacy of individuals each of whom has a fundamental natural-law right to existence. Following from this, they have additional supporting rights to those possessions which are necessary to secure their existence and a right to choose on matters which affect their individuality.

Locke's starting point is a *prima facie* case against absolute governments and he postulates a minimal role for the State or Commonwealth. For Locke, the State is an institution for the protection of individuals. It is not and does not have, in the Hegelian sense, an entity with a prior existence to which individuals owe an overriding obligation.

In his *Letter on Toleration*, Locke (1689 and 1956: 128) states that 'The Commonwealth seems to me to be a society of men constituted only for the procuring, preserving and advancing of their own civil interests'. These interests are defined as 'liberty, health and indolency of body; and the provision of outward things such as money, lands, houses, furniture and the like'. Furthermore: 'It is the duty of the civil magistrate, by the impartial execution of equal laws, to secure unto all people in general and every one of his subjects in particular, the just possession of these things belonging to this life.'

In effect, Locke has committed himself to a political platform which has to be theoretically justified. His justification is derived initially from Biblical texts, but the underlying principles, which are to be seen as *a priori*, do not necessarily depend upon Biblical authority. What Locke tries to demonstrate is the existence of 'rights' possessed by all individuals which are antecedent to the establishment of society. These rights are the product of social contracts agreed by individuals of equal status.

The idea of antecedent natural rights requires Locke (1689 and 1956: 4) to postulate a natural state of man prior to any form of social organization. He claims that men are in a 'state of perfect freedom to order their actions and dispose of their possessions and persons as they think fit within the bounds of the law of nature, without asking leave or depending upon the will of any other man'. Locke also considers it 'reasonable and just' to be allowed to destroy that which threatens an individual with destruction.

It might be objected that, in claiming antecedent rights, Locke is already drawing upon social concepts and that 'rights', 'freedom' and 'property' pre-suppose the existence of rules which define and protect them. We might say that a wild animal has a right to 'kill' but to talk in terms of property rights in such contexts is to use the terms metaphoric- ally.

In order to escape from such objections, Locke (1689 and 1956: 14) is obliged to introduce the idea of the right to self-preservation based on God's law. We are deemed to possess 'natural reason' as a gift from God which 'tells us that men being born have a right to their preservation and consequently to meat and drink and such other things as nature affords for their subsistence'. We have therefore 'a property' in our own person and in those things necessary to our preservation. Furthermore, we have a duty to God to preserve ourselves.

These are no more than *a priori* assumptions but they are logically necessary in support of Locke's political position. If it is not accepted as a starting point that all individuals are worthy of preservation then further claims about their welfare become irrelevant because there is no basis on which to justify them.

It should be noted that Locke has introduced a strongly normative element into his case in the concept of 'property'. The term includes both material possession and health and liberty. The right to self-preservation is thereby extended to cover not merely the right to exist but the right to exist in a particular qualitative sense for which material possessions and other forms of property are necessary. It is not even enough to be pro- vided with such things. Ownership must be vested in them. As society becomes more sophisticated and things like education are added to what is deemed necessary for a qualitative or normative view of 'existence' it is easy to see how they are then assimilated into the list of things to which we are said to have a right. Politically speaking, therefore, Locke has cleverly secured his position.

Because Locke's State is concerned only with the protection of indi- viduals and the maintenance of justice, it is not necessary for him to con- sider any other possible ends or purposes. Each individual is free to choose his own 'good life' and it is in no way incumbent upon the state to provide for people beyond a framework of 'justice'. For the State to play any part in defining social policy would be regarded as an infringement of individual liberty; therefore the powers of government must be contained within very strict limits.

The idea of a 'minimal State' has been reviewed and restated in recent years by Richard Nozick in his book *Anarchy, State and Utopia* (1974). It has attracted a good deal of attention, partly because of the rigour of the argu- ment presented, and also because it is so much in tune with present-day political thinking.

What is significant about such views, and it is central to the deontologi- cal philosophy, is that the absence of governmental influence in social policy is regarded as a virtue which over-rides considerations of general welfare. It is regarded as more important that individual freedom should be extended and maintained even though this might lead to reductions in publicly provided welfare services, including education. The furtherance of 'the good' is seen as a personal rather than a collective concern, and the defence of 'rights' is more important than, say, the amelioration of poverty.

Rawls and Nozick

Although each of these writers arrives at different political conclusions, they both start from similar philosophical presuppositions about the 'rights-based' ethic. Both writers draw upon the Kantian view that as 'centres of consciousness' each person should be regarded as an end and never as a means. We can never meaningfully ask 'for what purpose should a person be allowed to choose?' or 'why is self-development important?'. These are ends deemed to be self-evidently worthwhile.

The relevance of this to liberal adult education should be obvious because it too is defended as a worthwhile end which need not be justified by reference to instrumental purposes. On this view 'education' is a 'good', not something which furthers the good.

For Nozick (1974: 93), as for Locke,

> there is no *social entity* with a good to which individuals contribute. There are only individual people, different individual people, with their own individual lives. Using one of these people for the benefit of others, uses him and benefits the others ... To use him in this way does not sufficiently respect and take account of the fact that he is a separate person, that his is the only life he has.

This robust defence of the individual has to be reconciled with the fact that in most situations, an individual's decisions about his own life are likely to react upon the interests of other people. Locke in fact recognized this point and qualified an individual's right to possession and the fruits of his labour except in conditions where there is an abundance of resources. We can only claim an absolute right to possessions such as land 'where there is enough and as good left in common for others'. In most cases, we find ourselves in a competitive situation and it is there that the need for fairness and distributive justice arises. Constraints are then imposed in order to regulate competition and to resolve conflicts of interest. The theoretical problem is to provide a justification for the constraints upon individual actions which must themselves be arrived at in such a way that individual freedom is respected. What Rawls tries to do is to explain how the regulating principles of 'rights' and 'justice' can be arrived at and accepted by free agents. One possible solution would be the utilitarian one which assumes that the regulating principles would lead to the maximization of some general good such as 'happiness' or 'economic welfare'.

Utilitarianism, however, deals in generalities and it is in principle possible to maximize the general good in such a way that some individuals are left worse off. The rich might have to be heavily taxed, for example, or some people might be denied important freedom in the interests of the common good.

On the deontological principle, however, the common good cannot be allowed to become the prime concern from which policy is derived. Personal autonomy and the right to choose are primary and it is 'the good' which must be compromised if need be. Therefore Rawls, as did Locke before him, resorts to the idea of a social contract to establish the State and the principles which will regulate it. But Rawls wished to succeed where Locke had failed.

In justifying his principles of 'rights' and 'justice', Locke had introduced the notion of a duty to preserve oneself derived from the premise that 'God should be obeyed'. That in effect was a conception of the 'good'. Rawls sought a stronger position which, as Sandel (1982: 2) puts it, requires that 'principles of justice are justified in such a way that does not depend on any particular vision of the good. To the contrary, given the independent status, the right constrains the good and sets its bounds'.

The basis of this view is in Kant's claim that any conception of the good will be a purely contingent matter arrived at in the light of various 'interests', and can never be universal. It would be wrong, therefore, to commit ourselves to a particular contingent end. The universal moral imperative is the idea of morality itself and our ability to be moral depends upon our status as autonomous agents. A necessary requirement for being autonomous is the absence of any constraints which affect our capacity for making rational judgements. Kant therefore postulates 'selves' as centres of consciousness and reason, which are prior to and independent of any interests or attributes which we happen to have as a contingent fact. The individual is conceived as the irreducible 'I', who chooses in a way analogous to Descartes' 'self' which thinks and has experiences but which is not itself the object of an experience. This is a very rarefied conception of the 'self' but Rawls commits himself to a similar view.

In arriving at his version of the social contract, Rawls (1972: 11) asks us 'to imagine that those who engage together in social cooperation choose together in one joint act, the principles which are to assign basic rights and duties ... Men are to decide in advance how they are to regulate their claims against one another'. The choices made must be wholly rational but in Rawls' view (1972: 17–18), 'A problem of rational decision has a definite answer only if we know the beliefs and interests of the parties, their relation with respect to one another, the alternatives between which they are to choose, the procedures whereby they make up their minds, and so on'.

In real life, we cannot know all the beliefs and interests of all the parties and even if we did know, there is likely to be gross inequality between individuals, and their interests and beliefs are likely to conflict. Therefore in order that we might be sure that any social contract arrived at is rationally justified and therefore the 'correct' choice, we must be sure about the beliefs and interests of the parties to the decision. Moreover, there must be equality and a lack of contradiction between the various beliefs and interests, otherwise no determinate solution can be arrived at.

Rawls therefore introduces a set of simplifying assumptions and conditions which specify an 'original position' logically equivalent to Locke's 'state of nature'.

The 'original position' is called 'the veil of ignorance'. Behind this veil the participants are unaware of any interests, beliefs or other non-rational (that is to say 'contingent') influences which would cloud their judgement. Their only awareness is of themselves and they have no knowledge of how the various alternatives will affect their own particular case once they emerge from behind the veil.

Rawls (1972: 11–12) has set up a theoretical procedure which is intended to ensure that a wholly rational choice will emerge based upon no conception of 'the good', beyond 'the principles that free and rational persons concerned to further their own interest would accept in an initial position of equality. No one can "favour his particular condition" '.

What emerges, and what Rawls (1972: 124) intends should emerge, is the idea of 'justice and fairness' and a system of 'rights' based on two main principles of justice:

a   the principle of greatest equal liberty;
b   i the principle of (fair) equality of opportunity;
       ii the difference principle.

The difference principle is equivalent to Locke's qualification that one can only hold possessions if 'as much and as good is left to other men'. Rawls justifies any possible inequality in distribution if, and only if, the inequality makes the worst off individual better off than he otherwise would have been.

Capital accumulation in the hands of a minority is justified, for example, if the resulting output is higher than under any other distribution of capital and if even the poorest get goods at a lower price.

Taken together, principles (*a*), (*b*)(i) and (*b*)(ii) establish 'justice' as the first virtue of institutions, as truth is of systems of thought (Rawls 1972: 3), and justice alone can guarantee the defence of each individual's self-interest.

As Sandel (1982: 15–16) observes, 'justice is not merely an important value to be weighed and considered as the occasion requires but rather the *means* by which values are weighed and assessed. We need not ask whether a society or a social policy is 'good' but only whether it is 'just'.

Deontological liberalism establishes the 'right', i.e. what is 'just', as prior to and independent of 'the good'. It is concerned only with the procedures for the regulation of society and not at all with substantive issues which might be deemed to have a bearing on 'the good life', or what is regarded as worthwhile. Such things as public libraries, theatres, education, health services and so on may be provided only if to do so is consistent with justice and not because they are in some sense thought to be 'good'.

The concept of 'justice' also presupposes the concept of 'truth' because one cannot make judgements about particular cases without being sure of the facts of the case. These two concepts are therefore central regulators and they link social and political philosophy with epistemology, each of which has a strongly individualistic orientation. In the Cartesian tradition, individual self-consciousness is the basis of knowledge and rational empiricism depends upon the perceptions of individuals tested against the perceptions of other people. The concept of 'justice' is now brought into the liberal tradition in order to defend the integrity of the individual.

The 'self' is one individual in a 'plurality of individuals' to use Sandel's phrase, and is the most important concept as the source of knowledge and reason. 'Justice' is necessary as the ethical and legal concept to protect individuals *because* they are the source of reason and are seen as ends which require no further justification. Their rights to liberty should not be overridden in the interests of 'society as a whole' because to the deontologist this phrase is a meaningless fiction. What the Rawlsian argument ignores is that the rarified concept of the 'self' is itself a fiction, and the deontological case is based on claims about the status of individuals rather than on their ontological basis. The self-conscious centre of reason is a philosopher's invention and in common usage we tend to define 'persons' as 'individuals' in terms of describable attributes. It is these which give persons their individuality and enables us to distinguish between them. Disembodied 'selves' possess no distinguishing features and are thus deprived of individuality in any meaningful sense. Deontological theory removes the content from that which it sets out to protect. Rawls' individuals are reduced to the 'Archimedian points' which he says are required to assess the social system (1972: 261).

The deontological philosophy is intended to provide a liberating vision and its political purpose is to provide a formulation for claims to 'liberty'. What it is in danger of doing in practice is to establish a climate in which a jealous concern for 'rights' clouds all vision of what a society might become, and there are signs that this is happening in Western societies. On all sides, the right to choose appears to be regarded as more important than what is chosen. This view is manifest in politics and also in the arts where traditions and standards seem to be discarded in favour of individual expression, without too much concern for the worthwhileness of what is expressed.

This bring us back to adult education where the influence of deontological liberalism may be seen in 'andragogical theory'. 'Learning', which
is an undifferentiated concept, has tended to emerge in preference to the
value-based and normative concept of 'education'. It is regarded as more
important that individuals should learn what they choose, than that they
should learn something important and worthwhile. The refusal to make
judgements between different kinds and different areas of learning is
found even in official documents such as the ACACE Report on *Continuing Education: from Policies to Practice*. All learning might be of equal value if
personal choice is the major criterion but it should be asked whether this
view is helping to trivialize adult education. Do we need a philosophy
which helps us to identify what is most worthwhile and to establish priorities in education?

Our liberalism could be a disintegrating philosophy instead of a liberating one. The 'self' can also be viewed as a 'social self', a part of a whole,
and the unity of society rather than the Rawlsian unity of the self might
well be re-asserted in order to counteract disintegrating tendencies.

Deontological liberalism has deep roots, but as a tradition it produces
societies which no longer debate or seek 'the good'. It is a philosophy
suited to a society which has no vision. Its clearest manifestation is in a
free-enterprise monetary economy. It is less important to ask *what* is being
produced than to ask how much and of what monetary value is being produced. Profit and cost efficiency is what matters and these concepts are
the economic equivalents of 'rights' and 'justice'. They are impersonal criteria which enable us to concentrate on processes and to avoid the value
questions about what is good. Monetary values are the criteria by which all
subsequent values are judged and they must not be overriden by considerations of what is worthwhile. Monetary values *define* worthwhileness.

It may be worth asking ourselves whether liberal adult educators have
exacerbated the situation by apparently avoiding educational value questions. It is fashionable to say that adult education is about *process* not
content. This is eminently a deontological view. Is it an adequate one? Are
we trying to lead a culture into losing its way or are we following in a
society which has lost its way? These are big questions and they point to a
current lack of critical awareness at a number of points. Can we go on
without some conception of purpose and what is worthwhile? Such a
question should be a challenge to adult education. Is our liberalism in
the end too empty of content and concerned only with processes? If
so, should we try to redefine our philosophy in a more meaningful way
which respects individuals but defines them as part of a group and not
independently of it?

Bibliography

ACACE, 1982, *Continuing Education: From Policies to Practice*, Advisory Council for Adult and Continuing Education.

Griffin, C. 1983, '*Curriculum theory' in Adult and Lifelong Education*, London, Croom Helm.

Keddie, N. 1980, 'Adult education: an ideology of individualism' in Jane Thompson (ed.) *Adult Education for a Change*, London, Hutchinson.

Locke, John, 1689, *The Second Treatise of Government and A Letter Concerning Toleration*, edited by J. W. Gough, 1956, Oxford, Basil Blackwell.

Nozick, R. 1974, *Anarchy, State and Utopia*, Oxford, Basil Blackwell.

Paterson, R. W. K. 1979, *Values, Education and the Adult*, London, Routledge and Kegan Paul.

Rawls, J. 1972, *A Theory of Justice*, Oxford, Oxford University Press.

Sandel, M. J. 1982, *Liberalism and the Limits of Justice*, Cambridge, Cambridge University Press.

Wiltshire, H. C. 1976, 'The nature and uses of adult education', in A. Rogers (ed.) *The Spirit and the Form*, Department of Adult Education, Nottingham.

2   To a middle ground

Praxis and ideology in adult education

Arthur L. Wilson[1]
Ball State University

Whether we are lost to flagrant and groundless subjectivism or whether we can actually sustain and support our actions by appealing to discovered, transcendental truths is perhaps the chief ground of the modern and post-modern ages. In this paper it is argued that by seeking a middle ground through praxis, a ground neither lured by false foundationalism nor racked by relativism, we can sustain our social practices as educators only by critical encounters with the traditions and ideologies from which those practices emerge. To pursue this argument, it is suggested that because science does not well ground our practices we must therefore seek a sounder basis. To that end, a revitalized form of praxis is proposed, one that retrieves its central concerns with the moral dimensions of human action. Thus, in opposition to dominant interests in technical forms of educational practice based on empirically 'discovered' regularities, it is suggested that 'practical' reasoning provides a more useful understanding of how we conduct our practices as educators. In this respect we can understand our educational practice as requiring choice and deliberation in specific circumstances where courses of action are variable and debatable. Such a focus then allows us to consider the value-laden and community bases of practice and encourages improvement of practice through encounters with its normative nature. It is in this context that our views of what we believe to be right and why become the reasons for our actions as educators. Consequently, praxis has to be focused on the ideology of our practice. It is here that the final discussion of the paper considers the ultimate project of praxis which is to distinguish bad practice based on false beliefs from that which is sustained by continuing critical dialogue.

> ...we must understand the ways in which *phronesis* is nurtured by the *polis* or community.
>
> (Richard Bernstein 1983)

Introduction

To begin, I need to tell a quick but important story. It is a story with many possible beginnings, one for which there is no known ending so far, yet a story whose telling is crucial to our daily lives as adult educators. It is crucial because its central plot, its narrative structure so to speak, has come to dominate our lives whether we are aware of it or not. It is the story of Reason, whose most current proponents have it being 'born' in the Enlightenment and whelped by science. If the major project of the Enlightenment can be seen as the destruction of myths, superstitions, illusions and prejudices through the use of Reason (Bernstein 1986), then the sword bearer itself, the actual slayer of the Jabberwock, is instrumental rationality based on empiric science. This has led to a world in which everything is 'either grounded in scientific doctrine or method, or committed to the flames as sophistry and illusion' (Hollinger 1985: x). But under the accolades so often bestowed upon science is a dark side, one described by Weber as the 'iron cage' of instrumental rationality in which our lives become imprisoned in a technology based on science. If, as Gadamer (1975) claims, the central problem facing us in striving for moral imperatives for how to live is the continuing domination of technology, if Bernstein's paraphrasing of Nietzsche, Heidegger and Dewey is correct that 'logos ineluctably results not in illumination and Enlightenment, but the cosmic black night of nihilism' (1986: 199), then what are we to do about it?

In hermeneutic and pragmatic traditions, the answer lies in praxis. Certainly praxis has something to do with thinking about our educational practice, what we do with those thoughts, and how those thoughts inform our actions. And, no doubt, there are many adult educators who might easily agree with Gramsci's (1971) depiction, developed from Marxian thought, of praxis as having to be concerned with the inseparable link between theory and practice, between thought and action. The problem, at least as far as American adult education is concerned, is that few of us have any real sense of what that means, even if we advocate praxis in our classrooms and work sites. That is, as a field of professional practice, we don't really know what praxis is, nor, more importantly, do we typically understand the point of praxis, its *telos*.

One of the sources of this limitation, in the USA anyway, is our overly individualistic understanding of adult education (Rubenson 1989, Welton 1987) which prevents us from seeing the essential communal and tradition-bound nature of our practice as educators; what we typically fail to grasp is that reflecting on thought and action (theory and practice) is not simply an individualistic issue. It is not solely individualistic because our theory and practice are situated within and emanate from historical traditions; we don't practise as individuals but as members of those communities whose values, beliefs and norms about the means and ends of practice are reflected in and constitutive of our daily educational work. But what really limits our sense of praxis is the fundamental way in which we have misconstrued the nature of practical action in the USA. Despite our emphatic claim to emanate from the pragmatic traditions of Dewey and Lindeman, we have misunderstood some of their central concerns about 'practical action'. In the 'modern' practice of adult education from mid-century on, practical action in professional practice has been equated with the technical application of scientifically derived principles (Schon 1983, Wilson 1992a).[2] By focusing on technical issues such as needs assessment, planning models, instructional strategies and evaluation, what Cunningham pejoratively depicts as an 'ahistorical technology' (1989: 42), we have neglected what is really important about our practice as educators. By defining our practical action as technical, we have lost sight of its fundamental moral and political dimensions. Thus the focus of this paper is on a different notion of practical. Practical action, in the classic sense of Aristotle's notion of *phronesis*, is primarily concerned with the moral and political realm of our human action within its communities and traditions (Bernstein 1971), which is centrally concerned 'with the right estimation of the role that reason has to play in moral action' (Gadamer 1975: 278). We need to be concerned with more than technical know-how. We must be primarily concerned with the ethical know-how of practical action. This is the hard ground of praxis.

In the pragmatic and hermeneutic traditions upon which I am drawing for this paper is the shared perception that our 'social practices and traditions of a specific historical or cultural world are the horizons of existence' (Hollinger 1985: xiii). This central insight, evident in hermeneutic (Gadamer 1975), pragmatic (Bernstein 1983, Rorty 1979), and Marxian (Gramsci 1971) thought, argues that we cannot seek to ground our social practices in ahistorical and transcendental principles based on empirical investigations because 'our social practices are the given within which we must talk and act and improve things as best we can' (Hollinger 1985: xii). In other words, the tradition of praxis, which I seek to elaborate in this paper, rejects a foundationalist and Cartesian framework upon which to base our actions as human beings. It rejects the 'Cartesian Anxiety' (Bernstein 1983) that either there is some infallible way to warrant our truth claims (i.e., science) or else we are forever lost within the chaos of relativism. Instead, the tradition of praxis seeks to locate the justness of our actions, the moral imperatives of our practices, within critical encounters with the historical and cultural traditions which we both emanate from and contribute to. In order to appreciate the significance of such encounters, we have to realize the essential 'recursiveness' (Giddens 1979, Lave 1988) of our daily lives, for we live in and through social practices that are constitutively both the medium and the outcome of those practices. Thus the point I wish to make in this paper is that praxis should be the fundamental mechanism by which we construct our practice as educators precisely because our practice is neither transcendental or simply technical but constitutively bounded by, and constructed within, the cultural and historical traditions in which we work.

Consequently, I want to argue that normative discourse about the ends of practice is central to improving our practice. Without constant critical encounters with the cultural traditions that are constitutive of what we believe to be right (Bernstein 1985, Gadamer 1975, Rorty 1979), we cannot meaningfully seek to improve practice. What I will be arguing in this paper is that through praxis we can reintegrate the inseparable; that is, by coming to understand that thought and action are always practical – that practice is essentially moral and political, not just technical – we can better see what praxis is and how our practice will be better served by reflecting on it. This paper thus stands as an invitation (as intimated by others such as Bright 1989, Brookfield 1986, Cervero 1988, Usher and Bryant 1989) to consider the very essence of practice, its normative nature. Therefore, I want to use this paper to begin a conversation in adult education about the 'middle ground', a place that emanates from the varying social topographies of practice yet that recognizes a need to engage critically the communal values and beliefs upon which our practical action is predicated (Bernstein 1983, Gadamer 1975, Hollinger 1985). If we are to deal with the issue of the domination of science in practice, then we need to retrieve the essence of praxis as the critical consideration of the ends of our practice as well as the means.

In order to attempt this, I will first look briefly at the tradition of praxis in adult education thought. From there, I will begin to draw on certain contemporary philosophic arguments to show how praxis is more than just an act of individual reflection upon action; it needs also to be a critical and dialogic encounter with the norms, values and beliefs that inspire, inform and justify thought and action within specific, historical communities of educational practice. From this vantage, I will then argue both how individual and community forms of praxis are necessarily linked to a sense of practical reasoning (Aristotle's *phronesis*) which I believe better characterizes educational practice than the dominant hypothetical-deductive (i.e., scientific) model does. In this respect, by describing educational practice as a form of practical reasoning, we can more easily see its essential normative nature while also coming to realize that science cannot easily answer our questions about the ends of practice. Because our work as educators requires choice and deliberation in specific circumstances where courses of action are variable and debatable, such choices necessarily reflect the beliefs and ideologies of specific communities of educational practice. Our views of what we believe to be important, what we believe to be right, and why – our ethics – become the reasons for the choices we make as educators. Thus, if praxis is to have actual repercussions for adult education practice, then those choices and the beliefs that sustain them must be the object of praxic reflection, what pragmatists from Peirce to Bernstein describe as 'a community of inquirers committed to continuous, rational, self-critical inquiry' (Bernstein 1971: 199).

It is within these parameters that the presence of ideology[3] takes on expanded significance. Understanding the belief systems, assumptions and values by which educators define and justify their educational efforts can then be seen as a way of understanding how educators' thoughts and actions recursively contribute to the construction of particular historical circumstances and traditions. As Bernstein (1983) and Hawkesworth (1989) so eloquently indicate, the real point of praxis is to assist the judgemental process of determining the best course of action in specific circumstances, what Aristotle would refer to as actions of a moral-practical character. It is in this sense that adult education is the practice of moral endeavours – it is the putting into action of intentional prescriptions of what should be. As such, educational practice reflects a system of beliefs, however coherent, of how the world ought to be different because of choosing explicit educational action. Praxis, in this respect, has to be more than an indiscriminant process of reflection about thought and action. It has to be fundamentally concerned with revealing and considering the ethical appropriateness of educational actions as well as the standards by which we judge that appropriateness. Those standards by which we make such appraisals are themselves a function of historically evolving communities in which educational practice is conducted. Thus in order to understand and consequently to be able to judge our educational actions, we have to, through praxis, reveal and reflect upon the beliefs and ideologies which sustain, constrain, inspire and ultimately direct our actions as adult educators.

But the central polemic of this approach, its thorniest problem so to speak, is the very issue it wishes to address. That is, if the point of praxis is to take issue with the normative nature of both our individual and collective practical endeavours, if the point of praxis is to 'see through' scientific rationality to its underlying normative discourse in which the standards of judgement reside, then a very profound question arises: just how are we to distinguish among the multiple traditions available to us for guiding practice, how are we to distinguish between potentially moral practice and equally potential false practice? How do we know what good practice is and how can we distinguish it from bad? These resoundingly untechnical questions are at the centre of praxis. Thus to the issue of how to distinguish between 'vital and deformed traditions' (Hollinger 1985: xiv; see also Bernstein 1983, Gadamer 1975, Rorty 1979) is the answer to further the efforts of dialogue about our common practices. But as I will try to point out, the pragmatic tradition of praxis does not well provide answers, for it too, like technical rationality, seeks to determine ends by method. That is, we are asked the questions, through praxis, but it remains difficult still to determine the moral ground, to understand the standards by which to judge practice. Yet, far more than any instrumental form of technical rationality, praxis and practical reasoning enable us to better understand the moral and political dimensions of our practice as adult educators because they call for us to risk our values, beliefs and norms – our sense of certainty – in critical encounters with the traditions from which they emanate.

Praxis

Dialectical reflection on thought and action is the characteristic description of adult education notions of praxis. Brookfield, arguing that praxis is the central goal of facilitation, describes it as a 'continual process of activity, reflection upon activity, collaborative analysis of activity, new activity, further reflection and collaborative analysis' with the aim of fostering 'a spirit of critical reflection' (1986: 10) in which learners are challenged to confront the structures, values and norms by which they make sense of the world. Likewise, Mezirow emphasizes the process of critical reflection in perspective transformation (1981) and argues that individual (and possibly social) action is potentially an outcome of such reflection (1985). Praxis is an implicit thrust of Cervero's (1988) analysis of continuing professional educators. In his proposal for a 'critical viewpoint', reflection about the results of professional activity is as important a consideration as the means of achieving them: 'This viewpoint suggests that continuing professional educators must understand the political and ethical as well as technical dimensions of their work. ... Continuing profesional educators must continually – and critically – examines these means and ends' (Cervero 1988: 37). Brookfield focuses on the relationship of praxis to adult learning. Mezirow has developed the individual psychology of praxis (which Brookfield has employed) as well as entertained its socio-political ramifications. Cervero speaks directly to the ethical and political dimensions of praxis. All are largely concerned with delineating praxis as a reflective activity without enumerating any particular framework or set of standards for making such judgements, except to say that praxis is a necessary part of adult education practice both for educators themselves as well as for learners.

These are not new traditions in adult education. Lindeman (1926) described adult education as the process of helping adults find meaning in their experience by evaluating its significance, that is, reflecting upon its importance. That the social order could become rearranged in this process was an explicit but evolutionary effect for Lindeman, following somehow after individual 'self-improvement'. This theme is still evident in contemporary visions of praxis (for example, see Mezirow's work). Dewey (1938), whose views of pragmatism are easily seen in Lindeman and later adult education thought, also placed a critical reflectivity at the core of individual and social improvement. But clearly much of the current interest in praxis has been inspired by the visibility of Freire's (1970) work. Freire is expressly political. His use of Marxist notions of oppression often attests to that. Personal and political liberation are inseparable efforts. For Freire praxis is a central part of the liberatory struggle:

> The insistence that the oppressed engage in reflection on their concrete situation is not a call to armchair revolution. On the contrary, reflection – true reflection – leads to action. On the other hand, when the situation

calls for action, that action will constitute an authentic practice only if its consequences become the object of critical reflection.

(1970: 52)

Praxis, then, involves thought and action, critical evaluation of thought and action, and deliberate efforts to reconstitute further thought and action in terms of those considerations. Depending on the view, praxis can involve personal, social and political circumstances. Yet, with the exception of Freire whose version of praxis has explicit communal, political and ethical standards, the others, at best, only hint at a possible collective, communal nature of praxis. It is to that issue that I now wish to turn.

Praxis, community and the role of tradition

The foregoing took a brief look at variations of praxis that tend to have as their essential issue the thought and action of individuals. Bernstein (1983, 1985), in his attempt to fuse pragmatic and hermeneutical understandings of human activity, proposes an expanded vision for understanding the concept of praxis. For Bernstein, our individual thought and action is deeply, indeed inextricably, embedded in the social practices of the specific socio-historical communities which we inhabit. Grappling with the tensions between the Enlightenment's proposals for an ahistorical, generalizable, external view of truth and one founded on a form of subjectivism that views all forms of truth as essentially of equal merit, Bernstein suggests that we can move 'beyond objectivism and relativism' by coming to understand the ways in which our individual behaviour and social practices are dialectically combined in particular historical circumstances. Praxis is not just an interest in understanding individual thought and action. It is a process of coming to understand the community and historic fabric in which individuals play out their lives. Praxis is thus concerned with 'the highest form of human activity, manifested in speech and deed and rooted in the human conditions of plurality' (Bernstein 1983: 44). The essential human condition is therefore not one of absolute individual volition but rather a state in which humans irrevocably act within their relations to one another and within the continuities of their social practices (Kauppi 1991, Lave 1988).

In addition to this essential communality, the recognition and understanding of the force of tradition is also essential to an understanding of praxis. Our current communities, of course, do not exist *a priori*; they emerge through an evolutionary process from earlier communities. Gadamer (1975) has placed the concept of tradition in a central position for understanding who we are and what we are in the process of becoming. It is from these traditions that social practices emerge which are used in understanding and validating individual as well as collective thought and action. Bernstein, in his analysis of Gadamer, argues that 'we can take our historical situations and existing social practices seriously and at the same time develop a critical perspective on them that is informed by an understanding of our history and oriented toward an open future' (1983: 196). Praxis is thus a critical encounter with these traditions and how they affect our practice as educators. Praxis is only possible by appealing to these traditions; it neither exists in any transcendental fashion nor simply in a subjective sense.

Understanding the central role of community and tradition is crucial to understanding the power of beliefs and values on our practice as educators. Praxis is both a reflective and a judgemental endeavour and has to be seen in its socio-historical context. In his analysis of Arendt's views on human plurality, Bernstein argues:

> What Arendt is struggling to discriminate and isolate for us is a mode of thinking that is neither to be identified with the expression of private feelings nor to be confused with the type of universality characteristic of 'cognitive reason'. It is a mode of thinking that is capable of dealing with the particular in its particularity but which nevertheless makes the claim to communal validity. When one judges, one judges as member of a human community.
>
> (1983: 217)

This theme of the communal nature of judgement is important to see at this point because, if praxis is to have consequence for adult education, we must recognize the communal and tradition-based nature of adult education practice. Thus neither practice nor reflection about practice exists independently of our circumstances; nor is practice or reflection entirely idiosyncratic. Not only is praxis the reflection regarding our educational actions and thoughts within a historical community of practice, it is also reflection and action about these historical and communal circumstances. Bernstein refers to this as 'the sharing of criteria by communities' (1983: 74) and argues that particular communities are informed – that is, the appropriateness of action is judged – by the traditions from which they have emerged.

Praxis and practical reasoning

Now I wish to make a connection between this view of praxis as communally and traditionally bound and the idea of practical reasoning or phronesis first proposed by Aristotle. Aristotle originally differentiated theoretical knowledge (*theoria*) from technical knowledge (*techne*) from practical knowledge (*phronesis*). Practical knowledge is concerned with a type of situational and ethical know-how which involves making choices among available alternative courses of action, choices which reflect specific values and beliefs. This is what distinguishes theoria from phronesis:

theoretical knowledge is knowledge for its own sake whereas practical knowledge is in the service of action. Bernstein describes the nature of practical reasoning in this way:

> In speaking of the 'practical' character, I want to underscore the role of choice, deliberation, conflicting variable opinions, and the judgmental quality of rationality ... [which] allows for, indeed requires, interpretation, weighing, and application of these criteria to specific choices and decisions.
>
> (1983: 74)

This has very little to do with technical or instrumental rationality which is much more geared toward producing a product (such as building a house) and is far more concerned with performing an activity in a certain way (Bernstein 1971). Practice is more than instrumental because education requires us to commit to certain actions rather than others, actions which we choose to pursue based on what we believe to be right. Bernstein goes on to argue that this type of rationality is a process of 'rational persuasion' which is not easily assimilated in models of inductive/deductive proof and generalization and lacks, as well, a rule-determinate nature. This is remarkably similar to the types of discussion characteristic of the practical paradigm in curriculum theory (Carr and Kemmis 1986, Cervero and Wilson 1991). Reid (1979), Schwab (1969), and Walker (1975) all describe this deliberative quality as central to envisioning and implementing educational actions and reject a hypothetical-deductive model for conducting educational action. What we have to realize about this practical process is how important values and beliefs are in determining the choices we make as educators. These beliefs about how the world works and the way things get done are essentially embedded in the norms and values of our communities of educational practice.

Gadamer (1975) claims that hermeneutics is the way to this kind of situated and practical knowledge. Traditionally, the hermeneutic process has been separated into three distinct elements: understanding, interpretation and application (Hirsch 1967). Bernstein shows how one of Gadamer's major contributions has been the 'fusion of hermeneutics and *praxis*, and the claim that understanding itself is a form of practical reasoning and practical knowledge – a form of *phronesis*' (1983: 174). What Gadamer and Bernstein are attempting to show is that understanding, interpretation and application, which are perhaps more familiar to us in the terms of reflection and action, are a continuous praxic process inextricably bound in a pragmatic reality, one constantly buffeted by shifting social winds of community norms and values. They can neither be separated for analytical purposes nor in actual reality. What they both discuss is the notion of praxis as a constant mediation between social norms and values and idiosyncratic situations through a process of practical reasoning because there can be no scientific basis for our values. Bernstein's entire project is an attempt to see human activity as a rational process bounded by the deliberations embodied in the social and historical practices of the community in which they are embedded.

Thus our judgements about what to do in our practice as adult educators are irrevocably a symbiotic function of the historical and communal traditions in which that practice is conducted. As practitioners, we act within the parameters of our circumstances and our judgements about the appropriateness of our educational actions are a function of communally derived standards. Therefore, to understand – and to change, if necessary – our practice, we have to come to know the historically defined community of standards. These standards about the appropriateness of educational action are in turn a function of what the community of practitioners have historically believed to be the right thing to do.

As Kauppi argues, teaching (and I would include all professional endeavours) is a social activity taking place in a specific historical context: 'It can be argued that through their history teachers socialize into members of a professional community, and acquire its values, norms, and cultural models of action' (1991: 4). What this means is that values and norms underlying the practical choices we make as educators are located in the social structures and ideologies of our professional communities. If we are to understand why we do what we do, then praxis has to focus on how our communities of practice, representing more or less coherent visions of how the world is and how to act in it, contribute dynamically to our thoughts and actions as educators. Finally, this suggests that praxis is essentially concerned with reflecting on the ideologies justifying educational action.

Praxis and ideology

At this point I have tried to suggest an evolving set of themes for understanding praxis: It is a dialectical process of critical reflection and action; it is inextricably bound up in the norms and standards within specific historical communities; and it is directly tied to a practical view of rationality. But I am also trying to push this discussion toward an outline of Bernstein's argument for a larger, more dynamic context in which to understand praxis. What I will try to do now is show how reflection on ideology is crucial to our understanding of praxis in adult education.

Part of the argument I wish to make is concerned with the relation of thought and action. For quite some time there has been a steady and active gnawing at a 'foundational' understanding of knowledge, reasoning and action in the real world (see, for example, Apple 1979, Berger and Luckmann 1966, Bernstein 1971, 1983, Gadamer 1975, Gramsci 1971, Hawkesworth 1989, Kuhn 1979, Lave 1988, Rogoff and Lave 1984, Schon 1983, Wardhaugh 1986, Wertsch 1985, Winch 1958). Bernstein's 'postempiricist' argument suggests instead that our action in the world is informed by the beliefs and norms of specific socio-historical communities rather than the existence of some Archimedian structure or the availability of transcendental principles predicated on science. Hawkesworth (1989), using both Bernstein's analysis and arguments from human cognition analysis, presses essentially the same points. She describes the human condition as one of being 'theory-dependent' by which she means that our understanding of and action in the world are based on our idea of what the world is (this is a theme that echoes back through time to Berger and Luckmann and eventually back to Mead and Vygotsky). It is impossible for us to have an unmediated understanding of the world (the central claim of hypothetical-deductive models of rationality), for so much of our perception of the 'world' is constrained by the language and culture we have for understanding it, that is, the historical and communal nature of our circumstances. These various lines of analysis argue persuasively for an understanding of human action as practical and belief-driven. Therefore, praxis has to be an analysis of beliefs – that is, the ideology of the community of practice – and how these beliefs constrain, enhance, contrive and ultimately define our actions as humans. In other words, in order to reflect on practice, to engage the process of praxis, we have to reflect on the ideologies that enliven and sustain our practice as educators.

But there is a missing element that is important for investigating the relation of ideology to educational practice. Much of the work in this 'neopragmatic' tradition attempts to elucidate the conscious conditions of rational action. That is, while this tradition eschews the hypothetical-deductive model of Enlightenment rationality as falsely portraying how people think and act in the real world, it still proposes a practical rationality, underlain though it is and subject to the values of the reasoners, that is none the less based on consensual validation of argument and evidence. There is, however, a feature of the relation between thought and action that this analysis only addresses implicitly. While making the case for human discourse as fundamentally practical, pragmatists underplay the 'taken-for-granted' (see, for example, Apple 1979, Mezirow 1989, Schutz 1967, for discussions of this concept) aspects of beliefs working in the real world, which Apple characterizes as the 'unquestionable' (1979: 13). Gramsci (1971) describes the same phenomenon as 'common sense' by which he means the communally shared but typically uncritical and largely unconscious way of perceiving and comprehending the world that is common to any given historical period. For many of us, our real-world actions are an amalgamation of conscious thought and deed based on often uncritically considered and typically invisible assumptions and beliefs about the way things are; and this is what Hawkesworth means by being theory-dependent, Gramsci by common sense, and Apple and Schutz by taken-for-granted. Quite simply, we cannot meaningfully understand the world or even act in it without a view of how we believe it to be.

This is the place of praxis, for it has to get behind the rationalizations that drive practice to the ideology, the common sense, from which the reasoning emanates in order to reveal the standards by which we define our actions as educators.

But I need to go a step further. Not only has the taken-for-grantedness of ideology remained an implicit issue in these discussions, the rationality of the practical approach lacks, I believe, an accurate theory of human action, or, perhaps better put, a theory of the 'acting subject' (Giddens 1979). In his theory of structuration, Giddens shows the 'interdependence of action and structure' (1979: 3) by describing the 'central recursiveness of social life, as constituted in social practices: structure is both medium and outcome of the reproduction of social practices' (1979: 5). This central depiction has a major corollary that 'every social actor knows a great deal about the conditions of reproduction of the society of which he or she is a member' (1979: 5). This is a crucial understanding for a theory of praxis, for it gives us a way to understand how we both act in the world as well as construct its historical conditions. It gives us a way to understand the recursive connections between thought and action that are central to a pragmatic and hermeneutical understanding of social practices. But a key to understanding this in relation to the critical dialogue of praxis is Giddens's 'psychology' of social actors which he describes in three categories: the unconscious, the practical consciousness and the discursive consciousness. The important distinction for this paper lies in the latter two terms. Discursive consciousness is that which we are able to articulate at 'the level of discourse' (the level at which praxis is typically placed). Practical consciousness, on the other hand, is that tacit stock of 'knowledge which actors draw upon in the constitution of social activity' (1979: 5) which is the kind of knowledge that we use daily in constructing our social practices but rarely articulate because it is so informed by and constitutive of our ideological common sense (this is the level at which Freire's understanding of praxis operates). This is often what guides our practice as educators and therefore requires the kind of scrutiny praxis warrants. Thus Giddens's theory of structuration portrays the central recursiveness of social life as a unitary vision rather than the traditional subject-object model of scientific rationality. What Giddens's view allows us to do is to have an understanding of human social actors as reflectively and actively monitoring their interactions with each other in the social practices which their actions both constitute and are constituted by. This crucial set of insights means we have a way of both conceptualizing and accessing the very fabric of our actions.

It is here that praxis and ideology meet. The point of praxis is to examine critically those beliefs and values that inform our thought and action and how thought and action inform the constitution of our beliefs and values; it is to unveil their taken-for-grantedness, their commonsensicalness, their practicalness in order to see what their effect is on how we practise as educators as well as how we construct those beliefs through our practice. Mezirow, Brookfield and others have argued much the same, albeit by tending to focus on their relation to the structures of meaning in culture. But I am trying to push this notion in a different direction as well as reconstitute the view of rationality upon which to base praxis. This is why understanding the relationship ideologies have in forming the historical conditions is actually an important part of educational practice. It is not just what we 'discursively' think about our practice, but what our 'practical' thinking, which is constitutively linked to what we have thought in the past, tells us about what we do as well as what our 'recursive' doing tells us about what we think. Thus the inseparableness of thought and action is relinked. This is the hard ground of praxis, that nexus of mind, community, history, beliefs, values and action. Those who instrumentally employ the Tyler Rationale in curriculum planning, for example, uncritically, and perhaps unconsciously, assume its instrumental production-like values (Barone 1988, Cervero and Wilson 1991, Egan 1988, Posner 1988); they assume and act on the assumption that the world of curriculum works like the Tyler Rationale says it does. The project of praxis is to reveal, critique and evaluate how such assumptions and ideologies affect our practice as educators. But we have to do so as a community of inquirers who are willing not only to challenge our individual practices but the standards, located historically and subscribed to communally, by which we judge the appropriateness of our educational actions.

Praxis and educational practice

In the beginning I suggested that I hoped to use this paper to show how retrieving the Aristotelian notion of practical wisdom in moral action is crucial to improving adult education practice. Given this revived view of praxis, there are three ways in which the reflection upon the ideology of specific forms of practice can inform the praxis of adult educators. In the typical sense, as utilized by Brookfield and Mezirow for example, praxis is concerned with a critical consideration of individual thought and action. While it is implicit in Brookfield's generic sense of praxis, considering the effect of ideologically distorted perception on individual meaning structures is an explicit target in Mezirow's view of praxis. Both Mezirow and Brookfield, however, understand well that our acting and the meaning we derive from it are quintessentially affected by how we perceive that relationship. Understanding and perspective transformation for Mezirow is an inner, personal journey that may ramify beyond the action of individuals. But Mezirow and Brookfield are primarily interested in the learning psychology of adults. As educators, though, we can use their insights in the critical reflection on our practice. Perhaps the most important point for us to consider is the way in which ideologically construed meanings inform the intent and consequence of our educational practice. How do our world-view, our beliefs, our ideology of practice shape our sense of what is possible in an educational situation? What do our actions tell us about the way we think the world is or should be? Following this theme, our individual thought and action as practitioners become the object of praxis. This is more or less the contemporary view of praxis. I want to make the ethical ramifications of practice, as Cervero argues, the explicit thrust of such encounters. Then, asking such questions allows us to investigate and judge the ethical nature of what we intend as educators and why we believe what we do. This moves us away from the dominant focus on technical practicality to what I think is the more important one of moral practicality.

In a second sense, reflection on the ideology of practice can contribute to an understanding of the traditions and professional communities which we inhabit. The pragmatic view of the communal and traditional nature of values and norms is particularly poignant for educational practice. That there are 'schools' of thought and practice in education is, of course, an understatement. They are so prevalent (behaviouralism, scientism, cognitivism, humanism, constructivism, etc.) that we perhaps sometimes take their plurality for granted. In the day-to-day of educational practice, it is perhaps also forgotten that each of these many views has a particular set of beliefs that informs its system of thought and action. Coming to understand how these ideologies form boundaries around the educational actions of individuals within these specific communities can be seen as a form of praxis. For example, elsewhere (Wilson 1992b) I have begun to outline tentatively the development of pragmatism in Peirce's and Dewey's thinking and trace its emergence in American adult education as a primary philosophical footing for the practice of American adult educators. In that context the very issue of critical reflection is one bound up in the discourse of pragmatic thought. In that paper I have tried to show how critical reflection emerges in Dewey's and Lindeman's thought, tends to disappear in American adult education's period of technical emphasis, and reappears as a major focus in the movement of thought beyond those technical interests (which is a subtheme in this paper). In each period, responsible adult education is viewed differently because the beliefs, about what should be, differ. How does a praxic concern with these traditions inform adult education practice? Essentially it helps to reveal the range of beliefs and ideologies that contribute rationales to our intentions and practices; it gives a sense of what relations have existed between thought and action and how those have changed or remained the same over time. Such a consideration gives practice scope and reveals the traditions which have emerged as norms and values for the judgements we make in practice. Finally, by dealing with this side of the question, we have to return to the first theme because it allows us to ask ourselves as educators working from a particular point of view whether this is really what we believe is the right thing to do. Thus to understand our individual thought and action as practitioners we have to reflect on and examine the ideologies of the educational communities in which we practise. In other words, individual praxis is not possible without this dimension.

A third sense in which an understanding of ideology can inform praxis has to do with the discourse on practical reasoning. Much of the current discussion points to a view of rational action as practical and deliberative, a judgemental view that is based on the central beliefs we hold for acting in the world. We have also seen how the traditions of evolving communities bound the range and provide the valuation of that action. What an understanding of ideology can contribute to this is the specification of particular beliefs in particular socio-cultural circumstances. Ideology informs the very range of choices we make available to ourselves in deliberating about alternative courses of action; it becomes the common, but uncritical, sense by which we act. This is the central import of seeing educational activity as a process of practical reasoning. Praxis in this sense focuses on the nature of actual reasoning about what to do in specific situations and the way in which our beliefs constrain as well as inspire our decisions. Thus our personal beliefs, constituted by our location in historical ideologies, tell us what is possible, indeed, even imaginable. Once this fundamental relation becomes the object of praxis then as practitioners we can determine whether the actual and ethical consequences of our actions are what we wish and intend.

The telos of praxis

What I have suggested up till now may easily be construed as instrumental uses of praxis. The point of looking at these various perspectives, all bounded by a practical view of reality, has been to begin to grasp an expanded view of praxis and ideology. There is perhaps a *telos* for praxis that has lain dormant in much of the discussion so far. Thus I need to bring in one of the significant conclusions of the pragmatic debate regarding the nature of rationality.

One of Bernstein's chief concerns is not only a plea to recognize the influence of community and tradition in our thought and action but also a call 'to foster and nurture those forms of communal life in which dialogue, conversation, *phronesis*, practical discourse and judgment are concretely embodied in our everyday practices' (1983: 229). He refers to this as the *telos* of praxis which for him means dedicating 'ourselves to the practical task of furthering this type of solidarity, participation, and mutual recognition that is founded in dialogical communities' (1983: 231). Discovering and sustaining these communal tendencies is the important end point of praxis for Bernstein. Thus the project of praxis is to make explicit and overt the standards, norms, values, beliefs – the ideological common sense, values and beliefs – that form our educational practice. Why is this important? Hawkesworth states it plainly:

> It would be premature to conclude ... that all other accounts are ...
> equally valid or that there are no objective grounds on which to distin-
> guish between truth and falsity in divergent interpretations. The
> important point here is not that it is easy to make these determina-
> tions or that they can always be made in particular cases but that
> standards related to the range of human cognitive practices allow us
> to distinguish between partial views ... and false beliefs.
>
> (1989: 555)

This is the central ethical concern. In order not to be engulfed by the
Cartesian Anxiety, we have to recognize that our practices are, or can be,
rationally governed by ourselves: 'There can be no self-control or self-
criticism unless there are norms by which we distinguish the true from the
false' (Bernstein 1971: 191), which makes plain the normative nuances of
reasoning. But, and this is the major issue, 'there can be no dialogue, no
communication unless beliefs, values, commitments, and even emotions
and passions are shared in common' which means we have to be willing
'to really listen, to seek to understand what is genuinely other, different,
alien, and [have] the courage to risk one's most cherished prejudgments'
(Bernstein 1986: 205). Understanding and fostering the community and
coming to scrutinize critically the standards by which the community
judges then becomes praxis (it is this orientation that is missing in American understandings of praxis). But this expanded view still sounds instrumental because it has yet to confront the real issue. As Hawkesworth and
Bernstein claim, we have to distinguish between partial views and actual
falseness, for practice based on false beliefs is wrong. Clearly, if ideology is
understood as the taken-for-granted and common sense beliefs operating
in such communities, then the understanding of their intricate relations
with these judgemental standards becomes all the more important. If we
are to understand these standards which Bernstein and Hawkesworth
seek, we must also understand the beliefs that embody them. But understanding is not enough. We must also, through praxis, reject false beliefs
guiding practice and, in turn, critically justify our educational actions.

The major point is that practice and the reasoning necessary to embark
on courses of educational action are essentially and fundamentally normative, not scientific. Our educational practices can never be grounded
solely in instrumental rationality because the foundationalism upon which
that sort of reasoning depends does not well suit the varying ethical
topographies of practice. Practice is not simply a matter of choosing
appropriate means to well-understood and agreed upon ends, it is
fundamentally about choosing what ends to pursue. Praxis has to be concerned with how those choices are legitimated: whose choices they are, to
what ends, and who has been silenced in the choosing. The point of the
pragmatic and hermeneutic traditions is that we don't have fixed boundaries by which to be certain about what we are doing. Because of this lack

of a firm ground, it therefore takes a critical-practical approach to challenge constantly our intentions. If the central issue is to determine how we will chose and act, then we have to recognize that:

> The search for a 'foundation' for moral choice and action is part of a misguided search for a 'foundation' of knowledge. Once we give up the quest for certainty, once we recognize the impossibility of an 'absolute' justification, and the fallibility of all beliefs, including our moral beliefs, we need not despair. … If we are serious about this task, then we must direct our activity toward the realization of a genuine community of inquirers in which all share and participate. We must engage in those forms of praxis that can effect a genuine social reconstruction in which the quality of each unique individual's life is transformed.
>
> (Bernstein 1971: 227)

So where is the middle ground? It is coming to understand the transcience of our standards for right action but realizing they can be rational within a communal and dialogic context. By seeking to challenge constantly our actions and beliefs, then we can hold to a slippery middle ground where we have neither transcendental certainty nor the chaos of extreme subjectivism, but we do have a practical (i.e., Aristotelian) sense of what we are doing.

Even though the point of this paper is to mark out some lines on that slippery ground, there are some obvious omissions in this image. First, it must be clear that I am slipping into the same trap I adumbrated in the beginning – too much on what to do and not enough on doing it. That is, the pragmatic and hermeneutic traditions are long on talking about critical encounters but short on elaborating the standards of judgement. But maybe the medium is the message. Since the argument is that we inhabit horizons of existence of our own making, we then must be constantly (re)making them. So what makes the middle ground slippery is the transitoriness of standards. Therefore what these traditions offer us as educators are pleas to respect plurality and to risk our certainty in dialogic encounters with 'the other'. Yet, because of the essential practicalness (in the Aristotelian sense) and recursiveness (in the Giddensian sense) of our social lives, we must constantly be willing to encounter ourselves. Specifically, in adult education this means no issue can be allowed to become platitudinous, for to do so means we forfeit our becoming. Nor have I considered directly any specific set of beliefs and values in adult education, except for this limited encounter with the idea of praxis itself. Elsewhere (Cervero and Wilson 1994) I have been part of such encounters in going face to face with long-held systems of thought and belief in an attempt to reconstitute adult education as explicitly normative, political and practical; there we argue for, among other things, a specific set of standards by which to understand and judge practice. The point of this paper has been to offer an invitation for such encounters to continue in our field of moral and social endeavour and to suggest ways of framing those important conversations.

Consequently, at this point I am drawn back to Cervero's (1988) discussion of a 'critical viewpoint' in which he makes it clear that as educators we have critically to examine our methods and our intentions and by implication their social, political and ethical consequences. I have tried to suggest some ways in which such a critical encounter might be focused. That praxis ultimately has to do with ideological issues must be a question of actual practice. If our actions as adult educators are to be consciously motivated and not just actions of habit, then we must recognize that our intentions are directed by our understanding of the world. That such understanding itself may not be well articulated is why praxis is so important. This leads to examining what those beliefs, assumptions and understandings are. Examining the ideologies bounding practice can inform the praxis of adult educators from individual, community and practical perspectives. Such a consideration of ideology provides the specifics on which to reflect. It also leads to an understanding of those values which underlie the very reasons we put forth to support our actions as well as the taken-for-granted assumptions and common sense that define what is possible. That these reasons reflect the judgemental standards of the communities in which we live and work becomes the final point of praxis, for, as Hawkesworth and Bernstein argue, distinguishing false beliefs from partial views is the central ethical issue facing practitioners. Bringing those standards into view for critical reflection becomes a questioning of those very beliefs that form the basis for action in the world. It raises essential issues to consider. Are we as educators doing what we think we are? On what grounds are we judging the rightness of those actions? And where do those standards come from? Do we understand the consequences of our decisions and actions? Whose silence do we foster in our choices? Praxis is thus fundamentally concerned with the ethical consequences of adult education practice.

Both Bernstein and Hawkesworth argue that we neither know things in a 'foundational' sense nor that all knowledge is relative, and it is upon this central insight that a theory of praxis must rest. But it is a slippery place from which to see the world, a middle ground of ultimate precariousness. Their essential position draws on the notion that as communities and traditions come to define the values we live and reason with, and which through our social practices we contribute to, we must investigate those communities and traditions in order to understand those values and judgemental standards. But most importantly, as we become aware of these values, we must constantly be critical of their consequence for our educational action. Thus our theory-dependence about the way the world is and how we are in it becomes critically conscious, deliberative and intentional, rather than sublime and assumed. Thus our social, political and ethical practice becomes explicit so that we can more critically scrutinize its consequences. Praxis is reflecting on what we do, the ends to which action is intended, the means by which it is achieved, the context in which it occurs, the standards by which it is judged, and finally, most importantly, the essential rightness or wrongness of our practice as adult educators. In order to understand those values and traditions which bound our best judgements about what is appropriate in particular educational circumstances, we must examine the belief systems that embody our social practices as educators.

Notes

1   *Arthur L. Wilson* is an assistant professor of adult education in the Department of Educational Leadership at Ball State University in Muncie, Indiana. He has worked as a literacy instructor, has designed and instructed literacy staff development projects, and has worked in continuing education for the professions. He is co-author, with Ronald M. Cervero, of *Planning Responsibly for Adult Education* as well as consulting editor for the *Adult Education Quarterly* and the *Journal of Adult Basic Education*. His research interests include programme planning practice in adult education, the history and philosophy of adult education, and adult earning.
2   This is, of course, but one definition of 'practical'. See Bernstein (1971) for a discussion of 'high' and 'low' notions of the term in which he depicts 'high' as referring to Aristotle's view of the ethical wisdom for moral action, the definition at issue in this paper, and 'low' as referring to the American tradition of common sense and anti-intellectualism.
3   This typically confused term is of course immediately problematic. While the point of this paper is not to sort out its complexities, it none the less is an important concept to understand the significance of just what it is we have to reflect upon in praxis. Consequently, further along in the paper, I attempt to get a transitory 'fix' on the notion, at least in so far as it is possible in order to discuss its crucial connection to praxis.

References

Apple, M. (1979) *Ideology and Curriculum*, London: Routledge & Kegan Paul.

Barone, T. (1988) Curriculum platforms and literature, in J. Gress (Ed.), *Curriculum: An Introduction to the Field*, Berkeley, CA: McCutchan, pp. 140–165.

Berger, P. and Luckmann, T. (1966) *The Social Construction of Reality: A Treatise in the Sociology of Knowledge*, New York: Doubleday.

Bernstein, R. (1971) *Praxis and Action: Contemporary Philosophies of Human Activity*, Philadelphia: University of Pennsylvania Press.

Bernstein, R. (1983) *Beyond Objectivism and Relativism: Science, Hermeneutics, and Praxis*, Philadelphia: University of Pennsylvania Press.

Bernstein, R. (1985) From hermeneutics to praxis, in R. Hollinger (Ed.), *Hermenutics and Praxis*, Notre Dame, Indiana: University of Notre Dame Press, pp. 272–296.

Bernstein, R. (1986) The rage against reason. *Philosophy and Literature*, Vol. 10, No. 2, pp. 186–209.

Bright, B. (Ed.) (1989) *Theory and Practice in the Study of Adult Education: The Epistemological Debate*, London: Routledge.

Brookfield, S. (1986) *Understanding and Facilitating Adult Learning*, San Francisco: Jossey-Bass.

Carr, W. and Kemmis, S. (1986) *Becoming Critical: Education, Knowledge and Action Research*, London: Falmer Press.

Cervero, R. (1988) *Effective Continuing Education for Professionals*, San Francisco: Jossey-Bass.

Cervero, R. and Wilson, A. (1991) Perspectives on program planning in adult education, in *Proceedings of the 32nd Annual Adult Education Research Conference*, Norman, OK: University of Oklahoma, pp. 39–48.

Cervero, R, and Wilson, A. (1994) *Planning Responsibly for Adult Education. A Guide to Negotiating Power and Interests*, San Francisco: Jossey-Bass.

Cunningham, P. (1989) Making a more significant impact on society, in B. A. Quigley (Ed.), *Fulfilling the Promise of Adult and Continuing Education*, New Directions for Continuing Education, No. 44, San Francisco: Jossey-Bass, pp 36–46.

Dewey, J. (1938) *Experience and Education*, New York: Collier.

Egan, K. (1988) Metaphors in collision: objectives, assembly lines, and stories, *Curriculum Inquiry*, Vol. 18, No. 1, pp. 63–86.

Freire, P. (1970) *Pedagogy of the Oppressed*, New York: Continuum.

Gadamer, H. (1975) *Truth and Method*, New York: Continuum.

Giddens, A. (1979) *Central Problems in Social Theory: Action, Structure and Contradiction in Social Analysis*, Berkeley: University of California Press.

Gramsci, A. (1971) *Selections from the Prison Notebooks*, (Q. Hoare and G. N. Smith, Eds and Trans.), London: Lawrence and Wishart. (Original text written between 1929 and 1935.)

Hawkesworth, M. (1989) Knowers, knowing, and known: feminist theory and claims of truth. *Signs: Journal of Women in Culture and Society*, Vol. 14, No. 3, pp. 533–557.

Hirsch, E. (1967) *Validity in Interpretation*, New Haven: Yale University Press.

Hollinger, R. (Ed.) (1985) *Hermeneutics and Praxis*, Notre Dame, Indiana: University of Notre Dame Press.

Kauppi, A. (1991) (October), The methodological basis for developing teacher education in Finnish businessmen's commercial college, paper presented at the annual conference of the American Association of Adult and Continuing Education, Montreal.

Kuhn, T. (1979) *The Structure of Scientific Revolutions*, 2nd edn, Chicago: University of Chicago Press.

Lave, J. (1988) *Cognition in Practice: Mind, Mathematics and Culture in Everyday Life*, Cambridge: Cambridge University Press.

Lindeman, E. (1926) *The Meaning of Adult Education*, New York: New Republic.

Mezirow, J. (1981) A critical theory of adult learning and education. *Adult Education*, Vol. 32, pp. 3–24.

Mezirow, J. (1985) Concept and action in adult education. *Adult Education Quarterly*, Vol. 35, pp. 142–151.

Mezirow, J. (1989) Transformation theory and social action: a response to Collard and Law. *Adult Education Quarterly*, Vol. 39, pp. 170–176.

Posner, G. (1988) Models of curriculum planning, in L. Beyer and M. Apple

(Eds), *The Curriculum: Problems, Politics, and Possibilities*, Albany, New York: State University of New York Press, pp. 77–97.

Reid, W. (1979) Practical reasoning and curriculum theory: in search of a new paradigm. *Curriculum Inquiry*, Vol. 9, No. 3, pp. 187–207.

Rogoff, B. and Lave, J. (Eds) (1984) *Everyday Cognition: Its Development in Social Context*, Cambridge, MA: Harvard University Press.

Rorty, R. (1979) *Philosophy and the Mirror of Nature*, Princeton, NJ: Princeton University Press.

Rubenson, K. (1989) The sociology of adult education in S. Merriam and P. Cunningham (Eds), *Handbook of Adult and Continuing Education*, San Francisco: Jossey-Bass, pp. 51–69.

Schon, D. (1983) *The Reflective Practitioner*, New York: Basic Books.

Schwab, J. (1969) The practical: a language for curriculum. *School Review*, Vol. 77, pp. 1–23.

Schutz, A. (1967) *The Phenomenology of the Social World* (G. Walsh and F. Lehnart, Trans.) Geneva/New York: Northwestern University Press. (Original work published 1932.)

Usher, R. and Bryant, I. (1989) *Adult Education as Theory, Practice, and Research: The Captive Triangle*, London: Routledge.

Walker, D. (1975) Curriculum development in an art project, in W. Reid and D. Walker (Eds), *Case Studies in Curriculum Change: Great Britain and the United States*, London: Routledge & Kegan Paul, pp. 91–135.

Wardhaugh, R. (1986) *An Introduction to Sociolinguistics*, London: Blackwell.

Welton, M. (1987) 'Vivisecting the nightingale': reflections on adult education as an object of study. *Studies in the Education of Adults*, Vol. 19, No. 1, pp. 46–68.

Wertsch, J. (1985) *Vygotsky and the Social Formation of Mind*, Cambridge, MA: Harvard University Press.

Wilson, A. L. (1992a) Science and the professionalization of American adult education, 1934–1989: a study of knowledge development in the adult education handbooks, in A. Blunt (Ed.), *Proceedings of the 33rd Annual Adult Education Research Conference*, Saskatoon, Saskatchewan, Canada, pp. 260–267.

Wilson, A. L. (1992b), Pragmatism and social action in American adult education. *International Journal of Lifelong Education*, Vol. 11, No. 3, pp. 181–189.

Winch, P. (1958) *The Idea of a Social Science*, London: Routledge & Kegan Paul.

3 Thematization of power, the search for common interests, and self-reflection

Towards a comprehensive concept of emancipatory education

Mechthild Hart

As readers familiar with Habermas's work will know, the distinction between communicative and strategic or 'purposive-rational' action is at the core of his critical theory, signifying the one major unifying concern of all his writings: to discover and grasp the rationality behind processes of social rationalization in their entire scope and depth. Seen within the entire context of Habermas's work, the comprehensive concept of rationality he develops in conjunction with an analysis of speech and interaction therefore serves primarily a critical function. The general intent of critical theory to reveal ideological obfuscations of inequality and injustice is behind Habermas's specific attempt to counter the prevailing fetishization of scientific and technological rationality as the only form of true rationality (Habermas, 1969). This critique derives support and nourishment from the rationality built into the very structure of human speech and interaction, i.e., the rationality of mutual understanding based upon reciprocal, symmetrical relationships (Habermas, 1973a).

The deviations and violations of this ideal of unlimited intersubjectivity can be attributed to the underlying systematic, socially produced and maintained mechanisms of control and coercion which lead to 'systematically distorted communication' (Habermas, 1970). This term does not refer to the many ordinary disturbances which are typical for everyday communication and for which speech itself provides a number of rectifying means (Habermas, 1976), but rather to distortions which arise from the internal structure of communication itself, thus consistently, and self-perpetuatingly, denying or violating its own ideal.

Here ideology critique merges with a critique of systematically distorted communication since the social forces and contradictions which lead to a fetishization of technological rationality are reflected in the distorting operations and mechanisms of predominant forms of communication and interaction. In the case of ideology as well as in the case of systematically distorted communication the distinction between strategic and communicative action is at the core of critique. In the case of 'science and

technology as "ideology"' it serves to reveal the untruth behind the impe-
rious reign of instrumental rationality as the single paradigm for all rational action. In the case of systematically distorted communication it
elucidates the violation of the rationality of speech due to the unrecognized usurpation of communicative by strategic behaviour. Thus, technological rationality becomes irrationality when it dictates the character and
the forms of regulation of the many social, i.e. non-technological,
processes of society's ongoing reproduction and renewal of its own social
reality, its identity, and its stock of interpretations which give meaning to
and regulate social intercourse. Such reproduction becomes blind,
because society's members can neither understand nor critically reflect
upon the forces that regulate social intercourse since 'understanding' and
'reflection' are produced in the medium not of technological, but only of
communicative rationality.

Adult education, which forms a vital part of the general process of
social reproduction, therefore fully falls within the sphere of influence of
ideology, and of distorted forms of communication. This is symptomatically revealed in the fact that adult education literature has to a large
extent reduced problems related to social reproduction to technically
soluble questions and has relinquished theories and knowledge which
cannot be reduced to technically utilizable knowledge. At the same time,
adult education understands itself as an important part of liberal traditions and as a bulwark of Western democracies. Owing to the prevailing
reduction of educational interests in enlightenment to technological
rationalization, however, it does not make room for a critical reflection on
the nature and quality of our democracy. Consequently, adult education
literature operates mostly on the basis of implicit assumptions about what
comprises democratic forms of education and learning, placing its main
emphasis on methods and strategies which assume a clear sense of
achieved autonomy and independence of adults. Structures of communication and interaction among adults which reveal the continued existence
of unfreedom and dependence are not acknowledged as problems or
research priorities; at the same time, unrecognized power relations are
carried into, as well as being reflected by, educational situations involving
adults. Thus, procedures which on the surface appear to be democratic
may be imposed upon a lopsided or constrained intersubjective structure,
thereby contradicting or even mocking the explicit claims of freedom and
autonomy. In other words, in such adult education theories the nature
and quality of the intersubjective structure of the educational situation,
i.e., the entire net of relations that exist among all the participants, including the relation of the participants to themselves, is not investigated in
terms which would reveal limitations and distortions which are due to the
effect of power.

In my paper I want to focus attention on this neglected aspect of the
educational situation, taking the social and individual reality of power as

the point of departure. The empirical material is drawn from two major organizational forms of the women's movement: consciousness-raising groups and women's collectives. Although some of the problem constellations addressed in the following essay are specific for the reality of women's oppression, these groups provide a laboratory for adult education inquiry which is interested in unfolding all implications of democratic education. Within the context of female oppression, power is defined in terms of male-supremacist structures and ideologies, expressed and sustained by the normative systems of 'femininity' and 'masculinity' which organize the female life-context in ways which directly and unilaterally benefit the interests of men. Although power manifests itself only in concrete and specific ways, it always has the same purpose: to keep individual autonomy within strict and narrowly defined boundaries. This can occur either through direct, open power in the form of violence (or the permanent threat of violence), or through the mechanism of a false consciousness in the grips of beliefs and assumptions which reflect and cement power relations. Seen from this perspective, consciousness-raising groups and collectives provide exemplary material for adult education to study the distortions built into typical forms of social interaction, as well as ways of unlearning power-bound habits of perception and communication. Because the reality of unfreedom and dependence is unflinchingly acknowledged, the view is opened up for a realistic and critical assessment of the effects of power on human action and consciousness. The study of consciousness-raising groups and collectives is further particularly well suited for an illumination of the systematic nature of power settled into the structure of communication and interaction because the experiences of the participants (including myself) of such groups reveal how power stubbornly reasserts itself even against the deliberate, conscious intentions of the people involved. If the acquisition of a practical consciousness that is capable of rationally addressing moral-practical questions is accepted as a major educational objective, consciousness-raising groups and collectives can be considered genuine adult educational situations. The shaping of such a practical consciousness can only be an explicit goal for any education which claims to prepare or help students to participate in their society as autonomous members. A mature form of participation inevitably includes the capacity to reflect critically upon the values and norms guiding social behaviour, and to shape new or better ones in co-operation with other members of the society. Critique of established social norms and the shaping of new ones are precisely the two learning processes characterizing consciousness-raising groups and collectives which typically work by consensus rather than by majority rule. These processes are aimed at a dissolution of the effects of power on consciousness and interaction. As I shall describe in the following, not only are these two learning processes closely related, but both also contain a third learning process in which the group participants reflect upon the motivations and needs underlying their own individual action. To each learning process there correspond levels of human engagement of capacities. The critical calls into play the intellectual-cognitive; to the shaping of new norms that correspond to interpersonal and social virtues; the individual self-examination requires attunement to one's own needs, associations and motivational forces and the readiness to let dissolve perverting and self-deceiving mechanisms.

Thematization of power

All human action is guided by norms which take the form of reciprocal behaviour expectations. The force of norms governing human action derives from an underlying, taken-for-granted consensus about the validity of those norms. Because action is informed by these reciprocal behaviour expectations it is communicative and is therefore 'grounded in the inter-subjectivity of mutual understanding and secured by the general recognition of obligations; it is sanctioned conventionally' (McCarthy, 1981: 26). Further, such a tacit, unquestioningly presupposed background consensus automatically implies that the norms in operation '*deserve* the acceptance of all those concerned' (Habermas, 1981: 133). In other words, there is always the implication that the norms are legitimate. Habermas discovers in this implied legitimization at the basis of action and speech 'a gentle but obstinate, a never silent, although seldom redeemed claim to reason' (Habermas, 1979: 96). Reason, and rationality, move into two directions. First, they point to the dimension of criticizability of norms, i.e., to the dimension where legitimacy claims can be explicitly thematized, questioned, and tested. Second, as the above-mentioned quote already indicated, such discursive testing or 'redeeming' raises the previously tacit consensus, the backbone of ordinary communication situations, to the level of conscious, deliberate consensus of all those who are – at least potentially – affected by certain norms.

The problem of false consciousness, and of an ideological system producing and cementing the confines of false consciousness, can be formulated in similar terms. In societies characterized by an unequal distribution of power, and thus by unequal access to social and material resources, norms and normative systems regulate and sanction social behaviour which is a reflection of, and in turn helps to consolidate and maintain, structures of inequality and injustice. Explicit ideological justifications of such inequalities serve the dual function of 'proving that the validity claims of norm systems are legitimate and of avoiding thematization and testing of discursive validity claims. The specific achievement of such ideologies consists in the inconspicuous manner in which communication is systematically limited' (Habermas, 1975: 112–113). Systematically limited communication thus refers to the silent effect of dominance on the way people see, experience and act in the world they share with others, and where they do not recognize what really shapes and determines their experience. Such limitations are systematic because they are subject to well-entrenched, self-perpetuating mechanisms which prevent thematization of certain needs and interests, generally the needs and interests of those most affected by unequal distribution of power. Ideologies therefore supply patterns of interpretations of needs and interests which explain, justify and therefore mask the whole structure of inequities and injustice. Thereby does ideology benefit those who hold power and who have greater access (or sole access) to society's resources.

The women who joined consciousness-raising groups in large numbers during the early '70s gave in to the doubt that the thus far taken-for-granted explanatory systems of 'femininity' and 'masculinity' had adequately explained women's experience. In a way, we can consider the moment where doubts begin to stir already a moment of breakthrough cracking the rigid shell of a 'normalized today' (Freire, 1979) with its taken-for-granted assumptions and procedures. Mezirow made a similar observation by noticing the important catalytic effect of 'disorienting dilemmas' for a transformation of one's 'meaning perspective' (Mezirow, 1981). In all cases, whether through the more quiet moment of nagging doubt, courageously given into, or through the emotional turmoil of disorienting dilemmas, power is thematized already by naming the problem as one of the discrepancy between 'woman's consciousness, man's world' (Rowbotham, 1974). The recurring feminist themes of 'women's speechlessness' (Dietze, 1979), the 'problem that has no name' (Friedan, 1963), or 'the line of fault' of women's experience (Smith, 1979) – all refer to the expropriation of women's experience and interests by a male-supremacist social system and its ideological justifications. The power of ideologies to suppress contents of experience and corresponding interests is especially relevant for women, since it has taken a hold on female consciousness, producing 'effects on the level of desire' (Foucault, 1980: 59) and thus preventing women not only from pursuing their interests, but also from perceiving them. As a result of this insight women located the point of departure for a critique of the effects of power in everyday life. This was the sense of the early feminist slogan 'the personal is political'. Precisely because of the experience of patriarchal power relations as a suppression or dispossession of female experience, the women participating in consciousness-raising groups could not start from an already established categorical framework which would describe and explain their experience, but they had to start 'from within':

> The distinctive and deep significance of consciousness raising at an
> earlier period of the women's movement was precisely this process of
> opening up what was personal, idiosyncratic, and inchoate and discovering with others how this was shared, was objectively part of women's
> oppression, finding ways of speaking *of* it and ways of speaking it

politically. It is this essential return to the experience we ourselves have directly in our everyday worlds that has been the distinctive mode of working in the women's movement – the repudiation of the professional, the expert, the already authoritative tones of the discipline, the science, the formal tradition, and the return to the seriously engaged and very difficult enterprise of discovering how to begin from ourselves.

(Smith, 1979: 144)

However, not all experiences prove equally useful for consciousness-raising. This may be one of the reasons that consciousness-raising manuals quickly appeared despite early warnings that they would endanger the methodologically necessary spontaneity and once again prescribe to women what they were supposed to think and feel. The topics listed in these manuals were often collections which in previous consciousness-raising groups had already proved to be generative, i.e., able to open up into a 'thematic fan' (Freire, 1970: 107) thus gradually disclosing more and more facets of the reality of oppression, letting more and more elements emerge, and revealing more and more how those elements interact. Such a gradual process of disclosure is possible only if the individual scenes recalled during consciousness-raising contain and reflect typical patterns of interaction as well as particularly dense packets of these patterns. Many of the requirements Freire stipulates for the 'existential situation' to be decoded during *conscientizaçao* are relevant for the scenes recalled during consciousness-raising as well (Freire, 1970: 106–118).

In this context we can identify one of the major differences between consciousness-raising and group therapy with which it appears to share the same concern for the personal and for personal experiences, and to which consciousness-raising frequently degenerates. In group therapy the personal, generally accorded little social value and kept confined in the sphere of the purely private, is injected with instant importance. This valorization of the personal discards the non-personal or political reality of the world 'out there' as a falsifying influence on the therapeutic process. In a consciousness-raising setting which does not lose sight of its feminist and hence political goals and principles, the personal is not simply 'raised' to the level of the political, but it is disclosed as being endlessly mediated by the political, i.e., the larger context of subordination.[1] The work of disclosure cannot be an individual effort but requires a collective medium, since only through an intersubjective recognition of shared experience can previously simply private and idiosyncratic feelings be validated as subjective experiences of a general impersonal, objective context of oppression.

During consciousness-raising, women recall individual scenes as small units of experience whose meaning emerges in the process of remembering and understanding. In the past, the real meaning was present only in the form of a vague or diffuse experience of misery, of unarticulated frustration or disappointment, but since it had no legitimate means of expression, i.e., no *social* means of expression, it could not become concrete or real. Very similar to peasants in the Chinese consciousness-raising groups during the Cultural Revolution (Cell, 1977; Hinton, 1966; Whyte, 1974), women 'speak bitterness' not sweetness, because at issue is the painful denial or violation of individual autonomy and self-determination. But power is present in these scenes not only as the mute symptom of pain or unease, but also in the form of rigid, stereotyped behaviour which the woman blindly acted out in the past, according to her prescribed 'role'. In the process of understanding and recalling the scene, its ritualized order becomes strangely fluid, and the scene is both completed and opened up. It is completed because the previously suppressed or silenced contents of experience are allowed to emerge. It is opened up because the possibility of unexplored interpretations of experience, and of new kinds of action and interaction becomes visible. Thus, the past is not simply recalled, but reconstructed, and remembrance is inseparable from an orientation towards the future. Freire describes a similar process of attaining a genuinely historical consciousness, a 'temporalization of space', where the scenic arrangement of the 'limit-situation' is turned into a conscious experience of the past in the present pointing towards the future (Freire, 1970: 81).

Such an open view towards the future carries its own practical implications. Thematization of power unveils the supremacist relation between the norms of 'femininity' and 'masculinity', thereby unmasking the underlying consensus as false. To determine or discover ways of interaction which are not characterized by inequality and injustice, reflected in corresponding norms, is a different kind of work although the critique of power-bound norms already implies the principles on which such a search has to be grounded: the principles of mutual agreement, or a true consensus about which norms should govern social conduct. As the history of the women's movement reveals, this is as much a work of theory as of practice. An adequate language system which would truly represent and explain female experience is an ongoing collective effort. New, dominance-free forms of interaction need to be practised. The efforts and experiences of women who formed their own collectives and deliberately submitted themselves to the laborious effort to make decisions by consensus, i.e., by unanimous agreement rather than by majority vote, probably constitute the most systematic attempt to shape new ways of interacting, and to push forward our understanding of the deep-seated effects of power.

The search for common interests

To work by consensus means to make decisions based on unanimity or agreement. Such an agreement is the outcome as well as the supporting force of reciprocal, non-hierarchical relationships among the members of the group. Consensus therefore signifies a state of unity and agreement as well as a conscious, rational procedure orientated towards the creation of unity.

Many collectives therefore fluctuate between full involvement in day-to-day activities and in the making of numerous short-term decisions, and setting aside special sessions where evaluation and critique of the process of working together takes place (Batchelder and Marks, 1979). During those 'mutual self-criticism' sessions daily business, and with it the pressure to act and to make decisions, are deliberately put aside in order to free the members for the work of criticism. Such sessions have two main purposes: first, to check whether a formerly reached consensus is still valid, or whether it was perhaps the result of misunderstandings and unintended deceptions; second, to restore unity or agreement when serious disagreements have arisen and mutual understanding is no longer guaranteed. Consensus therefore refers to the foundational level of the collective, i.e., to the shared convictions and beliefs which have already been negotiated. It refers also to the level of the bonding of the collective, i.e., to the ongoing task of and procedure employed for reaching consensus. Likewise, criticism sessions take place with respect to both levels. Potentially, all aspects of collective reality as they affect unity and agreement (on either of the two levels) can become a focus for criticism. It can therefore be called successful only if it broadens the consensual base or strengthens the procedure, or, finally, if it restores unity when that has fallen apart.

Regardless of the concrete concern at issue during criticism sessions, conflicts and agreements always touch the complex and sensitive relationship between individual and collective interests (where the meaning of the latter is yet to be defined). For instance, behaviour may on the surface look like a violation of mutual behaviour expectations. When looked at more closely, however, and when seen within the entire context of interaction, the problem may lie in this context rather than in the behaviour of the individual woman alone. To give an example: in the two collectives I participated in we often ran into the problem of quasi-automatic volunteering of some members for too many tasks which tended to create a rather competitive atmosphere as to who was giving more to the cause. A woman who was criticized for not assuming enough responsibility may in reality have been quite fair and realistic in her assessment of her own abilities and time commitments. Mutual self-criticism can therefore not mean simply to match individual behaviour with a certain established collective behaviour code, but it must always take the entire situation, which is the established intersubjective structure, into account. In cases where there indeed exists a dichotomy between individual and collective interests, the opposing interests and beliefs have to be thematized and evaluated in order for the collective to come to an agreement about what could be accepted as generally valid for everybody. It is therefore not a matter of trying to reconcile individual with collective interests, whether through a compromise, or through individual sacrifice, but rather of scrutinizing and evaluating the implications of all interests, whether expressed by a minority or by a majority. Those interests whose 'validity and ... domain of application find general recognition' in the process of such a scrutiny are called 'generalizable interests' by Habermas (1973a: 251).

We can now deepen the understanding of the suppression of interests discussed in the previous section. Interests which are suppressed by the normative power of ideologies may well be truly generalizable, i.e., they may find the acceptance of all members of society if they would be allowed to be thematized and rationally considered by all those concerned. Ideologies function in a way which precisely prevents such thematization. Moreover, ideological justifications of unequal distribution of power 'assert counterfactually and suppose a generalizability of interest' (Habermas, 1975: 112). A perfect illustration of this ideologically burdened assertion is the slogan 'what is good for General Motors is good for America'.

If we apply Habermas's model of the suppression of generalizable interests to the female life-context specifically, we can see the problem of expropriation of women's experience in a new light. The differences in female and male life-contexts, and in the correlative modes of experience, are first of all determined by their hierarchical relationship to each other. Women and men see and experience the world differently because they are differently situated within the social structure as a whole. This difference in position is not due to sexual (or biological) difference, but due to a power-bound interpretation of this difference which transforms it into a source for inequality.

During consciousness-raising the prevailing interpretations of sexual difference are challenged by unveiling them as misinterpretations of women's experiences and interests because this defining context is one which subsumes them under the interests of men. What emerges in the process are, however, not simply 'women's issues', but experiences and concerns which contain potentially generalizable interests, i.e., ones which could be 'the same for all' and thus be of public or general concern. The prescriptive association of 'women's proper sphere' with the sphere of purely private matters adds an additional twist to the problem of suppression of generalizable interests. Because women's experiences are generally relegated to the so-called private sphere, they are therefore irrelevant or trivial over against those matters that enter the public or political realm and those that become part of the political decision-making process. The intent to find ways of publicly articulating and revealing the political or general relevance of the themes and interests contained in female experience is also behind the proclamation that 'the personal is political'. It announces a relationship between the political and the personal where the political does not exclude vital human interests by stigmatizing them as irrelevant, purely private, or 'simply' women's issues.

If power characteristically suppresses and excludes the thematization and pursuit of generalizable interests, a process orientated towards determining or defining them must be free from power's distorting influence. What is to be considered truly common or valid for all can only become evident in a co-operative, dominance-free process, and cannot be unilaterally determined in advance. Generalizable interests can therefore be neither 'empirically found to already exist nor simply posited; rather, they are in a non-contingent way, both *formed* and *discovered*' (Habermas, 1973b: 177).

In principle, the women participating in collectives precisely attempted to form and discover generalizable interests by collectively and bindingly interpreting their needs (Habermas, 1975: 113). We need to distinguish two steps involved in establishing and discovering generalizable norms. One is the co-operative effort itself, exemplarily found in the collective, the other is the outcome of such a will-formation in discourse, in reflection on what the necessary assumptions and commitments are for argumentative truth-seeking. Clearly, not everyone need be a technical philosopher in order to be able to participate in truth-seeking; but everyone must see the basic point that one is responsible for one's views and for one's rejections of others' views.

We can see that the work of such discursive will-formation and truth-seeking contains the work of consciousness-raising but carries it a step further. Norms are now proposed with the hope that they may prove to be useful for a just interpretation and regulation of interests. They are thematized and criticized on a higher plane, so-to-speak, but the possibility of injustice contained in those proposed norms necessitates the continuation of thematization and critique of power. The actual process requires a much more stringent form of communication than was necessary in consciousness-raising. Thus, the discussions around collective interpretations of needs bear the major characteristic of Habermas's concept of practical discourse where the main form of speech is argumentation, a type of speech 'in which the participants thematize contested legitimacy claims and try to redeem them or criticize them argumentatively. An argument contains reasons which are systematically related to the validity claim of a problematic utterance' (Habermas, 1981: 40). If the problematic utterance concerns the legitimacy of norms, argumentation is inherently critical. Consequently, argumentation cannot be confined to the formal requirements of deductive reasoning but must be extended to the realm of moral-practical questions, and it is thus fully inserted in the critically explicated horizon of the everyday world of the participants. The accountability and responsibility of people for their actions, only tacitly (and mostly counter-factually) presupposed during ordinary communication, is now systematically enacted, bringing to light the rational base of human speech. Responsibility is reflected in the kind of evidence brought forth in support of justifications of norms which describe 'the consequences and side-effects that the application of a proposed norm can be expected to have in regard to the satisfaction or non-satisfaction of generally accepted needs and wants' (McCarthy, 1981: 313). What is accepted as a sound or cogent argument is one which is capable of persuasion. This form of argumentation, i.e., critical argumentation, is therefore characterized by a supporting mode: 'Even if something cannot be deduced by virtue of logical argument it can be supported or weakened by arguments, it can be rationally considered and judged' (Habermas, 1974: 210).

The validation of arguments cannot be established without presupposing in principle a community of thinkers who are capable of an intersubjective understanding and formation of a consensus. Even lies and the refusal to participate partake of this presupposition of such a community. This is not an irrational belief in reason as a decision or a blind postulate. It is not irrational or blind because the completely meaningful question about the justification of this presupposition, just as the question about the presupposition of the principle of morality, is already participating in the discursive situation and already offering the basic principle which this question puts into doubt. Everyone who speaks or who acts already and at each moment of her or his life partakes in a virtual discussion and this participation *nolens volens* is a voluntary endorsement of the transcendental communicative society (Apel, 1973).

The use of arguments, and the entire process of argumentation, requires specific and highly developed communicative competencies, and it presupposes a number of logical and empirical conditions. Above all, it necessitates a 'virtualization of the constraints of action' (McCarthy, 1981: 291), i.e., a break with the normal context of interaction. Such a break has to occur on two levels. First, the pressure to act and to make decisions has to be temporarily suspended. We have already mentioned that the collective dealt with this requirement procedurally by setting aside special meetings for its criticism sessions. Second, it requires a 'putting out of play of all motives except that of a willingness to come to a rationally grounded agreement' (McCarthy, 1981: 292). In ordinary communication situations people's motivations, their individual or personal needs and interests, are unproblematically integrated into their actions and experiences. In order to allow for thematization, evaluation, and critique of norms which regulate socially acceptable pursuits of interests, and to determine which interests are generalizable and which have to remain particular, the link between motivations and actions has to be temporarily suspended. This does not mean that individual interests are discarded or suppressed as irrelevant, rather they themselves, their interpretations, and the claim of norms which regulate them, are under scrutiny. Or, put in another way: here the theoretical, truth-seeking interest is allowed to prevail. Thus, it is the compulsory force of needs and interests themselves which is put out of play in order to enable the participants of critical argumentation to look at them and to question them. They remain in the centre of attention because an agreement is sought in regard to their truth and meaning but they are lifted out of the context of everyday urgency to the level of discourse.

To be able to disentangle critique of needs from the conditions of those needs would signify the existence of a 'rational will', i.e., both in the form of a willingness to submit to a process of rational persuasion, and in the form of a capacity to keep the strength of needs and interests in guiding action at bay. This means not only that the participants have to present themselves truthfully, but also that they have to be able to do so by knowing what motivates their actions and whether their expressed intentions converge with their real ones. The whole enterprise of determining common interests is seriously endangered if mechanisms of deception and self-deception, however unintended, prevail. This is a problem all the more difficult to address and to control because by its very nature it eludes the influence of discursive speech or argumentation.

Self-deception and self-reflection

Speech and action which are guided by motives that remain opaque and impenetrable to individual consciousness function very much in the same way as lying. In terms of the underlying communicative structure, lying is a form of strategic action which consciously employs deception for the sake of private benefit. Similarly, compulsive action based on unconscious intentions is a form of deception and self-deception. On a conscious level, the members of the collective may sincerely believe that their action is orientated towards mutual understanding when in reality they follow the purely private dictates of their own unrecognized needs and interests. In other words, they act strategically where they believe that they act communicatively, thus directly contradicting the collective's overall orientation towards mutual understanding. Habermas calls this specific illusion or deception a 'communicative pathology' where the pathological character is measured against the ideal of undistorted communication (Habermas, 1981:445). One may say that such a pathological form of communication signifies the effect of oppression on the deep structure of individual identity and personality, if needs are understood not as quasi-natural entities lodged in the deep recesses of the non-social self, but as fully steeped in the matrix of established social norms. Because norms 'regulate legitimate chances of need gratification' (Habermas, 1973a: 251), they regulate which needs are allowed to be gratified and by whom, and which ones are subject to various censoring and repressing mechanisms. The normative systems of 'femininity' and 'masculinity' can be called such a highly lopsided, unjust system of regulating chances for need gratification. Moreover, norms not only regulate what is considered a legitimate chance of need gratification, but also the production and reproduction of certain need structures and need dispositions which are the result as well as the sustaining force of such regulatory systems.

It can be said that such a regulatory system is truly successful only when it has become a permanent fixture of the human psyche, i.e., when the ban on the pursuit of certain interests has become an internal censoring mechanism, organizing all experience according to its own inexorable logic. In a stunting, if not perverting sense, it makes for a certain consistency in human behaviour which is, owing to its undiscerned and mashed nature, symptomatically expressed in the rigidity of stereotypical behaviour. In her consciousness-raising group Manuela Freire observes the way 'the conditioning of our emotional lives' appears in the form of a 'consistency with which the same woman reacted in the face of the various situations of her life, and also by the way she repeated several attitudes with regard to the group' (Freire, 1979: 115). This description is reminiscent of the problem of stereotypical acting out of certain experiential 'scenes' discussed earlier. Such acting out then expressed the effect of normative expectations crystallized into 'roles', and the problem was posed primarily in terms of the power of ideologies to seal off or diffuse the dimension of criticizability of norms. This primarily cognitive difficulty could be addressed and rectified through a methodical enactment of 'systematic doubt' over against the legitimacy of such ideological systems of explanation and justification, and over against prevailing interpretative schemata of experience. In this section we are concerned with the underlying individual-psychological deep structure of norms and normative systems as reflected in a certain need disposition and self-identity. As such it eludes and is a prelude to the direct, conscious intervention of discursive speech. Cognition remains a problem, however. Although unconscious motivations are by definition beyond the control of consciousness, the communicative situation implies the rational will-power to render them accessible. Furthermore, because the relevant repressed motivations are entangled in a common social structure, the explication of this public matrix unmasks *ipso facto* these motivations, even if the mechanisms remain functioning. Not only do such motivations, and the unrecognized (repressed) needs and desires, organize experience, they themselves were at some point of individual development organized by experience in the sense of coming into conflict with established norms and taboos, and became 'de-symbolized' in the process (Habermas, 1970: 208). To render them accessible to consciousness therefore means to reinsert them into the linguistic structure, i.e., into the symbolic universe of meaning and interpretations. Regardless of the specifics of the method or procedure employed for such re-symbolization, it cannot be modelled after the characteristics of discursive speech but will have to be some kind of 'creative language extension', however 'guided by theoretical propositions' (Habermas, 1970: 209; McCarthy, 1981: 201). Thus, a procedure aimed at a dissolution of the reified and alienating determinants of individual self-identity is, in a peculiarly contradictory fashion, dependent on the cognitive work of plausible, theoretical systems and explanations. Without an adequate theory there is no hope that the state of self-estrangement created by unconscious motivations could be overcome.

From consciousness-raising we are familiar with a similarly close relationship and mutual dependency of availability of adequate interpretations and descriptions of needs and interests, and the ability to recognize them. Women were and still are struggling with the implications of an established discourse which has prescribed and imposed upon them what they are supposed to think, feel and want, thereby excluding or suppressing the reality of women's experience and interests. In consciousness-raising groups women tried to overcome this 'line of fault' which separates women's experience 'from the social forms of thought available in which to express it and make it actionable' (Smith, 1979: 1981). They tried to shape the first building-blocks towards correct and critical articulation of female experience. The present debates taking place in the women's movement on the structure of sexual desire testify to the extraordinary practical as well as theoretical difficulty with what can be called irrational needs and impulses as expressed, for instance, in sado-masochistic fantasies and desires (Linden *et al.*, 1982: Snitow *et al.*, 1983). Bartky (1983), who investigated and evaluated a great number of theories of sexual desire, likewise comes to the conclusion that it is as much a problem of adequate theory as of adequate praxis to rationalize sexual desire.

To be sure, the analysis has now shifted the focus from the problem of unconscious needs and desires, i.e., a problem of transparency of self, to the problem of a contradiction between one's need-economy and one's conscious beliefs and convictions. Such a contradiction where 'the structure of one's desire is at war with one's principles' is itself a result of damage done to the self, signifying the effect of coercion and violence on form as well as content of psychosexual dynamics, where the forces that produce the mechanisms of repression are the same as the forces that produce irrational needs (Bartky, 1983). What can be perceived as stereotypical behaviour from the standpoint of an observer is now painfully experienced as the obsessional character of deep-seated needs and desires. In a context like the collective, where the principle of conscious control, and consequently of conscious creation of rational forms of action and interaction is embraced, such a contradiction produces anxiety and guilt and may in turn lead to a variety of conscious and unconscious manoeuvres to avoid emergence or thematization of this conflict. We are therefore not only dealing with a problem of pseudo-communication where the force of unrecognized needs and interests to shape behaviour 'produces a system of reciprocal misunderstandings which, due to the false assumption of consensus are not recognized as such' (Habermas, 1970: 206). But we are also dealing with the additional related problem of inadmissability of certain needs and interests because they would come into conflict with the emotional and motivational requirements of the collective situation.

Within the framework of this paper I cannot sufficiently illustrate this complicated, multifaceted difficulty without myself running the risk of over-simplification and stereotyping. In general, the gravest conflicts seemed to arise out of the contradiction between the demands for criticism, i.e., the setting of distances and the laying bare of divisions and conflicts, and strong tendencies towards building harmonious, even symbiotic relationships. Those tendencies can – with some reservation – be considered a result of typically feminine socialization. Such a specifically female emotionality has been observed and investigated by several feminist authors (Batchelder and Marks, 1979; Freire, 1979; 'Der lange aufgestaute Mut', 1978).

In the course of describing the nature and the dynamics of the problem some elements, and some conditions, have already emerged for a process specifically orientated towards elucidating the obscure economy of needs, and of overcoming their tyranical rule. Because dominance has the two-sided reality of a mechanism of force which self-perpetuatingly banishes certain contents of experience from consciousness, and which lives on in the irrational nature of the needs themselves thus branded with the mark of power, such a process of elucidation and overcoming must likewise be two-pronged.

It is not a shortcoming that the women's movement has not developed a separate organizational form of self-reflection but rather has predictably degenerated into a form of psycho-therapy with its individualistic and ultimately conformist assumptions wherever it attempted to do so. It rather testifies to the principle that a process of self-reflection on behalf of personal identity cannot be severed from questions of morality to which the normative dimension of needs and interests is fully tied. Self-reflection can only be one moment in the overall process of questioning the mechanisms, and the theoretical explanations of these mechanisms, which produced irrational needs and need structures. In other words, it must be fully embedded in the process of methodically thematizing and overcoming the effects of power, itself adding an important dimension, and an important conscious concern, to that process.

M. Freire's description of the conscious analysis taking place in her consciousness-raising group provides us with the proof[2] that women can through the medium of consciousness-raising disentangle themselves from the conditions of their needs and come to an understanding about the nature of those needs. Although without the initial moment of conscious recognition such understanding would be impossible, the actual behaviour-guiding force of the needs and need dispositions recognized will have to be unlearnt slowly and over a long period of time. To wrench the individual person out of the grips of compulsion beyond the control of consciousness requires a different kind of interaction and process than critical argumentation or discourse. In other words, the prerequisite of 'unimpaired self-representation' (Habermas), i.e., of the absence of deception of self and others, and thus of a truly reciprocal relationship between autonomous human beings cannot be achieved through discourse itself.[3]

The collective damage done to the psyche of all women, however combined with personal and idiosyncratic disturbances, must be met with a collective cure. Because the problem of unconscious motivations is relevant within the context of interaction it must be addressed within the same context. As Bartky points out, some damages may not be able to be undone, and the best women can do is to try to alleviate the practical strength of those damages by embedding them into a collective culture which systematically fosters the progressive and rational tendencies of collectivity. This means that a counter-environment has to be created which would stop nourishing and reinforcing neurotic disturbances by systematically opening up dimensions of and capacities for experiences which are potentially present or rooted in feminine identity. Those experiences, and corresponding forms of interaction, will gain motivational strength only over a prolonged period of time where feminist practice is initiated and sustained.

Summary

In terms of the present concern with a concept of emancipatory education we can now describe it as a way methodically to deconstruct and systematically to organize everyday experience, opening up the dimension of criticizability of norms, and introducing forms of interaction which are based on mutual understanding. In other words, the practice and theory of the dissolution and reordering of experience faces the ideal of dominance-free communication. The implications of this practice and theory are translated into processes based on the rationality of communicative action. The three moments of thematization, formulation of common interests, and self-reflection are analytically distinct, because they address power on the three different levels of cognition, interaction, and motivation. In the lived experience, however, they are fully intertwined. Moreover, the all pervasiveness of power itself calls for a unified analysis, and for an all-embracing, comprehensive cure. I based my proposal for a three-dimensional concept of emancipatory education on experiences of women in the organized women's movement because they supply us with examples for emancipatory processes which a theory and practice of liberatory education has much to learn from. The experiences of women in consciousness-raising groups and feminist collectives served as illustrations for all practical attempts to recognize power in all its pervasiveness, thus throwing light on difficulties, obstacles, and problems any theory of liberation, including educational theory, has to grapple with. The premises which are to underly such a theory cannot be completely dissimilar from the premises underlying the various forms of organization of the women's movement.

In this paper the main emphasis was placed on the encompassing dimension of power as anchored in everyday experience, and branching out into the interior of the individual psyche, and into the exterior of ideological systems and explanations of this experience. The complex structure of communication, its normative fabric, and its deep structure of individual needs and need dispositions created and reinforced by prevailing patterns of interpretation, has to be reflected in the complexity of the concept of emancipatory education.

The question remains whether the institutions and institutional requirements of formal education allow for experiments with emancipatory education in the comprehensive sense developed here. Not only because of the systems requirements of those institutions but also because of well-entrenched, institutionalized expectations of students and teachers alike they provide little leeway for a fundamental questioning of social priorities inside and outside of educational institutions. Under these circumstances the simple act of providing factual information which has been suppressed or silenced because it would reveal the facts of social violence and injustice may bounce off the borders of a hermetically sealed consciousness which has a whole barrage of mechanisms at its disposal to avoid such thematization (Leithäuser *et al.*, 1977). I believe it is one of the most fundamental challenges for education to come to grips with such a situation theoretically, as well as practically. Precisely because education deals with cognition and aims at a maximum degree of differentiation of cognitive structures, socially and historically prevailing forms of total (not merely cognitive) consciousness must be studied. This is of special relevance for the field of adult education, since it deals with the results of many years of socialization in the form of well-entrenched habits of perception and experience. On the other hand, it is the adult working population which most keenly experiences the contradictions in society and the educational institutions.

Within the existing institutions emancipatory education may function primarily as a critical concept, generating a categorical framework for the study of power structures in the educational process. The limitations and constraints of formal educational institutions should therefore not be translated into limitations and constraints of educational inquiry which investigates the reality of power as well as the implications and concrete possibilities of liberatory education.

Notes

1 Probably every feminist is familiar with the problem of collapsing the distinction between political and personal in favour of the latter. In my interpretation, the original slogan 'the personal is political' denounced a false relationship between the two, and announced a new or different one, rather than extinguishing the distinction between personal and political altogether.

2 A West German social worker collective which met over a period of one and a

half years and analysed its own dynamics in relation to the general state of women's oppression provides us with another interesting and persuasive example of the close interconnectedness between interaction, self-reflection, and thematization. See 'Der lange aufgestaute Mut', 1978.

3 Habermas's own model of 'therapeutic discourse' is such an example of a fully separate, methodically enacted process of self-reflection modelled after the psychoanalytic method. While useful and illuminating in many respects, it must be rejected for a number of reasons. Not the least of these reasons is the obvious dependence of the psychoanalytic method on its concrete content which is highly problematic, if not altogether useless in terms of adequately capturing or explaining female experience. The patriarchal, and hence authoritarian, paradigm of psychoanalysis is repeated in the principally power-bound relationship between psychoanalyst and client, which comes to a peak in the – methodologically crucial – moment of transference. I am inclined to argue that the psychoanalyst/client dyad cannot do justice to the collective underside of neurotic disturbances. Granted that the psychoanalytic method may cure some isolated symptoms, we are here essentially talking about different kinds of neurotic disturbances, i.e., about a kind of 'collective neurosis'.

References

Apel, Karl-Otto 1973, *Transformation der Philosophie*, Vol. I, Frankfurt, Suhrkamp.

Bartky, Sandra Lee 1983, 'Feminine masochism and the politics of personal transformation'. Unpublished paper. University of Illinois at Chicago, Department of Philosophy.

Batchelder, Eleanor Olds and Marks, Linda Nathan 1979, 'Creating alternatives. A survey of women's projects', *Heresis 7*, Vol. 2, No. 2, pp. 97–127.

Cell, Charles P. 1977, *Revolution at Work: Mass Mobilization Campaigns in China*, New York, Academic Press.

'Der lange aufgestaute Mut' 1978, *Sozialmagazin*, September, pp. 20–33.

Dietze, Gabriele (Ed.) 1979, *Die Uberwindung der Sprachlosigkeit*, Darmstadt and Neuwied, Luchterhand.

Foucault, Michel 1980, *Power/Knowledge*. Selected interviews and other writings, edited by Colin Gordon. New York, Pantheon Books.

Freire, Manuela 1979, 'How the mother/daughter relationship influences the method of women's liberation', *The Second Sex – Thirty Years Later: A Commemorative Conference on Feminist Theory*, mimeographed, New York, Institute for the Humanities.

Freire, Paulo 1970, *Pedagogy of the Oppressed*, New York, Seabury Press.

Friedan, Betty 1963, *The Feminine Mystique*, New York, Dell.

Habermas, Jürgen 1969, *Technik und Wissenschaft als 'Ideologie'*, Frankfurt, Suhrkamp.

Habermas, Jürgen 1970, 'On systematically distorted communication', *Inquiry*, Vol. 13, No. 4, pp. 360–375.

Habermas, Jürgen 1973a, 'Wahrheitstheorien', *Wirklichkeit und Reflexion, Festschrift für Walter Schulz*, edited by Helmut Fahrenbach. Pfullingen, Verlag Günther Neske.

Habermas, Jürgen 1973b, 'A postscript to knowledge and human interest', *Philosophy of the Social Sciences*, 3, pp. 157–189.

Habermas, Jürgen 1974, 'Rationalism Divided in Two: A Reply to Albert', *Positivism and Sociology*, edited by Anthony Giddens. London, Heinemann, pp. 195–223.

Habermas, Jürgen 1975, *Legitimation Crisis*, Boston, Beacon Hill.

Habermas, Jürgen 1976, 'Some distinctions in universal pragmatics', *Theory and Society*, 3, pp. 155–167.

Habermas, Jürgen 1979, *Communication and the Evolution of Society*, Boston, Beacon Press.

Habermas, Jürgen 1981, *Theorie des kommunikativen Handelns*. Vol. I: *Handlungsrationalität und gesellschaftliche Rationalisierung*. Vol. II: *Zur Kritik der funktionalistischen Vernunft*, Frankfurt, Suhrkamp.

Hinton, William 1966, *Fanshen*, New York, Vintage Books.

Leithauser, T., Volmerg, B., Salje, G., Volmerg, U. and Wutka, B. 1977, *Entwurf zu einer Empirie des Alltagsbewußtseins*, Frankfurt, Suhrkamp.

Linden, Robin Ruth, Pagano, Darlene R., Russel, Diana E.H., and Leigh-Star, S. (Eds.) 1982, *Against Sado-Masochism*, East Palo Alto, Frog in the Well.

McCarthy, Thomas 1981, *The Critical Theory of Jürgen Habermas*, Cambridge, The MIT Press.

Mezirow, Jack 1981, 'A critical theory of adult learning and education', *Adult Education*, Vol. 32, No. 1, pp. 3–24.

Rowbotham, Sheila 1974, *Woman's Consciousness, Man's World*, Baltimore, Penguin Books.

Smith, Dorothy, 1979, 'A sociology for women', in Sherman, Julia A. (Ed.) *The Prism of Sex: Essays in the Sociology of Knowledge*, Madison, The University of Wisconsin Press, pp. 135–187.

Snitow, Ann, Stansell, Christine and Thompson, Sharon (Eds.) 1983, *Powers of Desire*, New York, Monthly Review Press.

Whyte, Martin King 1974, *Small Groups and Political Rituals in China*, Berkeley, University of California Press.

4 Adult literacy and the mode of production

Frank Youngman

The problem of the eradication of illiteracy has dominated international adult education since the establishment of UNESCO after the Second World War. The period has been characterized by different approaches in the field (such as fundamental education, functional literacy, the psychosocial approach) and by international declarations, such as those of the World Conference of Ministers of Education on the Eradication of Illiteracy in 1965 and the International Symposium for Literacy in 1975. But the statistics on illiteracy have given continued cause for concern because although the percentage of illiterate adults in the world has been falling (1950: 44.3%; 1960: 39.3%; 1970: 32.4%; 1980: 28.9%), the total number has risen with the increase in population (from 700 million in 1950 to 814 million in 1980). Also the global totals mask the particular problem of the Third World – in 1980 the estimated percentage of illiterate adults in Africa was 60.6% and in Asia 38.4% (UNESCO, 1982).

The achievement of universal literacy is therefore a major concern of adult education and this concern is reflected in the vast literature on the subject. However, much of this literature is descriptive and even where analysis has been attempted it has failed to explain statisfactorily the successes and failures in the struggle to eradicate illiteracy. In my view this is because such analysis has usually been derived from approaches which are empiricist and which do not theorise adequately the relationship of education to society. I believe that this relationship is most comprehensively conceptualized within Marxist theory and that a Marxist approach can provide insight into the question of universal literacy.

In this article I put forward the suggestion that a key concept of Marxist social theory – the mode of production – provides a useful analytical tool for a better understanding of the development of literacy in society (and thus furnishes the theoretical basis for an improved practice of adult literacy work). This suggestion is made within the context of the renaissance of Marxist theory that has taken place during the last twenty years and its increasing application to the field of adult education (Youngman, forthcoming). In particular, useful foundations for this analysis have been laid by the International Council for Adult Education's project on the political economy of adult education (Healey, 1983).

The article is essentially a theoretical one, putting forward a hypothesis that needs to be verified by the investigation of specific historical and contemporary societies. The hypothesis is this: the rate of literacy in any given society is conditioned by the extent to which the pre-capitalist modes of production have been transformed by either capitalism or socialism. This is a proposition rooted in the theory of historical materialism which, while according a certain degree of autonomy to education, asserts that in the end its nature (like that of other social institutions) is shaped by the economic basis of society (Engels, 1890). It is my contention that this hypothesis has greater explanatory and predictive power than current reasons given for the spread of literacy and it can therefore clear away some of the confusion which clouds the issue. In order to establish this position, I will first introduce the relevant Marxist concepts and then relate them to education and the development of literacy.

The mode of production

The concept of the mode of production is a central element of Marxist theory. Considered abstractly, a mode of production is a combination of the forces of production and the social relations of production. The forces of production include the means of production (such as land, raw materials, tools, machinery) and human labour (embodying knowledge and skill). The relations of production are the social relationships people enter into in the process of production, and are defined by who owns and controls the means of production.

In concrete terms, several different modes of production can be identified historically. They are differentiated according to the way in which products are distributed within society. In the earliest mode, primitive communalism, production through hunting and gathering and basic agriculture was at a very low level, land was held communally, and products were shared among the members of society. But once the development of settled agriculture had enabled the production of a surplus beyond immediate subsistence needs, the possibility arose of a social division of labour with one class appropriating the surplus product from the class of direct producers. The way this appropriation takes place is used to define subsequent modes of production:

> What distinguishes the various economic formations of society – the distinction between for example a society based on slave-labour and a society based on wage-labour – is the form in which this surplus labour is in each case exorted from the immediate producer...
>
> (Marx, 1867: 325)

The form of appropriation is determined by ownership of the means of production and therefore the nature of the relations of production provides the key to identifying a particular mode of production.

Marx used the concept to differentiate historical epochs, regarding the different modes as stages in the evolution of higher forms of society. In a famous passage he wrote:

> In broad outlines Asiatic, ancient, feudal and modern bourgeois modes of production can be designated as progressive epochs in the economic formation of society.
>
> (Marx, 1859: 329)

It is important to note that he did not regard these stages of social evolution in a unilinear way. Although human society began with the primitive communal mode of production, its evolution globally and historically has taken several different directions from that starting point (Gandy, 1979; Melotti, 1977). Sometimes a mode has remained relatively static for a long period, such as the Asiatic mode in China. Sometimes external forces have extinguished a mode, as in the case of the ancient mode of the Roman Empire. One mode, feudalism in Western Europe, underwent an internal process of development from the thirteenth century, resulting eventually in the capitalist mode of production. By the late nineteenth century this mode had spread so that it had made an impact on the rest of the world. During the twentieth century, it has been superseded by the socialist mode of production in several parts of the globe. The historical development of modes of production, therefore, has been an uneven process.

To summarize: the concept of the mode of production provides an analytical tool for the historical differentiation of societies. There have been the following modes: primitive communalism, a variety of pre-capitalist modes, capitalism and socialism. The central feature of all pre-capitalist modes is that they are based primarily on agricultural production and the mass of direct producers work on the land and produce their own means of subsistence. The ownership and control of land therefore shapes the mode of production by determining forms of appropriation of the surplus. However, capitalism is distinguished above all by the separation of producers from the land, so that their existence is dependent on selling their labour for wages. The owners of the means of production appropriate surplus labour in the form of profit. Socialism, on the other hand, is characterised by forms of collective ownership of the agricultural and industrial means of production and by socially regulated distribution.

The social formation

Although it is possible to define the historical existence of different modes of production, none of them has ever existed on its own in isolation. At any given time, there may be several modes evident in a society, although one will be dominant and thus define the character of the society. The totality of varying economic relations forms the basis of the social entity which Marx called the 'social formation'. As Gandy expresses it, this includes a configuration of modes: 'A formation embraces both the past and the future: dying modes of production; the dominant, defining mode; and seeds of coming modes' (Gandy 1979: 151).

The major focus of Marx's own analysis was the capitalist mode of production. He showed how it arose from pre-capitalist modes and how it would be superseded by socialism. The nature of the transition from one mode to another has been a centre of debate since Marx's time, not least because of its practical consequences for political activity. Since the 1960s, two particularly relevant debates have been going on. One has centred on the development of capitalism in the Third World. The other has considered the nature of socialist societies.

The first debate has been concerned with the character of the Third World societies which have been incorporated into the world capitalist system. Investigation has focused on the survival of pre-capitalist modes and the relationship between these internal structures and the external penetration of capitalism. Controversy has arisen over whether the expansion of capitalism immediately eliminates pre-capitalist modes or whether it interacts ('articulates') with them to the extent of sometimes reinforcing them. The debate (Foster-Carter, 1978) has been complex and in my view it has often been misconceived.

It is clear that Marx did not dichotomise the above alternatives. Rather he conceived the transition from one mode of production to another as a lengthy historical process of transition in which both internal factors, such as class contradictions, and external ones, such as conquest, might play a part. Different modes of production compete and overlap, so that at any given historical point a social formation has not only a dominant mode but also subordinate modes. His own detailed study in *Capital, Volume 1* illustrates the process. Here he shows how capitalism arose within the feudal mode of production (so that in sixteenth century England it was therefore a subordinate mode), and how it passed through several phases of development from handicraft production to large scale industry, finally displacing feudalism and becoming the dominant mode in the nineteenth century. But even with capitalism dominant, aspects of feudalism remained:

> Peasant agriculture on a small scale and production by independent artisans, both of which, on the one hand, form the basis of the feudal mode of production, and, on the other hand, appear alongside capitalist production after the dissolution of the feudal mode...
>
> (Marx 1867: 452)

Also the basis of a new socialist mode of production had been laid by the creation of the working class. A social formation must therefore be analysed in a historical perspective that grasps the process of change in modes of production that is taking place. Taylor's book *From Modernization to Modes of Production* (Taylor, 1979) is an example of one approach to this kind of analysis of Third World capitalist social formations.

The second of the current debates has not been explicitly related to the first but in fact is concerned with a different aspect of the same problem. This debate has considered the character of those societies in which a socialist mode of production may be said to be emerging from both capitalist and pre-capitalist modes. It has been provoked by the theory and practice of Mao Tse Tung since the revolution in China in 1949. Mao stressed the continuing influence of capitalist and pre-capitalist modes of production on China's attempts to establish socialism. In his analysis he identified the basis of this influence in forms of individual ownership of land and capital which had not been eliminated; in ways of thinking developed prior to 1949 which persisted in adults; and in the impact of foreign capitalism. He was emphatic that classes and class struggle exist within socialism. Other Marxists have applied this approach to the variety of existing socialist societies – for example, Bettleheim in his monumental work on the USSR (Bettleheim, 1976: 9–55).

What has seldom been clear in this second debate, is that it is really only an attempt to grapple with the concrete application to certain twentieth century social formations of Marx's concept of socialism as a transitional period between capitalism and communism. He had characterized this period as one 'which is … in every respect, economically, morally, intellectually, stamped with the birthmarks of the old society from whose womb it emerges' (Marx, 1875: 17). The nature of the effects of the old society on the new socialist society can in fact be helpfully studied with the analytical tool of the mode of production.

Both these debates have been highly controversial and have generated a lot of heat within Marxism. But they have also thrown light on important issues and it is possible to draw conclusions on which to base research hypotheses. For my purpose here, I conclude that it is possible to undertake the concrete analysis of a particular social formation (whether capitalist or socialist) using the concept of the mode of production. As we shall see, an identification of the different modes of production which are present can provide a key for understanding the nature of education in the given social formation.

The reproduction of modes of production

For a mode of production to continue its historical existence, it must have the capacity to reproduce itself. Indeed, the dominance of any one mode in a social formation can be gauged by the exent of the conditions necessary for its reproduction and the correspondingly restricted conditions of other modes.

Reproduction basically means the continual repetition of the cycle of production and consumption, a cycle which has a typical form according to the mode of production. It is based on the reproduction of the forces of production, so that the means of production used up in the labour processes (such as tools and raw materials) are replaced and the human labour power is maintained and renewed from generation to generation. It is also based on the reproduction of the social relations of production, so that the existence of the different social classes must be continually renewed. In feudalism, for example, the cycle is based on the serf spending part of his time producing for his own consumption and part of his time producing tribute for consumption by the lord. The destruction of crops, animals, seeds and so on through war or natural disaster would endanger reproduction. Similarly, the abolition of the social relation of serfdom would break the cycle. The necessary conditions for the reproduction of a given mode of production can therefore be specified and their presence or absence in a social formation identified.

The pre-requisites of capitalism are generalised commodity production (i.e., the production of goods for sale rather than personal use), the accumulation of capital, and above all the existence of free wage labour. The fundamental condition for the establishment and reproduction of capital is therefore the separation of producers from the means of production, so that they are forced to work for wages. It is essential to note the role of the state in this process. Marx wrote of its role in England in the seventeenth century:

> ...the power of the state, the concentrated and organised forces of society, to hasten, as in a hothouse, the process of transformation of the feudal mode of production into the capitalist mode, and to shorten the transition. Force ... is itself an economic power.
>
> (Marx, 1867: 915–916)

This is important because the penetration of capitalism in the Third World is very much associated with the role of the state in creating the conditions for capitalist reproduction. Arrighi's classic essay on Rhodesia gives an example from colonial Africa on state measures such as forced labour, taxation and land expropriation in creating a proletariat (Arrighi, 1973). The existence of the proletariat (i.e., working class) is the basis of the reproduction of capitalism.

The pre-requisites of socialism include the collective ownership of the means of production, the socialisation of labour, and the social (rather than individual) regulation of decisions about production and consumption. For industry, this is achieved by nationalisation and central planning. Industrial production requires a working class separated from the land

and working for wages defined as a share of the social product distributed according to work undertaken. Agricultural production requires co-operative ownership of the means of production and therefore an end to individual possession of land, animals and so on. Myrdal's book *Report from a Chinese Village* illustrates the process of socialist development in agriculture in one area of China between 1948 and 1958 (Myrdal, 1975). It began with the expropriation of landowners and the distribution of land to individual peasants, passed through the formation of labour exchange groups and mutual aid teams to a basic co-operative of thirty households and a higher co-operative of four villages, and culminated in the establishment of a commune comprising fourteen hundred households. The process consisted of a movement away from individual production towards collective ownership and social decision-making about the use of the products (divided into an accumulation fund for new means of production, a reserve fund, and a consumption fund for personal income and social services).

The significant point here is that the reproduction of both capitalism and socialism is based on the destruction of pre-capitalist modes of production which depend for their reproduction on the producers remaining tied to the land. In particular this means that the peasant class, which by definition is composed of those who work on the land and possess their own means of production (such as implements, animals and land itself), is essentially a transitional class which is ultimately broken down by the expansion of capitalism or socialism within the social formation.

In this section I have discussed the reproduction of modes of production primarily in terms of its economic dimension. But in fact the process also takes place at other levels and I turn to this next.

Education and reproduction

The mode of production constitutes the economic basis of society. But the social whole also included political and ideological institutions. Marx's formulation of this is well known:

> The sum total of these relations of production constitutes the economic structure of society, the real foundation, on which rises a legal and political super-structure and to which correspond definite forms of social consciousness. The mode of production of material life conditions the social, political and intellectual life process in general. It is not the consciousness of men that determines their being, but, on the contrary, their social being that determines their consciousness.
>
> (Marx, 1859: 503)

The nature of education must be considered within the context of reproduction and with the recognition that it is 'conditioned' by the mode of production. It is important to stress that the Marxist analysis of education is not one of crude economic determinism and that there is a complex relationship between the economic basis of society and the institutions of the super-structure (Williams, 1977: 75–94). Thus the word 'conditions' has the sense of limiting and influencing the nature of education rather than determining its precise form. However, in broad terms it is possible to identify a correspondence between different modes of production and different forms of education.

Education in pre-capitalist societies was primarily undertaken within the family. Training in craft and agricultural skills was acquired through practical work experience in family-based production. Social roles were inculcated in the home. But various forms of institutional education did exist. In modes with a limited social division of labour, these forms were restricted to short periods of instruction, as in initiation schools in Africa. But where the division of labour was more advanced, longer term education was provided for specific groups, such as the members of the ruling class, like the mandarin bureaucracy in China, or skilled workers, like the apprentices of feudal Europe. However, in no pre-capitalist society was there any form of universal institutional education.

This kind of mass education first arose to meet the reproduction needs of capitalism. The clearest exposition of this is to be found in the writings of Bowles and Gintis, particularly in their book *Schooling in Capitalist America* (Bowles and Gintis, 1976). Here they develop theoretically an analysis of the relationship of education to the capitalist mode of production and illustrate it in terms of the experience of the USA, paying particular attention to how developments within this mode (such as the shift from competition to monopoly) affect education. Since the dominance of capitalism in the nineteenth century, the characteristic form of education has been mass public education. Bowles and Gintis argue that mass education was developed not only to provide the skills and expertise to reproduce the forces of production but also to prepare people ideologically and culturally to work under the prevailing social relations of production.

They focus on the USA but their analysis is also relevant to forms of education accompanying capitalist penetration of the Third World. The previously noted process of proletarianisation in Rhodesia gave rise to education that was concerned with legitimating the new relations of production. The Rhodesia Chamber of Mines Report of 1905 argued that:

> ...the form of education suited to the status of the native and the requirements of his position is one which inculcates in the first instance habits of order, discipline and obedience with a view to rendering the native actually useful to his employer and accustoming him to look upon work as the natural means of earning a livelihood.
>
> (Van Onselen, 1980: 182)

The expansion of capitalism has invariably been accompanied by the expansion of educational institutions designed to contribute to reproduction by developing the differentiated intellectual capabilities required by the labour market and by engendering the ideology and social practices which legitimate the social order. (Of course because of the essential class antagonism at the basis of capitalism, educational institutions have also reproduced this inherent conflict (Apple, 1982: 12–35).) In general the development of capitalism has involved a process of de-skilling, as producers with craft and agricultural skills have entered into increasingly fragmented and unskilled jobs. Thus although some areas of capitalist production require high levels of skill, most jobs do not. However the formation of attitudes is crucial (as the quotation above from Rhodesia indicates) and appropriate forms of consciousness have to be established and then reproduced. (The replacement of pre-capitalist concepts of time because of work which has an even intensity throughout the year and which is accounted for in hours provides a fascinating example (Thompson, 1967).) Also, cognitive skills like literacy are important. Education within a social formation in which the capitalist mode of production is dominant is therefore characterised by general education for all, vocational training for a small group of skilled workers, and higher education for an even smaller group of owners, managers and bureaucrats.

The socialist mode of production has also been accompanied by the development of mass education. Here widespread education has been designed to raise the level of the productive forces (particularly through scientific and technical education) and to develop the attitudes and skills necessary for the new social relations of production which are based on co-operation and participatory decision-making. Bowles has written on this in his study of education in Cuba, which looks at the correspondence between education and the economy before and after the revolution of 1959 (Bowles, 1971). He illustrates how the process of superseding capitalism is reflected in changes in the education system. It needs to be added that the conflict between the two modes is also reflected within education. For example, Castles and Wustenberg (1979: 101–138) provide an account of the development of education in China between 1949 and 1976 which shows clearly how the continuing class struggle within the Chinese social formation led to a series of contradictory changes in educational policy.

To conclude: education is part of the super-structure of society and is an important aspect of the reproduction of modes of production. Its nature reflects the nature of the particular social formation. The specific question we can now address is this: how does literacy relate to the mode of production?

Literacy and the mode of production

Although in many pre-capitalist social formations there was no written language, in others there was the technology of writing. Indeed the first written codes appeared in Mesopotamia five thousand years ago. This fact requires a more lengthy and rigorous differentiation between pre-capitalist social formations than I am able to undertake here. However, it is clear that the technology of literacy only arose when the dominant mode of production had a marked social division of labour (including the basic division between mental and manual labour) and had therefore developed away from the communal stage. Those social formations closest to the communal mode – such as much of pre-colonial Africa south of the Sahara – did not have written languages. But other modes, such as the Asiatic mode in China and India, and the ancient mode in Greece and Rome, provided the conditions for the development of writing. The main characteristic of literacy in these modes is that it remained in control of the ruling class – aristocrats, priests, administrators and traders.

As Goody put it in *Literacy in Traditional Societies* (Goody, 1968), literacy remained 'restricted' to a relatively small group in society and did not become 'widespread'. (It should be noted that he argues that literacy was in fact wide-spread in ancient Greece, but this seems to me as dubious as considering ancient Greece a democracy – both ideas rest on ignoring the slave population whom the Greeks defined as 'non-citizens'.) This phenomenon of restricted literacy in what he calls 'traditional' societies led him to consider a key question:

> The factors that restrain the full development of literacy are many. As in other fields, social restrictions continue despite the release from technological limitations. What specific factors prevent the realisation of the full potentialities of literacy?
>
> (Goody, 1968: 11)

However, his own attempt to answer this question seems to me unsatisfactory precisely because he lacks a materialist theory of society. The identifications of factors such as 'the tendency to secrecy, to restrict the circulation of books' (Goody, 1968: 11) is superficial and lacking in explanatory power. Rather the explanation must be sought in the nature of the mode of production. Until there were changes in the social relations of production, the technology of literacy could not become widespread.

Historically, the spread of literacy beyond the restricted access of a ruling class was in the first instance a result of the development of the capitalist mode of production. Capitalism made economic demands for a work force with appropriate cognitive skills and, just as importantly, ideological demands for new values and behaviours. Literacy provided an important means of meeting these reproductive demands and it spread as the social relations of capitalism spread. To the extent that the development of capitalism has been uneven in terms of displacing pre-capitalist modes, so the spread of literacy has been uneven. Thus in Europe, the literacy rate is higher in England than in Eire, and in northern Italy than in southern Italy. In the Third World, it is higher in Chile than in Chad. But the historical tendency is that when capitalism achieves dominance within a social formation there is movement towards universal literacy, as in northern Europe, North America and Japan.

However, widespread literacy is also a consequence of the socialist mode of production. In the previously cited book on China by Myrdal, time and again the adult informants he interviewed refer to how the change in their social existence brought about by the collectivisation of agriculture changed their consciousness. In particular, they speak of the need to have the skills of literacy in order to undertake the tasks of organising production and participating in decision-making about their society. As one man said:

> I have never went to school for more than one winter, when I was nine; but since then I have attended several reading courses. In addition, I have learned by doing the work. I was compelled to learn quite a bit, while I was keeping the work journal and the record of labour points for the labour group for mutual help ... I can now read the newspaper and write letters.
>
> (Myrdal, 1975: 99)

The development of the productive forces (especially through industrialisation and the mechanisation of agriculture) and the changed social relations of production make literacy a necessity. Therefore the historical tendency of socialism is also towards universal literacy.

The development of this tendency within socialist societies depends on the exact nature of the social formation and particularly the extent to which precapitalist modes of production persist. Where capitalism has not penetrated deeply, as in Russia in 1917, the transformation of the existing relations of production takes a lengthy time and consequently the achievement of universal literacy is slow. For example, in the Soviet Union it took from 1917 to the early 1940s to reduce the adult illiteracy rate from around 70% to nothing. On the other hand, in Cuba in 1959 capitalism had already displaced pre-capitalist relations of production to a large extent. Thus the illiteracy rate amongst adults was only 24% and it was possible to reduce it in eight months of 1961 to 4% (Bhola, 1981).

At this stage I am able to formulate my hypothesis based on the foregoing discussion: the rate of literacy in any given society is conditioned by the extent to which the pre-capitalist modes of production have been transformed by either capitalism or socialism. In other words, the main factor restraining the development of universal literacy is the continuation of pre-capitalist relations of production (and, in particular, the persistence of the peasantry).

Universal literacy

The statistics quoted at the beginning of the article showed that the percentage of illiterate adults has fallen from 44.3% in 1950 to 28.9% in 1980 but that the total number has risen from 700 million in 1950 to 814 million in 1980 (UNESCO, 1982). It was noted that the extent of illiteracy amongst adults is not evenly distributed throughout the world but in fact high illiteracy rates are concentrated in the Third World (with Africa, for example, having 60.6% of adults illiterate in 1980). The practical problem of achieving universal literacy is therefore essentially the pre-occupation of adult educators in the Third World. Elsewhere it is a marginal concern which only occasionally takes on importance, as in Britain in the 1970s.

What significance, then, does my hypothesis have for the practice of adult education in the Third World? Fundamentally, it implies that the problems of spreading literacy are not primarily technical ones, rather they must be situated in the socio-economic context. Drop out, for example, must be seen in a perspective which regards motivation as a social product rather than an individual characteristic. (As the Chinese man quoted above says, he was 'compelled' by the changes in his social existence to become literate.) Thus the idea of a positive literacy climate, for instance, cannot be conceived abstractly. Even issues of teaching materials and techniques are secondary. Fernando Cardenal of the Nicaraguan literacy programme records Freire making this point:

> He stressed the importance of providing opportunities for learners to practise their creativity and added that within a liberating revolutionary process people would learn to read and write even with mediocre materials. The revolutionary context and methodology were more important than any isolated study programme or particular teaching techniques.
>
> (Cardenal and Miller, 1981: 17)

In fact although the attention given to Freire's work usually focuses on his method it is also necessary to consider the importance of its context. In Brazil in the early 1960s adult literacy programmes grew up in the context of the expanded capitalist penetration of the post-war period, and as a result of the development of the industrial and agricultural working class. In Guinea-Bissau in the late 1970s his work took place in the context of the development of socialist relations of production. It was this experience which has led Freire to put more emphasis on this aspect of the literacy process. The IDAC report *Guinea-Bissau '79-Learning and Living by Doing* draws attention to this change in thinking. It documents how the IDAC team reversed their approach, giving the example of how literacy was linked to a village's decision to establish a banana field to be cultivated collectively:

The diversification of the collective work in the field confronted the population with needs which constituted various areas of knowledge and skill to be explored ... It is interesting to emphasize here the reversal of the educational process. Thus, as the population's experience of changing the environment progresses, it becomes motivated to learn and to know more ... Writing reality precedes linguistic literacy. And it may be hoped that the objective conditions in which linguistic learning becomes possible and useful may in the future be established precisely through this deliberate and creative influence exerted by the community on its social environment...

(IDAC, 1979: 49)

The implication of my hypothesis is that the potential of purely educational measures in the field of literacy must be questioned and adult educators should locate their activities within the objective conditions of the social relations of production. Close analysis of the different relations of production in the particular social formation will clarify the potential for literacy and explain the differences between classes, regions and sexes, as well as between historical periods. (For examples of careful analysis of the production relations in different kinds of Third World social formation, see the *Review of African Political Economy* (1981) on Kenya and Houtart (1980) on Vietnam). Literacy programmes in, say, urban areas, agricultural co-operatives or the army, will be more successful than amongst nomads or peasant women not because of innate differences amongst people but because of the different socio-economic contexts. Literacy programmes must be linked to changes in the relations of production or they will flounder. It is the political character of these changes which finally raises the question of literacy for what – for better incorporation into an inherently unjust capitalist society, or for the capacity to build the egalitarian society envisaged by socialism?

Conclusion

In my opinion a lot of the writing on literacy exhibits considerable confusion about its socio-economic context. Dichotomies such as pre-industrial/industrial or traditional/modern are unhelpful categorisations. Indeed, so is the usage of the concept of the Third World if it fails to differentiate social formations as dissimilar as Vietnam and India, Mozambique and Kenya, Nicaragua and Brazil (all of which are of great interest in terms of their recent adult literacy programmes). This confusion stems from the theoretical inability to distinguish clearly between capitalism and socialism, and between them and the social formations which preceded them. Failure to do this leads to very unsatisfactory explanations of the factors in the achievement of literacy. For example, a recent international review of literacy research cites 'national will' (IDRC/ICAE, 1979: 12) as an important factor but it fails to specify what the concept means or to clarify its material basis in different societies such as early twentieth century Japan or contemporary Vietnam. Such explanations remain superficial because they are not derived from a theoretical framework which provides a coherent approach to the differentiation of societies and to the conceptualization of the relationship of literacy and society.

Similarly, Bhola in his recent book on adult literacy campaigns, *Campaigning for Literacy* (Bhola, 1981), tends to focus on political, ideological and technical issues and give an inadequate account of the underlying economic structures of the societies he is discussing. The book contains eight case studies from different countries but does not satisfactorily identify the nature of their different social formations. Thus in his study of the Brazilian Literacy Movement, which is his only example of a campaign from a non-socialist country, he fails to characterise Brazil as a specifically capitalist social formation. His advocacy of mass campaigns as a solution to the problem of literacy is therefore seriously weakened by his failure to theorise the socio-economic contexts of literacy.

This article has been deliberately theoretical. Its brevity and its intention of challenging prevailing idealist and technicist interpretations of literacy mean that it has presented a rather schematic argument on the basis of what is in fact a much more complex and subtle body of theory. However, I have tried to put forward a hypothesis for research which, by application to concrete situations and by further theoretical refinement, might improve our understanding of how to achieve a fully literate world.

References

Apple M. W. 1982, *Education and Power*, London, Routledge and Kegan Paul.

Arrighi, G. 1973, 'Labour supplies in historical perspective: a study of the proletarianisation of the African peasantry in Rhodesia', in Arrighi, G. and Saul. J. 1973, *Essays on the Political Economy of Africa*, New York and London, Monthly Review Press.

Bettleheim, C. 1976, *Class Struggles in the USSR First Period: 1917–1923*, New York and London, Monthly Review Press.

Bhola, H. S. 1981, *Campaigning for Literacy*. Report of a study submitted to unesco, 5 April 1981 on behalf of the International Council for Adult Education.

Bowles, S. 1971, 'Cuban education and revolutionary ideology', *Harvard Educational Review*, Vol. 41, No. 4, pp. 472–500.

Bowles, S. and Gintis, H. 1976, *Schooling in Capitalist America*, London, Routledge and Kegan Paul.

Cardenal, F. and Miller, V. 1981, 'Nicaragua 1980: the battle of the ABC's', *Harvard Educational Review*, Vol. 51, No. 1, pp. 1–26.

Castles, S. and Wustenberg, W. 1979, *The Education of the Future*, London, Pluto Press.

Engels, F. 1890, 'Letter to Bloch', in Marx, K. and Engels, F. 1969, *Selected Works, Volume 1*, Moscow, Progress Publishers.

Foster-Carter, A. 1978, 'The modes of production controversy', *New Left Review*, No. 107, pp. 47–77.

Gandy, D.R. 1979, *Marx and History*, Austin and London, University of Texas Press.

Goody, J. (Ed.) 1968, *Literacy in Traditional Societies*, London, Cambridge University Press.

Healey, P. 1983, 'The political economy of adult education', *Convergence*, Vol. XVI, No. 4, pp. 49–55.

Houtart, F. 1980, 'Problems of social transition – an example from Vietnam', *Ideas and Action*, No. 137, pp. 4–10.

IDAC 1979, *Guinea-Bissau '79. Learning by Living and Doing*, Geneva, IDAC.

IDRC/ICAE 1979, *The World of Literacy*, Ottawa, International Development Research Centre.

Mark, K. 1859, 'Preface to a contribution to the critique of political economy' in Marx, K. and Engels, F. 1969, *Selected Works, Volume 1*, Moscow, Progress Publishers.

Marx, K. 1867, *Capital, Volume 1*, Harmondsworth, Penguin, 1976.

Marx, K. 1875, 'Critique of the Gotha Programme', in Marx, K. and Engels, F. 1970. *Selected Works, Volume 3*, Moscow, Progress Publishers.

Melotti, U. 1977, *Marx and the Third World*, London, Macmillan.

Myrdal, J. 1975, *Report from a Chinese Village*, London, Pan Books.

Review of African Political Economy 1981. 'Kenya: The Agrarian Question', *Review of African Political Economy*, No. 20.

Taylor, J. G. 1979, *From Modernization of Modes of Production*, London, Macmillan.

Thompson, E.P. 1967, 'Time, work discipline and industrial capitalism', *Past and Present*, Vol. 38, pp. 56–97.

UNESCO 1982, *Literacy 81*, Paris, UNESCO.

van Onselen, C. 1980, *Chibaro*, London, Pluto Press.

Williams, R. 1977, *Marxism and Literature*, Oxford, Oxford University Press.

Youngman, F. 1985, (forthcoming). *Adult Education and Socialist Pedagogy*, London, Croom Helm.

5 Against modernity

Gandhi and adult education

Tom Steele[1] *and Richard Taylor*[2]
University of Leeds

Gandhi was one of the first life-long educationalists. Through his concept of Basic Education he tried to create a mode of learning which was both deeply spiritual and holistic. In this he was at odds with the western-inspired vocational approach advocated by Nehru and the Congress Party. Nehru privately regarded Gandhi as a reactionary 'magician' but stood in awe of his power over the people and subtly incorporated him into the nationalist project. Little remains of the craft-based decentred system Gandhi outlined at Wardha except for a few experimental ashrams. Drawing on some of the new Indian historiography we argue that Gandhi's inscription into the nationalist agenda maintained the division between an elite and the masses his educational system was designed to dissolve.

Since independence in 1947, Indian adult education has been dominated by an ideology of modernization. Inspired by western socialist ideas, Nehru and his successors have seen education as one of the key tools for transforming a backward, illiterate and predominantly rural society into a modern, industrial and materially productive national state. The main Indian educational perspectives of importance came from Gandhi and Tagore. Although ultimately unsuccessful, Gandhi's educational programme and arguments remain of considerable importance, for two interrelated reasons. Gandhi's general influence was so important a factor – symbolically as much as actually – in the course of Indian independence that his views on any aspect of Indian society are of interest. Second, because of Gandhi's coherent and in some respects extreme anti-colonialism, his educational philosophy is a part of a general ideological position which was fundamentally opposed to the culture, structures and practices of British colonial rule.

Gandhi's ideas on adult education cannot be separated from his ideas on education as a whole. Gandhi viewed education in a wholly ideological way, in the sense that he saw educational theory and practice as central to the life or death struggle of India (and other subject, colonial peoples) against western industrial civilization. He was opposed root and branch to the values embodied in and proselytized by mainstream western society as he argued in his most important writing on education, *Hind Swaraj,* in

1906 (Gandhi 1944[1906]). But Gandhi also pragmatically advocated the need for retaining practical elements of western education. For example, Brown (1989:91) notes that as late as 1908, 'he argued that an English education including study of English and the Sciences, was essential in the contemporary world. Without it they would be crippled and backward.' Education was viewed by Nehru and the nationalists primarily as vocational training in order to provide an increasingly skilled work-force to facilitate greater industrial progress and thus material welfare. This was anathema to Gandhi. He was opposed on fundamental philosophical grounds to western capitalism's culture of selfish, individualistic materialism. For him, the machine culture of industrial capitalism was the enemy of everything of value in human existence. This western culture threatened to destroy human spirituality and distract humanity from its rightful concerns of truth-seeking and communal, non-violent and harmonious social living. Gandhi was thus implacably opposed to developing an education system in India that was geared to replicating western 'progress'. As Krishna Kumar has put it, Gandhi located the 'problem of education in [the] dialectic ... of man versus machine' (Kumar 1989: 591).

The British system had created a rift between the educated elite, which was largely urban, and the massive rural population. One result was that the educated villagers left the rural areas and went to work in the towns as clerks or other functionaries. Villages were thus systematically deprived of their potential leadership cadres. In the end, the net effect of the British education system was the creation of an army of clerks whose only function was to administer the continuation of colonial ruling structures. It was hierarchical and elitist, and top heavy with higher education at the expense of primary education.

Nor was this Gandhi's only criticism. He also rejected the abstract and arts basis of western education. For Gandhi the real business of education was 'learning how to control the senses, and acquiring an ethical basis to life. Character-building, not the acquisition of a foreign language or irrelevant knowledge, was the need for India's millions' (Kumar 1989: 591). Although Gandhi did not develop his campaign for Basic Education programmes until the late 1930s (see below), the elements of his approach to education were clear by the end of the first decade of the 20th century. Education, both for children and for adults, should concentrate upon 'character-training rather than accumulation of knowledge, vernaculars as opposed to English, and learning through practical skills rather than book-based study' (Kumar 1989: 592).

It was Gandhi's conviction that the Congress movement was dominated by western-orientated, socialist, modernizing politicians that led him to give a new and urgent priority to education based upon rural India. Only through grass-roots reconstruction in the villages could a viable, independent and free India be created. Gandhi believed that the key to India's future lay in the villages, in rural India, and not in the towns.

The Wardha scheme

Gandhi's system of Basic Education was outlined at the Wardha National Education Conference of 1937:

1 There should be free compulsory education for seven years of all children on a national scale.
2 The medium of instruction should be the mother tongue.
3 The education should centre on manual and productive work and all other abilities to be taught should be related to the central handicraft.
4 The education should be self-financing through the production of some necessary material item like *khadi* which could pay the cost of the teacher and materials.

The Wardha conference was a direct response to the India Act of 1935, which, although not inaugurated until 1937, transferred substantial governmental power to eight of India's eleven provinces. Gandhi saw this as the opportunity to reconstruct the British imported educational system which had served the Indian people so poorly. Thus it was a consciously anti-imperialist strategy which anathematized, rhetorically at least, 'western' educational aims. Gandhi proposed that in the place of the British primary and secondary stratifications of education there should be one continuous schooling of at least seven years which should be called 'Basic' education. Whatever else followed would be based on this foundation. Gandhi believed that the artificial divisions imposed by the British system of primary and secondary education were both socially and personally divisive. Not only did secondary education depend on a rough division of children by social class but it broke the organic continuity of learning for the children themselves. He proposed that Basic Education should therefore be both universal and continuous.

Education should be clearly related to the needs of Indian independence and autonomy, to recognize her cultural difference from the West and the importance of maintaining the traditional practices of everyday Indian life. But Gandhi did not intend this to be a purely functional exercise in creating the efficiency state beloved of both Communist and western industrialized countries and insisted instead on inspiring the system with spiritual value. Central to this was the doctrine of non-violence:

> If we want to eliminate communal strife, and international strife, we must start with foundations pure and strong by rearing our younger generation on the education I have adumbrated. The plan springs out of non-violence. ... We have to make our boys true representatives of our culture, our civilization, of the true genius of our nation. Europe

is no example to us. It plans its programmes in terms of violence
because it believes in violence. I would be the last to minimise the
achivements of Russia, but the whole structure is based on force and
violence. If India had resolved to eschew violence, this system of education becomes an integral part of the discipline.

(quoted in Shrimali 1949: 84)

This clear signalling of educational value in the shape of non-violence
underlined the importance for Gandhi of maintaining Indian independence of all political systems based on violence and thus claimed a kind of
non-religious secular spirituality. The aims of education were to promote
a society based on common interest and equality inspired by the values of
solidarity, democracy and non-doctrinal learning.

Though opposed diametrically to Bolshevized Marxism, Gandhi nevertheless believed in the centrality of labour to the process of self-
knowledge and understanding (although he may well have relied more
on Ruskin than Marx for this understanding). Basic Education placed the
learning of a craft at the centre of the system and stressed the importance
of common productivity. Zakir Hussain, who chaired the drafting committee, noted that the scheme was above all designed to produce workers,
but not workers as mere extensions of the machine. He proposed that
education should produce workers who looked upon all kinds of useful
work as honourable and who desired to be self-sufficient rather than
dependent on society or the state for a living. 'Thus the new scheme
which we are advocating will aim at giving the citizens of the future a
keen sense of personal worth, dignity and efficiency and the desire for
self-improvement and social service in a co-operative community' (Shrimali 1949: 87–88). Hussain saw Basic Education as based on a triadic relation between the physical and social environment in which craft work was
pivotal, so that through the reflexive learning of a craft the student would
begin to grasp the relations between himself and the broader social
world.

Gandhi, who also believed that British arts education was positively
harmful in that it bore no relation to lived experience, insisted that all
learning was to be related to experience rather than based on abstract
principles. Information or ideas which bore no relation to personal
experience were useless and quickly forgotten. Mechanical rote learning
was equally useless. Instead, the curriculum should be problem-centred
and should encompass the actual personal and social difficulties the child
would meet in everyday life, enabling him or her to react intelligently to
new conditions. The curriculum laid stress on self-activity in the belief that
unless the child was gripped by the learning project and its outcome
he/she would not accept the enterprise as his/her own. Stimulated in this
way, the child would develop the spirit of scientific inquiry. It may be
important to note here that Gandhi was not opposed to this aspect of sci-

entificity, which encouraged intelligent activity on the part of the student rather than passive assimilation of information, although he was opposed to the uses to which scientific inquiry had been put by the British and other imperialist nations.

Similarly, Gandhi was not opposed to the idea of social progress as such and saw it as a goal. However, he did not encourage competitive individualism, another unpleasant imperialist import, and instead insisted that genuine social progress had to be based on co-operative action which thus became a curricular emphasis.

Basic Education was to contain a number of major curricular elements: craft learning, mother-tongue tuition, maths, social studies, general science and music and drama. Craft learning was to be the primary element upon which everything else hinged. Moreover, it had to be a basic craft which should equip a child with a means for independent occupation and depended upon the social and geographical context. Clearly, spinning and the production of *khadi* would be taught in cotton-growing areas, fruit and vegetable growing in producing areas, pottery in clay areas, carpentry in the forests and agricultural cultivation in appropriate areas. The craft had to be appropriate to the child's environment. However, it was crucial that the craft should not be taught in a mechanical fashion as a series of physical movements unrelated to intellectual application. 'The teaching of the craft should', Gandhi argued:

> ...be a medium of education not just vocational training. Craft teaching ... should be the means of intellectual training. ... A carpenter teaches me carpentry. I shall learn it mechanically from him and as a result I shall know the use of various tools but that will hardly develop my intellect. But if the same thing is taught to me by someone who has taken a scientific training in carpentry, he will stimulate my intellect too. Not only shall I then have become an expert carpenter, but also an engineer. For, the expert will have taught me the mathematics, also told me the difference between different kinds of timber, the place where they come from, giving me thus a knowledge of geography and also a little of agriculture.
>
> (Shrimali 1949: 97)

There were very good reasons why the mother tongue would replace English as the medium for instruction. The neglect of local languages by the British had the effect of increasingly alienating Indians from their own culture. Gandhi regarded the mother tongue as a reservoir of the accumulated hopes and aspirations as well as the wisdom of the people. Learning it would inspire pride in the historic achievement of the people and in their traditions and culture. Thus it would have an important place on the curriculum. It was proposed that Hindustani should replace English as the language of administration and government.

Pride in traditional culture was to be complemented by a third element of the curriculum, social studies, which aimed to make Indians aware of the injustice and privilege inherent in many of the old ways. They would concentrate on the non-violent solution to these problems in the context of learning about democracy and citizenship. Emphasis would be laid on the ideals of love, truth and justice, co-operative endeavour, national solidarity and the equality of the brotherhood of man. Nationalism would also be celebrated and encouraged but in a non-arrogant and non-exclusive way so as not to encourage sentiments of xenophobia and intolerance of foreigners. Within social studies, geography would also be taught but again in a reflexive way so as to encourage an ecological understanding of, and relationship with, the land. Civics, too, would be taught, though not with the intention of people being encouraged to become the passive servants of the state, but rather instilling the notion of citizenship, involving human and democratic rights. Schools should as far as possible echo the new republic by becoming self-governing institutions with democratically elected parliaments. There would be no religious instruction of any kind, this being seen as a private matter.

General science and maths were also curricular elements in Gandhi's schema. The same reflexivity applied there too and the emphasis would be on experiment and faith in the scientific method as a way of discovering the truth. The curriculum would contain elements of nature study, botany, zoology, physiology, hygiene, physical culture and chemistry, all of which would be taught in relation to the basic craft and the everyday needs of the child.

Thus, in summary, the scheme proposed by Gandhi at Wardha was one which gave education a purposively social orientation which aimed at developing children as citizens of a society based on non-violence and co-operation. It was also a profoundly practical education which focused unashamedly on the needs of the emergent independent India. Gandhi believed that Beauty would follow Truth: 'Whatever is useful to the starving millions is beautiful to my mind. Let us give today the vital things of life, and all the graces and ornaments of life will follow' (Shrimali 1949: 108).

Pedagogically, it stressed the value of work disciplines and the importance of students being given real work in a school context which would give them a sense of reality. Work would make them purposeful and develop habits of critical enquiry. Work was thought to develop moral qualities of self-discipline, co-operative activity, endurance of hardship and the value of order. Not the least value of work was that it would provide an income for the child's family who might not otherwise agree to sending children to school. Privileged classes would learn the value of labour while the mass of the people would learn increased control through understanding. For Gandhi, the use of craft training and work formed the foundation of education. They would be 'the spearhead of a silent social revolution fraught with the most far-reaching consequences. It will provide a healthy and moral basis of relationship between the city and the village and thus go a long way towards eradicating some of the worst evils of the present social insecurity and poisoned relationship between the classes. ... And all this would be accomplished without the horrors of a bloody class war' (Shrimali 1949: 114).

Thus, what on the surface appeared to be a functionalist, vocation-orientated training was actually conceived by Gandhi as being the instrument of social transformation. How far this could have been the case, history was not, however, allowed to divulge, because ultimately it conflicted with the plans of the nationalists.

Thus craft work was central and everything else should be built up round a scientific understanding of the craft. The student would get a good general education from what the hands and mind come into contact with. The craft need not necessarily be spinning, though Gandhi thought of this as the pre-eminent craft, but whatever it was it should be chosen for its educational potential.

The first Basic experimental school was founded at Sevagram in Autumn 1938 under Gandhi's supervision. The children would learn about nature from nature, about cotton production, spinning and cloth making, responsibility for equipment, cleanliness and practical hygiene, arithmetic from counting threads, and reading and writing. Gandhi insisted on no distinction between caste or creed, no competition and co-educational learning. There were also to be dyeing and weaving, carpentry to make equipment, maths and geometry for accounts and scientific principles of spinning. Vegetables were to be grown for the community and education given in food and diets. At Sevagram the course for teachers lasted nine months in which they had to master spinning and Hindustani. The school was run as a democratic body with ministers elected from the students at monthly elections. Self-expression was encouraged through painting and dancing and the great festivals of all religions were celebrated with village people joining in. Through the Kasturba Trust (named after Gandhi's wife) the education of women was emphasized: this included maternity and childcare, personal care and family maintenance. The aim was to draw together all work into a multipurpose co-operative society. Through this, Gandhi envisaged a return to true intelligence and the establishment of societies based on truth and non-violence (*ahimsa*).

An important element of Gandhi's Basic Education scheme was his insistence that all developments should be self-supporting financially, and autonomous. There were, as always with Gandhi, practical reasons for this: a poor society like India could not afford to resource, from the public purse, the huge programme he envisaged. However, there was also a less obvious ideological reason: Gandhi was deeply opposed to state financing and thus state control of education. One of the guiding political principles of Gandhi's life generally was opposition to the coercive state, and an assertion of decentralized, autonomous and free political structures. In many senses Gandhi was an anarchist; hence his admiration for Tolstoy, for example (Kumar 1989: 591–596). For Gandhi, truth and non-violence were the essential values, and dependence upon the state negated both. He adhered to the anarchist precept that 'war is the health of the state'. A state system of education was thus a contradiction of Gandhi's view of education.

As Kumar has noted (Kumar 1989: 592) Gandhi's idea of productive schools was clearly based upon his South African experience, where he had established Phoenix Farm in 1904 and Tolstoy Farm in 1910. It would be a mistake, however, to see Gandhi as wholly anti-western in his educational views. There is, in fact, a close correlation between Gandhi's ideological position and that of western romantic, anti-industrial, humanist and libertarian thinkers: Ruskin, Tolstoy, Carpenter and Dewey, for example. Gandhi often acknowledged his debt to Ruskin in particular:

> The thought expressed in these letters (Ruskin's letters to the working men of the West Riding, published as *Unto This Last*) are beautiful and resemble some of our own ideas, so much so that an outsider would think that the ideas which I set forth in my writings and which we try to put into practice in the Ashram, I had stolen from these letters of Ruskin.
>
> (Gandhi 1959–84: 242)

Both Dewey and Gandhi were products of early capitalist development and both believed in the small-scale rural community, composed of 'industrious, self-respecting and generous' citizens (Gandhi 1959–84: 593). Kumar also argues that Gandhi's proposal reads like a plea 'for delaying the growth of capitalism, for buying time to strengthen the capacities of men and women to live with machines'.

Surprisingly, like Dewey, Gandhi advocated a *secular* pedagogy. Despite the centrality of religion to Gandhi's perspective he felt that 'religions as they are taught and practised today lead to conflict rather than unity' (Gandhi 1979: 20). For Gandhi, the role of the teacher was that of a spiritual guru (rather than professional educator) who would convey the basic truths of all religions.

Basic Education was criticized by the Congress Party's National Planning Committee under Nehru, and by the industrialists (whom it increasingly represented). The subcommittee showed great reluctance in moving from the existing system to Basic Education. They objected to the emphasis on vocation and child labour, and offered instead:

> A broad liberal curriculum for elementary education, and expansion of facilities for technical education. Financial responsibility for compulsory primary education was assigned to be that of the state. This

was indeed the staple diet of modernist thought, compared to which Gandhian ideas looked obsolete and conservative. In contrast to Gandhi's Utopia of village republics enjoying considerable autonomy but offering a modest standard of life dependent on rudimentary production processes, the modernist Utopia featured a strong centralized state responsible for building an industrial infrastructure in order to ensure a high standard of living for all.

(Kumar 1989: 595)

In *The Discovery of India* (Nehru 1960 [1946]) Nehru almost paraphrases Gandhi's argument about the centrality of crafts to education but for 'craft' he substitutes 'machine'. He begins by agreeing with the basic principle that a craft or manual activity stimulates a child's mind but then proceeds to challenge the main economic assumption of Basic Education without ever identifying it.

There was a fundamental ideological difference between Nehru and the nationalists, and Gandhi. As argued earlier, Gandhi, whilst not anti-western, was wholly opposed to the industrial capitalist society. 'It is difficult to measure the harm that Manchester has done to us: the more we indulge our passions the more unbridled they become' (quoted in Chatterjee 1986: 87). Gandhi rejected not only the *politics* of western imperial power: he rejected also the system of social production that the West had developed.

The key factor was industrialization which he believed would inevitably lead to the exploitation of the villages. Gandhi criticized Nehru for believing that mere socialization of industry would solve the problems. Evil was inherent in industry. The villages therefore had to become self-contained and produce their own small-scale manufacturers. For Gandhi, *khadi* was the only sound economic proposition for India.

In governmental terms, Gandhi proposed popular sovereignty over representative democracy. Political power should be dissolved into the collective moral will, a kind of 'enlightened anarchy', though this comes close to enlightened despotism on occasion. 'The utopia is Ramarajya, a patriarchy in which the ruler by his moral quality and habitual adherence to truth, always expresses the collective will' (Chatterjee 1986: 92).

Gandhi also opposed the manner of British rule. He believed that the secularization of education had made a fetish of the knowledge of letters which had exaggerated and rationalized social inequalities. Moreover, payment for mental labour was in itself immoral since bodily sustenance should come from bodily labour, and the division between mental and physical labour should be abolished.

What then, was Gandhi's unique contribution? He was certainly not within the mainstream of Indian (or general Third World) nationalism. But he was no 'mere' peasant intellectual either: his objections to western industrialism were not simple anticolonial Luddism. Still less was Gandhi a replica of the post-Enlightenment Romanticism of Western Europe, although he adopted its critique of industrialism. Gandhi's unique combination of non-violent nationalist politics with a genuine and deep spirituality, constructed an ideology and a social movement which acted as the critical catalyst for mobilizing a mass movement for independence. The problem for the nationalist leadership (Nehru *et al.*) was that they were almost without exception members of a small, western-educated *and* orientated, vanguard or elite, with no real point of contact with the rural masses of India. Through Gandhi the nationalists were able to mobilize *and absorb* the masses. His effect was to mobilize the masses and articulate their gievances, without giving them access to actual political power. Chatterjee provides a detailed and sophisticated elaboration of these linkages (Chatterjee 1986).

By reconciling populist aspirations with the new bourgeois nationalist constitutional order, Gandhi provided for the first time an ideology for including the whole people within the political nation. He both challenged the fundamentals of nationalist thought through his attack on western civilization and yet inserted his political perspective within the process of nationalist politics. There is a fundamental incompatibility between the Utopianism of the moral conception and the realities of power. It created a national framework of politics in which the peasants were mobilized but did not participate, and of a national state from which they were distanced.

Using Gramscian language, Chatterjee, in his study of this relationship, described Gandhi's nationalist politics as the 'moment of manoeuvre'. The next stage was the 'moment of arrival', which Chatterjee ascribed to Nehru and what he called 'the passive revolution'. An historical compromise was made between the dominant and subaltern classes. After 1932, when Nehru reacted against the stand Gandhi took on behalf of the harijans, nationalism became situated in the domain of state ideology. The discourse was then about the process of effectively governing the state rather than satisfying popular aspirations. The autonomy of the state became the central organizing principle and its legitimizing principle was social justice. The old colonial framework was seen as antiquated and incapable of delivery. Modernity required new institutions with primacy given to economic affairs, whereas the colonial state was outmoded because it could not assume a centralized co-ordinating role.

Nehru denied any essential split between East and West and argued that the only difference was the fact of industrial society (which the West had developed first, for historical reasons). India's subsequent backwardness was because colonialism had interrupted its normal historical development, which would have led to an industrial and materially prosperous society.

Nehru believed, however, that India could and should adopt humanism and the scientific spirit from the West – precisely what Gandhi was sceptical about – and he saw socialism as the most advanced expression of the rationalism of the European Enlightenment. The need for industrialization was paramount, for without it poverty would be eradicated and the political foundations of national independence would be threatened. This could only be done by a sovereign, non-colonial state. He dismissed Gandhi's small scale as economically unrealistic; what was wanted was bigness and big business. For Nehru the nation-state lay at the heart of nationalism and had to embrace the whole people with equal citizenship irrespective of sex, language, caste, wealth or education.

For both men, therefore, education was seen as an essential ideological tool. For Gandhi, it was the key, through his Basic Education programme, for creating a decentralized alternative to the modernizing, western-orientated society which India was fast threatening to become. And for Nehru, education, conceived as vocational, technological training, was a key means of bringing about the modernization he and the nationalists thought was essential.

Chatterjee argues that Nehru found Gandhi 'incomprehensible' because he acted on emotive impulse and appeared to be able effortlessly and intuitively to sense the mass mind, while Nehru and the nationalist politicians were powerless. Although he found Gandhi's economic and social ideas obsolete and in general reactionary, Gandhi had shaken up India more than any other revolutionary before him. He was literally 'a magician'. Nehru incorporated Gandhi's 'truth' into the nationalist project while rejecting his metaphysics and language. Nehru found the ideas in *Hind Swaraj* an 'utterly wrong and harmful doctrine' (Chatterjee 1986: 157). Gandhi was a philosophical anarchist whose ideas were functional in arousing the masses but useless for creating the new state. As Chatterjee has commented:

> The relentless thrust of its [the new nationalist leadership] rationalist thematic turned the Gandhian intervention into a mere interlude in the unfolding of the real history of the nation.
>
> (Chatterjee 1986: 157)

So Gandhi was incorporated into the new nationalism as if he did not represent an absolute alternative to it. No longer in need of magicians the new nationalism emphasized expertise. The new state would stand above conflicting interests and dispassionately judge with the technical expertise at its command.

For good reasons, given India's potential for religious and communalistic conflict, Nehru and the nationalist movement tried to create a secular, technocratic state, embodying the best elements of the Fabian, centralist socialist ideology within whose framework they had been reared politically in the West.

How does this ideological conflict appear, about half a century on? There can be no doubt that India has developed – educationally, socially and politically – broadly along the lines envisaged by Nehru and the nationalists. In almost all spheres, Gandhi's visions of a future India have not materialized. As far as education is concerned, the 'new values inculcated through mass education ... in form and content reflect Western values and practices in a way which would have horrified Gandhi who had formulated such distinctive and Indian plans for Basic Education' (Brown 1989: 391).

Modern India has problems as grave as any faced at the time of independence. Violence, communalism, and economic and social dislocation have soured the nationalist dream. And Bombay, undoubtedly the most westernized and modern of Indian cities, also has some of the greatest disparities of wealth, some of the most abject poverty (and the most depressing general ambience) of all the great Indian urban centres.

In retrospect, Gandhi's insistence upon non-violent and spiritual values as the foundations of the new India seem eminently sane. His Basic Education programme certainly had its reactionary side: the authoritarian role of the teacher/guru (a tendency towards authoritarianism is a charge that can be levelled at Gandhi generally); the determined exclusion of abstract and particularly (western) scientific knowledge; and the eccentricity of his almost obsessive concentration upon village crafts (especially the symbolic concern with spinning). All these are tangible and weighty criticisms. And yet Gandhi was essentially far more of a radical than a reactionary, in educational as in other spheres. The *values* he espoused were socialist – though he was implacably opposed both to socialist, certainly Marxist, *methods* of conflict and violence, *and* to the socialist assumptions of industrialization and economic, consumerist growth. Again, who is to say in the light of the sorry history of both Stalinist communism and milk-and-water capitalist social democracy, that he was wrong? His critique of state control of education is positive and libertarian, while not being simply individualistic. It prevents education being used as a vehicle for party or state ideology while at the same time asserting communalistic values and social relevance. The continuing appeal of Gandhi and Gandhian philosophy to both East and West lies precisely in his espousal of the pure, idealistic values which underlie both religion and socialism, and in his equally vehement rejection of the increasingly materialist criteria of both eastern and western society.

It is mistaken, though, to try to analyse Gandhi in predominantly political terms. He was not primarily a political activist, still less a political theorist. He was 'fundamentally a man of vision and action, who asked many of the profoundest questions that face humankind as it struggles to live in community. It was this confrontation out of a real humanity which marks his stature and makes his struggles and glimpses of truth of enduring significance' (Brown 1989: 394). Whether his specific blueprint for Basic

Education is, or ever was, viable or even desirable, is a moot point. But adult educators, East and West, will continue to identify with at least some aspects of his reassertion of the fundamentally humanistic bases of adult education's objectives.

Notes

1 *Tom Steele* is currently Research Fellow in Adult Education at the University of Leeds and was previously WEA Organising Tutor for Leeds. His study *Alfred Orage and the Leeds Arts Club* was published by Scolar in 1990.
2 *Richard Taylor* is Professor of Adult Continuing Education at the University of Leeds. He is the author of studies of university adult education and the liberal tradition as well as a full-length study of CND. This article is the first of two to be published by *IJLE* and is the forerunner of a full-length study of the politics of Indian Adult Education to be completed later this year.

References

Brown, J. (1989). *Gandhi: Prisoner of Hope*, Yale University Press.
Chatterjee, P. (1986). *Nationalist Thought and the Colonial World – a Derivative Discourse*, London, Zed Books.
Gandhi, M. K. (1944). (first published 1906), *Hind Swaraj*, Ahmedabad, Navijivan Publishing House.
Gandhi, M. K. (1959–84). *Collected Works*, Vol. XLIX, New Delhi, Government of India.
Gandhi, M. K. (1979). *Documents on Social, Moral and Spiritual Values in Education*, New Delhi, NCERT.
Kumar, K. (1989). Profiles of Indian educators: Mohandras Karamchand Gandhi, 1869–1948, *Prospects*, Vol. 19, No. 4, pp. 591–596.
Nehru, J. (1960). *The Discovery of India*, London, Meridian Books.
Shrimali, K. L. (1949). *The Wardha Scheme*, Udaipur, Vidya Bhawan Society.

6 Gender and the curriculum of adult education

Sue Blundell[1]

In spite of the prominence of women as both students and teachers in adult education, there has to date been little discussion of the significance of the adult curriculum with regard to the reproduction of gender relations. This paper employs the perspectives of four feminist discourses – liberal, radical, Marxist and socialist – as a means of analysing the predominantly reinforcing role of the adult curriculum as it is currently constituted; and assesses the potential for change presented by the strategies associated with these discourses. The liberal discourse has probably been the most effective in terms of its ability to penetrate the adult education institutes and to bring about reforms which are aimed at breaking down sex-role stereotypes. But among feminists whose aim is the transformation rather than the selective amelioration of gender relations, it is recognized that an approach is called for which can encompass both an analysis of the social and economic roots of women's oppression, and a radical reworking of patriarchal definitions and distributions of knowledge. It is through a combination of the strategies devised by the radical feminist movement, in particular with regard to the development of a women-centred, women-only methodology, and the theoretical framework contributed by the Marxist/socialist discourse that the transformation of the adult education curriculum is most likely to be achieved. But it cannot be said that this process has even begun, and it is vital that feminists involved in adult education engage in the detailed discussions which must precede the creation of an effective and liberating programme for women.

In the field of adult education, curriculum theory is for the most part conspicuous by its absence, although the work of Colin Griffin (1983) has gone some way towards filling this significant gap. But Griffin would be the first to admit that his analysis takes little or no account of the issue of gender. Since women constitute a majority of both the students and the teachers in adult education, this omission would appear to be a serious one. To date, much has been achieved by women scholars in terms of hauling gender into the debate about the school curriculum;[2] and some very useful studies of the patriarchal bias within the curriculum of higher education have been undertaken.[3] But as yet there has been no detailed research which has focused on gender issues in relation to the curriculum of adult education, although books by Thompson (1983) and Hughes and Kennedy (1985), which set out to define and describe the essential characteristics of adult women's education, have offered some very helpful insights. In this article I shall be building on the work done by all of these women in outlining some basic analytical approaches to the gender implications of the adult curriculum.

My discussion will be structured around the four major discourses – liberal, radical, Marxist and socialist – which exist within the social and political theory of feminism. These discourses, which Sue Middleton (1984) among others has distinguished, seem to me to offer the most useful way into this subject if we are to examine the fundamental question which it raises: the question of whether the curriculum of adult education has any contribution to make to the liberation of women.

There is no doubt in my mind that this is the ultimate goal which an adult education programme for women should be aspiring to achieve; equally, I am convinced that as it is presently constituted adult education has very little to offer in this direction. There are, I think, two basic reasons for this failure: first, because the 'little home-maker' approach to women's education has by no means been eradicated from our adult centres; and second, because that part of the curriculum which on the face of it appears to be gender-blind is in fact profoundly male-centred. At present, what the traditional adult education curriculum is offering to women is either a reinforcement of their time-honoured domestic role, or selective admission to a system of knowledge which is defined, transmitted and controlled by men. It is through the medium of the four discourses that I shall be assessing the significance of the adult curriculum for women, and exploring the strategies for transforming it.

The liberal feminist discourse

Liberal feminism is the discourse of those feminists who seek equality with men within existing capitalist hierarchies, including the hierarchies constructed both within and by our education system. Many liberal feminists recognize that equality is denied to women not merely as a result of discriminatory legislation, policies and practices, but also by virtue of processes of socialization which condition them into accepting male-constructed definitions of 'femininity'. For them, true equality of opportunity can only be achieved when the sex-role stereotypes which so severely limit women have been demolished. Clearly, education can play a crucial part in this demolition process. Eileen Byrne, who provides us with the most comprehensive statement of the liberal feminist view of women and education, sees the persistent 'underachievement' of girls in school as resulting from 'the stereotyping of expected roles for men and women and the translation of these into curricula. The most pervasive inherited unexamined assumption is the alleged inferiority of women' (Byrne 1978: 34).

This is a perspective which points, albeit implicitly in some cases, to a psychological origin for women's lack of equality – women do not get what men do out of the education system because they have been conditioned mentally not to want it. It does not examine the historical basis for the construction of sex-role stereotypes, or suggest that their roots lie in a hierarchical economic and social structure which must be transformed before the stereotypes can be eradicated. As Bunkle has said, what this discourse is seeking is 'a slice of the capitalist action without changing its structure. All women's rights wants, and all it will get, is a change in the genitalia of the people at the top' (Bunkle 1979/80, part 1: 27).

Apart from 'a slice of the capitalist action', what liberal feminists are aiming to achieve is the removal of discriminatory policies and practices, the active encouragement of women into areas of study and employment which are non-traditional to their sex, and equality for women within the career structures of education. Goals such as these might also appear desirable to feminists of other persuasions; but liberal feminists see equality on this level as an end in itself, and do not relate it to social transformation on a wider scale. To adopt the perspective employed by Griffin (1983: 65–91) in discussing adult education in general, education within this discourse is conceptualized in terms of needs, access and provision. Women's prime educational need is identified as the need for educational opportunities which are equal to those enjoyed by men – in other words, women need the kind of education which men receive. In this context, access becomes a major concern: the access of women to courses which are normally followed by men, or to areas of knowledge or skills normally associated with men; access to levels of educational provision (most notably, higher education) which have in the past been dominated by men; and access to managerial positions within the education profession. The implication here is that the existing provision is satisfactory where curriculum content, methods and organizational structure are concerned; what is needed is an extension of the existing provision, on equal terms, to women.

In so far as feminist strategy has penetrated adult education at all, it is predominantly a liberal feminist strategy, and for this reason it is worth examining the aims outlined above in relation to the existing provision for adults. The position of women in adult education, when it is analysed in terms of those aims, appears in some respects to be quite satisfactory. Access to adult education provision as a whole does not appear to be a problem for women, since women students outnumber male students[4] Indeed, the access issue here *could* be said to be one of male access: I have on a number of occasions heard concern expressed by male managers in adult education about the low number of men attending – the feeling here seems to be that adult education will never be taken seriously as long as it is packed out with women. Jenny Scribbins, principal of Putney and Wandsworth Adult Education Institute, has described how, in an institution where 75% of students are women, discussion forums on equality tended to see attracting more men into the college as an important aim (Scribbins 1989: 49). The major problem here is not one of access, but of combating the notion that when women are equal in numbers, equality has been achieved.

The picture where access to managerial positions in the profession is concerned is not quite so seductively rosy. The DES does not publish figures showing the breakdown by sex of full- and part-time staff in adult education, but statistics relating to full-time teachers in further education as a whole show that, on 31 March 1988, the percentages of posts occupied by women were as follows: principal – 5.5%; vice-principal – 10.9%; head of department – 12.6%; principal lecturer – 13.4%; senior lecturer – 19.3%; lecturers 2 and 1 – 36.4% – (Statistics of Education: teachers in service, England and Wales, DES 1987/8). It seems certain that if statistics were available on part-time teachers, these would show women to be clearly in the majority. The picture which emerges here is of a service which operates largely for women, which is staffed at the lower levels largely by women, but which is managed largely by men.

On the face of it, adult education seems to erect few barriers where access to knowledge and skills is concerned. Women can enrol for any of the courses which men enrol for, and in adult education there are no teachers or careers advisors who steer them towards the 'feminine' subjects, or towards the courses which are likely to be useful in gaining 'women's work'. To many liberal feminists, the traditional adult education curriculum, with its tendency to reproduce the categories of schooling, probably appears to be perfectly adequate. Indeed, the presence of so many women students in adult education could go some way towards explaining its conservative curriculum: if women are seen as trying to 'catch up' on what they missed out on at school, then school knowledge is validated and strengthened. This is an outcome which is made all the more likely by the needs-meeting ideology of liberal feminism: what, in the analysis of Hilary Friend, is true of continuing education as a whole is certainly true of the liberal feminist approach to it – it 'cannot imagine women having any needs other than the need to be in the system' (Friend 1982: 12). Such an ideology, to use Griffin's words, 'will function overwhelmingly to reinforce prevailing definitions, distributions and evaluations of knowledge' (Griffin 1983: 80). What Griffin has not made explicit in his account is that those definitions, distributions and evaluations have been constructed, not just by the ruling class, but by a *male* ruling class. Men may now be prepared to give women a share in their knowledge, but they are not prepared to reconstruct it. It has served them so very well in the past.

It would be misleading to suggest that all liberal feminists are perfectly happy with the traditional curriculum of adult education. It is a curriculum which, like that of the school, neglects women in some fairly obvious ways; and much useful remedial work has been done along the lines of 'filling in the gaps' where women ought to be – for example, slotting into a history course a class on 'the position of women'. This work *has* been useful, I believe, but it should be viewed only as an interim measure. Only when the full implications of 'the position of women' are grasped will women's education transcend the liberal approach and become genuinely transforming. As Dale Spender, writing from a radical feminist perspective, has observed, 'adding women on to men's education' does not produce any radical changes in the curriculum:

> If 'great women' are inserted into the history books, women writers studied in the literary courses, women's jobs included in the sociology of work, women's customs included in anthropology, and women's contributions in the sciences acknowledged, then I shall express my approval. ... But I do not classify this as women's studies.
>
> (Spender 1982: 148)

'Adding women on' by itself, without following through the full implications of the addition, could be considered to contribute towards the validation of the traditional disciplines ('Art history is OK as long as we remember to include women painters'). Similarly, I believe that the liberal feminist strategy of attaching a 'women only' tag to courses where 'masculine' subjects like science and technology are being taught could serve to reinforce the male-centredness of those subjects. Certainly, it seems to be very often the case that little is done to challenge it: offering, for example, courses on 'Mathematics for Women', where the subject is taught in a traditional manner and there is no attempt to explore in what ways its basic structure contributes towards the exclusion of women, could help to ensure that maths continues to be a male preserve where women are expected to have to 'catch up'.

Liberal feminism, as well as 'adding women on' and creating reserved spaces for women, has also challenged the sex-role stereotyping which has been shown to play a major part in shaping the curriculum of adult education. Ammunition for their strategy is provided, for example, by the study of local authority adult provision conducted by Mee and Wiltshire (1978: 41). In this, they found that although in theory adult education institutes could teach what they liked and had a large amount of freedom to introduce innovations, three-quarters of the 22,761 courses they examined were basically similar – that there was in practice a common core curriculum. Their research showed that one-third of courses were related to 'personal care and household economy' – in other words, to the 'feminine' pursuits of cookery, dress-making, flower arranging, beauty culture, etc., etc. A survey conducted by the Advisory Council for Adult and Continuing Education in 1982, in which people were asked what new subjects they would like to study, showed a similar tendency to go for the stereotypical courses: 33% of women and only 2% of men said that they would like to study domestic science; whilst 18% of men and only 6% of women opted for carpentry and do-it-yourself classes.

In view of the lack of external constraints on the construction of the adult education curriculum, and the potential for experimentation which it appears to offer, the traditional character of much of its teaching is depressing, if not altogether surprising. The dominance of the needs-meeting ideology goes a long way towards explaining this conservatism; and certainly when the service is managed very largely by men, one would not expect there to be a high level of innovation where courses for women are concerned. One of the strategies of liberal feminists within adult education is still, quite justifiably, the breaking down of stereotyped expectations and the redefining of the boundaries of male and female roles. But as Kessler *et al.* have suggested (in relation to sex-role stereotyping in secondary schools), a strategy which seeks to shape individual identities through administrative changes in the curriculum is probably tackling the problem in only a superficial way:

> Talking about gender relations in terms of roles, internalised expectations, attitudes, and traits directs attention away from larger structures and focuses explanations of inequality on what is going on inside the heads of the subordinated group. It is a classic case of blaming the victim. ... The idea of sex roles exaggerates the importance of individual attitudes and minimizes the importance of the economic and social forces to which those attitudes are a response.
>
> (Kessler *et al.* 1985: 35)

The notion that tinkering with the curriculum could help to eradicate inequality ignores the reality of patriarchal power and the economic structures with which it is intertwined. In adult education terms, getting rid of domestic science and flooding the programme with computing-for-women-type courses will never be sufficient to liberate women.

To sum up, the liberal feminist prescription for education, with its stress on access to provision, access to men's knowledge and access to management roles, can be seen to conform to the residual model of adult education as outlined by Griffin (1983: 96–97): it treats women by and large as members of a temporarily disadvantaged group who must be handed out compensatory courses in order to permit them to 'catch up' with men. The reforms which it seeks, if treated as ends in themselves, can have the effect of validating and reproducing the traditional, male-centred categories of schooling; and at the end of the day, because of the failure to tackle the social and economic roots of women's oppression, this can only lead to a sweetening rather than a transformation of women's position.

The remedial aspect of adult education for women is likely to become more pronounced in the future, as the present demographic crisis and the demand for skilled labour produce a growing focus on women as a 'target group'. This is creating a situation which is very similar to the one that existed in this country during the two World Wars – once again 'the reserve army' of women is being kitted out, and adult education institutes are at last beginning to see a way of making themselves really useful. This type of provision is fuelled, of course, not by a concern for women's equality, but by the demands of the capitalist economy. As such, it can be seen to correspond to the functional model of education outlined by Acker (1984: 25), which sets up as the objective of education the production of appropriately qualified people to meet the needs of the economy. From the liberal feminist perspective, this is a model which in present circumstances very much answers their wishes, since it should greatly enhance the prospects for women's access to all levels of post-compulsory education.

At present, of course, the recognition of this need for access is not being accompanied by the legislative and policy changes which will make it really meaningful: the government, for example, has made it clear that it is not prepared to fund state nurseries or to legislate for career breaks. It is also true that the improvement in access is likely to last, like increased opportunities for women during the two World Wars, for only as long as the crisis lasts: once the labour shortage is over, women's services will be dispensed with. The outcome in the long term could be a reaction against the presence of women in an 'overmanned' workforce, and yet another return to the ideal of Woman as Homemaker. Yet even if the necessary policy changes are made which will help to establish equality of access to educational provision, and even if that equality of access were to become a permanent feature of our education system, true equality for women would still not have been achieved. Ultimately, the functional model of education can never work for women. It can never work because in accordance with the 'rational' economic criteria under which it operates women are always going to be less 'useful' than men on account of their need to take time out for child-rearing – the return on the investment in their education will always be lower than the return on the investment in men's education. Above all, it can never work for women because it is bound up with the functions of capitalism, and the reproduction of capitalism is inextricably related to the reproduction of women's oppression. It is with this view in mind that I turn now to the more radical perspective on women in education.

The radical perspectives and the patriarchal construction of knowledge

The radical perspectives on women embrace three major discourses – the Marxist feminist, radical feminist and socialist feminist discourses. Though these differ in their broad analyses of the nature of women's oppression and in some aspects of their prescriptions for change, they do have certain fundamental points in common. One is their belief that women *are* oppressed (as distinct from the liberal view that they are 'disadvantaged'), and that this oppression is one way or another intrinsic to our social structure, so that some kind of social transformation will be required before women can be liberated. Another point in common, more specifically linked to the discourse on education, is the view that one facet of the oppression of women is their subordination within a knowledge system which is patriarchally constructed. Before examining these discourses separately and giving some account of their differences, I shall set out the main features of the view of knowledge which they share.

No one has done more than the radical feminist Dale Spender to illuminate the multifarious means by which male power in our society gets translated into male control of the definition and distribution of knowledge – means which include the control of language and the 'power of naming' (Spender 1980), the patriarchal bias of academic subjects (Spender 1981b), and the stranglehold on powerful positions within the academic professions (Spender 1981a). Under the last heading, she notes the way in which all the agencies that have a hand in the generation of academic knowledge – publishers of books and periodicals, professional associations, conferences, academic boards, examination boards, and of course the academic departments within the universities – are dominated by men. As a result, Spender says, 'men are able to exclude women from the construction of knowledge: they can exclude them as subjects when they set up research which is problematic to men, they can exclude them as researchers and theorists by not allocating funding to projects which are perceived as problematic to women, and by "disallowing" women's unfunded research' (Spender 1981a: 159).

The construction of academic knowledge is not just an issue within higher education: academic definitions influence what counts as knowledge in secondary schooling; and adult education, to the extent that it either reproduces the knowledge categories of schooling or delivers a watered-down version of what is taught in universities, is thoroughly permeated by this male-centred knowledge. It is, moreover, a knowledge which successfully masks its patriarchal bias: in many if not all of the academic disciplines, male experience is represented as constituting universal experience,[5] a distortion which the strategy of 'adding women on' cannot fundamentally alter. The typical analytical scenario which this procedure produces goes something like this: 'people say, do or think (a), (b), or (c) (but oh, by the way, women on the other hand say, do or think (x), (y), and (z))'. Not only does this offer no challenge to the universalizing of male values (i.e. men = people) but, by making a special case out of women, it helps to reinforce the impression that women are 'deviants' who do not conform to the norm of human experience.

What is true of the academic world at large is also true, needless to say, of the discipline of education. Sandra Acker (1981) draws attention to the way in which sociologists of education have used data derived from predominantly male sources in constructing general theories, and is highly critical of the 'new' sociology of education for failing to tackle this masculine bias. Theorists like Michael F.D. Young,[6] who have been instrumental in developing new approaches to the sociology of education, have been at pains to point out the way in which the construction of knowledge serves to legitimize the existing relations of production within capitalist society; but they have produced little or no discussion of the role which knowledge plays in legitimizing existing *gender* relations. Much the same could be said of Griffin's theoretical work on adult education (1983). Like the new sociologists, Griffin is primarily concerned with knowledge construction as a function of the social relations of production: in spite of the important role which adult education plays in the education of women, gender relations are not accorded a single mention.

This said, I have to admit that the analysis of the relationship between the patriarchal construction of knowledge and the reproduction of gender relations, and of the relationship between gender relations and the relations of production, is a thorny and controversial area of theory. It is at this point that the three remaining feminist discourses begin to part company, so I deal with this topic under the separate sections devoted to them.

The radical feminist discourse

Radical feminists see patriarchy as the root cause of women's oppression: for them, the domination by men is not a function of capitalism; rather, it precedes capitalism and is one of the principal elements in its evolution. According to this analysis, patriarchy is a universal and enduring facet of human social organization because it is grounded in woman's capacity for child-bearing and in the sexual division of labour to which this has given rise. The resulting separation between the female domestic sphere and the male public sphere has placed political and cultural power in the hands of men, and they have used this power to assign a high value to their own social role, and a low value to the role of women[7]. In this discourse, then, gender division is seen as the basis for a system of oppression – patriarchal oppression – which is quite independent of class division.

For this reason, the radical feminist analysis of the education system is a reasonably straightforward one, since it tends to concentrate on the manifestations and reproduction of patriarchal power, and can, by the criteria of its own analysis, safely ignore the interconnections between patriarchal power and the relations of production. The deconstruction of the knowledge content of education in this discourse relies heavily on identifying the areas of direct male control, and on assembling the evidence for overt and hidden male bias in the curriculum. On the positive side, radical feminists are concerned with constructing a new, women-centred knowledge to replace the old male-centred variety; and with getting women into a position where they can distribute and reproduce this knowledge. Thus, according to Spender,

> while males control education there is no direct means for women to pass on their understandings. What women know frequently dies with them, until feminists periodically rediscover them and their writing and attempt to reconstruct women's heritage and tradition. Each generation of women forges understandings about subordination, within their own lifetime and from the circumstances of their own lives, but because these meanings do not become the general currency of the culture they are not passed on to the next generation with the result that neither women nor men know about the women who have gone before.
>
> (Spender 1982: 18)

Although writers like Spender are certainly not without hope that the male-centred knowledge system at present dominant in education can ultimately be changed, they see change as something that will be generated through the construction of the 'viable woman-centred alternative' (Spender 1982: 144); and it is on the latter that their attention is naturally focused. Moreover, so far as Spender is concerned, the changes which are envisaged for men's education do not apparently involve any radical transformation of its knowledge content, but rather a recognition of its lack of objectivity – an abandonment, in fact, of the *concept* of objectivity. Men will have to accept the limits of their own subjectivity, and in so doing they will be immediately stripped of much of their assumed authority: 'If there are to be men's "truths" which originate in men's subjectivity, and women's "truths" which originate in women's subjectivity, then it is obvious that there must be more than one "truth" ... No one group will have a privileged way of knowing...' (Spender 1982: 148–9).

In constructing a curriculum for women's education, radical feminists build on the separateness of the male and female identities and make it into a virtue. One important feature of their prescriptions has been to advocate the setting up of separate, women-controlled institutions for the education of women, or, as the next best thing, of women-only, women-taught courses within our existing educational institutions.[8] In both cases the areas of knowledge explored can be subsumed under the general heading of women's studies.

There are many different ideas about how precisely the knowledge content of women's studies should be constituted, but most writers agree that one vital element is their interdisciplinary nature, and the challenge which this offers to the patriarchal definitions of knowledge. Many are also anxious to dispel the notion that women's studies involves the study only of women and not of men. According to Evans (1982), many liberal male academics assume that the objective behind women's studies is the examination of a neglected bit of the world, and for this reason they do not see it as offering any challenge to either the traditional disciplines or the traditional methods of enquiry. It is only through the recognition of the crucial role which the deconstruction of male knowledge has to play in women's studies that this marginalization can be avoided. As Fitzgerald has written, 'women's studies ... challenges the ways in which social structures (the curriculum very much included) create and foster ideas about ourselves and the world ... Questioning the underlying assumptions about the truth and supposedly objective knowledge of academic fields is to recognise that the very chopping up and categorising of knowledge in the academy is itself a political act' (Fitzgerald 1978: 3).

Few radical feminists, however, would go so far as Mary Evans does when, in acknowledging that there are some aspects of the patriarchal disciplines which women can turn to their own uses, she warns of the danger of refusing the accumulated knowledge of the past 2,000 years (Evans 1982: 70). Generally speaking, other radical feminists have not followed Evans in her emphasis on the knowledge content of the women's studies curriculum, or in her insistence that the significance accorded to women's subjective experience should not lead to a downgrading of theoretical and analytical research (Evans 1982: 67). In most of the discussions of the philosophy of women's studies, there has been a tendency to concentrate on its methodology, as presenting the most obvious contrast to the operations of the patriarchal curriculum. Spender, in describing the way in which women's studies developed out of the women's movements of the late 1960s and early 1970s, gives a telling account of this practice:

> Unlike men, we had no received tradition in which to operate ... There were no established authorities whose reputations were vested in a particular theory and who sought to initiate us into seeing things their way. In short, there was no hierarchy.
>
> In the absence of experts, courses, books, models, theories, we were all on an equal footing. No-one was more learned, no-one had access to a privileged way of knowing; there could be no division into teachers and students, for we were all engaged in the same process of trying to generate knowledge about women, and the venture was co-operative, not competitive ... there could be no privileged or authoritative group who could rule that the knowledge of some women was valid, while that of others was not ... If we were to have descriptions and explanations about the existence of women, then *all* women should be included in the frame of reference, *all* women had to have a voice and be accommodated.
>
> (Spender 1982: 144–145)

What Spender is outlining here is a perfect example of the concept of the learner-centred curriculum which writers like Knowles and Freire were fostering in the 1970s[9] As in the prescriptions of Knowles, we get the same stress on self-directed learning, applicability to the learner's role in life, the problem-centred approach, and above all the importance of personal experience: to quote Spender once more, 'by demonstrating that all those who are involved in women's studies can *make* knowledge and are not passive dependents waiting to *receive* it, we have challenged some of the foundation stones of education and of male supremacy' (Spender 1982: 146). We are also very close to Freire here, with his strictures on the banking concept of education, and his insistence on breaking down the contradiction between teacher and learner. His notion of the 'teacher-student' (Freire 1972: 53) comes to mind when we read Janet Robyns's account of her experience of a women's studies group: 'The "teacher" did not remain the same person. In sharing our knowledge, our thoughts and experiences, the "teacher" rotated among us. Each functioned as teacher at times because each had something to offer. There was no knower/non knower, judge/judged hierarchy' (Robyns 1977: 3).

To my mind, one of the most striking *differences* between these feminist accounts and the writing of Knowles and Freire is that they are describing something that actually happened, while Knowles and Freire seem to remain very much on the level of theory. My own experience of the feminist consciousness-raising groups of the 1970s tells me that the absence of the teacher/learner distinction was a reality among those groups, and that this was linked with the 'bottom-up', non-institutional character of the movement. No experience which I have had in adult education, either as teacher or student, has ever matched this. And it is difficult to imagine how in an institutional setting it ever could. Certainly in the works of Freire and of Knowles's disciples there is no shortage of accounts of how theory has been translated into practice; and in my own work as a teacher I have attempted to follow some of their principles. But I have never been convinced by anything that I have read or done that someone who enters a room as a 'teacher' (or, even worse, an 'investigator', to pick up on one of Freire's terms) can leave it as 'just one of the girls'.

Spender is well aware that, with the development of a body of knowledge and the entry of women's studies into the educational institutions, there is a danger that the practice will no longer match up to this non-competitive model of education developed by the early women's movement: 'where the possibility of "transmission" exists – with all its concomitant attributes of hierarchies and competition – it may be very important for feminism to focus on past achievements and to keep the co-operative model in mind ...' (Spender 1981a: 171). Nevertheless, as Spender says, the feminist model of education can still make itself felt in institutionalized courses. The stress which is placed on the value of personal experience, the abandonment of sterile and dishonest notions of objectivity, and the non-hierarchical social conditioning which many women have received all make it likely that, even if the teacher cannot entirely disappear, her role can at least be minimalized. Women-only classes in adult education, in my experience, come far closer to the learner-centred model of the curriculum than do mixed classes. At the same time, the relative informality of adult education classes, the large numbers of women attending them, and the potential for innovation which they offer are all factors which make the adult education institute fruitful territory for the introduction of women's studies.

To appreciate what women on an individual level have to gain from learning in a women-only environment, we need only refer to the experience of one of Dale Spender's interviewees:

> After institutionalised education you feel worse. After feminist educa-
> tion you feel better. I left university convinced I was dim, I was always
> sure everyone around me was brighter than I was, and I was always
> frightened of being found out. I was frightened of the world. I felt
> incompetent. I had the mentality of a victim. All that changed after
> my women's studies course. I felt much more in charge of my own
> life, though I was more aware of the things that were against me. But I
> felt capable, I thought it was possible to do something about them.
>
> (Spender 1981: 171)

These words evoke perfectly the way in which a patriarchal education can terrorize and demoralize women, and the way in which, on the contrary, a women-only education can empower and gladden them. They represent, I think, a huge indictment of our current education system.

The concept of women-only courses does, however, throw up a number of problems. First, there is the obvious, organizational problem that at present the law permits the advertisement of women-only provision in only two instances: where it provides for women 'who have not been in regular full-time employment for some time because of domestic or family responsibility'; and where it provides training for employment in work in which women are locally or nationally under-represented. Clearly, we have to campaign for a change in the law if general women's studies courses are ever to be provided on an effective basis. A second problem is the one that Evans (1982) highlights: in stressing the tremendous value of the learner-centred methods of feminist education, we should not lose sight of its knowledge content. If we immerse ourselves in the subjective experiences of subordination, and do not apply any hard analysis to the political and social structures which determine that subordination, then we run the risk of producing only individual responses to a collective oppression. Women's education, in other words, can easily become depoliticized, and for this reason it is important to develop a theoretical perspective for women's studies which endeavours to integrate method with content.

Maggie Coats (1989: 33–34) has drawn attention to other problems which are intrinsically linked to the separatism of women's studies. One is the danger that women-only provision might seem to imply identical provision for all women – that all women experience the same conditions of existence and have identical needs. This would be to ignore the effects of class, race, sexual orientation, disability and age. The second difficulty arises from the fact that for many women, women-only provision is transitional, since they are going to move on to education or training in mixed situations. It is important, therefore, that issues of transition and progression should be addressed within all-women groups – we cannot afford to ignore the existence of the other sex.

What these two difficulties highlight is the fundamental danger inherent in women-only provision, the danger that it might lead to the ghettoization of women's education. Our education system does not exist in isolation, but is an element within social and cultural structures which persistently undervalue women. If a significant number of women were to opt for the total separatism which seems to be advocated by Spender, then we could end up with a kind of educational apartheid, involving a traditional, high-status curriculum for men, and an innovative but low-status curriculum for women. To guard against this, we will need to foster the kind of theoretical perspective which can address questions of patriarchal domination. But we will also need to ensure that there is a continual flow of women out of separate provision and into the mainstream of education, where they must hold on to what they have learnt from each other and struggle to achieve the transformation of patriarchal definitions and practice.

The Marxist and socialist feminist discourses

There are many features of the radical feminist analysis of women's oppression with which Marxist and socialist feminists would find themselves in broad agreement; and some of the radical strategies for change in education (including the importance of some form of women-only provision) would similarly meet with their approval. Their main criticism of the radical feminist perspective is that it fails to take into account the system of class relations to which patriarchy is wedded: one result of this weakness is a simplistic account of the processes by which knowledge is defined and distributed in our society, an account which seeks only to describe and not to explain the reality of patriarchal control. This has produced a rather naive conception of what education can achieve in the way of women's liberation.

The basic problem for Marxist and socialist feminists is one of constructing a model of society which incorporates both class and gender relations. There are some significant differences between the two discourses where this is concerned; but in subsequent analysis there are many overlappings, and for this reason I shall deal with them in the same section.

The major source for the classical Marxist position is a treatise by Engels (1891) which relates the origins of the subordination of women to the gradual emergence of production for exchange as a basic organizing principle in society: with the development of industrial capitalism, this form of production (practised largely by men) came to dominate the economy, and women's production for use within the home was accorded a secondary and socially subordinate role. In this analysis, then, gender relations are seen as a function of wider social and economic relations, and not as a direct product of biological difference. For classical Marxists, it is through the struggle against capitalism, and not against patriarchy as such, that the liberation of women will be assured.

Many Marxist feminists would argue against the view which I have just outlined, pointing out that it takes no account of oppressive gender relations within the family: for them, the subordination of women cannot be analysed solely in terms of a male-defined class system, since it predates and cuts across economically determined class differences.[10] Some would agree with the socialist feminist analysis, according to which patriarchal domination is structurally independent of the capitalist system, and will not automatically come to an end when this is dismantled; nevertheless, in the present social formation it constitutes one of capitalism's central organizing principles. As MacDonald has written in an important article, 'In the capitalist economy, patriarchal relations have a specific material base in, for example, the separation of the family from the production process, in the economic dependence of women on men'. Capitalism, MacDonald argues, produces people who are 'classed' as well as 'sexed', who are to take their place in a 'social division of labour structured by the dual, yet often contradictory, forces of class and gender relations' (MacDonald 1980: 13).

This complex debate is intrinsic to any discussion of curriculum theory, since it involves questions of the reproduction of gender relations and its link with the reproduction of capitalism. According to MacDonald, any theory of education which seeks to account for the form of schooling in terms of the mode of reproduction of the work-force must recognize the structure of male-female dominance as an integral and not a subsidiary organizing principle of the capitalist system. It is for this reason that she criticizes the influential work of Louis Althusser (1977) who, in his analysis of the role played by schools in transmitting an ideology of class domination, takes no account of the way in which this is mediated by an ideology of patriarchal domination. MacDonald herself sees the stratification of knowledge and the structuring of school relations as crucial elements within the process of a gendered work-force reproduction: the former involves a hierarchy of 'male' over 'female' subjects; while the latter reproduces the gender relations which exist within the workplace, with regard to both the sexual division of labour (hierarchy of boys over girls) and the male stranglehold on management positions (hierarchy of male head-teachers over girl pupils).

This is not to say that distinctions of class among women are not significant. Here MacDonald brings in 'the dual and contradictory role' of women as domestic and wage labourers. The education which working-class girls receive focuses on the former role, and this contributes to their seeing work outside the home as peripheral. So education becomes one of the ways in which the conditions are ensured for 'the continued existence of a female reserve army of labour and an unskilled, cheap, female labour force' (MacDonald 1980: 17). At the same time, the creation of a female domestic labour force is guaranteed, so that the biological reproduction and nurturance of workers on which the reproduction of capitalism depends is also ensured. The education of middle-class girls is different but, according to MacDonald, no less contradictory. For them, there is an overt ideology of equal opportunity and equality between the sexes, which is apparently realized in the equal range of curriculum options available to girls. This, however, runs counter to the hidden curriculum of the school (bolstered by the construction of gender relations within the family), which perpetuates an ideology of femininity as synonymous with the role of wife and mother. Middle-class girls are still likely to see this as their main role in life; and where work outside the home is accorded equal value, they tend to opt for the typically 'feminine' professions, like medicine, education and social work, which fit in to the ideology of 'the caring woman'. This does not, of course, prevent a conflict developing between the domestic and the workplace functions. In the education of middle-class girls, then, there is not such an overt ideology of sex difference brought to bear; but for girls of both classes there is an ideology of femininity which produces an acceptance of the sexual division of labour both within and outside of the home.

The concept of hegemony, developed by the Marxist philosopher Gramsci, has been used by other theorists to describe and account for the experience of women within the education system. The belief that the reproduction of existing social relations depends on the acceptance of the dominant system of beliefs and values by groups of oppressed peoples is clearly relevant where women are concerned: their willingness to assume their subordinate social role stems not just from their initiation into 'feminine' pursuits, but also from their acceptance of men's culture as a universally recognized and therefore 'natural' entity. Writers like Valli (1986: 181) and Kessler *et al.* (1985:35) have noted that there is a strong strain of functionalism in most reproduction theories: people are seen as passively receiving and reflecting the structures imposed on them through ideology and culture, and no account is taken of the role of consciousness as an active medium in this process. Kessler and her co-authors, in exploring the ways in which this consciousness is shaped within schools, discuss the part played by relationships between pupils and teachers and by the academic curriculum in creating dominant patterns of 'hegemonic masculinity' and 'emphasised feminity'.

In their analyses of the role played by education in the reproduction of gender difference, the Marxist and socialist feminist discourses have concentrated to a very high degree on the school as the key institution in this process. It is probably true to say that by the time women arrive in adult education classes, they have already been thoroughly schooled into an acceptance of their subordinate position in the family and workplace, and that adult education serves only to reinforce that acceptance. Certainly, the findings of Mee and Wiltshire (1978) and of ACACE (1982) suggest that the sexual division of labour, and the relegation of women to the domestic sphere, are strengthened by the curriculum of adult education, with its concentration on subjects related to household management and childcare. In this way, adult education can be seen to be completing the job of the school, and contributing to the process of social reproduction by teaching women to be better reproducers, servicers and repairers of the labour force. It may even be the case that courses outside the domestic category are seen as helping to enhance women's expertise as supporters of their families, if, as Bridget Barber has suggested, a significant number of them are drawn to more academic classes by an interest deriving from their children's secondary school work.[11]

But we should not forget that adult education is fulfilling this function of reinforcing the domestic role largely in relation to middle-class women. If MacDonald is right in saying that working-class girls are educated into seeing domestic labour as their most important role in life, while middle-class girls are more likely to accord equal value to work outside the home, then there is a contradiction here, since working-class women stay away from adult education in droves. It seems that we need a more sophisticated interpretation of the reinforcing role of adult education. I think this is provided in part by Keddie, when she identifies an ideology of individualism as a crucial element within the value system purveyed by adult education:

> ...many of these subjects provide for the socially sanctioned ways in which women, especially middle-class women, can express individuality in managing and servicing the home, through the special dinner party recipe or the colour blends of the furnishings or the arrangement of flowers. In this respect the mainstream curriculum of local authority provision not only underpins the status quo and services the traditional roles of women, but it is uniquely geared to meet the notions of individualism which those roles require
>
> (Keddie 1980: 56)

Keddie maintains here that adult education is seen by middle-class women as providing them with an opportunity to restate their sense of themselves as individuals against the demands made on them at home to service the needs of others. But at the same time the gender conditioning which they have received ensures that the outlets which they seek are ones that support rather than contradict their role as household managers. Even courses which are not obviously related to this role – courses like painting, literature, art appreciation – may have a reinforcing effect in that, by meeting the need for self-expression, they help to reduce the sense of frustration experienced within the home. In this way, the bourgeois ideology of individualism is met, but without disturbing the sexual division of labour. In the words of Keddie, adult education can be seen in this light as 'enabling women to become more satisfied consumers of their own oppression'.[12] But the ideology of individualism has less meaning for working-less women, possibly because, as Paul Willis (1977) believes, the collective counter-school culture to which many working-class children subscribe militates against its development. At the same time, the schooling which these women have received has placed less emphasis on achievement outside the home. Hence working-class women do not feel the same need to express themselves as individuals through the 'competent, lively and intelligent housewife' persona which is being fostered in adult education classes.

Adult education still responds to a very high degree to the limited and prescribed needs of middle-class women. But since Nell Keddie expressed this view in 1980, there have been *some* changes (although not as many as we generally like to think). There has been an increase in the number of middle-class women studying more academic subjects. This can be interpreted as the result of the penetration of a liberal feminist perspective into education in general, which has strengthened the residual, 'catching up with men' character of adult education. To the extent that the teaching of these academic subjects conforms to the student-centred ideology of adult education, then it underscores the individualist approach to learning, which once again tends to exclude working-class women, and which masks the system of gender relations by which middle-class women too are ultimately constrained. To the extent that it embraces the traditional model of the curriculum, then it reproduces the categories of secondary schooling, and exposes women to the diverse hegemonic pressures distinguished by Kessler and her co-writers.

Another change has been the appearance in recent years of the computing/plumbing-for-women-type courses. The residual character of these is a varied one. In some cases, it permits the entry of selected women into the management hierarchies previously monopolized by men, while doing nothing to challenge the oppressive system of gender relations to which these women are often subjected in their domestic lives. In other cases, it seems to invite women to become even better managers of their homes, by providing them with the skills they need to do the jobs around the house traditionally performed by men. The growth in courses of this kind could well be linked to the increase in the number of single-parent families; in any event, the outcome of them could be an even more complete polarization of gender roles, with women absolutely self-sufficient in the domestic sphere, and men completely redundant there. Finally, there is the growing likelihood that, in response to the demographic crisis, the residual character of adult education will make itself felt in the encouragement it offers to working-class women to become skilled labourers, and to see their role in the workplace as more than a peripheral one. While this is an eventuality to be welcomed, since it offers the best hope we have of attracting working-class women into adult education, we must not lose sight of the fact that these changes will increase the pressures on them as household managers, and will not substantially alter their exploitation within the labour market. In all cases, it is open to doubt whether adult education will succeed in transforming the male-centred categories of schooling; rather, it can be seen as responding to a shift in gender relations which is the function of a changing but ever-present patriarchal hegemony.

Conclusion

The Marxist/socialist feminist discourses are much stronger on analysis than they are on prescriptions for change, and in this respect they are less satisfying than either the liberal feminist or the radical feminist discourses. To the extent that they offer alternative programmes, these are broadly in line with those which emerge from the radical feminist approach to education, with the proviso that the total separatism advocated by writers like Spender is unacceptable to theorists who recognize the integration of systems of gender reproduction within the overall process of reproducing the social relations of capitalism. What these discourses do offer – and what to my mind makes them indispensable to any feminist strategy for transforming the adult curriculum – is a theoretical framework which enables us to analyse and transcend the problems inherent in the other two discourses. The liberal feminist perspective, which through its detailed criticisms of discriminatory policies and practices has highlighted some worthwhile short-term goals for women in adult education, cannot ultimately generate any transformation in gender relations, since it fails to challenge the basic social and economic structures in which the subordination of women is rooted. The radical discourse has developed the most effective agenda for a liberating education programme, but in its most extreme form it would isolate the challenge to patriarchal control within women's studies courses, and so run the risk of creating a separate anti-male subculture, which in spite of its overt resistance to patriarchy ultimately accepts its subordinate position within society.

The various pressures which are making themselves felt in adult education at the present time – the external demand for a return of women to the labour market, coupled with the campaigns of both liberals and radicals inside the system for more women-centred or women-only courses –

are creating a situation which yields a great deal of potential in terms of transforming the curriculum. But it remains to be seen whether this potential can be realized. What the Marxist/socialist discourses demonstrate is that no fundamental change will come about unless we can transcend the needs-meeting and ultimately reinforcing ideology into which adult education is currently locked. If women's studies are to be a medium through which this can be achieved, then their analysis and alternatives to the patriarchal construction of gender must be brought back into the mainstream of adult education, and located within an overall challenge to the social systems for the reproduction of difference.

Clearly, with women's studies still very much in their infancy as far as adult education is concerned, a great deal of work has to be done before we can begin to put this into practice. On one level, it is vital for feminists involved in adult education to engage in detailed discussions about the curriculum for women. They must consider how all the strands which at present make up adult women's education – the household management subjects, the 'catching up with men' or 'surviving in a man's world' courses, the traditional academic subjects, the 'discovery of women' classes – can be subsumed within a programme whose methods and knowledge content are directed towards tackling the root causes of women's oppression. They must campaign for the institutional reforms – such as more flexible teaching hours, creches, educational guidance – which are essential to an effective service for women. They must devise strategies both for the introduction of women-only provision and for ensuring a continual process of interaction between the women-only and the mainstream curriculum. What they must aim for is nothing less than the transformation of the adult curriculum as a whole. But on another level, what feminists must also bear in mind – and this above all is the lesson of the Marxist/socialist discourses – is that a struggle for women's liberation which is situated entirely within educational institutions is doomed to failure. The integration of women's oppression within a broader system of social domination makes it imperative that the struggle be carried out of the institutions, not just into the private lives of women, but into every area where the forces of oppression are at work. Adult education must at the end of the day recognize its own limitations.

Notes

1 Sue Blundell has degrees in Classical Civilization from the University of London. She teaches Greek history to adult students at Birkbeck College, London, and for the Open University, and has just completed a book about women in Ancient Greece. This paper is based in part on a dissertation which she wrote in 1989 for a Diploma in Continuing Education from Goldsmith's College, London.

2 See Middleton (1984) for a perceptive and critical survey of some of this research.

3 See Spender (1981b), and Acker, in Acker and Piper (1984: 25–48).
4 In 1988/9, of students enrolled on part-time day and evening adult education courses, 26.3% were men, and 73.7% were women (*Statistics of Further and Higher Education*, Department of Education and Science, 1988/9).
5 A number of papers have been published which examine the patriarchal bias of particular disciplines: see, for example, a paper by Kelly (1985), in which she puts forward the view that science is masculine not merely because it is perceived as such, but also because it is packaged as such; and an influential article by Ardener (1972), in which he claims that the analytic tools which a male-oriented intellectual tradition has supplied to social anthropologists equip them only to respond to the world views of male informants, and neither to hear nor to understand the views held by women. Probably the most successful and detailed critique of a patriarchal discipline has been the one that Ann Oakley (1974) has applied to sociology. More recently, Jean Grimshaw (1986) has examined some of the basic tenets of philosophy from a feminist perspective.
6 Young's *Knowledge and Control* (1971) is generally seen as the definitive work which helped to launch the new sociology of education. To be fair to Young, he has in a recent paper (Young 1988: 10) set out as one of the weaknesses of the new sociology of education the fact that it has neglected questions of race and gender.
7 See Firestone (1979), Ortner (1974) and Rosaldo (1974).
8 See Rich (1975) and Spender (1981b: 127).
9 See Freire (1972) and Knowles (1978).
10 See, for example, Bland *et al.* (1978).
11 Barber has suggested this in a private communication to Nell Keddie: see Keddie (1980: 232, n. 21). A number of my own students have given this as their reason for attending adult education classes.
12 From an unpublished paper by Nell Keddie – 'Adult education – a women's service?' – quoted in Thompson (1983: 84).

References

ACACE 1982, *Adults: their Education Experiences and Needs*, Leicester, ACACE.

Acker, S. 1981, No-woman's-land: British sociology of education, 1960–1979. *Sociological Review*, Vol. 29, No. 1, pp. 77–104.

Acker, S. 1984. Women in higher education: what is the problem?, in Acker and Piper (1984), pp. 25–48.

Acker, S. and Piper, D. (Eds) 1984, *Is Higher Education Fair to Women?*, Guildford, SRHE & NFER-Nelson.

Althusser, L. 1977, Ideology and ideological state apparatuses, in *Lenin and Philosophy and Other Essays*, trans. Ben Brewster, London, NLB, pp. 123–173.

Ardener, E. 1972, Belief and the problem of women, reprinted in S. Ardener (1975).

Ardener, S. 1975, *Perceiving Women*, London, Deni.

Bland, L., Brunsdon, C., Hobson, D. and Winship, J. 1978, Women 'inside and outside' the relations of production, in *Women Take Issues*, London, Hutchinson, with the University of Birmingham, Centre for Contemporary and Cultural Studies, Women's Studies Group.

Bunkle, P. 1979/80, A history of the women's movement, in five issues of *Broadsheet*, September 1979 to January/February 1980.

Byrne, E. 1978, *Women and Education*, London, Tavistock.

Coats, M. 1989, The case for women-only provision and a women-centred curriculum, in Cole (1989), pp. 33–36.

Cole, S. (Ed.) 1989, *Women Educating Women: Exploring the Potential of Open Learning*, Conference Papers, National Extension College, Cambridge.

Deem, R. 1980, *Schooling for Women's Work*, London, Routledge.

Engels, F. 1891/1940, *The Origin of the Family, Private Property and the State*, London, Lawrence and Wishart.

Evans, M. 1982, In praise of theory: the case for women's studies. *Feminist Review*, No. 10, pp. 60–74.

Firestone, S. 1979, *The Dialectics of Sex*, London, Women's Press.

Fitzgerald, A. 1978, Teaching interdisciplinary women's studies. *Faculty Newsletter*, Great Lakes College Association, 27 March.

Freire, P. 1972, *Pedagogy of the Oppressed*, Harmondsworth, Penguin.

Friend, H. 1980, *Continuing Education: from Policies to Practice*, Leicester, ACACE.

Friend, H. 1982 Second chance for women in British adult education? *Women Speaking*, Vol. 5, No. 12, October–December.

Griffin, C. 1983, *Curriculum Theory in Adult and Lifelong Education*, London, Croom Helm.

Grimshaw, J. 1986, *Feminist Philosophers: Women's Perspectives on Philosophical Traditions*, Brighton, Wheatsheaf.

Howe, F. (Ed.) 1975, *Women and the Power to Change*, New York, McGraw-Hill.

Hughes, M. and Kennedy, M. 1985, *New Futures: Changing Women's Education*, London, Routledge.

Keddie, N. 1980, Adult education: an ideology of individualism, in Thompson (1980), pp. 45–64.

Kelly, A. 1985, The construction of masculine science. *British Journal of Sociology of Education*, Vol. 6, No. 2, pp. 133–154.

Kessler, S., Ashenden, D., Connell, B. and Dowsett, G. 1985, Gender relations in secondary schooling. *Sociology of Education*, Vol. 58, pp. 34–48.

Knowles, M. 1978, *The Adult Learner: A Neglected Species*, Houston and London, Gulf.

MacDonald, M. 1980, Socio-cultural reproduction and women's education, in Deem (1980), pp. 13–25.

Mee, L. G. and Wiltshire, H. C. 1978, *Structure and Performance in Adult Education*, London, Longman.

Middleton, S. 1984, The sociology of women's education as a field of academic study. *Discourse*, Vol. 5, No. 1, pp. 43–62.

Oakley, A. 1974, *The Sociology of Housework*, London, Martin Robinson.

Ortner, S. B. 1974, Is female to male as nature is to culture?, in Rosaldo and Lamphere (1974), pp. 67–87.

Rich, A. 1975, Towards a woman-centred university, in Howe (1975), pp. 15–46.

Robyns, J. 1977, Reproductive versus regenerative education; the extension of English education through reference to feminism, unpublished Associateship Report, University of London, Institute of Education.

Rosaldo, M. Z. 1974, Woman, culture and society: a theoretical overview, in Rosaldo and Lamphere (1974), pp. 17–42.

Rosaldo, M. Z. and Lamphere, L. (Eds) 1974, *Woman, Culture and Society*, Stanford University Press.

Scribbins, J. 1989, Winning and developing equal opportunities in education – a practitioner's viewpoint, in Cole (1989), pp. 49–52.

Spender, D. 1980, *Man Made Language*, London, Routledge.

Spender, D. 1981a, Education: the patriarchal paradigm and the response to feminism, in Spender (1981b), pp. 155–173.

Spender, D. (Ed.) 1981b, *Men's Studies Modified: The Impact of Feminism on the Academic Disciplines*, Oxford, Pergamon.

Spender, D. 1982, *Invisible Women. The Schooling Scandal*, London, Writers and Readers Publishing Co-operative.

Thompson, J. (Ed.) 1980, *Adult Education for a Change*, London, Hutchinson.

Thompson, J. 1983, *Learning Liberation: Women's Response to Men's Education*, London, Croom Helm.

Valli, L. 1986, *Becoming Clerical Workers*, Boston, Routledge, pp. 137–182.

Willis, P. 1977, *Learning to Labour: How Working Class Kids get Working Class Jobs*, Farnborough, Saxon House.

Young, M. F. D. 1971, *Knowledge and Control: New Directions for the Sociology of Education*, London, Collier-Macmillan.

Young, M. F. D. 1988, *Curriculum and Democracy: Lessons from a Critique of the 'New Sociology of Education'*, Occasional Paper No. 5, University of London, Institute of Education, Centre for Vocational Studies.

Part 2
...to lifelong education

7 Basil Yeaxlee and lifelong education

Caught in time

Angela Cross-Durrant

Introduction

Basil A. Yeaxlee, CBE, MA, B Litt (Oxon), BA, PhD (London) was born in 1883 and died in 1967. He was deeply involved in adult education and religious education, as manifest by the following posts, amongst others, which he held during his working lifetime: 1915–18 Editorial Secretary of the National Council of Young Men's Christian Associations; 1917–19 Member of the Ministry of Reconstruction Adult Education Committee, which issued the famous 1919 Report; 1920–28 Secretary, Educational Settlements Association; 1930–35 Principal, Westhill Training College, Selly Oak; 1933–57 Editor of *Religion in Education*; 1935–49 University Reader in Educational Psychology, and Lecturer and Tutor in the Department of Education, Oxford; 1940–48 Secretary, Central Advisory Council for Adult Education in HM Forces; 1949–51 Secretary, Education Committee, British Council of Churches.

It is clear from some of his published work, viz. *Spiritual Values in Adult Education*, Vols. I & II (1925), *Towards a Full Grown Man* (1926), and *Religion and the Growing Mind* (1939), that religion was the spring from which he drank, the source of his interpretation of life, and the vehicle he used to convey his views about the meaning and purpose of education.

This discussion, however, whilst drawing on the works already cited to contextualize Yeaxlee's notions of education and growth (in accord with Dewey's definition), will concentrate on Yeaxlee's significant contribution to the notion of lifelong education.

His book, published in 1929, entitled *Lifelong Education*, is one of the earliest expressions of a vision of regarding all of life's resources and experiences as playing a related and meaningful part in an individual's education, and of education as being seen as truly life long. Yeaxlee viewed education at school as merely the start of the process, and in that sense projected education for adults beyond a compensatory, or occupationally expedient, activity. He also wished to unite the various 'realms' of education (primary, secondary, 'technical', university) in order to embark upon the joint enterprise of education for, through, and throughout life. (This plea for reform of the entire enterprise is echoed today by writers such as Flude and Parrott, who express dismay at the lack of progress made towards lifelong or recurrent education, and who point to 'existing institutions of education and training ... as impediments to recurrent education because they stem from an historical development which has tended to split them apart rather than bring them together' (1979: 25).)

Yeaxlee seems not to have received the recognition that he perhaps deserves, and this paper attempts to highlight his contribution to lifelong education, despite the arguably somewhat restrictive religious framework within which he worked out his ideas. Whereas his religious beliefs provided the vehicle, which today may be regarded as inappropriate, the message conveyed lives on, and is as significant – if not more so – now, as we face a future in which it could be argued that lifelong education is (ironically) regarded as socially and economically imperative to contend with an exponential rate of societal change, as it was when the UK looked to mobilize its social, political, educational and economic forces for reconstruction after the 1914–18 War.

The context

The history of adult education is signposted through the centuries by clergy wanting all members of society to be able to understand and ultimately read the Bible. From the 18th century, the rise of and progression from Sunday Schools, to Mechanics' Institutes, Working Men's Colleges, University Extension and the WEA, reflected the ideological thrust of people like F. D. Maurice, and later, A. Mansbridge, who firmly believed in the personal and social well-being (spiritual and physical) and emancipation that education could bring to the ordinary working man and woman. From a desire to share in the teachings of the Bible (i.e., a widening of the interpretation of its hitherto 'mystical' texts) grew also a desire to understand the political, economic and social forces of which they were victims in an attempt to change the condition in which they found themselves. The context of education gradually changed from the interpretation of religious and traditional dogma to effecting a forward surge of evolution to a better future, to social justice and the recognition of man's rights. The earlier considerable influence of religion and of the Anglican Church was seriously eroded by the Great War, because of the impact of Christian fighting Christian. When the government of the day set up committees for reconstruction after the war, the mood was one of relentless disillusionment. The battle in which people were caught up became one fought at the material level; the level of the spiritual or metaphysical was gradually abandoned. Whereas people in Britain had to an extent accepted the mediation of organized religion – in the form of the Christian church – between man and the idea of God, the search for social and personal emancipation brought with it a 'man-centred' (humanistic) response to life which no longer required a mediator between man and God, if it required the idea of God at all.

Self-reliance replaced faith in Christianity, since Christianity in the outer world had failed to produce what it had promised – love, peace and brotherhood. The bitter evidence of the Great War could not be denied. At this time – 1920s and 1930s – the heightened interest in the inner workings of the psyche (e.g. Freud, Jung) suggested that people expected 'something from psychic life which [they] had not received from the outer world' (Jung, 1966: 237). 'I do not believe that I am going too far when I say that modern man, in contrast to his nineteenth century brother, turns his attention to the psyche with very great expectations;' (239).

Some Christian educators recognized and acknowledged the supremacy of the 'humanistic socialism' pervading the day, e.g. R. H. Tawney (1964: 103).

> We have to revise the work not of four years but of a century and a half. The quarrel is not merely with the catastrophic changes of 1914–1919, but with the economic order of the age which began with the spinning-jenny and ended with the great war ... Social Reconstruction either means Social Revolution, or it means nothing.

These men sought to legitimize large-scale economic and social transformation for economic and social liberty and responsibility.

Yeaxlee, on the other hand, argued for transformation of education to prepare everyone for, and provide everyone with, continued lifelong education, so that having thereby gained his intellectual and, consequently, his spiritual freedom, man would find his way back to the Christian fold, better acquainted with himself, his fellows, the world and the metaphysical. He saw education as clarifying the image of man for man; that image not being simply a passive victim of his condition, but rather a vital, responsive, interactive agent capable of generating the right attitudes and future conditions for the flourishing of self-fulfilment and perpetual growth of harmony and of love, until all were united in a 'wholeness' of humanity and Christian faith. He saw education as the means of allowing everyone the wherewithal to enter the causal process of his environment and act upon it. By concentrating on the full development of individuals whilst emphasizing collective life, he argued, we can hope to seek freedom and claim responsibility. 'The aim, then, is a philosophy and a way of living, an insight and a joyous purpose, with some power of achieving it' (Yeaxlee, 1929: 165). He would have everyone develop 'his own individuality to the utmost, no longer as a separated and conflicting being but as a part and contribution to one continuing whole' (H. G. Wells in Yeaxlee, 1929: 164).

When referring to Robert Peers' similar views, Yeaxlee wrote:

> There all the distinctive notes of lifelong education are struck – know-
> ledge, experience, wisdom, harmony and the giving of self in service.
> All of them are rooted in the practical affairs of ordinary men and
> women. Each of them reaches out into the infinite. They are mean-
> ingless apart from the growth and the activities of the individual
> personality. They are impossible unless that personality is in perpetual
> living relationship to the whole – the whole of truth and the whole of
> life, immediate reality and ultimate.
>
> (165)

It is here that Yeaxlee's concern with the 'ultimate' and 'the whole', of
which he might have said we are all a part, comes to the fore. Whilst some
educators (e.g. Tawney and Dewey) and others with strong social con-
sciences and commitment looked to educational, social and politico-
economic reform or revolution for the betterment of the human
condition, Yeaxlee sought to use educational reform to lead people back
to God, thereby putting themselves at the (social) service of their fellows.

Yeaxlee's proposal was to induct children into metaphysical thinking
(i.e., direct them away from just the 'here and now', and the obvious
and physical), and to make explicit the metaphysical or spiritual
enquiry in adult education. He claimed that what was wrong with the
world was that it had 'lost sight of spiritual values' (Yeaxlee, 1925: 8);
that 'we have not found, or even set ourselves to find, that philosophy
which sees everything as part of one harmonious whole', using education to help young people and adults alike to develop personalities
'rightly and consciously related to society and the universe' (7). This
philosophy, or metaphysical quest, he argued, is a natural goal of every
person – 'In the depths of every mind there is a philosophy' (G. Gentile
in Yeaxlee, 1925: 9).

According to Yeaxlee, then, philosophy or seeking answers to metaphysical questions about the purpose, meaning and value of life, is not
beyond the 'shop and market place', nor 'beyond the ken of the common
people'. (Yeaxlee, 1925: 8–9). In psychological terms he speaks of this
capacity as an integral part of personality.

> The problem of knowledge, the problem of thought, the problem of
> unified moral action, are all problems that spring out of the greater
> problem of the nature of personality. How do we remain ourselves
> and yet go out of ourselves? How can we retain our identity and yet
> enter into innumerable relationships with others? To this Bergson
> offers an answer: 'Obviously there is a vital impulse ... something
> which ever seeks to transcend itself, to extract more from itself than
> there is – in a word to create. Now a force which draws from itself

more than it contains, which gives more than it has, is precisely what is called a spiritual force.

(Yeaxlee, 1925: 21)

It is this immanent force which Yeaxlee sought to uncover and develop throughout life (in the same sense as Dewey explored 'growth'; 1964: Chapter 4) in order to have it propel mankind toward values which would interpret and ennoble all of life, and place each individual, society and nation in a universal setting, thus enabling understanding of what makes life worth living.

Not *what* he is or does will be taken into account so much as *why* his life is of that quality or his actions of such a kind. The supreme question about him is not *whether* he can attain to the best men know in character or relationships, conditions of life or power of service, but *how* he is to be helped to attain them.

(Yeaxlee, 1925: 34)

Now no man is compelled by any force outside himself to take this view or to accept and live by these values.

(ibid.)

Why should we make any leap [in any one particular direction] at all, why not confine ourselves to the little bit of reality we have seen? The answer is that we are not only spectators of reality, we are also makers of reality. When we *act*, we create a new bit of reality ... The movement of time compels us, whether we want to or not, to act. But for action we need to form some hypothesis as to the universe in which we act, as to what lies beyond the range of previous experience.

(Mackenzie in Yeaxlee, 1925: 35)

Yeaxlee argued that education cannot escape the universal, the metaphysical dimension to the quality and meaning of life: questions such as: What is personality? How is each person related to other persons and to the universe? What is the meaning and purpose of human life? Where can we find a scale of values that is ultimate and universal? (He did not question that there was such a universal and ultimate 'scale'.) Education, he claimed, 'being inevitably concerned with them, should both implicitly and explicitly direct enquiry and thought towards them' (Yeaxlee, 1925: 54). On this point, he further argued that adult education could be envisaged as a spiritual activity because earlier schooling had failed to remove most people from the 'here and now'. Adults were capable of reevaluating their lives. 'Education as a weapon, or as an elevated form of recreation, appeals readily to many a man who has never conceived it as integral to life itself. The revelation of spiritual values and the adjustment of personal and social life to them ...' had not been seen as the 'supreme gains' of education (57). However, as adults, bringing with them wider experience of the rigours and 'practical wisdom' of, say, adult social and working life, such enquiry acquired relevance and perhaps urgency.

There are those today who, to an extent, would echo Yeaxlee's sentiment with regard to 'religious studies' forming an important part of individual cognitive development. See, for example, Jarvis' exposition of man's questions of meanings changing as he advances from childhood to youth to adulthood, and the way that changed circumstances or 'biography' can produce a situation 'in which the individual recommences his quest for meaning' (Jarvis, 1983a: 22).

> Since man's religious quest begins with the individual, then the aims of an adult education course [in religious studies] should relate to the facilitation of the growth of the ... participants and to assist them in discovering or rediscovering beliefs and ideas that they regard as relevant to their questions of meaning. In no way should the educator seek to inculcate ideas ... Finally, this approach recognizes no conflict between the process of exploring knowledge discovered in different disciplines and exploring beliefs articulated by various religions ... Hence the more we explore the meaning of life the more we may grow and develop – and that, surely, is an aim of adult education.
>
> (22–3)

Yeaxlee would go further, and say that the

> relationship between adult education and religion is not only close, but organic ... Either the relationship follows directly from the nature of personality, the meaning of spiritual values, and the necessities intrinsic to the educational process, or it is indeed negligible.
>
> (1925: 60)

> On the other hand, it is equally indisputable that a spiritual attitude towards life and the universe does not necessarily imply possession of definite religious faith...
>
> (62)

He did claim, however, that Christianity may be used as a vehicle for formalizing the relationship between education and religion because he argued that it was less open to superstition and misunderstanding than, say, Stoicism, Buddhism and so on.

Thus Yeaxlee claimed that by reflecting purposively upon man's own nature, the purpose of life 'and the nature of the power that controls the universe' (1926: 27) he would become 'full-grown', by having 'felt desperately the necessity and gained some glimpse of the possibility of such a view of life – nay, until he has began to test it, and found that he can live by it. His philosophy must become his religion' (28). This could be achieved, he argued, by referring to gestalt psychology. Perceiving outward objects, actions, etc., in patterns 'each part of which owes its significance to its relationship to the other parts, while the whole is more than the sum of the parts' (Yeaxlee, 1952: x) was the start. 'Furthermore, we are constantly aware of incomplete patterns and we find ourselves impelled to try to complete them ... by insight' (ibid.). This is how man might perceive the 'wholeness' or the 'universal'. This process, he argued, should begin in childhood, with education aimed at developing to the full the sentient and sentimental (in the truly psychological sense) personality or disposition of every child, and was best achieved by including Christian religious study in the school curriculum to provide the best model for understanding and for behaviour. (The effect of this view on his notion of lifelong education will be discussed later.)

This, then, was the religious inspiration of Basil Yeaxlee. He quite clearly believed that study of, and reflection upon, the Christian way of life, as part of the educative process would lead to a 'better' life for all. In a world far more secularized now than at the time of his earlier writing, his inspiration appears somewhat confined. On the other hand, there are those who would commend a 'philosophical' stance (as opposed to a religious one) in education on the grounds that 'Philosophy ought to transform those who pursue it. People ought to be better, by being philosophical' (Sprague, 1978: 5). The point might be said to be made, grandiloquently admittedly, by Sir Thomas Browne: 'The world was made to be inhabited by beasts, but studied and contemplated by man'. Contemporary philosophers might enlarge upon this by explaining the world, philosophically, at any rate, as all that

> anyone might perceive. The effect ... is to bring out that we expect to get in touch with the sum of all that is, by perceiving what we can of it, and understanding that there is still more to it than we can perceive at any one time. These considerations will lead one to say that we do not see the world, but only bits of it; so the world is not a perceptible thing, but a notion we have that there is a system that contains all we have seen, and can see, and more.
>
> (Sprague: 84)

This enquiry and perception has then to made meaningful.

> Generally, things become meaningful to us as we attach values. Family, community, church, nation are meaningful to us because they represent certain values. Would that be equally true of mankind? Is not mankind meaningless to most of us because we do not attach any particular value to it? This may be a matter of indifference rather than intent. Some may

also question whether the survival of mankind is worth the effort involved. But suppose we had determined that civilization must not perish, that we want to make a better world for our children if not for ourselves, that through education we must try to create a better understanding of our world. Would mankind not then become meaningful?

(Hirschfield in Ulich, 1964: viii)

Though a secularized sentiment, there is much in these views which is in sympathy with Yeaxlee's ends.

Unfortunately, the irrational behaviour of man is caused not only by his psychological limitations; it has its cause also in our intellect itself. For purposes of clarity, the intellect has to isolate the object of its attention from the whole within which it stands. Even when we try to extend the span of our interest as far as possible, the whole is beyond our grasp; it exists only in our vision, or intuition. Yet, without a picture of the whole we cannot even comprehend the single ... behind every person is also his society, his nation, and its history, mankind, and finally the universe. It is good to remind ourselves from time to time of all this infinity in order to acquire this healthy relativism, which should prevent us from idolizing ourselves and our nation, our creeds, our truths, and our little knowledge.

(Ulich, 1964: 22–3)

It serves no purpose to quibble over whether there is something beyond the universe; it is the sentiment that should herald reflection upon mankind and its destiny. 'The point of reflection is to minimize the risks involved in acting inappropriately' (Kekes, 1980: 33). Whereas Kekes looks to philosophers to interpret, criticize, defend or develop 'world views', Yeaxlee would argue that, with appropriate education, everyone could contribute to that process. Others might well point to the fact, however, that 'In the face of violence and destruction that have come upon us this century, a philosophy based on the fundamental goodness of man seems altogether naïve' (Kitwood, 1970: 86).

It would seem, nonetheless, that the quest for meaning and purpose has endured throughout time, in all segments of the globe. Sometimes it has been conveyed or interpreted through myths, through religions or through philosophy. The questions remain; they remain unanswered yet seemingly pertinent to each generation. (Perhaps the reason we are now, particularly, failing to answer questions about our humanity is because, tied as we are to 'the scientific method' and to 'objectivity', we cannot cope with questions which concern us most, and in which we are inextricably involved. However, 'We must ... try to understand what is human for the very simple reason that we have a human life to live (Kitwood, 1970: 8)). Whereas Yeaxlee articulated his possible solutions in religious vocabulary, his attempt is no less worthy than that of philanthropists, politicians and philosophers who came after him and who made the attempt in 'secularized language'. Yeaxlee's book on lifelong education may be fairly described as 'before its time', for despite its religious roots, his vision stretched beyond his times, beyond the contemporary boundaries of educational practice, to what is regarded today as a boldly speculative (though in some countries being actually introduced) notion of a reformed educational scene. It is to this particular publication, containing forward-looking pedagogic and andragogic ideas, that this discussion now turns.

Lifelong education – then and now

In his book published in 1929, Yeaxlee looked to the education of adults to help a nation to 'grow up', to seek the twin ideals of freedom and responsibility. 'We begin to seek quality in living – more life and fuller' (Yeaxlee, 1929: 23). Based on a notion of 'knowledge as the mother of understanding and thus of creative enjoyment' (24), he saw the adult education movement as a means of achieving a harmonized world and a more democratic lifestyle. He would have all adults aware of and responsive to 'industrial disputes and social crises', rather than subject to 'crass ignorance and culpable narrowness of outlook ... They are the fruitful irritant sources of malignant disease in the body politic. The less we are conscious of them the more, like repressions and complexes in the individual personality, they work desperate mischief' (22). He pointed to improved, and prolonged, education of children and young adults as an optimistic and positive step in achieving the wherewithal to generate such understanding and behaviour, and looked particularly to what he described as 'within sight', the full-time education for all to the age of 15 or 16, and 'a great increase in the facilities for higher education given as a right of citizenship, independently of social status or financial circumstances' (ibid: 26). He then addressed himself to a question which, it seems, even today has considerable currency – a view which has long influenced the paucity of resources trickled into adult educational provision.

> Shall we not then grow out of the need for adult education – and perhaps sooner than we anticipate? Ought we not to avoid exaggerating the importance of it, and to recognise that it is a transitory social phenomenon, a medicine for a social weakness which we are rapidly overcoming rather than a part of 'human nature's daily food'?
>
> (26)

This is followed shortly afterwards by what could be viewed as the linchpin of the modern Lifelong Education movement, as outlined, for example, by Dave and his colleagues (1976).

We discover more, and not less need of adult education as we make progress. It will not have a fair chance until better preparation is made for it during the years of adolescence. On the other hand, we are unlikely to achieve a thoroughly sound and complete system of primary and secondary education until the adult members of the community, by continuing their own education, realize how mischievous a thing it is to abbreviate or mishandle the school-education of boys and girls. But adult education, rightly interpreted, is as inseparable from normal living as food and physical exercise.

(Yeaxlee, 1929: 28)

Educare, he reminded his readers, was used to refer to the healthy physical development of children. 'By a natural transition the idea was applied to the process of mental growth. The needs we have indicated are universal ... incessant and lifelong' (28). Thus he claimed that all adults had these same requirements. Adult education, he further clarified,

may have its special value ... as an aid to the realization of political or economic freedom, a resource for the pleasurable and profitable employment of leisure time, a means of gratifying personal tastes and ambitions ... If it is regarded as nothing more than a manner of 'finishing' one's education, ... it is completely travestied...

(28–9)

Inasmuch as we are all involved in political and social strife, changes and interpretations, 'it becomes obvious that we all stand in need of much wider and fuller lifelong education' (34). 'The enjoyment of expansion, of growth and exercise', he claimed, was to be found in the love of sport, exciting music, dancing and so on.

Education does not imply any detraction of the sparkle and the sting from these expressions of vitality. It sends them on fresh ... voyages of discovery, with more reliable compasses and with better charts – which they are to take their share in completing ... When, therefore, we interpret adult education in terms of life and people, and not merely in those of books and subjects of formal study, we shall see fresh opportunities and stimulating challenges everywhere ... The distinction between 'highbrow' and 'lowbrow' ... will no longer possess meaning.

(36)

'Education', he affirmed, 'involves knowledge, experience and fellowship. For that reason it is never finished, and cannot be more than begun in childhood and youth' (39). As he saw it, because we continue – or have the capacity to continue – to grow intellectually (and he cited Spearman's and Thorndike's work to support his claim) long after leaving, and outside, formal education, he was at pains to establish the view that adult education ought not to be regarded as compensating for earlier deficiencies, or as a rival to technical (now perhaps 'professional' or 'vocational') education, or as the 'poor sister' of higher education. Nor did he accept that people received all the education they were ever likely to need or want by the time they left formal education. (Incidentally, he was one of M. Knowles' (1978) precursors in drawing attention to motivating factors in adult learners. 'It is largely in order that he may answer the questions or satisfy the hungers stimulated by the experience of daily life that he [the adult learner] turns to the resources of class, lecture-room, or library' (Yeaxlee, 1929: 44).)

He also heralded a much-vexed issue of parity of esteem for 'vocational' and 'liberal' education.

> Clearly, it is not a matter of superiority or inferiority ... The two are simply different – but also complementary ... The consideration of motive and aim is relevant and helpful only when we agree that in both fields the governing impulse may and should be a worthy one, and that in the complete personality, fulfilling a proper function in society, the two will blend harmoniously.
>
> (129)

The solution to this enduring dualism, he argued, was for the agencies of education to 'attain this unity of spirit and purpose [i.e. the full bloom of personality and growth] amidst differentiation of functions' (141). He urged society to keep in mind that in a democratic community, everyone has a distinctive contribution to its well-being and progress; that difference is not to be equated with inferiority. 'Humanistic studies ... must surely include all that for them lends living a deeper significance and a more abiding joy, whichever of the senses or of the areas in the grey matter of the brain may happen to be the gateways whereby it finds entry' (153). In closing, 'humanistic studies', he claimed, can have no finality. 'If we ask ... "When is his (a man's) education complete?" the only true answer is "Never while he lives." ... There all the distinctive notes of lifelong education are struck ...' (164).

Many of Yeaxlee's sentiments are echoed by writers such as R. H. Dave (1976: 34): 'Lifelong education is a process of accomplishing personal, social and professional development throughout the lifespan of individuals in order to enhance the quality of life of both individuals and their collectives'. They are reflected also in A. J. Cropley's articulation of 'self-actualization' (in Dave (Ed.) 1976: 191), or H. Janne's sociological perspective of education being a 'dimension of the whole life' in which individuals would 'evolve along a continuum where study, work, leisure, responsible decision-making will at all times be present, any one of these preponderating temporarily and largely irrespective of age' (ibid: 174, 175). Certainly, clear echoes may be heard in R. Boshier's account of a learning society, which dismisses the idea that education for adults as an 'intermittent peripheral activity only engaged in by people with the necessary time, money and energy' (1980: 2), but rather views adult education as a normal, integral part of a lifetime of learning, living and working. These echoes may also be detected in E. Faure's recommendations for 'lifelong education as the master concept for educational policies in the years to come' (1972: 182), and in A. J. Cropley's 'stocktaking' of lifelong education (see Cropley (Ed.), 1979). The current movement imagines the whole in order to execute the parts, just as Yeaxlee did. And Yeaxlee would have concurred wholeheartedly with P. Lengrand: 'While waiting for spectacular decisions concerning the whole of society, everyone can, and should, see to it that in his own position, at his level of responsibility, the principles of lifelong education are applied, even if only in parts' (Lengrand in Cropley, 1979: 35).

Yet for all this, Yeaxlee receives a mention by Suchodolski (in Dave, 1976: 58), but is otherwise a silent influence in the growing interest in the concept of lifelong education. Of course, it could be argued that his vision of lifelong education was restricted by his somewhat narrow parameters, and that his notions did not burgeon and mature, but remained rather tight-budded. It could also fairly be said that his views were prescriptive compared with the 'largesse' of today's multifaceted, humanitarian, all-embracing, pervasive notion of education and life being fully integrated – with the individual self-actualized, able to stand in his own right, his own personality, rather than the pale reflection of a perceived perfect entity (however defined). Today, the nature of the plurality of lifestyles perhaps precludes 'an answer' – there has to be scope for a number of answers. Interestingly, however, there remain enduring questions about meaning, purpose and goals, and their relationship to education. There also remains the struggle to persuade those with power and with control of resources that the learning process in adulthood is very active, and that learning and living are inseparable in an unfolding lifelong developmental process.

Yeaxlee recognized man's innate quest for meaning; his ever-present capacity for learning. He wished to channel them in one direction throughout life; the modern movement allows for many directions. They both seek to help man reach out beyond the exigencies of survival to a meaningful existence, because both perspectives respect man's capacity to do so.

Conclusion

'The unexamined life is not worth living.' (Socrates)

It appears that when 'throwing out the bathwater', posterity may well have (temporarily) 'lost the baby'. Religion as an educative vehicle gradually lost its supremacy as secularization gained popularity. Perhaps this is why a writer so committed to religious inspiration and design was lost to a society increasingly looking to man and 'humanness' as opposed to 'superman' and the religiously metaphysical. Nonetheless, a metaphysical perspective on human life still has currency – albeit largely but not exclusively in the philosophical realm. Many people would, perhaps, prefer to use the term 'philosophical' rather than 'religious', but Jarvis (1983b) does make the point that religion is one element in man's response to the process of questioning, that the questioning endures, and has endured throughout time. In his sociologically slanted discussion on religiosity, he makes a powerful case for regarding any process of the questioning for meaning as 'religious': 'Religion is, therefore, regarded as an element in man's response to this fundamental process of questioning ... the provision of answers to questions of meaning suggests, at the very least, that the person has pondered upon the problem of human existence and may thus be described as being religious' (Jarvis, 1983b: 55). Human beings have always sought universal meaning beyond merely detailed knowledge. The language or medium of religion, once popular, used to convey the collective and personal search may seem inappropriate now, but the process – as argued for example by Jarvis – when analysed, can offer great insight into personal development and the realization and nourishing of the 'self'.

Yeaxlee phrased his similar outlook in terms of individual personality in interaction with society. He wished to emphasize religion as an educative tool in this respect; others (e.g. Jarvis) emphasize 'religiosity'; philosophers emphasize 'metaphysical' thought.

What Yeaxlee attempted was to suggest a plan to draw upon man's inherent quest (in a process of lifelong education), to help equip him with the intellectual and affective instruments to guide him to a truly democratic, benevolent society, committed to Christianity. Whilst some looked to government and politics for potentially sweeping changes in society, Yeaxlee focused his attention on each individual in a universal setting. He would have had everyone understand him/herself and the concept of the universe, in order to unite to concert collective effort towards an ultimate goal. He was not alone in expecting that each individual could reach out beyond his/her inheritance to seek out the question of meaning and quality of life and explore its possibilities. But this enterprise simply withers in irrelevance if the 'religious' or 'philosophical' investigations are not related to the task of clarifying in which way the examined life is worth living. It is laden with individual value judgements, whilst at the same time searching for a sharable, or universal and enduring, meaning.

Lifelong education, if it means anything at all, is an attempt to reconcile the search for a potent self in relation to a potent, democratic and ever-changing society. There have been many attempts at scaling this phenomenological mountain – from ideologists (e.g. Marx), religionists (e.g. Yeaxlee), religious ideologists (e.g. Freire), philosophers (e.g. Dewey) and 'global' educationists (e.g. Dave, Cropley, Janne *et al.*). In its evolution, mankind has drunk from many springs to sustain its (sometimes dubious) progress, to improve its understanding of itself, its condition, environment and purpose. Too often, whilst advocating harmony it has brought about destructive polarization.

There is always the danger of vagueness when an holistic view of all these attempts is taken, in order to select what is best in each. The movement of Lifelong Education makes a determined effort by drawing from historical, sociological, anthropological, economic, psychological, 'theoretical' and methodological fields. Some of these perspectives embrace ideologies; rarely do religious aspects enter the discussions, if only even from the historical or philosophical viewpoint. It is perhaps a pity that Yeaxlee's contribution rarely features in the discussions since he so clearly embraced all its major principles. His perspective may well be described as solitary, or too sharply circumscribed by his Anglican beliefs to register in the current school of thought. Nonetheless, his view of education and educability was prophetically optimistic; he gave expression to reform of education to prepare the way for a lifetime of learning; and he sought to bridge the unnecessary elitist divide between 'academic' and 'vocational' education, some 50 years before UNESCO embraced the movement for Lifelong Education. The spring from which he drank may be running somewhat dry now, but the inspiration it gave him to explore an educational plan, which today is gaining ever more respect as the movement clarifies its philosophy, ought not to be unrespected or ignored.

Whether a religious, philosophical or ideological microscope/telescope or perspective is used to 'examine' life, the one linking strand is that education sets the sights, and that a lifetime of education ensures continuous examination.

Yeaxlee wished, through education, to ennoble man in the image of God; humanists, on the other hand, wished to ennoble him in his own right. Either way, both perspectives allow for ennoblement; it is just that one seeks the qualifying adjective and attendant ideals of 'Christian' (or other religious outlook), and the other no qualifying adjective at all, except perhaps 'humanitarian'. Currently, in the struggle for survival, the aspects of life with which man tends to wrestle are those that pertain to the social, economic and physical well-being of existence. The battle is fought at the immediately human level; the level of the spiritual or metaphysical tends to be largely set aside. This is perhaps a 'sign of the times', times which are 'realistic' and 'pragmatic'. But just because 'times' change it does not mean that earlier educational contributions or theoretical approaches to the battle should be forgotten. They, too, are inextricably woven into the tapestry depicting the history of the fight, always challenging injustice, bigotry, oppression, class war, and so on. And if it can be accepted that the distinction may be made, whether it comes from the spirit, heart or mind, part of the ennoblement may lie in that very challenge.

References

Boshier, R. (Ed.) 1980, *Towards a Learning Society*, Vancouver, Learning Press.

Cropley, A. J. (Ed.) 1979, *Lifelong Education: A Stocktaking*, UIE Monograph, Paris, UNESCO.

Dave, R. H. (Ed.) 1976, *Foundations of Lifelong Education*, Paris, UNESCO.

Dewey, J. 1964, *Democracy and Education* (first publ. 1916), New York, Collier-Macmillan.

Faure, E. (Chairman) 1972, *Learning to be*, Paris, UNESCO.

Flude, R. and Parrott, A. 1979, *Education and the Challenge of Change*, Milton Keynes, Open University Press.

Hirschfield, G. 1964, 'The Council for the Study of Mankind' in R. Ulrich (Ed.) *Education and the Idea of Mankind.*

Kekes, J. 1980, *The Nature of Philosophy*, Oxford, Blackwell.

Kitwood, T. M. 1970, *What is Human?*, London, Inter-Varsity Press.

Jarvis, P. 1983a, 'The lifelong religious development of the individual and the place of adult education: in *Lifelong Learning: The Adult Years*, May, 15, 9, pp. 20–23.

Jarvis, P. 1983b, 'Religiosity – a theoretical analysis of the human response to the problem of meaning', University of Birmingham, *Bulletin for the Institute for the Study of Religious Architecture*, pp. 51–66.

Jung, C. G. 1966, *Modern Man in Search of a Soul* (first publ. 1933): London, Routledge and Kegan Paul.

Knowles, M. 1978, *The Adult Learner: A Neglected Species*, Houston, Gulf Publishing Co.

Sprague, E. 1978, *Metaphysical Thinking*, New York, Oxford University Press.

Ulich, R. (Ed.) 1964, *Education and the Idea of Mankind*, University of Chicago Press.

Tawney, R. H. 1964, *The Radical Tradition*, Harmondsworth, Penguin Books.

Yeaxlee, B. A. 1925, *Spiritual Values in Adult Education* (2 vols.), Oxford University Press.

Yeaxlee, B. A. 1926, *Towards a Full Grown Man* (The John Clifford Lecture), London, The Brotherhood Movement.

Yeaxlee, B. A. 1929, *Lifelong Education*, London, Cassell.

Yeaxlee, B. A. 1952, *Religion and The Growing Mind* (first publ. 1939), London, Nisbett and Co.

8 Lifelong education and adult education

The state of the theory

Kenneth Wain[1]

Some years ago when the concept of lifelong education was in vogue and when there was a constant flow of literature about it being published by a core of writers gravitating around or employed by UNESCO, the constant warning was not to confuse the concept of lifelong education with adult education because this would unduly limit the concept and distort the educational philosophy it represented. This warning has not, generally, been heeded by writers and the expression 'lifelong education' has consequently lost the distinctive meaning writers like Dave, Cropley, Gelpi and Lengrand tried to give it in the 1970s and early 1980s. In 1979 Cropley edited a book called *Lifelong Education: A Stocktaking* which, in fact, tried to take stock of the state of the theory and to identify the problems with its promotion. Gelpi took up the latter task in some detail in a subsequent article but failed to address certain problems with the concept of lifelong education itself, raised earlier by Lawson. This paper goes over all this ground and then tries to clarify some confusions with the concept of lifelong education by examining two different interpretations or views of lifelong education, the 'maximalist' and the 'minimalist', which have evolved through the literature of the subject, identifying the former with the core of writers mentioned above. It then examines the role of adult education within the two interpretations, arguing that the 'maximalist' view has largely disappeared to the detriment of adult education, and reproposing it anew to adult education writers and practitioners.

In 1979 A.J. Cropley edited a book called *Lifelong Education: A Stocktaking* which included papers in it by some of the most established names in the lifelong education literature. The authors had reviewed that literature over the previous five years. My intention in this article is to repropose, roughly 12 years later, the theoretical problems for the concept of lifelong education and the issues that were identified in that report with the object of restating and reassessing them. At the same time I shall be especially interested in one particular issue/problem: the common identification of lifelong education with adult education and the detrimental consequences of this identification for both. Finally, I shall be reproposing a particular theoretical frame, that of the 'education research programme', which would establish some order in the field thus avoiding some of those consequences.

The Cropley report was concerned with four broad and general questions: (1) what clarification has so far been achieved in thinking about lifelong education? (2) What are the major unresolved issues? What problems still exist? (3) What are the major implications of lifelong education for educational practice? (4) What are the prospects for the future? Where should effort now be focused (Cropley 1979: 2)? It was the co-operative product of seven authors (Cropley himself, Suchodolski, Lengrand, Richmond, Stock, Carelli, Pfluger), five of whom also attended a meeting on the subject.

The concept of lifelong education, they decided, could be approached at three levels: (a) as a 'philosophy' of education; in which case the analysis would be in terms of its ultimate goals, moral and ethical basis, internal consistency, degree of fit with more general philosophical systems, and so on; (b) as a theory either derived from observation or educational experience or else suggesting the general nature of practices which could be adopted, in which case discussion would turn on comprehensiveness, effectiveness, responsiveness to perceived deficiencies of practice, feasibility, etc.; (c) in terms of specific practices, longstanding or novel, said to define it; the evaluations here would be formal, 'experimental' (Cropley 1979: 4–5). Thus, they held, two sets of questions could be separated and asked; theory questions, and questions about actual practices. The theoretical questions they identified were:

1   Is lifelong education a philosophy of education, a set of operational principles, both of these or neither?
2   Is lifelong education compatible with any social or political philosophy, or does it imply a particular model of human nature, accept only certain ultimate goals as good, and so on?
3   What is the typical and unique contribution of lifelong education to existing educational theory?
4   What agreement has been reached concerning the notion of lifelong education? What are the key issues and problems which need to be investigated? What kinds of approach hold the most promise?

With regard to the meaning of lifelong education, Pucheu (Cropley 1979) had attempted to simplify things by reducing the issue to five questions: lifelong education for whom? by whom? of what? how? and had judged that they had not been answered at the time. His view then was that lifelong education was an 'elastic concept' with no precise meaning, and that it would remain so until these questions were answered. What seems to have been the scope behind Pucheu's list of 'practical' questions was to bring 'an end to concentration only on global abstractions' (Cropley 1979: 21) which was typical of the early theorizing about lifelong education (Wain 1987). Cropley's own view in 1979 was that 'no single answer exists for each' (1979: 21) of Pucheu's questions and that only 'general guidelines' were possible and available from the literature since 1974, which was the material considered for the 'stocktaking' report. Cropley proceeded to identify these 'guidelines', and this is probably the limit any attempt to answer them should be ambitious to achieve. Also, while sympathizing with Pucheu's frustrations with the early theory of life-long education, the point to be made against his own simplification of the issue is that too narrow a conception of the 'practical' can carry the yen to simplify too far. What is required to render a concept less 'elastic' is its sys-tematic clarification and this need not require its 'simplification'. Indeed simplifying issues to a few cryptic questions like Pucheu's can be a way of cutting corners rather than effectively distilling the analysis for the sake of clarity. Besides, epistemologically there is no question of escaping 'theory' in a search for 'practicality'; one can harbour the illusion of being able to do so, but it is a dangerous illusion to harbour. The dichotomy between the practical and theoretical is unreal; even the most 'practical' of judge-ments presupposes a relative theory. Meta-questions of these kinds identi-fied by Cropley and the team of theorists who discussed them cannot be avoided as Pucheu seemed to want to suggest.

Lengrand, in fact, began his own written contribution to the report by declaring that 'the principal danger threatening lifelong education is to forget that it is a concept' (1979: 28). He continued to say that its 'signific-ance and range' was, in fact, already clear, that it 'does not float in the clouds of Utopia, but is based on an analysis of real situations' (1979: 28). And he repeated the same claim ten years later (1986). For Lengrand 'life-long education' has come to play a similar role to other key concepts that have appeared at certain points in history, 'notions such as liberty, justice and the rights of man' (1979: 18). In other words, Lengrand saw 'lifelong education' as not only already established but as located among those con-cepts that have served humanity as a radical rallying call for reform. Suchodolski similarly described it as 'a notion which has triumphantly resounded throughout Europe and the entire world' (1979: 36). At the same time he conceded actual divergence in the 'diagnoses and prognoses concerning lifelong education'. The fundamental issues that underlay these divergences, he continued to say concern 'social and metaphysical conceptions(s) of life'. Thus, 'if it is true that our civilisation stands at the crossroads – as it undoubtedly does – then lifelong education necessarily stands at the same crossroads' (1979: 37). Quoting Comenius, Suchodol-ski described lifelong education as 'a struggle seeking to make all people more human' (1979: 39). In this context, he complained that 'there is no evidence that contemporary societies are evolving towards the ideal' which he referred to as the 'educative society'. His view was that the 'apostles and prophets' of lifelong education 'wander alone on this land shaken by social conflicts and political tensions, a land of plenty and of famine, of heroic struggle for national liberation, social progress and elementary education, and of the satiation, lassitude and degeneration which characterizes the beginning of the post-industrial epoch' (1979; 40). For Suchodolski, the question regarding the future of lifelong education is identical to the question of the future of our civilization. Which will triumph, he asks without much optimism, the 'educative society' or the 'ecospasm' of our civilization?

Richmond and Stock showed a typically Anglo-Saxon difference of approach to the subject from their European colleagues. Richmond opened ambiguously and controversially with the statement that 'in discussing lifelong education the verbal label is not important: on the other hand, it is not unimportant'. He opined that the best English usage is 'continuing education' rather than 'lifelong education'. But, at the same time, he argued further that the concept of 'continuous education' is at once a philosophy and a theory, both of which find their expression in ongoing practices in contemporary society (1979: 63). Stock, on the other hand, was concerned with certain 'post-school educational developments' in the UK and elsewhere, partly in reaction 'to the neglect, damning-with-faint-praise or outright dismissal of this diverse but increasingly powerful sector of provision, which denigration has often appeared in the literature of lifelong education' (1979: 78) mainly, if I understand Stock correctly, through the confusion over different nomenclatures or 'labels' used in the sector; 'lifelong education', 'adult education', 'recurrent education' and 'career education', which are often misunderstood and regarded as virtually synonymous.

Cropley closed the account with the discussions during the meeting, which was attempted by five of the writers (those not attending were Richmond and Stock), plus Gelpi, and which focused on the two sets of questions mentioned earlier: those regarding lifelong education as a way of theorizing about education and as a set of practices. He distinguished two ways in which the concept and its practices could be theorized. One begins with theorizing about the nature of man and society and leads to the subsequent working out of the implications of the theory for practice; Cropley called this the 'pure' theoretical approach. The other takes the form of an after-the-fact rationalization of existing educational trends. The former 'emphasizes values and goals, and looks to the theoretical analysis of education for answers', the latter 'places more emphasis on the forces in society which have permitted the emergence of certain kinds of change in both theory and practice, or the identification of the underlying theoretical concordance between existing practices, and looks to the analysis of practice as the main source of answers' (Cropley 1979: 100–101). Both approaches were regarded as valuable by the participants but there were no proposals about how, if at all, they could be utilized together in a single, unitary approach. Cropley contented himself with the unexplained assessment that they involve only a difference in emphasis, though the former, he commented, appears more provocative from the point of view of discussion. Moreover, he pointed out, both are present in the literature on lifelong education. Later in this paper I shall show that, in fact, either 'emphasis' is insufficient by itself and requires the other too for its completion. I shall also, as I said in my opening paragraph, propose a paradigm which will synthesize them effectively into a single theoretical approach.

In the next section Cropley discussed 'lifelong education and philosophy'. Consideration of lifelong education as a philosophy of education, he said, 'opens the discussion to the question of its ultimate goals. What is it really for?' (1979: 101). At the beginning of his discussion he put the question as to whether lifelong education is, in fact, a philosophy of education aside, arguing that, 'for present purposes, looking at the ideas and practices encompassed by the label "lifelong education" in terms of some of the things which could be expected from a true philosophy of education would be a useful approach, regardless of whether or not they actually comprise a philosophy' (1979: 101). He did not say how one can decide whether ideas and practices constitute 'some of the things that could be expected from a true philosophy of education' without entering into the question of what constitutes a philosophy of education. But his conclusion was 'that the majority of writers in the area have indeed accepted, implicitly if not always explicitly, certain beliefs about the nature of man, good, society and education'. He continued to say that if such agreement constitutes having a philosophy, then 'there is an identifiable "philosophy" of lifelong education', and this is 'loosely humanitarian and humanistic in nature'. Its main tenets are that education should:

1   involve learners as actors in their own learning rather than as passive recipients;
2   foster the capacity to play the role just mentioned;
3   lead to democratization of society;
4   improve the quality of life of men and women.

At the same time, after identifying this 'philosophy' (the reason, given this list, why he felt the need to put the words in inverted commas is obvious), Cropley hastened to add that practices involving lifelong education 'have developed in settings reflecting many different philosophies, either in the scholarly sense or in the socio-political sense' (1979: 103). He further pointed out, with reference to the list above, that 'these values and goals are not unique to lifelong education, although they may be given special significance in its context' (1979: 104).

Where the crucial matter of the relationship between the theory of lifelong education and educational practice was discussed in the report, Cropley distinguished two approaches: one 'minimalist', which 'equates lifelong education with inservice training, recurrent education, and the whole domain of adult education in general', the other 'maximalist'

which 'sees lifelong education as involving a fundamental transformation of society so that the whole society becomes a learning
resource for each individual, and is aware of its educational responsibility' (1979: 105). Other ways of distinguishing different approaches to
practice he identified were in terms of their instrumental/non-
instrumental and process/activity orientations. Though these orientations should not be regarded as constituting dichotomous distinctions,
Cropley argued, the non-instrumental process orientation of theory is
clearly compatible with the 'maximalist' position, while the instrumen-
tal-activity orientation is compatible with the 'minimalist'. Although
there are a number of well-defined operational principles that express
the practical implications of lifelong education and that must be
common to all, Cropley continued, there is no 'universal blueprint' in
lifelong education. The common view, on the contrary, is that an
'anthropological' approach to the concept is necessary to correspond
with the fact that 'educational practice in differing countries occurs in
many different contexts, which depend upon factors such as a country's
geography and history, technological development, socio-political and
economic system, and many more' (1979: 106).

Opportunities and obstacles

In 1984, five years after Cropley's 'stock-taking' publication, Gelpi, who, at
least up to that time, was probably in the best position to assess them
because of his post with UNESCO, wrote about the current opportunities
and obstacles for lifelong education as he saw them. Opening on, and
retaining throughout, a note of guarded optimism, which it is doubtful he
would now retain, given his own subsequent tribulations with UNESCO
and the folding up of his lifelong education unit there, he nevertheless
identified two general difficulties with the concept that had not, he said,
disappeared with the years. One was 'that lifelong education is still conceived in merely tautological or prescriptive terms, without any actual
progress or challenge'. The other concerns 'the "subversive" practice of
lifelong education which raises issues about the content, method, and,
above all, aims of the educational process' (1984: 79). Gelpi's more
general lament in his paper, however, was that even if the notion is
increasingly accepted at the theoretical level, the actual policies and practices that should operationalize it are still very limited because of obstacles
in the system of production and in the educational system itself. His analysis was typically generic and impressionistic but useful none the less, given
his international experience. It was made on two dimensions: those of
'social and international relations', and those evidently inspired by the
leftist socio-political orientations of his own thought.

The practical obstacles to policies and practices he identified were to:
(a) lifelong education at the work-place where lifelong education takes

the form of self-management (and thus calls into question the power structure); (b) lifelong education by means of mass communication in a two-way direction between consumers and producers; (c) lifelong education of people for active participation in international affairs on a basis of equality between countries; (d) lifelong education inside and outside the apparatuses of the state, the church, the parties, to involve everyone actively in these institutions and in civil society. He also identified more direct resistances on the part of teachers concerned with a larger workload and the loss of opportunities for promotion, social groups opposed to the democratization of schooling and the introduction of real educational equality, and political elements who fear the loss of hegemonic control over their members and, eventually, on society itself as a whole. To these obstacles he added the 'incapacity of certain social tendencies' (unions, political parties, social movements, etc.) which are otherwise 'positive', to grasp the educational issues and become involved with reform. And, finally, naked repression against educational activities that demonstrate 'individual and collective creativity' and that take different forms in different countries (1984: 837).

Gelpi went on to lament 'the ephemeral character of definitions of lifelong education, which needs to be sharply defined' and expressed his fear of the concept's use in this 'unhistorical way'. He then turned to 'research methods' in lifelong education, rightly pointing out that 'the choice of one definition or another of lifelong education has consequences for the methods to be used in research, in the evaluation of lifelong education policies and activities and for the evolution of the concept itself' (1984: 847). His own view was that 'operationalising the concept' of lifelong education at the level of educational policies and structures has made it possible to locate it better in a historical, social and economic framework' (1984: 85). This places him squarely within the latter 'pragmatic' strain of the literature rather than the earlier 'utopic' or 'philosophic' one (Ireland 1978). Thus, he went on to say about this approach that it requires research dominated not by 'theory and philosophy' (as it has in the past) but centred on 'the policies and strategies of education'. Research, in other words, which is empirical and historical (Gelpi 1984: 85). Finally, he closed by giving some instances of what he called 'the manipulative possibilities of lifelong education' (1984: 86–87) and expressing the hope for 'co-operative and interdisciplinary work among researchers, practitioners and users of educational structures' in opposing them (1984: 87).

Gelpi's justified distrust of 'philosophical' approaches to lifelong education (not shared, however, as we have seen, by Cropley and the contributors to his report), was really a distrust of the 'utopic' theorizing which characterized the earliest lifelong education literature as a search for abstract global 'models' of lifelong education. But his own solution was too radical, and, as I have argued elsewhere (Wain 1987) even counterproductive to one of his central intentions, which is to identify and disown 'subversive' or 'manipulative' practices of lifelong education. For concentrating on the pragmatic and the empirical means depriving oneself of the very theoretical tools needed to combat these practices. More, it deprives one of the deeper analysis and justificatory arguments that one needs to vindicate one's own practices and to show that they are not 'subversive' or 'manipulative' (Wain 1987). Finally, pragmatic and empirical arguments cannot even ensure, by themselves, the satisfaction of that historical relevance in practice which Gelpi mentions, which is so dear to the pragmatist, and which lies at the heart of his/her objection to 'abstract' theorizing. For the satisfaction of relevance requires a preliminary account of what one will consider as 'relevant': conditions, objectives, standards or criteria of some kind. The argument that something is relevant and, therefore, justified just 'because it works' is incomplete without further account of what 'works' means in the context. And that account cannot be restricted to instrumental evaluations if one is also concerned with the issue of 'subversion' and 'manipulation'. 'Arguments about relevance, [then], are not,' in fact as one writer has noted, 'separate empirical or pragmatic arguments; they can only provide a kind of constraining framework within which problems arise to be settled by other kinds of justificatory arguments' (Bailey 1988: 123). And these 'other kinds of justificatory arguments' are normative or philosophical.

The Cropley report and Gelpi's paper together create a reasonably accurate picture of the theoretical and practical difficulties with the concept of lifelong education. The first is whether 'lifelong education' is a *concept*, and, if not, how it should be considered. Notwithstanding Lengrand's confident assertion that there is a concept of lifelong education, Lawson (1982) has argued that there is not; that 'lifelong education' is simply a label for certain policies and no more. Second, there is the question of the definition of lifelong education. Is it important or not? Richmond, we have seen, is ambiguous but tends to think that it is not; Gelpi, on the other hand, is certain that it is and wants a 'strict definition' of lifelong education. A third and more general question emerges from the first two, without which they cannot, in fact, be answered; this is how to deal with the notion of lifelong education theoretically, the question raised in the Cropley report. Finally, to complete the evolution of this line of analysis, the fourth question is how to conceptualize the relationship between the theory and practice of lifelong education. Here the possibilities outlined by Cropley were either 'minimalist' or 'maximalist'. What I propose to do in the rest of this paper is to take up these questions one at a time, hoping that at the end the waters will be clearer.

Concept or policy?

First, why does Lawson want to deny that there is a concept of lifelong education? This is what he says:

> The concept of 'lifelong education' is difficult to delineate, and exposition of the concept touches on most of the major questions concerning the nature and purposes of education. It is difficult to apply to 'lifelong education' the kinds of linguistic analysis which can be used on many of the more traditional educational concepts because there is no established tradition of common usage from which to elicit examples and counter-examples in order to work out the 'logical geography' of the concept. Indeed, it can be questioned whether we are dealing with a concept at all, because from many points of view 'lifelong education' can be seen to be less of a concept of education and more as a policy for education.
>
> (1982: 99)

In effect notwithstanding the truth of the claim made by its theorists that the idea of lifelong education is an old and practically universal one, and that it is natural to pre-industrial and pre-literate human societies, Lawson is right in affirming that, unlike the traditional educational concepts ('liberal education', for instance) there is 'no established tradition of common usage' of the term 'lifelong education' which can be analysed linguistically in order to work out its 'logical geography'. Comenius may have been a kindred spirit, as Suchodolski pointed out, but he did not use the expression 'lifelong education'. Does this all mean that there is no concept of lifelong education? The question obviously turns on the further question, what is required for a term to qualify as a 'concept'? Lengrand's argument is that there is a concept of lifelong education because the term has 'significance' or 'meaning'; its 'range' is clear. And, indeed, this is what, in ordinary, everyday, terms, is required of concepts. Does an expression need a 'tradition' which can be analysed linguistically to have 'meaning', as Lawson claims? The question shifts the issue into the realm of 'meaning' where it actually belongs. Lawson's insistence on a 'tradition' indicates that he would want a concept to have the logical properties of a 'universal' to qualify as such, that is if I deduce his position correctly.

But the contrary theory is that the 'meaning' of a term is not its 'tradition but the use that is made of it in actual everyday use, in a 'language'. According to this version of the matter being a concept means precisely having a role to play in some 'language game' such that it is understood and used as a tool of communication by players (Wittgenstein 1972). Within this nominalist version of 'meaning' lifelong education is indeed a concept, notwithstanding the lack of a tradition of use, if it can be shown that there are 'players' who use it with understanding as a communicative tool. I have already argued elsewhere (Wain 1987) that the criterion of having a 'tradition' is necessary only for a particular understanding of philosophy, as conceptual analysis, an understanding which identifies the search for 'meaning', for a 'concept', with the identification of a fixed 'core' of use within the language. Against it I identified a contrary philo-sophical approach which is content to localize 'meaning' or the under-standing of a concept socio-historically in a flux of 'conversation' between different contemporary partners, and which refuses the idea that there is need for a fixed universal 'core' to 'establish' a term's meaning or to define it as a 'concept'. I also conceded that Lawson's criticism is sound within the philosophical paradigm from which it is made, but irrelevant from this other one. But it seems to me that the paradigm of conceptual analysis (though not the technique of linguistic analysis) has had its day and that its 'essentialist' approach to the question of 'meaning' has been subverted epistemologically by different nominalist approaches, relativist (hermeneutical) or absolutist (critical theory).

Evidently this is not the place to go into the argument again. That there are a large number of people around who use the words 'lifelong educa-tion' is scarcely in doubt. The crucial question is, do they all mean the same thing by the term? The answer is no, except at the most superficial level of agreement that education does not stop with schooling. Other-wise, as is generally acknowledged, lifelong education means different things to different persons and is most generally identified either with adult education *tout court* or some form of it. This is what Lawson means when he says that it does not have a 'tradition', and there is no doubt that this fact constitutes a handicap in the sense indicated by Gelpi, that the expression consequently demonstrates a certain fragility of meaning on a 'universal' scale. The problems with definition expressed also by Gelpi and by everyone in the Cropley report are only a symptom of this fragility and they will only disappear with time and use and, it is hoped, with the aid of the kind of theoretical work which this article is engaged in.

So what does Lengrand's insistence that there is a concept of lifelong education amount to? Obviously, Lengrand is referring to the agreement on the meaning of lifelong education shared by himself and the other contributors to the Cropley report, and by a number of other theorists whose work they examined. These do, indeed, form a group of 'conversa-tional partners' who negotiate a common understanding of the expres-sion, and it is this common understanding that Lengrand refers to as the concept of lifelong education.

The maximalist and minimalist views

The first step towards clarifying matters is to recognise that referring to the concept of lifelong education is inaccurate. That what exists is a concept of lifelong education shared by theorists who do indeed use it with the significance and range of meaning Lengrand had in mind. But that there are also other popular uses of the term that simply identify it with different adult education policies, as Lawson contended. Lengrand and his fellow theorists also constitute what may loosely be regarded as a 'movement', inasmuch as their understanding of lifelong education is also underpinned by a common 'philosophy', in the sense described by Cropley, that they share a common, if loose, understanding of 'the nature of man, good, society and education'. The movement's understanding of lifelong education is 'maximalist', in the way described by Cropley, in that it aims for a reconceptualization of the whole of education as compared with 'minimalist' views of different kinds. Some of these 'minimalist' views, but not all, though they constitute policies and strategies that correspond to the idea of 'lifelong' education, are rationalized in their own ways, and their users distinguish themselves by using different labels like 'recurrent', and 'continuing' education, others do not. What all 'minimalist' views hold in common, and what also distinguishes them from the 'maximalist' view is that they are all concerned exclusively with adult education and use the term 'lifelong education' interchangeably with 'adult education'. Consequently they also differ from the 'maximalist' position in the way they regard adult education itself, as either a 'stop-start' provision of vocational opportunities throughout adult life, or as a 'topping up' of professional or academic programmes on the traditional school provision. The 'totalizing thrust' of the 'maximalist' view, on the other hand, as the Cropley report rightly points out, finds its ultimate expression in the concept of a 'learning society' or, as Suchodolski calls it, an 'educative society' which is marked by a total and co-ordinated mobilization of institutional and personal resources for learning and by a particular mentality.

The other distinguishing characteristic of the 'maximalist' position of the movement, openly acknowledged by its members, is its reformist, even 'missionary' or revolutionary thrust. Suchodolski described it as a 'struggle'. That is, in fact, what really makes it a 'movement' rather than simply a collection of writers attached to a common understanding or ideal. My earlier summary of some of the central concerns of Suchodolski's paper, Lengrand's ambitions, and the critical thrust of Gelpi's analysis of current opportunities and obstacles shows these to be a perfect illustration of this fact, but one could just as easily have quoted from the works of other writers. The writers of the movement, in sum, are plainly out for more than the simple expression of adult education or even its improvement or reform; they are out to reform society itself through reforming its educational philosophy, structures and policies. Gelpi, who shares Suchodolski's description of education as 'a struggle', goes even further in his reformist ambitions, extending them to the international order as well, even retaining the 'utopian' belief that even this can be reformed through education. The difference between the earlier 'utopic' writers and the later 'pragmatists' like Gelpi is, in fact, a difference of strategy occasioned by a number of considerations that had intervened onto the scene by the time they were writing, and nothing more. Among them are the heavy criticism addressed against the former approach, characterized mainly by the Faure Report of 1972 (Elvin 1975), the need to concede the 'subversive' possibilities of the bare idea of lifelong education referred to by Gelpi, the perception that 'abstract theorizing' in general was, as a theoretical approach, inconsistent with the demand of the theorists themselves for the 'institutionalization' of lifelong education, and the reaction of those in what Gelpi calls 'the peripheral countries' who rejected the concept of lifelong education because it tended to be projected as one 'belonging to Northern societies' (Gelpi 1984: 17).

Lifelong education and adult education

Not only is the 'maximalist' view of lifelong education of the movement not universally shared, judging from the literature it has advanced very little if at all since 1979 and may be on its way out; there are few new theorists and writers supporting or even discussing it, and very little new theoretical work within its perspective being published. One of the reasons for this may be the apparent withdrawal of much of that Unesco support which was crucial for the earlier sponsorship of the movement which was, in fact, Unesco-based. Although that sponsorship may also have handicapped the movement in many ways (Elvin 1975), it provided different opportunities to meet and to publish and gave the concept itself a certain international prestige and currency. Among Anglo-Saxon theorists the style, tone and reformist ambitions of the movement's literature may be off-putting, while the extent to which the whole 'maximalist' approach may appear alien to them is exemplified in a recent paper by Richard Bagnall (Bagnall 1990). Bagnall, like Lawson, finds problems with the permissive use of 'education' which lies at the heart of the 'maximalist' position and which includes informal as well as formal and non-formal learning. He also finds problems with the central notion of a 'learning society', which is outside the dominant tradition of liberal educational theory which focuses on the individual, and with which he associated different repressive possibilities none of which is, however, either necessary or advocated in the movement's literature. There cannot be any comparison either in the history of political and social events or in the history of ideas, as Lengrand claims extravagantly, between the notion of lifelong education and those of liberty, justice and the rights of man. Even the more limited reformist cry to action on behalf of adult education, as he himself notes elsewhere (Lengrand 1975) is a fairly recent one, while the other notions he mentions are central to the history of human struggles from the 17th century on and have been persistent themes of different writers since then.

True, the popularity of the expression has grown considerably everywhere over the past 30 years or so, as Gelpi noted. But Suchodolski's statement that it has 'triumphantly resounded' through the world is more than a trifle immodest. In any case it is not, if anything, the movement's conception of lifelong education which has 'triumphed' but the expression itself; otherwise it continues to mean, as was pointed out earlier, different things to different people. The impression one gets, in fact, is that it is the different 'minimalist' conceptions that have won popularity rather than the 'maximalist' one of the movement. That it is the tendency referred to of identifying lifelong education with adult education *tout court* by non-theorist and theorist alike that is growing. For the former, the simplicity of this identification is clearly attractive. Also it often corresponded in the past with what may have been the main concern of many: selling adult education, mainly vocational or professional, to the unwilling or the unenlightened. In general, in fact, for many the utility of interchanging the term adult education with lifelong education has been: (1) to make a stronger case for adult education through the pragmatic case for lifelong education; and (2) to revitalize adult education by using a new and trendy term.

Witness to the strength of this identification of lifelong education with adult education among theorists is the pages of the *International Journal of Lifelong Education* itself which, in the years of its existence, has not carried more than a very small handful of articles that have really been about 'lifelong education' and not directly about adult education, never mind being concerned with the issues raised by the literature of the movement. Witness also is the periodical bibliographical publication edited by Ursula Giere, which is also becoming less and less a locus of information on publications about lifelong education as such and more and more generic in character. Finally, Titmus's recent publication of an 'international handbook' on 'lifelong education for adults' is an eloquent comment, in itself, on this state of affairs (Titmus 1989). There is one extremely short token section on 'lifelong education' in the book including brief articles by Cropley and Lengrand ploughing up old ground again, otherwise not only is there no attempt to study the relationship between lifelong education and adult education, as the title of the book would seem to promise (there is not even a gesture in this direction in the 'introduction'), there is only the very scantiest use of the expression 'lifelong education' itself throughout the texts, and there are virtually no references to any lifelong education literature in the bibliographies of the contributors. In sum, the book is really about adult education and lifelong education barely comes into it at all; the title is simply another instance of the exploitation of the term's currency among those whose interest is, in reality, only confined to 'adult' education.

'Minimalist' accounts of lifelong education range between treating the expression as a slogan bearing the simple idea that one should continue with one's education after school and throughout one's life to the more sophisticated theories of 'recurrent' education. Promoting it as a slogan for personal initiative leaves one in the realm of considering the methods of efficient propaganda and, possibly, support. Considering it as an adult education programme, on the other hand, may mean either debating it in terms of the effectiveness of narrow vocational and professional goals, as often happens, or in broader personal, socio-cultural and political terms, and being concerned with the strategies to operationalize them. Of the two approaches it is clearly only the second broader, and more 'ideological', approach that corresponds in spirit to the movement's view of lifelong education. Otherwise, adult education theorists who have used the label 'lifelong education' have been prone to regard adult education as a phenomenon that can be isolated or hived off separately and dealt with theoretically and practically without any consideration of the earlier phases of childhood or youth, without any interest in schooling in particular, as Titmus's book amply shows.

The writers of the movement, on the contrary, are interested in adult education as a phase located within lifelong education. They understood the commitment of lifelong education literally, as a commitment to education as a whole, as a totality of learning experiences ranging over the whole of life, not specifically adulthood. Adult education they regard as part of that totality, with its own characteristics and concerns, certainly, but incapable of being understood or dealt with coherently outside the general context of lifelong education as a whole. In conformity with this holistic thrust schooling was an important concern for the movement from the start, and a lot of its literature has dwelt on the subject, mainly critically, of what it regards as the predominantly traditionalist character of contemporary schooling and even pre-schooling, in many societies. The notions of 'vertical integration' and 'horizontal integration' were introduced by writers of the movement as tools to theorize this totality on the level of the individual and his/her life, and at the level of the 'learning society' respectively.

My contention is that this interchange of meanings between the two terms 'lifelong education' and 'adult education', has certainly been detrimental to the scope of lifelong education as proposed by the theorists of the movement. It is also arguable that it has been detrimental to the cause of adult education itself which has equally deep theoretical problems and is also, like lifelong education, in what commentators have referred to as 'a semantic quagmire' (Titmus and Kidd 1989: xxviii). The latter were certainly against it from the start, and warned against it repeatedly. It is also my contention that it would be a loss not only for education in general but for adult education itself if the trend towards the growing popularity of 'minimalist' approaches continued; if the 'maximalist' approach eventually disappeared with the movement, to be replaced completely by the 'minimalist's' generic identification of lifelong education with adult education. Were the 'maximalist' view to disappear one danger is that the implications for the earlier phases of education in childhood and youth, of regarding education as a lifelong process, would be lost completely or cease to be an issue, chief among these the need to work on cultivating 'educability' at these stages rather than working towards some finished product of the 'educated person'. It is clear, also, that the 'maximalist' interpretation of lifelong education, especially its concept of a 'learning society', enriches the notion of adult education considerably by extending the interests of adult education into the region of informal learning, of that learning which comes from the environment, and by extending the responsibility of educating to all society's institutions rather than restricting it to a specialized few in the 'post-school sector'. From this point of view it is clear that the exclusion of the 'maximalist' view would be a net loss to the development of adult education itself. Finally, with its emphasis on the continuity of the educational process, the 'maximalist' approach highlights the importance of examining and planning the integration between the different phases of education, including the transition from childhood and youth into adulthood, something which is lost completely to 'minimalist' approaches.

Lifelong education as research programme

Gelpi's argument that the way one defines a term or understands an expression, the way one conceptualizes it, determines the research methodologies one chooses to theorize it with, is a crucial one I have also made elsewhere myself (Wain 1984). A possible approach to the question of definition (for those who are interested in 'lifelong education' as a concept, not simply as a convenient label for a number of policies) is suggested by Dave who points out that the meaning of the expression 'lifelong education' turns on how one understands three key words: 'life', 'lifelong' and 'education' (Dave 1975). Once one has made the initial separation of the expression 'lifelong education' from 'adult education' (an equivalence which is, in any case, not even borne out semantically since 'adult' distinguishes a particular, restricted phase of life rather than its totality), one needs to recognize that, technically, one can have as many theories of lifelong education as these words lend scope to. The only technical requirement for each to qualify is that it should declare itself as following the basic principle of regarding education as a 'lifelong' process. Otherwise a particular theory could be 'liberating' or 'repressive', 'liberal' or 'vocational', 'maximalist' or 'minimalist', or different combinations of these qualities. The movement's 'maximalist' theory of lifelong education is technically one theory of lifelong education, distinct from others in the interpretation it gives them. We have seen from the Cropley report that the interpretation of 'life' it loosely adheres to is 'humane and humanistic', its technical definition of education is that of a process which includes formal, non-formal and informal learning, and its interpretation

of 'lifelong' education, following from its technical definition of education which includes informal learning, is that of a continuous process, a
process with no pauses, no 'gaps'.

The way to approach the current confusion over the use of the expression 'lifelong education' (as also to approach any view of education whatever, theoretically, I have argued elsewhere) is by regarding the whole
field of education, whether in its explicitly theoretical form or in its practical form, as a number of competing paradigms. The healthy ones, those
currently flourishing in dynamic form, one could then regard as ongoing
research programmes. What distinguishes each programme from the
other is its 'ideological core', which embodies its particular view of 'life',
its socio-cultural and political norms, values and aims, and its 'operational
belt' which furnishes the programme's technical definition of education
and prescribes and evaluates its practices.

Representing different approaches to education as 'research programmes' of this kind, because of the holistic structure of the programmes, establishes their composition clearly. It also provides a clear
framework for research into the relation between the 'theoretical' and the
'practical' aspects of education, and enables one to bridge the different
approaches identified by Cropley uniting them into one powerful theoretical frame. It also indicates the kind of research that is required in educational theory in general. The 'theoryladenness' epistemological thesis,
which seems to meet with universal consent, says that no approach to education is innocent of theory, that ideological presuppositions underlie any
practice or can be read into it. So the movement, in declaring its reforma-
tive interests, simply makes its own ideological position, Cropley would
call it 'philosophy', explicit, though not explicit enough as I have argued
elsewhere.

On the other hand, the 'operational belt' itself is the creation of different factors. As a set of policies and practices it lies in perpetual tension
between the demands of consistency made on it by the 'ideological core'
on the one hand, and by the pragmatic demands made upon it by the
world, the locus to which the policies and the practice are addressed and
where it takes place, on the other. Therefore, of its nature, it is both
dynamic and adaptive. Gelpi's theoretical approach to education, mentioned earlier, is appropriately historical. It addresses itself to the operational belt and defines the research appropriate for 'lifelong education' as
one addressing 'opportunities and obstacles', in particular socio-cultural
and political settings, but it is open to the criticism made earlier of ignoring the ideological 'core' explicit or implicit which must underpin any
understanding of education. The earlier lifelong education theorists, on
the other hand, concentrated on ideology and abstract solutions and
ignored the pragmatic historical requirement of context. Not only does
the 'research programme' paradigm respond to the deficiencies of each
and synthesize into a unitary project the three different ingredients

identified by the Cropley report; its emphasis on the importance of recognizing the ideological significance of one's practical project combats the danger of conscious or unconscious subversive practices; its emphasis on context ensures the pragmatic 'relevance' of the practice. Its emphasis on regarding the whole of education as a single research programme ensures the desired correspondences between the two and requires one to regard adult education in the context of a holistic approach to education in general.

Adult education as lifelong education

With regard to theories of adult education these can, but need not, be theories of lifelong education. If they are simply theories of adult education then they are not theories of lifelong education. Technically, theories of adult education need not be parts of theories of lifelong education either. Theories of lifelong education, on the other hand, must include theories of adult education. This point also needs to be very clear. Theories of adult education are only theories of 'lifelong education', or parts of them, if they are consciously regarded as such, if the theorists and practitioners who adhere to them demonstrate a sensitivity to the fact that committing oneself to the idea and practice of lifelong education means committing oneself to regarding education as a continuum over life. This commitment is consistent with the recognition of the peculiar needs and characteristics of each phase but introduces the principle that no phase can be hived off and understood, or researched outside the continuum of phases constituted by the life-span of an individual person. It means recognizing that adult education must be theorized within a holistic framework which gives due regard to the continuity, consistency and integration of the different phases. If 'adult education' is viewed, and theorized, in this way, as a stage in lifelong education, not as some separate free-floating entity, then its proper locus of research and discussion is in the operational belt of an education research programme which includes adult education as part of its integral whole. The different theories of adult education will find their proper places in different education programmes according to their ideological commitment and their particular technical definitions of education. Some theories of adult education, from this point of view, will be located in a research programme that defines education in minimalist, others in maximalist terms.

The lifelong education theorists argue, with some justice, that the current practice of not locating adult education anywhere, of discussing and researching it as though it could be separated from the rest of the process of education, is incoherent. But their own contribution in the area of working out the meaning of adult education within their own 'maximalist' concept of lifelong education, and in the area of critiquing actual adult education theories to work out their implications for lifelong education strategies has itself been very scant, to say the least. And this has led theorists like Griffin (1983: 158) to complain that:

> ...lifelong education theory has ... replicated the theoretical failure of adult education. For just as it was suggested that adult education theory has often become bogged down in sterile attempts to 'distance' it from schooling, so lifelong education theorists have overstressed the difference between it and adult education. There is little sense of the dynamic relationships between the knowledge-content of schooling and that of adult learning at all, so that paradoxically in curriculum terms lifelong education is often identified with (progressive) schooling itself.

The immediate challenge of the future for those who really believe in the case for lifelong education must be to work for clarity; to ensure, in particular, that those working in the field of education in general, and of adult education in particular given the present circumstances, are aware of issues and consequences like those raised and discussed in this paper. That will not be easy among adult education theorists because the field of adult education itself shares the same theoretical difficulties as lifelong education theory (Titmus 1989). It will be even more difficult for those who theorize education exclusively in terms of schooling because, in their minds, as in most people's minds, 'lifelong education' stands for adult education, a field to be set apart as *sui generis* and left to other interested theorists. The difficulties in promoting a 'maximalist' view of lifelong education will be equally formidable for the reasons mentioned earlier. In either case the 'stocktaking' cannot indicate a very promising future.

Note

1 *Kenneth Wain* is a professor and lecturer in philosophy and the Head of the Department of Educational Studies at the University of Malta. His publications on lifelong education include articles in different journals such as the *International Journal of Lifelong Education, Educational Theory* and *Educational Philosophy and Theory*, the introductory essay and editing of the book *Lifelong Education and Participation* (Malta University Press, 1985), and his book *Philosophy of Lifelong Education* (Croom Helm, 1987). He is currently doing philosophical work on the notion of a 'learning society' or 'educated public'.

References

Bagnall, R. E. 1990, Lifelong education: the institutionalisation of an illiberal ideology? *Educational Philosophy and Theory*, Vol. 22, No. 1, 1–7.

Bailey, C. 1988, Lifelong education and liberal education. *Journal of Philosophy of Education*, Vol. 22, No. 1, 121–126.

Cropley, A. J. (ed.) 1979, *Lifelong Education: A Stocktaking*, Hamburg, UIE Monographs, 8.

Dave, R. H. 1975, *Reflections on Lifelong Education and the School*, Hamburg, UIE Monograph.

Elvin, L. 1975, Learning to be … *Education News*, 15.

Gelpi, E. 1984, Lifelong education: opportunities and obstacles. *International Journal of Lifelong Education*, Vol. 3, No. 2, 79–87.

Griffin, C. 1983, *Curriculum Theory in Adult and Lifelong Education*, London, Croom Helm.

Ireland, T. D. 1978, *Gelpi's View of Lifelong Education*, Manchester University Press.

Lawson, K. 1982, Lifelong education: concept or policy? *International Journal of Lifelong Education*, Vol. 1, No. 2.

Lengrand, P. 1975, *An Introduction to Lifelong Education*, London, Croom Helm.

Lengrand, P. 1979, Prospects of lifelong education, in A. J. Cropley (ed.), *op. cit.*

Lengrand, P. (ed.) 1986, *Areas of Learning Basic to Lifelong Education*, Oxford, Pergamon Press.

Richmond, R. K. 1979, The concept of continuous education, in A. J. Cropley (ed.), *op. cit.*

Stock, A. K. 1979, Developing lifelong education: post-school perspectives, in A. J. Cropley (ed.), *op. cit.*

Suchodolski, B. 1979, Lifelong education at the crossroads, in A. J. Cropley (ed.), *op. cit.*

Titmus, C. J. (ed.) 1989, *Lifelong Education for Adults: An International Handbook*, Oxford, Pergamon Press.

Titmus, C. J. and Kidd, J. R. 1989, Introduction, in C. J. Titmus (ed.), *op. cit.*

Wain, K. 1984, Lifelong education: a Deweyan challenge. *Journal of Philosophy of Education*, Vol. 18, No. 2, 257–263.

Wain, K. 1987, *Philosophy of Lifelong Education*, London, Croom Helm.

Wittgenstein, L. 1972, *Philosophical Investigations*, Oxford, Blackwell.

9 Globalization and lifelong education

Reflection on some challenges for Africa

Akpovire Oduaran[1]

University of Botswana

The global phenomenon called globalization frequently offers justifications for socio-economic and political actions aimed at bringing rapidly into fruition the 'Global Village' which Marshall McLuhan had anticipated decades ago. Both the 1972 UNESCO sponsored Commission Report chaired by Edgar Faure and that of 1996 chaired by Jacques Delors produced important documents which, as at other times, reviewed issues and priorities in education worldwide, in spite of the obvious extreme diversity in socio-economic, political and educational situations, conceptions and structures. As always, UNESCO had been concerned about the numerous and vibrant challenges the future holds in store for everyone. In doing so, lifelong education has been identified as one of the indispensable assets available to us in the pursuits which regularly bring into the fore the concern for equality, equity and, indeed, human reasonableness. As the world pursues the ideals and objectives of globalization, the need arises for a timely reassessment of positions especially in the context of consequences and challenges that are inherent. This paper seeks to examine globalization in the context of some of the major challenges it poses for Africa. In particular, it proposes how lifelong education might be structured to assist Africans in comprehending, evaluating and possibly, participating comparatively effectively in the relations implied in globalization rather than standing aloof and becoming hapless objects.

Introduction

The main thesis of this paper is that in spite of the current outcry against some of the unintended consequences of globalization as depicted by Campbell (1993: 7), Korten (1995: 6–14) and Beveridge (1996: 68) the phenomenon is seemingly inevitable and raises some challenges for the implementation of lifelong education legislation and policies in Africa. In fact, the so-called dangers inherent in the unequal distribution of capital between the First and Third Worlds which Frank (1981: 1–18) had attributed to globalization some 17 years ago and which seemed to inform the basis of the arguments by critics of the phenomenon today, cannot easily be wished away by the peoples and leaders of Africa. If anything, Africa must do well to comprehend and embrace the challenges induced by globalization in order to compete quite competently in a rapidly changing world.

On the basis of this conviction, the focus and argument in this paper would be that globalization as principle and practice has become a reality and, indeed, a driving socio-economic, cultural and political force, which we cannot afford to ignore. Indeed, it is being argued that the relevance of Africa as a continent to be reckoned with in this millennium would depend significantly on how much its peoples have become subjects and not hapless objects of globalization.

To achieve the goals intended in this paper an attempt has been made to examine briefly the contextual differences and commonalities that exist among African nations. Secondly, it is realized that there is need to conceptualize globalization and lifelong education. Thirdly, the basic assumptions of globalization and some of its manifestations in Africa are examined. Finally, suggestions are made as to how lifelong education might be structured to be of use in helping Africa to compete favourably in the relations implied in globalization.

One obvious difficulty in articulating the debates on globalization manifests in its divergent connotations. For example, the application of globalization to the economy and its merits tends to be easily blurred by criticisms of social globalization. Yet, we know that the effects of economic globalization have been somewhat overwhelmingly positive. As Sutherland (1998: 1) noted, economic globalization has led to unprecedented liberalization of international trade, inducing increased productivity and efficiency and creating millions of jobs. Economic globalization has also induced a significant increase in international investment. Consequently, in the 1990s alone, foreign investors are known to have invested US$1 trillion in developing economies, leading to improved living standards in some countries much faster than many people would have thought possible (Sutherland 1998: 1). This may be a welcome development.

Even at that, there are those who contend, advancing convincing reasons as they do, that economic globalization has actually impoverished the South ever more than before (Bhola 1998: 488, Brock *et al.* 1996: 4–5, Deutscher *et al.* 1996: 2–8, Holtz 1995: 7). Such positions should naturally question an attempt like this one which proposes that lifelong education needs to be really relevant in striving to equip Africans for effective competition in the global economy. In fact, Bhola (1998: 502) has been concerned that to globalize lifelong education would become lifelong bondage to the free market whilst the gap between the already unequal rewards in the market place would grow wider and wider.

These are wrong significant fears and suspicions being expressed by several scholars. They see in globalization a kind of socio-economic and political 'monster' that is capable of traumatizing nations that cannot or are unable to compete on equal terms.

The fears already expressed about globalization may not be unfounded; but the reality of our situation is that in the present circumstances it may be difficult for anyone to undermine the vigorous presence of the phenomenon. Worst still, no one can really halt globalization by preferring to pretend that the phenomenon need not exist. The fears being expressed about globalization, especially in Africa, have found roots in the unimpressive performance of our economic, social and political indices of development.

The rising advantages of economic globalization have not been unfortunately profound in Africa, especially Sub-Saharan Africa. Many of the Sub-Saharan African nations have recorded disappointing economic performance. This fact is reflected in their failure to integrate into the world economy and thus, to trade successfully and attract investment (Sutherland 1998: 1). In such situations as those in which many African nations have found themselves, it is necessary to examine and comprehend the phenomenon called globalization with a view to articulating how Africa's educational structures can be modified to be of much more relevance in the competition both in the long and short terms.

It is true that nations, including those in Africa are not equal as far as globalization is concerned. Nevertheless, the whole essence of development is to move away from one stage of development to a better one and globalization appears to be one of such shifts.

One fact we cannot run away from is that no nation, advantaged or disadvantaged from any perspective, can possibly ask the other not to develop. Within continents, there is always room for competition. Indeed, the emergence of complex and advanced manufacturing technology typified by the use of computer numerically controlled (CNC) machine tools, flexible manufacturing systems (FMS) and robot systems has meant that there must be a need for maintenance staff with higher level skills in many instances (Clarke 1996: 66–67). It would seem that every nation has had to wake up to these new realities of competition.

If Africa must move away from the periphery of influence and begin to cope with the realities of the present situations, the need arises for us not only to comprehend fully the phenomenon called globalization but to commence examining the challenges it poses to the people with a view to developing strategies which might better arm them for competition in the comity of nations. We must not fail to take urgent steps in identifying and developing as many strident strategies as could provide us side-bets. In the context of this discussion, lifelong education has been singled out for consideration as one of such strategies. But we cannot possibly reflect effectively on how lifelong education should help Africa in dealing with the challenges posed by globalization without first of all examining some of the basic differences and commonalities that exist among African nations since this should help to contextualize our discussion.

Differences and commonalities

The comprehension of how phenomenon affect Africa and the proposition of possible solutions for obviation obviously negative ones are frequently compounded by the existence of multiple histories, traditions,
realities, approaches and practices. These would influence considerably
how African nations respond to different phenomena, including globalizing processes. But this does not rule out the fact that there are at the same
time very many significant commonalities, which may permit describing
Africa's problems and solutions in some homogenizing way with allowance
for specificity.

Africa has had contacts with peoples from almost every other continent.
Historically, the colonization of Africa and whatever so-called gains, losses
and problems arising therefrom have been ascribed largely to Britain,
France and Portugal. Today, the continent has been 'polarized' along
three major language blocs, namely anglophone, francophone and lusophone Africa. But much more than this superficial language 'divide', the
socio-economic and political impacts of colonization have been noticeable
in the way African nations respond to phenomena and, indeed, their comprehension and state of preparedness to reject, modify and adapt same. It
might not be possible within the limits of our discussion to explore, in a
profound way, the intricate manifestations of the responses.

Whatever differences that might appear to hinder describing and discussing Africa in a homogenizing way seem to be reduced significantly by
what we might term as the commonalities. Indeed, in its 1995 report on
the state of education in Africa, UNESCO's regional office in Dakar pin-
pointed some of the major commonalities (UNESCO 1995: 1–8). We can
only attempt to highlight just a few of these commonalities.

Africa's harsh geographic and climatic conditions appear to be
common. For many countries within the equatorial region, there are
violent rainstorms and high humidity. For others striding the tropics of
Cancer and Capricorn there are records of extreme periods of heat and
cold. Countries bordering the deserts frequently experience draughts,
and these are just a few of the simplistic descriptions.

By far the most obvious commonalities in the context of this discussion
are overdependence. Many African nations have continued to remain
overdependent on their former colonizers for many things. And this has
permeated socio-economic and political matters. For instance, African
economics depend largely on a limited range of export products. In 1990,
for example, Nigeria depended by almost 90% on the exports of crude oil
just as cotton accounted for 50% of the exports in Chad, coffee for 75% of
the exports in Burundi, oil for 80% of the exports in Gabon and the
Congo, and bauxite for 86% of the exports by Guinea.

Rapidly growing population, illiteracy, diseases, high mortality rates
and political instability are some of the major commonalities for many

African nations. We cannot explore all of these, but Africa's external debts and the industrialized countries preference for protectionism has contributed to the marginalization of Africa. And the process of marginalization will continue if Africa is not alert enough to understand what is happening and its people equipped to compete effectively.

It is perhaps true that Africa's debt burden is the heaviest in the world. In 1991, the external indebtedness for sub-Saharan Africa was 110% of the GNP and comparatively 58% for the Middle East and North Africa, 41% for South America and the Caribbean and 34% for South Asia (UNICEF 1994). The prices of raw materials, the mainstream of most African economies, have been unstable with consequences for growing rates of prostitution, unemployment, crime and poverty. Furthermore, World Bank reports that since 1988, Sub-Saharan Africa has been involved in the long negative flow of capital in the form of payment of the principal and of interest on debt, to the tune of US$0.7 billion in 1988, $3.5 billion in 1992 and an estimated $2.1 billion in 1993 (World Bank 1994). The point being made here is that whatever heterogeneity African nations seem to have are homogenized significantly by the commonalities, some of which have been cited in the context of the present discussion. These commonalities certainly compel some unity of purpose or practice on the continent. Contrary to the impressions anyone might hold, African nation-states are more united in the crusade against poverty, illiteracy, diseases and bliss. Semblance's of the uniting efforts are clear in the emergence of economic and political blocs like the Economic Community of West African States (ECOWAS), the Southern African Development Community (SADC) and the umbrella body known as the Organization of African Unity (OAU). But the application of the ideas implied here can be made meaningful only by detailed conceptual clarification of the major concepts in focus.

Lifelong education

Lifelong education as a concept is very old and almost ageless. Part of its early expositions are located in the philosophical views of Socrates, Plato and Aristotle. For these ancient philosophers could be credited with pioneering in their individual discourses of intellectual development the view of the importance of the application of the human mind throughout lifespan. And Plato and Aristotle, in particular, advanced metaphysical arguments to back up their ways of thought and to lend credence to their practical initiation of sequences of studies aimed at developing the powers of reasoning.

Since the times of Socrates, Plato and Aristotle, scholars have continued to refine the concept of lifelong education. Thus far, strong views continue to be proposed which are asking for the structural modification of the education system such that we make learning societies into realities.

Gass (1996) describes the main features of such learning societies to include continuous investment in people; overcoming the fragmentation of life into education, work and retirement; forging new routes to equal opportunities; diversifying education and training opportunities; reconciling cultural, social, and economic goals; building on past achievements; and devising a new 'systemic' logic.

There are such other features as the strategic movements toward bringing about a more flexible 'architecture' or structure of learning institutions and opportunities wherein the processes of education are learner-centred and learner driven. Lifelong education has induced modifications to institutional frameworks such that people can learn in a relevant manner throughout life. It has prescribed as well the need for new pathways from school to work while deliberately developing and renewing adult person's intellect via continuing education. In all, lifelong education is being better comprehended and strongly accepted as the fulcrum around which education systems ought to be built.

The meanings ascribed to lifelong education are many, each of which is seemingly right in its own environment. In spite of these variations, lifelong education has its social, political, economic, personal and educational dimensions. Whichever dimension is emphasized and adopted depends on the individual who is free to make a choice.

The diversities of meaning ascribed to lifelong education notwithstanding, it is the view of this author that it is useful to accept the recommendation by Longworth and Keith Davies (1996: 21–37) to the effect that Elli's words provide a working definition of lifelong learning which fits aptly to lifelong education:

> Lifelong learning (education, *sic*) is the development of human potential through a continuously supportive process which stimulates and empowers individuals to acquire all the knowledge, values, skills and understanding they will require throughout their lifetimes, and to apply them with confidence, creativity and enjoyment in all roles, circumstances, and environments.

In the conceptualization highlighted above, there is obvious reference to the elements of human potential which needs to be regularly explored by ensuring that education systems offer a variety of organized and systematic opportunities for learning throughout life. And this is what rightly advocates lifelong education and draws attention to it, in demanding for the horizontal and vertical integration of education such that in-school education is integrated with other components of society promoting learning, for example, the public libraries, archives, museums, the media and so on. In its vertical integration, education can be structured so that learning events at various age levels become really interactive and complementary. Even though we cannot go to more lengths within the limits allowed in this discussion, it is clear that the other elements of support, process, stimulation, empowerment, individuals, knowledge, values, skills, understanding, confidence, creativity and enjoyment, roles, circumstances and environments generally implied in the working definition can be applied to coping with some of the challenges induced by globalization. Indeed, the position adopted in seeking solution to the challenges lies in bringing into fruition a human development model for Africa which is aimed at making its peoples willing and able to comprehend and compete in globalization processes which could alienate them for a long time unless they embark on timely interventions such as the one intended in the present discussion.

Globalization

Lifelong education has been touched by globalization. Again the concept of globalization is not new in any way. For globalization is often linked with colonialism, and it confines the old patterns of power between the core (usually the North) and the periphery (usually the South) as identified by the dependency theorists (Bhola 1998: 488). At present, there are hundreds of definitions of globalization that we cannot altogether examine. It is understandable that the concept has been used indiscriminately, and this only compounds the confusion built around the different connotations.

Johnston (1990: 18) defines globalization as the increasing interdependence and interconnectedness of people of the world in their request to improve the general condition of life for all human beings. This way, it seems the main purpose of applying globalization is the improvement of the living conditions of all human beings.

The search for ways of improving living conditions cannot be easy. Consequently, Beveridge (1996: 69) urges us to take globalization as a revolutionary transformation process which seeks to dismantle all barriers to international trade and free capital movement in order to create a single, global market. This definition emphasizes the economic slant of the concept featuring, among other things, the following:

1   Instant movement of capital from one country to another.
2   Corporations' management of production on a global scale, leaping national borders in search of lower costs and higher profits.
3   The raising ratio of world trade, compared to other forms of trade.

But the economic intentions of globalization should actually be seen as being encompassed by geopolitical manifestations.

Harris (1996: 5–10) and Bowers (1992: 11–126) propose that the networks of modern technoscience go beyond the reach of nation-states and become global in the topological sense that a globe has more varied possibilities. What emerges out of this conceptualization is the fact that globalization entails the maximization of opportunities available to us such as that our living conditions might be improved, all other things remaining equal. The maximization of opportunities, as we know, is only meaningful to the extent that competitors enjoy comparative advantages reflecting elements of equality.

Historically, the forces which drive globalization have been in operation for many years. If, indeed, globalization is a political and socio-economic phenomenon with global unification for different purposes, we must see it as sprouting, for example from attempts to bring into form the League of Nations in 1917. Subsequent developments led to the formation of the United Nations with all its organs and agencies geared towards making the world a better place to live in.

Since 1950, the economic forces driving globalization have become so powerful that it has tended to influence almost every sphere of concern. Beveridge (1996: 70), quoting Campbell (1993), has identified the major forces driving globalization since 1950 as follows:

1   Simultaneous technological revolutions in computers, telecommunications and transport;
2   Changes in government policies both domestic and foreign (especially policies aimed at the liberalisation of trade and capital flows);
3   Corporate and individual investor strategies; and
4   A powerful *liases-faire* ideology of deregulation, privatization and liberalization.

These forces have acted together to establish persons and nations with similar interests and goals, and who, therefore, try to unite for obvious gains.

We do know as well, that globalization has emerged from the union of the 1970s and 1980s resurgent neo-classical economic theory which stimulated corporate interests and indeed, from the privately financed forum established in 1972 became known as the Trilateral Commission. The Commission represented American, European and Japanese corporate business interests and was meant to devise means of managing the global economy and, in particular, dismantle the so-called Keynesian welfare state. Actually, these moves were supposed to 'midwife' the birth of the 'triumph of capitalism'. The consequences of these moves are obvious to us.

As would be obvious in the views already expressed the consequences are firstly economic. Economic because globalization has often evolved in rapid structural economic change that requires fast and huge capital transfers, and, as Brown (1999: 3–17) notes, the rapid development of information technology, new opportunities for international production and exchange of services amidst the declining role of the nation state and the deregulation of economic systems.

Globalization has had its geopolitical meanings as well for economic policies do impact on politics, because any political system has to be secured so that the global capital transfer, investment and production processes are not endangered. The internationalization, which is depicted in globalization, implies that environmental and population threats are becoming too broad and menacing to be left to one nation state. And beyond this there is need for the establishment of transnational identities and a new international 'civil society' that can effectively cater for the world citizenry (Mann 1997: 473–474). The optimism implied in the socio-economic and political manifestations of globalization has been questioned by 'pessimists' who are reminding us about the need to be wary about the unintended negative consequences of the phenomenon.

To really comprehend and contextualize globalization, it might be useful to examine some of its basic assumptions.

Basic assumptions of globalization

One basic assumption that may have propelled into action the present globalization schemes throughout the world is the slow rate at which the development gap between and among nations is being bridged.

In the economic context, for example, there is serious concern that the special distribution of income across societies is getting ever more uneven. This is a situation Peet (1991: 6) has lamented thus:

> The high-income people of the First World, constituting 15% of global population, have 75% of the world's income; the low-income countries of the Third World, with 56% of the global population have less than 5% of the world's income...

This imbalance may be rapidly addressed by deliberately sharpening the abilities of Third World nations to enter into globalization. For example, the people could be empowered socio-economically such that they can pool their resources together in an efficient manner to invest on-and-off-shore. Moreover, it is probably time for Africans to accept that state-run economic activities in the form of corporations may not be the best way to promote rapid economic development. The example of several African nations prove this point. Nigeria which is supposed to be the sixth world largest exporter of crude oil is perpetually battling with an energy crisis. That crisis has virtually paralysed Nigeria's economy. Yet, there are public corporations such as the Nigerian National Petroleum Corporation (NNPC) with its subsidiaries and the National Electric Power Authority (NEPA) which are not functioning satisfactorily.

In the socio-political context, the dividing line between the First and Third Worlds is even more obvious than ever before. Whereas in the First World, the skyline is inundated with towering skyscrapers, the Third

World continues to exhibit growing numbers of squatter locations and homelessness, to take just one example. Politically, whereas the First World appears to enjoy political stability that invites investors, the Third World continues to be bedevilled by political instability, coups and counter coups and, sometimes, endless political transition programmes.

In the light of these imbalances, academics continue to propose theories of uneven development aimed at comprehending realities so that solutions leading to equality might be critically examined and applied. Peet (1991: 9) proposes two systems supporting theories of uneven development, namely:

1   that based on evolutionary biology for explanatory power and lending weight to the strong or deterministic thesis and the weak or possibilistic thesis; and
2   that based on dependency.

While not seeking to pursue both theories to any significant epistemological conclusion here, it might be useful for us to rely considerably on Peet (1991) in distilling the kernel inherent in both theories in order to provide some basis for the positions that might eventually emerge in our analysis of Africa's proper status in globalization.

The evolutionary biology theory argues that geographic differences in human achievement are the inevitable effects of prior variations in natural environment. To that extent, human achievement and the differences, which are observable, are determined more by vocational natural endowment than by anything else. This is what has lent credence to two emerging versions of this theory, namely:

1   the strong (deterministic) thesis which posits that nature creates and nurtures people with unequal potentials of consciousness and effective action; and
2   the weak (possibilistic) thesis, which posits that nature, endows people with superior resource environments, which allow for easier or quicker development in some places than in others.

Eventually, this theory of natural inevitability and environmental determination declined in importance. Conversely, there is a neo-marxist oriented dependency theory, which emerged after the failure of modernization theory, which tends to explain regional differences in terms of the diffusion of modern institutions from original cores of Euro-America. But the dependency theory, which posits that contact with Europe may really bring 'modern' elements to the societies of the Third World, has also connected them to an exploitative social order.

Considering the theories highlighted above, one is bound to propose the need to examine the objectives and clear manifestations of globalization.

Manifestations of globalization in Africa

Political globalization

The political manifestation of globalization in many countries in Africa is visible. The political systems of Africa have undergone profound militarization and civil dictatorships. For example, Nigeria, Ghana, Niger, Benin, Togo, Algeria, Libya, Uganda, Sudan, Ethiopia and the Gambia have at various times been under military dictatorships. Togo has been under civil dictatorship just as has been Kenya under Arap Moi and Malawi under Kamuzu Banda.

Good as the intentions of political globalization have been in Africa, there has been profound ambivalence and prevarification in some cases. The overthrow of the legitimate government in Congo Brazzaville went ahead without vigorous opposition just as the winner of the democratic elections of June 1993 in Nigeria, Chief Moshood K. Abiola was pressurized to abandon his popular mandate until he died in jail in July 1998.

The political globalization of Africa is alleged to have introduced the fear of the erosion of political sovereignty and the enthroning of what Harris (1996: 5) describes as corporate power. Harris (1996: 6) has quoted Estabrooks (1988) as having argued that now it is the Multinational Corporations (MNCS) and Trans-national Corporations (TNCS) and not governments that are at the helm of global politics. The TNCS and MNCS are held by Estabrooks (1988) and others to be in power economically and politically. It remains to be argued convincingly whether this is for good or for bad.

But the fact which emerges from this fear is that African leaders need to be competent enough to manage the politics of globalization.

One other obvious fact is that the quest for economic control often goes hand-in-hand with that of securing democratic legitimacy. It is, therefore, natural that those who are investing capital for economic control must of necessity demand appropriate forms of governance which can bring about appropriate civil society wherein socioeconomic goals can be pursued with certainty. Where this is not the case, appropriate actions, including sanctions and social ostracization, tend to be generated.

Socio-cultural globalization

This form of globalization in Africa has actually preceded other forms. Aided by the explosion in communication technology, much of Africa had been laid bare to all manner of influences.

Socio-cultural globalization in many countries in Africa has been criticized for some negative consequences. For example, the style of dressing, speaking, conduct, music and eating among others are largely foreign. Values like respect for the elderly have been dashed. Instances of declining utility and the role of the African extended family systems are obvious. But one must resist the temptation of being over-sensitive since some might argue that there have been some good in this form of globalization. This might well be so but the fact is that the African social system is in grave danger of being completely eroded. However, African values can only be better reassessed and preserved through regular schemes of research, dissemination and preservation.

The monoculture anticipated in social globalization has meant for Africa the readiness to explore values which should be exported. For instance, the African virtues of communal living and sharing, the upholding of the dignity of humankind, good neighbourliness, humanness, avoidance of racism and ethnic chauvinism, among others, that are obviously lacking in some other continents are valuable and could be diffused globally for global peace, love and unity. As a matter of fact, the unique closeness that had been the lot of Africans could be introduced and 'sold' to the world. The world could be taught to understand, appreciate and adopt the African warmth and kind-heartedness, which is lacking in many other cultures.

Economic globalization

We earlier stated that the phenomenon known as globalization is driven more by economic motives than by any other consideration in terms of intensity. It is necessary to remind ourselves that economic globalization is an economic revolutionary transformation on a global scale. This transformation is aimed at increasing the tempo of economic operation and the promotion of consumerism.

For economic globalization to work, it is required that every barrier to export competitiveness, free trade and free capital movement must be demolished in the attempt to create a single global market. Indeed, instant capital movement across boundaries without any hindrance in the quest for lower costs and higher profits is the guiding principle. Integration and deregulation are the grease required for economic locomotion. Africa has been exposed to the effects of economic globalization. The gains are there in the opening up of the economy for competition even if it meant doing so on unequal terms. Problems have emerged and as a result there have been the problems of the inability of many African nations to control their monetary and fiscal policies. The debt burden has tended to become ever more burdensome as there are at the same time increases in job losses, downsizing of government corporations and government labour forces, retrenchment with its potency for enhancing political and social disintegration and the intensification of impoverishment. In some instances it seems that economic globalization is ending up by providing material abundance to some while the masses continue to wallow in poverty, misery, ignorance, disease and hopelessness. These problems pose challenges to our leaders and scholars. But we cannot afford to erect barriers to globalization in an attempt to protect ourselves and recapture an earlier era of independence. To do so is to confuse the cause and effect of globalization (Sutherland 1998: 2).

Globalization in education

Education cannot be isolated from critical influences. Globalization in education has taken the form of compelling the schools and other education sectors to prepare for the competition in the global economy. Beveridge (1996: 70) laments that education has been converted into a commodity for trade and subject to the new international trade deals and services.

Beveridge (1996: 70) and other scholars in his line of argument have alleged that sometimes African nations must downsize expenditure on education and engage in the harmonization of standards so as to facilitate the mobility and the portability of professional skills or that tertiary institutions downsize their staff strengths or even close down if necessary as was the case in the Edo State College of Education in Nigeria in 1997. Fortunately, these expectations have been successfully countered by African scholars who have resisted the political manipulation of the education systems with some degree of success even under military dictatorship regimes, as was the case in Nigeria.

Globalization in education has posed challenges to scholarship in Africa. The flow of academic information from European and American institutions of higher education into Africa continues to reveal the weaknesses in Africa scholarship. It may be argued that conditions for scholarship in Africa are years behind those prevailing in the Northern Hemisphere. Even so the realities of the African situation are a challenge to organize more collaborative initiatives aimed at enhancing standards in research, scholarship, training and scholarly development such that Africa can compete favourably and successfully. African academics cannot lament the Northern Hemisphere dominance of scholarship and training without identifying the root cause of the problems as well as viable solutions for overcoming them.

What should lifelong education do?

It is true that lifelong education, as a movement, process, programme and method, has no supermacro economic, social and political structures with which it can deal directly with the globalization challenges confronting Africa. But it has a vision and can infuse people such that they can comprehend the objectives and process of globalization. Law and Low (1997: 113) confirm the conviction among some scholars in the South that lifelong education is an essential capability in a people, workforce and a society in the determined effort to compete effectively and successfully in a global economy.

An assessment of the 'Africaness' of the present drive for globalization must leave one unimpressed. For example, how much input of the people of Africa can one see in global economic corporations like Natwest, Merrill Lynch, Deutsche Morgan Granfell, J. P. Morgan, Ing Barrings, the Swiss UBS Securities, SBC Warburg Securities among a host of others?

African nations cannot expect any revision of the principles of globalization; it is not reasonable to expect any other nation to slow down the process of becoming a strong competitor. If anything, globalization requires greater competitiveness from developing economies. Any nation's capability in this direction could be enhanced by reinvigorated management capabilities. This is possible through providing opportunities for effective human resource development programmes. This is where lifelong education has the greatest potential for a meaningful contribution towards coping with the challenges.

We are aware that lifelong education is a specialization and as a specialization, it is limited by its tendency to provide fragmentary or what Peet (1991: 30–40) calls aspect biased disciplinary approaches to dealing with problems emanating from a variegated subject like globalization. For example, how can lifelong education alone offer strategies for dealing with the challenges facing Africa particularly as this phenomenon is concerned unless contributors are inviting economic, socio-cultural and political studies. Limited as specialization's might seem to be when dealing with global schemes such as this, they are capable of providing fruitful insights. This article takes the view that lifelong education can help many countries in Africa as far as this phenomenon is concerned.

The first task lifelong education must undertake in this particular instance is that of generating awareness. It must utilize its structures to educate the people from the top to the grassroots levels about the nature, objectives, structures and processes of globalization. There is profound ignorance as to what globalization is all about, and how it will affect the people. For example, do people understand the slogan 'think globally, act locally'? It is meaningless to the illiterate, hungry, unemployed, homeless, hopeless and sick masses of the people. It can only make meaning to them if directed against the cause of their frustration.

An important component of this endeavour to create awareness will mean incorporating the tacit understanding of globalization in a subtle way into the popular education programmes like the national literacy campaigns, empowerment schemes and income generation. Another foundation we can build is the integration of globalization principles and processes into the curricula used in formal schools. Creating an awareness of the nature, objectives and operational mechanism of globalization at the level of basic education is an irreducible minimum for building up the continent's reserve of expertise needed for coping with the challenges.

A related vital task would require that scholars in Africa step up movements for the better funding and promotion of all forms of education. In particular, there is need to ensure that the lifelong education programmes we have initiated are strengthened in such a way as to illicit favourable spontaneous response from our peoples. For studies have proved that the lower the initial education, the less likely the learner will be to continue learning in the adult years (Law and Low 1997: 114). All categories of people (including the workforce) need to upgrade continuously their knowledge and skills.

The second task relates to the stimulation and provision of fora for academic discussions emphasizing self-criticism on the part of all stakeholders. This differs from the first approach in the sense that the stakeholders in this case should comprise of the present '*winners*' and 'winners-to-be' in the game pattern of globalization. The self-criticism intended here is that which is capable of fostering deep understanding of the forces at play in globalization and of how best a balance can be struck in the interest of all. If, for example, the poorer and disadvantaged African nations understood the root cause of their disadvantage, they might well be motivated into undertaking liberators action.

The third task for lifelong education is that of using the social action programmes in community development to ease the pains of transition from the local realities of existence to global ones. Globalization entails a gestation period during which the people must understand, experiment and adopt (or reject) new alternatives in all spheres of international exchange. When lifelong education acts in a manner that eases this transition it might reduce the incidents of tension and, sometimes, disruptive behaviours.

The fourth task relates to that of using lifelong education structures to accelerate community beaming through placing emphasis on beaming centres, and what Harris (1996: 9) calls, community 'narrowcasting' which open doors for voices from the South as far as this subject is concerned. Socio-cultural globalization has prompted the saturation of Africa's cultural environment with media products up to the point that the people's culture is becoming almost totally irrelevant and extinct with all the attendant grave consequences. Lifestyles and patterns of thought are so negatively influenced that whatever cultural advancement Africa made in the last three decades is dwarfed. Indeed, we now have to contend with the so-called global citizenship in which there is hardly any foothold for Africa's cultural traits. The suggested community – 'narrowcasting' programmes geared towards promoting Africa's cultural traits would require the intellectual attention of academics from diverse disciplines.

Lifelong education, in the fifth task, can initiate linkages, which would mediate the building up of relevant African research and knowledge bases, which can prepare the people for global competition. Concern here will be about practices that have worked and which can be developed for entry into global competition with good chances of success.

To date, balanced information exchange in scholarship is glaringly lacking among the Lusophone, Francophone and Anglophone blocs within Africa. Exchange can be facilitated through the breaking down of communication barriers. This becomes the sixth task. For example, relevant learning packages on globalization could be simultaneously translated for more rapid dissemination across the blocs.

The seventh task consists of the need for lifelong education in Africa to open up linkages with those in the North with a view to working out areas of co-operation and collaborative research. This establishment of linkages must also be extended to staff and student exchanges. But if this linkage proves to be rather slow in coming, then African nations with appreciable technological foundations could through their relevant government ministries, well-meaning private companies and non-governmental organizations bring into reality a much more vigorous borderless, versatile, multifaceted scientific and technological competency based training than the continent has ever witnessed.

The eighth task relates to human capital review, formation, modernization and acceleration. The ability to compete depends, to a great extent, on human capital since all other advantages may remain inert without this one. This means that the programmes of lifelong education in the sphere of professional continuing education must be streamlined to reflect globalization in terms of enhancing the people's capability to enter into the competition (Oduaran 1997: 99). For example, it might be possible to run a continental workshop on how the people can enter safely into offshore investment. Furthermore, the trend towards skill enhancement instead of deskilling, pre-production technology instead of mere production, and mental skilling instead of manual skilling has obvious implications for human capitalization programmes. Lifelong education needs to reflect this reality.

In this regard, many African countries like South Africa, Botswana, Namibia, Zimbabwe, Egypt, Libya, Ethiopia, Nigeria and Ghana to name but a few, that are at the basic level of technological development may choose to lead the way in preparing our peoples for effective competition in globalization. Towards realizing this goal, African nations have a lot to borrow from Singapore, a country in the South. The Singaporean model of entry into globalization has required political will and commitment as well as the mounting of vigorous national training programmes made up of Basic Education for Skills Training (BEST), Worker Improvement through Secondary Education (WISE), Modular Skills Training (MOST), Training Initiative for Mature Employees (TIME), the Adult Co-operative Training Scheme (ACTS) and the Certified On-the-Job Training Centre (COJTC), all of which have complemented formal education initiatives to produce a solid basis for competitiveness. The experience here seems to prove that nothing is impossible for any nation and, indeed any continent that is committed to striving to be subject rather than mere object of the global historical process.

Finally, there should be a deliberate effort to enforce policies on life-long education in the continent. So far it seems that existing policies are a mere expression of intentions. In several African countries, less than 2% (instead of the minimum of 5%) of the GNP is allocated to education in general and much less to the education of adults. The problem here is that when allocation to education declines, human capital suffers and our chances of facing up to real competition globally are in jeopardy. This is our real technical crisis.

Conclusion

We have tried within the context of this paper to selectively examine the phe-nomenon of globalization; its challenges and the role lifelong education could play in strengthening Africa in the process of entering into the implied competition. Since the proper comprehension and the application of the concept of globalization should depend on the articulation of several issues, we had examined summarily Africa's differences and commonalities. This was what we did in the context of how globalization and lifelong educa-tion may apply in homogenizing and heterogeneous ways. Furthermore, we applied lifelong education to the technique of how we might enhance Africa's participation in globalization. For we believe that it is possible to bring about the needed variety of organized and systematic opportunities for learning throughout the lifespan by legislating education systems with equal access for all. Towards achieving the goal of applying lifelong education to globalization, it was recommended that there is need to integrate education systems horizontally and vertically in Africa. In exploring the origins, basic assumptions, objectives and principles of globalization, we highlighted its political, socio-cultural, economic and educational manifestations in Africa. Based on these manifestations, we offered propositions as to what lifelong education could and should do in order to enhance Africa's capability to compete favourably in the global phenomenon called globalization.

Note

1 *Akpovire Oduaran*, Professor of Adult and Community Education, was Professor and Head of the Department of Adult Education at the University of Benin, Nigeria, for five years. He is the founding Executive Secretary of the Community and Adult Education Research Society of Nigeria (CARESON). Professor Oduaran now lectures at the Department of Adult Education, University of Botswana, where he takes responsibility for co-ordinating the higher degree pro-gramme   and   academic   staff   research   and   seminars;   e-mail: oduarana@mopipl.ub.bw

References

Beveridge, D. (1996) Globalization and sustainability: issues and options for adult education. *Convergence*, XXIX, 68–74.

Bhola, H. S. (1998) World trends and issues in adult education on the eve of the 21st century. *International Review of Education*, 44, 485–506.

Bowers, J. (1992) Postmodernity and the globalization of technoscience: the computer, cognitive science and war. In J. Doherty, *et al.* (eds) *Postmodernity and Social Sciences* (London: Johnston).

Brock, L., Albert, M. and Hessler, S. (1996) The dematerialization of the world economy. *Development and Cooperation*, 1, 4–5.

Brown, T. (1999) Challenging globalization as discourse and phenomenon. *International Journal of Lifelong Education*, 8, 3–17.

Campbell, B. (1993) *Moving in the Wrong Direction* (Ottawa: Canadian Centre for Policy Alternatives).

Clarke, A. (1996) Competitiveness, Technological Innovation and the Challenge to Europe. In P. Raggat (ed.) *The Learning Society: Challenges and Trends* (London: Routledge), pp. 66–67.

Deutscher, E., Jahn, T. and Moltmann, B. (eds.) (1996) *Development Models and World Views* (Bonn: German Foundation for International Developments), pp. 2–8.

Frank, A. G. (1981) *Crisis in the World* (New York: Holmes and Meier Pub. Inc).

Gass, J. R. (1996) The Goals, Architecture and Means of Lifelong Learning. *Eric: No:* ED418268.

Harris, E. (1996) Revisioning citizenship for global village: implications for adult education. *Convergence*, XXIX, 5–10.

Holtz, U. (1995) Towards a new development paradigm. *Development and Cooperative*, 6, 7.

Johnston, G. G. (1990) *Globalization: Canadian Companies Complete* (Ottawa: Conference Board of Canada).

Korten, D. (1995) *When Cooperations Rule the World* (West Hertford: Kumarian Press).

Law, S. S. and Low, S. H. (1997) An empirical framework for implementing lifelong learning systems in M. J. Hatton (ed.) *Lifelong Learning: Policies, Practices, and Programs* (Toronto: School of Media Studies, Humber College), pp. 112–114.

Longworth, N. and Keith Davies, W. (1996) *Lifelong Learning: New vision, New Implications, New Roles for People, Organizations, Nations and Communities in the 21st century* (London: Kogan Page Limited).

Mann, M. (1997) Has globalization ended the rise and rise of the nation-state? *Review of International Political Economy*, 4, 472–496.

Oduaran, A. B. (1997) Professionalism, training needs and institutional capacity. In A. Fajonyomi and I. Biao (eds) *Policy Issues in Adult and Community Education* (Maiduguri: Mai-Nasara Pub. Co).

Peet, T. (1991) *Global Capitalism: Theories of Societal Development* (London: Routledge).

UNESCO (1995) *Report on the State of Education in Africa* (Dakar: Breda).

UNICEF (1994) *La Situation des Enfants Dans le Monde* (Geneva: UNICEF).

World Bank (1994) *Rapport Annuel 1994* (Washington, DC: World Bank).

10 Education and work

Preliminary thoughts on the encouragement of productive work in the educational process

Ettore Gelpi

Head of Lifelong Education Unit UNESCO

Abstracts

English

Since there should be no gap between initial education and productive work, it is essential that the latter is not divorced from the curriculum of the former. Similarly the educational content of productive work should not be overlooked. Therefore the relationship between the two is explored and the concepts of work and educational space expanded. Finally, factors leading to resistance and receptiveness between the two systems are discussed.

Français

Afin d'éviter toute faille ou interruption entre l'enseignement initial et le travail productif, il est essentiel de ne pas séparer celui-ci des programmes d'études; mais il est également important de ne pas ignorer le contenu éducatif du travail productif. Ainsi il convient d'explorer la relation qui doit exister entre ces deux activités, et d'élargir les concepts de travail et de formation. Pour terminer, nous étudierons les facteurs responsables de la résistance ou de la réceptivité entre les deux systèmes.

Deutsch

Da es zwischen Allgemeinbildung und produktiver Arbeit keine Kluft geben sollte, ist es von entscheidender Bedeutung, die letztere nicht vom Curriculum der ersteren zu trennen. In gleicher Weise sollten der Bildungsinhalt bzw. -gehalt der produktiven Arbeit nicht übersehen werden. Deshalb untersucht der Aufsatz die Beziehungen zwischen den beiden Faktoren und erweitert die Begriffe "Arbeit" und "Bildung". Abschließend untersucht der Verfasser Beweggründe, die einerseits Widerstand, andererseits aber auch Aufgeschlossenheit gegenüber beiden Faktoren auslösen können.

Definition and problems

1

Any definition of productive work in schools must necessarily be linked with a particular view of the purpose of education. Within an open view of education, productive work contributes to man's individual and collective development and aims to develop all his physical, moral, aesthetic and intellectual appreciation and abilities, stimulates the individual's social conscience, his creativity, his acquisition of knowledge and skills, to prepare him for his working life and for transforming his life. That being so, the aim of what is done in workshops, laboratories, work placements, in factories, in the country, in public services (hospitals, libraries, forestry etc.) and in leisure time should be to make the child and the young person better able to deal with production, social life, affective life, etc.

Why productive work? Traces of new activities can be found in school programmes over the years but, characteristically, they have had no social or productive relevance. Talking of productive work means going beyond this stage and introducing activities which are economically and socially significant. However, productive work must not be interpreted restrictively. Encouraging productive work does not just mean engaging pupils in activities which are socially and economically useful, but also developing the whole range of educational activities towards a scientific training, within which theory and practice are integrated in a balanced way and we go beyond the ideas of 'manual' and 'intellectual' activities.

2

The introduction of productive work into the educational process has been associated with the idea of education contributing to development; new approaches to the concept of development, even with all their contradictions, call into question education (and productive work in school) fulfilling the requirements of a type of production which is often foreign to the overall economic development and social and cultural reality of a particular country. Overall development, taking into account the cultural, social, economic and scientific dimensions, requires the introduction of a type of productive work which can contribute to the enrichment of man and the society he lives in along all those dimensions.

There can be no one single way of approaching and implementing productive work in the educational system because there are different requirements for development in each country and also because the ideological framework, the socio-economic system and the relationships of production vary from one country to another and, over the years, within any particular country.

New relationships between work and education must start from the specific, educational, productive and cultural systems of each individual country. If this individuality is not respected, pupils could be faced with totally useless exercises: having to carry out tasks which are already part of their day-to-day experience, increasing production beyond the country's requirements, lowering the quality of things already produced (shoddy handicraft, worthless art etc.). These could result from the thoughtless introduction of productive work. For example, according to the statistics of the International Labour Office (BIT) fifty-two million children are forced to go to work at an early age (it must not be forgotten that, in many countries, they represent a significant percentage of the population), often contrary to every international convention. In this case, improving the relationship between education and work means doing away with the exploitation of child labour and giving children the right to education.

3

The discovery of a relatively new area of educational research (productive work in the educational process) has led to some confusion over terminology and competence. Education and work, education and employment, education and productive work, teaching technical and vocational subjects, vocational training and job training, organizing scientific and technological activities, all have points in common, but they are also different and require different types of expertise. The study of the relation between education and work is the framework into which all the others fit, being economic, social, scientific, psychological and pedagogical problems. The fact that they are all distinct areas of study does not mean that there is no interrelationship, for example, between education and employment, teaching technical and vocational subjects and organizing scientific activities; but the fact that they are different implies a range of different types of expertise.

4

The structural characteristics of each educational system must be studied: number of years of schooling, integration or segregation of the various branches, relation between initial and continuing education, access to education for teachers and taught. Take for example the increase in the numbers of years of schooling which is a common factor in many countries: experience of work means that the extension of education must be matched by an extension of productive work, as it is a common non-discriminatory experience across the whole range of pupils.

The life-long character of the educational process and the frequent changes in vocational tasks create a new demand for educational institutions attended by a wide range of different types of people. After primary or secondary school the young people do not necessarily find skilled jobs: there is often unemployment, under-employment, unskilled work or work which does not match their qualifications; initial training and work experience in school could be training for future vocational tasks only in fairly exceptional cases. That is why productive work must be closely associated with general education and the vocational training dimension is only one aspect of it and not necessarily the most important one.

5

Workers plan and participate in things like self-management, workers' councils, etc. which require competence which is not restricted to technical training. Preparation for these management functions includes initial training in which the social, associational and management dimension is just as important as the technical and vocational dimension. There is also a tendency in firms to give certain groups of workers a greater say in decisions about their work (a power of decision which, however, does not necessarily mean economic power – in some cases just the opposite). Co-operatives, independent worker-producer organizations, sub-contracting are structural aspects of these tendencies which cover both the rich and poor sectors of the labour market. Also, a high percentage of people in rural areas are either independent, or independent collective producers (capitalist or State exploitation is only a part of agricultural production).

These facts about the types of working structures could influence both initial and life-long education. Management might be one of the basic subjects, with education and work meaning education for management.

6

As regards a typology of the work/education relationship the following situations could be distinguished:

a   Activities promoting artistic, scientific and technological creativity in school.
b   Laboratory work in school.
c   Production units in school.
d   Training courses within the production system.
e   Vocational training both in school and at the place of work.
f   Working placements supervized by teaching staff.
g   Production cooperatives developed by schoolchildren and students both inside and outside the educational framework.
h   Artistic, technological and scientific experience in leisure time within the various structures (educational system, production system, community, associations).

The types of experience of productive work covered by this typology call for changes in educational structures, methodology and content; new educational spaces; recruitment and training of different types of educators; application of educational criteria in setting up production units; coordination between educators and directors of work-place training; combined training of teachers of theoretical subjects and those in charge of various practical and work activities; defining common objectives in the preparation of theoretical and practical type programmes; overall evaluation of various types of activity rejecting any dichotomy between productive work and academic and vocational orientation; support for artistic, scientific and technological leisure-time activities.

The educational value of work lies in intellectual stimulation, the integration of study and practical activity and the social usefulness of the product. Stressing certain aspects and ignoring others has led to incomplete and often disappointing experiences.

7

Evaluating experience of work within an educational framework implies its own criteria of evaluation not limited merely to economic return or learning how to perform the activity. Before productive work is introduced into the pupil's curriculum there must be an evaluation of the parameters of the work: the pupil's level of knowledge and previous experience; the overall training programme. If these are not considered in detail productive work may be educationally meaningless. On the other hand, what is produced is part of the educational value of the experience of production. The process and the product must be evaluated together. There is nothing more anti-educational than an aesthetically and functionally bad product.

The contribution of educational sciences (history, sociology, anthropology, etc.)

1

With a critical historical approach we may be able to benefit from the thinking and experiments which have taken place in countries having different types of social and productive structures. During the nineteenth and twentieth centuries, Pestalozzi, Owen, Marx, Dewey, Krupskaya, Blonsky, Karschensteiner, Montessori, Makarenko, Decroly, Freinet, among others, have included educationally oriented work activities in their socio-educational experimentation and in their pedagogical thinking – i.e. work which, apart from its economic value, contributed to training in sociability, aesthetic appreciation, creativity and cooperation.

These authors reflected the transformation of societies towards industrialization. Parallel to them there is the thinking and encouragement of productive work in countries struggling to free themselves from colonial domination (Marti, Gandhi, Mao-tse-tung, Boubou Hama, Nyerere and others). It is useful to study these authors and the context of their writings because they illustrate (a) certain theoretical premises for a pedagogy of work and (b) the influence of culture and society on the problems of work and education. However, interesting as these authors are, we must not forget what is now outdated in their writings and the changes which have come about in the systems and relations of production.

Side by side with pedagogical thinking and the encouragement of productive work, there are continuing educational, work and cultural traditions (in Asia, Africa, Europe and America) which have rejected the separation of life, creation and production from education. Such traditions have come up against, and been wiped out by, colonial domination from outside or inside the country introducing educational schemes which have not always been relevant to the overall development of the individuals or the society. The history of the relationship between education and work also includes non-formal education which has been handed down by peasants, workers, craftsmen, unofficial political leaders, artists, village associations, musicians, fishermen, hunters, etc. to succeeding generations, whether or not they took part in the activities of the formal educational system. There is also another history of education and work written by teachers, underground groups, technicians and artists who, in often very difficult conditions, have trained young people for immediate action in hostile situations or in contexts where there was little encouragement for creative production.

2

Disciplinary and interdisciplinary research (history of education, anthropology, sociology of work, sociology of work culture, ergonomics etc.) have been ignored by educationalists and educational planners, who have often restricted themselves to an analysis of educational institutions. Pedagogical exploitation of this research and the setting up of research projects to find out more about the implications of work for education and education for work should be actively pursued. The sociology of work and the sociology of work culture contribute to the study of work and education. It may be possible to exploit the working environment for educational purposes if we know about it from the technical, social and cultural point of view. Admittedly, sociology of work and sociology of work culture have paid more attention to adults than children, but they have shown what the working environment is like and this concerns not only adults. Teachers are not very familiar with the world of work, but one of the prerequisites for the introduction of productive work into schools is familiarizing teachers with the working environment.

3

In an enquiry carried out in November 1977 into the establishment of life-long education, Unesco's National Commissions were asked 'Is there any experience of productive work within primary education?'. Fifty-four replies were analyzed and 31.5 per cent answered 'yes' (for 14 per cent it is compulsory). To the question 'Is there any experience of productive work in secondary education?' 74 per cent answered 'yes' (and for 45 per cent it is compulsory).

The trends which emerge in the member states are towards the introduction of productive work in education, but aims and methods are often very different. There are two main directions in the use of productive work in school: (a) productive work which reinforce educational dualism (productive work for technical/vocational streams); (b) productive work as a means of overcoming the dichotomy between general and vocational education, intellectual work and manual work. These two directions are not always clear-cut or explicit and there are often contradictions between declared aims and practice.

Theoretical and empirical research indicates that there is no single reason for the administration and productive structures taking an interest in linking education to work: the need to increase production and/or productivity, excessive cost of educational provision, unemployment, class struggle, raising of the school leaving age etc. are the causes of pressure on the educational system to turn its attention to the system of production. So many contradictory interests in linking education and productive work make all generalization impossible. For example, if productive work becomes an instrument for reinforcing educational and social dualism (culture for some, work for others), it would be an instrument for reinforcing social and class hierarchies and consequently in contradiction to education as a tool for social equality.

Strategy for the encouragement of productive work

Extending the concepts of work and educational space

The introduction of productive work can be seen as an element of the integration of general and vocational education, either with a view to subsequent separation or with education dependent on the productive system and looking to be cost effective. It is important, then, that the way in which productive work is introduced makes it possible to use this experience for educational purposes linked to the development of an analytic mind, concept learning, the ability to synthesize and a creative attitude. These aspects must be taken into consideration in the choice of productive work, as well as the age of the child or young person, his level of knowledge and the purpose of introducing him to production.

Aesthetic and physical education is also an important factor in training, and experience of work which develops aesthetic taste and physical ability should be favoured in the framework of integrating general and vocational education. Stressing the different purposes of work and not merely the economic objective helps to make man master rather than slave of what he produces.

The poverty or richness of scientific or work experience influences initial training. Any enrichment of this experience in the environment (parents, community, school, etc.) is stimulating for children and young people. Because of this there is a close link between adult experience and the training of the young.

The relationship between education and work is easier if there is a positive relationship between the school and the community. If the community has a reserved or fearful attitude towards the school, the contribution from work will be affected. If, for example, the school seems to be trying to take advantage of professional competence or to set up in opposition to local craftsmen, they will not be prepared to make their contribution to the school.

Looked at from the standpoint of a close relationship between education and work, educational space is a combination of several areas inside educational establishments (classrooms, laboratories, workshops and school fields) and outside (production, services, associations etc.). It is important not only for these various places to be used but for the different experiences gleaned from the various segments to be related. Internal and external geographical mobility (migrant workers and their children) and the job opportunities point to a relationship between education and work in which the work aspect changes frequently during the lifetime of the future worker.

Leisure time and working time

Non-formal work, creative scientific, technological and artistic activities during leisure time, creativity in solving every-day technical problems are often ignored by educational systems and not encouraged by the centres of decision making for scientific and educational policies. A positive approach to these activities is required to stimulate scientific and artistic creativity in close association with meaningful productive work.

The development of each person's body by physical exercise, sport, dance etc. can also contribute to study and scientific training. There is a considerable investment of time in these activities, but there is often no awareness of their educational implications. The leisure dimension is too often separated from education and nothing is made of all the scientific knowledge acquired during leisure time.

There are obstacles to getting children to overcome the rigid separation between work and play in societies in which play and leisure tend to be a response to alienation from work and education. On the other hand, enrichment of educational and work experience gives a new dimension to leisure and play. The separation between these different facets of human life becomes blurred and new relationships appear: creativity, sociability and production, spirit of analysis and synthesis become associated with these different activities.

Originally, there was no division in function for mankind, and a child would not distinguish between leisure, productive activity and learning if this division was not imposed on him. In early childhood, a certain continuity could be achieved by integrating production, learning and leisure, although with an opportunity provided to step back and give the children a critical appreciation of their experience.

Manual and non-manual work

Another of the aims of introducing productive work in school is to get away from the contrast of manual and non-manual work. Faced with the wide range of different types of work, young people may be made aware of the fact that in all manual activity there are some areas which involve thinking on a theoretical level. This may stimulate links between manual and non-manual work, between theory and practice.

Within the educational framework it is possible to give permanent scientific, artistic and technological training by introducing technology and equipment on which children and young people can acquire practical scientific skills and learn to handle simple technology.

Resistance and receptiveness of the system of production

The receptiveness of the system of production to education beyond its internal requirements of vocational training is often quite limited. In general, it is difficult to obtain work placements for young people and to ensure that they are supervised. There are a few new regulations as a result of laws or union negotiations but they are still very recent.

In most countries the structures of production are not available for education activities because the logic of immediate cost-effectiveness and efficiency often make it difficult to provide educational experience in the work place. Resistance is found particularly in certain sectors of production such as service industries and technologically advanced industries (although they are very concerned about training their own management). On the other hand experience of agricultural work within the educational framework seems to be the most widespread, but the cognitive value of this experience is often very modest because the technology is rudimentary, there is no innovation and limited scope for theoretical thinking.

Considering work and education without taking into account conflicts over work and the gap between young people's expectations and job opportunities means once again getting caught up in pedagogical rhetoric producing fine words and avoiding the problem.

In many countries not only young people leaving primary and secondary school but also those with technical and professional qualifications will be faced with unemployment or unskilled work. So, rather than saying what a good thing work is it would be preferable to present young people with a critical analysis of the realities of work both present and future.

Productive work within the framework of education must be analyzed from the economic standpoint; unemployment or, on the other hand, the need to employ young people, may make it inadvisable or essential to have intensive high productivity work programmes. In addition, there is nothing more pointless than involving children and young people in work activities which are illogical either economically, educationally or culturally. Educational policies associating work and education must take into consideration several variables: (a) the dynamics of the labour market and job opportunities (segmentation of the labour market, under-employment, unemployment) locally, regionally and internationally; (b) the educational or non-educational dimension of the structures of production in the various countries (by sectors of production and categories of employment); (c) labour organizations and the strength of young and adult workers in negotiations about their work; (d) cultural traditions about the value of work; (e) the social, physical and cultural marginality of individuals and groups, not in order to perpetuate it but to go beyond it, etc..

Science, technology, worker participation, the relationships of production, social and international division of labour are some of the variables which contribute to the modification of work and educational demand. Restricting oneself to a consideration of the technical variable alone could greatly reduce the content of initial training.

Resistance and receptiveness of the educational system

Bringing together work, research and training may lead to an upheaval in educational and social practices with which the social and educational system could not cope. This explains why the educational system resists or adapts only superficially, stressing the value of work but actually rejecting any challenge to the social hierarchy, giving preference to talk and reinforcing the discrimination between 'theoretical' and 'practical' subjects.

Recognizing the value of scientific knowledge wherever it occurs, in formal or informal situations, means recognizing the contribution of those who possess this know-how: the introduction of productive work in schools; organizing cultural, scientific and technological activities; building into education creative experiences in the fields of science and technology; all these require the use of different types of expertise drawn from all areas of education, industry and social life.

As far as structural changes are concerned, there is one in particular which must be considered: the possibility of bringing educators who are not teachers but who are in outside work into the educational system without breaking their work link: often normative or economic obstacles prevent the use of such highly qualified personnel.

The recruitment and training of teaching staff with a view to integrating education and productive work must also be reviewed; people directly involved in production and teachers of theoretical subjects are both important in training; any separation between these two types of educator must be avoided. The combined training of skilled workers and vocational teachers will be organized around experience in the workplace and in laboratories.

In relating production and education, the contribution of group organizations (professional associations, unions, local communities etc.) to education is also important because they can play a useful role in enabling young people to participate in social and cultural experiences within the framework of productive activity.

The role played by the family in vocational training, particularly in rural communities, is also important. That is a parameter of adult education as an investment for future generations. Considering family education as vocational training means that the educational structures must contribute to extending the family vocational training experience which is often narrow.

No hasty conclusions must be drawn about productive work and education but it might be as well to remind ourselves that productive work in school (and to some extent education itself) is determined by the nature and quality of work in the society and that any change in work will have consequences on productive work in school and on education in general.

Translated by Portsmouth Polytechnic French Studies Translation Workshop and revised by Bob French and John Bourne.

11 Professional practice, learning, and continuing education

An integrated perspective[1]

Ronald M. Cervero[2]

University of Georgia Athens, Georgia

The popular wisdom among professionals is that the knowledge they acquire from practice is far more useful than what they acquire from more formal types of education. This observation contradicts the dominant viewpoint in society and the professional education establishment that has given legitimacy to knowledge that is formal, abstract and general while devaluing knowledge that is local, specific and based in practice. This viewpoint has strongly influenced continuing education, which has followed the model set at the preservice level in focusing on the transmission of formal, abstract knowledge. In this paper, I describe and provide evidence for three propositions that build on the importance of knowledge gained from practice. These are: (1) the goal of professional practice is wise action; (2) knowledge acquired from practice is necessary to achieve this goal; and (3) a model of learning from practice should become the centrepiece of systems of continuing education for the professions.

A grizzled, and I might add astute, educator recently offered the following description of the most frequently encountered form of continuing professional education: 'a single instructor lectures and lectures and lectures fairly large groups of business and professional people, who sit for long hours in an audiovisual twilight, making never-to-be-read notes at rows of narrow tables covered with green baize and appointed with fat binders and sweating pitchers of ice water' (Nowlen 1988). Furthermore, these simple activities are expected to improve the performance of professionals whose practices are characterized by complexities, uncertainties and conflicting values. Given these conditions, the widespread concern in the professions over the effectiveness of continuing education seems quite justified.

Although the landscape of continuing professional education is dotted with a number of innovative educational approaches, these are distressingly few. We should not be surprised, then, that the popular wisdom among practising professionals is that the knowledge they acquire from practice is far more useful than what they acquire from the more formal forms of education.

Of course, current practitioners and researchers are not the first to observe that learning from practice (or experience) is a central way that people create their world and give it meaning. John Dewey most recently made this point, and David Hume before him and Aristotle before him (Dreyfus and Dreyfus 1986). However, for the better part of this century, our society has given legitimacy to knowledge that is formal, abstract and general, while devaluing knowledge that is local, specific and based in practice (Benner 1989). For this we owe a debt to Plato and Socrates, who believed that for something to count as knowledge, it had to be de-contextualized, generalized and abstracted to cover a range of situations.

Although everyone agrees that professionals learn from practice, the debate becomes interesting when a model of learning from practice is juxta-posed against other models of learning in the fight for the hearts, minds and dollars of those who control professional education programmes. Bruner (1985) has forcefully made the point that there is no naturalistic way to decide which model of learning we should enshrine at the centre of our educational practice. To make this decision, in the end we must make a political choice about how the mind should be cultivated and to what end.

My bedrock assumption is that many of the shortcomings of continuing education are due to inappropriate choices about the ends to which the minds of professionals should be cultivated. Specifically, most continuing education has followed the model set at the preservice level in focusing on the transmission of formal, abstract knowledge. In the rest of this paper I will describe and provide evidence for three propositions, which offer a basis for the improvement of continuing education for the professions. These are:

1   The goal of professional practice is wise action;
2   Knowledge acquired from practice is necessary to achieve this goal;
3   A model of learning from practice should become the centrepiece of systems of continuing education for the professions.

The goal of professional practice

My view is that the distinguishing characteristic of practice is its action-orientation. Professionals reason toward the goal of wise action, rather than describing what it is (Buchmann 1984). They attempt to put matters right rather than uncover the truth. Thus, practice is a normative, not a descriptive, enterprise. If practice is normative, then wisdom must be seen as socially constructed, taking its meaning only within the particular ethical framework of those who have the power to define wisdom for a profession. We all saw a particularly vivid example of this during the nomi-nation process of Robert Bork for the Supreme Court of the United States. It was clear that his judicial wisdom was seen as deficient not because of his technical ability but rather because of the moral framework in which it was embedded.

This view of practice implies that professionals constantly make judgements about the appropriate course of action in a given situation. Wise action means making the best judgement in a specific context and for a specified set of ethical beliefs. These judgements are evaluated as best against what is possible in the specific circumstances in which they occur and what is desirable within a particular ethical framework. Thus, to improve practice, professionals' ability to make the best judgements must be facilitated (Cervero 1988).

The centrality of judgement in professional practice has recently been noted for a variety of professions including medicine (Bok 1984), teaching (The Holmes Group 1986), nursing (Benner 1984), architecture (Gutman 1985), urban planning (Alonzo 1986), public policy (Wildavsky 1985), journalism (White 1986), and the ministry (Carroll 1985). In providing the rationale for Harvard's New Pathway Medical School curriculum, the president of Harvard University notes the growing change in perception of how physicians go about making their characteristic decisions of diagnosis and treatment. He says: 'Few doctors are now inclined to think of themselves as simply arriving at logically determined conclusions by applying scientifically tested truths to experimentally derived data. ... Considerations of many kinds are often jumbled together to form a picture full of uncertainties, requiring the most delicate kinds of judgments and intuitions' (Bok 1984: 37–38).

These judgements have as much to do with what problem needs to be solved as about how to solve it. Thus, problem setting is as important to practice as problem solving. Take for example the teacher whose student is having difficulty learning how to read. He may be uncertain about how to think about the cause of the problem: is there a neurological problem? Is the student not applying him/herself fully? Is a different language spoken in the home? Is the student developmentally delayed? The teacher may also experience conflict between a number of values. For example, in choosing how to teach reading to this child, he may be torn between the views of his teacher colleagues, his graduate school advisors and textbooks, and his own personal experience. What if the student is a member of a minority group? Does the teacher worry about evaluating students using culturally biased forms of criteria? This teacher is not simply selecting means to clear ends, but also must 'reconcile, integrate, or choose among conflicting appreciations of a situation as to construct a coherent problem worth solving' (Schon 1983: 6).

These judgements are complicated by the fact that professions are not homogeneous communities with shared sets of values that work toward common ends. Rather, they are 'loose amalgamations of segments pursuing different objectives in different manners and more or less held together under a common name at a particular period in history' (Bucher and Strauss 1961: 326). This implies that individual professionals may have different if not conflicting values about what constitutes wise action.

The existence of internal dissension and value conflict within the professions is supported by a good deal of evidence (Abbott 1988). For example, law is traditionally seen as a form of altruism in which the legal and judicial systems are the guardians of the rule of law for the benefit of society in general. In this view judges apply legal principles dispassionately, free of political bias and personal prejudice. Another view believes that the legal system has a vested interest in a given social order and that lawyers support an exploitive system in which only a few benefit (Heraud 1973). Using this as a starting point, the critical legal studies movement assumes that legal decisions are really policy choices and that we should dismiss the idea that law is an objective process (Unger 1986).

This view of professional practice assumes that professions are necessary because important structures and functions in society depend on their special knowledge and competence. However, it recognizes that professionals' 'special knowledge is embedded in evaluative frames which bear the stamp of human values and interests' (Schon 1983: 345). In other words, professionals' actions are never value-neutral; they must be judged as wise with respect to an ethical framework.

The necessity of learning from practice

In this section I provide evidence that supports my second proposition, namely, that the knowledge acquired from practice is necessary to achieve the goal of wise action. A compelling body of research has accumulated in a variety of fields over the past 15 years supporting this belief. I will synthesize evidence from three of these areas: the literature about cognition, Schon's writings on the 'reflective practitioner', and the literature on professional expertise.

Let me briefly highlight the logic of this evidence. The first point is that the systems of practical knowledge are distinct from the systems of abstract knowledge for each profession. Second, in their work professionals actually use practical knowledge systems. Eliot Friedson (1986) states this most directly when he says: 'To assume ... that textbooks and other publications of academics and researchers reflect in consistent and predictable ways the knowledge that is actually exercised in concrete human settings is either wishful or naive' (p. 229). These knowledge systems are used because of two defining characteristics: they are situated and oriented toward action. Finally, this knowledge is best learned through practice or reflection on practice.

Cognition

Schema theory (Glaser 1984, 1985, Sternberg 1986) describes how acquired knowledge is organized in the mind and how cognitive structures facilitate the use of knowledge in particular situations. In this theory, schemata are prototypes in memory of frequently encountered situations that people use to construct interpretations of related situations. One of the most fundamental distinctions among schemata types, which was first proposed by philosopher Gilbert Ryle (1949), is between declarative and procedural knowledge (Anderson 1983, Shuell 1986).

Declarative knowledge is knowledge *that* something is the case, whereas procedural knowledge is knowledge of *how* to do something. Although declarative knowledge varies in scope (that is, it can be facts, generalization, attitudes), it is relatively static. Procedural knowledge, in contrast, is dynamic. When these knowledge structures are activated, the result is not simply a recall of information but a transformation of information.

Both forms of knowledge are necessary for skilled performance, with declarative knowledge at first providing the data to perform some procedures. However, after the procedures have been performed a number of times, they can be applied directly without accessing the declarative knowledge. This means that procedural knowledge is acquired only when executing a skill; or in the vernacular, one learns by doing (Anderson 1983, Kyllonen and Alluisi 1986, Lesgold *et al.* 1988). A major difference between experts and non-experts in any field is that experts have far more procedural knowledge (Gagne 1985). That is, they *know how* to perform their craft.

The major insight in this view of how the mind works is to offer strong evidence for two systems of knowledge structures; that procedural knowledge underlies skilled performance, and that procedural knowledge is acquired through practice. These conclusions support my three points.

However, we have to turn to the relatively new research area of culture and cognition to understand fully why the knowledge acquired from practice is viewed by most professionals as the gold standard. This research by cognitive anthropologists (Holland and Quinn 1987, Lave 1988) and psychologists (Resnik 1987, Scribner 1986, Sternberg 1986) has examined the knowledge used in practice. These researchers have sought to understand the nature and processes of what is variously termed practical intelligence (Sternberg 1986), practical thinking (Scribner 1986) or everyday cognition (Lave 1988, Rogoff and Lave 1984).

Although these researchers accept the importance of procedural knowledge, they critique the assumption that the mind can be understood in and of itself (Scribner 1986). The proponents of this viewpoint argue for a more contextualized view of thinking and learning. In summarizing the main differences between learning in school and in practice, Resnik (1987) illustrates the central characteristics of the knowledge used in practice. This knowledge is created and made meaningful by the context in which it is acquired. This is what is meant by situated knowledge. Further, the use of this knowledge is not simply a matter of pattern recognition but rather is oriented toward action. It is embodied in the process of practical reasoning where problem solving occurs in an open system that includes objects and information in the environment and the goals and interests of the problem solver and of others in his context. Because of these two characteristics, Resnik concludes that the packages of knowledge and skill provided by formal instruction in schools seems unlikely to map onto the clusters of knowledge people use, even for highly technical professional training.

If, in fact, professionals' everyday cognition represents a set of processes different from the formal reasoning processes taught in most professional schools and continuing education programmes, it is clear why learning from practice is held in such high regard by professionals. It is where they acquire the knowledge they actually use in practice.

One does not need to resort to the extreme empiricist point of view that anything of consequence can only by learned through practice or reflecting on practice. That is, the knowledge acquired from practice is not both necessary *and* sufficient for wise action. There clearly is a role for systems of abstract professional knowledge. However, the research in cognition strongly supports the proposition that without the knowledge acquired from practice, wise action is not possible.

Schon's model of the reflective practitioner

Donald Schon has developed a model of professional practice based on detailed studies of several professions, including architecture, town planning, management and teaching (1983, 1987, 1988). His viewpoint has received wide currency across the professions and has recently been the subject of a number of thoughtful critiques (Abbott 1988, Fenstermacher 1988, Liston and Zeichner 1987, Selman 1988, Shulman 1988).

As noted by Shulman (1988: 37) there is a remarkable similarity between Schon's work with his goal of seeking to understand the 'artistry' of professional practice and the work in cognition, particularly that which focuses on thinking in practice. Schon's starting point is that there are two kinds of knowledge systems. Further, the knowledge professionals use in practice is not the same as the professional knowledge taught in the schools. Like the cognitive psychologists, he argues that the use of research-based (read declarative) knowledge does not distinguish the excellent practitioner from the merely adequate. Rather, there are two forms of knowing (read procedural knowledge) that are central to professional artistry: knowing-in-action and reflection-in-action.

These forms of knowing have the two characteristics that make them particularly useful in practice: they are situated and action-oriented. Schon's model assumes that knowing is in the actions of professionals (read situated knowledge). Most of the spontaneous actions that professionals take do not stem from a rule or plan that was in the mind before acting. Schon calls this process *knowing-in-action*.

Many important situations of professional practice are characterized by uniqueness, uncertainty and conflicting values. Therefore, more often than not, knowing-in-action will not solve a particular problem. Rather, one needs to construct a situation to make it solvable. The process of doing this, of *reflecting-in-action*, is the core of professional artistry. Professionals reflect in the midst of action without interruption; their thinking reshapes what they are doing while they are doing it. The goal of reflection-in-action is to change indeterminate situations into determinate ones, and the key to successfully completing this problem-setting activity is to bring past experience to bear on current action.

Through their past experience, professionals have built up a repertoire of examples, images and understandings (Schon 1983: 138). When practitioners make sense of a situation considered uncertain, they see it as something already present in their repertoire. It is important to note that Schon does not see this as simply mapping a template onto a situation, but rather the creation of a representation of the situation, in interaction with other people (Boreham 1988). Thus, like the cognition researchers, he sees practical reasoning (what he calls a reflective conversation with the situation) as a central component of reflection-in-action.

How are these processes of knowing acquired or learned? Knowing-in-action may be an application of research-based knowledge taught in the schools, may be overlapping with it, or may have nothing to do with it (Schon 1987: 40). Its primary source, however, is the reflection-in-action undertaken in the indeterminate zones of practice. Schon suggests that professionals learn to reflect-in-action by going through a developmental sequence (1987: 40) in which: first, they learn to recognize and apply standard rules, facts and operations; second, to reason from general rules to problematic cases, in ways characteristic of the profession; and third, only then to develop and test new forms of understanding and action in practice.

With Schon's nearly total emphasis on procedural knowledge, his description of how professionals become reflective practitioners is consistent with that of schema theory. However, in Schon's model, reflection is not a purely individual, psychological process; rather, it is social process that is action-oriented. Thought and action are not separate; they occur simultaneously in a social context where both ends and means must be considered. In this, he echoes the themes of the culture and cognition approach with its emphasis on situated knowledge and practical reasoning.

Professional expertise

The work in this area attempts to understand the nature and development of professional expertise through a careful examination of practice. In addressing the questions of how experts know and how they acquire their knowledge, the literature on professional expertise supports the central themes reviewed above.

In the past two decades, researchers have studied the development of expertise in many types of human activities, such as playing chess and doing physics (Chi *et al.* 1988). Only recently has attention turned to the study of professional expertise. In a comprehensive review of this area, Kennedy (1987) identified four different conceptions of expertise: (1) technical skill, (2) the application of theory or general principles, (3) critical analysis, and (4) deliberate action.

There is a substantial amount of disconfirming evidence for the views of expertise as technical skill or the application of general principles. Both assume that expertise consists of prescriptions of what to do based on knowledge that has been developed by others and is transmitted to practitioners. Although most practitioners do not follow these prescriptions, they should if they are to become expert. As Kennedy observes (1987), these views do 'not address the complicated judgments involved when practitioners adjust general principles to specific circumstances, select the most appropriate principle from several that apply, or merge multiple applicable principles into a single integrated formulation' (p. 143) of the situation.

An example of this disconfirming evidence comes from the literature on medical problem solving. In recent critiques of the literature both Berner (1984) and McGuire (1985) conclude that the dominant model used to understand how physicians solve problems does not account for what real doctors do in real situations. They both call for a new way of conceiving of clinical reasoning that accounts for the multiple problem types, the situational constraints, and the conflicting values that characterize actual practice situations.

Kennedy's description of expertise as deliberate action, which is the ability to analyse situations in the context of action, is most consistent with the goal of practice as wise action. Within this conception of expertise there is widespread agreement on the importance of practical knowledge. The small, but growing, body of work on practical knowledge can be seen in teaching (Eisner 1985, Feiman-Nemser and Floden 1986, Clark 1988, Clark and Peterson 1986), nursing (Benner 1984), medicine (Dowie and Elstein 1988), business management (Dreyfus and Dreyfus 1986, Isenberg 1984, Wagner and Sternberg 1985, Weick 1983), and the judiciary (Lawrence 1988). In studying decision making by experts, a distinction is made between two forms of knowledge, what the cognitive psychologists call declarative and procedural.

Although the latter goes by several names, it clearly forms the basis of expert practice. In these various research efforts, procedural knowledge has been called implicit theory (Clark 1988, Spodek 1988), practical knowledge (Benner 1984, Feiman-Nemser and Floden 1986), know-how (Dowie and Elstein 1988, Dreyfus and Dreyfus 1986), and intuition (Isenberg

1984). The point is repeatedly made that the use of practical, not abstract, knowledge is the basis of expertise. For example, Lesgold *et al.* (1988) have found that radiologists interpret X-rays using mental processes different from those taught in medical courses, textbooks and even hospital teaching rounds. In another example, Dreyfus and Dreyfus (1986) show that when expert pilots try to use the rules they are teaching to apprentice pilots, their performance regresses. They must rely on the practical knowledge acquired through years of practice.

In summarizing the literature in teaching, Feiman-Nemser and Floden (1986) remind us that philosophers have long recognized that the value of practical knowledge stems from its two main features: it is time-bound and situation-specific and it is personally compelling and oriented toward action. These features are consistent with the findings from the culture and cognition literature: the knowledge people use in practice is situated knowledge that is used in the process of practical reasoning. These characteristics also map well onto Schon's description of professionals' repertoires of examples, images and actions that are used to reflect-in-action.

Given these features of practical knowledge, it obviously can only be acquired by engaging in practice or at least simulations of practice (Kennedy 1987). The literature is unified in support of this finding. For example, Benner (1984) found in her research with nurses that 'expertise develops when the clinician tests and refines propositions, hypotheses, and principle-based expectations in actual practice situations' (p. 3). Nearly all the researchers in this area are clear that although expertise evolves as professionals practice, the correlation between the two is nowhere near perfect. There are clearly some people who learn from practice better than others, and this ability distinguishes experts in a particular profession.

Let me now summarize the logic of the evidence that supports my second proposition, which is that the knowledge acquired from practice is necessary to achieve the goal of wise action. There are two kinds of knowledge that are called variously: declarative and procedural, abstract and practical, and knowledge that and know-how. In practice, professionals use procedural or practical knowledge. This results from its defining characteristics: it is situated in time and context and oriented toward action. Finally, because of these characteristics, it is acquired through practice or reflection on practice.

Implications for continuing education

I now move on to my third proposition, which suggests that a model of learning from practice should become the centrepiece of systems of continuing education for the professions. At the outset I must reiterate my earlier point that the choice of a model of the learner to use in a given situation is a value choice about the ends one wishes to achieve. I believe the primary goal of continuing education should be to improve professionals' ability to engage in wise action.

The choice of which model of the learner to use must be situation-specific, for the improvement of wisdom requires both abstract and practical knowledge. However, as the training of professionals has retreated from the locations of practice (e.g., hospitals, law offices) over the past century (Resnik 1987, Clifford and Guthrie 1988), to locations of research and instruction (e.g., universities), we have witnessed the delegitimization of practical knowledge in favour of abstract knowledge.

The theory and research I have reviewed provides a strong rationale for the importance of practical knowledge. Although it would be inappropriate to use a model of learning from practice in all situations, it should become the dominant model when the goal is to develop practitioners who engage in wise action. This model of the learner is one in which professionals engage current practice situations using a repertoire of practical knowledge and reasoning processes that has been acquired primarily through experience in prior practice situations. This model has implications for what must be learned in continuing education as well as how it can most effectively be learned.

First, the focus must be on the development of practical knowledge, which is generally understood as a repertoire of examples, metaphors, images, practical principles, scenarios and rules of thumb that are used in a professional's practice. Because most professionals are not fully aware of the knowledge in their repertoires, it is as important to help them make this knowledge explicit as it is to help them develop new knowledge. In making this knowledge explicit, we must recognize that professionals are reporting social constructions of reality that are subject to the limits of what can be expressed in language.

The second focus should be on the processes by which professionals use their practical knowledge in their practice contexts. This process of thinking in action has been called reflection-in-action and practical reasoning. Unlike the practical knowledge that is unique to their own practice, the processes by which knowledge is used are a universal cognitive act. Continuing education can help the learner make these processes more explicit and thereby open them up to evaluation and improvement.

The starting point of developing educational strategies to foster these forms of knowing most effectively must be that what the learner does is more important in determining what is learned than what the teacher does. Instructional strategies should be designed to give professionals the opportunity to observe, engage in and discover these kinds of thinking in action. Such an approach would enable them to see how this knowing fits together with their abstract knowledge and how they make use of a variety of resources in their social and physical environment (Brown *et al.* 1989, Collins *et al.* 1989).

Many specific methods have been proposed and used, including discovery methods (Glaser 1984), case studies (Dreyfus and Dreyfus 1986), and coaching (Schon 1987). A typology of these methods has been proposed (Collins *et al.* 1989) that suggests a developmental sequence for their use. This sequence maps well onto the appropriate learning strategies for the different levels of expertise that have been identified in previous research (Benner 1984, Dreyfus and Dreyfus 1986).

The first three (modelling, coaching and scaffolding) would help the learner develop their practical knowledge in an area in which they were unfamiliar through processes of observation and guided and supported practice. The next two (articulation and reflection) are designed to help learners gain conscious access to and control of their own knowledge and reasoning processes as well as that of experts. The final method (exploration) is aimed at encouraging learner autonomy in defining and formulating problems to be solved.

All of these methods assume that learning advances through collaborative social interaction and the social construction of knowledge within a community of practitioners and a context of practice. Thus, it is important in these methods to involve groups of practitioners, for it is only within groups that social interaction and conversation can take place.

This leads to one of the risks of this model of the learner that must be avoided. One view of professionals' practical knowledge is that it cannot be very effective because it is not justified by theoretical underpinnings and empirically based research. In this view even experts do not practise very well (Eddy 1988). However, the model I have just described should not be used to glorify professionals' practical knowledge and reasoning simply because they are used in daily practice. In doing so, we would make the mistake of believing that the way things are is the way they should be.

What is the role of abstract, academic, or declarative knowledge in this scheme? We must recognize that the primary use of academic knowledge is to legitimize professional work by clarifying its foundations in relation to major cultural values such as rationality, logic and science (Abbott 1988). However, it also has a role to play *vis-à-vis* practical knowledge because of its ability to generate new diagnoses and treatments. It can make connections that seem nonsensical within practical professional knowledge, but that reveal underlying regularities that can reshape practical knowledge altogether. The introduction of antibiotics is but one of a legion of examples in medicine. Another example is how the cognitive revolution has changed the ways that teachers act in classrooms. The challenge is to be able to integrate this form of knowledge into professionals' repertoires of practical knowledge and reasoning.

So the paper ends where it began because it could have been given as a speech in which I, the single instructor, lecture and lecture a large group of people sitting for a long time at rows of narrow tables covered with green baize. The reader may point out the discontinuity between the thesis of this paper and its mode of transmission. Where does this paper stand in relation to its own message? It should be clear that this is an example of abstract knowledge and scientific reasoning. And as such it has a role to play in the development of practical knowledge and reasoning. The mistake is to assume that it is superior to practical knowledge or that it is necessary and sufficient for wise action.

Continuing education has a great advantage over other stages of professional education in seeking to promote wise practitioners. It occurs when professionals are most likely to be aware of a need for better ways to think about what they do. But if educational practitioners are to exploit this natural advantage, they must better understand how they learn and think in practice. In our efforts to help professionals become wise practitioners, we should begin with ourselves.

Notes

1 *Ronald M. Cervero* is a professor of adult education at the University of Georgia. He has written extensively in the areas of adult basic education and continuing professional education. His book *Effective Continuing Education for Professionals* was awarded the 1989 Cyril O. Houle World Award for Literature in Adult Education.

2 This paper was previously presented as an invited address for Division I and Division J at the annual meeting of the American Educational Research Association, San Francisco, 31 March 1989.

References

Abbott, A. 1988, *The System of Professions*, Chicago, The University of Chicago Press.

Alonzo, W. 1986, The unplanned paths of planning schools. *The Public Interest*, Vol. 82, Winter, pp. 58–71.

Anderson, J. R. 1983, *The Architecture of Cognition*, Cambridge, MA, Harvard University Press.

Benner, P. 1984, *From Novice to Expert: Excellence and Power in Clinical Nursing Practice*, Menlo Park, Addison-Wesley.

Benner, P. 1989, Performance expectations of new graduates. Paper presented at the AACCN Invitational Conference, 'Critical Care Nursing at the Baccalaureate Level – Strategies for the Future', San Antonio, Texas.

Berner, E. S. 1984, Paradigms and problem solving: a literature review. *Journal of Medical Education*, Vol. 59, pp. 625–633.

Bok, D. 1984, Needed: a new way to train doctors. *Harvard Magazine*, May-June, pp. 32–43, 70–71.

Boreham, N. C. 1988, Models of diagnosis and their implications for adult professional education. *Studies in the Education of Adults*, Vol. 20, pp. 95–108.

Brown, J. S., Collins, A. and Duguid, P. 1989, Situated cognition and the culture of learning. *Educational Researcher*, Vol. 18, pp. 32–42.

Bruner, J. 1985, Models of the learner, *Educational Researcher*, Vol. 14, pp. 5–8.

Bucher, R. and Strauss, A. 1961, Professions in process. *American Journal of Sociology*, Vol. 66, pp. 325–344.

Buchmann, M. 1984, The use of research knowledge in teacher education and teaching. *American Journal of Education*, Vol. 92, pp. 421–439.

Carroll, J. W. 1985, The professional model of ministry – is it worth saving? *Theological Education*, Vol. 21, pp. 7–48.

Cervero, R. M. 1988, *Effective continuing education for professionals*, San Francisco, Jossey-Bass.

Chi, M. T. H., Glaser, R. and Farr, M. J. (Eds) 1988, *The Nature of Expertise*, Hillsdale, NJ, Lawrence Erlbaum.

Clark, C. M. 1988, Asking the right questions about teacher preparation: contributions of research on teacher thinking. *Educational Researcher*, Vol. 17, pp. 5–12.

Clark, C. M. and Peterson, P. L. 1986, Teachers' thought processes, in M. C. Wittrock (Ed.) *Handbook of Research on Teaching* (3rd edn.), New York, MacMillan, pp. 255–296.

Clifford, G. J. and Guthrie, J. W. 1988, *Ed School: A Brief for Professional Education*, Chicago, The University of Chicago Press.

Collins, A., Brown, J. S. and Newman, S. E. 1989, Cognitive apprenticeship: teaching the craft of reading, writing and mathematics, in L. B. Resnik (Ed.) *Knowing, Learning, and Instruction: Essays in Honor of Robert Glaser*, Hillsdale, NJ, Erlbaum (in press).

Dowie, J. and Elstein, A. (Eds) 1988, *Professional Judgment: A Reader in Clinical Decision Making*, Cambridge, Cambridge University Press.

Dreyfus, H. L. and Dreyfus, S. E. 1986, *Mind over Machine*, Oxford, Basil Blackwell.

Eddy, D. M. 1988, Variations in physician practice: the role of uncertainty, in J. Dowie and A. Elstein (Eds) *Professional Judgment: A Reader in Clinical Decision Making*, Cambridge, Cambridge University Press.

Eisner, E. (Ed.) 1985, *Learning and Teaching the Ways of Knowing*, Chicago, The University of Chicago Press.

Feiman-Nemser, S. and Floden, R. E. 1986, The cultures of teaching, in M. C. Wittrock (Ed.) *Handbook of Research on Teaching* (3rd edn.), New York, MacMillan, pp. 505–526.

Fenstermacher, G. 1988, The place of science and epistemology in Schon's conception of reflective practice?, in P. P. Grimmett and G. L. Erickson (Eds) *Reflection in Teacher Education*, New York, Teachers College Press, pp. 39–46.

Friedson, E. 1986, *Professional Powers*, Chicago, The University of Chicago Press.

Gagne, E. D. 1985, *The Cognitive Psychology of School Learning*, Boston, Little, Brown.

Glaser, R. 1984, Education and thinking: the role of knowledge. *American Psychologist*, Vol. 39, pp. 93–104.

Glaser, R. 1985, All's well that begins and ends with both knowledge and process: a reply to Sternberg. *American Psychologist*, Vol. 40, pp. 573–574.

Gutman, R. 1985, Educating architects: pedagogy and the pendulum. *The Public Interest*, Vol. 80, Summer, pp. 67–91.

Heraud, B. J. 1973, Professionalism, radicalism, and social change. *Sociological Review Monograph*, Vol. 20, pp. 85–101.

Holland, D. and Quinn, N. (Eds) 1987, *Cultural Models in Language and Thought*, Cambridge, Cambridge University Press.

The Holmes Group 1986, *Tomorrow's Teachers: A Report of the Holmes Group*, East Lansing, MI, Author.

Isenberg, D. J. 1984, How senior managers think. *Harvard Business Review*, Vol. 62, pp. 81–90.

Kennedy, M. M. 1987, Inexact sciences: professional education and the development of expertise, in E. Z. Rothkopf (Ed.) *Review of Research in Education, 14,* Washington, DC, American Educational Research Association, pp. 133–167.

Kyllonen, P. C. and Alluisi, E. 1986, Learning and forgetting facts and skills, in G. Salvendy (Ed.) *Handbook of Human Factors,* New York, Wiley, pp. 124–153.

Lave, J. 1988, Expertise on the bench: modeling magistrates' judicial decision-making, in M. T. H. Chi, R. Glaser and M. J. Farr (Eds) *The Nature of Expertise,* Hillsdale, NJ, Lawrence Erlbaum, pp. 229–259.

Lesgold, A., Rubinson, H., Feltovich, P., Glaser, R., Klopfer, D. and Wang, Y. 1988, Expertise in a complex skill: diagnosing X-Ray pictures, in M. T. H. Chi, R. Glaser and M. J. Farr (Eds) *The Nature of Expertise,* Hillsdale, NJ, Lawrence Erlbaum, pp. 311–342.

Liston, D. P. and Zeichner, K. M. 1987, Critical pedagogy and teacher education. *Journal of Education,* Vol. 169, pp. 117–137.

McGuire, C. H. 1985, Medical problem-solving: a critique of the literature. *Journal of Medical Education,* Vol. 60, pp. 587–595.

Nowlen, P. M. 1988, *A New Approach to Continuing Education for Business and the Professions: The Performance Model,* New York, Macmillan.

Resnik, L. B. 1987, Learning in school and out. *Educational Researcher,* Vol. 16, pp. 13–20.

Rogoff, B. and Lave, J. (Eds) 1984, *Everyday Cognition: Its Development in Social Context,* Cambridge, MA, Harvard University Press.

Ryle, G. 1949, *The Concept of Mind,* Chicago, The University of Chicago Press.

Schon, D. A. 1983, *The Reflective Practitioner,* New York, Basic Books.

Schon, D. A. 1987, *Educating the Reflective Practitioner,* San Francisco, Jossey-Bass.

Schon, D. A. 1988, Educating teachers as reflective practitioners, in P. P. Grimmett and G. L. Erickson (Eds) *Reflection in Teacher Education,* New York, Teachers College Press, pp. 19–30.

Scribner, S. 1986, Thinking in action: some characteristics of practical thought, in R. J. Sternberg and R. K. Wagner (Eds) *Practical Intelligence: Nature and Origins of Competence in the Everyday World,* Cambridge, Cambridge University Press, pp. 13–30.

Selman, M. 1988, Schon's gate is square: but is it art?, in P. P. Grimmett and G. L. Erickson (Eds) *Reflection in Teacher Education,* New York, Teachers College Press, pp. 177–192.

Shuell, T. J. 1986, Cognitive conceptions of learning. *Review of Educational Research,* Vol. 56, pp. 411–436.

Shulman, L. S. 1988, The dangers of dichotomous thinking in education in P. P. Grimmett and G. L. Erickson (Eds) *Reflection in Teacher Education,* New York, Teachers College Press, pp. 31–38.

Spodek, B. 1988, Implicit theories of early childhood teachers: foundations for professional behavior, in B. Spodek, O. N. Saracho and D. L. Peters (Eds) *Professionalism and the Early Childhood Practitioner,* New York, Teachers College Press, pp. 161–172.

Sternberg, R. J. 1986, All's well that ends well, but it's a sad tale that begins at the end: a reply to Glaser. *American Psychologist,* Vol. 40, pp. 571–573.

Unger, R. M. 1986, *The Critical Legal Studies Movement,* Cambridge, MA, Harvard University Press.

Wagner, R. K. and Sternberg, R. J. 1985, Practical intelligence in real-world pursuits: the role of tacit knowledge. *Journal of Personality and Social Psychology,* Vol. 49, pp. 436–458.

Weick, K. E. 1983, Managerial thought in the context of action, in S. Srivasta and Associates, *The Executive Mind: New Insights on Managerial Thought and Action*, San Francisco, Jossey-Bass, pp. 221–242.

White, S. 1986, Why journalism schools? *The Public Interest*, Vol. 82, Winter, pp. 39–57.

Wildavsky, A. 1985, The once and future school of public policy. *The Public Interest*, Vol. 79, pp. 25–41.

12 Beyond legitimacy

Facing the future in distance education

T. R. Morrison

In a time of drastic change, it is the learners who inherit the future. The learned find themselves equipped to live only in a world that no longer exists.

Eric Hoffer

A good deal of meaning in any society is a function of context. The status and meaning of distance education is no exception to this rule. To understand what is occurring in distance education and what meaning we as professionals, or society at large, should ascribe to this phenomena, it is important to come to grips with the context in which it is developed and practised.

Distance education is emerging to prominence in all quarters of the globe. This is reflective of a number of fundamental changes occurring in the relationship between higher education and the societies in which it is placed. Historically, most change in higher education has come as a result of forces at work outside institutions. Court decisions, demographic patterns, public policy imperatives, social problems, development priorities, immigration movements, wars and global competition – all of these, and more, have produced changes, over time, in the role of higher education. It is ironic that the so-called Ivory Tower has been one of the institutions most affected by societal change. One should not confuse the persistence of academic mores, with institutional stability.

The changes to which we bear witness in our world today are sufficient in scale and breadth to call for a new perceptual framework through which to view the role of higher education in society. That new framework is expansive and open, encompassing a great variety of educational providers and an unprecedented diversity of learners of all ages. Using such an enlarged framework, I outline below a number of postulates which relate to the changing role of higher education in society and which help to explain the place of distance education in that environment.

Postulate One is that formal institutions of higher education no longer control the market for the provision of educational services. In the USA, for example, higher education provides slightly more than one-third of the organized learning opportunities for adults – the remaining two-thirds, according to a recent major study (Carnegie Commission 1985), is provided by a vast array of schools and non-collegiate institutions. Industry, for example, spends billions of dollars annually on the education and training of employees. It has been argued by Cross (1986: 217) that in the USA, business allocates more money for education and training than all 50 states combined spend on higher education. Large companies such as Boeing, IBM, Xerox, and Aetna have built campuses and residence halls within their systems. Professional associations of all kinds are joining business in the development of this 'in-house' and 'brokerage' capacity.

This intensification in the development of an in-house training and education capacity by business and other agencies not only signals the rise in importance of training and education but also reflects a dissatisfaction with the ability of mainline public institutions to respond to changing needs. More often than not, this dissatisfaction focusses on the perceived inability of institutions to provide adaptive, flexible, relevant and problem-centred approaches to training and education and, moreover, at a reasonable cost. Whether this is true or not, a new reality faces public higher education institutions: there will be a rise in competition for the training and education dollar, not only within the public sector, but also between that and the private and voluntary sectors. If these trends continue, higher education will be forced increasingly to test its hypotheses and long-standing normative principles in a live market environment.

Postulate Two is that the roles and function of various educational providers, once reasonably clear, are increasingly blurred. It is no longer clear what courses deserve credit, who may offer them, and who needs them. Indeed, the classical distinction often made in the West between 'education' offered by public higher education institutions and 'training' offered by industry is increasingly difficult to maintain. Educational programmes in many corporations concentrate as much on theory, research, and personal development as those of any college or university. This focus is evident because, in the light of the emergence of new rules of trade in a global economy, private and public corporations have had to rethink a number of basic assumptions. The classical business paradigm in Western economies has been seriously challenged, for example, one result of which has been the emergence of a fundamental intellectual ferment in business which has increasingly made the academic discussion of universities just that – academic.

Consider, for example, this description of IBM's Systems Research Institute:

> The Institute's educational philosophy is in many ways that of a university. It stresses fundamental and conceptual education and allows students to choose those courses that will best nurture their own

development. The intent is to stimulate and challenge, to teach the theoretical and the practical, to discuss and argue differing viewpoints, to broaden the individual, focussing on his or her special skills.

If one were provided with a blind sample of course outlines today, it would be difficult clearly to discern whether they emanated from industry, universities, professions, unions or museums. This blurring of distinctions is further muddied by the intermingling of credit and non-credit learning: a concept which, beyond institutional imperatives, has never made logical or educational sense. The point underlying this postulate, then, is that the role of educational providers in the learning society is far from clear and that an increased blurring of functions rather than clarity is the trend. For universities, this blurring of functions has brought forth responses which range from defensive territoriality to blind entrepreneurism; a fact which has further blurred roles.

Postulate Three is that higher education no longer is assured the full-time commitment of students. One of the most significant trends of the past 15 years has been the rise in the number and percentage of part-time students. If the exponential growth of continuing education programmes is added, as I believe it should be, then this growth rate has been phenomenal. Formal education is, as noted by Cross (1986), changing from a full-time commitment for four years of a student's life to a part-time commitment for 40 years.

The driving priorities of this new generation of adult part-timers is not a single minded passion for higher learning but a desire to enhance their competitive position in the job market and the resultant need to balance such adult resposibilities as child care. Higher education, as a result, now faces unaccustomed competition for the time and attention of students, in a situation where a host of options exist. Much to the dismay of the professoriate, the 'age of instrumentalism' has arrived and is being championed by the new adult student.

Postulate Four is that, while learning has become a lifelong necessity, there remains a basic incongruence between that reality and the public and institutional policies within education. In today's world, the phrase 'lifelong learning' is used as a rationale for changes which encompass a wide spectrum of reform proposals. The phrase is used with such off-handed ease, moreover, that it is my sense that we have lulled ourselves into believing that it is a living reality within our institutions. But is it?

The concept of lifelong learning was legitimated and injected into public consciousness through a 1972 UNESCO report entitled *Learning To Be*. The very fact that such a report could be produced was revolutionary itself and provides a useful commentary on our times. Representatives from seven nations formed the commission: France, Chile, Syria, Peoples' Republic of the Congo, USSR, Iran, and the USA. If one reflects somewhat upon the political events which followed, this mix of nations is truly remarkable. Indeed, this report may have been the last major effort in which the two superpowers collaborated and agreed.

In re-reading the report, it is evident that the commission (Faure 1972) had a very clear idea of what was meant by the concept of lifelong learning. This concept embodied six strategic principles:

1   That dimensions of living experience must be restored to education by redistributing teaching in space and time.
2   That education should be dispersed and acquired through a multiplicity of means – the important thing is not the path an individual has followed, but what he has learned or acquired.
3   That the concept of a general education must be broadened so that it definitely includes general socio-economic, technical and practical knowledge.
4   That educational action to prepare for work and active life should aim less at training people to practice a given trade or profession than at equipping them to adapt themselves to a variety of jobs, at developing their capacities continuously.
5   That lifelong education, in the full sense of the term, means that business and industrial firms will have extensive educational functions.
6   That access to different types of education and professional employment should depend only on each individual's knowledge, capacities and aptitudes and should not be a consequence of ranking or below experience gained during the practise of work.

If taken seriously, the concept of lifelong learning is a revolutionary idea, perhaps the only significant educational idea of this century. Those who advocate it are arguing in favour of the implementation, on a systems basis, of a number of subsidiary ideas: accessibility, institutional openness, needs-based learning, competency-based education, co-operative education, mastery learning, paid educational leave, and credit for prior learning.

To talk seriously about developing educational institutions as centres for lifelong learning, then, is to talk of change of a most fundamental order. Given the hypothesis, suggested by Clark (1983), that the primary imperative of any institution is to control rather than liberate those within, it may be a false hope to assume that any institution *per se* can be founded upon lifelong learning principles. But a learning system can, since it has a range and impact greater than the sum of its parts.

In this context, then, what we are experiencing today is a pressure against the internal and external boundaries of our formal learning system brought about not by creative educational or policy thinking but by the aspirations and actions of people themselves. If this pressure continues, as I believe it will, then one can argue that we shall witness either an accommodation within or a basic reconfiguration of our learning system. The shape, structure and degree of openness of our learning system not, as many argue, the financing of it, will be the policy issue of the future. This is so, since answering the former question inevitably begs an answer to the latter. To date, leaders in higher education have focussed upon the level of financing without realizing that this has energized an even more intriguing feedback loop: financing what?

Postulate Five is that current and planned developments in communications technology clearly challenge the long-standing assumption in higher education that information is a scarce commodity. In fact, information, when linked to newer technologies is, as argued by Cleveland (1985: 1–25), a shareable, expandable, compressible, substitutable and transportable thing. The zero-sum informational games of traditional market economies, upon which universities rest, need to be re-thought. While all around us we see the emergence of sharing rather than exchange transactions in information, most universities jealously guard credit as the sacred element in their educational rituals.

This altered informational world, characterized by a multiplicity of interrelated and increasingly integrated channels for the flow of ever larger amounts of information, poses serious questions for higher education. In this expansive informational environment, it is true to say that no institution or agency dominates or controls the flow. The strength of a university in the late 20th century, in this regard, does not reside in the way it transmits information, but on what it can contribute to the selection and interpretation of what is received. And yet, universities continue to talk of teaching hours as a key ingredient in their economic planning. I would suggest that learning hours is a better concept, for it opens up the possibility of self-directed and other forms of learning and growth.

The decentralization of information technology to the work place and other locations, moreover, poses new issues related to basic skills. Whereas in previous periods it was possible to train the mind apart from action, the new information technologies bring thought and action together, particularly in the work setting. What Edward de Bono (1986: 1–10) calls 'reactive' and 'map-making' thinking are brought together in these situations where the availability of information demands informed action on a constant basis. The divorce of learning from action, which still pervades formal higher education, is being made redundant by the integration of information, theory, and action in the work setting. In this context, in addition to such skills as numeracy and literacy, a new type of action-thinking is required. In de Bono's terms, this style of thought can be called 'operacy' – the skill of doing and the thinking that goes with it. Operacy, to be developed, requires that thought be developed in an action context. If universities are not to be merely the contexts for the development of literacy and numeracy, which can be developed in other ways, or the custodians merely of intellectual tradition, which again can be preserved in other ways, then their challenge is to find new ways to bridge the gap between thought and action in a person's development.

To understand distance education and its rise to prominence at this time it is important, as I noted at the outset, to understand the context in which it exists. In this regard, I have outlined five postulates regarding the changing relationship between higher education and the broader society. I have suggested that:

1   higher education no longer enjoys a monopoly on the provision of learning services
2   the roles and functions of educational providers are increasingly blurred
3   higher education no longer can claim the full-time commitment of students
4   there is a continued incongruence between the reality of lifelong learning and institutional and systems responses to it
5   higher education's basic assumption of an information deficit in society in being seriously challenged by new technology.

Distance education has risen to prominence precisely because it has the potential to address these societal changes. First, distance education is an alternative system for the provision of learning services. Second, the blurring of roles and functions allows distance-learning systems, through flexible networks, to link students with learning opportunities. Third, distance-learning systems are designed precisely to accommodate the varying time and space realities of part-time adult learners. Fourth, as a process-based learning system, distance education is not bound by time, age or location and can provide lifelong learning opportunities in the real sense for people. Last, distance education, of all areas in education, utilizes a range of ways of transmitting information, most of which are independent of face-to-face teaching contact, and are increasingly guided by new communication technologies.

Due to the confluence of societal trends, the discontinuity of these trends with traditional educational systems, and a growing cost-consciousness, distance education has come out of the closet and found that it is increasingly legitimate. Broadening the idea of distance, within distance education, to include cultural, social and economic distance from the mainstream of society, as well as geographic distance from the source of teaching, adds further to its appeal.

This very success of distance education, underpinned by a growing social legitimacy, however, contains within it the danger that distance educators will become complacent and fail to realize that the world is changing and that they too, face difficult choices and challenges. In this regard, there are at least six challenges facing distance education today:

1   The need to broaden the concept of distance education in order that it can enhance not only access to but success in learning

2   The need to move from an institutional to a systems level in planning, needs assessment and delivery
3   The need to develop a learning approach to organizational ethos and management
4   The need to develop a model for the appropriate use of technology
5   The need to globalize its vision
6   The need to balance quantity with equity in its contribution to development.

From access to success

Distance-learning systems of all kinds have been successful in demonstrating that increased access to learning can be obtained through such processes. This claim should perhaps be tempered somewhat by asserting that most distance-learning systems have, in fact, broadened access to learning for reasonable well-schooled and academically prepared individuals (Athabasca University 1986a). This pattern is not surprising, since most distance-learning systems are still predominantly print based and, therefore, assume those literacy skills which are often lacking in so-called 'disadvantaged groups' (Anisef 1982). The challenge of broadening the social basis of accessibility to distance learning, therefore, remains as an unsolved problem. In bridging this 'cultural gap', distance-learning systems will face challenges more profound and difficult than those encountered in its efforts to overcome spatial barriers to learning.

Beyond access, increasing success in distance learning still stands as a formidable challenge. The same groups succeed in distance learning systems as other learning systems and the differential dropout rate, within distance learning, is varied and high.

Distance educators are prone to argue and, indeed, herald increasing accessibility as the social mission which guides their activities. Is access alone, however, a sufficient criterion to employ in the design and evaluation of distance-learning systems? Surely, access begs at least three subsidiary questions: Access by whom, to what, and with what result?

The attraction of distance educators to the principle of access is understandable, since that concept has been traditionally linked to the idea of equality of opportunity. Policy-makers, for instance, have tended to believe that the goal of educational equity is attained when the conditions exist in which no person is denied access to higher education because of race, gender, income or social status. Distance educators, of course, add to this list the facts of geographical location.

Equality of access, however, relates primarily to the number of places available: Are there opportunities open for everyone who wants a university education and are they affordable? This form of access is unquestionably a necessary but insufficient condition for equity. So, too, is access an insufficient basis upon which to build a distance-education enterprise which hopes seriously to address equity.

In distance education, the concentration on access has resulted in a front-end and input-focus in programme and systems design. Removing barriers to access, be they of time, space or life circumstance, has been the abiding concern of distance education. Flexible registration procedures, the use of communications technologies, regional centres, tutorial support systems, and educational counselling services have all been used to remove access barriers and, judging by growing participation rates, they have achieved a good deal of success.

Equalizing access, however, does not necessarily equalize the chances of success for learners. The barriers which block a person's access are not those which prevent success following admission. Access barriers relate primarily to such factors as time, space, lifestyle, income and a person's perception of competence. Success barriers also relate to these factors but, as argued by Jencks (1975) and Astin (1984), also encompass such variables as preferred learning style, cultural assumptions within curricula, the labelling process, and power relationships. A distance-learning system which is geared, not only to increasing access, but also to altering the social pattern of success must address the barriers which block success. Such a success-based system must be prepared to be evaluated, not only on its ability to broaden the social basis of access but also in terms of the social pattern of its outcomes. Equality of opportunity, in other words, must be linked to equality of results. Most importantly, this linkage must be forged in ways which recognizes what Amy Guttman (1987) postulates as the twin principles underpinning a just approach to education: non-discrimination and non-repression.

The idea of equality of results often brings forth counter-arguments regarding a presumed decline in equality or excellence. In other words, is it true that an outcomes orientation, and the changes required to achieve it, leads inevitably to a decline in quality and, hence, works against the egalitarian ideal itself?

An outcomes orientation, contrary to the criticism it suffers, does not alter the substance of what is learned. Rather, it concentrates on the processes of learning – on how that substance is acquired. Much of the debate about a presumed decline in quality, in the face of an equality of results scheme, wrongly assumes that quality is a function of how one learns as opposed to what is learned. If, for example, the learning time for X is enlongated to accommodate a cultural difference, and if the student, as a result, learns X, then has there been a decline in quality or a rise in efficacy?

Moreover, a concept of quality in education, which is not tied to the developmental capacities of a person and to the socio-cultural context in which these are expressed, is ultimately a mask shielding the fact that bias is the operative principle. The function of such concepts of quality is not

education – that is, the development of the talents of those who participate – but exclusion, selection and tracking.

Any real social impact of distance learning must occur at the level of
outcomes. It is at this level, as argued by Psascharopoulus & Woodhall
(1986), that the potential redistributive function of education occurs. In
order for distance-learning systems to redistribute real opportunity in
society they must increase both their efficiency in guaranteeing access and
their efficacy in producing success. To accomplish these twin goals means
that distance-learning institutions must undertake a thorough examination of their processes and models to determine whether or not they
provide for maximum access to success. Such an examination, I would
suggest, would be challenging, if not intimidating to most institutions. But
if the rhetoric is to match reality, it needs to be done.

Given that problems of access and success are linked to social, cultural
and economic factors, no distance-learning system alone will be sufficient
to broaden access or increase success. The difficulty embedded in this suggestion is that some distance educators have become so wedded to
particular concepts of distance education, and the belief system which it
engenders, that they have become the 'new traditionalists' in an innovative field. They resist the idea that distance education alone may be
inappropriate to the attainment of social goals. Instead, as other educators, they insist on forcing all needs and goals within a distance-education framework. The model, in other words, not only confuses, but
dominates reality.

At this point in time, distance education needs to be understood for
what it is: a technique to overcome, primarily, spatial barriers to learning.
It is not, in its current stage of development, a process which overcomes
cultural, economic and educational barriers to learning.

If it is to fulfil this wider mission, distance education needs to be recast
conceptually within the broader and more normative concept of an open-
learning system. An open-learning system is characterized by five features:

> the absence of a discriminatory entrance requirement
> a results-driven concept of equality
> a success-based concept of programme and service design
> a multiple strategy and matching model approach to programme
> delivery
> a developmental concept of quality.

When assessed against these criteria, it is apparent that a distance-
learning system is not necessarily an open-learning system. This distinction, and the failure of most distance-education institutions to assess its
implications for change, explains why distance-learning systems have not
achieved a broadening of the social base of access or significantly
increased levels of success for diverse students. This is not to criticize the

achievements of distance learning but to suggest that, if its exponents intend to take broadened access and success seriously, then these systems must take the next step towards the development of open-learning systems. In taking the next step, it is paradoxical that not only will external forces be obstacles to change but so, too, will there be resistance within distance-learning institutions and systems. If distance education is not to remain embedded in its own technique and wedded to the ethos which surrounds this, drawing farther and farther from its true social purpose, then a paradigm shift is in order.

From institutional to systems thinking

In a remarkably short period of time, distance education has become institutionalized. This has occurred in two areas: within traditional educational institutions and through the development of institutions specializing in distance education. This development was and is essential to the legitimacy of distance education and the concentration of a body of expertise. As with all processes of institutionalization, however, the ever-present danger is that the concerns of the institution will predominate over the issue of providing equality and success in learning. I need not recite the many examples of this pattern in the conventional education sector to make this point. Distance education institutions thus have a special obligation to be ever watchful that institutional imperatives do not swallow up and envelop the creative engagement with learning which is the *raison d'être* of the enterprise itself.

The latent danger in distance-learning institutions is that they will, as in Baudien's terms (1973), reproduce, albeit in somewhat different form, the educational order in relation to which they ostensibly provide an alternative. Being watchful alone, however, will not prevent the processes of cultural reproduction from taking hold in distance-learning settings. Watchfulness must be supplemented by a mode of perception and thought which ensures that development rather than reproduction is the norm. In this context, distance education is well suited to the adoption of a systems perspective in the conceptualization and design of its work and social role.

In technical terms, a system, as argued by Rosensleuth & Wiener (1950), is a set of two or more elements which satisfies the following three conditions:

> the behaviour of each element has an effect on the behaviour of the whole
> the behaviour of the elements and their effects on the whole are interdependent
> however subgroups or elements are formed, each has an effect on the behaviour of the whole and none has an independent effect.

A system thus is a whole that cannot be divided into independent parts. The essential properties of a system, taken as a whole, derive from the interaction of its parts, not their actions taken separately. When a system is taken apart, it loses its essential properties. Because of this, a system is a whole which cannot be understood by analysis.

Synthesis, or putting things together, is the key to systems thinking; just as analysis or taking them apart was the key to machine-age thinking. Analysis focusses on structure; it reveals how things work. Synthesis focusses on function; it reveals why things operate as they do. Thus analysis yields knowledge; synthesis yields understanding. There are considerable differences between analytical and synthetic approaches to planning and management. One such difference is based upon the following systems principle: the performance of a system depends more on how its parts interact than on how they act independently of each other.

Distance-learning enterprises, particularly when cast within the larger concept of open-learning systems, are ideally suited to planning and management within a systems perspective. These enterprises can be seen as parts of a larger learning system: the varied processes through which people acquire knowledge, values and skills on a formal, non-formal and informal basis. The meaning and function of distance education, as a result, derives from the pattern and processes of the larger learning system and its interrelationship to it and its other parts. It follows that distance education is best construed, in the words of Arthur Koestler (1980: 7), as 'a whole part of a whole'.

Within such a systems perspective, a primary goal for distance-education institutions is to contribute to the larger learning system and to consciously build interrelationships and connections to it. The more interconnected distance-learning institutions are, the more effective they are. The identity and legitimacy of distance institutions, within a systems perspective, derives not from isolation and uniqueness, but from relationship and a linkage to the community of learners. A clear implication of this is the need for distance education to balance its current analytical obsession with its own nature and role – the part, if you like, with a broader focus on the learning system of which it is a part. This focus, rather than normative, in essence should begin with a simple descriptive question: What and how are people learning and what affects that process? An answer to this question should provide the appropriate context in which to locate distance education and provide a sense of cultural meaning to the enterprise. The construction of such an ecology of distance education would, at a minimum, place a moratorium on textual analysis and industrial production models of distance education (Holmberg 1983); each of which contribute a 'partial' understanding of the larger enterprise.

Distance-learning institutions, particularly when framed as open-learning systems, must maintain fluid boundries and be open to the society at large. Without such openness, distance-learning institutions, rather than being facilitative vehicles, will emerge as yet another institutional barrier to learning. How can this be done? At this point, I would argue that it can be partly achieved through collaborative models of programme development and networking.

True collaboration in programme development goes beyond adversarial functions and moves towards real power-sharing with external groups and agencies. Moreoever, it is premised upon the assumption, as argued by Botkin (1979), that knowledge is socially constructed and, therefore, its transmission must be evolved in a social context. At Athabasca University, our recently developed special access project provides, in my view, an example of collaborative programme development, with all the give and take and mutual learning which that entails (Athabasca University 1986a).

Networking means that an institution accepts the fact that, in certain cases, it is not the whole but a whole part of a whole. The process expertise of distance-learning institutions can provide a necessary and vital link in many areas where the components exist in isolation. This approach, in marketing terms, is called 'nichemanship' and conforms to the ways in which, as described by Levitt (1986), many people are finding solutions to personal, social and business problems.

From the management of learning to a learning organization

Distance education, when conceived as an open-learning system, is unique in our educational world and requires, accordingly, an organizational and managerial concept which is appropriate to its mission. If learning is the *raison d'être* of open-learning systems, then organizations involved in that process should be learning organizations.

There is no right way to manage all organizations at all times. There is no monolithic theory or single set of rules that is appropriate in all nations or to all organizations. This is the lesson of history and the real lesson underpinning the recent outpouring of 'managerial fixes' from the corporate world. To accept this reality is both daunting and refreshing. In the absence of a single ideology which will magically solve the 'management problem' – a strange term for the description of how people come together to engage in work – the only viable alternative for an organization is to become a learning organization.

For any organization to succeed, in the long run, managers and others must abandon the search for the one right way to manage. Instead, they must adopt a learning attitude in which they constantly derive inspiration from changes in the environment and apply what they learn to the continuous recreation and renewal of the strategies and practices in their organizations.

The linchpin of a learning organization is its posture towards uncertainty. Under conditions where uncertainty is pervasive and unrelieved, a learning organization founds its survival and development not upon its ability to control outcomes but on its ability to be resilient. This demands an on-going effort to discover what is going on inside and outside the organization as a basis upon which to adjust to and influence events. An open-learning organization needs the ability to unlearn and relearn successfully. Being resilient means responding to the world as if it were both this and that rather than either this or that.

Donald Michael (1978) has described the attributes requisite to performing effectively inside and outside the organization, in the face of uncertainty, as the 'new competence'. Although space does not permit a full elaboration, this new competence includes an ability to live with and acknowledge high degrees of uncertainty, a willingness to embrace and learn from errors, an attitude which is responsive to alternative futures, the personal ability and organizational undergirding required to span information and normative boundaries, and a high degree of interpersonal competence. It is interesting to note that Michael's prescription for the learning organization conforms, at the personal level, to the reported life experiences of adults in the modern world. The new competence, in other words, far from creating a vanguard organization in society, will merely draw that organization into confluence with life as it is being lived today, and with this generate an enhanced vitality and relevance within it.

Distance education is an educational innovation. More specifically, it is a process, rather than product, innovation. Its uniqueness rests in the management of how people learn, not primarily in what they learn. Models of distance education, then, reflect models of learning. Given the developing state of theory and research into human learning, particularly as that applies to learning in live social and cultural contexts outside formal educational settings where most distance learners are located, models of distance learning and education must be seen in exploratory and evolutionary terms. Of all educational enterprises, then, distance learning must be constantly innovative, exploring regularly new ways to link learners through process to content.

The strategic management principles most appropriate to distance education, especially when conceived as open-learning systems, are not those drawn from either the industrial or traditional academic worlds but from innovation and entrepreneurship. Distance-education organizations must, by definition, be willing to move beyond accepted wisdom to combine ideas from unconnected sources, to embrace change as an opportunity to test limits. More of the resources and attention of distance-learning organizations should be focussed upon what they do not yet know than on controlling what they already know. These organizations should measure themselves not only on the standards of the past (how far they have come) but also by visions of the future (how far they have yet to go).

If the business of distance-education institutions is innovation in learning, then it follows that such institutions must be innovative on an ongoing basis. The challenge for many distance-education institutions, particularly those at the university level, is to find ways to accommodate the conservative tendency within the academic culture with the innovative norms demanded by the organizational culture. The irony is, however, that process innovation can co-exist with content conservatism. For distance education institutions, more so than for traditional universities, the need to develop appropriate and effective ways to manage this duality is of paramount importance. Failure to do so means that these institutions face one of two equally undesirable options: a blind retreat to the past or a headlong and random engagement with the future. In opposition to these stark alternatives, the management of this duality paves the way for the challenge of confronting the 'radical middle'.

From a technological fix to an appropriate model of technology

Yet another problem facing distance education is the need to develop a framework through which to make judgements concerning the appropriate use of technology. A sense of perspective is a useful lens through which to perceive the 'new' as it unfolds in the present. In this regard, champions of new technology in distance education are prone to disregard the past, even though that must be the benchmark against which to locate and assess the future. In all quarters of the globe today one hears of the promise of new technology – from a revolutionizing force in education to the saviour of economies. Unquestionably, new technology opens up countless opportunities for human learning and material betterment. But so, too, did the invention of print and printing. What has been the legacy of print? What will be the legacy of new technology? In each case, the jury is out.

The imprint on a culture of any technology is never clear and uniform. In the industrial revolution machinery both liberated and enslaved humankind. Nuclear technology in the modern era both serves humankind and yet could be the ultimate source of its destruction.

Embedded within any technology, indeed as part of its very logic and the fact that it must be applied in a social context, are processes which can lead to the benefit or detriment of human society. All claims in relation to new technology, therefore, whether they be claims of positive or negative impact, need to be assessed through the eyes of a sympathetic sceptic: to do otherwise is to deny history. The case of new technology in distance education is no exception to this rule.

In this regard, the starting point must be a definition of technology. What is meant by the concept of technology? Is technology, as many people assume, merely a synonym for machinery of various kinds? Is it a branch of knowledge which deals with applied science and engineering? Is it a process of invention or a method? Or is it, as social scientists claim, the sum of the ways in which social groups provide themselves with the material objects of their civilization? To a certain extent, technology is all of these and more.

Technology, for the purposes of this discussion, is defined as the process of transforming inputs into outputs. This concept of technology, although sparse in the use of words, has several critical implications. The first is that technology is not a thing, but a process. In particular, it is a transformational process and, as a result, change is inherent in its very essence. Thus, when one is talking about technology one is also talking about change, and this has serious implications for the exploration of technology in the context of distance education.

The second implication of the above concept of technology is that it is a social as well as mechanical process. Inputs which can be transformed through technology do not come exclusively from the mechanical world, but can include human beings and the various social organizations which they create. Genetic manipulation and various planning models, for example, are technologies.

Technology is also more than a mechanical process in that all transformations of inputs into outputs occur in a social context, whether recognized or not. The history of technological change and development – attempts to improve or alter the transformation of inputs into outputs – is rife with examples of the failure to see that technological change does not occur in a vacuum.

When discussing the impact or potential of technology in distance education, then, it is vital to recognize that we are dealing primarily with a process and one which is inherently social as well as mechanical. Any decisions taken or plans proposed for the introduction of new technology to the educational process must be undertaken with the social context of technology clearly in mind. In fact, it can be argued that what is really needed today are not more machine technologies but more creative social technologies, which often provide the acceptance envelope of the machine technologies. This acceptance envelope, which defines the ways in which new technologies are diffused and implemented, also affects the type of impact they will exert, both positive and negative. In this regard, distance-education systems themselves can be seen as both machine and social technologies.

With the concept of technology as a transformational process in mind, in what way can we talk of our current technologies as new? Technologies developed in the industrial period in Western history primarily extended the physical capacity of man and, as a result, led to a substantial change in the ways in which physical resources could be transformed into material goods. This process was aided by new social technologies, such as assembly line mass-production systems. The result was an increased ability to transform natural energy sources into a host of material outputs, some of which, as demonstrated by Noble (1983), had social value and some of which did not.

The newer technologies, which have emerged in the last half of this century, are qualitatively different from those of the industrial era. These newer technologies, computer and telematic systems of various kinds, extend not only the physical power of human beings but their mental power and capacity. One of the major results of this transformation has been to shift somewhat the thinking of people with regard to what the key economic resource will be in future. In this context, many people argue that information, the product and ambient culture so to speak of the new technologies, will be equal to, if not more important than, natural energy as the driving force of future economic growth and development. Not only is information a resource in its own right but, as argued by Hawken (1984), increases in productivity, based upon earlier technological processes such as manufacturing, are traceable to a changed ratio between information and raw energy in the production process. This is precisely what new information technologies such as CAD-CAM are doing to the production process; that is, they make it a 'smarter process' and hence a more efficient one.

As noted above, the history of technological development in the world has left a trail of unintended consequences, unfulfilled expectations, and intellectual confusion. In addressing questions such as the use of new technology in distance education – a field which because of its nature is particularly prone to easy and blind adoption of technology – it is vital that distance education should avoid falling into the trap of looking for a 'technological fix' for its problems. Technologies are created by human beings, even those applied to the transformation of the person and, as such, must be guided in their use by a basic humanism – a sense of what is most appropriate to and beneficial to the person. To do otherwise is to dehumanize the person. In an educational context, surely dehumanization cannot be a morally acceptable goal.

It is wise to remind ourselves not only of the potential of technology for educating but also of its limitations. The new information technologies, in essence, bring four elements together: the ability to store information in vast amounts, the ability to process that information in obedience to strict logical procedures, the ability to display such information in multiple formats and the ability to send such information simultaneously to multiple receivers. Because the ability of new technology to store, process, display and send data corresponds to similar processes in human beings, several of its exponents conclude that this new technology can indeed perfectly simulate human thinking. There is, however, a vital difference between what new technologies do when they process, store, send and display information and what human minds do when they think. Not to recognize these differences will lead, in the introduction of new technology in education, to a tragedy rather than a triumph.

At the heart of this caution is the basic postulate that the mind thinks with ideas not with data. And the development of the thought process of the person, regardless of the content to which it is applied or cultural variations in its mode, is surely a universal goal of education.

Data may helpfully illustrate or decorate an idea; it may, where it works in cooperation with a contrasting idea, help call other ideas into question. But data does not create ideas in itself, nor does it validate or invalidate them. An idea can be generated, revised or unseated only by another idea. A culture survives, flourishes or declines through the imaginative and uniting power of its ideas. Ideas come first because they define, contain and produce data. Ideas are integrating patterns which satisfy the mind when it asks the question: What does this mean? What is this about?

As Theordore Roszak (1986) has noted, all cultures contain what one can call core ideas – the great moral, religious and metaphysical teachings which are the foundations of culture. These core ideas are often based upon very little data and, in some cases, no data. They are often born out of absolute conviction or a sense of the ideal. These are a sampling of such core ideas:

> The Tao that can be named is not the true Tao
> Man is a rational animal
> The mind is a blank sheet of paper
> God is love
> God is dead
> Life is a miracle
> Life is an absurdity.

These core ideas are not statements of fact, but are metaphors which represent another reality. These core ideas give order to experience. Core ideas, moreover, can be humane or brutal in their implications for society and this is precisely why they are important. The dramatic turning points in culture happen when a new core idea rises up against an old core idea and judgements must be made. Ironically, today, we face just such a situation in the emergence of newer technologies.

The suggestions has been proposed (Feigenbaum & McCorduck 1983) that new technologies can not only assist human thought in education but also supplant it. Whether this is possible practically or theoretically is not the concern at this point. The real issue is whether, in our use of new technologies in education, we will implement these with this goal in mind. For example, is the goal in distance education to use new technology to assist in a human-based learning process or to use technology to factor out the human element? If the goal is the former, then human factors must always guide decisions related to new technology. If the goal is the latter, then technological factors alone can be used. Given the fact that education entails much more than learning – that is, it is guided by values, culture, and a sense of the ideal – the latter case must prevail.

The point of this reservation regarding new technology is to ensure that, regardless of the many positive benefits which can flow from its reasoned adoption in education, a basic blurring of the distinction between ideas and data does not occur; nor the confusion of data processing with human thought. New technology can, if over-emphasized, bury even deeper the substructures of ideas upon which information stands, placing these ideas further from our consciousness and critical reflection.

Distance-education technology is part of the larger issue of the relationship between inputs and outputs in education. Outputs can be evaluated in terms of learner impact (as measured by tests regarding knowledge, skills, behaviour, attitude) or social impact (the ability of people to be socially and economically productive). In each case, the factors which affect outcomes are not restricted to a specific educational intervention alone. Figure 1 illustrates this ecological effect in terms of distance education technology. As the chart shows, both learner and social outcomes are affected by individual and situational factors. A substantial body of research exists to document this web of relationships (Psascharopoulus & Woodhall 1986, Carnoy & Levin 1985).

The injection of new technology into an existing distance-education system should not be undertaken without due attention to the fact that this will not only change the distance-education system but affect, as well, the larger ecological system of which distance education is a component. In changing this larger relationship between distance education and the ecological system of which it is a part, a number of impacts are possible:

1 The distance-education system itself may acquire a new meaning and function within the larger ecological system.
2 Non-distance-education factors can be converted from barriers to development, to facilitators of development, or vice versa.
3 The distance-education system may involve major impacts on the non-distance-education factors and change their impact on learning.

Planning for the introduction of new technology in distance education, therefore, should not be restricted to the distance-education system or to technology itself. The larger ecological system should be the context in which such planning occurs. New technology, for example, has the potential to make the work setting not only a place for earning and producing but also for learning. The realization of this potential would give a fundamentally different reality to the work setting and its role in distance education. New technology can also lead to a reassessment of the place of initial schooling in affecting a person's opportunity and access to benefits. These larger system effects are further complicated by the fact that they exist in a situation where the principle of mutual feedback loops operate.

While countless examples can be given of the failure to take such an ecological perspective on education, distance education, due to its relative

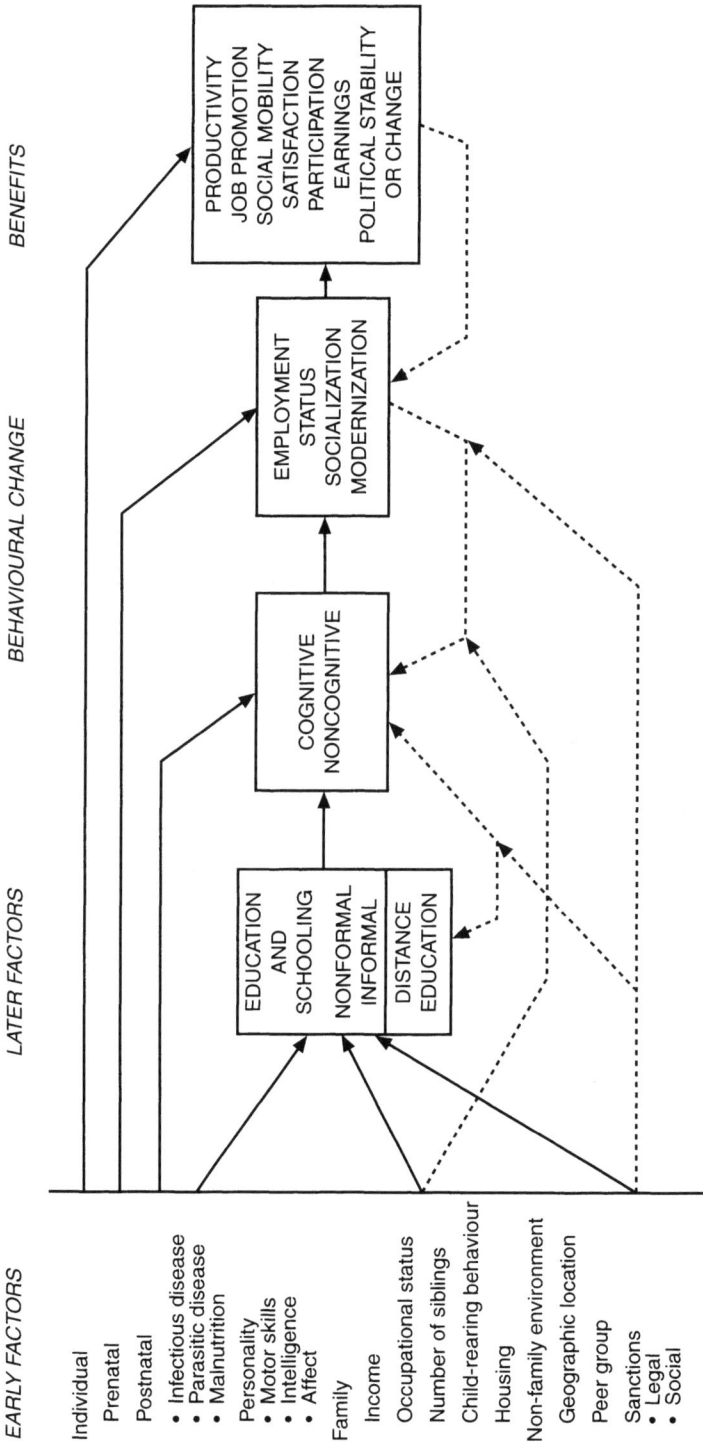

Figure 1 The learning system: causes, consequences and interaction.

newness, has the opportunity to learn from this experience, particularly in relation to new technology. This learning begins by recognizing the age-old principle that 'the whole is greater than the sum of its parts'.

Since it does not have the advantage of the face-to-face encounter and the situational adjustment capacity which that allows, distance education must be a field which takes learning seriously. All distance-education systems, therefore, are mirrors of deliberate learning designs. In the early development of distance education, these learning designs focussed upon text. As technology has developed and research in adult learning and distance education matured, it has been increasingly recognized that a textual design is not a learning design. It is surely a necessary but not sufficient condition.

The challenge, both conceptual and social, facing distance education today is how to match the person, content, process, and context in such a way as to increase both accessibility to and success in learning. In any effort to develop such congruence or match, it becomes clear that no single core strategy will prove sufficient. Indeed, distance education today needs to foster and promote a multiple strategy approach to its task. This is required if, for no other reason than the fact, as argued by Ornstein (1986) and Gardner (1983), that learning and cognitive functioning are multi-dimensional and multi-modal. In the pursuit of such a multiple-strategy approach, new technologies should be seen as one strategy among many possible strategies. No new technology, in its own right, nor any textual design, can provide that match between the person, what they learn, where they learn and how they learn, let alone guarantee access to and success in learning. This is the meta-principle in distance education and, if it is grasped, will guide new technology in finding its appropriate and enabling place in the ecology of human learning.

From a territorial to a global vision

Another challenge facing distance education relates to its vision – its conception of the future, if you like. Today, two vectors operate simultaneously to drive the world: the vector of technology and the vector of globalization. Developments in technology have established a new law of convergence: the tendency for everything to become more like everything else. In the world of business, for example, this has translated into global markets with global corporations (private or state-based) selling the same single standardized products – autos, steel, chemicals, petroleum, cement, agricultural commodities, banking, computers, telecommunications, to mention a few of the obvious – largely in the same ways everywhere. World standardized product lines compete on the basis of appropriate value – the best combinations of price, quality, reliability, and delivery for products that, in respect of design, function and even fashion, are globally identical. This does not mean the end of choice or market segments. It means, though, as described by Levitt (1986), the beginning of price competition for quality products aimed at fewer but larger global market segments.

If convergence is a basic, long-term, multifold trend in the world today, then the vision of distance educators must be informed by this. And if technology is one of the key driving forces behind this pattern, then distance education, given its natural alignment with technologically mediated learning, must globalize its vision.

Recently, under the auspices of the World Bank and the government of the Peoples' Republic of China, I had the opportunity to observe and assess the world's largest learning system – the Radio and Television University System of China. To obtain a sense of the scale of this system, consider the following features. The RTVU system has over 2.5 million students, 30,000 staff, 28 separate universities, over 550 learning centres, and delivers programmes on a nationwide basis, using print, tutors, radio, television, computers and satellite systems. Moreover, the system is intimately linked to the manpower rquirements of the nation as a whole and specific industries within it. This system has been fully developed in less than ten years. There is literally nothing in the West to which it can be compared, neither in terms of scale nor effectiveness. It is revolutionary in its societal and global implications.

China is not alone in the development of open-learning systems. Thailand, India, Pakistan, Indonesia, Holland, Columbia, Bolivia and many other developed and developing nations have, as a matter of public policy priority, established open-learning systems as a major principle in development. Distance and open-learning systems, in fact, are emerging as a major development strategy on a worldwide basis. Even panglobal initiatives are under-way. The Massachusetts Institute of Technology, along with several large corporations and universities, for example, has announced the establishment of an International Space University – one objective of which is to have a global university in orbit by the early twenty-first century.

The combined impact of four factors – cost, scale, flexibility and technology – has led governments throughout the world to look to open-learning systems as a major option in human resource development. This development alone is of significance. Of even more importance, however, is the fact that these developments are laying the groundwork, or infrastructure, for what until heretofore was only a dream: a global learning network. The linkage in this network, what makes it possible, is the use of a common process of providing learning.

Imagine, if you can, collaborative course teams drawn from several nations, developing programmes in areas of common concern, and showing the perspectives of each of their cultures. Image a collaboratively produced course being offered simultaneously in 20 nations, with the delivery strategy adapted to local conditions. Imagine as well, a student in Canada taking this course – a cross-cultural experience itself – with an international network of tutors, and receiving credit in 20 universities in 20 nations. Imagine the personal mobility and cultural understanding which flows from such an experience. Imagine the contribution to trade and peace that such a network can render.

Today, the world stands on the precipice of a quantum leap in the scale and context of learning. The infrastructure for a globalization of learning is currently being put in place and the process is being led by the developing world. The implications of such a development for economies and cultures are as yet unstudied and unseen, but will be profound. This globalization of learning may offer humankind its last chance to live peacefully and productively in the global commons. It requries, to be realized, first and foremost, a shared global consciousness. Some may say that this is a 'distant' hope, but surely not those involved in 'distance' education.

From quantity to equity in development

The development challenge of the last years of this century can best be summed up as achieving integrated growth with equity. While economic growth based upon increased productivity is still fundamental, an equal sharing of the fruits of that growth is not only a moral imperative but provides an ongoing contribution to economic health. This new challenge also rejects the traditional notion that economic and social development are distinct and must proceed in a way in which the latter follows upon the former. Social and economic development are interlocked and must proceed hand in hand. This principle applies to any educationally based development effort.

Distance and open-learning systems are uniquely equipped to contribute to and, in fact, lead in the development of new strategies which flow from the goal of integrated growth with equity. The first such emergent strategy involves focused measures to increase economic output and a process of implementation which will involve the entire nation in the development process with a resultant equitable distribution of the benefits. Distance- and open-learning systems, because of their ability to increase the scope of coverage, extend access and adapt to change, can be both targeted to sectoral priorities and provide learning systems which involve a range of people in the process and results.

The second emergent strategy involves large-scale, integrated efforts to accelerate rural development, with local people playing key decision-making roles. Distance-education systems, particularly when linked to new decentralizing telecommunications technologies, can provide the means of taking expertise to rural areas as well as developing a rural-based system for the sharing of that expertise.

The third emergent strategy requires a frontal attack on the roots of mass poverty, designed to meet basic needs of disadvantaged people for education, food, health and family planning. This area is perhaps the greatest challenge facing distance learning. Current print-based models of distance learning, in this regard, are inappropriate, since they presume the very skills disadvantaged groups often lack. However, a networking strategy, in which distance-learning systems link teachers, helpers and learners to local communities and their needs, provides an alternative path.

The fourth emergent strategy centres on efforts to increase the opportunities for particularly disadvantaged groups such as women and ethnic minorities. Special access programmes using distance-education techniques, underpinned by community involvement, can form an integral part of this strategy. For such strategies to be workable, though, real power-sharing with the groups concerned must be the norm.

For the better part of this century, development has been misconstrued as achieving an increase in the national incomes of so-called 'developing countries'. These are usually formalized in targets, such as the 5% growth rates set for the first development decade. This focus on national income is, of course, convenient. Policy makers find a single, all-encompassing measure useful. Economists are provided with a variable which can be quantified and a set of dynamics which can be analyzed into changes in sectoral output and categories of expenditure. This energizes economists' natural tendency towards model-building.

It is confusing, if not misleading, however, to confuse development with economic development, and economic development with economic growth. The only hope in such reasoning is to suppose that an increase in national income, if it is faster than population growth, will trickle down to those in need and sooner or later lead to the solution of social and political problems.

It is singularly unhelpful for those involved in the establishment of distance and open-learning systems to define their development mission in terms of its contribution to the gross level of national income. Since many of these distance-and open-learning systems are closely attuned to the development policies of the nations in which they exist, and will be judged within these policies, it is important to strip away the macro-economic gloss around the idea of development and to be more precise about what we mean.

Development is inevitably a normative term, since it implies a direction, a sense of the worthwhile. Without canvassing the endless definitions of that term, I would suggest that development, whether in a Western or Third-World context, is essentially a process through which the potential of human beings can be realized.

If one asks what is an absolute necessity for this, one answer is obvious – enough food. Below certain levels of nutrition, a person lacks not merely bodily energy and health, but is rarely interested in things other than food, learning included.

Another basic necessity, in the sense of something without which human potential cannot develop, is an active role in society. This does not mean just employment; it can include studying, serving others and care-giving roles. To be denied access to active roles in society is to be in a situation of dependency – the antithesis of development.

Both poverty and unemployment, it is true, are associated with per capita income. If per capita incomes are falling, poverty cannot be much reduced. But increases in per capita income are far from enough, as petroleum economics shows. A rise in per capita income can, in fact, be accompanied by rising unemployment. The direct link between per capita income and the numbers living in poverty is income distribution. Equality, then, is the third element in development.

The questions to ask about any nation's development are therefore: What has been happening to poverty? What has been happening to employment? and, What has been happening to inequality? For open and distance-learning systems, if they are designed as contributors to development, these very same questions apply. What has been happening to poverty, active roles, employment and inequality as a consequence of distance education? For distance- and open-learning systems to be truly part of the development process, these questions must inform how these systems are designed and, more importantly, how they are judged. Some will say that it is unfair to hold distance and open learning accountable in this way. This is, in part, true. But a continuation of poverty, restrictions in roles, inequality and unemployment, regardless of where the pattern persists, is equally and profoundly more unfair.

References

Anisef, P. Okihro, N. (1982). *Losers and Winners*, Toronto, Butterworths, pp. 19–52.

Astin, A., (1984), *Achieving Educational Excellence*, San Francisco, Jossey-Bass.

Athabasca University (1986a), *Study of Graduates*.

Athabasca University (1986b), *Student Motivation Study*.

Baudien, P. (1973), Cultural Reproduction and Social Reproduction, in Brown, R. (ed.) *Knowledge, Education and Cultural Change*, London, Tavistock Press, pp. 71–112.

Botkin, J. (1979), *No Limits to Learning*, London, Pergamon Press.

Carnegie Commission on Higher Education (1985), *The Corporate Classroom*, New York, Carnegie Foundation.

Carnoy M. & Levin, H. (1985), *Schooling And Work In Democratic Society*, Stanford, Stanford University Press.

Clark, B. (1983), *The Higher Education System*, Berkeley, University of California Press, pp. 107–135.

Cleveland, M. (1985), *The Knowledge Executive*, New York, Dutton, pp. 1–25.

Cross, P. (1986), New Students in New Bottles, in Neilson, W., Gaffield, C. (Eds.) *Universities in Crisis*, Halifax, Institute for Research On Public Policy, p. 217.

de Bono, E. (1986), *Six Thinking Hats*, New York, Oxford Press, pp. 1–10.

Faure, E. (1972), *Learning To Be*, Geneva, UNESCO.

Feigenbaum, E. & McCorduck, P. (1983), *Fifth Generation*, New York, Addison-Wesley.

Gardner, M. (1983), *Frames of Mind*, New York, Basic Books.

Guttman, A. (1987), *Democratic Education*, Princeton, Princeton University Press, pp. 44–45.

Hawken, P. (1984), *The Next Economy*, Toronto, Holt Rinehart, Winston, pp. 74–90.

Holmberg, B. (1983), *Status and Trends in Distance Education*, New York, Oxford Press.

Jencks, C. (1975), *Inequality*, New York, Doubleday.

Koestler, A. (1980), *Janus*, New York, Abacus.

Levitt, T. (1986), *The Marrketing Imagination*, New York, Free Press.

Michael, D. (1979), *On Learning To Plan On Planning To Learn*, San Francisco, Jossey-Bass.

Noble, D. (1983), *The Forces of Production*, New York, Alfred Knopf.

Ornstein, R. (1986), *Multi-Mind*, New York, Dutton.

Psascharopoulus, G. & Woodhall, M. (1986), *Education for Development*, New York, Oxford Press.

Roszak, T. (1986), *The Cult of Information*, New York, Pantheon, p. 221.

Rosensleuth, A. & Wiener, N. (1950), Purposeful and Non-Purposeful Systems, *Philosophy of Science*, Vol. 17, pp. 318–326.

13 Athene in academe

Women mentoring women in the academy[1]

Joyce Stalker[2]

University of Waikato, Hamilton, New Zealand

Increasingly, adult educators are expressing interest in the activity of mentoring in the academy. The literature discusses it as primarily a positive adult learner/adult teacher connection. This is evident in its discussion of the structural and personal relationships and of the multiple outcomes associated with the process. A feminist critique of mentoring, however, reveals that these analyses are androcentric. They ignore women academics' unique location as both 'same' and 'other' within patriarchal academe. Theoretical consideration of this location yields new understandings of the potentials and problematics of the role of the women as mentors.

Introduction

The activity of mentoring has a long history. It orginates from Homer's *Odyssey*, in which Athene, goddess of wisdom, took the image of Mentor, Odysseus' loyal friend, and was given the responsibility for guiding Odysseus' son Telemachus. It was Mentor's task to direct Telemachus in a comprehensive way in each element of his life. In this role, Mentor nurtured and guided the holistic development of Telemachus' skills, and personal and civic abilities.

Increasingly, the field of adult education is expressing interest in the mentoring process (Bolton 1980, Daloz 1991, Merriam, 1983, Merriam *et al.* 1987). It is seen as a unique adult learner/adult teacher connection which has positive implications for the learner and teacher. However, definitive empirical evidence about the activity of mentoring – particularly in academic settings – is lacking. Some research suggests that it is a vague process with no measurable outcomes. Other research lists step-by-step procedures and argues that it is a 'necessary part of successful growth in any walk of life' (Lively *et al.* 1992: 82).

Merriam notes that the inconsistencies in the literature are due to the 'idiosyncratic nature of available studies' (1983: 163) and 'the lack of a distinct line of research' (1983: 168). Before any line of research into mentoring is extended, however, it is essential that the process is conceptualized adequately. Thus, the purpose of this study is to inform the current conceptualization of mentoring by critiquing it from a feminist perspective.

In order to accomplish this, I first define the notion of mentoring. I do this by discussing the relationships and outcomes of the mentoring process as presented in the literature. I then undertake a feminist critique of that literature, first from a general perspective. Second, and most importantly, I reject the literature's basic underlying assumption that women mentors produce and reproduce the patriarchal academe. I present an alternative view and explore the theoretical limitations and possibilities of women academics' location on the boundaries of academe. I then examine the implications of that location for the mentoring process. I conclude by highlighting the need to consider the mentoring process in a way which reflects the unique nature of our location as women mentors.

Mentoring

Although the concept of mentoring can be traced back to Homer's writing, no clear definition of the term exists. Numerous words have evolved as synonyms for the term. Words such as teaching, coaching, advising, training, directing, protecting, sponsoring, guiding and leading are among the terms used. Similarly, words such as mentee, protégé, apprentice, learner and novice, used to describe the person being mentored, hint at the diverse nature of the mentoring activity.

This diversity results in part from our understanding being derived from a combination of different settings. Since mentoring occurs in day-to-day interactions as well as in institutional settings, its forms are varied. Common-sense understandings of the activity exist side by side with more formal, institutionalized understandings.

In instances which focus on the formal institutionalized understandings, the definitions are derived primarily from business/management and higher education settings and the field of psychology (Jacobi 1991, Merriam 1983). Although there is a loose acknowledgment that each of these areas is distinct from the others, the studies inform each other and are almost inextricably interwoven. Furthermore, in the case of articles written about academic mentoring, distinctions are not necessarily drawn between mentoring within settings where the education of children occurs and within settings where the education of adults occurs. Thus, clear definitions of mentoring in academic settings are difficult to establish.

Given the confusion in the literature about the term 'mentoring' the next section of this paper explores it in terms of its relationships and outcomes. These two dimensions are incorporated into most mentoring literature. They will thus help to explicate the nature of the term as it is commonly used in the research community. To the extent that it is possible to extricate the literature about academic mentoring from the literature about other kinds of mentoring, this section focuses on mentoring within academic settings where the education of adults occurs.

Relationships

A dimension of mentoring which is seen to be essential to the process concerns relationships – both structural and personal. These relationships define the connections through which interactions occur and outcomes are achieved.

Structural: In terms of structural relationships, the dominant representation in the literature is of a hierarchical mentoring relationship. Normally, an older, wiser person advises, counsels and acts as role model to a younger person on a one-to-one basis. The activity is a top-down, 'didactic' (Daloz 1991: 206) one in which a neophyte academic is chosen or 'anointed' (Sandler and Hall 1983: 2) by an experienced and senior academic who has 'high organizational or specific career status' (Bova and Phillips 1982: 7) and the power associated with that status. Some authors (e.g., Daloz 1991) suggest that the asymmetrical, hierarchical relationship can evolve toward a more symmetrical one, but the implication is that the relationship is then no longer a mentoring one.

This hierarchical relationship is deemed to arise usually more or less spontaneously out of the day-to-day teacher/learner situation. Like the alternative models below, however, it can be part of a formal, planned induction programme in which the mentee is assigned to the mentor or mentoring programme.

An alternative, but much less frequently used model of mentoring suggests structural relationships which are based in lateral, multiple connections rather than hierarchical dyads. Within the academic settings, this model accepts lateral faculty–faculty, student–student and administrator–administration relationships. It also presents mentoring as usefully undertaken through networks, career cooperatives, written materials and multiple helping relationships with subordinates as well as peers (Sandler and Hall 1983; Hill *et al.* 1989). Some authors seem uncomfortable with this latter notion and, in what appears to be an attempt to reimpose the traditional hierarchical model, distinguish between mentors and the 'significant' mentor (Lively *et al.* 1992).

Personal: In terms of personal relationships, the literature discusses mentoring as an activity which involves an intimacy or intensity which transcends friendships and 'supervisory relationships' (Burke *et al.* 1991: 459). This intensity varies within and between mentor(s) and mentee relationships (Schockett *et al.* in Bush Wilde and Garrett Schau 1991). The possible ranges of that intensity have been well represented by Shapiro *et al.* (1978: 57). They suggest a continuum that moves from peer pals, through guides and sponsors to mentors. Their model traces the developmental nature of the mentoring relationship from sharing through explaining and protecting to promoting and shaping the mentee. Overall, the mentoring process requires a delicate balance between intimate and impersonal challenges and support.

Together, the structural and personal dimensions of mentoring create the foundations upon which the outcomes of the mentoring activity are built. It is to those outcomes that this paper now turns.

Outcomes

This section reflects the literature's acknowledgement that ideal mentoring relationships are reciprocal and that the mentor as well as the mentee derives specific outcomes from the relationship (Bush Wilde and Garrett Schau 1991, Daloz 1991, Jacobi 1991, Merriam 1983). Although these outcomes are inextricably interwoven, for the sake of discussion they are presented here in three separate categories: career advancement, personal development and professional identification.

Career advancement: Researchers who explore mentoring consistently stress the connection between mentoring and an outcome of career advancement (e.g., Sandler and Hall 1983, Jacobi 1991, Levinson 1978, Messervy 1989). This outcome is the accumulated result of several related outcomes. One such outcome is the mentee's acquisition of the practical, technical skills and formal scientific knowledge required in academe (Reskin 1979). These include writing ability, logical thinking (Berger 1990) and research skills connected to theories and methodologies (Lyons *et al.* 1990).

Similar outcomes accrue to the mentor, since the mentee may provide 'technical support or new ideas [and] new knowledge' (Wright and Wright 1987: 205). As well, they may undertake the more 'mundane tasks' of the mentors' jobs and free them for 'more creative pursuits' (Lyons *et al.* 1990:279).

A second related outcome is the mentees' raised visibility in the academic community. This may occur as mentors encourage their mentees to establish a research programme. Such a programme results in the mentees making contact with other academics and in the increased possibility of publications (Jacobi 1991). Similarly, a raised visibility occurs when they are introduced by the mentor into formal and informal academic networks at professional meetings.

Once again this outcome is a reciprocal one. According to research, mentors can build new links through the mentee's contacts. They can also be rewarded for discovering and developing new talent. As well, they may enhance their own reputations and visibility vicariously through the mentee's publications and research programmes (Phillips-Jones 1982).

Personal development: The second outcome of an ideal mentoring activity concerns personal development (Schockett and Haring-Hidore 1985, Wright and Wright 1987). In this instance, mentoring results in the mentees' heightened self-esteem, confidence and self-assurance. This improved personal self-assessment occurs in both intellectual and emotional aspects of the mentees' lives (Schockett and Haring-Hidore 1985). Processes of mirroring and reflecting ensure that mentees come to see and understand their own thoughts and behaviours in new ways. Consequently, they understand and value their intellectual and personal strengths and weaknesses more clearly (Daloz 1991).

A complementary notion is that mentees acquire stronger 'risk-taking behaviours [and] communication skills' (Bova and Phillips 1984: 18). These in turn are seen to enhance the mentees' career advancement and professional identification.

From the mentors' point of view, mentoring may produce similar outcomes. Mentoring ideally provides insights into personal issues and helps mentors to define their own strengths and weaknesses more clearly. The personal satisfaction and excitement of involvement with mentees as they grow and develop is a form of development for the mentors as well (Daloz 1991). Indeed, Phillips-Jones (1982) suggests that mentoring helps mentors to move through an ego stage of adult development. It helps them to leave behind childhood and assume the responsibilities of adulthood.

Professional identification: The third and final major outcome of ideal mentoring concerns the mentees' enhanced understanding of their professional identity within academe. Research reveals that those who have mentors feel much more integrated into the functioning research university (Lyons *et al.* 1990). In other words, mentoring moves the mentee into the 'ecology of the workplace' (Sands *et al.* 1991: 179). This notion suggests that mentees' survival is dependent on their ability to adapt to the academic environment.

This 'goodness of fit' (Sands *et al.* 1991: 179) ensures that the mentee is socialized into the institution. The mentor is thus 'a guide in the rites of passage' (Lyons *et al.* 1990: 278) who shares information and strategies which enable the mentees to 'succeed' within the specific environment (Jacobi 1991: 513). Mentors thus ensure mentees' integration into the language, norms, values, attitudes and beliefs of academe. Mentors provide a personal connection into an 'often impersonal and threatening world' (Daloz 1986: 220) which is composed of unwritten rules and politics (Bova and Phillips 1982).

From the mentors' point of view, mentoring may reaffirm their commitment to academe, or be a way in which they repay debts to the field (Phillips-Jones 1982). The fostering of mentees with a sense of loyalty and commitment to the organization or field ensures its continuity. This,

in turn, provides mentors with a reassuring sense of professional regenera-
tion and endurance (Wright and Wright 1987).

A feminist critique

From a feminist's point of view, there is a major problem with the traditional conceptualization of mentoring as portrayed above. It is androcentric, that is, it has a male bias and orientation. It expresses this in several
ways: in its construction of research designs, in its avoidance of the problematics of men mentoring women and in its underlying assumption that
women mentors act as producers and reproducers of the patriarchal
academe.

Research designs

It is clear that the majority of the mentoring research has a male orientation. It does not consider gender as a major variable. Most research is
based on, and findings are generalized from, mixed-sex populations. The
majority of research projects are conceptualized in a way which does not
recognize the experiences of women mentors as unique from those of
men. This gives the impression that the nature of male and female
mentors and of the mentoring process is homogeneous.

On the other hand, among those studies which *do* consider sex as a
major variable, there is a tendency 'to cast in stone what differences do
exist and to view females as aberrant or deficient when and where they fail
to comply with male "norms"' (Collard and Stalker 1991: 76). Bushardt *et
al.* even go so far as to suggest that 'mentors regardless of their gender
utilize predominantly masculine sex role behaviour' (1991: 620).

Ignoring the problematics

The majority of the mentoring literature also ignores the problematics of
men mentoring women. To a certain extent, this merely reflects the tendency throughout the literature to assume that mentoring is a process of
mutuality and congruence (O'Neil in Bush Wilde and Garrett Schau
1991) which provides 'a lifetime of colleagueship and supervision' (Houle
1979: 112). A few authors have acknowledged the possibility of tension
and dissension in the relationship (Daloz 1991, Merriam 1983, Bush Wilde
and Garrett Schau 1991) and suggest that it may end abruptly and unhap-
pily (Levinson 1978). Others (Daloz 1991, Wright and Wright 1987) state
that the mentoring activity can be counterproductive and negative for
both the mentor and mentee and identify issues of excessive demands for
time, unrealistic expectations, manipulation, jealousy, over-dependency,
over-protectiveness or inappropriately sexual intimacy (Phillips-Jones
1982).

Although few researchers acknowledge that mentoring may be exploitative and dysfunctional as well as challenging and supportive, fewer still acknowledge the issues in terms of gender. For insights, it is necessary to turn to specific projects and studies which have focused on the problems inherent in men mentoring women.

The Project on the Status and Education of WOMEN (Sandler and Hall 1983), for example, suggests that male mentors' behaviours are connected to women's traditional roles as helpers rather than as achievers. They propose that deeply embedded paternalistic views ensure that male mentors treat women mentees as 'teacher's pet' (p. 8) more than as potential heirs or worthy academics. Further, because women are viewed too often as sexual partners rather than professional colleagues, they are overlooked as potential mentees.

Studies do exist which confirm the problems associated with men mentoring women (Bolton 1980, Lyons *et al.* 1990, Sands *et al.* 1991, Simeone 1987). Among their findings are that male faculty affirm male students more than female students; more frequently give both informal and formal encouragement to male students; treat male students as colleagues and select them above women for teaching or research assistants. These situations are exacerbated when the women are also aged, handicapped, lesbian, of colour or of ethnic origin. It appears that mentors relate best to mentees who share their values, and attitudes. Thus, mentees who are women and who also have one of these attributes are less likely to be mentored in North American academic settings. In sum, the mentoring literature, while not declaring these kinds of mentoring relationships 'unworkable', clearly stresses the problems inherent in them (Jacobi 1991). This literature, however, remains marginal to the mainstream conceptualization of mentoring.

Underlying assumption

The third and theoretically most important critique of the mentoring literature concerns its assumption that women mentors socialize mentees, most of whom are women (Busch 1985), into acceptance and accommodation of the patriarchal academic system. This view must be critiqued for its simplistic interpretation of women mentors as producers and reproducers of the patriarchal academe. It bears an uncanny similarity to theories of social and cultural reproduction, prominent in the 1970s but brought under heavy scrutiny by resistance theorists in the 1980s.

Like those early reproduction theories, this assumption displays an overly deterministic and reductionist view of the mentoring process. It ignores women mentors' simultaneous location as 'same' and as 'other' – a location on the boundaries of academe. This location ensures that women mentors act out complex and often contradictory roles of resistance, contestation, mediation and reproduction of patriarchal institutional and societal structures. The theoretical implications of this location for women's mentoring are considerable, yet, to date, they have not been considered in the mentoring literature. Thus, they will be explored in depth in the discussion which follows.

Mentoring on the boundaries

At first glance, women mentors appear to engage in a delicately balancing act. On the one hand, we accommodate the patriarchal institution of academe which threatens to consume and subsume us. On the other hand, we resist those structures and risk the consequences of anonymity and marginality. Women mentors' work in the 'interstices' (Farwell Adams 1983: 135) is much more complex than this dichotomous representation, however. Women who are within 'the sacred grove' (Aisenberg and Harrington 1988) are simultaneously and dynamically involved in the processes of being both 'same' and 'other'.

'Same'-ness

Women mentors in academe experience being 'same' in a variety of ways. As Talpade Mohanty (1983) notes, the hierarchical nature of academe forces an unavoidable homogeneity and sameness on those within the institution. Through its clearly defined relationships it creates a conformity and similarity of connections throughout the organization. Within that context academic women, like all academics, possess a measure of the privileges and power of the élite who produce and legitimate knowledge and language. In addition, as 'same' we engage in structured competition for recognition of publications, research, scholarship, teaching, influence and power. Indeed, new opportunities opening up in academe for women increasingly 'tempt women into complicity with these arrangements through individual careerism' (Fisher 1982: 61).

Women academics also exhibit 'same'-ness to the extent that they exemplify the norms, values and beliefs of the male academic culture within which they work. Henry suggests that this is often the case, since women academics are those 'who filter through the rigorous screening system and satisfy their [male academics'] criterion for admission to the inner circle of academe' (1990: 129).

As 'same', women accept that professional work supersedes both personal relationships and interests outside the academic world (Jensen 1982). We understand that the spheres of our public lives and private lives must be kept separate. We engage in the authoritative, assertive, abstract style of 'rational' 'phalloreferential/reverential' (Hardy Aiken *et al.* 1987: 270) discourse which dominates academe (Aisenberg and Harrington 1988).

'*Other*'-*ness*

At one level, women who practise 'same-ness' successfully become invisible – that is, they present no problematics within the academe. This 'same'-ness, however, is illusionary. For although women academics may be inside, they are simultaneously, inevitably and irrefutably 'other'. As Farwell Adams says, 'Thirteen years of teaching in universities has at last disclosed to me the secret that there is no second sex in academe. There is only one sex: male' (1983: 135). It is self-evident that they are a group who are in the minority, do the least prestigious teaching, take the majority of part-time positions and staff 'women's specialties' and 'women's fields.' Less obviously, they are also 'other' relative to the patriarchal academic structures, to the expectations for women, to other women and to themselves.

In terms of the patriarchal structures, women's criticisms of the patriarchal bases of research and theory locate them as 'other'. This situation may be an inevitable one for women (Aisenberg and Harrington 1988), for, even if they enter their discipline without the explicit intent to critique it, their 'outsider experience and status ... [will] sooner or later' drive them to express 'values counter to the established definition of the subject' (p. 86). These discourses of dissonance are oppositional to the 'Eurocentric male dominance of academic discourse' (Carty 1991: 17) and become by that definition 'other'. This sense of 'other'-ness is exacerbated by the subordination of these areas of discourse to domains of lower status and power.

Further, when women academics display these assertive, vigorous behaviours and challenge the male norms they may be penalized and denied access to resources – and thus be restricted to the margins as 'other'. (The irony of this is, of course, that those very behaviours indicate 'same'-ness.) Alternatively, if they act in stereotypically female ways and are compliant, co-operative and nurturing, they are allocated to teaching and service roles (Simeone 1987) – roles which once again identify them as 'other' in an environment where scholarship and publishing records are valued over teaching and service.

Women also remain 'other' in terms of stereotypical expectations. These expectations suggest that there is a women's culture distinct from a men's, and thus academic, culture. The works of Belenky *et al.* (1986), Gilligan (1982) and Noddings (1984) are among those which highlight the unique nature of women as concerned with connectedness and caring. This view of woman as separate and unique has been 'extremely helpful in baring some of the roots of masculinist liberal capitalism' (Fox Keller and Moglen 1987, p. 511), but it also reinforces the view of academic women as 'anomalies' (Roland Martin 1990, p. 13). As they acquire the skills of academe, such as rule-making or speaking with authority, they enter the territory which usually is viewed as 'properly the province of men' (Aisenberg and Harrington 1988: 65). At the same time, their engagement with academe is limited by the extent to which they can create non-traditional partnerships within their private spheres in order to accommodate the time, energy and resource demands of their public spheres. These relationships also reinforce an 'other'-ness relative to expectations for women. In the face of this 'other'-ness, women still assume the major responsibility for the household and family. Even in circumstances where their partners are supportive, they tend to see those responsibilities and functions as their own (Simeone 1987). They are caught between the demands of the public and the private spheres – two 'greedy institutions' (Acker 1983: 191). This in itself might not create women as 'other'. However, it is combined with an academic structure which acts as if each family member had supportive and responsible partners at home. In the case of women with children, this is evident in the lack of institutional support for comprehensive child care.

Women academics are also 'other' relative to women within the academy who have less power, status and authority. This is particularly relevant in their relationships to women who differ in colour, class and ethnicity. Women of colour have explored their location as a 'double minority' (McKay 1983: 144) most eloquently. They note that too often white, middle-class women who dominate academe consider issues directly related to their own experiences and ignore the inseparability of racial and sexual oppression. For women who differ in colour, class ethnicity and sexual orientation, their differences are reified as an inescapable 'other'-ness relative to white, heterosexual women as well as to white men and black men.

The dominant group of women academics thus play a role in creating the very experiences of isolation and invisibility which they experience and condemn. Through their 'same'-ness with those in privileged positions, they exercise power and authority in hiring, firing and shaping the nature of the academy. They are simultaneously the oppressor and the oppressed, the creators of 'other'-ness and the 'other', within the male domain.

Finally, women academics may be 'other' in relation to themselves. By locating themselves within patriarchal structures, they may risk losing themselves (Aisenberg and Harrington 1988). They may have 'cooperated in [their] own defeat' (Farwell Adams 1983: 140) as they are absorbed, admitted and shaped by the patriarchal structures. There is a sense of a 'bifurcated consciousness' (Acker 1983: 198) in which they experience the lack of fit between the theoretical and their personal life world experiences. In other words, to be a successful woman academic and to achieve in educational institutions is somehow not to be a woman (Collard and Stalker 1991).

Implications for women as mentors

This, then is the location of women academics – simultaneously both 'same' and 'other' – caught in the web of 'same'-ness, but never able to transcend their 'other'-ness. As noted earlier, the theoretical implications of this location for women's mentoring have not been considered in the mentoring literature. On one hand, it can be interpreted as a location of paralysis. After all, in structural relationships women as 'other' are engaged in their own struggles to establish high organizational or specific career status. Lacking the power associated with that status, most women might appear to be inadequately placed to be effective mentors.

In terms of personal relationships, women who establish sensitive, caring and concerned personal relationships with their mentees risk confirming views of themselves as located primarily within the women's culture, rather than within the male academic culture. In that environment, such caring relationships are associated with increased professional and political vulnerability.

Women academics' location similarly confuses their role of mentors in ensuring the traditional outcomes. To the extent that they enter into discourses of dissonance which are oppositional to the 'Eurocentric male dominance of academic discourse' (Carty 1991: 17), they exist outside the dominant academic structures. They are thus poorly located to facilitate mentees' entry into the dominant academic networks, ways of producing knowledge and research methodologies. Similarly, some may judge that women are not well placed to heighten mentees' self-development in the struggle to find value for their own ideas and behaviours within the patriarchal academe. Finally, some might argue that, in view of woman's inevitable critique of their disciplines (Aisenberg and Harrington 1988), they are not orientated to facilitate mentees' movement and integration into the 'ecology of the workplace' (Sands *et al.* 1991: 179).

This view of women mentors' unique location as one of paralysis is unacceptable. It portrays women in academe as passively receiving the inherited and imposed nature of the patriarchal academic culture. It depicts women as 'lacking an consciousness' (Moglen 1983: 131). It represents women mentors as victims of the male academic culture, as deficient relative to the 'norm' of male mentors. Finally, this view confines its understanding of mentoring to the institution. It does not extend its analysis to the wider system of patriarchy in society.

The alternative view of women academics presented below represents their location as one of possibility and transformation. Their location in the interstices is viewed, not as marginal, but rather as a site of 'vigor and life' which will survive as 'the Patriarchy, like any overstabilized system, is collapsing inwards' (Farwell Adams 1983: 141). It emphasizes the strength of women who come 'from outside, without allegiances to the Men's Club'

(p. 138). It stresses the transformative potential of women who simultaneously understand and oppose the patriarchal structures.

In the earlier discussion, women's location was conceptualized as a
narrow boundary line between being subsumed and consumed by, or
being marginalized and separated from, the male academy. This alternative conceptualization expands women's razor's edge existence into a
viable space within which they can move collectively, and thus re-create
and re-form institutional and societal structures. It portrays women as
groups of active agents; actors who are able to take and shape space to
their own ends. It acknowledges the dialectic ability of women academics
to react, resist and act on the social world they inhabit. It acknowledges
women's ability self-consciously to critique their experiences of oppression
and together to act on them.

Within this framework mentoring is not merely a tool for socialization
into and accommodation of the current patriarchal, classist and racist
structures. Rather, it is an active mechanism for transformation. As Fisher
suggests:

> ...the exhilaration stems from success in destroying the sexual stereo-
> types and myths students bring with them, in helping women to
> become more independent, self-determining people, in offering an
> alternate view of an intellectual discipline, and/or in conveying a
> more radical view of the society and the potential of feminist action to
> change its underlying structure.
>
> (1982: 57)

Recalling that women academics mentor primarily women mentees, they
thus play a particular role in fostering resistance to the male academy.
Sensitive to the power structures which limit their activities, they emphasize the importance of empowerment of women. Some mentors actively
encourage their mentees to be something other than 'good girls'. As one
woman academic said, 'Their environment is saying, be good and stay still
and I'm saying be loud and make waves and do what you want and be free'
(Aisenberg and Harrington 1988: 18).

Embedded in this view of women mentors as actors is the notion that,
located within this unique space, they can transform the nature of society.
There is the suggestion that through their activities within the institution,
they can extend their influence beyond its boundaries and act on larger
social issues. The assumption is that they carry with them different views
which are congruent with the conscientization of their mentees to political and economic oppressions.

This view of women mentors as transformers of institutions and society
is problematic if it stands on its own. Fundamentally, it is impossible to
ignore women mentors' reality of being simultaneously both 'same' and
'other' and the consequences which flow from that location of being the

oppressor and oppressed, powerful and powerless, paralyzed and trans-formative. None the less, it is clear that women academics are uniquely located and possess a mentoring potential which is not acknowledged in the literature.

A reconceptualized, thoughtful view of mentoring acknowledges the unique location of women mentors. It notes both women's accommoda-tion of and separation from patriarchal structures. It values the unique nature which allows them to mentor within the walls of academe at the same time that they reformulate the structure of those walls. It critiques the assumptions of static hierarchical power and authority which underlie the dominant model of mentoring. It adds to the literature a dynamic view of power in which the mentor's location plays an important role.

An alternative view of mentoring endorses the resistance and transfor-mations that women mentors bring to patriarchal cultures. It critiques the existing power bases and explores the ways in which power can be used to challenge the status quo. In sum, a reconceptualized view of the mentor-ing process moves away from the dominant androcentric conceptualiza-tion toward a more widely based, critical view which is informed by the experiences of women and women mentors.

Notes

1 Selected portions of this paper were presented at a joint conference of the Aus-tralian Association for Research in Education and the New Zealand Association for Research in Education, 22–26 November, 1992, Geelong, Australia.

2 *Joyce Stalker* is a Senior Lecturer in the Department of Education Studies at the University of Waikato, in Hamilton, New Zealand. Her research interests include sociological, gender and equity issues related to adult, community and tertiary education in international settings.

References

Acker, S. 1983, Women, the other academics. *Women's Studies International Forum*, Vol. 6, No. 2, pp. 191–201.

Aisenberg, N. and Harrington, M. 1988, *Women of Academe. Outsiders in the Sacred Grove*, Massachusetts, University of Massachusetts Press.

Belenky, M., McVicker Clinchy, B., Rule Goldberger, N., and Mattuck Tarule, J. 1986, *Women's Ways of Knowing*, New York, Basic Books.

Berger, M. 1990, Getting published: a mentoring programe for social work faculty. *Social Work*, Vol. 35, pp. 69–71.

Bolton, E. 1980, A conceptual analysis of the mentor relationship in the career development of women. *Adult Education*, Vol. 30, pp. 195–207.

Bova, B. and Phillips, R. 1982, The mentoring relationships as an educational experience, ERIC Document Reproduction Service No. ED224944.

Bova, B. and Phillips, R. 1984, Mentoring as a learning experience for adults. *Journal of Teacher Education*, Vol. 35, No. 3, pp. 6–20.

Burke, R., McKenna, C. and McKeen, C. 1991, How do mentorships differ from typical supervisory relationships? *Psychological Reports*, Vol. 68, pp. 459–466.

Busch, J. 1985, Mentoring in graduate Schools of Education: mentors' perceptions. *American Educational Research Journal*, Vol. 22, No. 2, pp. 257–265.

Bush Wilde, J. and Garrett Schau, C. 1991, Mentoring in graduate schools of education: mentees' perceptions. *Journal of Experimental Education*, Vol. 59, No. 2, pp. 165–179.

Bushardt, S., Fretwell, C., and Holdnak, B. 1991, The mentor/protege relationship: a biological perspective. *Human Relations*, Vol. 44, No. 5, pp. 539–642.

Carty, L. 1991, Black women in Academia: a statement from the periphery, in H. Bannerji, L. Carty, K. Dehli, S. Heald, and K. McKenna (Eds) *Unsettling Relations: The University as a Site of Feminist Struggles*, Toronto, Women's Press.

Collard, S. and Stalker, J. 1991, Women's trouble: women, gender and the learning environment, in R. Hiemstra (Ed.) *Creating Environments for Effective Adult Learning*, San Francisco, Jossey-Bass.

Daloz, L. 1986, *Effective Teaching and Mentoring*, San Francisco, Jossey-Bass.

Daloz, L. 1991, Mentorship, in M. Galbraith (Ed.) *Adult Learning Methods*, Malabar, Kreiger.

Farwell Adams, H. 1983, Work in the interstices: women in academe. *Women's Studies International Forum*, Vol. 6, No. 2, pp. 135–141.

Fisher, B. 1982, Professing feminism: feminist academics and the women's movement. *Psychology of Women Quarterly*, Vol. 7, No. 1, pp. 55–69.

Fox Keller, E. and Moglen, H. 1987, Competition and feminism: conflicts for academic women. *Signs: Journal of Women in Culture and Society*, Vol. 12, No. 3, pp. 493–511.

Gilligan, C. 1982, *In a Different Voice. Psychological Theory and Women's Development*, Massachusetts, Harvard University Press.

Hardy Aiken, S., Anderson, K., Dinnerstein, M., Lensink, J. and MacCorquodale, P. 1987, Trying transformations: curriculum integration and the problem of resistance. *Signs: Journal of Women in Culture and Society*, Vol. 12, No. 2, pp. 255–275.

Henry, M. 1990, Voices of academic women on feminine gender scripts. *British Journal of Sociology of Education*, Vol. 11, No. 2, pp. 121–135.

Hill, S., Hilton Bahniuk, M., Dobos, J. and Rouner, D. 1989, Mentoring and other communication support in the academic setting. *Group and Organization Studies*, Vol. 14, No. 3, pp. 355–368.

Homer 1963, *The Odyssey*, trans. R. Fitzgerald, New York, Doubleday.

Houle, C. 1979, *Continuing Learning in the Professions*, San Francisco, Jossey-Bass.

Jacobi, M. 1991, Mentoring and undergraduate academic success: a literature review. *Review of Educational Research*, Vol. 61, No. 4, pp. 505–532.

Jensen, K. 1982, Women's work and academic culture: adaptations and confrontations. *Higher Education*, Vol. 11, No. 1, pp. 67–85.

Levinson, D, 1978. *The Seasons of a Man's Life*, New York, Knopf.

Lively, B., Barnett, C., Berger, B., Greer, M. and Holiday, M. 1992, Mentoring of faculty. Summary and bibliographic report. *American Journal of Pharmaceutical Education*, Vol. 56, pp. 82–83.

Lyons, W., Scroggins, D. and Bonham Rule, P. 1990. The mentor in graduate education. *Studies in Higher Education*, Vol. 15, No. 3, pp. 277–285.

McKay, N. 1983, Black woman professor – white university. *Women's Studies International Forum*, Vol. 6, No. 2, pp. 143–147.

Merriam, S. 1983, Mentors and proteges: a critical review of the literature. *Adult Education Quarterly*, Vol. 33, No. 3, pp. 161–173.

224 *Joyce Stalker*

Merriam, S., Thomas, T. and Zeph, C. 1987. Mentoring in higher education: What we know now. *Review of Higher Education*, 11, pp. 199–210.

Messervy, P. 1989, *Mentoring: An Aid to Career Development for Women*, Wellington, NZ, Health Services, EEO Development Unit.

Moglen, H. 1983, Power and empowerment. *Women's Studies International Forum*, Vol. 6, No. 2, pp. 131–134.

Noddings, N. 1984, *Caring: A Feminine Approach to Ethics and Moral Education*, California, University of California Press.

Phillips-Jones, L. 1982, *Mentors and Proteges*, New York, Arbor House.

Reskin, G. 1979, Academic sponsorship and scientists' careers. *Sociology of Education*, Vol. 52, pp. 129–146.

Roland Martin, J. 1990, The contradiction of the educated woman, in J. Antler and S. Knopp (Eds) *Changing Education. Women as Radicals and Conservators*, New York, State University of New York Press.

Sands, R., Parson, L. and Duane, J. 1991, Faculty mentoring faculty. *Journal of Higher Education*, Vol. 62, No. 2, pp. 174–193.

Sandler, B. and Hall, R. 1983, *Academic Mentoring for Women Students and Faculty: A New Look at an Old Way to Get Ahead*, Washington, DC: Project on the Status and Education of WOMEN.

Schockett, M. and Haring-Hidore, M. 1985, Factor analytic support for psychosocial and vocational mentoring functions. *Psychological Reports*, Vol. 57, pp. 627–630.

Shapiro, E., Hasletine, F., and Rowe, M. 1978, Moving up: role models, mentors and the 'Patron system'. *Sloan Management Review*, Vol. 19, pp. 51–58.

Simeone, A. 1987, *Academic Women, Working towards Equality*, Massachusetts, Bergin and Garvey.

Talpade Mohanty, C. 1983, On salvaging difference: the politics of black women's studies. *Women's Studies International Forum*, Vol. 6, No. 2, pp. 243–247.

Wright, C. and Wright, S. 1987, The role of mentors in the career development of young professionals. *Family Relations*, Vol. 36, No. 2, pp. 204–208.

14 Education for sale – at what cost?

Lifelong learning and the marketplace

Patricia A. Gouthro[1]
Mount Saint Vincent University, Canada

This paper examines the influence of the marketplace on discourses in lifelong learning and raises questions about the future direction of these discussions, drawing upon critical and feminist analyses. A brief overview of how the notion of lifelong learning has shifted from an emphasis on cooperation and shared development to a discourse of competition and individualism is given. Drawing upon the works of various educators, an overview is given of some of the ways in which the marketplace has influenced lifelong learning discourses and has become a pervasive presence in academia. Both critical and feminist analyses are used to examine how justice, equity issues, and critical thinking are suppressed when the marketplace becomes a predominant influence in education. An assessment of questions raised by educators working to challenge this marketplace orientation in lifelong learning and suggestions for further areas of research conclude the paper.

In recent years there has been a resurgence in interest in the concepts of lifelong learning and lifelong education that have garnered broad social, government, and corporate support. This support is often linked with a marketplace orientation that centres on learning primarily as a means to upgrade vocational and professional skills (Shipley 1997, Hatton 1997) and serves to reduce the dominant discourse in lifelong learning to a form of propaganda for industry that excludes many important educational and societal concerns. This agenda has been enthusiastically embraced by government and is shaping the educational policies of our universities and colleges to develop a narrowly constructed concept of lifelong education that benefits capitalist interests in industry by encouraging people to compete as educational consumers and producers. Within this context, the wider concept of lifelong learning has been conflated to mean lifelong training. Education that focuses on the broader goals of democratic citizenship or attends to the concerns of women and minorities is given low priority. Increased participation in adult education programmes is motivated primarily by the widespread perception that continuing education is needed within a globally competitive economy. A discourse of cooperation and development has been replaced with one of competition and profit (Delors 1996). That this orientation has emerged within the private sector is not surprising, but in recent years the encroaching influence of the marketplace has also become clearly evident within academia (Downey 1996, White and Hauck 2000).

This narrow focus limits the potential for lifelong education to foster democracy and fails to address the underlying ethical concerns that are often given low priority on the corporate agenda. Lifelong education becomes yet another item for consumption that demarcates the difference between those who are 'successful' in life, and those who are not. The marketplace focus undermines the critical orientation that has long been associated with the field of adult education. When industry and government assume responsibility for defining the types of curriculum and programmes that will receive financial support and funding, academic autonomy and freedom may be threatened. Despite discussion over the need for employees to have 'critical thinking skills', in vocational and professional training programmes students are usually not encouraged to develop the capacity to be truly critical. Issues such as sustainable development, the exploitation of human rights, and discriminatory practices are rarely explored in depth (Hart 1992).

Rationale for lifelong learning

The rapid rate of change created by modernization is the main justification that has been given to support the need to develop lifelong learning or a 'learning society' (Edwards 1997). Methven and Hansen (1997: 5) argue that traditional attitudes towards learning must be changed because 'the inherent weakness of a system in which it is assumed that one can be educated for life is that life itself changes'. The effect of globalization and rapid advances in technology indicate that change will continue at an even more rapid rate, thus intensifying the need for lifelong learning (Longworth and Davies 1996).

Over the years, UNESCO has taken an active role in promoting the concept of lifelong education. Regarding the 1947 Universal Declaration of Human Rights, Dave (1976: 17) argued that 'for the first time in history, education has been universally and officially accepted as a human right'. The term 'lifelong education' gained widespread usage and popularity after the UNESCO Faure (1972) report, *Learning to Be*, was published in which lifelong education was heralded as the answer to the multiple problems plaguing non-Western countries and was seen as an effective way to adapt to the rapid social and economic changes created by the swift technological advances of the twentieth century. Limiting educational efforts to primary levels for children was seen as insufficient as many dropped out before attaining adequate literacy levels. Instead, it was argued that educational opportunities should continue into adulthood

(Faure *et al.* 1972). Finger (1995: 111) writes about the UNESCO discussions in the sixties and seventies, stating that, 'adult education was to be part and parcel of the humanizing process'. Through lifelong learning, disadvantaged and developing nations could strive towards educating their populace, improving the quality of life for all citizens and enabling each individual to develop his/her unique potential. By sharing education between nations, we would have a more integrative and cohesive global community.

Unfortunately, the initial enthusiasm for lifelong learning as a solution to world problems seems to have largely dissipated. The optimism of the seventies has given way to a more pragmatic, some would say cynical approach to attending to global issues. The recent Delors (1996: 92) report for UNESCO notes that today education is often used to further divide the rich and the poor, North and South, by increasing the know-ledge gap and limiting access to learning technologies. It states that:

> the general climate of competition that is at present characteristic of economic activity, within and above all between nations, tends to give priority to the competitive spirit and individual success. Such competition now amounts to ruthless economic warfare and to a tension between rich and poor that is dividing nations and the world, and exacerbating historic rivalries.

Within the context of globalized capitalism, support for lifelong learning is not to lead to a more democratic and egalitarian world, but rather to situate individuals, groups, and even nation-states to gain a competitive advantage.

Lifelong learning that is defined by the profit oriented goals of industry, corporations, government, and policy makers is increasingly visible in academia. There is a trend towards vocationalism in post-secondary institutions and support for 'professionalization' which requires continuous educational upgrading and certification (Collins 1991). Within higher education there is a movement towards privatization (Rae 1996). Adult education literature and government policies discuss an agenda for adult educators that is defined by the need to prepare students to adapt to the exponential increase in information technologies (Shipley 1997, Hatton 1997). Discourses in lifelong learning often focus primarily on connections between adult education and the paid workplace and are based on the underlying assumption that the value of education is largely determined by how useful it is in training people to successfully participate in and adapt to the evolving global marketplace. The primary motive governing educational policy decisions is the rendering of greater financial profits, which are perceived to be beneficial for industry, government and society as a whole (Tasker and Packman 1994). Competition is the driving force behind this rationale for lifelong learning, whether it is the individual motivation that encourages a particular student to upgrade his or her academic qualifications for the workplace, or the funding support provided by industry or government to academia in order to provide specialized training programmes.

Chapman and Aspin (1997: 156) note that recent policy papers (the European Parliament 1995, Nordic Council of Ministers 1995, UNESCO, Delors 1996, OECD 1996) support a broader definition of the concept of lifelong education. Lifelong learning is perceived to have intrinsic value, in which

> people engaging in educational activities are enriched by having their view of the world and their capacity for rational choice continually expanded and transformed by increasing varieties of experiences and cognitive achievements that the lifelong learning experiences offers (Chapman and Aspin 1997: 156).

The marketplace orientation in lifelong education is rejected as too narrow a conception of the potentiality for human learning. Yet at the same time, the interests of the marketplace continue to be the predominantly represented within political and economic discourses. Quite often only 'lip service' is paid to other focuses for educational attainment. Educators working from critical and feminist perspectives raise a number of serious issues that need to be addressed as we examine the future direction of lifelong learning.

The corporate climate in academia

Throughout academia, the influence of the corporate sector is growing in an insidious and pervasive manner. Hartley (1995: 412) noted that 'in education, as in other parts of the welfare state, the maxim of the hour is "doing more with less", or "optimising resources"'. Education is being pressured towards a competitive rather than cooperative mode and is linked with national success. As funding is being cut back from government sources, universities are forced to look closer to the private sector for financial assistance. Corporate sponsorship is creeping into universities, affecting everything from the soft drink beverages offered on campus, to control of the bookstores, the names of buildings, and the constant barrage of advertisements displayed everywhere from the margins of web course sites to televisions running constant commercials in student lounges (White and Hauck 2000).

Tasker and Packman (1994: 182) point out that for many people, 'the relationship between higher education, industry and the government is still seen by many as unproblematic: industry needs highly trained employees and it is the function of government to see that universities provide them'. Turning to the private sector in order to fund higher education is perceived by many to be a practical alternative in the face of huge government deficits (Downey 1996). Students who are worried about employment prospects when they graduate are anxious to obtain job-related skills and information.

Universities are under increasing pressure to attend to the needs of the marketplace. Ryan and Heim (1997) argue that with increased competition and change, it is inevitable that universities will work in closer alignment with industry. This can be a mutually beneficial arrangement, providing financial supports for the institution, employment opportunities for students, and research funding for faculty. Ryan and Heim (1997: 46) note that 'universities are often viewed as a reservoir of intellect and often aggressively market technology to potential users in the private sector', while in industry-driven partnerships the initial approach is made by the industry that is looking for research targeted to a specific problem. In government-supported university-industry relationships, 'the state and the university often team, projecting a seamless set of attributes that make an attractive package to an expanding or relocating industry' (1997: 49). Corporate sponsored research is becoming a thriving business. Huber (2000: 107) notes that 'according to a report from the Association of University Technology Managers, universities in the United States and Canada made $592 million in 1996 from licences and royalties from research sold to corporations.'

Downey (1996: 74) describes the university as a trinity composed of three interrelated components; corporation, collegium, and community. He argues that financial cutbacks will lead to the corporate aspect of universities being emphasized. The demands for accountability will increase since universities will have to rely more upon student tuition and private sector funding in order to operate (1996: 78). As a consequence, universities will foster stronger relationships with industry.

Suggesting that universities need to attract more business clientele, Moser and Seaman (1987: 228) suggest that 'it would behoove educators to be as flexible as possible in structuring activities, while at the same time conveying this willingness to members of the training community.' In this way, they may be able to attract more opportunities to provide training for businesses and corporations. Cooper *et al.* (1995: 79) argue the importance of developing flexible courses, suited to various 'customer needs' and suggest that adult and community education can be perceived as 'essentially consumer-driven and client-responsive'. Developing research initiatives to better understand 'consumer needs' in education will lead to the goal of 'achieving organisational effectiveness, that is, high quality in courses and in teaching' (1995: 80)—whereby the determination of 'high quality' is assessed according to the needs of the marketplace. Francis Hill (1997: 212) argues that universities need to examine the discrepancies between consumer expectations and experience to ensure 'customer satisfaction'. To assure 'quality control', students need to be guaranteed consistency with regards to performance and dependability, and it should be made clear 'to all personnel, that student satisfaction is an institutional priority' (1997: 228).

Challenging corporate values

There are numerous concerns in attempting to follow a narrowly deterministic economic agenda. First of all, there is a practical difficulty with regards to determining what is 'valuable' education, even within the context of the marketplace. Collins (1991: 45) writes that 'in the present political climate, so-called competency-based education defines useful knowledge in the light of bureaucratic and corporate needs'. One of the problems with this approach, however, is determining the needs of industry. As Dyke (1997: 5–6) has pointed out, 'defining the needs of industry has proved to be quite elusive'. Prickett (1994: 174) also notes that 'historically we have rarely been able to predict in advance what subjects may turn out to have practical value'. Even if educators chose to follow this route, it is not as clearly marked out as one might initially think.

Moving beyond this initial critique of determining educational 'value' to a broader analysis, educators raise numerous points about the limited context of an education oriented towards the marketplace. Morley (1997: 234) argues that this approach undermines any commitment to social justice or equal rights, stating that 'as concepts of consumerism and individual rights and choice gain currency, questions arise as to how equity values can be sustained in the increasing emphasis on economic/ efficiency models' which educational institutions are currently being based upon. Within this context, the demand for accountability is based upon maximizing profit and serves to reinforce rather than challenge inequalities in the distribution of wealth and power in society. Morley (1997: 234) notes that 'the new culture in the public services obscures the fact that what counts as efficiency and effectiveness is itself both a political judgement and a social construct'. Determining what is an efficient or effective means of educating people is subjectively defined.

Increasingly, academics are held 'accountable', so that 'advocates of educational reform' are required 'to provide economic legitimacy for their policies' (Dyke 1997:8). Under an economic agenda, the value of an education is closely linked with how effective it is in providing the student with employment opportunities. Huber explains (2000: 109):

> As universities accept the corporate mandate of the market, students have watched departments such as anthropology, French, Spanish, comparative literature, cultural studies, and a variety of history, art, and social science courses cut because administrators would rather use the resources to expand the business school. Using 'supply and demand' as a justification, administrators who make sweeping staffing

and curricular changes claim that they are acting in accordance with what the job market requires, and that their responsibility is to prepare students for the job market. In the process, the idea that every student is more than just a worker-to-be is lost.

Allman and Wallis (1997: 115) give an example of this, noting that when enrolment for their Freirian courses declined, they were cancelled, as their department decided to offer more 'market friendly' courses. Students may not be initially interested in critical disclosures because they have never been exposed to them. But if the purpose of a liberal education is to broaden students' perspectives they need to be exposed to alternative theoretical perspectives. It is doubtful this will happen if programs are determined largely by market interests.

Henkel found many academics are leery of new approaches to assuring 'quality' in university education as it is linked with 'market values: consumerism and the idea of customer-led higher education' (1997: 141). She summarizes their concerns, that 'quality assurance' is 'connected with an under-valuing of individualism, excellence and risk, espousing instead a "predictable mediocrity"' (1997: 141).

Barrett (1996: 70) warns against the idea of treating students as 'customers', arguing that 'the term "customer", unlike "student", "scholar", "learner", and "intellectual" involves no implication of engaging in the life of the mind, and embodies no preference for making intelligent rather than unintelligent choices, or for proceeding in a disciplined rather than a desultory or capricious manner'. Barrett argues that customers do not have to be responsible for their actions in the same way as students or learners do. He writes:

> A customer can be satisfied simply because of the end-use features of what has been purchased in the mall. This is entirely compatible with total ignorance of the product's method of fabrication or of any externalities, such as pollution or resource depletion, or of any attendant issues, such as the use of foreign labour. The satisfied customer can then be a model of contented narcissistic superficiality. This is hardly the inspiration for improvements in education.
>
> (1996: 70–71)

While one would hope that all customers and consumers are not as blandly ignorant of issues such as environmental degradation as Barrett implies, his point is a valid one in that there is no onus on the customer to develop this awareness. As educators, however, we would hope that developing a more acute critical awareness of the global nature of our society would be a key and important issue to address in teaching our students. If education is designed primarily to provide students with credentials to advance themselves to a more competitive position in the paid workplace, however, it might very well overlook some of these more profound and disturbing issues that should be addressed.

The private funding of research in universities may influence the kind of research that is supported, as well as in some instances, limiting academic freedom. Research for profit may benefit corporations, but may not be the most beneficial for the larger society. A recent CAUT (Canadian Association of University Teachers) bulletin discusses an incident where David Healy, a medical scholar, was recruited to become a professor at the University of Toronto and the clinical director of the mood and anxiety disorders programme at the Centre for Addiction and Mental Health. Healy gave a conference presentation where he expressed concerns that some medical research may be suppressed because it may impact on pharmaceutical sales. He gave the example of how there has been considerable medical controversy that suggests some antidepressants such as Prozac may lead to suicides in patients—but no research has been done on this topic. The following week Healy was fired. The University of Toronto president denies that Prozac's manufacturer, Eli Lily and Co., a private donor to the centre, exerted any pressure in this case. However, in the email to Healy that explained why he was not a good 'fit', it stated, 'This view was solidified by your recent appearance at the Centre in the context of an academic lecture ... We do not feel your approach is compatible with the goals for the development of the academic and clinical resources that we have' (CAUT May 2001). Clearly, there is a cost to private funding for research, but if it is the price of academic freedom, then we need to reconsider if it is too steep to support.

Educational inequalities

Education that is based on a marketplace agenda may serve to perpetuate rather than eradicate inequalities. People who are most likely to participate in adult education programmes tend to have higher levels of education to begin with (Merriam and Cafferella 1991, Shipley 1997). Those at the lowest end of the social spectrum are less likely to be involved in formal types of education in adulthood. Critical theorists note that while it is important for industry to have workers who possess a high level of technical skills, they do not need for everyone to have it (Apple 1990, Hart 1992). Dyke (1997: 5) examines the historical tensions created by having an educated citizenry, arguing that 'education is viewed as essential to the reproduction of the economic structure, yet feared as a potential source of individual empowerment'. For the elite to maintain existing power relations, workers must attain the skills required to function in a highly technical workplace. To go beyond that, however, may create dissatisfied populace.

Forrester *et al.* (1995) argue that access to lifelong learning creates a schism between the core and peripheral workforce. The core workforce has greater educational opportunities and supports than marginal workers who are frequently unemployed or underemployed. Women and minorities are more likely to occupy the peripheral workforce and the effect of multinationals on developing the global economy has further perpetuated these divisions. Forrester *et al.* (1995: 294) argue that 'the influence of multinationals is far from benign. While they may be functional from the abstract point of view of capital, they are dysfunctional for both marginalized sectors of society in the North and whole national economies in the South which have inherited the mantle of colonialism'. Hart (1992) discusses how within global capitalism capital is able to be mobilized and transported to countries which provide 'cheap labour'. She argues that 'By undermining the bargaining power of workers, this global dispersement contributes to a reduction of labor costs, or the "cheapening" of labor in industrialized countries themselves' (1992: 28).

As the power of multinational corporations continues to evolve, an uneven playing field emerges across which nation-states compete to situate their economies in the most advantageous position. Countries in the South have fewer options than those in the North and this is revealed in the types of labour practices emerging. As Naomi Klein (2000) notes, the shift in production is no longer easily defined by clear-cut jobs moving from one country to another. Instead it is 'orders' that define what employment opportunities will be available in the production sector. 'Free zones' where local labour and environmental laws can be ignored spring up in the periphery of less developed nations. Large industries such as Nike, the Gap, or Reebok find local companies that employ a marginalized labour force consisting primarily of young women from poor, rural areas. Sometimes sleeping on floors between spray painted lines, treated with the same consideration as cars in an urban parking garage, these young women become a disposable labour force that displaces them as soon as they become pregnant, disabled by poor and unsafe working conditions, or too old to withstand the gruelling 10–12 hour days. This is one aspect of the gritty reality of the 'new economy' rarely acknowledged by either the big corporations or governments that espouse the ideals of life-long learning and the consumer economy.

Globalized capitalism has created an environment of cutthroat competition, leading to corporate restructuring and downsizing that establishes a climate of uncertainty. Within countries in the North, those who are employed often do not have permanent jobs or careers, but sustain a tenuous existence on short-term contract positions or part-time forms of employment. Klein (2000) talks about the whole generation of young people who work at places such as Walmart or Starbucks where they are permanently part-time, without benefits or long-term job security. This peripheral workforce is poorly represented by unions and have little access to the benefits of full-time employees, such as funding for education (Forrester *et al.* 1995). The trend towards outsourcing employment means that a wider pool of casual contract employees has become the norm. As Hake (1999: 84) notes, with this comes the increasing expectation of 'the willingness of employees to accept individual responsibility for investing in education and training'. Rifkin (1995) speculates that the world of work, with regular, full-time employment as the norm for most individuals, will eventually cease to exist.

The fractured workforce is one driven by constant competition and the need to 'upgrade' skills in order to survive. While the overall material wealth of many nations continues to evolve, a smaller proportion of the population will control a larger percentage of these assets. Thomas Frank (2000) discusses how shareholder capitalism has served the interests of the elite by perpetuating a myth that everyone is able to share in ownership of companies, thereby redistributing the wealth that is generated by these companies. The reality, however, is that the bulk of corporate shares are clustered in the hands of a privileged few. Frank (2000: 96–97) points out that even a strong supporter of the 'new economy', Lester Thurow, has noted that 'a full 86% of the market's advances in the last four years of the bull market ... went to the wealthiest 10% of the population. The majority of the population, not owning any stock at all, shared in the great money handout not at all'. The consequence of this, argues Frank (2000: 97), is that 'the booming stock market of the nineties did not democratize wealth; it concentrated wealth'. Despite overall increases in profits from global capitalism in the last couple of decades, most people have not benefited. The rich are indeed becoming richer, while the poor become poorer.

The ideal of lifelong education as a means to ensure a more equitable world seems impossibly naive in the current context of globalized capitalism. The logic of the marketplace urges competition over cooperation, personal advancement over social justice. Within this context, adult educators must ask themselves, is it possible to address issues of equity, equality and democracy in lifelong learning?

Developing critical and feminist analysis

Rising support for the notion of lifelong learning will provide opportunities in higher education and adult education to provide programs for increasing numbers of mature students and adult learners. Coldstream (1994: 167) seductively discusses the number of opportunities for adult educational ventures, noting 'What a market for trainers, distance-learning packages, college and universities'. Educators are no more immune to the challenges of working in an increasingly globalized workplace than any other sector is. Few full-time academic positions are coming open, and competition is stiff (Caplan 1994). The temptation to reap the profits from new academic ventures is a very tantalizing prospect. However, as adult educators we need to examine the underlying values which determine the thrust of these educational opportunities. As Jack Mezirow (2000: 30) notes, 'adult educators are never neutral'.

Critical and feminist theorists serve to challenge the predominant influence of the marketplace in lifelong learning. While the perspectives of these theorists represents diverse viewpoints, the shared focus is the commitment towards developing an educational agenda that is attentive to issues of social justice, equitable practice, and democratic ideals. By examining some of these different perspectives, insights into an alternative framework for lifelong learning may be explored.

Wilson (1993) argues that the professionalization of the field of adult education has meant that the field has been largely shaped by a technical-rational influence. The trend towards professionalization is a movement away from the critical perspective of adult education movements that were interested in initiating social changes. In assessing the role of the educator, Michael Apple (1990: 10–11) points out that:

> It is in understanding these hegemonic relations that we need to remember something which Gramsci maintained – that there are two requirements for ideological hegemony. It is not merely that our economic order 'creates' categories and structures of feeling which saturate our everyday lives. Added to this must be a group of 'intellectuals' who employ and give legitimacy to the categories, who make the ideological forms seem neutral.

Educators who promote programmes that support the dominant economic paradigm are an important part of the process of legitimating this approach to education. Collins (1991: 68) argues that educators need to develop a critical approach that challenges students to view education as more than a commodity and to look beyond their own needs. He states:

> Even though true needs cannot be identified by merely asking people what they want, it is not the role of adult educators to make the actual distinctions on behalf of others. Rather, their task is to organize pedagogical situations where it becomes possible to understand more clearly how needs are constituted, whose interests are served, and in what ways they emerge in the context of their everyday lives.
>
> (1991: 68)

To do this, educators need to have a broader understanding of adult education theory. Students need to be actively engaged and involved in defining the educational agenda, not as consumers selecting the best product on the market, but by questioning their own underlying assumptions and beliefs in order to develop greater critical capacities as reflective learners.

Stephen Brookfield argues that ideology critique needs to become central to critical reflection if important learning is to occur. Brookfield (2000: 128) states that 'critical reflection as ideology critique focuses on helping people come to an awareness of how capitalism shapes belief systems and assumptions (ideologies) that justify and maintain economic and political inequity'. Unless educators strive to develop in people the capacity to understand how ideology is constructed and sustained, learners will have a limited comprehension of the forces that are shaping their lives.

Frank (2000) points out that people in positions of corporate power have an incredible array of advertising and marketing resources at their disposal to shape images of a benevolent and democratic marketplace. Tara Fenwick (1998) assesses how the type of workplace education that is often fostered today encourages an almost spiritual level of commitment from the employee to contribute to the corporation's need for productivity and innovation, without assessing the individual risks and uncertainty of employment that are an only too real aspect of the 'new economy'. This creates a number of paradoxes for employees in the so called 'learning organizations'. Fenwick (1998: 151) argues that 'employees, told to trust in the corporation's benevolent human-growth-centred agenda, are invited to confess and transform their innermost desires and beliefs, to stick out their necks and keep learning and forget that they are in constant danger of being summarily ejected'. Workplace education that is only directed by a marketplace agenda fails to assess many of the real needs and concerns of employees.

Developing a critical theoretical assessment of the influence of the marketplace on lifelong learning, Michael Welton (1995: 132) questions how 'liberal democratic countries have now adopted the rhetoric of "lifelong learning" and speak of the need for massive "job training"'. Drawing upon Habermasion theory, he argues that the 'lifeworld'—the communicatively shaped sphere encompassing home and community, is under siege by the system—the political-economic structure, as evidenced by the increasing impact of the marketplace on education. The effects of mass media and culture can be seen in how 'the newly inflated roles of consumer and client channel the influence of the system to the lifeworld' (1995: 147). Values are taught through a constant barrage of media and advertising, rather than being constructed within families and communities. The traditional roles of worker and citizen are disempowered, thus limiting the potential for emancipatory types of learning.

While not discounting the importance of assessing how we can develop workplace learning that is truly beneficial to employees, Welton argues that we also need to broaden the purposes of lifelong learning to include consideration of learning for citizenship. Civil society is an essential component of this type of learning, as it is the arena of grassroots political discourse that can serve to challenge the predominant influence of the marketplace. He writes (2001: 20):

In the 21st century lifelong learning has emerged as the regnant paradigm for the global era. The design of a just learning society, scarcely begun, requires social learning theory that can offer necessary conceptual elements for policy makers and practitioners. Work, state and civil society comprise the fundamental domains of lifelong and lifewide learning.

Through civil society movements, it may be possible to raise issues of equity and justice, environmental concerns, and political representation that tend to be left out of marketplace and workplace learning. The grassroots organizations of civil society encompass various activist groups that represent the needs of citizens and different communities.

In her discussion of women and citizenship, Jane Elliott (2000: 16) argues that 'lifelong learning can encourage a greater participation in civil and political society through a curriculum focusing on the nature of our civil society and its institutions'. Taking a critical feminist approach to help understand the potentiality of civil society movements, I have suggested in previous writing (see Gouthro 2000) that we also need to consider connections to the homeplace. The participation of women in activist groups to address safety and environmental issues, both at local and global levels, has often been linked with concerns connected to the homeplace, whether it be birth defects caused by contaminated drinking water to laws that do not adequately address issues of domestic abuse.

Feminist writers often address the life demeaning and life destroying activities of the marketplace that lead to dehumanizing labour practices and threaten the sustainability of the environment (Bhasim 1994). As Angela Miles (1998: 251) argues, 'everywhere, the exigencies of global competition and the global market are used to enforce policies that put priority on unfettered transnational profit making at the expense of people and the planet'. Drawing upon both critical and feminist perspectives, Mechthild Hart (1992: 89) argues that 'a narrow, instrumental view of work translates into a view of education which places 'immediate relevance' and efficiency above concerns for overall human development and well-being'. Hart (1992) argues that subsistence forms of labour, such as motherwork, are traditionally overlooked or devalued in educational discourses. Giving primacy to education that is always linked with returns in the marketplace contributes to a value structure that undermines the lifeworld. Hart argues for the need to develop an educational agenda that focuses on issues about life rather than just profit.

Reclaiming lifelong learning

If lifelong learning is to be more than some vague and ubiquitous term that has no real meaning or impact, educators must strive to reclaim some of the sense of agency that first gave meaning to the notions of lifelong

learning, lifelong education, and the learning society. A more holistic
approach to lifelong learning needs to be advocated that attends to issues
of social justice, access, and inequalities. Both feminist and critical theoretical discourses reveal some of the limitations of the marketplace orientation to lifelong learning. Educators need to continually reflect upon
how they conceive of and understand the notion of lifelong learning to
incorporate a broader understanding that encompasses learning that
occurs outside of the marketplace. Issues around citizenship, subsistence
labour and learning, and inequalities in educational access are examples
of some of the topics that require further exploration to develop a
broader conception of lifelong education. Educators need to be vocal
about their concerns to ensure that the 'logic' of the marketplace will not
be the primary directive for discourses on lifelong learning.

Note

1 *Patricia Gouthro* is currently the head of the Graduate Adult Education programme at Mount Saint Vincent University in Halifax, Nova Scotia, Canada,
B3M 2J6. Her most recent work includes an article in *The Canadian Journal for the
Studies of Adult Education* (2002) called 'What Counts? Examining academic
values and women's life experiences from a critical feminist perspective' and an
article in *Convergence* (2000) called 'Globalization, civil society, and the homeplace'. She may be contacted at patricia.gouthro@msvu.ca.

References

Allman, P. and Wallis, J. (1997) Commentary: Paulo Freire and the future of the
radical tradition. *Studies in the Education of Adults*, 29, 113–120.
Apple, M. W. (1990) *Ideology and Curriculum* (New York: Routledge).
Barrett, L. R. (1996) On students as customers – some warnings from America.
Higher Education Review, 28, 70–73.
Bhasim, K. (1994) Let us look again at development, education and women. *Con-
vergence* XXVII, 5–13.
Brookfield, S. D. (2000) Transformative learning as ideology critique. In Mezirow,
J. and Associates (eds) *Learning as Transformation: Critical Perspectives on a Theory
in Progress* (San Francisco: Jossey-Bass).
Caplan, P. J. (1994) *Lifting a Ton of Feathers: A Woman's Guide to Surviving in the Aca-
demic World* (Toronto: University of Toronto Press).
Canadian Association of University Teachers (CAUT) Bulletin (May 2001) Acade-
mic freedom in jeopardy in Toronto, 48, 1.
Chapman, J. and Aspin, D. (1997) Schools as centres of lifelong learning for all. In
M. J. Hatton (ed.) *Lifelong Learning: Policies, Practices, and Programs* (Toronto,
Ontario: School of Media Studies, Humber College) pp. 154–167.
Coldstream, P. (1994) Training minds for tomorrow: a shared responsibility.
Higher Education Quarterly, 40, 160–167.
Collins, M. (1991) *Adult Education as a Vocation: A Critical Role for Adult Educators*
(London: Routledge).
Cooper, T, Velde, C. and Gerber, R. (1995) A survey on the education and train-

ing of adult and community educators for the workplace. *Studies in the Education of Adults*, 27, 79–91.

Dave, R. H. (ed.) (1976) *Foundations of Lifelong Education.* (Oxford: UNESCO: Pergamon Press).

Delors, J. (chairman) (1996) *Learning: The Treasure Within – Report to UNESCO of the International Commission on Education for the Twenty-first Century* (Paris, France: UNESCO Publishing).

Downey, J. (1996) The university as trinity: balancing corporation, collegium, and community. *Innovative Higher Education*, 21, 73–85.

Dyke, M. (1997) Reflective learning as reflexive education in a risk society: empowerment and control? *International Journal of Lifelong Education*, 16, 2–17.

Edwards, R. (1997) *Changing Places? Flexibility, lifelong learning and a learning society* (London: Routledge).

Elliott, J. (2000) The challenge of lifelong learning as a means of extending citizenship for women. *Studies in the Education of Adults*, 32, 6–21.

European Parliament (1995) *Commission of the European Communities: Amended Proposal for a European Year of Lifelong Learning.* Brussels: European Parliament Publications Office.

Faure, E., Herrera, F., Kaddouila, A. R., Lopes, H., Petrovsky, A. V., Rahnema, M. and Ward, F. C. (1972) *Learning to be: The world of education today and tomorrow* (Paris, France: UNESCO).

Fenwick, T. (1998) Questioning the concept of the learning organization. In Scott, S. M., Spencer, B. and Thomas, A. M. (eds) *Learning for Life: Canadian Readings in Adult Education* (Toronto: Thompson Educational Publishing, Inc.) pp. 140–152.

Finger, M. (1995) Adult education and society today. *International Journal of Lifelong Education*, 14, 110–119.

Forrester, K., Payne, J. and Ward, K. (1995) Lifelong education and the workplace: a critical analysis. *International Journal of Lifelong Education*, 14, 292–305.

Frank, T. (2000) *One Market Under God: Extreme Capitalism, Market Populism, and the End of Economic Democracy* (New York: Doubleday).

Gouthro, P. A. (2000) Globalization, civil society and the homeplace. *Convergence*, XXXIII, 57–77.

Hake, B. J. (1999) Lifelong learning in late modernity: the challenges to society, organizations, and individuals. *Adult Education Quarterly*, 49, 79–90.

Hart, M. (1992) *Working and Educating for Life: Feminist and International Perspectives on Adult Education* (London: Routledge).

Hartley, D. (1995) The 'McDonaldization' of higher education: food for thought? *Oxford Review of Education*, 21, 409–423.

Hatton, M. J. (1997) *Lifelong Learning: Policies, Practices and Programs* (Toronto, Ontario: School of Media Studies, Humber College).

Henkel, M. (1997) Academic values and the university as corporate enterprise. *Higher Education Quarterly*, 51, 134–143.

Hill, F. (1997) The implications of service quality theory for British higher education: an exploratory longitudinal study. *The Journal of General Education*, 46, 207–231.

Huber, S. (2000) Tough customers: business' plan to corner the student market. In White, G. D. and Hauck, F. C. (eds) *Campus Inc.: Corporate Power in the Ivory Tower* (New York: Prometheus Books) pp. 106–118.

Klein, N. (2000) *No Logo: Taking Aim at the Brand Bullies* (Canada: Alfred A. Knopf).

Longworth, N. and Davies, W. K. (1996) *Lifelong Learning* (London: Kogan Page).

Merriam, S. B. and Caffarella, R. (1991) *Learning in Adulthood* (San Francisco: Jossey-Bass).

Methven, P. J. B. and Hansen, J. J. (1997) Half a revolution: a brief survey of life-long learning in New Zealand. In Hatton, M. J. (ed.) *Lifelong Learning: Policies, Practices, and Programs*, (Toronto, Ontario: School of Media Studies) pp. 2–17.

Mezirow, J. (2000) Learning to think as an adult. In Mezirow, J. and Associates. Learning as transformation: critical perspective on a theory in progress (San Francisco: Jossey-Bass) pp. 3–34.

Miles, A. (1998) Learning from the women's movement in the neo-liberal period. In Scott, S. M., Spencer, B., and Thomas, A. M. (eds) *Learning for Life: Canadian Readings in Adult Education* (Toronto: Thompson Educational Publishing, Inc.) 250–258.

Morley, L. (1997). Change and Equity in Higher Education. *British Journal of Sociology of Education*, 18, 231–142.

Moser, K. and Seaman, D. (1987) Implications for potential linkages between business-industry and higher education. *Adult Education Quarterly*, 37, 223–229.

Nordic Council of Ministers (1995) *The Golden Riches in the Grass: Lifelong Learning for All*. Copenhagen: Nordic Council of Ministers.

OECD (1996) *Making Lifelong Learning a Reality for All*. Paris: OECD.

Prickett, S. (1994) Enterprise in higher education: nice work or ivory tower versus exchange & mart. *Higher Education Quarterly*, 40, 169–181.

Rae, P. (1996) New directions: privatization and higher education in Alberta. *The Canadian Journal of Higher Education*, XXXVI-2, 59–80.

Rifkin, J. (1995) *The End of Work: the Decline of the Global Labour Force and the Dawn of the Post-market Era* (New York: G.P. Putnam's Sons).

Ryan, J. H. and Heim, A. A. (1997) Promoting economic development through university and industry partnerships. *New Directions for Higher Education*, 97, 42–50.

Shipley, L. (1997) An overview of adult education and training in Canada. In Shipley, L. (ed.) *Adult Education and Training in Canada* (Human Resources Development Canada) pp. 1–25.

Tasker, M. and Packman, D. (1994). Government, higher education and the industrial ethic, *Higher Education Quarterly*, 48, 3, 180–187.

Welton, M. R. (1995) In defense of the lifeworld: a Habermasian approach to adult learning. In Welton, M. R. (ed.) *In Defense of the Lifeworld: Critical Perspectives on Adult Learning* (NY: State University of New York Press) pp. 127–156.

Welton, M. R. (2001) Civil society and the public sphere: Habermas's recent learning theory. *Studies in the Education of Adults*, 33, 20–34.

White, G. D. and Hauck, F. C. (eds) (2000) *Campus, Inc.: Corporate Power in the Ivory Tower* (New York: Prometheus Books).

Wilson, A. L. (1993) The common concern: controlling the professionalization of adult education. *Adult Education Quarterly*, 44, 1–16.

Part 3

... and lifelong learning

15 The concept of experiential learning and John Dewey's theory of reflective thought and action

Reijo Miettinen[1]

University of Helsinki, Finland

The conception of experiential learning is an established approach in the tradition of adult education theory. David Kolb's four-stage model of experiential learning is a fundamental presentation of the approach. In his work *Experiential Learning*, Kolb states that John Dewey, Kurt Lewin and Jean Piaget are the founders of the approach. The article discusses Kolb's eclectic method of constructing his model of experiential learning. It studies how Kolb introduces and uses the Lewinian tradition of action research and the work of John Dewey to substantiate his model. It is concluded that Kolb generalizes a historically very specific and unilateral mode of experience – feedback session in T-group training – into a general model of learning. Kolb's interpretation of John Dewey's ideas is compared to Dewey's concepts of reflective thought and action. It is concluded that Kolb gives an inadequate interpretation of Dewey's thought and that the very concept of immediate, concrete experience proposed by the experiential learning approach is epistemologically problematic. The theory historical approach of the article discusses both substantial questions related to experiential learning and the way concepts are appropriated, developed and used within adult education theory.

Introduction

Experiential learning is an important approach within the theoretical tradition of adult education in Europe, North America and Australia (see e.g. Boud *et al.* 1985; Boud and Miller 1996; Weil and McGill 1989). The approach, or movement, has a special nature as a cognitive enterprise and it can also be seen as a kind of ideology needed to confront the diverse challenges of adult education. Its theoretical frame has diverse sources of inspiration: the T-group movement, the learning style technology, humanistic psychology and critical social theory. It has been influential in the literature of management training as well as adult education *per se*. Without doubt, the two concepts that characterize the approach most clearly are experience and reflection.

In this paper, I shall evaluate the concept of experience, primarily from an epistemological point of view, that is, as a representation of learning and the process of gaining new knowledge. I will argue that in the light of the philosophical studies on the ways of gaining new knowledge of the world, the model of experiential learning is inadequate. Through its humanistic connection, the concept of experience also has an ideological function: faith in an individual's innate capacity to grow and learn. This is what makes it particularly attractive for adult education theorists and for the idea of life-long learning. The humanistic connection is also epistemologically significant, since it strengthens the methodological individualism of experiential learning. To fully evaluate the legacy of the experiential learning approach, the concept of reflection and its roots in critical theory should also be analysed. In this paper, I shall focus on the concept of experience. These two concepts are, however, interrelated. It is experience that is reflected. If the conception of experience is problematic, so is the possibility of its reflection.

David Kolb's book *Experiential Learning* (1984) is perhaps the best known presentation of the approach. Kolb's four-stage model of learning elaborated in the book is regarded as classical and as a foundation for experiential learning. It is used routinely as a source in the literature of the field and in the theses of adult education students. It has been an important starting point for several attempts to develop adult education theory (Jarvis 1987; Weil and McGill 1989). It has been used as a foundation for formulating a theory of organizational learning (Dixon 1994). It also has been widely used in management consultation, leadership training and in research on cognitive processing styles. There are, therefore, good grounds for studying carefully the theoretical foundations of Kolb's work. That will help in a more general way regarding some of the basic tenets of experiential learning.

Within the scope of an article, it is impossible to discuss all the various themes and concepts presented by Kolb in his book. Therefore, I shall follow the following procedure. First, I shall discuss Kolb's method of constructing the model. Second, I shall study how Kolb derives his model, which he claims to be a Lewinian model, from the tradition of Lewinian action research and small group research. Third, I will study how Kolb introduces and uses the work of John Dewey to substantiate his own model. I compare this interpretation to the recent interpretations of Dewey specialists in philosophy concerning Dewey's concept of experience and reflective thought (e.g. Burke 1994; Campbell 1995; Welschman 1995) and to the idea based on my own reading of Dewey's theory. This critical method will elucidate both the substantial questions related to experiential learning and the way Kolb uses historical sources in his book. In more general terms, it also deals with the problem of how concepts are appropriated, developed and used within adult education theory.

Kolb's eclectic method and its consequences

Evaluation of Kolb's model and book is a problematic task. The book represents a special genre of writing, which could be characterized as consultancy literature. It was originally formulated to state arguments for the utility of the sociotechnology previously developed by the author in the 1960s: the Learning Style Inventory (LSI). The first version of the model was presented to substantiate the use of the inventory in a book of exercise in *Organizational Psychology* (Kolb *et al.* 1971: 28). The main application of the model was to manage and gain control of individual learning by inventing one's learning style (Kolb 1976a, 1976b). By recognizing her or his own learning style profile and goals, an individual is meant 'to choose which set of learning abilities he will bring to bear in any specific learning situation'. In *Experiential Learning* (1984) Kolb tries to elaborate further both the foundations of the model and the extended societal application of the Learning Style Inventory. Because the author is the developer of this technology, the book can also be seen as a marketing promotion.

The social technological and practical background is reflected in the way theorizing proceeds in the book. The substantiation of the model combines widely different ingredients: ideas, terms and conceptions from many sources. The concepts are defined briefly and without adequate reference to the background literature. As a result, these concepts often remain unclear and open to many interpretations. On the other hand, the book has a programmatic nature. It claims to present solutions to many burning problems of adult education and working life in western, postmodern society.

Kolb starts his book by defining the historical roots of experiential learning. According to him, the founding fathers and developers of the conceptions are John Dewey, Kurt Lewin and Jean Piaget. Kolb presents in a graphical form the conceptions of learning of these three theoreticians (Kolb 1984: 22, 24, 25). After presenting the three founding fathers, Kolb states that the approach was further developed by therapeutic psychologies based on psychoanalysis (Carl Jung, Erik Erikson) and humanistic psychology (Carl Rogers and Abraham Maslow) as well as by radical educationists such as Paulo Freire and Ivan Illich. He also utilizes the results of neurophysiology which report the functional differences between the right and left hemispheres of the human cortex and to the theory of world models presented by the American philosopher Stephen Pepper. He further indicates (1984: 17) that techniques and methods such as those employed in T-groups and action research have contributed to the conception of experiential learning. Kolb says that he does not want to develop an alternative theory of learning, 'but rather to suggest through experiential learning theory a holistic integrative perspective on learning that combines experience, perception, cognition, and behavior' (1984: 21).

This procedure and method can be called eclectic. Kolb unites terms and concepts, extracting them from their idea-historical contexts and purposes and puts them to serve the motives of his own presentation. As a result, theoreticians with quite different backgrounds, motives and incompatible conceptions can be used as founders and 'supporters' of experiential learning. This happens when Kolb lumps together Carl Jung, Kurt Lewin and John Dewey with humanistic psychologists, as founders and developers of experiential learning. One cannot help concluding that Kolb's motive is not critical evaluation or interdisciplinarity but an attempt to construct an 'attractive' collection of ideas that can be advocated as a solution to the social problems of our time and to substantiate the usefulness of his learning style inventory.

Kolb uses in the development of his conception the theory of world hypotheses of the American philosopher Stephen Pepper. In his theory Pepper suggests that there are four basically different hypotheses of world, four ways of conceptualizing the reality: fornism, mechanism, contextualism and organism (Pepper 1972). Kolb fuses these hypotheses to his model and combines them with those findings of brain physiology that indicate functional differences between the right and the left hemispheres of the human cortex. Broad historical ways of conceptualizing the world, that is, a history of ideas, is combined with the physiology of the nervous system. Pepper rejects such a mixing of ingredients. Two central principles of his method are 'Eclecticism is confusing' (104–114) and 'Concepts which have lost their contact to their root metaphors are empty abstractions' (113–114).

Pepper evaluates the possibilities of the eclectic method as follows (1972: 106):

> It is a tempting notion, that perhaps a world theory more adequate than any other ... might be developed through the selection of what is best in each of them and organizing the results with a synthesis set of categories ... It is the eclectic method. Our contention is, that this method is mistaken in principle in that it adds no factual content and confuses the structures of fact which are clearly spread out in the pure root-metaphor theories; in two words, that is almost inevitably sterile and confusing.

Pepper argues that the concepts – when taken out of their theoretical context, the context where they come from – change into 'thin, little more than names with a cosmic glow about them' (1972: 113). The concepts and terms outside their theoretical context do not have intrinsic or ultimate value in themselves. It is a paradox that Kolb uses Pepper's basic metaphors exactly in a way that is contrary to Pepper's methodology, by taking them out of their context and by fusing them as auxiliary terms into his 'holistic, integrative perspective'. Kolb does not use Pepper's root metaphors to analyse the background presuppositions of his own synthesis.

The background of Kolb's concept of experience: the four steps

Kolb's theory is best known through the four-stage model of experiential learning (Kolb *et al.* 1971: 28, see figure 1). In 1976, he calls it 'the Lewinian Experiential Learning Model' and 'The Lewinian model of Action Research and Laboratory Training' (Kolb 1984: 21). This model is generally known as Kolb's model, and Kolb constructs his own theory with it as a starting point.

It is misleading, however, to call this model a Lewinian model. In his presentation Kolb does not refer to Lewin. Instead he uses, as his source, a report written by Ronald Lippit on the well known training and development enterprise organized by Lewin and his colleagues, in 1946, in the Research Center for Group Dynamics in the Massachusetts Institute of Technology (MIT). The theme and substance of the training intervention comprised an analysis and solution of the racial prejudices and conflicts in the State of Connecticut. Lippit's book (1949) is one of the finest and most careful reports ever written about an educational enterprise oriented to effect a change in the community life. However, Kolb uses it very selectively. He picks up from the variety of content and methods of the seminar only one aspect: direct feedback related to the group dynamics after the group sessions. The recollections of the participants in the feedback situation can be regarded as a 'here and now experience' to be analysed. It was these feedback sessions that, later on, developed into the heart of the laboratory and T-group training movement. It is this specific aspect of the seminar that Kolb picks up to formulate the basis of his concept of experience. He leaves out other, more important working methods without proper attention.

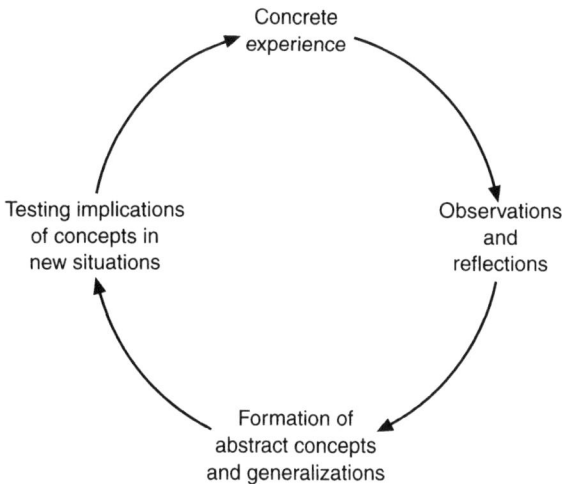

Figure 1 The Lewinian experiential learning model according to Kolb (1984: 21).

Table 1 Time distribution between the phases of the problem solving process in Benne's and Lippit's groups in the 1946 seminar (Lippit 1949: 169)

	Benne Group %	Lippit Group %
Defining the problem and getting facts about it	26	35
Formulating action possibilities in the problem situation	7	16
Practising human relation skills needed to carry out problem solutions	42	24
Formulating general principles of action	3	3
Planning specific steps of back-home action	21	18
Group self-evaluation of its own problem solving activity	1	4

The basic idea of the seminar followed the stages of Lewin's action research: diagnosing problems, finding solutions to them, exercising the solutions and planning carefully the actions to be taken 'back home'. The group dynamics exercises comprised a method in the third phase of Lewin's action research. The reflection on group experiences played a minor role in the seminar, as can be seen in table 1 where the time spans for the different parts of the seminar in the groups led by Kenneth Benne and Ronald Lippit are presented.

The table also shows the differences between the groups. As a matter of fact, the nature of Kolb's view of the 'here and now' immediate experience becomes visible, if we study how it was developed in relation to the historical transition from Lewin's community and action oriented seminar to the T-group movement. I can see four steps in this evolution. These steps roughly correspond to the important developments in the history of the T-group training and research practice (see Hirsch 1987).

1 The shared societal object of the group is eliminated and the 'group interaction as such' becomes the object of analysis

The objects of study in the 1946 seminar were the racial prejudices and social problems in the State of Connecticut. In the T-groups, this kind of societal, 'outside' object was replaced by the reflection of the interaction of the group members. In the 1946 seminar, the participants, community activists and leaders, had plenty of diverse knowledge and experience of racial problems and of attempts and ways of trying to solve them. This knowledge and experience was widely used in the 1946 seminar. It was, of course, not anything like 'here and now' experience. It comprised accumulated knowledge of and insight into the communities, community programmes as well as conditions and possibilities of various kinds of action. The selection of one mode of action of the seminar, the immediate recollection and analysis of what had happened in group sessions of the day, therefore, replaced the wide selection of working methods related to the solution of community problems. Kolb characterized this substitution in his analysis of 'the struggle of "here and now" and "there and then" knowledge'. Kolb cites Kenneth Benne (Kolb 1984: 10):

> There resulted a competition between here-and-now happenings, which of necessity focused on the personal, interpersonal and group levels; and discussing the outside case materials. This sometimes resulted in the rejection of any serious consideration of the observer's report of behavioral data. More often it led eventually to rejection of outside problems as less involving and fascinating.

The National Training Laboratories were founded in 1947 to carry on the work started in the Massachusetts Institute of Technology. Hirsch shows how the feedback sessions of the 1946 seminar were the invention that formed the basis for the development of the T-group method (1987: 20):

> The feedback data about interaction in the group provide rich learning experiences, presenting T-groups as a new and valuable tool in training and education.

Robert Farr presents an explanation of this substitution described above that took place in small group research and training. The small group research at the national Training Laboratories – the most important centre for the development of the T-group method – was mainly funded by the Office of Naval Research of the United States' Army. The office was interested in how autonomous small groups behave in circumstances of total isolation from the rest of the world (1996: 153)

> It was not clear at the time whether these small groups would be in midget submarines or space craft or just wintering over time in Antarctica during the international geophysical war.

Anyhow, in this context, the regularities of behaviour of groups encapsulated in a laboratory was relevant knowledge.

2 The collection and analysis of the data by the researchers is replaced by the discussion of the recollections of the group members

In Lewin's laboratory, the study of group behaviour was based on the data collected by the researchers. In each group, there was an observer who wrote down her observations on a form designed by Lewin's research group. It directed observation to the problems that were interesting to the group such as leadership, competition, orientation to action etc. The systematic and coordinated way of collecting data made the data comparable and analysable. In the T-group and laboratory training, this systematic collection of data based on hypothesis was replaced by the recollections of the participants of the day's group meetings. This replacement is in a curious way visible in Kolb's characterization of the relationship of the first and second phases of his learning model (1976a: 21):

> The process that begins with here-and-now experience ... followed by collection of data and observations about that experience.

If the recollections and interpretations about a group meeting by the group members are discussed, how will it be possible to acquire further data? What does it mean to observe the 'here and now experience'? Is it the same as introspection?

3 Individualization of experience

The 1946 seminar followed roughly the idea of action research as introduced by Lewin (1957): define the problem and make a diagnosis, draw up a total plan for solving the problem and plan the first step to implement the total plan. The versatile knowledge and experience of the participating community leaders, the outside specialists and the researchers of Lewin's group were widely used. The group planned action programmes for solving racial problems in their respective communities. The interviews conducted after the seminar showed that the course, indeed, gave rise to new networks of collaboration and projects in the communities (Lippit 1949: 171).

In the T-group training individuals are supposed to learn about the interaction in-groups, that is, develop individual 'human relations skills'. Accordingly, the creation of new joint activities and new ways of working, as well as networks of collaboration, is missing in the concept of experiential learning.

4 The concept of experience is tied to humanistic anthropology and values

The additional qualities given to the concept of experience, such as 'personal', or 'authentic' are based on a special social ontology and value system of humanistic psychology and existential-phenomenological conception of man. Hence, the concept of 'immediate', 'here and now', having a practical and technical background, can be given a philosophical meaning like 'existential'. Humanistic conceptions represent normative and philosophical arguments for methodological individualism and the 'subjective personal' nature of experience. The influence of these theories is not manifest in Kolb's work. It is more visible in the rhetorical value commitments than in the learning model itself. Kolb states that humanistic values offer 'new hope-filled ideas for the conduct of human relationships and the management of organizations' (Kolb 1984: 11). The humanistic and person-centred orientation grew prominent in the T-group training movement during the 1960s (Hirsch 1987: 65–69).

Understanding humanistic and Jungian conceptions of experience would require a separate theory-historical analysis. Suffice to say, in this context, that the 'peak experiences' revealing the biological true nature of man proposed by Abraham Maslow are religious experiences (Maslow 1970). To Jung, important experiences were based on connection to the collective unconscious, the archetypal primordial images from pagan times or to the species-historical primitive. Also Jung saw the psychological experience as an alternative to institutionalized religion (Jung 1933: 233):

> the psyche becomes something in its own right, which cannot be dealt with measures of the Church alone. It is for this reason that we need a psychology founded on experience and not upon faith or the postulates of any philosophical system.

To me, both of the approaches are, idea-historically, blends of romantic biologism and an attempt to create a new kind of world view or lay religion. That is why they can serve as a specifically ideological ingredient in the approach of experiential learning in adult education. To analyse the role of humanistic conceptions of experience in learning, one should analyse in what sense these kinds of 'peak' or mystical experiences – if they exist – could be the basis for learning and reflection.

The four steps characterized above in the elaboration of the concept of 'immediate experience' imply a radical impoverishment of the concept of experience. This kind of experience is based on the generalization of a very specific mode of action, a feedback session, which developed into a key procedure in the T-group training – combined with a highly individualistic and normative humanistic-existential anthropology. The rich variety and modes of human experience characteristic of various human activities are replaced by a narrow and particularistic conception of experience.

The dynamics of the model of experiential learning

Kolb states that each of the phases of the model is a 'different form of adaptation to reality' or a 'learning mode' (Kolb *et al.* 1971: 28). A separate individual ability corresponds to every phase of the model (1984: 30):

> Learners, if they are to be effective, need four different kinds of abilities – *concrete experience abilities* (CE), *reflective observation abilities* (RO), *abstract conceptualizing abilities* (AC) and *active experimentation abilities* (AE). That is they must be able to involve themselves fully, openly and without bias in new experiences (CE). They must be able to reflect on and observe their experiences from many perspectives (RO). They must be able to create concepts that integrate their observations into

logically sound theories (AC) and they must be able to use these theories to make decisions and solve problems (AE).

In the next section I shall return to the crucial point of the model, the theoretical and epistemological inadequacy of the concept of immediate personal experience which is meant to form the basis of reflection and of the whole model. The quotation above expresses well the eclectic quality of the model. The phases remain separate. They do not connect to each other in any organic or necessary way. Kolb does not present any concept that would connect the phases to each other. Rather he collects into his model historically and theoretically distinct ingredients. Kolb continuously speaks about 'dialectical tension' between experiential and conceptual. However, he resolves the tension simply by taking both as a separate phase to his model. There is surely no dialectics in this. Dialectical logic would show how these two are indispensably related to each other and are determined through each other. It would look for the origin of their interrelatedness. The separateness of the phases and corresponding 'modes of learning' are also based on the fact that the model is constructed to substantiate the validity of Learning Style Inventory. The construction of the distinct styles makes it necessary to postulate distinct modes of adaptation. In this way, the technological starting point partly dictates the mode and content of the 'theoretical' model.

John Dewey resolved the relationship and tension between experience and reflection by taking, as the basic point of departure, practical, material life activity. He regarded non-reflective experience based on habits as a dominant form of experience. The reflective experience, mediated by intelligence and knowledge grows out from the inadequacy and contradictions of the habitual experience and ways of action. For Dewey, the basis of, and reason for reflection was the necessity of solving problems faced in habitual ways of action. He also shows that hypotheses generated by reflection can only be tested in experimental activity, which might solve the problem that elicited the process of reflection. In contrast to Kolb's model in Dewey's conception (see figure 3), every phase is necessarily interconnected. It is the problems and dynamics of life activity that are the common denominator in both habitual and reflective experience for Dewey, and which made him a philosophical pragmatist.

The problem of induction and theory ladenness of observations

In his summary, Kolb presents a working definition of learning (Kolb 1984: 38):

> Learning is a process whereby knowledge is created through the transformation of experience.

Accordingly, the core of his model of experiential learning is 'a simple description of a learning cycle – how experience is translated into concepts, which in turn are used as guides in the choice of new experiences' (Kolb 1976a: 21). This characterization resembles the empiricist theory of scientific knowledge proposed by the logical empiricists in the 1930–1950s. This theory was a prevailing conception of the origins of knowledge until recently. Since then, it has been criticized in various ways in the philosophy of science. This epistemological criticism and discussion concerning man's possibility of obtaining new knowledge about the world, is the most relevant issue for any theory of experience.

According to the empiricist theory of science, true knowledge is based on perceptions. With his senses an unprejudiced observer can make unbiased perceptions of reality. These can be presented in the form of elementary observation statements; sometimes called 'protocol' statements. These statements form a foundation for true knowledge. Following the rules of formal logic, it is possible to infer laws and theories from these statements (induction). From these laws and theories, in turn, one can infer new propositions and forecasts concerning reality (deduction) that can be tested empirically, that is, to show their correspondence with unbiased observations. Although Kolb speaks about observation and reflection instead of observation and induction, the basic problems of his model remain the same.

Whereas empiricist philosophy regards observations of reality and nature as a starting point of knowledge, Kolb postulates observation of experience as a starting point. This resembles the method of introspection of idealist psychology in the 1800s, which made the inner states of mind an object of observation and reporting. Experience can be understood either as a stream of consciousness or subjective recollections of an interaction situation (compare T-group). The experiential model replaces the naive epistemological realism of empiricism with an individualist and subjectivist stance. What unites the two is the confidence in induction.

The conception of the formation of knowledge discussed above was denounced by several prominent philosophers in the 1960s and the 1970s (see, for example, Hanson 1965). They showed that the idea of objective, unbiased observation of facts was not tenable. They showed that observations were necessarily guided and laden by prior conceptualizations and cultural expectations. Ludwig Wittgenstein in his *Philosophical Investigations* describes an idea as follows (1997: 450)

> it is like a pair of glasses on our nose through which we see whatever we look at.

This was called the principle of theory-ladenness. It was substantiated by the results of comparative cultural psychology and the psychology of perception. People from different cultures see the same perceptual stimulus (for example a three-dimensional figure) in different ways. The picture projected on the retina does not explain the content of observation. John Dewey formulated the cultural mediatedness of observations already in 1925 in his book *Experience and Nature* as follows (L W 1: 40):

> Experience is already overlaid and saturated with the products of the reflection of past generations and by-gone ages. It is filled with inter-pretations, classifications, due to sophisticated thought, which have become incorporated into what seems to be fresh naïve empirical material. It would take more wisdom than is possessed by the wisest historical scholar to track all of these absorbed borrowings to their original sources.

Dewey considers that one of the purposes of reflection is to be conscious of the layers of cultures weaved in the observations. They can be preju-dices and carriers of the circumstances of past time, therefore being an obstacle for sensible action in the present circumstances. Once made visible and critically transformed by reflection, they can turn into means of enriching thought and action. In the 1990s, philosophers have stressed that observation is not only laden with theory but also mediated by instru-ments and practices. A scientific observation, as an Australian philosopher of science Allan Chalmers states, is a practical accomplishment. It is a result of getting a whole arsenal of instruments to work (Chalmers 1990). It is laden with local cultural traditions and resources (Barnes *et al.* 1996). Any scientific observation already includes an interpretation whether the organization of observation and experimentation was satisfactory or not.

Chalmers elucidates the principle of theory-ladenness using the follow-ing example: What do a philosopher and a biologist see on the screen of a microscope? Where an experienced microscopist sees a cell dividing, a philosopher can see nothing but a 'nebulous milky substance' (1990: 42). Had a group of philosophers or adult educators collected beside the microscope, they would not have been able to make any kind of sensible or usable generalization. Similarly helpless would be the philosopher in the control room of a paper machine, beside the concrete casting of a cellar, or in the inspection of the errors of a firm's accounts. Observation necessarily takes place in a certain activity; context or thought-community, using the concepts, instruments and conventions historically developed in that context. They steer the observations, and with them the observer interprets and generalizes what is seen and regarded as problematic and important.

Philosopher Michael Polanyi characterized the communal origin and theoretical and historical mediatedness of observations by analysing how students of medicine learn to interpret X-ray pictures (Polanyi 1964: 101). In the beginning, the students see practically nothing in the pictures. It is only after months of practising, discussions and analysis of hundreds of pictures together with an experienced analyst that the capability of seeing and interpreting the pictures develops. Therefore, there is every reason to acknowledge that concepts and hypotheses based on them precede adequate observations. Accordingly, the reinterpretation of conceptions and practices is an essential part of reinterpretation of observations and learning. Learning can, therefore, be regarded as a relationship between culturally appropriated conceptions, ways of action and hypothesis and empirically new ways, deviating from previous and problematic elements in practical activity.

In the light of our knowledge on observation and knowledge formation it is highly unlikely that an individual could, as Kolb stated above, 'be able to involve themselves fully, openly and without bias in new experiences' let alone draw any generalizations from such experiences. Karl Popper calls the assertion of such a possibility absurd (1981: 72). A student of Dewey's logic, Tom Burke, crystallizes Dewey's conception of the issue (1994: 43):

> the problem is not only how to formulate hypotheses on the basis of given data ... but how to reformulate hypotheses, based on the given data and on prior hypotheses that suggested how and why to gather those particular data in the first place.

Dewey, therefore, asserts that hypotheses are drawn from observations, from the hypothesis and conceptions that directed the observations and, if necessary, from the totally new cultural resources and conceptions that are mobilized to interpret the observation data.

A solution to this problem was proposed by the founder of pragmatism Charles Peirce. He analysed the difference between induction and a hypothesis as forms of logical inference (1992/1878). Induction leads to the recognition of a fact on the basis of the similarity of facts. Hypothesis, instead, often suggests something that cannot be inferred from immediate perception at all. Peirce resumes (ibid.: 194) 'Induction classifies, hypothesis explains'. Peirce calls the inference that proceeds through hypotheses an abduction. Dewey further elaborated this logic and applied it to social practice.

Dewey's naturalistic model of reflective thought and action

Having presented the 'Lewinian model', Kolb introduces briefly, with a few sentences, John Dewey's model of experiential learning (1984: 22, see figure 2). He states that it is remarkably similar to the Lewinian model. According to him, Dewey studies in his model 'how learning transforms the impulses, feelings and desires of concrete experience into higher-order, purposeful action' (op. cit.: 22). This interpretation is based on a lengthy citation that the author has taken from Dewey's small book

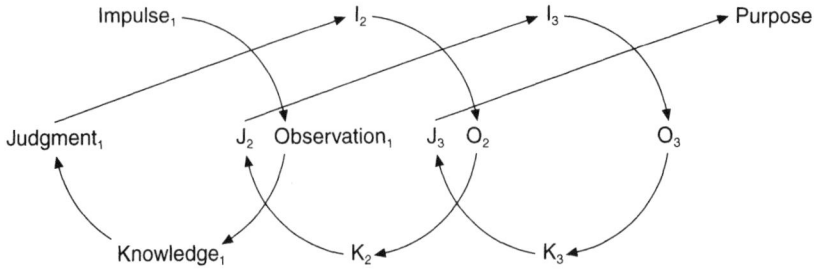

Figure 2 John Dewey's concept of experiential learning according to Kolb (1984: 23).

Experience and Education (1938). This book is based on a series of lectures that Dewey gave on the state of the school, in 1937. The quotation is the only reference to the work of Dewey in the presentation. This fragment of text is selected because it supports the author's agenda. The text from which the citation is taken deals with the problem of pupil motivation at school. However, from the point of view of Dewey's general theory of experience and thought, it is marginal. As a matter of fact, the excerpt and Kolb's interpretation of it gives a unilateral and erroneous picture of Dewey's theory on experience and reflective thought and action (see figure 3).

Dewey developed the conception of experience in his works *Experience and Nature* (1925) and *Art as Experience* (1934). His conceptions of reflective thought and learning he presented most clearly in his works on thought and logic: *How We Think* (1909), *Essays in Experimental Logic* (1916) and *Logic, Theory of Inquiry* (1938).[2] Dewey's approach is a naturalistic one. On the basis of Darwinian biological theory of evolution, it takes the adaptation of the organism to its environment as its starting point (see Dewey 1976). In adapting to the environment, individuals form habits – routine ways of doing things. When these habits do not function, a problem, uncertainty and a crisis emerges and calls for reflective thought and investigation into the conditions of the situation. As in experimental research in natural science, a hypothesis is formulated and tested in practice. The central issue in Dewey's conception of experiment is whether an authority-bond and routine ways of thinking and action can be replaced by a 'reconstructive' and reflective way.

Dewey makes a distinction between a primary and a secondary experience. The primary experience is composed of material interaction with the physical and social environment. For Dewey things are – as he says in *Experience and Nature* (L W 1: 28):

> objects to be treated, used, acted upon and with, enjoyed and endured, even more than things to be known. They are things had before they are things cognized.

The secondary experience is a reflective experience that makes the environment and its things as objects of reflection and knowledge. It is the failure and uncertainty of the primary experience that gives rise to reflective thought and learning.

The phases of reflective thought and action

The phases of reflective learning as defined by Dewey are presented in figure 3. In the following, I shall briefly deal with the content and significance of each of the phases.

1 The indeterminate situation: the habit does not work

Routinized ways of doing things are mostly accomplished without reflection. When the normal course of activity is disturbed, a state of uncertainty and indetermination emerges. The starting point of the experience is not experience understood as an internal representation or recollection of an individual but as a disturbance in the human, material activity or in the man-environment system. Some kind of obstacle or resistance in the situation makes the normal flow of action difficult. The inhibition of direct action is a necessary precondition of reflective thought bringing about 'hesitation and delay that is essential to thinking' (L W 8: 201). Reflective thought starts with studying the conditions, resources, aids, difficulties and obstacles of action.

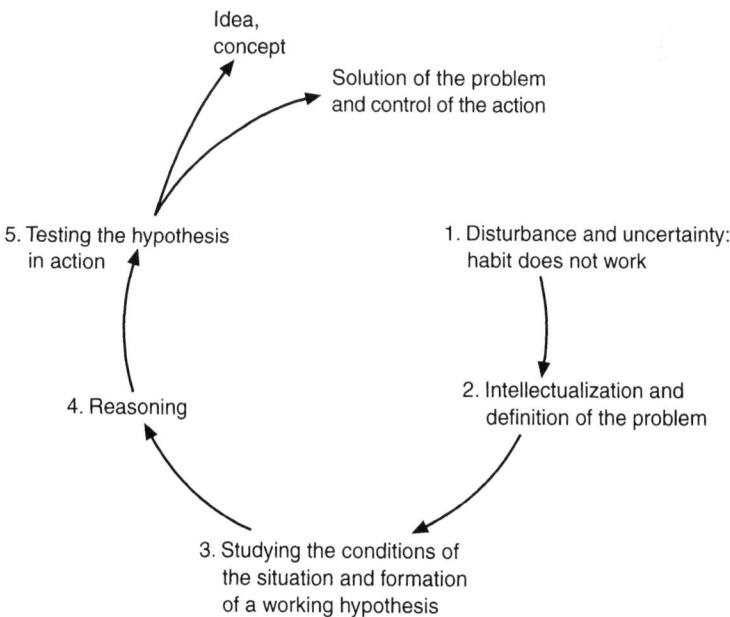

Figure 3 Dewey's model of reflective thought and action.

2 Intellectualization: defining the problem

The process of reflective thought starts with an attempt to define what is wrong in the situation. The actor forms a tentative conception of the difficulty and defines the problem. The formulation of the problem already presupposes the studying of the conditions of the situation and transformation of the problem-situation itself. Dewey underlines the significance of the problem definition for thought. The problem that directs the acquisition of knowledge and further studies of the conditions of the situation (L W 12: 112):

> Without a problem, there is blind groping in the dark. The way in which the problem is conceived decides what specific suggestions are entertained and which are dismissed; what data are selected and which rejected; it is the criterion for relevancy and irrelevancy of hypotheses and conceptual structures.

3 Studying the conditions of the situation and formation of a working hypothesis

In the following phase the analysis and diagnosis of the conditions takes place. The conditions include both material and social conditions and the means and resources with which the problem is supposed to be resolved. The presupposition of the possible solution is called a working hypothesis. A working hypothesis also can be characterized as a guiding idea or a plan. The working hypothesis – like the problem – is tentative.

4 Reasoning – in a narrower sense

Reasoning is composed of the elaboration of the meaning of ideas in relation to each other. In reasoning, thought experiments can be done. In it the tenability of the working hypothesis can be evaluated and tested in the light of the knowledge and resources available for an individual or a community. These thought experiments are important because they allow the return to the beginning again. The results of material and practical experiments are non-recursive. The thought experiments can lead to the reformulating of a working hypothesis.

5 Testing the hypothesis by action

The working hypothesis is tested by trying to realize it in practice, by reconstructing the situation or the man-environment relationship. Dewey says that only the practical testing of the hypothesis in material activity makes it possible to draw conclusions of its validity. That is why he calls the reasoning in the previous phase as reasoning in a narrower sense.

Proper reasoning takes place as a part of the process of testing of the hypothesis in practice. The situation is reconstructed according to the requirements of the hypothesis, to see whether the consequences deduced from the hypothesis become real in practice. Thought is not armchair activity. Overt, material actions are needed. Actions that use cultural artefacts constitute an essential part of thought (M W 9: 328):

> Upon this view, thinking, or knowledge-getting, is far from being the armchair thing it is often supposed to be ... Hands and feet, apparatus and appliances of all kinds are as much a part of it as changes in the brain. Since these physical operations (including the cerebral events) and equipment's are a part of thinking, thinking is mental, not because of a peculiar stuff which enters into it or of peculiar non-natural activities which constitute it, but because of what physical acts and appliances do: the distinctive purpose for which they are employed and the distinctive results which they accomplish.

Dewey does not include the outcomes of this process as an independent phase in his model. He, however, deals with them. The testing of the hypothesis does not always lead to the confirmation of the hypothesis. But the hypothesis makes learning possible, because the outcome can be compared to the initial suppositions implied in the hypothesis. This differentiates the process from bare trial and error.

What is important is Dewey's statement that the process has two kinds of result. The direct, immediate outcome is that the situation becomes reconstructed in such a way that the initial problem becomes resolved. This outcome means the increased control over the activity. Another, indirect and intellectual outcome is the production of a meaning that can be used as a resource in forthcoming problem situations. Dewey says (1916: 22–23):

> And it may well be that this by-product, this gift of the gods, is incomparably more valuable for living a life than is the primary and intended result of control, essential as that control to having a life to live.

None of the phases of Dewey's model of reflective activity are included in Kolb's model of Lewinian experiential learning. None of them is included in the model (figure 2) that Kolb presents as Dewey's model of learning either. The essence of Dewey's thought disappears in Kolb's treatment. There is no reflective learning for Dewey outside problem, hypothesis and its testing in practice. The difference becomes even more pronounced if we look at how Dewey differentiates between non-reflective and reflective experience and between empirical and theoretical thought.

The two-edged nature of experience: empirical 1 and theoretical thought

Habit has a twofold meaning for Dewey. It is, on the one hand, the great flywheel of society. It is necessary, in this society, to have stabilized ways of doing things that function well and in a predictable way in the recurring situations of life. On the other hand, the act of following these habits can turn into a conservative factor, an obstacle for change and innovation. In *How We Think*, in a short passage 'The meaning of experience' Dewey defines the dual nature of experience (L W 8: 277):

> The term experience may thus be interpreted with reference either to the empirical or to the experimental attitude of mind. Experience is not a rigid and closed thing; it is vital, and hence growing. When dominated by the past, by custom and routine, it is often opposed to the reasonable, the thoughtful. But experience also includes the reflection that sets us free from the limiting influence of sense, appetite, and tradition.

Experimental and theoretical thought liberates us from intellectual laziness and from the tyranny of tradition. Dewey compares empirical and theoretical thinking in the 13th chapter of *How We Think*. Empirical thinking is based on observation of regularly occurring or coinciding things and phenomena. It does not imply hypotheses of the causes of mechanisms. As such, empirical thinking is useful in many everday situations. But empirical thinking entails, according to Dewey, three obvious disadvantages (L W 8: 269–270).

- It leads to false conclusions. Empirical experience does not contain any criteria for evaluating which of the conclusions might be right and which wrong. That makes empirical experience a veritable source of many false conceptions.
- Empirical experience is helpless in confronting and explaining change and the emergence of the new (L W 8: 270): Empirical inference follows the grooves and ruts that custom wears and has no track to follow when the groove disappears.
- Empirical experience is often accompanied by mental inertia and dogmatism. Dewey is quite relentless in characterizing this feature of empirical thinking: laziness, conformism, slave-like dependence on authority. 'Passivity, docility, acquiescence, come to be primal intellectual virtues'. Scientific thinking is necessary for liberating the thinker from the tyranny of habit and perception, and this liberation is a precondition of progress (L W 8: 277):

> When dominated by the past, by custom and routine, it is often opposed to the reasonable, the thoughtful. But experience also includes the reflection that sets us free from the limiting influence of

sense, appetite, and tradition. Experience may welcome and assimilate all that the most exact and penetrating thought discovers.

Dewey presents here the fact that the testimony of experience often means seeing things through the lens of the established and traditional, the self-evident. Therefore, 'it follows that it would be impossible to over-estimate the educational importance of arriving at conceptions ... Without this conceptualization or intellectualization nothing is gained that can be carried over to better understanding of new experiences' (L W 8: 238–329).

Dewey, however, thinks that concepts and meanings are not con-structed in the head alone. They are generalizations of the interactions between humans and the entities of environment, in practical activity. It is the regularities of these interactions – including the properties of things involved – that make the transfer of concepts from one situation to another possible.

Hypothesis and models as plans of action

Why does Dewey not speak much about concepts in his model of reflective activity, although he underlines the significance of scientific concepts? There are at least two reasons for that. First, he wanted to stress that con-cepts are always tentative and have the nature of the hypothesis. That is why he often uses the terms hypothesis, working hypothesis and guiding idea instead of concept. Second, Dewey wanted to stress the functional and practical significance of concept and make a distinction from classical idealistic theories that regarded concept as mirror image of reality, as reflections of the pregiven and eternal structures of nature (Dewey 1916: 312–313):

> From the standpoint of the idea of working hypothesis, the chief func-tion of philosophy is not to find out what difference ready-made for-mulae make, *if true*, but to arrive at and to clarify their *meanings as programs of behaviour for modifying the existent world.* From this stand-point, the meaning as a world-formula is practical and moral, not merely in the consequences that flow from accepting certain concep-tual content as true, but as regards that content itself.

The continuity of a situation is realized through hypotheses and conceptions as plans of action. They are formed in one situation and are then transferred as 'programmes of behaviour' to other situations as tools of reflection, analy-sis and anticipation. Reflection and reconstruction of the environment are inseparable. This connection between thought, practice and the properties of things involved in actions has a profound epistemological significance. Thought is a part and an expression of the individual-environment system.

The value of thought lies in what can be accomplished by it. The content of thought is about the interactions of the many entities of the system, not the experience of the individual when understood as recollections of events or immediate perceptions (Dewey M W 9: 339):

> Thinking is what some of the actual existences do. They are in no sense constituted by thinking; on the contrary, the problems of thought are set by their difficulties and its resources are furnished by their efficacies; its acts are their doings adapted to a distinctive end.

Dewey's idea of concepts as tools or plans of actions resembles Ludwig Wittgenstein's metaphor of words as tools, as well as Marx Wartofsky's theory of secondary artefacts. Wittgenstein uses in his *Philosophical Investigations* an example of a complete simple language game – the interaction of a mason and his helper constructing a house. Vocabulary is a tool kit that is instrumental in communication needed in practical activity, the construction of the house (Wittgenstein 1997: 3). Marx Wartofsky has a theory of different kinds of artefacts. Ordinary material tools are primary artefacts. Secondary artefacts, models and concepts, are generalizations of the ways of using the primary artefacts, that is the ways of man-environment interaction in practical activity (Wartofsky 1979: 142).

Dewey's conception is also a forerunner of modern practice-oriented, heterogeneous constructivism in philosophy and sociology of science (Pickering 1992)[4]. It resembles closely the idea of Ian Hacking presented in his *Representing and Intervening* (1983) according to which phenomena are constructed in a laboratory and do not exist as such in nature. It has also many similar features with actor network theory developed by Bruno Latour. Latour proposes that agency is distributed among humans and the non-human artefacts in networks (Latour 1993). The non-human entities also do things, react and contribute to the accomplishment of the aims of activity (Latour 1994).

Conclusions

We have to conclude that Kolb does not give an adequate interpretation of Dewey's concept of experience and reflective thought. Kolb speaks about experiential learning. Dewey speaks about experimental thought and activity. These terms are phonetically close. However, they are theoretically and epistemologically quite far apart. For Dewey, there is no reflective thought without a disturbance in the habits and ways of doing things, without hypotheses and testing them in practice. In his thinking, experience includes the objective forms of interaction between humans and the environment including all the artefacts and things involved in the interaction. To Dewey, experience is not a matter of psychological state, nor anything in the minds of individuals.

In 1949, Dewey started to write a new introduction to his main meta-physical work *Experience and Nature*. In this unfinished introduction, Dewey expressed his disappointment about the nondualist conception of experience – covering the individual and the world – being interpreted mainly in an individual and psychological way.[5] Dewey says that had he an opportunity to rewrite *Experience and Nature* he would give it a new name *Culture and Nature* (L W 1: 361). He would use culture 'in its anthropologi-cal sense'. He regarded it as philosophically important that culture com-prises both artefacts and humans in their mutual interaction. The concept of culture also covers the large variety of human activities and practices necessary for understanding the thinking and actions of individuals. Dewey cites Bronislaw Malinowski (L W 1: 364): 'Culture is at the same time psychological and collective'. In this late text, Dewey comes very near the cultural psychology of the 1990s (Shweder 1990, Cole 1996) that regards the interaction between an individual and culture as the basic unit of analysis.

It appears to me that the concept of experiential learning, in the form used by Kolb and the adult education tradition, represents the kind of psy-chological reductionism that Dewey considered a misinterpretation of his antidualist conception of experience. This conception is based in Kolb's book on the model of a very particular historical incident – or habit: the immediate feedback in human relation training. Although this procedure has developed into one of the tenets of T-group training, it is epistemolog-ically highly problematic and cannot be generalized as a way in which people learn and gain understanding of the world and of their own possi-bilities in it. When the romantic biological and therapeutic ideas of humanistic psychology are combined with it, a thoroughly individualistic conception of learning emerges.

Why is this conception so popular within adult education? Why is the language it uses set apart from the philosophical theorizing of man's possibilities of gaining knowledge in the philosophy and sociology of knowledge? Perhaps the idea of experiential learning forms an attractive package for adult educators. It combines spontaneity, feeling, and deep individual insights with the possibility of rational thought and reflection. It maintains the humanistic belief in every individual's capacity to grow and learn, so important for the concept of life-long learning. It comprises a positive ideology that is evidently important for adult education. However, I fear that the price of this package for adult education research and practice is high. Along with that package, adult education is at risk of remaining a quasi-scientific academic field without connection to the philosophical, anthropological, sociological and psychological studies of learning and thought. Moreover, the belief in an individual's capabilities and his individual experience leads us away from the analysis of cultural and social conditions of learning that are essential to any serious enter-prise of fostering change and learning in real life.

Notes

1 *Reijo Miettinen* is Professor in the Department of Education at the University of Helsinki, and Vice-Director of its Centre for Activity Theory and Developmental Work Research. He is leading a research group that studies learning in innovation processes and research work.
2 In this paper, I refer mainly to the critical edition of Dewey's writings edited by Jo Ann Boydston, abbreviated as: E W = The Early Works 1882–1898, five volumes; M W = The Middle Works, 1899–1924, 15 volumes; and L W = The Later Works 1925–1953, 17 volumes. For a good presentation of Dewey's conception of experience, see *Art and experience*, chapter three, 'Having an experience' (L W 10, 42–63).
3 On the phases of reflective thought and learning, see *How We Think* (L W 8: 199–208) and *Logic, a Theory of Inquiry* (L W 12: 105–122). On page 157 of *Demacracy and Education* (1916) Dewey has concisely presented the key characteristics of reflective thought (M W 9: 157). For recent philosophical interpretations of Dewey's theory of logic and thought, see Burke (1994), and Campbell (1995).
4 A philosopher of science, Sergio Sismondo, makes the distinction between three different meanings of constructivism: social constructivism, Neo-Kantian constructivism and heterogeneous constructivism (Sismondo 1996). Because the material entities are an essential part involved in Dewey's reconstruction of the situation, Dewey represents heterogeneous constructivism as also in actor-network theory (Latour 1993) and cultural historical activity theory, that regards consciousness always as mediated by artefacts, tools and signs (Vygotksy 1978).
5 '"Experience" had become effectively identified with experiencing in the sense of the psychological, and the psychological had become established as that which is intrinsically psychical, mental, private. My insistence that "experience" also designates what is experienced was a mere ideological thundering in the Index for it ignored the ironical twist which made this use of "experience" strange and incomprehensible' (L W 1: 362).

References

Barnes, B., Bloor, D. and Henry, J. (1996) *Scientific knowledge: A sociological analysis* (London: Athlone).
Boud, D. and Miller, N. (1996) *Working with experience. Animating learning* (London and New York: Routledge).
Boud, D., Keogh, R. and Walker, D. (1985) *Reflection: turning experience into learning* (London: Nichols Publishing Company).
Burke, T. (1994) *Dewey's new logic. A reply to Russell* (Chicago: The University of Chicago Press).
Campbell, J. (1995) *Understanding John Dewey. Nature and cooperative intelligence* (Chicago: Open Court).
Chalmers, A. (1990) *Science and its fabrication* (Buckingham: The Open University Press).
Cole, M. (1996) *Cultural Psychology* (Cambridge: Cambridge University Press).
Dewey, J. (1938) *Experience and education* (New York: MacMillan).
Dewey (1976/1909) *The influence of Darwin on Philosophy. The Middle Works of John Dewey* Vol. 4 Edited by Jo Ann Boydston. (Carbondale & Edwardsville: Southern Illinois University Press).
Dewey, J. (1985/1916) *Democracy and education. The Middle Works of John Dewey* Vol.

9 Edited by Jo Ann Boydston (Carbondale & Edwardsville: Southern Illinois University Press).

Dewey, J. (1988a/1925) *Experience and nature. The Later Works of John Dewey* Vol. 1 Edited by Jo Ann Boydston (Carbondale & Edwardsville: Southem Illinois University Press).

Dewey, J. (1989a/1909) *How we think. The Later Works of John Dewey* Vol. 8 Edited by Jo Ann Boydston (Carbondale & Edwardsville: Southern Illinois University Press).

Dewey, J. (1989b/1934) *Art as experience. The Later Works of John Dewey* Vol. 10 Edited by Jo Ann Boydston (Carbondale & Edwardsville: Southern Illinois University Press).

Dewey, J. (1991/1938) *Logic. The theory of inquiry. The Later works of John Dewey* Vol. 12 Edited by Jo Ann Boydston (Carbondale & Edwardsville: Southern Illinois University Press).

Dixon, N. C. (1994) *The organizational learning cycle. How we can learn collectively* (London: McGraw-Hill Book Company).

Farr, R. M. (1996) *The roots of modern social psychology* (Cambridge, Mass.: Blackwell).

Hacking, I. (1983) *Representing and intervening. Introductory topics in the philosophy of natural science* (Cambridge: Cambridge University Press).

Hanson, N. R. (1965) *Patterns of scientific discoveries: An inquiry into the conceptual foundations of science* (Cambridge: Cambridge University Press).

Hirsch, J. I. (1987) *The history of the National Training Laboratories 1947–1986. Social equality trough education and training* (New York: Peter Lang).

Jarvis, P. (1987) *Adult learning in the social context* (London: Croom Helm).

Jung, C. G. (1933) *Modern man in search of a soul* (London: Routledge & Kegan Paul Ltd).

Kolb, D. (1976a) Management and the learning process. *California Management Journal*, 18(3), 21–31.

Kolb, D. (1976b) *The learning style inventory: Technical manual* (Boston: McBer and Company).

Kolb, D. (1984) *Experiential learning Experience as the source of learning and Development* (Englewood Cliffs, NJ: Prentice Hall).

Kolb, D., Rubin, I. and Mcinture, J. (1971) *Organizational psychology – an experiential approach* (Englewood Cliffs, NJ.: Prentice-Hall).

Latour, B. (1993) *We have never been modern* (Hertfordshire: Harvester Wheatsheaf).

Latour, B. (1994) On technical mediation. Philosophy, sociology, genealogy. *Common Knowledge* 3(2), 29–64.

Lewin, K. (1957) Action research and minority problems. In G. W. Lewin and G. Allport (eds) *Resolving social conflicts. Selected papers on group dynamics* (New York: Harper & Brothers), 201–216.

Lippit, R. (1949) *Training in Community relations. A research exploration toward new group skills* (New York: Harper & Brothers Publishers).

Maslow, A. H. (1970) *Religions, values, and peak experiences* (New York: Penguin).

Peirce, C. (1992/1878) Deduction, induction and hypothesis. In N. Houser and Kloesel (eds) *The essential Peirce. Selected Philosophical writings* Volume I (1867–1893), 186–199.

Pepper, S. C. (1972) *World hypotheses. A study in evidence* (Berkley: University of California Press).

Polanyi, M. (1964) *Personal knowledge, Towards a post-critical philosophy* (New York: Harper & Row).

Popper, K. (1981) The myth of inductive hypothesis generation. In R. D. Tweney, M. E. Doherty and C. R. Mynatt (eds) *On scientific thinking* (New York: Columbia University Press), 72–76.

Schweder, R. A. (1990). Cultural psychology – What is it? In J. W. Stigler, R. A. Scweder and G. Herdt (eds) *Cultural psychology. Essays on comparative human development* (Cambridge: Cambridge University Press), 1–43.

Sismondo S. (1996) *Science without myth. On constructions, reality and social knowledge* (Albany: State University of New York Press).

Wartofsky, M. (1979) *Models: Representation and scientific understanding* (Dordrecht: Reidel).

Weil, S. and McGill, I. (1989) *Making sense of experiential learning: Diversity in theory and practice* (Milton Keynes: Open University Press).

Welschman, J. (1995) *Dewey's ethical thought* (Ithaca and London: Camell University Press).

Wittgenstein, L. (1997) *Philosophical Investigations* (Padstow, Cornwall: Blackwell Publishers).

Vygotsky, L. S. (1978) *Mind in society: the development of higher psychological processes* (Cambridge, Mass.: Harvard University Press).

16 Adult education

A Sartrean-based perspective

Bonnie Burstow

Toronto

Introductory remarks

For some time now I have felt that the adult education movement was in need of firmer philosophic grounding. When I hear the terms that have become our hallmark – terms like 'self-directed learning' and 'ongoing learning' – I am aware that these imply some sort of image of the learner that is libertarian and emergent. The image appeals to me because it seems sensitive to what we really are as human beings. This appeal notwithstanding, I always end up feeling that it is a vague free-floating image at best. It is not rooted in ontology. That is, it is not rooted in an understanding of what is fundamental to existence generally and human existence in particular. And what relates to this, while it involves some sort of commitment to emergence, it does not tell us what human emergence really is. This being the case, it does not give us the help we need in our ongoing attempt to understand our own educational practices and to correct misdirections.

For the last few years I have been turning to existentialism for grounding. Other adult educators have also seen promise here. Indeed, we are already drawing on Buber, and I value what has been gained. Who stands out for me in particular is the French existentialist Jean-Paul Sartre.

The possibility of a Sartrean foundation first presented itself to me a number of years ago while I was working on my doctoral thesis on Sartre. My method or approach to the texts was dialogical, with dialogue understood in the Buber sense.[1] As I dialogued, as I opened myself up to what presented itself, as I brought myself and my concerns to what I read, I came to feel that Sartre's understanding of human existence generally and authentic human existence in particular had powerful implications for our field. After I finished the thesis, I continued to probe Sartre. I continued to ask questions about adult education and to piece together. The purpose of this article is to share what I have come up with.

To be clear about the status of what I am presenting, I am not suggesting that Sartre explicitly held the position on adult education that I am explicating. Besides the fact that dialogue as method and as epistemological grounding prohibits such a claim, I have clearly gone beyond Sartre in my construction. What I am doing is offering the beginning of a foundation and a direction for adult education based on:

a   my understanding of Sartrean ontology;
b   my dialogue with Sartre;
c   my understanding of adult education.

My hope is that it is a beginning which other educators will find viable.

I shall begin by explicating my understanding of Sartre's theories on existence and authentic human existence. I will go on to discuss the meaning I see for adult education *per se*.

Sartrean theory

As I have come to understand it, Sartre sees existence as divided into two realms, one of which is more primordial than the other. Sartre calls the more primordial realm the 'in-itself', though he also refers to it more generally as 'Being'. The second realm – the realm with which human existence is primarily associated – he calls the 'for-itself'. The picture he gives of the in-itself is a dense mass which has no intrinsic meaning. The for-itself, which creates the meaning, is a derivative of the in-itself. It comes into existence as for-itself by separating itself from 'what is' and defining itself as a 'not-that'. It secretes, as it were, a nothingness between itself and other existents and it hides behind this nothingness. Its being, correspondingly, is the being of nothingness. It is a not-that, a negation. It is also, notes Sartre, consciousness, for to be conscious of something is to separate yourself from that thing and distinguish yourself as a not-that. Its ultimate being, however, is the being of freedom, for freedom is precisely this ability to secrete and hide behind a nothingness. Being-free, to put it another way, is the very being of the for-itself. While the in-itself has an essence, the for-itself or consciousness exists as freedom; out of this freedom it determines what it and its situation will be.

Asked how the human being determines what he and his situation will be, Sartre answers that he determines it by his 'projects'. The human being, Sartre notes, projects himself toward what does not exist; that is, he establishes goals about which he organizes things and he works toward these goals. It is precisely this organization of means in terms of goals which gives meaning to the in-itself and which creates world. Given the centrality of his projects, the human being can change himself and his world by changing his projects.

Just as the for-itself separates itself from the in-itself, it separates itself from itself; in fact, it is this very separation from self which allows it to separate itself from other entities, to project itself toward what is not, and to create world. There are two dimensions to this more inward separation. The for-itself, says Sartre, separates itself both from its past and from its future. These separations, like the separation from the in-itself, are what is meant by its 'being-free'. Secreting a nothingness which separates itself from itself, the for-itself is always free to determine what it will be.[2]

It is in and through anxiety or anguish that the for-itself discovers these separations, this freedom. Just as there are two separations from self – separation from the self that was and separation from the self that will be – there are two modes of anxiety – anxiety in the face of the past and anxiety in the face of the future. The first is typified by the gambler, the second by the mountain climber. The gambler discovers in anxiety that the decision he made yesterday – the decision not to gamble anymore – will not save him from the gambling tables today. What he discovers is that he is not bound by his previous decision. He is separated from it, and so it fails in the mission he has given it. He is separated from it by a nothingness. This nothingness, notes Sartre, is impassable *just because it is nothing.* By the same token, the mountain climber who decides that he is going to walk more carefully when he comes to the narrow turning up ahead realizes in anguish that it is not certain that he will walk carefully. His present self can determine to walk carefully later on, certainly, but this present self cannot determine the decision or actions of the self which he *will* be when he actually arrives at the turning. It cannot, because this future self is separated from his present self. What the gambler and climber are discovering is the permanent rupture in determinism. What they are discovering is their being as being-free.[3]

If the being of the human being is freedom, Sartre hastens to point out, it is not free-floating freedom. It is freedom in-the-world. As such, it is conditioned by 'what is' or, as Sartre puts it, it is conditioned by 'facticity'. Facticity plus the meaning given by freedom combine to create the situation. The situation is always concrete, is always individual, though it partakes of certain universal structures. These structures, in turn, are part of the human being's facticity. Examples of facticity are: the past which cannot be changed, the environment, and so forth.[4] These are important. Most important of all, however, is the existence of others. Through the other, the for-itself acquires an outside and thereby becomes a human being. Without other subjects, it would be for-itself pure and simple. It would be pure subjectivity. With the emergence of the other, it acquires a dimension which exists for the other – a dimension from which it personally is alienated. With the emergence of others, correspondingly, it ends up with a general social dimension – a being which is for-others. It ends up, accordingly, significantly determined from without. Everyone, Sartre notes, is so determined. Nonetheless, he adds, there are different degrees of determination. More or fewer of a person's choices may be sabotaged; more or fewer qualities may be imposed upon him from without; more or fewer projects may be stolen from him. People are likely to meet with more determination if they are part of a scapegoated minority and/or live in a society which thrives on victimization and scapegoating.[5]

Authentic existence is predicated on a lucid awareness of one's situation in all its concreteness. It contrasts with self-deception or the obscuring of awareness. In so far as a person is inauthentic, Sartre contends, he is virtually hiding from or denying his own awareness. Sartre calls this hiding – this denial – 'bad faith'. Essentially, bad faith is a process of self-deception. In bad faith, I keep myself from knowing what I am aware of. I do this by keeping myself from focusing or reflecting on both my awareness of 'what is' and my awareness of the self-deceit I am engaged in. In bad faith, the human being denies aspects of his facticity he would rather not own. What he is particularly intent on denying, however, Sartre claims, is his awareness of his own freedom. He does this by looking at himself as if he had the solidity of a thing and stopping himself from reflecting on his awareness that he is not a thing. Essentially, he takes on the project of being a thing. A more complex project a person may also take on is the project of having the solidity of a thing – that is having an absolute nature like the in-itself – while at the same time being the absolute freedom which posits this nature. Sartre calls this project 'the project to become in-itself-for-itself'; he sees it as the for-itself's fundamental project. Sartre sees it, that is, as underlying all the person's other choices. The fundamental project is adopted and maintained prereflectively, that is, without explicit awareness. The upshot is, the person goes through life making choices without any reflective awareness of what his choices are really about.[6]

Every instance of bad faith, Sartre contends, is a flight from anxiety and the recognition and responsibility which anxiety brings. If inauthenticity is flight, authenticity, correspondingly, is a cessation of flight. If a person is to be authentic, to put it another way, he must stop fleeing and become reflectively aware. Whether by himself or with the aid of a helper, he must rid himself of bad faith. He must rid himself of individual instances of bad faith. Beyond this, he must come to terms with the original lie or project and acknowledge himself for the being that he is. This process Sartre refers to as a 'radical conversion'.

The early Sartre saw the fundamental or original project as something that could be utterly removed once identified. This being the case, he advocated a procedure designed to identify the original project, and he asked nothing but analytic skills and objective detachment of the 'helper'. Gradually he came to see the authenticity process as something gradual, as something subtle, as a process of transcendence. Attempting to explicate the process, Sartre writes:

> This process is not an instantaneous movement; it is a long work; each movement of this work is at once the surpassing and to the extent that it is posited for itself, the pure and simple subsistence of deviations at

a given level of integration. For this reason a life develops in spirals. It passes again and again by the same points, but at different levels of integration and complexity.

(1958: 106)

Change, meaningful growth or authenticity is absolute in the early Sartre. In this late Sartre it is relative. Change or meaningful growth is instantaneous in the early Sartre. In this late Sartre it is gradual.

Asked what he now sees as facilitating meaningful growth, Sartre responds that he still sees value in analysis and in identifying instances of bad faith, but it is not this which is pivotal. It is *willing to the end*. It is *persevering through the concrete*. A person must try to realize his choices just as far as they can be realized in the concrete situations he is in. In so far as he does, Sartre claims, there is growth in meaning and authentic spiralling occurs. In this regard, he writes:

One must will an act to the very end. But the act is alive, it changes. The goal one sets at the beginning is abstract and consequently false. Little by little it is enriched by the means employed to attain it, and ultimately the concrete goal, the true goal, is what one wants at the finish.

(1964: 626)

Given this later understanding of change and change facilitation, the detachment and reductionism described earlier will not do. The external helper is now asked to engage more. He is asked to call attention to the concrete, to what is there. He is asked to help the other 'will to the end'.

If the helper is to do this, Sartre points out, he must gain an intimate understanding of the other. Asked what promotes such understanding, Sartre answers love and esteem. With love and esteem, the helper understands the other not as an object but as a subject, not as a thing but as a Thou. With love and esteem, he is brought into encounter with the other – he meets the other. To this love, this esteem, this meeting, Sartre gives the name 'dialogue'.[7]

Radical conversion, in the first model, has an end. In the second, it never really ends. This difference notwithstanding, there comes a point at which the human being may be seen as authentic or aware. At this point, Sartre suggests, the human being will value freedom above all other values as he will recognize it as the source of all values. He will value and commit himself not only to his own freedom but to the freedom of others, for he will see the connection between them. He will fight, accordingly, against whatever limits or alienates freedom. He will join political groups which address the political issues of the day. He will look at how he personally alienates and scapegoats, whether as an educator, a member of the privileged class, or what have you, and will alter his situation as best he can. And he will strive to meet the other in an attitude of mutuality and love.[8]

Sartre's theory seen as a theory of learning

What, then, is learning? And what is authentic learning? Sartre does not answer directly. An answer is implicit, though, in what I have already stated. Human existence, note, is defined as a consciousness which *moves*, which *projects*. Noting this, I asked myself what term educators use for this movement of consciousness. The term I came up with, the term I am suggesting, is 'learning'. When our consciousness *moves*, when we *go where we are not*, we are *learning*. By this token, existence may be defined *as a consciousness which learns*, or, to put it another way, as *a learning which is aware of itself*. Consciousness is associated with *projects*, with *projection*. Learning, then, is associated with *projects*, with *projection*. Learning occurs as the human being attempts to realize his projects. Learning occurs as the human being chooses ends and organizes means in relation to them. Learning occurs as the human being projects himself futurally. Learning occurs as the human being projects himself toward what is not yet and helps bring it about. Learning, by this understanding, is *a leap into nothingness and an ordering*. It is predicated on the separation of self from Being. It is predicated, more internally, on the separation of self from self; and it is rendered unpredictable by this same predication. I cannot know what I will end up learning for the learner that I am now is separated from the learner that I will be. It is separated by a nothingness. This nothingness is impassable just because it is nothingness.

Authentic learning, correspondingly, is a process in which consciousness spirals, a process in which the human being is forever transcending himself and enriching his means-ends network in the process. It is predicated on and it culminates in a lucid awareness of one's situation and an assumption of the responsibilities involved. This means an awareness of one's freedom, of one's separation, of the unpredictability of one's journeying. It means an awareness of facticity, of what is given, of what is to be accepted. It means committing oneself wherever freedom is at issue. It occurs through attending to the concrete, through persevering. It is facilitated by scrutiny, reflection and dialogue.

Sartrean theory and adult education

The position lends support to and grounds both the general idea of adult education and key tendencies in the field. As grounding, as fundamental understanding, it supports what we have already built. At the same time, as grounding, as fundamental understanding, it can be used to identify misdirections and to correct. Herein lies its contribution.

To spell this out, and to begin with the support, Sartre's vision of human existence or what I am calling 'learning aware of itself' is essentially a vision of ongoing growth and change. The human being, he suggests, is forever outside of himself and toward what is not. The vision is one of a being who projects himself outward and onward as he progresses in his spiralling from one project to another. This vision contrasts with the conventional understanding of early life as the time of major learning and change, of mid-life as a period of consolidation, and of later life as a period of decline. It contrasts similarly with the notion of institutions as the place where 'real' learning occurs. Correspondingly, it coincides with the views inherent in the adult education movement. As I see it, we adult educators are asserting that learning is:

a   a lifelong task;
b   a task that enters into all facets of existence.

It is not restricted to official institutions and certainly not to the institutions attended from age 7 to 25. Sartre's vision supports this. At the same time, it calls attention to the gradualness of learning, to the relationship between the learner and the world, and to the future orientation – to the standing ahead of oneself – which is inherent in all learning activity.

Just as Sartre's vision lends philosophic support to the notion of adult education as a whole, it lends support to fundamental principles and practices in the field. The most significant of these are:

a   the emphasis on self-direction;
b   the image of the facilitator as someone who respects, allows for, and facilitates self-direction.

In the Sartrean schema, the individual in his freedom establishes his priorities, values, and so forth. To rely on an authority from without to tell him what to learn and what to value is to be guilty of bad faith. Correspondingly, to impose a learning schema on another is to violate the other's freedom. In each case the person involved is acting contrary to the demands of authenticity.

Speaking more practically, Sartrean theory lends support to:

a   the stress adult educators now give to what is concrete;
b   the centrality given to the learner's actual situation;
c   the use of concepts like individual learning projects, especially the more liberal understanding of learning projects as put forward by educationalists like Allen Tough (1971);
d   the insistence by adult educators like Tough (1971) that the adult learner not only is morally responsible for his own learning projects but is in fact generally their principal planner and manager;
e   the emphasis on process and awareness of process;
f   the concept of education as a vehicle for social change, as put forward by educationalists like Freire (1970);
g   the emphasis on personal growth;

h   the appreciation of and commitment to accommodate differences in learning styles;
i   the use of problem-solving models and of group processes;
j   the use of learning contracts.

This support is matched with correction. As philosophical grounding for these tendencies, Sartrean philosophy involves a deeper understanding of them. As deeper understanding, it indicates where misunderstanding has occurred and points the way to correction. Misdirections could be specified and correction given for each of the tendencies touched on to date. To limit myself, however, to the most important of these, one very significant area in which change is called for is in the concept of the facilitator. As already indicated, a respect for self-direction is implicit in the facilitator paradigm and this, certainly, is consistent with Sartre. The extreme aloofness, the extreme pragmatism of the facilitator, however, is called into question. The link which Sartre establishes between authenticity, understanding and dialogue requires the facilitator to be *something more* than the resource person and/or technician which we often find today. Meaningful learning, meaningful change, according to the Sartrean paradigm, is not facilitated by detachment or technical know-how. It is not facilitated either by creating a vacuum or by bombarding the learner with highly adroit flipchart diagrams or multimedia presentations. It is facilitated by intimate understanding, by concern, by involvement. The helper – in this case the adult educator – is called upon to invite concretization and personalization. He is called upon to engage in dialogue, to love, to esteem. The learner's very understanding of himself depends on this interaction. What follows from this is that the notion of self-directed learning itself needs to be modified to make more room for the 'other'.

Correspondingly, the Sartrean notions of understanding, individuality and personal responsibility call into question our reliance on problem-solving models on one hand and group work on the other. To be clear on this, as I have indicated, problem-solving and group work are both sanctioned by Sartre. Indeed, the problem-solving model is well equipped for dealing with concrete problems. Group work, correspondingly, at once facilitates the feedback which Sartre sees as vital and lends itself to societal change. It is not the *use* of problem-solving models and groups but the degree and mode of use which is in question. To comment quickly on the first – on the problem-solving model – in many adult education centres problem-solving has been accepted as THE MODEL OF HUMAN THOUGHT, AS THE MODEL FOR HUMAN LEARNING. This acceptance or overacceptance clashes with the commitment to accommodate different learning styles. Problem-solving itself, after all, is inherently *convergent*, and it supports a *practical* mode of being-in-the-world. Groups pose a somewhat different problem. With our stress on group processes, learners tend to become functions of the group. Authentic selfhood, accordingly, is endangered. While encouraging the human being or learner to work in groups, Sartre asked him to safeguard his personal integrity. He asks the learner to remember that he is an individual with individual projects and responsibilities.

Change is also called for in our approach to projects. As noted earlier, the notion of learning projects is sanctioned by Sartre and even given an ontological foundation. Onus is placed on us, however, to approach it in a less piecemeal fashion, in a more personal fashion. Facilitators and other learners tend to offer a person the type of feedback on a project which befits a project that is 'everybody's and nobody's'. The project is approached by the learner and others as if it were discrete, as if it could be abstracted from everything else, as if it were impersonal. As Sartre makes clear, however, every individual project is part of the human being's *ongoing projection* into the future. It is part of his *emergence*, of his *spiralling*. This emergence is *unique* to him. This emergence has as its facticity all his earlier projecting and it is conditioned by that facticity. In light of this, we need to ask how any project fits with the *particular* learner's existence. We must help him to explore what part it plays or might play in his spiralling and to make the ongoing alterations which this exploration invites.

Finally, to end this section by highlighting a correction which I feel particularly strongly about, change is called for in our approach to learning contracts. The idea of learning contracts *per se* is clearly given sanction. Contracting, after all, is a way of concretizing, persevering, assuming responsibility. What are *not* sanctioned are:

a   our insistence on contracts;
b   our emphasis on tightly designed and administered contracts – contracts, say, in the Mager tradition, which come complete with highly specific behavioural objectives and absolute accountability (Mager 1962).

This insistence and this approach clash with the commitment to accommodate different learning styles, for contracts – and especially tight contracts – are inherently convergent. They clash with the commitment to freedom. Tight contracts, moreover, are incompatible with an understanding of and commitment to process in general, and the process which is the human being or human learner in particular.

The first two points seem clear. To spell out the last, if learning or existence is a leap into nothingness, tightly designed and administered contracts are an abnegation of learning or existence. IF I AM AUTHENTICALLY LEARNING, IF I AM TRULY SPIRALLING, I WILL NOT BE ABLE TO PREDICT WHERE I WILL GO WITH ACCURACY. IF I CAN PREDICT WITH ACCURACY, THERE IS A WAY IN WHICH I ALREADY KNOW WHAT I AM PURPORTING TO LEARN; THERE IS A WAY IN WHICH I HAVE ALREADY ARRIVED AT WHERE I HAVE DECIDED TO GO. At very least,

I am not giving myself fully to the process as indeed I must if authentic learning is to occur. The goal specified in the learning contract – do not forget – is not the *true goal.* The true goal, as Sartre had indicated, is what we desire at the *end,* not what we desire at the *beginning.* In so far as I as learner have come up with a detailed contract that has been agreed on by the person(s) with authority over me, however, my tendency is *to gear my 'learning' to fit the contract, to make the end match the beginning, to do precisely what I said I would do.* This, in fact, is what is expected of me. Spiralling, movement, authentic learning is sacrificed.

The upshot is that we adult educators are called upon to approach learning contracts more flexibly. In this regard, what might be helpful are:

a   a greater willingness to dispense with contracts where the learner finds them oppressive;
b   a greater acceptance of open-ended statements about objectives and procedures;
c   a vision of the proposal or contract as an emergent design or a projective statement which the learner is likely and indeed *encouraged* to transcend.

This said, to end this article by clarifying the general direction which I see as underlying these specific corrections, the Sartrean paradigm is calling upon us to be more process-orientated, more concrete, more reflective, more wholistic, more vigilant, more relational, more personal, more caring, and more trusting. The dutiful side of this is that we need to modify our practices and to rethink our way of being-with-the-learner. The liberating side is that it frees us to be ongoing learners ourselves and to do our own emerging.

Notes

1 For an enunciation of what pertains to Buberian dialogue, see Buber 1979: 17–59 and 1970: 1–222.
2 For a discussion of these and related ontological issues, see Sartre 1956: 3–84 and 55–238.
3 For a discussion of these two forms of anxiety, see Sartre 1956: 50–84.
4 For discussions of both facticity and the universal structures, see Sartre 1956: 127–133 and 619–707.
5 For his discussion of being-for-others, see Sartre 1956: 301–470. For pointers on overdetermination, see Sartre 1965 and 1964.
6 For Sartre on the original project, see Sartre 1956: 712ff. For an analysis of someone who lives his life backward, see Sartre 1967.
7 For Sartre on the significance of love, esteem, mutuality, see Sartre and Contat 1977: 3–91.
8 For Sartre on the commitment to freedom, see Sartre 1957: 9–51.

References

Buber, M. 1970, *I and Thou* (Walter Kaufman, Ed. and Trans.), New York, Charles Scribner's Sons.

Buber, M. 1979, *Between Man and Man* (Ronald Gregor Smith, Trans.), London, Font Paperbacks.

Freire, P. 1970, *Pedagogy of the Oppressed* (Myra Bergam Ramos, Trans.), New York, The Seabury Press.

Mager, R. 1962, *Preparing Instructional Objectives*, Belmont, California, Fearnon Publishers.

Sartre, J.-P. 1956, *Being and Nothingness: A Phenomenological Essay on Ontology* (Hazel E. Barnes, Ed. and Trns.), New York, Pocket Books.

Sartre, J.-P. 1957, 'Existentialism', in Sartre, J.-P. *Existentialism and the Human Emotions* (Hazel E. Barnes, Ed. and Trans.), New York, Philosophical Library.

Sartre, J.-P. 1964, *Saint Genet: Actor and Martyr* (Bernard Frechtman, Trans.), New York, Mentor Books.

Sartre, J.-P. 1965, *Anti-Semite and Jew* (Berge J. Becker, Trans.), New York, Mentor 1Books.

Sartre, J.-P. 1967, *Baudelaire* (Martin Turnell, Trans.), New York, New Directions Paperbacks.

Sartre, J.-P. and Contat, M. 1977, 'Self Portrait at Seventy', in Sartre, J.-P., Contat M. and Rybalka, M. *Life/Situations: Essays Written and Spoken* (Paul Austen and Lydia Davis, Trans.), New York, Pantheon Books.

Tough, A. 1971, *The Adult's Learning Projects*, Toronto, Ontario, Institute for Studies in Education.

17 Making judgments as the basis for workplace learning

Towards an epistemology of practice

David Beckett

University of Melbourne, Australia

Paul Hager

University of Technology, Sydney, Australia

Workplace learning has emerged as a significant site of adults' informal experiential learning, with implications for the provision and shape of formal education. There are, however, a prohibitive number of variables encumbering research into such learning. We can bypass the variables by focusing on phenomenal accounts of how professionals (in this instance) make judgements at work, underpinned by an organic logic derivable from Dewey. This article shows how to characterize a new epistemology of practice through both empirical and conceptual innovation, and thus advances the detail of this new informal workplace learning. This epistemology deals in five characteristics central to lifelong learning anyway, namely: the contingent (rather than exclusively formal, sustained, and systematic studies); the practical (rather than exclusively the theoretical); the process (rather than exclusively the assimilation of content); the particular (rather than the exclusively universal and a priori as the 'context'); and the affective and the social domains (rather than exclusively the cognitive domain). Our fieldwork so far shows, through interview findings, how these are prominent in professional workplace judgments, and what prospects there are for further research on judgment as a site of 'organic' learning for adults.

Learning during daily work: beyond tacit knowledge

Workplace learning offers a powerful way in to exploring connections between lifelong learning and education of various kinds. What do practitioners actually do at work from which they can learn? In this article some empirical evidence is shown and this is connected with education. In *International Perspectives on Lifelong Learning* (Holford *et al.* 1998), it was argued for a new epistemology of practice, centred on the dissolution of the old dichotomies bedevilling education and training (*sic*) (Hager and Beckett 1998). It is believed that such a project is necessitated by the closer attention being given to lifelong learning, because that attention calls into question the reliance upon, and epistemological dominance of, formal learning (such as in award courses) as the best way to perform. If 'experience is the best teacher', the time has come for experience – that great 'given' of adult learning theory and practice – to show what it is made of, insofar as workers find they are taught by it, in the very conduct of their daily work. Up until now, there has been a tendency to call such learning at and through work some mysterious tacit capability. This is not an adequate characterization, even if there is some intuitionistic element that is retained as more forensic attempts are made to ascertain just what and how workers learn from the experience of work.

As has been already claimed, then, research into the phenomenal spectrum of daily workplace experience – how decision-making and judgments go to make up a certain practical wisdom (or, in Aristotle's term, *phronesis*) – is showing a basis for a new and integrative epistemology of practice (Hager and Beckett 1998: 224). Thus, it was argued, lifelong learning in the workplace, structured by mapped experience, is more accurately regarded as lifelong education in the workplace. We claimed to be interested in research which maps site-specific experience, which therefore shows that workplace education emerges from the following:

1   the contingent (rather than exclusively formal, sustained, and systematic studies);
2   the practical (rather than exclusively the theoretical);
3   the process (rather than exclusively the assimilation of content);
4   the particular (rather than the exclusively universal and a priori as the 'context'); and
5   the affective and the social domains (rather than exclusively the cognitive domain).

These five characteristics are features of life experience itself, so could be expected to feature in accounts of learning in the workplace, since workers spend so much time and energy undergoing experiences at work. The further, more radical claim, was that the organic nature of those experiences – that is, the way they are presented as human experiences – strongly indicates that theorizations and research activities centred on (lifelong) workplace learning should recognize and advance that phenomenological holism. Thus the five characteristics listed are organic in that they incorporate their traditional binary opposite, to create a new organic education logic. Support from Dewey (1916) is claimed in this. If organic logic is feasible, then (lifelong) workplace learning can be regarded as lifelong education, albeit an educational experience rather different from that which was, hitherto, and traditionally, the exclusive preserve of formal schooling (including universities) and of traditional on-the-job training. Organic logic does not concern itself with the demarcation of concepts by exclusion, so much as by inclusion. There is an integrative purpose in the application of organic logic in lifelong education – not so that anything can be claimed at whim, as 'lifelong' grist to the mill, but so that specific sites of learning, and all the judgements and decision-making that can occur at these sites, can be shown to generate powerful education, albeit under-recognized until the late twentieth-century. The place to look for the new organic logic in operation is simply at workplaces where some professionals are overtly learning from their work (as is expected of professionals, but of course not only professionals), and who can articulate this to some extent (Beckett 1998a, 1998b). Consider this fragment of an obituary:

> Grant was not a 'lawyer's lawyer'. He would not want to be remembered for his technical abilities or craftsmanship in the law, although it has to be said that he was a most accomplished lawyer. His talents lay more in his use of masterful judgment and tactics in litigation. He always had an uncanny 'feel' for a case.
>
> (Obituary, *The Age*, November 20: 1998: 22)

When a lawyer demonstrates a 'feel' for a case, then, as in many similar situations, there seems to be a reliance on what has become known as 'tacit knowledge', arising from the recognition it has been given by Polanyi, and then by Schon, and then by many other writers concerned with the power of informal learning, arising in experiences. Underpinning these analyses has been the abiding influence of the later Wittgenstein, Ryle, and of course Dewey.

In this article, the more detailed analysis is taken up of this sort of knowledge as a way into the new more organic epistemology of practice referred to above, but without resort to the temptation of the labelling of informal learning in some situations of ordinary experiences as 'tacit'. In attempting to de-mystify such knowledge, the danger is that ascription of 'tacitness' re-mystifies it. Clearly the use of 'tactics' and the reliance on the tacit are related, at least etymologically. In what follows, we want to preserve the centrality of the empirical activity that lies with, for example, a lawyer's 'use of masterful judgment', by enquiring of busy professionals what it is they find themselves doing, at work, in the midst of the 'hot action' (Beckett 1996). This is taken to be significant in the light of the renewed interest in workplace learning, particularly in its informal manifestations (Garrick 1998; Hager and Beckett 1998; Boud and Garrick 1999).

One of the clear findings of this work is that an unusually large number of variables influence workplace learning (Hager 1997b). Such variables include:

- the workplace environment/culture;
- authentic learning experiences;

- quality of learning materials;
- role of language and literacy; and
- company/business size.

This creates the problem of 'far too many variables' for researchers wanting to investigate workplace learning. What is needed is some manageable way of conceptualising workplace learning that draws attention to the main characteristics listed earlier, while at the same time being sensitive to the potential contributions of the many variables that have been shown to influence workplace learning. Learning beyond the simple recognition of tacit knowledge requires, we believe, close attention to the presentation of the learning in the very experiences of the work. This article reports some empirical research which does just that, and therefore fleshes out this conceptual argument in favour of a new epistemology of (lifelong) workplace learning – one which arises in practice.

Judgments and the professional's workplace

In looking to the main features of the phenomenal (that is to say, the organically-presented) nature of workplace learning, a central activity of people learning in the workplace is concentrated upon, namely making judgments. The hypothesis is that making better judgments represents a paradigmatic aim of workplace learning, and that therefore growth in such learning is represented by a growing capacity to make appropriate judgments in the changing, and often unique, circumstances that occur in many workplaces.

Of course, the extent to which workers make judgments during the course of their work depends, amongst other things, on the way that the work is structured and organized. An assembly line, for example, is organized so that workers will exercise minimal judgment, therefore there will be little or no workplace learning. The much discussed 'learning organization' maximizes the exercise of judgment, and, hence, learning. Most jobs fall somewhere between these two extremes. This research project argues further that by theorizing workplace learning in terms of what people actually do (make judgments), we can then take account of the effects of the many variables that influence workplace learning via their influence on such judgments. It turns out that the many variables that influence workplace learning are just the kinds of factors that are taken into account when judgments are made.

The empirical study of the performance of work in a range of occupations with a view to identifying and analysing the main judgments involved in individuals' work performance requires a definition of a judgment. For our purposes, we can say that judgment involves deciding what to believe or do taking into account a variety of relevant factors and then acting accordingly. More generally and technically, according to Lipman '[t]o judge is to judge relationships, either by discovering relationships or inventing them' (Lipman 1991: 16).

The research methods used to study work performances could include:

- observations of work performance;
- interviews with workers about the judgments they make in critical work situations;
- asking workers to account for judgments that others make in critical work situations; and
- examination of holistic competency-based assessment strategies that are in current use in some occupations to determine the nature and extent of judgment in these assessment situations.

For this article, only the second of these methods – interviews with practising professionals (five in Sydney; five in Melbourne) – were utilized. These interviews were each of one hour and were taped, transcribed, returned for 'trustworthiness' revision and then coded and gridded. For the present stage of this project, only some of the details were selected from the first three interviews. Women and men are equally represented in the ten interviews, and the professional work covers, for example, a psychiatrist, a private school principal, a nurse-turned-ambulance officer, a lawyer, a corporate consultant with education/training expertise and two senior public servants.

Ethnomodological research needs to be supplemented by strategies which 'get beneath the surface' of experience, rather than merely report it. Thus, reflective interviews, loosely shaped by common questions, which had not been revealed beforehand, with practitioners on their work performance, can be methodologically informed by Ferry and Ross-Gordon's (1998) 'think aloud' approach. At a more profound level, such interviews draw upon the development of a Dreyfus/Benner interpretive phenomenology, but we are mindful of the debate over the resort to phenomenological analysis in research activity (see Crotty 1996). The ontological implications of a Husserlian 'thing-in-itself' would raise for us some substantial philosophical objections (but not in this paper: basically, like Carr (1998), the traditionally ontologically objectivist view that there is a mind-independent reality is taken).

Workplace experiences as learning

The beginnings of a model of a workplace learning via judgments have been suggested in previous work (Hager 1996a, b and 1997a). This model possibly can be extended by ideas from Dewey's hitherto neglected logic (Burke 1994) and its account of judgments. Traditionally, logic was concerned centrally with universal propositions, which were also the mark of the highest forms of knowledge. In this scheme, judgments were also propositions. On this approach, workplace learning is of little interest, since, at best, its particularities are but distantly connected to the ideal of universal knowledge. Thus the problem becomes one of accounting for how practice is connected to theory. Notoriously theory/practice accounts of workplace judgments have repeatedly failed (Hager 1996b).

Dewey's logic, however, is a logic of action, which repudiates the theory/practice dichotomy (and cognate dichotomies such as discursive vs. practical). It also distinguishes propositions from judgments. With the development of artificial intelligence, robotics, etc. the field of logic is finally turning its attention to the logic of action and Dewey's ideas are starting to receive serious scholarly attention (Burke 1994). In a logic of action, vocational (or professional) knowledge is no longer placed at the periphery of knowledge. Such a logic does not invert the order of traditional logic and privilege the particular over the universal and the practical over the discursive. Rather it incorporates all of these and rejects as false dichotomies theory/practice, universal/particular, discursive/practical, etc. (Hickman 1990).

A model of workplace learning via judgments that is proposed to be developed and in this research builds on the work of Lipman (1991) and Nonaka and Takeuchi (1995) as well as that of Dewey (1916), in that it focuses on the whole lived experiences of workers, not merely their skills, attitudes, and outcomes of these. In this sense, the research is based on an organic logic of action. Such experiences of working life are manifest in daily practices, particularly in decisions where the worker is caught up in and expresses those decisions in what can be called 'hot action' (Beckett 1996, borrowing the term from Marshall McLuhan). These experiences are typically judgmental in that a series of actions issue from deliberations over 'what to do next', when faced with the usual routines and contingencies across the working day. If these actions are 'right' (efficacious, appropriate and so on) it is perhaps mainly because they achieve what was contextually suited. There is in all of this what psychologists are now exploring as 'situated cognition' (Billett 1995, McLellan 1996), but our research picks up the increasing interest in the social and affective aspects of these judgments (Mumford 1993, Karpin 1995, Bowman and Jarrett 1996), especially the idea of 'flow' (Csikszentmihalyi 1992, Goleman 1996), and of the role of 'attention' in human learning (Winch 1998).

In these judgments, individuals 'attend' to their total perceptions of their workplace: cognitive (reason-based), affective (feelings, wants) and social (group and team allegiances) dimensions of these perceptions are only artificially separable. We want to maintain the integrated, organic nature of these perceptions, so that their (literal) 'integrity' is the focus of the empirical investigation of practical judgments. To that end, phenomenological analysis – the imputation of meaningfulness in experience – will be an essential part of the methodology.

However, while these propositions and others like them (which can be grouped as broadly 'cognitive') no doubt contributed to the judgments, there were also other factors that were not wholly propositional. These are conative ('of the will'), emotive and ethical factors. The rest of this article will explore these latter factors, as follows: to what extent and in what ways do interviewees adduce these (non-propositional) factors to their growth in capacity to make judgments?

Three scenarios and discussion

Taking the nurse-turned-ambulance officer as an example, in this scenario below a whole series of 'decisions' (i.e. judgments) are found which are saturated with conative, emotive and ethical considerations. Moreover, in this first paragraph, the respondent's own feelings are clearly not uppermost in her reporting of the scenario – her ambulance-officer partner, and the family are significant here. Later on, when she is asked about that, she is able to articulate three-stage growth in how her non-propositional experiences have related to her judgments.

RESPONDENT: …And the little baby certainly wasn't breathing. The first decision is – do you start resuscitation or not? And there's a whole set of rules that we have about when you do and when you don't start resuscitation. So I made the decision to start … My partner was more frazzled by the situation than I was. He and I had an interesting relationship at that time because he was in a superior position, theoretically, but in practice and knowledge I was ahead of him. So that made it awkward, and he knew that. He felt very uncomfortable about it, and I did too – because of the way he treated me because of that. So the relationship was on the face of it harmonious, but it had some undercurrents that made things difficult. And this resuscitation brought those out because I'm used to resuscitating children, and so I just went into that role. And he wasn't, and he didn't. So we resuscitated the little baby, and we actually got an output, which means that we got some heart rhythm back – which in these circumstances was very unusual and quite unexpected – well not unexpected but unusual. And so another crew arrived, which was the intensive care crew, and so they helped us to continue to resuscitate. Eventually we had to stop.

So I suppose decisions that I made were things like – which equipment to use and when; how to help my partner through it, because he obviously wasn't coping very well with it. He had little kiddies the same age, so apart from the conflict he and I had, I could see it was hard for him anyway. Then dealing with the family obviously was difficult. It is very difficult in the ambulance world because they actively encourage the family to stay around for resuscitation, whereas in nursing they are not as progressive in that way. So it is very difficult doing resuscitation with the family watching, than it was in a hospital where you put them out the door and when it's all over you bring them in again. So during the resuscitation, I had to decide when to speak to them – and when you know, when you're pretty sure that you're not going to get the little baby back – you give them a warning before you stop. And so you have to decide when to do that and how to phrase it. And there's a decision that we've made collectively as a group of officers about whether to stop the resuscitation or whether to keep it going or not.

INTERVIEWER: You do that collectively?

RESPONDENT: Yes. Once it's all finished, you talk to the family about it, and give them some time with the baby. And there's a whole set of protocols about where you take the baby's body and call the police.

INTERVIEWER: So the police arrive while you're there?

RESPONDENT: Yes they did, and that's routine ... it's difficult dealing with the death of children obviously. But I've developed some techniques for dealing with that.

INTERVIEWER: How have you done that?

RESPONDENT: Through exposure I suppose and exploring how my feelings play a part, particularly in my decisions, because after I've been in a situation where I make judgments about things, or just my everyday job – this is from quite a few years ago I started doing this. Looking at what role my emotions played in it, and I found that the more dissatisfied with how I performed, I was, the more my emotions had a played a less than constructive part in the job. So I don't believe you can keep your emotions right out of it or have your emotions controlling the situation. And I think you need to have a balance somewhere in between, and so I'm getting to the point – and I'm practising it – I don't say I do it that well – actually I like to think I do it pretty well. I find it easy to do a job now and keep my emotions right out of it, and think about it later on. And I think that's a step up for me from having my emotions play a part and affect my judgments. And that's a step up from not having your emotions in there at all.

So now I'm getting to the point where I like to be able to feel my emotions at the time, and still have them not impact upon the appropriate judgments and the decisions that I make – and that's complex.

Notice that this is a long way from support for anything like tacit knowledge (inarticulate, ineffable arcana) in judgment, but it does acknowledge a rich array of conative, ethical and emotional factors in the 'hot action' of the scenario outlined.

If the action is cooler (where there is more time for reflection), does tacit knowledge gain a toehold? In the following scenario, it initially appears – as instinct – but then it is substantially qualified by growth in experience, with conative and emotive ('feelings') factors acknowledged but corralled. The interviewee is principal of a large private school.

INTERVIEWER: Where you get resistance to decisions – perhaps with staffing implications – that people wouldn't be comfortable with, or parents not comfortable with, and people land on your doorstep with a gripe, what do you bring to the resolution of these situations?

RESPONDENT: I bring to it an instinct – an instinctive feel for how it fits within our culture and how it fits within our future. Now of course I don't think that I'm conceited because I actually argue with myself all the time but obviously I think my instinct is right...

INTERVIEWER: And you'd have a series of these decisions across several days or across the working year, which could be routine for you, because they are utterly consistent with the way in which you read the situation, or read the culture.

RESPONDENT: Yes.

INTERVIEWER: Where the organization has faced external constraints such as the planning difficulties I read about with your extensions and development – that kind of thing – when you have to make judgments of an overtly political nature involving the media, the local press, and so on, what do you bring to those sorts of judgments?

RESPONDENT: Well you already know what your own plan is in term of you seek advice what you're prepared to do. What is right to do – what is ethical and appropriate. And you may have noticed if you are local that I made a decision very early on that I wasn't going to talk to the press. So that was the end of it. But it has been in the press with the comment that the principal hasn't returned a call or wasn't available. That's fine ... You have to know what you're doing for your own organization is right in the first place. You have to be very sure about that...

INTERVIEWER: I wanted to build on the idea of what I take to be reliance on intuition.

RESPONDENT: Right. Huge, huge.

INTERVIEWER: So when I say, and you say, 'the reading of the culture', a lot of that is intuitionistic?

RESPONDENT: And a build up of that experience. If you'd interviewed me say six or seven years ago – different, different totally.

INTERVIEWER: But can we formalize that more in knowledge-based terms so that you can say – 'Look I'm the principal and I've got this depth of experience': It's different from when I started the job. I'm able to say just by rule of thumb. I can exercise judgments that I know are going to be more or less effective.

RESPONDENT: Oh yes.

INTERVIEWER: So even against the odds you might pull something off with the council, staff, or people within the community because you backed a hunch that you could really formalize this knowledge.

RESPONDENT: Oh. I do that quite a bit and I'm always pleased when it's something that is my idea, that a lot of people didn't want at the time. We just sort of say OK well we'll try it and the people find they actually *do* like it. However we also try and work in a team way on a whole variety of decisions but another thing I'd say, I can't remember in my ten years working with the school council (and their culture has changed too and some of that would be my influence ...), I can't remember anything that I've asked for that doesn't happen...

INTERVIEWER: Now, based on that, I'm picking up the feeling that it's important for you that a challenging judgment is something that shouldn't really arise in an *ad hoc* or unforeseen fashion. It's very important to have it thought through, deliberated upon, well-resourced, justified, and so on. So I'm wondering if in the daily course of your work there is very much reliance on the emotions, feelings.

RESPONDENT: What sorts of feelings?

INTERVIEWER: Trusting them.

RESPONDENT: When it comes to trusting them?

INTERVIEWER: Yes, instinct is fine, but this sort of warmer, fuzzier idea of feelings.

RESPONDENT: No I don't think so – not if it's got to be cool objective thinking ... I think I'm being utterly objective when I can disassociate myself from feelings, friendships, and other alliances and say look at the big picture, look at this, look at that. So no I don't think so.

INTERVIEWER: So if somebody walked in to see you and they had a particular problem and they dissolved into a flood of tears – would you be less likely to modify the point of view that you had?

RESPONDENT: I don't know. I'd – depending on who it was – I'd put my arm around them and want to solve their personal problem first and then deal with the rest of it ... Two other things, unrelated but maybe not, I love it when someone walks through my door and says 'I've done something terrible: I've got the most dreadful problem you can imagine', because I instinctively know it's going to be the most easy thing to solve of the lot.

But secondly, if someone – as will happen today – walks through my door for an interview – then when I'm choosing people for interview to come and work here, as you know from research, the CV goes out the window the minute they come through the door and instinct takes over but also a little bit of that is feelings. And even though they may not fit your criteria, they're some of the most critical judgments I ever make for the school – picking the right people ... It's my principal job – getting the right people into this school.

What seems to be emerging is a distinction between the role of, and evidence adduced towards, making a judgment, in, first, an initial situation where the need to make a judgment is presented, and, second, a continuous situation where the actual judgment is made. Interviewees seem to be able to distinguish between a cluster of conative, emotive and ethical factors relevant to the framing of the initial situation (instinct comes in there, but so does propositional knowledge, presenting as past experiences), and a cluster of these factors relevant to the framing of the judgment itself.

In this third scenario, the action is midway between the heat of the emergency resuscitation, and the cool of the private school: the interviewee is a psychiatrist. She carefully separates the two situations (diagnosis and treatment, in this case) drawing on several conative, emotive and ethical factors, but packaging these adroitly as sociopolitical considerations, which actually determine the clinical response to the medical diagnosis.

INTERVIEWER: When you need to make a decision, how do you decide what you're going to do? I have a few examples. Do you decide based on intuition – perhaps a feeling? Do you have an ethical response? Is it a cognitive principle? Or is it possibly a blend?

RESPONDENT: It's obviously a blend of all three ... The first information I have is theoretical knowledge of the situation – of someone who has a psychotic illness – I know a lot about that. I know what is optimal, and I know what is necessary. Now what I actually do has to be based on an ethical system as well, and it has to be based on the legal implications and responsibility, in terms of the care. So there are many factors in this. But the major thing that directs what you do in this clinic – the clinic in which I work – is the facilities that we actually have for carrying out what is necessary. And so it's a blend of all those things – the practicality of it, the needs of the patient in the given situation. Now if you wish to speak optimally for the young man who was in withdrawal, the optimal situation would be for him to be placed in reasonably long-term care – and quickly, treated medically, withdrawn from his drugs, and then put into a programme which would protect him to a degree from his capacity to use drugs further. So he couldn't in fact get them, and would be given long-term rehabilitation. Now none of these things exist at the moment. So these are the things that you have to weigh up, but what you end up with is a totally unsatisfied arrangement where he was allowed to go – allowed to leave, and then overdosed, shortly afterwards...

INTERVIEWER: So you're saying that your judgments are curtailed by what's available?

RESPONDENT: What we can actually do, what positions we reach, are based on the practical availability of the services in the end.

INTERVIEWER: When you're presented with one of these situations, do you find yourself trying to fit this particular instance into a familiar pattern, or sometimes do you find you are trying to establish a new pattern to meet the specific instance?

RESPONDENT: There's a familiarity in the cases that are presented to us. They're all very much the same in many ways due by the nature of the illness these people suffer. There is familiarity at that level. The differences occur in terms of the social milieu from which the people come. Because we are accepting the most handicapped people, from the poorest level of society, there is also familiarity of the patterns because these people are all on welfare. They're all unable to work. The vast majority of them have got into the hands of people involved in drug use. So all these situations are becoming familiar and have become quite familiar over the last five years. But this is quite different to say ten years ago.

INTERVIEWER: Just thinking of the young man – the way you described how you coped with his situation. Do you think that was a spontaneous response? The way you described it, it was – it was very unfamiliar and you really had to come up with some 'out of left field' response.

RESPONDENT: Yes, that's unusual because the drug services have recently been cut back from that area. Once upon a time there used to be services for acute withdrawal patients – to help people with drug addiction. And now they don't exist. They only exist if people are capable of waiting, and capable of fulfilling all these conditions drug and alcohol services put down. Which in fact keep the people away from care because they can't fulfil the requirements. They can't wait till 5 o'clock and ring up every day to check whether there is a place or a bed to use for them in a particular institution. They don't have the money. They don't have the telephone. They don't have the capacity to do it...

INTERVIEWER: When you decided to give him those drugs, and you were thinking about it – did you find yourself thinking – if I do this, this might happen. Or if I do this, this will. Is there a certain scenario that's going on in your head?

RESPONDENT: A definite scenario because we knew he came in specifically to get benz. We knew that if we didn't give the benz, he'd be in worse withdrawal. We knew that it was illegal in crisis to prescribe the amount of benz that he was in fact taking. So we couldn't even prescribe a sufficient dose to cover his withdrawal. So we knew that by giving him a dose supply he'd take the lot at once, and probably go out and go to another doctor and get more, or steal them, or buy them in the street. We knew that would happen and we weren't surprised when we heard he had a major drug overdose shortly after. [pause]

    There is spontaneity in so far as you've seen most situations before and you're familiar with them and you know what the procedures are and the way to approach. Given unusual scenarios, like the situation with this drug victim, there's not much that we actually spontaneously do because we always discuss it. So that, for example, I had long discussions with another care worker at the time the young man presented. So it's very rarely that we do anything without considerable talk. So it's not spontaneous. It's usually mutually decided and agreed upon, and if there's any doubt about the ethical nature of the problem, or you're really concerned, you go to a more senior consultant, and discuss the situation before you actually act … There's not a lot of responding to the person and the problem. In fact that's what you have to make a lot of distance from. You really have to take into account lots of factors. The more factors you know, the more you take into account.

INTERVIEWER: So you don't believe that you act spontaneously – it's very much a calculated thought, based on your experience, most of the time.

RESPONDENT: Yes. With people who are working in a field – very specialized fields for a very long period of time. As I've had 35 years of experience, there's not a lot that's new. It's just variation and many of the responses that I would give now are thoroughly learned responses which have become a part of me. So that I don't have to think the way someone who's greeting the situation for the first time has to think. If you watch people coming into this and observing what we're doing, they're quite nonplussed. They're quite confused, disordered, distressed by it all because they tend to be more reactive to the patient who is often in extreme distress. But once you've been doing it for a long time you tend to distance yourself from that. You don't get involved at the distress level. So you're not reacting.

Conclusion

The three scenarios have dealt centrally with the five characteristics of life experience which (listed in section 1) fit a new (organic) model of workplace learning, namely:

1   the contingent – the informal, non-routine and capricious nature of daily work is overtly decisional;
2   the practical – the need to solve problems efficaciously (the Aristotelian 'good' result) is paramount;
3   the process – Schonian reflection-on-action has generated expectations of professional growth;
4   the particular – the need to address the here and now with compromise is accepted by our interviewees; and
5   the affective and the social domains – judgments are basically (but not entirely) value judgments; because which cognitive considerations are

entertained depends on how they can be made sense of, conatively, emotionally and ethically.

If our three professional practitioners were dealing in these five sorts of work-and-life-given experience, then the interview data shows that growth in capacity to make judgments occurs in three ways. These are: (a) an ability to separate the stage of the presentation of the initial need to make a judgment, from the stage of the contiguous actualization of that judgment; (b) an ability to 'read' the conative, emotive and ethical considerations in the light of that separability (such considerations will be factored in differently for each stage); and (c) the de-centring of the practitioner's sense of identity at one of these stages, but not in both of them.

Thus an epistemology of practice which unpacks (lifelong) workplace learning in an organic sense seems to require a growing (and growth-oriented) sophistication in the ability to discriminate (a), (b) and (c) – both between them, and within each of them. Now this ability to discriminate is frequently taken to be one of the hallmarks of the (formally) educated person. We believe that in daily work life, a sophisticated epistemology of practice will generate the ability to articulate the subtle discriminations required by the demands of the job, and that (a), (b) and (c) are necessary but insufficient criteria of that sophistication. An organic logic will acknowledge the strengths of this discrimination, as complementary to the traditional educational virtues of sustained formal studies. Such logic de-mystifies the obituary's epistemologically fascinating claim that 'Grant ... had an uncanny "feel" for a case'. Moreover, such logic connects life and work in ways that offer great educational promise.

Notes

David Beckett is a Senior Lecturer in the department of Vocational Education and Training at the University of Melbourne, Australia.
Paul Hager is a Professor in the School of Education, University of Technology Sydney, Australia.

References

Beckett, D. (1996) Critical judgment and professional practice. *Educational Theory*, 46, 135–149.
Beckett, D. (1998a) Past the guru and up the garden path: the new organic management learning. In D. Boud and J. Garrick (eds) *Understanding Learning At Work* (London: Routledge).
Beckett, D. (1998b) Anticipative Action and Its Contribution to An Epistemology of Workplace Learning. Papers of the *Annual Conference of the Philosophy of Education Society of Great Britain*. New College Oxford, April 3–5 1998.
Billett, S. (1995) Workplace learning: its potential and limitations. *Education and Training*, 37, 20–27.

Boud, D. and Garrick, J. (eds) (1999) *Understanding Learning at Work* (London: Routledge).

Bowman, C. and Jarrett, M. (1996) *Management in Practice*, 3rd edn. (Melbourne: Oxford University Press).

Burke, T. (1994) *Dewey's New Logic: A Reply to Russell* (Chicago and London: University of Chicago Press).

Carr, D. (ed.) (1998) *Education, Knowledge and Truth: Beyond the postmodern impasse* (London: Routledge).

Crotty, M. (1996) *Phenomenology and Nursing Research* (Melbourne: Churchill Livingstone).

Csikszentimihalyi, M. (1992) *Flow: The Psychology of Happiness* (London: Rider).

Dewey, J. (1916) *Democracy and Education*, 1966 edn. (New York: Free Press).

Ferry, N. M. and Ross-Gordon, J. M. (1998) An inquiry into Schon's epistemology of practice: exploring links between experience and reflective practice. *Adult Education Quarterly*, 48, 98–112.

Garrick, J. (1998) *Informal Learning in the Workplace* (London: Routledge).

Goleman, D. (1996) *Emotional Intelligence: Why It Can Matter More Than IQ* (London: Bloomsbury).

Hager, P. (1996a) Relational realism and professional performance. *Educational Philosophy and Theory*, 28, 98–116.

Hager, P. (1996b) Professional practice in education: research and issues. *Australian Journal of Education*, 40, 235–247.

Hager, P. (1997a) Knowledge and knowledge productivity. Unpublished paper for conference, *Knowledge Productivity*, University of Leiden, The Netherlands, November.

Hager, P. (1997b) *Learning in the Workplace*. Review of Research Monograph Series (Adelaide: National Centre for Vocational Education Research).

Hager, P. and Beckett, D. (1998) What would lifelong education look like in a workplace setting? In J. Holford, P. Jarvis and C. Griffin (eds) *International Perspectives on Lifelong Learning* (London: Kogan Page), 224–235.

Hickman, L. A. (1990) *John Dewey's Pragmatic Technology* (Bloomington and Indianapolis: Indiana University Press).

Holford, J., Jarvis, P. and Griffin, C. (eds) (1998) *International Perspectives on Lifelong Learning* (London: Kogan Page).

Karpin, D. (Chair) (1995) Enterprising nation: renewing Australia's managers to meet the challenges of the Asia-Pacific century. Report of the Industry Task Force on Leadership and Management Skills (Canberra: Australian Government Publishing Service).

Lipman, M. (1991) *Thinking in Education* (Cambridge: Cambridge University Press).

McLellan, M. (ed.) (1996) *Situated Learning Perspectives* (New Jersey: Educational Technology Publications).

Mumford, A. (1993) *How Managers Can Develop Other Managers* (Aldershot: Gower).

Nonaka, I. and Takeuchi, H. (1995) *The Knowledge-Creating Company* (Oxford and New York: Oxford University Press).

Winch, C. (1998) *The Philosophy of Human Learning* (London: Routledge).

18 Being and becoming

A student trajectory

Ronald Barnett[1]

Institute of Education, University of London

What is it to become a student? Higher education is an institution deliber-ately designed to sustain differentiated and public forms of human experience and seeks to enable individuals to get on the inside of those external forms of experience. The student experience of so doing is, however, a private affair. How do we make sense of this interaction of the private and public realms of the student experience? In coming into a proper relationship with an epistemological framework, the student dis-places herself into that framework. With educational displacement comes a trajectory. The trajectory can continue upward, with the student gaining more confidence; or it can flatten off; or it can fall away, with the student losing interest in her studies and with her cognitive powers diminishing. The trajectory offers a form of becoming: the student becomes herself in a new guise – her own new, and authentic, person. The being of the student is achieved through a process of becoming the student.

Introduction

What is it to be a student? Currently, there is an extraordinary gap in our conceptual understanding of the term 'student'. The gap has to do with the intersection of the private and public realms of human experience, at the intersection of which stands the student. 'Stands', of course, is an inadequate metaphor. The student is both partly constituted by and actively – to varying degrees – produces that *mélange* of experience.

The key problem before us is easily stated. Higher education, perhaps more than any other social institution, is an institution deliberately designed to sustain differentiated and public forms of human experience and, in its educational task, seeks to enable individuals to get on the inside of those external bodies of experience. The student experience of so doing, the totality of intellectual and emotional experiences which consti-tute an unfolding trajectory, is however partly a private affair. The ques-tion before us is: how do we make sense of this interaction of the private and public realms of experience?

Does one have priority over the other? Is it that the external has to be transformed into the internal for it to have significant meaning? Or is it that the internal has to yield to the external in order for the integrity of the external to be maintained and realized in the mind of the student? Things are of course more complicated than this either/or formulation seems to admit. But simply to ask the questions plunges us immediately into conceptual difficulties. They reveal a fundamental gap in our understanding of higher education. A shorthand characterization of this gap is that we do not understand how higher education works: inside out or outside in?

Postmodernism says that anything goes. But postmodernism has not yet been adopted by the academy. The university remains, indeed intensifies its function as, a social institution for sustaining technical and elaborate discourses around sets of communicative rules. Developed by the subcultures of the academic community, the disciplines still stand as the cognitive capital of the university. Certainly, the disciplines are changing as the relationship between the state and its universities become closer. Even more technical, but also experiential *and* policy oriented in character, the disciplines – to a greater or lesser extent – are eager to demonstrate their appropriateness for the modern society. Performativity is the name of this game, both in personal competences and in the use-value of the intellectual capital on offer.

The character of the disciplines comes under some strain, therefore. The human competences they deliver are said to be inadequate. What is now required by the ever-changing labour market is metacompetences (Fleming 1991), capacities to respond to unpredictable situations and to renew one's cognitive capital through one's lifespan. Cognitive capital is itself an inadequate characterization of the accoutrements now to be fastened on. Nor is cultural capital a helpful alternative formulation. Culture and traditions are seen as regressive, as resistant to change. Human orientations not just to enter but to create a brave new world are called for. 'Flexibility' becomes one of the key code words of our time; and its core lies in its attitudinal aspect. This is not yet postmodernism, but an advanced form of modernism. Society both retains structure and calls for high-level expertise; but the specific structures of postmodern society and its associated expertise change with increasing rapidity.

The university finds itself called forth to assist these transformations in human capital. Currently, we are in the midst of changes and new demands on the educational functions of the university that we can scarcely comprehend. High-level disciplinary knowledge and skills, wider societal and work competences turning especially on advanced forms of interaction and communication ('transferable skills'), new attitudes to change and innovation, and even ethical development all crowd into the curriculum. The student is confronted with all of this and more.

Much, then, stands externally to the student, to be mastered, comprehended, and exhibited in performance. To academic competence have been added societal competence and work competence; to narrow skills have been added general metaskills to sustain the graduate in a world of unimaginable change.

So fulfilling the role of student is more demanding than ever. And the students, being rational persons wishing to make their way in the world, know this and respond to it. Precisely because of the press of the totality of the external demands, students may all too easily adopt coping strategies to enable them to get through. No longer is the role construed as the development, in interaction with one's peers, of an oppositional role to society. The external demands on the students are considerable. Instead, the challenge is construed as acquiring the degree, preferably with as little effort as possible. If the notion of 'student' is framed by the external world, if students are expected to become this or to do that or to acquire these competences, it is hardly surprising if students feel that their becoming is not of their making. The task of being a 'student' accordingly becomes one of meeting others' agendas as painlessly as possible.

The acquisition of the required competences is seen by the students for what it is: the demands of a real external world. 'Real' in the sense that its externality and its demands are *there*, even if those demands and the future that they represent are literally uncertain.

Yet responsiveness to external demands cannot be the full story of what it is to be a student. There are internal demands, too, at least in the archaeology of the idea of 'student'. Realms of thought and action both supply internal demands, 'internal' in the sense of being internal to the forms of thought and action which partly constitute student being.

Thought, for example, is itself a complex so far as the student experience is concerned. Learning, cognition and understanding are only some of the relevant concepts. Each is an achievement term as well as having task components (Peters 1967). They point to processes which are intellectually demanding in themselves; they may be painful, arduous, even perplexing. But they also point to processes which have their own inbuilt standards.

We can point to mental processes as involving learning, cognition or understanding when certain kinds of states of mind are achieved. We could not talk of understanding if the student was not able to form ideas and propositions which had some kind of verisimilitude. We could not talk of learning unless the student had reached changed his/her state of mind and was now able to say new things coherently or do things anew. We could not talk of cognition unless the insight that accompanied it had some kind of internal anchoring and structure.

So forming an understanding of the kind appropriate to higher education is to yield to epistemological demands. Even more active forms of demand bear in on the notion of student, however.

While not a logical part of the mental states they pick out, understanding, learning and cognition reveal themselves in time in action. I mean action here in a particular sense. Expressing a point of view, analysing a compound, interrogating a text, bringing together different theories in a synoptic offering, critically examining one's own utterances and coming up with a counter claim: all these – and many others – are forms of action. They require the student to act, to say implicitly this is where I am in my understanding and to offer personal significations for possible evaluation. These acts are interventions in the world: in making utterances of this kind, propositions are formed and offered to the world.

Originality has nothing to do with this point. What is at issue is that the act of making a statement is itself to intervene in the world. The student becomes active, more fully herself and no longer a passive recipient of encountered experiences. There is difficulty here for the student, since to make a statement of one's own requires a certain toughness. It is to take a risk.[2] No longer willing to hold onto others' quotations or computations, the student does it or says it for herself.

These difficulties are not the intellectual difficulties mentioned a moment ago. These difficulties are personal, and ontological. They arise out of the nature of truth telling. Following Habermas (1991), we can say that participation in a truth-orientated discourse imposes a range of ethical demands. First, in offering a proposition of her own, the student is submitting herself to others' evaluations. Second, the proposition has to be offered in such a way that it can be understood by the prospective listener or reader; there has to be a receptiveness to the discourse at work. Third, there has to be a coherence or orderliness about the interventions; *ad hoc*cery or a sequence of unconnected offerings will not do. Lastly, the student has to have a degree of personal commitment to what she says or does; there have to be components of sincerity and ownership at work. Otherwise, we could say at best that we were in the presence of duplicity; at worst, in the presence of plagiarism or cheating.

In short, being a student in its fullest sense imposes internal demands on both thought and action which arise out of entering and beginning to participate in a truth-orientated community. No wonder that students, especially when faced with the external demands we noted earlier, opt for the easy life. Playing the game, getting by, engaging in conspiracies to buck the system, towing the line, and simply doing the necessary to acquire the degree award: these are understandable stances of students in the modern age.

There is, therefore, both an internal student and an external student. On the one hand, we have the student grappling with the interior demands of understanding, of inner conceptual struggle, of formulating coherent thoughts and ideas, and of definite and bold expression. This is a virtually invisible student. Sometimes, we catch such students as they show themselves in their hesitant responses and uneasy formulations or, indeed, their silences. On the other hand, we have the external student, the student picking up the messages of the wider world and responding more or less to them. This is the student occasionally mentioned in policy documents, whether of the state or even of the university itself. This external student also has, we should note, an invisibility about it; or rather, a fictive character. It is a hypothetical student, an assumed student, a two-dimensional student largely passive in the face of the external demands which press themselves forward, simply acquiring uncritically the prescribed transferable skills and providing the sought-for human capital for the economy.

Inside out or outside in? How can we bring these two images of 'student' into a relationship with each other? What *is* their relationship? Does either side of the relationship have priority? Is it a case of the external world impinging on an otherwise pure inner life and distorting it; or is it a case of the inner life taking its bearings and, indeed, shape from the external world? To reply that it is neither of these and that the relationship is much more subtle, or dynamic or dialectical is no answer at all. Responses of that kind are evasions unless they can give us some insight into the structure of the relationship.

On understanding 'the student experience'

It should be noted that what is in question here is not in essence an empirical matter but a conceptual matter of what we take the nature of 'student' to be. What is at issue here is the doubtless perplexing issue of what it is to be a student in its fullest sense. Certainly, we can conduct inquiries into 'the changing student experience' or 'student satisfaction' or students' 'approaches to learning' (to cull some contemporary examples from the current scholarly and policy discourses).[3] But empirical inquiries of this kind do not and cannot shed light on the fundamental issue before us. Indeed, those empirical inquiries are largely groundless unless we have some answer to the conceptual question here.

We can hardly mount a serious empirical inquiry into student life and consciousness unless we have a prior notion of 'student'. First, we shall not know what to look at. And second, we shall be devoid of any critical standard against which to assess our findings. That empirical inquiries of the kind just mentioned do usually end by making implicit critical evaluations (of the character of the learning or of the experience) and yet have not usually embarked on a prior conceptual examination of the kind being suggested is an indication that prior and implicit judgements have been entered into about the ideal nature of 'student'. This absence – of an explicit conceptual inquiry – is not an indication that it is not necessary.

The inquiry required here, however, cannot be purely conceptual. If it is to be adequate to its object, it has to take into account the dominant features of the external world. If it is to say anything of substance about the interplay of the inner life with the outer world, it has to be sensitive minimally to the character of that external world with which the typical student has to cope. In understanding higher education, philosophy does real work only when it is sociologically informed.

Two worlds

Let us start in an entirely schematic way by picking out, without any pretence at comprehensiveness, features of the internal and external worlds of being a student (table 1). The 18 pairs of terms in the two columns are not intended to be polar opposites. If they appear to resonate with each other across the columns, that is an additional value in the table; its first purpose is simply to put flesh on my earlier claim, that there are two students before us, the external and the internal and that they are different from each other. It is possible to weave an apparently coherent story about a fictive student drawing only on the terms in one of the columns, even if it would be an improverished account of what it is to be a student.

In fact, most policy documents – in so far as they do mention students – limit themselves just to the sense of 'student' drawn from the left-hand 'external' column. The public accounts of what it is to be a student are fictive in a double sense. First, they imply that a student is just an amalgam of the external requirements of students called for by modern society: if a student can respond positively to all those demands represented by the left-hand column, the task of being a 'student' is complete.

The second fiction is even more serious. It is the implicit characterization of 'student' as merely responsive, as fulfilling others' agendas. The fiction is that, as we have seen, this view is epistemologically naïve. Entering actively a truth-orientated discourse calls forth action. This fiction is no accident, however. It buttresses an ideology, a view that this is how the life of the student should be construed. The ideology at work is a silence:

Table 1 Features of the two worlds of a student

External	Internal
Higher education structures	Person
Policies	Self
Universities as organizations	Personal projects
Disciplines	Beliefs
Research	Meaning
Objective knowledge	Personal knowing
Received 'truths'	Own effort towards verisimilitude
Institutions	Ideas
Institutional culture	Own values
Courses	Experiences
Staff	'I'
Libraries	Own struggles at articulation
Teaching	Understandings
Institutional resources	Inner strength
Discourses	Making sense for oneself
Outcomes	Personal achievements
Competencies	Meeting one's own targets
Degrees and awards	Becoming

no longer is the prospect entertained that the student might offer an oppositional source in the shaping of modernity. The outcomes are defined in advance. The task of the student is to fall in with the specification.

But silences are to be found in notions of student which stand essentially on the other side of the table. Notions of andragogy, of experiential learning, of reflection, of group-based learning and of learning contracts are, in certain formulations, attempts to be sensitive to the inner world of the learner and can result in curricula which are largely based in the right-hand column. Adult learning and some forms of professional education exhibit this *Weltanschauung* among others. The starting point is the student as learner with experiences which are valuable in themselves. The next claim is that learning has personal meaning and, therefore, personal power and longevity, when based on experiences in the curriculum which are owned by the student herself. *En route*, it is suggested that peer interaction – and, thereby, a minimization of the presence of authorial presences – is a key to enabling this concrete learning to become embedded in one's cognitive strata. The concluding destination is that of particular kinds of personal development marked out by such terms as authenticity, self-realization, empowerment, transformation and even emancipation.

This, too, despite its best endeavours to do justice to the real, to the inner struggles of students, to their human-ness, is another set of fictions. It pretends that students and their learning can seriously be understood independently of the external world in which they are placed. Here, the task of teaching is construed as enabling, as facilitating and as supporting. Mentoring, for some time a term with currency in professional fields and in adult education, now makes its appearance in higher education proper. Indeed, the idea of teaching is itself skewed. Command over a discipline, a national or even an international reputation in scholarship or research, are not to be paraded. Authority arises out of skill in interactions which produce self-becoming and self-authorship on the part of the student.

It will be said that this is to confuse two things: the internal experience of being a student, as caught in the right-hand column of our earlier table, and a certain *Weltanschauung* coming into higher education from adult and professional education in which the student's pysche takes centre stage.

The point being made here, however, is that the latter, the consciousness-focused *Weltanschauung*, finds a home in higher education today because of the new receptivity that the emerging curricular offer. The ideology of life experience is welcomed precisely because of its resonance with the new internalism in curriculum thinking now arising as higher education becomes a quasi-market. Both exhibit a sensitivity to the student as a human being with an internal consciousness of her own, as someone engaged in a personal struggle to make sense of the world, and as someone with her own legitimate offerings. The incoming ideology adds a sensitivity to feelings, experiences, worthwhile beliefs and personal values. In other words, the ideology tells us that students are adults with full personalities of their own and not just an assembly of cognitive processes.

And never the twain

We have, then, two rival versions of what it is to be student: one that takes seriously the necessary personal components of participating in a truth-orientated discourse; the other that underlines that participation in higher education itself in the modern age is not just a personal whim but is a deliberate result of state policy. The one requires individuation; the other treats students – as the term makes clear – simply as a unit within a largely undifferentiated mass.

This double vision of the student is hardly new. 'According to Kant, [in understanding the university] a sharp distinction was to be made between the private and the public spheres' (Liedman 1993: 76). What is new are the tendencies towards polarization of the two spheres. Whereas the German concept of *Bildung*, in its combination of personal development and intellectual acculturation, offered a bridge between the two senses of 'student' (cf. Rothblatt 1993), now we are seeing signs of the two senses splitting off from each other with little apparently to bring them together.

On the one hand, the planners, in their eagerness to forge a mass higher education system to meet the requirements of the economy within an ever leaner resourcing envelope, forget that even to have the capabilities sought by modernity calls forth deep personal qualities. On the other hand, the experientialists implicitly deny the brute facts of the external world. And they do so not only by neglecting the policy framework which has led to the students' presence; they also even downplay the reality of the academics' discourses and the fine-grained conceptual worlds already constructed and which students have to come to inhabit if they are to make any serious sense of the academic world.

I said that the gap between these two worlds, the public and the private, is growing. The reasons are clear enough. As the higher education system grows, so it becomes internally more differentiated. To the sub-cultures of the academics are added the interests of the wider society – mediated in more or less benign ways by the new corps of university managers – and the claims of new constituencies such as the adult learners. In some of its forms, notably mid-nineteenth century Germany, the traditional gap between teacher and learner was slight. All were learners on a philosophical journey. That gap has become more pronounced in an age of mass higher education and has been compounded by the new interests that have emerged. In some perceptions, the student simply is a product of the system that enters or does not enter the labour market; in others, the student is a pure centre of consciousness, engaged on a journey of self-discovery.

How, conceptually, might these two worlds be brought together? Or, to phrase the question differently, how is higher education possible? What is the relationship between the internal and external worlds of becoming a student?

The use of the term 'worlds' in the last sentence may seem to point us in a helpful direction. Both Popper (1975) and Leavis (1969), for example, spoke of the different worlds of World I, the external world of spatio-physical objects; of World II, the world of the inner consciousness; and World III, the world of objective knowledge. But, unless we can begin to fill in the ways in which those worlds interrelate, we are no better off. Admittedly, both made some schematic remarks on the matter. Popper insisted that World III acts on World I, but only through World II; but he left the nature of those interactions elusively open.

The matter is of some practical importance. What is it to teach in higher education? The teacher has to have some conception of the kind of integration being aimed at between the internal and external worlds if the necessary integration is to be brought about. The practical motivation suggests less a philosophical inquiry into the concepts of either 'teaching' or 'learning' but a more psychological path. Talk of integration perhaps points us towards a Piagetian schema of assimilation and accommodation (1971). There, surely, we find the makings of a conceptual framework for comprehending how the two worlds come together. But even if the ideas of assimilation and accommodation can be filled out, that does not help us in the present situation. For we would only have insight into the internal psychological processes at work.

What is at stake, to repeat, is the relationship of the external and the internal. And the relationship in question here is a conceptual one. What is implied in our conception of 'student' for the external and the internal to come into a relationship with each other? How can personal becoming and external frameworks have *any* fruitful relationship with each other?

Perry's stage theory of ethical and epistemological development looks a promising candidate (Perry 1970). There, we see a model of student becoming which precisely involves the internal world of student consciousness and the external world of cognitive structures with which the student is struggling to come to terms. That theory, of progressive cognitive independency from epistemological frameworks, *is* helpful. There, we have a sense of an internal struggle over time, and a progressive process of student becoming. Ultimately, the student reaches a point of hard-won independence, an independence built on the epistemological frameworks which are now internalized but yet are objectified. In the end, the student declares and commits herself, makes the quasi-ethical stand of saying: here I stand.

Elsewhere, I have suggested that Perry's stage theory needs to be carried further if the student's independence is to be maximized (Barnett 1994). Stages of critique and displacement have to be added, to allow the student the space to see through both the framework's ideological and other limitations so as to have the personal power simply to call it up as a resource as and when required. The framework is *deployed* with a sceptical and even playful detachedness.

Yet such refinements of the Perry model carry us only so far. The Perry model is still, ultimately, psychological. It is concerned with the internal states of mind, albeit states of mind which are wrestling with the external world. The external world is taken as given.

The possibility, therefore, begins to arise that the problem is insoluble. The internal and the external worlds of the student are two worlds and we can give no coherent account of their relationship. Indeed, it could be argued that there is no relationship. The argument could run like this. The external and the internal worlds are separate in several senses. The first world is epistemological, economic and policy-driven in character; the second is private, personal and psychological. We understand these worlds, live in them, constitute ourselves (as teachers, policy makers and students) by resorting to different discourses in relation to the life of the student. There is a difference, then, in their logics. The inner and the outer worlds cannot be brought together. The twain does not and cannot meet.

On splitting the difference

Yet, we know they do come together. Whether in grappling with tedious lectures, in coming to terms with insufficient material resources, or making sense of the host institution which is termed 'university', students do in their mental states normally negotiate some kind of equilibrium with the epistemological, economic and policy worlds which they are obliged to inhabit. Their outer and inner shells fuse, even if they do not become one. And many are able to show their Perry-like independence from it all as well.

How is this possible? Unless we have some notion of how it *is* possible, we are devoid of any satisfactory account of what it is to be a student. One way forward may lie in beginning from the fact that, at least pragmatically, students do seem to be able to live both in the internal world which they construct and the external worlds imposed on them. But that, of course, in the absence of the empirical work, remains supposition. We just do not know to what extent students do in fact bring the internal and external worlds together coherently.

It should be clear that there is no easy middle position open to us. We cannot split the difference. There is no half-way house or world which students could be said to inhabit. It may be that students live uneasily in both their internal and others' external worlds. But there is no happy resting place between them. It would have no discourse, no language community and no inhabitants. There would be no home for it. We are back, therefore, to puzzling out the internal/external relationship.

On living in the third world

In this section, I want to proffer the outlines of what I believe is a solution to the problem I have been discussing. The solution lies in the idea of displacement. I raised earlier the idea of displacement in discussing Perry's stage theory of cognitive and ethical development. The ultimate stage, on that theory, is one in which the student effectively is able to stand aside from the disciplinary framework, because she can see it for what it is, warts and all. Here, though, I want to develop a contrary sense of displacement, in which the student displaces not the external framework (in forming a relationship to it) but herself. In coming into a relationship with an epistemological framework, in becoming intellectually independent, the student displaces herself *into* that framework.

Talk of a single framework is misleading here. There are at least two frameworks, one at a disciplinary level and the other at a metadisciplinary level. One concerns the discourse, the concepts, the conventions, the paradigms, the traditions and, indeed, the ideologies which constitute a particular disciplinary framework. The other concerns the way of going on that constitutes what it is to engage in any rational discussion. It involves a determination to reach towards truth, a willingness to yield to the better argument, a personal commitment to one's statements in time, and a preparedness to formulate one's utterances in a comprehensible fashion.

This distinction, between disciplinary and metadisciplinary framework, is profound and I shall return to it; but it is not of the essence here. The idea of displacement applies to *both* levels of discourse.

Displacement carries the idea of movement from one place to another. But it also carries a sense of taking up some kind of home in the new place. Admittedly, there is a slightly perjorative edge to the term; one is not usually displaced willingly. All of these senses come into play in an educational setting. In the end, the student leaves her life-world cognitively speaking and enters the new world of the intellectual framework.[4] The leaving and the entering are not without difficulties and, being new, may generate anxiety. But *this* displacement, to be effective, has to come under one's own volition in the end. Otherwise, reproductive learning is likely to be the result rather than meaning-orientated learning (Marton *et al.* 1984).

The leaving of one's life-world need not be permanent. Indeed, the educational value of the displacement being suggested here is likely to be enhanced if, having entered the new world, the old can be revisited with the perspective of the new. Of course, such a revisiting is not straightforward. In such a situation, one is inhabiting two discourses at once: the discourse of immediate experience of the life-world; and interpreting that life-world in a theoretical discourse. There is an awkwardness in inhabiting two worlds at once; but there is also a wisdom that comes with informed detachment.

Trajectory: its rise and possible fall

Richard Peters talked of education as initiation (Peters 1970); Michael Oakeshott of education as entering a conversation across the generations (Fuller 1989). Each of these metaphors is highly instructive. In each, we have a sense of traditions of thought and understanding standing outside of individuals; education is then the development of the capacity to participate in those traditions. 'Conversation' reminds us that knowledge is alive and is maintained through continuing dialogue, a dialogue that is being conducted now. 'Initiation' focuses on the transmission of the individual into those external traditions.

To repeat, both metaphors are helpful. But they are misleading in that they fail properly to recognize that the student is *already* engaged in her own conversations. They imply an unformed consciousness whereas educators, especially those of adults, are confronted with well-developed centres of consciousness among their students. These metaphors, instructive as they are, oversimplify the educator's task. But they also oversimplify the challenges in front of the student. It is not simply a matter of coming into a form of life mapped out for one. It is the much more challenging task of bringing one's own framework into some kind of relationship with a different one; and, in its conceptual integrity and procedural demands, markedly different at that.

The idea of displacement recognizes this challenge. The student has to displace herself, has to leave her home, in order to come fully into the new one. This need not be a permanent separation. On the contrary, as I mentioned, there might be continual movement between the student's life-world and her new theoretical systematized world. But there is no simple regression available. Once displaced, the life-world is liable to shatter. It will be seen anew.

With educational displacement comes a trajectory. Trajectory carries the sense of velocity and direction and taking off. All these are present in student becoming. The student comes into the role of student by displacing herself into particular forms of interaction, inquiry and truth-telling. Ultimately, the student comes to stand on firm ground, knows the intellectual territory, is at home in it and feels confident enough to strike out on her own. The student becomes herself, albeit within the epistemological and interactional framework which marks out the discipline or field of study. Here, there is a personal dynamic, a movement of self; but it is progressive, giving the student increasing power. It is a trajectory.

The trajectory can continue upward, with the student gaining more and more confidence, and acquiring more and more conceptual resource and veridical leverage. The trajectory can flatten off, with the student 'coasting along', secure in the knowledge that she has 'done enough to pass'. Or, even while on the course, the trajectory can fall away, with the student losing interest for some reason and failing to maintain her cognitive powers. This is a particular problem on part-time programmes or research degree programmes which are necessarily spread over a time-frame, and where other happenings in the life-world can intrude to command the student's attention.

The 'taking-off' implied by the idea of 'trajectory' is of two kinds. On the one hand, the cognitive journey is such that it gives the student a new view from above, as it were The notion of a '*higher* education' itself implicitly conveys this sense of a higher order of cognition. This metaphor of height has a long history in thinking about higher education. Newman considered that 'if we would improve the intellect, first of all we must ascend' (Newman 1976). The 'ascent' here is of a logical not a social kind; social superiority is not at issue. What is being alluded to is a level of conceptual inquiry, interrogation and reflection which enables the student to form a view of her cognitive experience.

We are in the presence of a higher learning when the conceptual resources have been acquired which impart this higher order capacity. In exercising it, the student is at a distance from her immediate experience in the domain in question. She has displaced herself and followed a trajectory in which the experience can be marshalled and examined. We are here in the presence of a hierarchy of cognition in which the elaborated form of thought yields the power to scrutinize, and so free one from, one's immediate experience.

The second sense of 'trajectory' which is at work here is that already implied. There is, ultimately, a sense of talking off and of flying under one's own power. Student becoming takes place in two modes. First, there is the coming into the formal structures of thought and understanding which mark out not just the territory but the ways of going on characteristic of the student's field or discipline. Second, the becoming has a personal aspect. The student becomes herself in a new guise. The academic who is a physicist or who is a historian is so in a continuing sense: she defines herself as a physicist or a historian. Those descriptions – 'physicist'/'historian' – describe persons. In coming to see the world as a physicist or a historian, the student is not alienated from herself but becomes that self more fully.

Admittedly, as an undergraduate, the student's trajectory may not take off fully. The student reaches simply the stage where she can understand fairly comprehensively the discourse, and is able to show a minimal mastery of it. But students' accomplishments are relatively reactive to experiences put their way on their course of studies. They do not reach the stage where they take off under their own power. Perhaps they just lack the personal confidence to open the throttle and attempt to take off. After all, taking off is dangerous; if things go wrong, one is in rather an exposed position. Mistakes are serious.

Conclusions: the disappearing gap

We began by suggesting that the central problem in front of us in this paper was straightforward. What account might be given of the relationship between the internal and the external domains in the making of a student? A student is a person, with her own life world and consciousness attaching thereto. But that same student is also, *by definition*, someone who is studying something external to herself.

In getting to grips with this relationship, we have *en route* indicated that there are separate externalities which impinge on the student. There is the world of objectified knowledge and the discipline(s) in which it is anchored; the programme of studies, which itself has course, departmental and institutional aspects; and the wider world of educational policy making and governmental decision, which frames the student's wider environment (but which has a very real impact, for example, both through the accessibility of staff within the course and the student's general financial and accommodation situation). It is precisely because the student intersects with these external frameworks that the idea of 'student' has public and semi-formal aspects. There is no job description but we can still legitimately talk of the role of student because of these social structures which have to be inhabited.

'Student', in the discussion here, has turned out to be a multi-layered construction. At its centre is the student struggling to bring her cognitive experiences into a coherent form and to understand them; then there is the organized programme of studies and, beyond that, its institutional context; and, beyond that still, the sphere of policy making. This paper has concentrated on the first layer in the onion ring, that of the student coming into a relationship with the ideas, concepts, theories and intellectual structures central to her programme. In short, the problem before us has been 'how is understanding possible?'.

The temptation might have been to conceptualize the matter of a student and an intellectual framework separately from each other, with the student in some way having to jump the gap to get on the inside of the form of thought. That has turned out to be a misleading way of construing the situation, the being of the student is achieved through a process of becoming the student.[5]

Duties and responsibilities fall on one who is a student. The student has to yield to the givenness of a form of thought or principles of right reason, even if she is to make her mark on it and perhaps develop it. Logically, there is something misleading about calling someone a student simply because she has registered on a programme of study and has just received the first grant cheque. The role of student is an achievement: 'student' is an appelation won as a result of coming into a form of thought.

Nor is the student constructed from without. The student is not simply one who assimilates the experiences put her way. The student constructs herself; comes into herself more fully. She does so through yielding to the demands of the discipline. Although the process can reasonably be called a displacement of the self, the student remains a self, in command of herself. She is starting on a trajectory over which she has control.

There is no gap, therefore, either existential or epistemological, between the inner and the outer student. It is a gradual but a definite process of becoming. The butterfly emerges from the chrysalis; and the butterfly *can fly.*

Notes

1 *Ronald Barnett* is Professor and Dean at the Institute of Education, University of London. He is a frequent author on higher education topics. His books include *The Idea of Higher Education* and, most recently, *The Limits of Competence.*
2 The notion of risk as employed here is not to be confused with the notion of 'risk' as currently being deployed in social theory (for example, in Beck 1992). The 'risk society' is a society peculiarly characterized by risk. The risk in question here is a personal form of risk. More importantly, it is a risk willingly entered into, whereas the risks inherent in the 'risk society' typically, do not enjoy any underwriting from citizens. A learning community is one in which participants willingly enter into situations of risk, since the response from the other participants cannot be predicted. On the other hand, since the utterances are offered in a framework of mutual listening, reflection and learning, the risks are limited. Utterances are preferred knowing that they will not be met with invective or even worse kinds of violence.
3 'The changing student experience' is the title of the 1994 annual conference of the Society for Research into Higher Education; 'student satisfaction' is the term given to an internal survey conducted by the University of Central England at Birmingham; students' 'approaches to learning' is a term used by Marton and others in developing a 'phenomenographic' research strategy in the 1970s and is still much in use today (Marton *et al.* 1984).
4 The concept of 'the life-world' I take from the work of Jurgen Habermas.
5 Implicit in this argument about education-as-being and as becoming is a repudiation of education-as-having as a form of 'education' (Jarvis 1992).

References

Barnett, R. (1994) *The Limits of Competence: Knowledge, Higher Education and Society* (Buckingham: Open University Press).

Beck, U. (1992) *Risk Society* (London: Sage).

Fleming, D. (1991) The concept of meta-competence. *Competence and Assessment,* No. 20 (Sheffield: Employment Department).

Fuller, T. (ed.) (1989) *The voice of Liberal Learning: Michael Oakeskott on Education* (London: Yale University Press).

Habermas, J. (1991) *The Theory of Communicative Competence,* vol. 1 (Cambridge: Polity).

Jarvis, P. (1992) *Paradoxes of Learning: On Becoming an Individual in Society* (San Francisco: Jossey-Bass).

Leavis, F. R. (1969) *English Literature in our Time and the University* (London, Chatto & Windus).

Liedman, S.-E. (1993) In search of Isis: general education in Germany and Sweden, in S. Rothblatt and B. Wittrock (eds), *The European and American University since 1800: Historical and Sociological Essays* (Cambridge: Cambridge University Press).

Marton, F., Hounsell, D. and Entwistle, N. (eds) (1984) *The Experience of Learning* (Edinburgh: Scottish Academic Press).

Newman, J. (1976) *The Idea of a University* (Oxford: Oxford University Press).

Perry, W. G. (1970) *Forms of Intellectual and Ethical Development* (New York: Holt, Rinehart & Winston).

Peters, R. S. (1967) What is an educational process?, in R. S. Peters (ed.), *The Concept of Education* (London, Routledge & Kegan Paul).

Peters, R. S. (1970) *Ethics and Education* (London: Routledge & Kegan Paul).

Piaget, J. (1971) *Structuralism* (London: Routledge & Kegan Paul).

Popper, K. (1975) *Objective Knowledge: An Evolutionary Approach* (Oxford: Oxford University Press).

Rothblatt, S. (1993) The limbs of Osiris: liberal education in the English-speaking world, in S. Rothblatt and B. Wittrock, op cit.

19 The adulthood of Buddhahood

Buddhism, lifelong learning and the education of desire

Sonia Macpherson[1]

University of British Columbia

This paper analyses Buddhism as a philosophy of education as opposed to a religion to offer an alternative model of lifelong education. The three trainings of Buddhism – ethics, meditative stabilization and special wisdom – are described and their implications for education are considered. The special case of Tantric Buddhism offers a further development in Buddhist discourse on the education of desire, a critical new area of educational inquiry required if we are seriously to address the current environmental crisis. The paper presents Octavio Paz's ideas concerning the differential development of Asian Buddhist culture and Western Protestant culture in terms of their relations to the signs 'body' and 'non-body', and concludes with his Utopian vision of the future.

Upon this gifted age, in its dark hour,
Rains from the sky a meteoritic shower
Of facts ... They lie unquestioned
    uncombined.
Wisdom enough to leech us of our ill
Is daily spun, but there exist no loom
    To weave it into fabric...
                    (Edna St Vincent Millay
                    in *Huntsman, What Quarry?*)

These prophetic words of Edna St Vincent Millary delineate one of the greatest shortcomings of lifelong education in our age: spinning endless, unconnected threads, we produce unfathomable bits of data and facts which remain suspended in (cyber?)space. This deluge of unprocessed information is the product of our compulsion to create in the absence of vision, wisdom and ethical intent, thereby impairing our ability effectively to apply our abundant knowledge to the suffering and need besieging contemporary society.

As I integrate myself in the academic community of a graduate school in education, I am troubled by this realization, perhaps because I have known something different. Having studied Buddhist philosophy over a

15-year period in Sri Lanka, India, the Himalayas, the USA and Canada, I have witnessed glimmerings of what an integrated and living wisdom is capable of contributing to our collective and individual human life. I also have learned to recognize the negative impact of this neglect of wisdom, a neglect that is barely cognized or acknowledged in our modern and post-modern times, except by those on the periphery of power – artists, poets, social critics, philosophers and the like. Wisdom is a subtle thing ... for it is not a thing ... just as compassion is not a thing. All the books, degrees, clerical collars, robes and other material signs suggesting these qualities say little about their actual presence or absence inside a person or culture; they are an inner reality known only inferentially by their outward mani-festations in actions and words.

Buddhism as a philosophy of education

My intention in undertaking the writing of this paper is twofold, both to introduce some of the foundations of Buddhist philosophy and to consider some of the possible implications of those foundations for lifelong educa-tion. Buddhist thought revolves around the education of both compassion and wisdom. Probably because it is assumed to be a *religion* as opposed to a *philosophy of education*, Buddhist philosophy has been marginalized from the intellectual and mainstream life of both Asia and the West, in spite of the fact that this century has led Western philosophers to pose the very ques-tions that lie at the root of Buddhist thought. Questions such as the relative and absolute nature of knowing; the multiple, relative nature of identity; being and becoming; compassion and freedom; the nature of and relation-ship between mind and matter; the interdependence of all forms in the natural world; all have been debated previously in the history of Buddhist philosophical development, and the conclusions of those debates could contribute substantially to our current discussions.

Professor Robert Thurman of Columbia University (1984: 6) cites four reasons why Western philosophy have largely ignored Buddhist philo-sophy to date: 'a sense of the superiority, rational and cultural, of the "West"; a sense of the intrinsic progressivity of history; a sense of the intrinsic value of originality; and a sense of the fundamental non-perfectability of human understanding. These four presuppositions prevent them even from seeking ... that which they would find interesting and helpful in their current philosophical malaises, for which the theories of emptiness and relativity are more than ever the needed medicines'.

In addition to the question of why Western philosophers have resisted turning to the centrist philosophy of Buddhism as a source in their current debates, is the equally perplexing fact that Asian states are now adopting Western colonial and materialist-orientated pedagogies instead of drawing on their own traditions for models of education. Thurman (1984: 7) also identifies some possible causes of this tendency of Buddhist practitioners to neglect to embrace the full, creative import of Buddhist critical thought: 'a sense of the religious and cultural superiority of the "East"; a sense of the inexorable degeneracy of the process of history; a sense of the intrinsic value of traditionality, especially as supporting the cultivation of quietistic states of withdrawal; and a sense of the vast difference between their own state of "ignorance" and the "enlightenment" of the Buddhas and Bodhisattvas. As a result, these practitioners consider the expression *Buddhist philosophy* a contradiction in terms, which view prevents them from engaging ... with the critical contemplation of the analytic insights of intuitive wisdom'. He then concludes:

> I shall trust that (those still reading) intend to explore the most useful philosophical and scientific teachings from "West" or "East"; that they face the fact that history is not predetermined as inevitably progress or degeneration, and so take responsibility for creating progress, whether it seems feasible or not; that they realize that there is an age-old 'tradition of originality', the enlightenment traditions that have flourished in all cultures. And most importantly, I shall trust that they suspend dogmatic prejudgment of the issue of the perfectability of human understanding, having realized the arbitrariness of either theistic or materialistic insistence on a fundamental imperfection in human genius, either dogma or 'fact' arising as a philosophical or 'scientific' buttress of authoritarian social structure, in ancient and modern cases, respectively
>
> (1984: 8)

An overview of Buddhist thought

Buddhist history spans 2500 years of formal existence. From the beginning, this formidable and radical education sought to provide thinking and questing minds with a refuge and safe haven from the overwhelming demands of secular life. These efforts focused on creating a religious context in which philosophical and liberative endeavours could be pursued peacefully. People of all castes, both women and men, were admitted into the process; it may be difficult for us in the late 20th century to appreciate just how radical such practices were for the then-entrenched patriarchal caste society of India. It was an education predicated on free and open inquiry, conducted from an ethical foundation of compassion. The notion of *blind belief* is anathema to the true spirit of Buddhist philosophical engagement, a process which implores practitioners to test everything heard against the litmus of experience and reason, as we might scratch a piece of gold to make certain it is real. Buddhism offers a view of education aimed at assisting the individual in his/her personal existential quest. The Buddha's final words reflect this radical path of individual religious inquiry (Komatsu 1989: 28):

Be your own masters, and depend upon on-one else.
Do not look for refuge anywhere beyond yourselves.
Be your own lamps.
Make the Law your lamp, your refuge, your master.
The teachings that I have given you will be your guide after I am gone.
Practice them wholeheartedly. Now remain a while in silence. My time
is already passed. Now I shall enter Nirvana. This is my final teaching.

Sakyamuni Buddha, the life

Buddhist philosophy is accessible through various forms – narratives, discourses, expositions and a panoply of meditative techniques. Buddhist
narratives consist of a biographical tradition which includes the life of the
historical Buddha, those of his previous incarnations (called the Jataka
tales), and those of his disciples through the ages. The biographies
provide a fascinating account of the evolution of critical inquiry within the
stream of Buddhist thought, from its Hindu precursors to today. The
following are the salient features of Sakyamuni Buddha's life (Komatsu
1989: 3–11):

> Gautama Shakyamuni was born as the Crown Prince of Kapilavastu, a
> small kingdom in what is now Nepal. Shortly after his birth, it was
> prophesied that this child would either take the throne as a universal
> ruler or walk the holy path with the universe as his kingdom. In his
> childhood, Gautama Shakyamuni was given every luxury imaginable
> to avert the possibility of his becoming religious and renouncing his
> throne; his father quite rightly surmised that if his son could be pro-
> tected from the encounter with or sight of suffering, old age, death,
> and religious practitioners, he would not have the opportunity to
> become religiously inclined. After marrying and having a son, Sakya-
> muni became curious about these aspects of existence from which he
> had been so assiduously sheltered. So, going beyond the four gates of
> his palatial city, he witnessed old age, illness, death, and a religious
> mendicant, respectively. Unaccustomed as he was to these realities, he
> was greatly disturbed by the sight of them. At the age of twenty-nine,
> disillusioned, he renounced his throne and family to seek freedom
> from these seemingly inalienable sufferings of existence.
>   After six years of asceticism, living among the forest-dwelling practi-
> tioners of his time, Sakyamuni came to renounce the ascetic path as
> well, just as he had once renounced that of sensual indulgence. Then
> and only then, after accepting milk from a young woman and kusa
> grass as a seat cushion, was he able to stabilize his mind sufficiently to
> produce the bliss and energy needed to subdue the demons of his
> mind. Touching the earth beneath him, he proclaimed, 'the earth
> bears witness to my right to be unmoved by desire or fear'. After a

week of meditating, he overcame all craving, the causes of ignorance and hence suffering, and there arose in his mind the clarity of a fully awakened human consciousness. On the evening of his Enlightenment, he saw the brilliant light of the stars in the eastern sky and exclaimed, *How magnificent! All sentient beings are without exception endowed with buddha nature!* For the next three weeks his insights continued to unfold, until he finally resolved to teach: *So long as even one sentient being exists with little dust on their eyes, I will teach.*

The Buddha's awakening as adult education

These insights and experiences, as remarkable and historically relevant as they are, describe a process of education as much as of religion, being reproducible by others and founded on many experiences common to adult learners everywhere. It is only as an adult that Sakyamuni was able to extricate himself sufficiently from his father's expectations to discover his own calling. Until then, he lived his father's desire, not his own, and as a consequence his life was constructed on false pretences and the illusion of harmony. The seeming accord between himself and his social world masked an underlying discord with the natural laws of existence. When his experiences beyond the four gates punctured holes in that illusion, his world as he had known it collapsed. The subsequent disjuncture provided the imperative to learn that led Sakyamuni to risk his physical and social comforts for the life of a homeless one. The magnitude of his learning was commensurate with his risk, a perfection of learning we now call *enlightenment* or *awakening* in Buddhist terminology, of which first he and then all the *we* these millennia since are the beneficiaries.

Renunciation

Like Sakyamuni, adults in contemporary society are often led to redefine or even abandon certain familial or employment roles, whether or not they wish to do so. Furthermore, as we age, we become more susceptible to the inevitabilities of illness, old age and death. In this sense, the Buddha's process can offer some insight into the insecurity and identity loss of living and ageing in these times of great upheaval. In the strictest sense, Buddhist *renunciation* is one of disciplined choice, turning one's attention away from coarse worldly aspirations to those more ethically based and sublime. However, sometimes the world helps us along in the process, *disillusioning* us until we let go. We tend to renounce something because we learn that it is suffering; what we assume to be pleasurable or permanent turns out not to be so. If we resist learning, then we need not renounce or change, but we may nevertheless *suffer* under an illusion of safety; when our house of cards collapses, we are ill-prepared to deal with the resulting transformation of circumstances. In understanding the means to transform consciousness as the Buddha did – as he taught – we become better adapted to live flexibly, creatively and in harmony with the inevitability of change.

Fundamental tenets of Buddhism

The four qualities that define a philosophical system as Buddhist are: *all products are impermanent* (anicca); *all contaminated* (by ignorance) *things are suffering* (dukkha); *all phenomena are empty and selfless* (anata); and *nirvana is peace* (Gyatso, Tenzin 1985). These four are related in that the imperma- nence of existing things is given, yet our minds are driven by desirous craving to try to make them permanent. Our ignorance of and resistance to this natural law of change creates suffering from which relief is found only by the realization of the lack of inherent identity – emptiness – of self and phenomena. This realization is the path to peace called *nirvana*. It is interesting to reflect that as our society experiences a dramatic accelera- tion in the pace of change, relativistic philosophical movements – i.e. con- structivism and deconstructionism – have developed, bearing a resemblance to the Buddhist conception of relativity, the manner in which phenomena can be said to exist and not exist.

However, we in the 'West' have yet to articulate relativity theory fully. We are currently either tending to the extreme of positing that all know- ledge is discourse, a view which contradicts experience, or to the more moderate but as yet ill-defined attempt to acknowledge some essential, precognitive, preverbal reality capable of being experienced, known and articulated. People advocating the latter are still wading through the murky waters of psychoanalytic theories to understand what that reality might be; their efforts are important, but it would be instructive to con- sider the Buddhist view of this gap between knowledge carried in cultur- ally relative discourses and knowledge from the semiotics of experience. In Buddhism, that gate, the necessary reference point that is no point, is *emptiness*. As the Dalai Lama explained in his Harvard lectures (Gyatso, Tenzin 1988: 194): 'Usually, I explain that emptiness is like a zero. A zero itself is nothing, but without a zero you cannot count anything; therefore, a zero is something, yet zero.'

The Buddha's first discourse, in Deer Park at Sarnath, introduced the foundation of his thought – The Four Noble Truths: the truth of suffering (or struggle), the truth of the cause of suffering, the truth of the cessation of suffering and the truth of the path to the cessation of suffering. This progression is founded on an understanding of causation or karma as a law of phenomena. *The Four Noble Truths* might be rephrased to read that in so far as suffering is constructed from a cause, that being desirous craving, it can be deconstructed from a cause as well, thereby liberating one from suffering; the cause of that liberation is the Eightfold Path: *right* understanding, *right* thought, *right* speech, *right* action, *right* livelihood, *right* effort, *right* mindfulness, and *right* concentration (Komatsu 1989: 11).

We in the West might balk at the notion of *right*; however, it is worth considering that these *rights* are not presented as dogmatic behavioural codes but rather as tried and tested conditions to bring about enlightened mind. They are the means by which enlightenment or awakening can be taught. In fact, in elucidating the respective qualities in terms of their *right* manifestation, the Buddha translated what came to him through the peculiar circumstances of his life and birth, providing a way for others to emulate his path regardless of their circumstances, even when they are overwhelmed with ignorance and suffering. However, it is helpful to bear in mind that in Buddhism the mind manifesting enlightenment is spontaneous and beyond prescriptive or proscriptive action, and to apply rules when they are no longer needed is considered an obstacle.

The three trainings

This eightfold path falls into three areas of endeavour: training in ethics, training in meditative stabilization and training in special wisdom (Gyatso, Tenzin 1985). Cultivation of all three areas is required if a full liberation of enlightened mind is to occur. These three trainings and all that has been mentioned so far are common to all schools of Buddhism; however, there are some subtle variations.

Training in ethics

Buddhist ethics can be subsumed under three categories: the ethics of individual liberation, Bodhisattva ethics and the ethics of Secret Mantra. The former is common to both the Theravadin and Bodhisattva Vehicles (therefore to all Buddhist schools), whereas the latter two are common to the Bodhisattva Vehicle alone (Gyatso, Tenzin 1985). The Theravadin Vehicle is found in places such as Thailand, Sri Lanka, India and Burma; the Bodhisattva Vehicle is found in places such as Singapore, Hong Kong, China, Japan and Tibet. Tibetan Buddhism incorporates the spectrum of all schools; inherited from India between the 8th and 12th centuries, it is the only extant example of the Secret Mantra tradition of Buddhism. All Bodhisattva Vehicles acknowledge compassion as the highest ethic of humanity, and it is in dependence upon that ethic that the perfectability of the human form and consciousness is posited as possible. In the Secret Mantra form of the Bodhisattva Vehicle, the attainment of that perfection is considered possible in a single lifetime through the cultivation of a more subtle consciousness with which to apprehend emptiness.

In Tibetan Buddhism, each of these three emanations of Buddhist thought – individual liberation, Bodhisattva and Secret Mantra – has a distinct ethical system, albeit interrelated with the other two. The ethics of individual liberation involve avoiding harming others, interpreted most fundamentally as the abandonment of the *ten non-virtues* – three non-virtues of body, four of speech and three of mind. The ten include training to avoid killing, stealing and sexual misconduct; lying, senseless talk, divisive speech and harsh speech; and covetousness, harmful intent and wrong view (Gyatso, Tenzin 1985).

As a Bodhisattva path, Tibetan Buddhism posits progress in the beginning, middle and end as contingent upon a compassionate intention, without which Buddhahood would not be possible ... and Buddhahood is considered possible for everyone endowed with a human body. *Compassion* is further defined in over 30 guidelines or vows. The Secret Mantra tradition, in turn, is a special case of the Bodhisattva Vehicle with elaborate vows to help inculcate and sustain the subtle mind required for this refined meditation technique. However, as with all Bodhisattva vehicles, Tibetan Buddhist ethics are reducible to one overriding ethic: compassion.

The ethical orientation of 'Western' adult and lifelong education tends to be proscriptive, concerned as it has been with restricting the harming of others. For example, ethical guidelines for adult educators generally concern questions of how to avoid offending students of diverse cultural backgrounds, how to restrain from seducing students of the opposite sex, and how not to distort the truth or exploit power in the classroom. As noble as these efforts are, on some level they remain preoccupied with *self* interest. To suggest actively carrying compassion into the classroom sounds idealistic, ideological and perhaps out of context, seeming to contravene the golden rule of *professional distance*. Consequently, introducing compassion as an overriding ethic in the adult world of the classroom, office or any environment is really quite a radical proposal. It calls for courage, and a willingness to cross the socially defined boundaries of what is generally considered to be *one's business*. If every *other* sentient being becomes my business, as much or more than *I* am my business, then I transform the public world into something personal. It does not mean that I help others at the expense of my own long-term happiness; such a tactic would not work in the end for I would become bitter, thereby constraining my ability to bring joy and pleasure into the lives of others. Compassion is full attention with interest, in which *I understand that another's happiness may be my best interest.*

Ethical education, especially that involving compassion, has been the perview of religious education in the past. As interest in religion dissipates, compassion needs to be wrested from its marginalization in religious discourses if it is to be of service to the world. Most of the crises facing human societies around the world can be said to emanate from a deficit in ethics, a deficit in compassion. If we could free up our energy to deal with the illnesses and natural disasters that really are beyond our control at present, we might be better prepared to reduce suffering in the world. I suspect that sufficient knowledge, resources and technologies are available to provide a quality of life for every sentient being on the planet today, but greed, hatred and ignorance – the failure of compassion – preclude our arriving at the necessary solutions.

Optimal learning occurs in an environment of compassionate interest, in which a learner feels safe to explore freely. If our motivation in educating another is tainted, if it is not founded on altruistic intention, then we may face the danger of perpetrating personal and cultural invasion, threatening students' well-being such that learning becomes restricted. Jarvis (1992) has outlined eight types of learning actions, three of which involve responses of non-action to potential learning experiences – *anomic, preventive* and *non-response*. Learning is unlikely if not impossible to occur in these circumstances. The education process is somehow perceived by the learner as a danger to their safety and well-being, in terms of their cultural, personal or economic interests. Or perhaps the social milieu is inhospitable to the learner in other respects, or the teacher or state prevents learning from occurring through censorship or force. All of these can be reduced to the problem of failing to establish trust, safety and compassion in the learning environment.

Training in meditative stabilization

The second area of training in Buddhist education concerns meditative stabilization or calm abiding. Most systems of Buddhist meditation involve cultivating this quality prior to and alongside special wisdom; before our minds can apprehend the subtle reality of emptiness, they must be stable in such qualities as clarity, concentration, interest, joy and equanimity. These meditations can include breathing meditation on a fixed point, emptiness meditation, deity yoga and meditations on living-kindness and compassion. To cultivate calm abiding, the mind needs an object of meditation, optimally itself as its own object, and then it must attempt to sustain attention on that object for as long as possible. When the mind wanders, it is gently brought back to its object.

The five obstacles to the cultivation of calm abiding once an object of meditation is taken to mind are (Gyatso, Tenzin 1985: 64):

1   laziness, which is a lack of enthusiasm for cultivating meditative stabilization;
2   forgetfulness, which is the loss of the object of observation itself;
3   the mind's falling under the influence of laxity or excitement, although the object of observation is not forgotten;
4   not making use of the antidotes to laxity and excitement, although one has identified that the mind has fallen under their influence;
5   even though laxity and excitement are absent, one still does not concentrate on the object but mistakenly continues to apply the antidotes to laxity and excitement.

The four antidotes to laziness are: faith, aspiration, effort and pliancy; the antidote to forgetfulness is mindfulness. *Laxity* refers to a coarse *sinking* experience or a more subtle dulling of the clarity of the mind, while *excitement* refers to the coarse loss of the object of concentration as well as more subtle distractions. The antidote to all types of laxity and excitement is introspection. In the case of laxity, the apprehension of the mind must be heightened; in the case of excitement, the apprehension of the mind must be lowered. The antidote to (4) – not making use of the antidotes – is an *intention of application*. The antidote to (5), (over) applying the antidote, is the equanimity to leave the mind abiding in its natural state.

The fruits of this training are meditative stabilization or calm abiding. Only with such a stable and calm mind are we sufficiently at ease to learn to change the way we think and behave. Even in a loving environment, our minds can be disturbed, and this feeling of insecurity can interfere with our ability to learn. When our minds are trained to abide in equanimity and calm, even in the middle of a highly stressful situation we can feel safe and thereby remain open to engaging creatively with our environment. Furthermore, this is a well-developed and tested method for cultivating both memory and concentration, without which learning is superficial at best. Television, advertising, consumerism and the fast pace of our contemporary life can have a distracting effect on the mind, such that people experience difficulty holding attention on one object for more than 10 minutes. In the training outlined above, the mind can learn to hold its object for four hours without interruption after only six months of practice. Then and only then, with an unshakeably calm and concentrated mind, are we ready to engage in the profound and subtle meditations leading to special wisdom.

Special wisdom

In Buddhism, wisdom refers to the discrimination of phenomena through investigation and analysis, a process which, when fully cultivated, can become the perfection of wisdom. There are three types of wisdom (Gyatso, Tenzin 1985):

1   The wisdom realizing the selflessness of persons and phenomena, either through analysis or directly apprehended.
2   The wisdom realizing conventionalities, defined as acquired skills in the *five sciences (linguistics, logic and epistemology, arts, medicine and inner sciences)*.
3   The wisdom realizing how to bring about the welfare of sentient beings. This is also known as *skilful means* and refers to knowing how to teach effectively *to achieve the present and future welfare of sentient beings without impropriety.*

Of these three, the most important is the first, the special wisdom which apprehends the selflessness of persons and phenomena. Only with this wisdom can we fully appreciate the existence of other people and phenomena and how to address their interests. If one ascertains the selflessness of persons, it is easier to apprehend the selflessness of phenomena; so, initially it is best to inquire into the selflessness of persons. The Indian Buddhist philosopher Chandrakirti wrote (quoted in Gyatso, Tenzin 1985: 78):

> Seeing with their mind that all afflictions and defects
> Arise from the view of the transitory collection of mind and body as inherently existent *I* and *mine*,
> Yogis, upon realizing that the self
> Is the object of this view, refute the inherent existence of self.

The suffering of *cyclic existence* refers to contaminated actions (karma) driven by afflicted emotions (greed, hatred, ignorance), both the state and the cause of suffering associated with worldly attachment. Another form of suffering elucidated in Tibetan Buddhism is referred to as the suffering of *solitary peace*, a state in which one achieves a limited form of individual liberation without regard to the suffering of other sentient beings. The former is a suffering caused by attachment to form, the latter suffering caused by a nihilistic attachment to formlessness. The root of these problems is said to be the same – the ignorance conceiving inherent existence, as well as its predispositions. The wisdom of selflessness is contradictory to ignorance; according to Buddhist thought, it is the only means effectively to eradicate the ignorance driving suffering. The means of realizing the understanding of selflessness is through making effort at extraordinary special insight (Gyatso, Tenzin 1985).

The insight into emptiness can be made directly through access concentration cultivated in meditative stabilization or analytically through methods of contemplation called *analytical meditation*. The analytical path to settle the selflessness of persons involves four essential contemplations (Gyatso, Tenzin 1985: 78):

1 ascertaining the object of negation;
2 ascertaining the entailment (of emptiness);
3 ascertaining the lack of oneness;
3 ascertaining the lack of difference.

To ascertain the object of negation involves the recognition of that which is (mis)conceived by an awareness conceiving true existence. In meditating on the selflessness of persons, the ascertainment of the object of negation is the (illusory) appearance of the inherently existing *I*. This misconception makes the *I* appear 'to be established as able to stand by itself – to be self-instituting – without depending on the collection of the mental and physical aggregates which are its basis of designation, or without depending on any of them individually, even though the *I* appears with those aggregates' (1985: 79). The *ascertainment of the entailment of emptiness* refers to the realization that the *I* must either be the same entity as or a different entity from the mental and physical aggregates if it is to be established as inherently existing. The *ascertainment of the lack of oneness* is the reasoning by which one establishes that the *I* is not the same as the collection of mental and physical aggregates, while the *ascertainment of the lack of inherently established difference* is the reasoning by which one establishes that the *I* is not distinct from the mental and physical aggregates.

Thinking thus, one establishes a disjuncture between the fact that the *I* appears to exist yet the *appearance* of this *I* is different from its *being*, as established through contemplative analysis. This disjuncture leads the inquiring mind to the realization that the self is not a valid phenomenon in either a relative or ultimate sense. The *I* is established nominally, but does not exist on its own side. In other words, it is a sign of the mind signifying an ambiguous variety of collections and units of *other* phenomena, i.e. body, mind, body parts, feelings, thoughts, sensations, perceptions, conceptions. In other words, it is a sign of the mind signifying ... nothing, really.

Similar reasoning is applied to phenomena; in this way, they are recognized as dependent-arisings existing both *interdependently* and also, by virtue of being imputed norminally, *merely*. This does not mean that the *I* or phenomena do not exist, but rather that they do not have an inherent identity separate from what gives rise to them, including human conception (Gyatso, Tenzin 1985: 83):

> Also, in dependence upon ascertaining merely nominally imputed dependent-arisings, ascertainment of the fact that phenomena are empty of being established from their own side arises in greater force. When such mutual reinforcement occurs, one has realized emptiness as the meaning of dependent-arising and dependent-arising as the meaning of emptiness – the correct view, the Buddha's unsurpassed thought – exactly as it is.

The aforementioned is one process of analytical meditation to bring about special insight into the nature of phenomena and the self. However, there are many different ways to conduct analytical meditation, of which the above is just one case. It is recommended to move between meditative stabilization and analytical meditation such that the space-like experience of emptiness is experienced in conjunction with the realization of dependent-arising and vice versa, thereby correcting any tendency for either attachment or nihilism. However, the path of Secret Mantra does not rely on analytical meditation, but rather involves a methodology whereby the union of emptiness and dependent-arising for both self and phenomena can be experienced directly through its unique visualization practice.

The resulting wisdom is called the *Union of the Two Truths*, referring to the realization of the simultaneous manifestation of the relative or conventional appearance of phenomena (as dependent-arisings) and their ultimate nature on analysis (emptiness). In the Secret Mantra tradition, this is called Buddhahood and corresponds with the establishment and union of the *Truth Body* with the *Form Body* of a Buddha. The Truth Body produces the liberation of a Buddha and the Form Body the omniscience. The Form Body in turn can be subdivided into the *Emanation* (Material) *Body* and the *Enjoyment* (Pleasure/Imagination) *body*. When these Three Bodies – Truth, Enjoyment, and Emanation – become united in Buddhahood, a fourth body is described as being established, that of a Buddha.

So, we might well ask what such a perfect liberated and omniscient state entails. A Buddha is said to know the *appearance* of inherent existence through the viewpoint of persons who have not overcome it; however, he/she has overcome and eradicated the appearance of inherent existence within his/her own mindstream (Gyatso, Tenzin 1988: 55):

> It is explained in both sutra and tantra that whatever appears to a Buddha appears as the sport of bliss. Then one could ask whether the sufferings of sentient beings appear as the sport of bliss to a Buddha? If the sufferings of sentient beings appeared to a Buddha to be the sport of bliss, then the Buddha's consciousness would be a mistaken consciousness. Also, if the sufferings of sentient beings do not appear to a Buddha, then a Buddha would not be omniscient. So how does such appear? They appear as the sport of bliss from a Buddha's own point of view; however, they also appear as suffering, but only from the point of view of, only through the force of, their appearing to other beings as sufferings.

Such a conception of perfection can lead to the realization of a viable Utopian vision for humanity if one understands that the quality of purity rests in the mind of the perceiver. It is not a Utopian peace imposed from above, from a social reconstruction, but rather from below and moving outward with compassion for sentient beings, empathically understanding their circumstances and perspectives. The question of whether such a purified perception is possible is difficult to prove; I have met people who manifest this quality or something approximating it, including the Dalai Lama, a quality recognizable in their words and actions, as well as in their effect on the states of mind of others. Such a state of perfection – Buddhahood – does not mean one is impervious to valid laws of nature, but that one is more cognizant of and in harmony with those laws. My understanding of this notion of perfection is that people who realize such an omniscient consciousness do not necessarily know all there is to know about specific information, but rather their faculty of special wisdom – their capacity to learn and to weave learning through the profound interrelatedness of phenomena – has been perfected.

The subject of Buddhist special wisdom is abstruse; it is a subtle truth and one attainable only after training in ethics and meditative stabilization. The illusion of inherent existence naturally arises in the mind as an adaptive strategy of organismic life; however, the need to defend this illusion of self and identity has carried us into a very maladapted condition, one inducing suffering both individually and collectively. The faculty of special wisdom involves critical inquiry; such critical inquiry cultivates both the ability to deconstruct the socially conditioned view of our selves and our environments and the ability to reconstruct them in a more compassionate and accurate view. In this sense, Buddhist education represents a method of enacting change from the most rudimentary level of human consciousness through ethical intention to the macro level of social organization and the environment.

The education of desire

Of the many problems facing humanity today, perhaps the most pressing are those concerned with production, reproduction and consumption, all of which could be subsumed under the rubric of *environmental issues*. What drives these three interrelated phenomena is desire. Given its import in human existence, desire remains a relatively ill-defined and undifferentiated phenomenon, especially in the West; it tends to have a positive or at worst a neutral connotation, while conjuring up images of sexual gratification. Freud and his neo-Freudian legacy in Lacan and the 'French' feminists have probably taken the Western discourse of desire the furthest. Yet their work is not well known outside select literary, psychoanalytic and academic circles.

Buddhism offers 2500 years of human reflections on desire; for example, its role in human existence, what stimulates and reduces it, how to recognize its manifestation in consciousness, and its contribution to both suffering and liberation are all taken up at different points in the evolution of Buddhist thought. The early teachings of Buddhism emphasize the negative aspect of desire, thereby focusing meditative and ethical action on the control and containment of desire. The wheel of suffering, *samsara*, is propelled by desire and so it is only through renouncing desire that the path to liberation from suffering is conceived to be possible. Given that they believe desire to be a feature of corporeal life itself, these early teachings contend that final liberation comes only with death – *parinirvana*.

This rather negative interpretation of the role of desire in human education became mitigated over time in Buddhist philosophy as the Bodhisattva and later Secret Mantra schools developed. The desire to help

sentient beings leads the (aspiring) Bodhisattva to vow to return to existence so long as space endures and even one sentient being remains in
need. In turn, Tantric Buddhism ascribes a role for *passion* in the cultivation of this (com) passionate view, a role in which desire is utilized as a
means to attain Buddhahood. Paradoxically, in Tantra, it is as if we trick
ourselves by using the enormous interest and energy of desire to overcome its deleterious effects. There is, after all, a precedent in the life of
the Buddha, who perfected his consciousness by learning moderation, the
path between sensual indulgence and asceticism. In fact, one factor
leading to Shakyamuni's enlightenment was his recollection of a memory
of being left alone in the sunshine as a child; he recognized the pleasure
and bliss of that moment as the very experience of happiness that he
sought.

Death education

Meditation on death is a salient feature of Buddhist thought in all its
various schools and forms. In differing instances, this emphasis is
explained in terms of the belief in reincarnation, *parinirvana*, or the
notion that enlightenment can be attained through various *gates* or trans-
itions of which death is one case. Yet, particular conceptions of post-
mortem experience need not be called upon to justify these reflections on
death. It is in the denial of death that the illusion of the permanent and
inherent self is most easily preserved; given that this illusion drives suffering, the denial of death is understood in Buddhist practice as a source of
suffering. It is only in acknowledging this component of lifelong
experience and incorporating it into lifelong learning that liberation from
the negative effects of desire and fear is possible. If left unconscious,
desire manifests unbridled lust and consumption, while death manifests
various forms of destruction. Tantric Buddhism brings both of these
unconscious drives – desire and death – into union through its meditative
method such that each serves as the corrective of the other, and each as
the reversible face of the other.

Secret Mantra or Tantric Buddhism

Secret Mantra is also known as Tantra, a term meaning *weaving*; perhaps it
is the weaving Edna St Vincent Mallay may have had in mind when she
wrote the poem that opened this paper. In the teachings of Tantra, the
education of desire finds its most sophisticated method and expression.
The site of its meditative method is the body – the imagination and the
word resonating in the body. I consider it to be the most poetic path of
Buddhism, and perhaps this poetic quality is the reason why one of its
early Western interpreters was Octavio Paz, the Nobel Prize winning
Mexican poet, philosopher and anthropologist.

Octavio Paz (1982 [1969]) compares the development of Christian and Tantric Buddhist cultures in terms of their different relations to the signs *body* and *non-body* in his book *Conjunctions and Disjunctions*. He contents that Christian culture evolved from an identification with the sign *body* – the *incarnation* in early Christianity and Catholicism – to the disincarnation and subsequent repression of the body – a preoccupation with the sign *non-body* – in Protestantism. Paz contends that the relationship between these signs in Protestantism became one of *disjunction* in which one extreme was preserved or adopted at the expense of the other. Contrasted with this is the case of Tantric Buddhism, in which the early Theravadin Buddhist *non-body* (i.e. empty) sign is evolved in Secret Mantra to incorporate the opposite, the *body* sign, through an understanding of corporeal pleasure. Unlike Christianity, Buddhism follows a path of *conjunction* in which the opposite is continually absorbed into the process. Eventually, the opposites are creatively combined, first in multiple then unified realities, whereby the path to emptiness and freedom is paradoxically discovered through the body, desire and the passionate:

> The language of the Tantras is a poetic language and its meanings are always multiple. It also has a quality that I would call reversibility: each word can be converted into its contrary and later, or simultaneously, turn into itself again. The basic premise of Tantrism is the abolition of contraries – without suppressing them. This postulate brings on another: the mobility of the meanings of the signs and their meanings. Flesh is mental concentration; the vulva is a lotus that is emptiness that is wisdom; semen and illumination are one and the same thing; copulation is, as Mircea Eliade emphasizes, *samarasa*, the *identité de jouissance*. ... The Tantric meal is a transgression. Unlike transgressions in the West, which are aggressions tending to destroy or to abolish the contrary, the transgression of Tantrism has as its aim to reintegrate – again, to *reincorporate* – all substances – including filthy ones such as excrement and forbidden ones such as human flesh.
>
> (Paz 1982: 65)

This notion of a reincorporation of the body is one of the most compelling reasons why Buddhist philosophy needs more serious consideration, especially in the context of 'Western' lifelong education. Because of our dissociation from the body, we are largely unconscious of our process of educating desire; we then seek fulfilment and gratification symbolically in sources that only encourage greater and greater dissociation through production and consumption. The current environmental crisis cannot be addressed in any meaningful way unless it is carried into an understanding of the education of desire. Rather than learning from alternative models such as Buddhism, we are exporting our cult of consumption around the globe, a cult which is symptomatic not only of a dissociation from the body but from nature in general. Paradoxically, it is in Tantra's seemingly extreme reinterpretation of pleasure as the epiphany of the sacred that the path to moderation in consumption may be found, for if we starve ourselves of a truly fulfilling pleasure, seeking it always where it will never be found, then that lack may drive us into a consumption frenzy and thereby into our collective grave. True (com) passion can only live in the corporeal body/mind, and it is only there that it can find its voice:

> The language of Protestant Christianity is critical and exemplary, a guide to meditation and action; the language of the Tantras is a microcosm, the verbal double of the universe and the body. In Protestantism, language obeys the laws of rational and moral economy and even-handed justice; in Tantrism the cardinal principle is that of wealth lavishly spent: an offering, a gift, and also luxury – goods destined to be consumed or dissipated. The 'productivity' of the Tantric language belongs to the realm of imitative magic: its model is nature, not work. In Protestantism there is a separation between language and reality: the Holy Scriptures are conceived of as a collection of moral principles; in Tantrism there is a union of language and reality: scripture is *lived* as a body that is an analogue of the physical body – and the body is *read* as a scripture.
>
> (Paz 1982: 78)

Tantric Buddhism, while intrinsically ethical, is really an education of desire as opposed to moral education. As Octavio Paz points out, morality is dualist, concerned as it is with good and evil, *here* and *there*, and right and left/wrong. 'But Tantrism is not immoral: it attempts to transcend all dualisms and thus not even the adjective amoral fits it. The Tantric attitude, precisely because it is extremely religious, is not moral. ... Tantrism is a superhuman effort to really go beyond good and evil. This lack of moderation may be mindful of Nietzsche. But Nietzsche's "nihilism" is philosophical and poetic, not religious. And it is solitary ... The center, the heart of Tantrism, is something Nietzsche rejects: ritual' (1982: 72). In Tantric ritual, the individual liberation becomes communal, and the individual transformation, universal.

Of course now I have been caught in a contradiction. I set out to discuss Buddhism as a philosophy of education, and I am now ending with it as a religion capable of claiming all secular and corporeal ground. Perhaps education itself would benefit from appropriating religious terminology in its self-definition; how about ... *the transformation of consciousness resulting from the dialogue between the corporeality of matter and the divinity of mind* ... where *divinity* is understood to mean *being or having the nature of a deity, supremely good, magnificent, heavenly, perfect* (Houghton Mifflin *Canadian Dictionary of the English Language*).

The role of the teacher

In Tantric Buddhism, this notion of *transformation* is accentuated, a transformation of consciousness and hence of society. The role of the teacher
in this process is extended from being a transmitter of information to
being a healer, a therapist and an essential catalyst of personal, social and
environmental transformation. In the dialogue between a well-motivated
student and an accomplished teacher, through a process comparable to
transference/countertransference in psychoanalysis, interdependence
finds one of its most poignant expressions. Both learner and teacher come
to appreciate that in every moment of our existence we are both a teacher
and a learner simultaneously, and that we have a profound responsibility
in both capacities. This relationship engraves on our consciousness not
only the radical egalitarianism needed for the free individual to manifest
the free society but an appreciation of the intrinsic reciprocity of existence that might assist us to live more in harmony with our social and
natural worlds.

This radical redefinition of the role of the teacher as healer, therapist,
political activist and educator is yet another aspect of Buddhist philosophy
we might benefit from considering. Our notion of the professional
specialization of functions within contemporary education has proved
ineffective in dealing with the mounting problems facing young and old
people alike. Perhaps if we broke down some of the divisions between our
conceptions of what education, psychotherapy, religion and life
experience are, we might find the means to better address the complexity
of our needs.

Conclusion

It seems to me that Tantric Buddhism is where science and poetry inter-
sect, making our cells resonate with the same music as our imagination.
Secret Mantra is both reasonable and inspirational; it is both pragmatic
and Utopian; it is reaching inside the imagination to create a fantastic
vision of perfection, while reaching outside with the body in spontaneous
play to make it real. Because Octavio Paz reminds me that I am not alone
in my vision, and because he articulates it so perfectly, so poetically, I will
close with his words:

> ...are [we] living *an end of time*? I have already expressed my belief:
> modern time – linear time, the homologue of the ideas of progress
> and history, ever propelled into the future, the time of the sign *non-*
> *body*, of the fierce will to dominate nature and tame instincts, the time
> of sublimations, aggression, and self-mutilation – is coming to an end.
> I believe that we are entering another time, a time that has not yet
> revealed its form and about which we can say nothing except that it

will be neither linear time nor cyclical time. Neither history nor myth. The time that is coming ... will be neither a future nor a past, but a present ... It is a negation of the sign *non-body* in all its Western versions: religious or atheist, philosophical or political, materialist or idealist. The present does not project us into a place beyond, any motley, other-worldly eternities or abstract paradises at the end of history. It projects us into the medulla, the invisible center of time: the here and now. A carnal time, a mortal time: the present is not unreachable, the present is not forbidden territory. How can we touch it, how can we penetrate inside its transparent heart?

... I see in the conjunction [of poetry and rebellion] the possibility of the return of the sign *body*: the incarnation of images, the return of the human figure, radiant and radiating symbols. If contemporary rebellion ... is not dissipated in a succession of raucous cries and does not degenerate into closed, authoritarian systems, if it articulates its passion through poetic imagination, in the widest and freest sense of the word poetry, our incredulous eyes may behold the awakening and the return to our abject world of that corporeal and spiritual reality that we call *the presence of the beloved*. Then love will cease to be the isolated experience of an individual or a couple, an exception or a scandal. The word *presence* and the word *love* have appeared in these reflections for the first and the last time. They were the seed of the West, the origin of our art and of our poetry. In them is the secret of our resurrection. (1982: 138–139)

Note

1 *Sonia MacPherson* is a PhD student in Education at the University of British Columbia in Vancouver. She is conducting a comparative study of the Indo-Tibetan Buddhist monastic curriculum and the Western-based secular model of education as encountered in various Tibetan refugee communities in India. Currently, she holds a Webster Fellowship at Green College and is a past recipient of the Shastri Indo-Canadian Fellowship. She has studied Buddhism for 16 years, and has received instruction on Buddhist thought from the senior-most lamas of each of the four branches of Tibetan Buddhism. However, her most extensive studies have been with His Holiness the Dalai Lama and the late Venerable Tara Tulku, both leading lamas of the Gelugpa school. Prior to commencing her graduate studies, she worked for 10 years in various educational settings.

References

Gyatso, Tenzin, The Dalai Lama (1985) *Opening the Eye of New Awareness*, trans. D. S. Lopez Jr. with J. Hopkins (London: Wisdom Publications).

Gyatso, Tenzin, The Dalai Lama (1988) *The Dalai Lama at Harvard*, trans. J. Hopkins (Ithaca, NY: Snow Lion Publications).

Jarvis, P. (1992) *Paradoxes of Learning: On Becoming an Individual in Society* (San Francisco: Josey-Bass).

Komatsu, Chiko (1989) *The Way to Peace: The Life and Teachings of the Buddha*, trans. Gaynor Sekimori (Kyoto: Hozokan Publishing). [Original work published 1984].

Paz, O. (1982) *Conjunctions and Disjunctions*, trans. H. Lane (New York: Arcade Publishing). [Originally published 1969]

Thurman, R. A. F. (1984) *The Central Philosophy of Tibet: A Study and Translation of Jey Tsang Khapa's ESSENCE OF TRUE ELOQUENCE* (Princeton, NJ: Princeton University Press).

Part 4

... to the learning society and beyond

20 The learning society

Hendrik Van Der Zee[1]

University of Amsterdam

There is a growing consensus that educational reform should focus on the goal of creating a learning society. This, of course, does not necessarily imply clarity about the criteria for the development of a learning society. In this article the author outlines five strategic issues: the need to broaden the definition of learning (education as a dimension of society); the need to redirect the goal of learning (growth towards completeness); the need to go beyond learning and instruction (increasing collective competence); the need to foster autonomy in learning (self-education); and the need to stress a political approach to learning (the right to learn). These issues represent the challenges facing all advanced industrial nations.

Charting criteria

Every community takes steps to ensure that its members acquire the different kinds of knowledge considered necessary for life. But societies vary considerably with respect to the importance given to learning, the specific aims that they try to satisfy through learning, and the way in which they attempt to support and reinforce learning. In the Jewish tradition learning occupies pride of place. Thus, in the twelfth century Maimonides wrote (according to Abram 1984: 64):

> Every Jew, whether rich or poor, healthy or sick, at the height of his powers or old and infirm, has the duty to study. Wood-cutters and water-bearers figured among their great scholars, even blind men. They studied day and night. (...) Until when should a person continue to learn? Until the day of his death. (...) Learning is the most important of all the rules of behaviour given in the Torah. Even stronger: learning is more important than all other rules of behaviour together. (...) Make learning a regular habit. Do not say: 'I'll learn if I have time'. You may never have time.

These words deserve noting in the light of the contemporary world-wide debate on educational standards.[2] The pedagogical assumptions on which present-day curricula are based, are increasingly coming under attack. However defective we may consider our curricula to be, we should bear in mind that criticism of education is not new. In the last century, for example, Friedrich Nietzsche (1872: 133–152) complained that educational institutions, far from seeking to civilize men and society, teach people to be functionaries and make them marketable. The same and similar complaints can be heard today.

Criticism of the functioning of our educational system should be seen in the context of the societal forces that affect learning needs. These forces include:

- the explosion of knowledge and technology;
- automation in companies and institutions;
- attempts to make labour and labour organizations more flexible;
- the economic and political unification of Europe;
- the innumerable people who have to scrape an existence on the edges of the labour market;
- the tendency towards individualization;
- the increase in the amount of free time we have at our disposal;
- the ageing of the population;
- the variety in sorts of households and forms of cohabitation;
- changes in the relationship between men and women and parents and children;
- the co-existence of different ethnic and cultural groups;
- the revaluation of the environment.[3]

Various suggestions are proposed to address the diverse and shifting learning needs which are emerging in response to the combined impact of these social and economic changes.

Some scholars seek the solution primarily in a *new approach to training and education.* Two different points of emphasis are discernible within this approach. In the one case, the introduction of a new or revised educational concept is stressed (self-directed learning, problem-orientated instruction, learning from experience, andragogy). In the other case, the emphasis lies on the methods that should be used in the design of instruction and for solving performance problems (instructional design, educational technology, course planning).

A second response to the new demands for education and training is the *effective school movement.* This research driven movement takes the organization of education as its point of departure. It is maintained that such factors as strong management, regular testing of learning achievements, getting back to basics and a secure and well-ordered school environment have a vital influence on the achievements of the pupils.

A third innovation in educational thinking is the *open learning movement.* Client orientation and flexibility in the provision of learning opportunities are the main theme here. In practical terms this means the setting up of cafeteria-style arrangements for education, doing away with entrance requirements, the application of technology (television, video, telephone, computers), the use of self-instructional material, the development of a support system.

A more radical proposal for reform comes from the movement for the *de-schooling of society*. This movement, which was prominent in the 1970s, highlighted the side-effects of attempts fixated on promoting the extension and perfection of educational facilities. The de-schoolers argue that, little by little, a colossal learning factory has been created from which everything resembling education in the original meaning of the word has disappeared. Our schools have become instruments of repression: they reinforce social inequality, keep people dependent, stub out initiative and creativity, and impede common action. Moreover, what people most need to learn, schools seem least able to teach. However valid this criticism may be, it can be said that the de-schoolers have paved the way for a discussion about our educational priorities, in particular about what the basics are, about principles of self-organization, and about informal and non-informal modes of learning.

The final theme for change which I would like to mention is the idea of *recurrent education*. The term recurrent education refers to an overall strategy aimed at restructuring the educational system, so as to distribute periods of study over the total life span of the individual in a recurring way, i.e., alternating with extended periods of other sorts of activity such as work, leisure and retirement. Although recurrent education has been a political hobby-horse for many years in the Netherlands, statistics on participation and time-budget studies show that the idea has not been put to work.

Of course, the above is not an exhaustive catalogue of new directions for education. None the less the survey does give an impression of the variety of proposals for reform. It is clear that the changes in society's demand for education have produced divergent reactions.

The more miscellaneous the chorus of critics and reformers, the more dire the need for an overall score, a concept which stresses the importance of harmony between the multitude of separate approaches.[4] A preferred score would provide room for a variety of initiatives to renewal, without justifying every proposal beforehand and so circumventing the need to choose. Rather it would act as a common source of inspiration. The metaphor of a *learning society* has the potential to fulfil this need.

However, at the present moment it is customary to sketch the society of the future as an *information society*. Why do I not take the availability of information (i.e., knowledge), but the acquisition of knowledge (i.e., learning) as the primary consideration? The reason is that an information society is still not an informed society. The evidence is otherwise. What is envisaged is a society in which the pressure from technology and the economy is so great that people, the users of the information, feel defeated. If we don't take action, an inhuman, highly technocratic society lies ahead of us (see, for example, Martin 1988 and Roszak 1986).

No matter how one regards an information society, one thing is missing in this metaphor: people. Roby Kidd (1983: 530) maintains that an important linking operation is needed which enables us to make our own sense out of information. The word learning guarantees this sort of linking operation. It directs attention to the dynamics of the relations between information and information technology on the one side, and the individual and the community on the other.

'The learning society is growing because it must', is the opening of Patricia Cross's inspiring survey of literature *Adults as learners* (1986: 1). This makes us curious about the characteristics of a learning society, or rather about the ideas and values to which the concept appeals. Defining a concept that has engendered a world-wide debate is tricky. Nevertheless, in this paper I will pinpoint five criteria (strategic issues) for the development of a learning society. These are:

1 The need to broaden the definition of learning (education as a dimension of society).
2 The need to redirect the goal of learning (growth towards completeness).
3 The need to go beyond learning and instruction (increasing collective competence).
4 The need to foster autonomy in learning (self-education).
5 The need to stress a political approach to learning (the right to learn).

Dimension of society

A learning society stimulates and allows all its members and groups continually to develop their knowledge, skills and attitudes. Education is anchored in culture as a primary condition of existence. It is high on the agenda of many societal institutions. Besides the educational system proper, numerous other agencies are involved – the mass media, the unions, industry and commerce, the health services, travel organizations, public information outlets, prisons, and so on. This is what I mean by education as a dimension of society.[5]

Education can be described as the manner in which persons and groups gain skills, extend their knowledge, receive impulses, define their attitudes: in short, learn things. I believe that a comprehensive strategy, aimed at opening up new opportunities for people to learn, should consist of the following three steps. First it is necessary to chart the existing forms of learning. Then we should examine how the potential of the suggested types of learning can be further developed. Finally we should take into account the unique contributions as well as the interdependencies of the many agencies of education and other learning resources. I will now discuss these three steps in order.

Forms of learning

The bewildering variety of modes in which human learning occurs can be viewed from various angles. The context determines what constitutes a meaningful classification and terminology. Here the first priority is to clarify the possibilities for strengthening the educational dimension of society. From this point of view it is essential to distinguish between three basic forms of learning.

The first, but not necessarily most powerful mode of learning, is *guided learning*. By guided learning I mean all sorts of learning activities which involve a measure of instruction or tuition. This includes following occupational training, attending a management seminar, taking part in a course via the television or going to dancing lessons.

The second basic form can be referred to by the term *do-it-yourself learning*. It covers all activities people undertake on their own initiative, without the mediation of teachers or course-makers, with the intention of broadening their horizons or improving their capacity to accomplish some task. Ferreting something out in the public library, doing a job 'with the social sciences', cracking a computer with the aid of a manual and mastering a physical handicap with the support of a patient's association are examples of do-it-yourself learning. It should be noted that self-learners often do not regard their behaviour as 'learning', and that only a fraction of their initiatives take the form of learning projects.[6]

The third basic form is *spontaneous learning*. Like do-it-yourself learning, spontaneous learning, as a rule, takes place without organized instruction. However, whereas do-it-yourself learning is deliberately designed to cope with a problem or to summon inspiration, one bumps into spontaneous learning without meaning to, as in the case of a serious accident (through which daily worries are put in perspective), a conflict at work (through which scales drop from the eyes), and a love affair (through which we come to look at ourselves and to reassess old relationships). At other times learning happens by the way, as a by-product of an activity which is primarily guided by other motives. Watching television, starting an own company and practising a sport are examples of activities from which a lot can be learnt in an unselfconscious fashion.[7]

To say that much learning takes place without recourse to teachers or producers of instructional materials is to state the obvious. Everyone concerned with the training and education of young people and adults acknowledges this phenomenon. Nevertheless, professional practitioners, policy makers and researchers continue to regard the school system as 'too separate, too all-sufficient and too effective an organization of provisions' (Fletcher 1984: 406).

Promoting learning

The forms of learning mentioned above offer as many points of contact for educational reform. With respect to the area of guided learning, at least three groups of initiatives deserve special attention:

1   Improving the quality of the existing school system. This category includes all activities which aim at more effective, efficient and appealing methods of instruction, improved instructional materials, greater differentiation, more skilful teachers, innovative management, and better amenities.
2   Developing new programmes and types of education, especially around questions and needs for which the present range of educational facilities does not, or does not fully, provide.
3   Enlarging access to courses and training by getting rid of all sorts of impediments which prevent people from taking part. Examples of such impediments can be: irregular working hours, transportation problems, not being able to afford the registration fee, lack of self-confidence, ignorance of the opportunities, insufficient studying skills, not satisfying the entrance requirements.

The problem of how to cope with the two remaining types of learning is less easily answered. This is due to a lack of knowledge about the processes involved. A framework for examining the tasks facing us in our daily practices is needed before more conscious action can be taken. Which tasks question our ways of thinking and behaving? How do we respond to the difficulties and opportunities these tasks represent? What sort of competence and wisdom will help us move ahead? In what way can the required proficiencies be obtained? With regard to the last question, I advocate keeping the perspective as open as possible. A multitude of sources and means deserve consideration.

- informal contacts: friends, neighbours, members of the family;
- the mass media: books, radio, television, newspapers, magazines, audio- and video-cassettes;
- labour organizations: the place of work as place of learning;
- cultural institutions: museums, libraries, theatres, cinemas, creative centres;
- utilitarian facilities: trade fairs, labour exchanges, banks, do-it-yourself shops.

Uncovering this educational potential is a daunting task. Recent studies on learning in the workplace, the public library as an open-learning centre, learning through television, and the educational possibilities of museums indicate a basis upon which we may proceed.

Harmony

Let flowers flower everywhere. However, the situation in which the diverse 'agencies of education' only care about their own back yard must be avoided. As Cyril Houle (1972: 6) sketched:

> The typical career worker in adult education is still concerned only with an institutional pattern of service or a methodology, seldom or never catching a glimpse of the total terrain of which he is cultivating one corner, and content to be, for example, a farm or home consultant, museum curator, public librarian, or industrial trainer.

The many sources and means available to learners must be brought into harmony. This requires co-operation, the formation of networks, the division of duties, a realization of the unique contributions one agency can make that other agencies cannot, continuous innovation and a common perspective. There may be no misunderstanding about who should judge the harmony: in the last analysis, the user of the facilities.

The fact that there is a negative side to teaching should never be forgotten. Lauren Resnick (1987: 13–20) has unravelled how knowledge gained at school relates to knowledge required in everyday life and at work. She discovered four differences:

1   At school individual achievements are tested, while in life you are judged by what you can contribute in a social context.
2   In school it is what is in your head that counts, while in life what matters is if you are good at using technology, aids and appliances and sources.
3   At school you learn to use meaningless symbols, while in life inventiveness in approaching meaningful problem situations is required.
4   At school you learn general skills and subject-dependent understanding, while in life you need knowledge and experience which is relevant to specific problems situations.

These findings may not be revolutionary. But it does not hurt to think about them once again. The failure of our schools to teach proficiencies that are essential for living challenges the pedagogical assumptions on which a lot of today's curricula are based.

It is a great mistake, however, to equate a society's broad educational goals with instrumental learning and an utilitarian bias. Genuine education teaches people to stand 'above the machine'. Moreover, schools share this responsibility with the media, literature and the arts, the public library, and many other institutions. This brings us to the second foundation of the learning society: education as the growth towards completion.

Growth towards completion

Now we proceed from the ferment in the learning society, its sources, means, and institutions, to the consideration of what is learnt. The creation of the opportunity to learn, irrespective of content, is not necessarily a positive virtue. At school and elsewhere we often learn things that do nobody any good, either directly or in the long run. Narrow-minded opinions, antiquated theories, ossified working methods, empty skills, disturbances of the motorial system, callous behaviour, ungrounded fears, docility – all are examples of the wrong kind of learning. In such cases education degenerates into, to use a word introduced by John Dewey, miseducation. But it is even worse than that. Much of the knowledge that would be most valuable to us no doubt goes unlearned, as Hirsch sets forth in his book *Cultural literacy: what every American needs to know* (1988). How, then, do we settle our educational priorities?

Here it is only possible to talk about the direction in which I think the answer should be sought. I am not really happy about the wording but am as yet unable to do better: we learn to become a *complete* person. The justification for any educational activity, therefore, lies in the following question: in what degree does the learning contribute to a person's completeness? All learning objectives are subordinate to this ultimate test. The concern for completeness has far-reaching implications, as I do Abram (1984: 69), who has made an extensive study on the role of learning in the Jewish community, indicates:

> The permanent pupil does not learn to be able to practise a profession, not even that of rabbi, in order to obtain power or authority, but to improve himself and his behaviour and thereby the world. The purpose of his learning is, in other words, to become a complete person. (...) But what is 'a complete person'? There is no straightforward answer to this question. The answer depends on the picture of the world and especially of humanity in the mind of the permanent pupil, on what he studies and appreciates in the culture, on how he digests the past and sees the future. (...) Each pupil has his own learning journey to make and the true significance and personal implications of the desired result, completeness, can only be revealed to him in the course of the learning process. The Torah rejects imitation both of learning method and of learning result.

This – selective – description of what 'completeness' means, of course, can only be a starting point. A connection must be made with the formation of present-day opinion on the purpose of education. When we make this connection, we notice that the concept of 'completeness' consists of two components: it encompasses a double aspiration.

Pursuit of quality

The first component is the pursuit of quality, an attempt to achieve improvement and ultimately excellence. In a certain sense this aim serves as a counterpoint to a point of view which dominated the discussion on the relations between education and society in the 1960s and 1970s: the ideal of equal opportunities. I am in no way advocating that the topic of social inequality and justice should disappear from the agenda. Further on the opposite will become apparent. But here I wish to emphasize a matter which, due to a misinterpretation of the egalitarian ideal, has been neglected time and time again: the human urge to be special.

Note that the pursuit of quality encompasses more than championing the very gifted. I would go even further; thinking in terms of the very gifted (and therefore also the less gifted) violates the idea of completeness as it is put into words in the Jewish tradition, for example. In this *Education in society: the Promethean fire* Ronald Fletcher (1984: 26) offers a more meaningful approach to the concept of quality:

> One task of education at least (...) is that of continually seeking to civilize men and society: to bring their level of life, feeling, thought and judgement *above* that of the market-place, the class struggle, the power struggles of the immediate political arena, even above the level of the vision of the narrow parochialism of the present – to levels of cultivated awareness of the world, and to skills of realizing and expressing that awareness, which are hard to attain.

The passion for quality is *in no way* connected with the formation of an elite and *hardly* with assessments and tests, inspection committees, diplomas and examinations. On the other hand, it is *very much* related to recognizing potential and the continuous search for conditions which stimulate potential.

Pursuit of all-round development

There is a second side to the emphasis on 'completeness': the pursuit of all-round development. This striving can be seen as a counterpoint to another dominant educational trend, i.e., the concentration of attention on the cognitive development only of human beings. Other aspects of personality – including the aesthetic, social, moral, emotional, physical and even technical/manual – are regarded by western culture as more or less peripheral to education.

The British education philosopher Louis Arnaud Reid is one of those who has repeatedly denounced this one-sidedness. In *Ways of understanding and education* (1986) Reid stresses that there are two basic forms of knowledge. One form is discursive. It involves propositional statements of fact about the world around us. The other form, which covers the area of intuitive experience, is called non-discursive. The arts are excellently suited as media for expressing non-discursive knowledge. According to Reid, there should be an interchange between these ways of knowing, since the rational-intellectual and the intuitive–creative need each other. However, in western culture in general, and in curricula in particular, human knowledge is identified with what can be expressed in propositional statements. This has led to a separation of the world of the intellect, science and technology from the world of feelings, values, emotions and creativity. A disastrous schism, as Reid (1986: 2) writes:

> The life of personal subjects, the life of feelings and emotions, of the creative urges, of obscure symbolisms, of moral urges and intimations, religion, personal relations – all these, cut off, on this divisive assumption, from the critical purgings of thinking and intellect, remain raw, chaotic, often infantile. The personal self is split down the middle.

More attention for the training of 'eye, hand and heart' and more recognition of the importance of history, languages and literature will not, it is true, halt the increasing encroachment of specialisms, but it could nevertheless provide some counterbalance.[8] To put it more positively, education is concerned with the whole human being and the whole culture. Does this mean that the medieval idea of the *homo universalis* is about to be reinstated? However much this ideal may appeal to us, circumstances are now very different to those of our distant forefathers. There is no demand for a *homo universalis* in the present day because of the abundance of collective competence constantly around us.

Collective competence

The expression 'collective competence' is taken from De Zeeuw (1984, 1985). Put simply, collective competence is the ability to act, given the availability of support systems. What, then, is a support system?

In this context I take the concept of a support system in its widest sense. Support systems are of all times and are part of the human tradition. Cultural artefacts such as songs, fairy stories, the Bible and a hammer can be regarded as support systems. The same can be said of manuals, spreadsheets, self-help groups, planning procedures, consultancy bureaux, radar installations, and data-banks. Thus, support systems are means, tools, sources, facilities, technology.

Some support systems augment our physical strength, others reinforce our senses or our thinking powers. Some support systems enable us to act collectively (forms of social organization), others inspire us and shake us awake (art, literature).

But all support systems have one thing in common: they embody the understanding, ideas and values of the past, and in this respect they are human projections. Thus, using a source or aid, or some other appliance, implies calling on experience which has often been built up painfully from generation to generation in tackling the problem with which the facility is intended to cope. The more competence a support system provides, the less competence the actor who makes use of it needs. As Resnick (1987: 14) shows, the history of navigation is a case in point:

> Sailors once navigated by the stars; in addition to recognizing the constellations, they needed to perform complex geometric calculations. Simple magnetic compasses dramatically changed the skill requirements for navigation, although computations to compensate for degrees of variation between magnetic and true north were still needed. Later, the invention of a compass with built-in compensations for variation provided a tool that pointed directly to true north, thereby eliminating most of the computational work. But it was still necessary to know the relationships between north and other points of the compass to determine direction of sighting. Today's gyrocompasses remove even that requirement, because they compute and name the direction of sighting. With each of these changes in technology, compasses in effect became 'smarter', and the user needed successively less skill. But the total system lost no intelligence or knowledge. Instead some skill and knowledge passed out of the hands of compass users and into the hands of compass designers and their products.

Sources, technology, and other facilities are a part of our environment. Our competence, therefore, stands or falls with the extent to which we can avail ourselves of the collective competence caught up in mankind's facilities. What does this mean from the point of view of education? Educators could try to teach the substitute knowledge incorporated in support systems. De Zeeuw (1984) calls this approach to education the *entrance model*. Schools often proceed from the entrance model. They act as if no support systems existed. In Resnick's words (1987: 13):

> In school, the greatest premium is placed upon 'pure thought' activities – what individuals can do without the external support of books and notes, calculators, of other complex instruments.

Here we have come up against a form of resignation of which the 'last of the idealists' Arthur Schopenhauer (1851: 210) was the most articulate protagonist:

> The pen is to thought what the stick is to walking; the lightest gait is that without a stick, and the most perfect thought proceeds without a pen. It is only with age that one gratefully makes use of stick and pen.

There can be no dispute that an approach to education which ignores today's support systems is out of touch with reality and, therefore, undesirable. A countervailing approach that stresses the importance of appropriating the human achievement embodied within support systems is badly needed. De Zeeuw (1984) suggests such an approach, and calls it the *participation model*. His model relies on the tacit knowledge that sources, tools and other facilities represent. We reveal this knowledge by using it, i.e., by participating in the culture in which we all have our stake.[9]

Currently there are, however, human, economic and technological obstacles to realizing this model. Let us look at some practical measures that could be taken to increase participation, thereby putting human achievement to work. These measures are centred around five critical points: (a) enriching the school environment, (b) redesigning the curriculum, (c) incorporating an educational element in the design of facilities, (d) making facilities more intelligent, and (e) removing restrictions on access to facilities. I do not have room to discuss these points at length here but will limit myself to a short explanation. In each case the explanation is confined to a single example of a support system; the community or office data-base.

Enriching the school environment

The school is still too much of an island. The sources from which pupils learn for the most part remain restricted to material that has been specially designed for educational purposes, and to teachers and fellow-pupils. Facilities which are available in society still do not penetrate far enough into schools. However, here and there things are changing. For example, new technology is now welcomed enthusiastically in vocational training, as are simulations of practice. But the situation is still unsatisfactory in more generally-orientated educational institutions. As society moves into the micro-electronic environment of the future, the installation of computers giving access to data-bases relevant to the subject being handled in classrooms would be a step in the right direction.

Redesigning the curriculum

Redesigning the curriculum is even more vital than the mere presence of present-day technological facilities in the school environment. Students need to be taught how to work from and with facilities. So no mental arithmetic, but a task performed with the calculator. No hand-written business correspondence, but straight into the computer. No prefabricated teaching material but 'real life' sources should be used.

The community and office data-base is such a source. As computerized knowledge systems become more accepted in educational settings, students will have to acquire new skills in order to cope with them. What can teachers do to help students in this respect? The solution which schools are beginning to develop is the provision of special programmes on subjects with such names as study skills, information skills, computer literacy, library skills and communication skills. An alternative is to integrate the training in the normal discipline-centred courses, which involves a different kind of pedagogy. In whatever way they are organized, the perspective – what are the lessons for? – must be clear. Explanation (of why), broadening (of the possibilities for application), coupling (of the various forms of computer applications in daily life) and recognizing 'the meaning of meaning' should be key areas of attention.

Embedded training

Few individuals like to invest a lot of time and energy in learning how to use facilities such as libraries or computers. By incorporating an educational element into the design of such facilities it is possible to avoid forcing the beginner to struggle through all sorts of manuals and instructions, or even to attend training courses before being able to start off. It makes instruction available when and where needed, on the job, in everyday settings. Furthermore, building education into a support system ensures that actors keep on developing their skills to a 'professional' level. Indeed, embedded training can best be seen as a form of learning by doing.

What are the implications for our case study, the computerized knowledge system? First, the information offered and the retrieval procedures must be clear. Second, support must be available at critical moments when decisions have to be made and steps taken. Third, this support facilitates reflection on the user's actions and the development of an own perspective on the subject. Fourth, the data file must contain valuable information which is attractively presented and tempts the user to proceed further. Fifth, there should be room for several methods of working.

Making facilities more intelligent

This measure lies in the extension of the previous one. However, here we are concerned not so much with the educational aspect, but rather with the desire for something that is referred to as 'user friendliness'. The criteria are, then, simplicity in use, accessibility, the appeal of working with the facility, efficiency. But there is more. The facility must not only be 'friendly' towards the user, it should also be designed from the users' perspective and not proceed from the demands of a specialized discipline or a programming language. There is even a further criterion. Most facilities are inclined to deteriorate over the years as, for example, when professionals come to dominate their use or when insufficient attention is paid to changing needs and circumstances. For this reason, facilities should be designed with mechanisms that ensure a permanent dialogue between the (projected) user and the professional.

Depite the fact that they may be regarded as wonders of sophistication by some, all the automated information facilities with which I am familiar seem depressingly inadequate with respect to the criteria just mentioned. Take one example from my own experience. I discovered part of the documentation for this study using the Online Public Catalogue which the Library of the University of Amsterdam recently installed. It had something to offer, undoubtedly. But to begin with, the layout on the monitor was so primitive: no pictograms, far too many words and codes, no attempt at all at a pleasing graphical presentation. And to think that this is a relatively advanced system. Contrary to the shining visions of the computer enthusiast, it is obviously still a long time till the micro-electronic era. Lessons on how to use information often deal chiefly with problems which would not exist if the system had been built more intelligently in the first place.

Increasing the availability of facilities

Modern society is rich in facilities. But not everything is within everyone's reach. Wealth – and consequently opportunities to learn – is unevenly distributed. It has been shown, for example, that children from prosperous backgrounds have a considerable head start at school, because they have access to a PC at home.

With regard to computerized knowledge systems there are signs that in the coming years increasingly more information on the most diverse topics will be (exclusively) stored in computers. But the public at large has no or no easy access to these electronic publications. It is a good thing that in several countries the public library is trying to do something about this problem. Two Dutch projects are worth mentioning, TACO (a national data-bank) and Biblitel (a local data-bank). However, the context in which a project such as TACO must function deserves more attention. Taking repercussions on existing ways of working, established responsibilities and hierarchies into account, there are three basic possibilities. First, the data-bank leaves everything as it is (and is probably hardly ever used). Second, the introduction of the data-bank requires some adjustments to be made in its environment (until a new equilibrium is reached). Third, the introduction of the data-bank leads to a restructuring of intelligence work and to adjustments at other levels of the institution and this, in turn, leads to special design requirements for the data-bank, and so on. Only in the last case can we speak of a true innovation, in the sense of a long-term increase in the collective competence embedded in public libraries.

So much for a number of measures connected with collective competence. I would add this: by regarding sources, equipment and other facilities as support systems, terms of reference are set within which a constructive discussion of our culture can be held. Such a discussion is constructive because it is directed to transforming our culture into a living possession with everyone participating in it. The notion of collective competence has brought the third premise for the learning society into focus. But more is involved in such a society.

Self-education

The achievement of self-education is the fourth key to the advancement of a learning society. Although different writers mean different things when they use the word self-education, the insight that the concept contains two elements is gradually emerging. First, self-education is the objective aimed at: encouraging people to keep on learning of their own volition. A general heading that applies to this aim is *learning to learn*. Second, self-education is a recommended *way of teaching*, an approach for helping people to learn. In educational practice self-education can be both the objective and the vehicle. However, to avoid confusion, I have unravelled these two strands.

Learning to learn

Learning to learn seeks to emphasize that, throughout life, human beings are what they are because of learning. The concept assumes a 'recursive framework', one that sees actors as potentially creative. At its heart is the achievement of autonomy; people taking the responsibility for their own learning.

Libraries could be filled with what has been written on these ideas, though not every writer goes under the same banner. Because of its utilitarian flavour, Robert Smith (1982: 19) prefers the phrase learning *how* to learn. His effort to come to terms with the slippery concept starts from the following definition:

> Learning how to learn involves possessing, or acquiring, the knowledge and skill to learn effectively in whatever learning situation one encounters.

Such a general definition looks attractive, but it is not adequate in this case, since it ignores the fact that the concept can be approached from various angles. Thus, learning to learn is variously described as:

1   acquiring skills in tracing and making sense of information;
2   becoming proficient in solving problems in varying situations;
3   obtaining a grasp of the principles of good research;
4   reinforcing self-regulation in school and training settings;
5   practising study techniques;

6   developing 'higher order' skills;
7   increasing one's ability to learn from experience;
8   nurturing the desire to become a complete person.

Admirable as these goals are, instruction to increase people's competence in learning is usually simplified into courses or lessons in studying skills (5th meaning). Often such efforts are dominated by a school-bound mentality, by helping students to survive in the educational arena. The chief concern is about coping with the system: tricks on how to get through examinations, learning material by heart, doing homework, marking study texts, making notes.

In my opinion, the study-skills movement should broaden its perspective and shift its focus from the reproductive to the productive aspects of knowledge. For that a link should be sought with the other approaches to improving the capacity to learn.

In addition, it is necessary to emphasize the crucial importance of the environments in which the skills one has learned are applied. What I advocate is an ecology of learning to learn. The ecological view may be premised with some thoughts on the problem of transfer, which is indeed a major deficiency in many study-skills programmes (Nisbet and Shucksmith 1986). But the ecology of learning implies more than simply taking care of transfer. It also involves being fully alive to the power relationships within the social structure. To paraphrase the Czech novelist Milan Kundera (see McEwan 1984: 26–32), we can say that in a world which has become a trap the struggle for inward independence (and against the monster within) should coincide with the struggle for outward independence (against the monster from outside).

How can this look at learning to learn be implemented in practical situations? Various suggestions have been made. Some, e.g. David Boud (1988: 8), advocate changes in the regular curriculum: 'They believe that it is the responsibility of all teachers to ensure that they construct their courses to foster autonomy and that this goal is compatible with the discipline-centred goals which often predominate'. Others take the existing curriculum as a fact of life but think that it should be enriched with supportive lessons, optional or otherwise, on subjects such as coping with self-instructional materials, working through projects, writing a thesis, using a library, and 'reading' media constructions. A third groups maintains that measures outside education are also needed; there is a task for broadcasting organizations, museums, libraries, publishers and creativity centres.

As I see it, a learning society will explore all possible avenues of promoting learning to learn. With one reservation. I have very little faith in initiatives determined from on high which do not take the day-to-day experiences of those involved into account. Emancipation – meaning inner and outer independence – is not granted, it has to be fought for and won.

Way of teaching

As I said, the word self-education stands not only for something to strive for, but also for a means, a way of teaching. This is another topic which has fuelled a lot of controversy and, again, polemicists do not all share the same background. This is expressed in the variety of concepts denoting the principles of good practice. Perhaps the issues at stake can be clarified by identifying two basic ways of helping people to increase their know-ledge and improve their qualifications. I have labelled these contrasting views the 'school approach', and the 'adult approach'.[10]

The school approach	*The adult approach*
transmitting a given body of knowledge	developing an own perspective on a subject
the teacher decides	the learner decides
a semantically poor context	a semantically rich context
learning without facilities	learning with facilities
learning as drilling	learning as a conscious activity
experience as condition	experience as foundation
directed to subject-matter	directed to problems
evaluation as a check	evaluation as a means of improving
compulsion and duty	voluntary basis, pleasure in learning
directed at achievement	directed towards completion
closed tasks	open tasks

It has to be admitted that this scheme is full of crass contradictions. But the descriptions help us to cut out the proverbial rigmarole that is so typical of the age-old discussion about the most appropriate ways of meeting learners' needs. It goes without saying that the approach advoc-ated here is the adult approach. Its principles characterize the spirit in which pupils – of any age – and teachers deal with each other in a learn-ing society.

For clarity's sake: an adult approach is also possible outside general forming and development work and group teaching. Its principles are viable everywhere: in study at a distance, in computer-assisted learning, in mathematical education, in in-house company training programmes, in occupational training, at universities, in museums, in public libraries, and elsewhere.

Right to learn

As a social issue education is the responsibility of the community. In a learning society, therefore, learning should be a right and not a privilege. All citizens – regardless of social status, income, initial training, descent, sex and affiliations – should be given equal opportunities to develop themselves and to improve proficiencies throughout their lives.

This goal is music to democratic ears. Is it then any wonder that since the 1960s such terms as lifelong learning, permanent education and recurrent education have occurred regularly in the introductions of official educational documents? Enough rhetoric to sink a ship.

But what are the implications for educational practice? Which attitude should the government adopt? What is entirely private domain, and how far should state interference reach? Kidd (1983: 530) sketches the alternatives:

> Is there a basic education that a citizen should have as a birthright and would the provision of such constitute the main conditions of a learning society? Or would something more be needed, such as national declarations or laws, or an ethos of learning, or an environment for learning?

It seems that, as far as the right of learning is concerned, the Dutch government does not wish to commit itself to more than guaranteeing a sort of minimum programme and even that is under review. The most important policy instrument is the general-proficiency schooling for 12- to 15- or 16-year olds. In addition there are plans for an educational voucher system.

General-proficiency schooling versus basic education

According to the Scientific Council for Government Policy (1986: 8) general-proficiency schooling is concerned with:

a   *basic* skills: proficiencies (knowledge, attainments, understanding) that are vital to be able to function as a member of society and which are the essential foundation and nucleus for further development;
b   education for *everyone*: in principle, the contents of the basic forming are the same for all groups;
c   *common* education: in principle, the schooling is directed to the common acquisition of the contents of a curriculum that is equally valid for all. Forms of differentiation between pupils in anticipation of their further education are, in principle, to be avoided.

How does this renewed interest in the myth of 'the common school, common programme, common core' (Holmes 1988: 246) fit in with the notion of a learning society? Getting back to basics, in keeping with the diversity of tasks that life has set aside for people, seems to me a viable idea, provided that general schooling allows for differential educational provisions to accommodate inequalities in pupils' capacities and backgrounds. As far as the belief in common public education appeals to the idea of equality as a principle of justice it cannot possibly mean equality of treatment. Rather it has to come to terms with the principles of equal consideration and equal opportunity (Fletcher 1984).

Whatever general-proficiency schooling may mean, my greatest fear is that we may claim to be achieving quality if everyone in this country can neatly answer a barrage of pre-set questions drawn up by experts in different fields. We will then be even further from the mark. Our educational system will not be truly worthwhile until schools succeed in motivating youngsters to keep on learning and asking critical questions about the world.

Another point which prompts criticism and concern is that adult education has been left out of the discussion. It is an obvious step to give not only young people but also adults the opportunity to acquire and cultivate basic proficiencies. The State Regulation on Adult Elementary Education could be applied to this end. In addition to higher priority for this branch of adult education, a more differentiated package of lessons with more choice, more quality, and less utilitarian bias is needed.

A third issue is also important. It must be recognized in word and in deed that it is not just schools that enable citizens to function in contemporary society. The involvement of companies, television, newspapers, museums, public libraries and other 'socializing contexts' is essential. A *National newspaper literacy day*, an American initiative, could be held up as an example.

Educational vouchers?

The second policy instrument that is expected to strengthen the right to learn is the educational bond. The idea has been broached that all young people should be presented with an educational bond at the end of their compulsory schooling at sixteen. The bond would consist of a fixed number of vouchers which would entitle each holder to the same number of years of full-time day education, to be filled in as they choose. The personalized vouchers would remain valid indefinitely, but when they are used up, that is it. Precursors of such a voucher system exist already. We only have to think of the time limits in higher education.

Much as support must be given (with reservations) to the idea of general-proficiency schooling, so the idea of an educational bond is hopeless. The introduction of a voucher system does not lead to an enlargement but to a contraction of the opportunities for learning. Will schooling soon only be available to ticket holders? Whatever ends this regulation meets, it certainly does not serve that of lifelong learning, even aside the question of practicality. Social security has proved to be beyond our reach in many ways; would educational security fare better? (Not to mention the containment of the expectations roused by the voucher system.) Should government credulity be trusted this time?

Looking further

A government which takes the right to learn seriously cannot limit its actions to seeing to it that skills 'which are an essential foundation and form the nucleus for further development' are taught. Attention must also be given to the quality of the learning environment. For this is often the difficulty, as can be seen from research into the background and reasons for (non-)participation in educational activities. Lists of the large number of barriers to learning have been drawn up time and time again. However, we are still waiting for a plan of campaign for tackling these obstacles. Unless it is accompanied by free access to the relevant sources of learning, the right to learn is just so many words.

Conclusion

The disturbing question of the future of education led an American government commission in 1983 to shake the American people awake with the report *A nation at risk*. The typical Dutch reaction was to conduct a 'trial investigation to establish if a periodical assessment study into the level of education in the Netherlands' was feasible. This unsentimental attitude appeals to me. But at the same time, I hope that a more creative answer will be found based on a sense of direction concerning the future of our culture and not on mourning for a lost past. An answer, moreover, which takes learning human beings and not educational institutions as its starting point.

The concept 'learning society', a society in which learning is the whole of life and the whole of life is learning, is a powerful stimulation to the formation of opinion. In this paper I have outlined what the cornerstones of such a society could be. I realize the risks involved in working with an abstract, even utopian, idea such as that of a learning society. On the other hand, it has to be said that it is impossible to work without a perspective – without sources of inspiration, aims, guidelines and norms.

A lack of commitment is one of the risks of the approach proposed above. Dimensions of society, growth to completeness, collectice competence, self-education, right to learn – all good publishers' blurb. But what are the practical implications of this way of thinking? The values to which the notion of a learning society appeals will indeed have to be embodied in the various situations in which people can learn. This is precisely the strength of the chosen concept: it enables us to gather a variety of approaches and social initiatives together at a higher level of abstraction, beyond immediate self-interests and parochialism.

Time is of the essence. The general climate has not become more hospitable to human learning in the last twenty years. Today the criterion is the return from educational institutions and not the contribution made to stimulating potential. Training courses increasingly benefit ambitious men in senior and top functions, while the training chances for those with only elementary education, for the unemployed and for women are decreasing. The school approach to learning and teaching is gaining the whip hand. Consumerism and cafeteria-style education is encroaching on all sides. But the cause for most concern is probably that the discussion about such a crucial public issue as educational reform is being conducted by the civil service, industry and commerce and educational specialists; there are not organized counterforces. Is this the culture we want?

Notes

1 *Hendrik van der Zee* is a lecturer in the Department of Education at the University of Amsterdam. His current research centres on educational design, with an emphasis on public institutions as promotors of self-directed and open learning. He is the author/editor of eight (Dutch language) books, including *Adult education: dilemmas and perspectives* (1984) and *Guide to using libraries and media* (1989).
2 Here I am concerned with the organization principle, without the restrictions on contents. For a Jewish believer the sources are fixed (the Torah), he only has to dig things out. In this paper, on the other hand, the selection of sources is under discussion.
3 This list gives salient examples. Its sole-purpose is to show that various societal developments should be involved in the considerations at the same time. In my opinion, the future of our educational institutions, not unlike that of other social institutions, is shaped at least as much by their own history as by external forces.
4 Instead of speaking of a *score*, we could talk of a *myth* as Mark Holmes does (1988:248). But then not of a myth in the sense of an antiquated, exaggerated or obviously unreal representation of things, but in the sense of 'a traditional narrative which serves to explain, justify and celebrate social norms and institutions'. According to Holmes, the lack of a *mesure commune*, a common myth founded on the premises of western culture, is the prime reason for the present crisis in the educational system.
5 As defined here, the *educational* dimension coincides with the *cultural* dimension (Zijderveld 1983) and the *moral* dimension (Etzioni 1987). Politics and the economy are examples of alternative perspectives for viewing societal processes. My position is quite close to Fletcher (1984).
6 The concept 'learning projects' has gained some popularity through the writings of Penland and Tough (see, for example, Penland and Mathai 1978, and Neehal and Tough 1983). But two related terms are increasingly found now: self-directed learning and independent learning. Strictly speaking, the word 'learning project' refers to sustained, planned and voluntarily-chosen major efforts to learn something that is fairly well defined. This meaning has been eroded. The idea that people are the active agents of their own education has led to a plethora of empirical studies. Yet the findings are still very modest. Cross (1986: 199): 'So far, most pioneer researchers on self-directed learning have left what happens during the learning project virtually unexplored territory. Whether one wants to know how to facilitate learning or how to present information to adults, more in-depth study of how learning takes places in everyday settings is a necessity, one that should receive first priority in the 1980s'. Cross has put her finger on the sore spot. But more work has to be done. There is also a pressing need for clarity about the theoretical basis of this line of thought and practice.

7 The unintentional lessons which accompany taking part in training programmes and courses are a special case of spontaneous learning. Asserting
yourself in a group, waiting your turn, getting used to discipline, and experiencing company culture are examples of this phenomenon. The occurrence of
such side-effects, whose importance should not be understimated, is called the
'hidden curriculum'.
8 The importance of general development cannot be sufficiently emphasized.
Nijk (1985: 127): 'Access to tradition, to the many stories, narrative schemes
and narrative genres is and will remain a precondition for the development of
human life and for the ability to act in the fullest sense of the word'. For a fascinating and at the same time controversial attempt to survey what is called
general development, see Hirsch (1988).
9 A theoretical framework that has kinship with De Zeeuw's ideas is Donald
Schön's concept of *knowing-in-action*. Schön (1987) uses this term to refer to
the sorts of know-how skilled practitioners display in their judgements,
decisions and other complex actions, usually without being able to state the
rules or procedures they followed. The knowing is part of the action.
10 There are many other terms in circulation at the moment which denote the
polarization of ways of (thinking about) teaching. To name but a few: pedagogy versus androgogy (Knowles), the dissemination orientation versus the
development orientation (Hodgson c.s.), the didactic model versus the communication model (Laurillard), the behavioural paradigm versus the normative paradigm (Pask).

References

Abram, I. (1984) *Permanent leren in de joodse samenleving* (Lifelong learning in the
Jewish community), in H. Van der Zee (Ed.), *Volwasseneneducatie: dilemma's en
perspectieven (Adult Education: Dilemmas and Perspectives)*, Meppel, Boom.

Boud, D. (Ed.) (1988) *Developing Student Autonomy in Learning*, London, Kogan
Page.

Cross, K. P. (1986) *Adults as Learners: Increasing Participation and Facilitating Learning*. London, Jossey-Bass.

De Zeeuw, G. (1984) *Verborgen vaardigheden* (Hidden skills), in H. Van der Zee
(Ed.) *Volwasseneneducatie: dilemma's en perspectiven (Adult Education: Dilemmas and
Perspectives)*, Meppel, Boom.

De Zeeuw, G. (1985) Problems of increasing competence. *Systems Research*, Vol. 2,
No. 1, pp. 13–19.

Etzioni, A (1988) *The Moral Dimension: Toward a New Economics*, New York, The
Free Press.

Fletcher, R. (1984) *Education in Society: the Promethean Fire*, Harmondsworth,
Penguin Books.

Hirsch, E. D. Jr, (1988) *Cultural Literacy: what Every American Needs to Know*, New
York, Vintage Books.

Holmes, M. (1988) The fortress monastery: the future of the common core, in I.
Westbury and A.C. Purves (Eds), *Cultural Literacy and the Idea of General
Education*, Chicago, University of Chicago Press.

Houle, C. O. (1972) *The Design of Education*, London, Jossey-Bass.

Kidd, J. R. (1983) Learning and libraries: competencies for full participation.
Library trends, Vol. 31, No. 4, pp. 525–542.

Martin, W. J. (1988) The information society: idea or entity? *Aslib Proceedings*, Vol. 40, No. 11/12, pp. 303–309.

McEwan, I. (1984) *Een gesprek met Milan Kundera* (Talking to Milan Kundera). *De revisor*, 6, pp. 26–32.

Neehal, J. and Tough, A. (1983) Fostering intentional changes among adults. *Library trends*, Vol. 31, No. 4., pp. 543–553.

Nietzsche, F. (1872) *Waarheid en cultuur* (Truth and culture) a selection from Nietzsche's early work, issued by the publishing house Boom in 1983.

Nijk, A. J. (1985) *De mythe van de zelfontplooiing* (*The Myth of Self-Development*), Meppel, Boom.

Nisbet, J. and Shucksmith, J. (1986) *Learning Strategies*, London, Routledge & Kegan Paul.

Penland, P. R. and Mathai, A. (1987) *The Library as a Learning Service Center*, New York, Marcel Dekker.

Reid, L. A. (1986) *Ways of Understanding and Education*, London, Heinemann.

Resnick, L. B. (1987) Learning in school and out. *Educational Researcher*, Vol. 16, No. 9, pp. 13–20.

Roszak, T. (1986) *The Cult of Information: the Folklore of Computers and the True Art of Thinking*, New York, Pantheon Books.

Schön, D. A. (1987) *Educating the Reflective Practitioner: Towards a new Design for Teaching and Learning in the Professions*, London, Jossey-Bass.

Schopenhauer, A., (1851) *Parrerga und Paralipomena.* I have used a selection from Schopenhauer's work *De wereld een hel* (*The World is a Hell*), published by Boom in 1981.

Scientific Council for Government Policy (1986) *Basisvorming in het onderwijs* (Basic Forming in Education), The Hague, State Publishing House.

Smith, R. M. (1982) *Learning to Learn: Applied Theory for Adults*, Milton Keynes, The Open University Press.

Zijderveld, A. C. (1983) *De culturele factor; een cultuursociologische wegwijzer* (*The Cultural Factor: a Cultural/sociological Guide*), The Hague, VUGA.

21 Social capital, human capital and the learning society

Tom Schuller[1]
University of Edinburgh

John Field
University of Ulster

Introduction

The idea of a learning society assumes that certain types of social arrangements are more likely to promote lifelong learning than others. Yet
although the idea of a learning society has been widely and enthusiastically embraced by politicians and educationists, there has been little
debate over the precise types of social arrangement which promote communication, reflexivity and mutual learning over time (Ranson 1994,
European Commission 1995). Specific studies of learning within social
institutions such as the family or the workplace have rarely been
accompanied by a wider conceptual framework on societal learning.

This paper considers the potential of one such conceptual framework,
that of social capital. As developed by James Coleman and others, the idea
of social capital has come to play an important role in helping explain
educational attainment (Coleman 1988, 1994). For Coleman, the concept
of social capital complements that of human capital; indeed, it helps
explain variations in the levels of human capital in any given society.
Coleman's conclusion is, briefly, that high levels of human capital tend to
arise when individuals can draw on:

> ...the set of resources that inhere in family relations and in community
> social organisation and that ... can constitute an important advantage
> for children and adolescents in the development of their human capital.
> (Coleman 1994: 300)

This is an appealing conclusion, not least because it directs attention to
such 'soft' variables as social networks and values, rather than focusing primarily upon the 'hard' variables that tend to form the bedrock of human
capital thinking. This paper therefore considers the relationship between
human and social capital, not only in respect of the educational attainment
of school-leavers, but more widely in the context of the learning society.

Human capital: a two-edged instrument?

It was in the 1960s that Theodor Schultz and Gary Becker developed Adam Smith's original notion that investment in education and skill formation was as significant a factor in economic growth as investment in physical plant and equipment, and the phrase human capital was born. It has been immensely influential at all sorts of levels, including that of political imagery.

James Coleman, one of the originators of the term social capital, observes that:

> Probably the most important and most original development in the economics of education in the past 30 years has been the idea that the concept of physical capital as embodied in tools, machines and other productive equipment can be extended to include human capital as well. Just as physical capital is created by changes in materials to form tools that facilitate production, human capital is created by changes in persons that bring about skills and capabilities that make them able to act in new ways.
>
> (Coleman 1988: S100)

Since Becker and Schultz, huge amounts of research and analysis have been built on the notion of human capital (see e.g. Carnoy 1995). In particular, economists have focused on rates of return to different types of investment in human capital, which may be calculated in such a way as to allow aid donors and other investors to make informed decisions about where to focus their efforts. But how appropriate is this approach, particularly when examined in the broad context of the learning society?

Measurement of human capital has always been a problem. Highly sophisticated econometric analyses of the effect of human capital investment are often founded on the assumption that human capital can be measured simply by the number of years' schooling. More plausible is the use of qualifications as a measure but here again there are serious question marks against the intrinsic validity of such measures (e.g. Mulligan and Sala-i-Martin 1995). The assumptions on which towers of statistical analysis about the relationship between education and economic success are built are often heroic to the point of stupidity. Given the power of human capital, in theory and practice, there is a remarkable dearth of serious instruments by which the nature and quality of the investment are measured.

It is important that we do not project onto human capital theory blame for a whole range of unpalatable developments which arise largely from political choices, and not from the nature of the theory. Nevertheless, there are serious objections. One is the intrinsic merit of education as a consumption good, to persist for a moment longer with the economic vocabulary. People do, and should, value learning as something which they enjoy, even if the value is consumed once the act of learning is over. Very obviously, people buy books, CDs, computers and the other accoutrements which designate the professional learner; and, happily for those of us working in continuing education, they still spend money on traditional courses and appear to enjoy them. We are not aware of any attempt to incorporate such educational consumption into the human capital model; rather, these activities are treated by economists primarily as a form of leisure spending with little relevance to productivity and competitiveness. This can be criticized on at least three grounds: first, that it ignores evidence of 'spillover' or transfer between one learning domain and another; second, that it is based on a partial picture of economic activity, excluding such areas as voluntary engagement or domestic labour; and third, that it treats quality of life issues as at best intangible, at worst peripheral.

The second major objection is more of a tactical one, but none the less important for that. The more the language of investment dominates, the more it is accepted not only as rational in its own terms but even as the only language, the more difficult it will be for learning activities which cannot show a visible return, and especially a quick return, to justify themselves. This is a serious problem in an accountancy-driven society. It incidentally adds a question mark against the otherwise very interesting, if somewhat impracticable objective – one of five – of the European Union's Year of Lifelong Learning, to make investment in human resources as regular a feature of company balance sheets as investment in physical assets.

These objections notwithstanding, human capital remains an immensely powerful analytical notion. But it is time to ask whether it may not have achieved, at least implicitly, a dominance which partially undermines its contemporary utility. The narrowness of its measures, of input and output, arguably has a distorting effect on real investment patterns. In particular, it concentrates on individuals, since it is individuals who spend the years in school and to whom qualifications are awarded, and to the extent that it does this it ignores the wider social context within which much learning takes place, and the relationships – personal and institutional – which actually constitute the vehicles or channels through which learning takes place. It is precisely this relational domain that forms the object of social capital analysis.

Social capital: three conceptions

The notion of social capital has already acquired currency in the USA, but is only starting to do so in the UK. Robert Putnam defines social capital as 'the features of social life – networks, norms and trust – that enable participants to act together more effectively to pursue shared objectives'

(Putnam 1996: 66). This is indeed broad, but he proceeds quickly to give this empirical substance, drawing on extensive time-budget surveys of Americans in succeeding decades: 1965, 1975 and 1985. Most forms of collective political participation, both in the direct sense of political such as working for a political party or more broadly such as attending meetings about town or school affairs, have declined by between a quarter and a half. These findings are complemented by opinion surveys which show a decline in the last two decades of social trust. Only nationality groups and hobby clubs are reported to run counter to this trend (for a fuller account, see Putnam 1995).

Putnam examines possible causes for this civic disengagement. He looks for a possible explanation to such items as longer working hours, participation by women in the workforce, or the decline of traditional communities through slum clearances. The main conclusion is that the 'culprit' is television. He contrasts newspaper reading, which is positively associated with participation, and television, where 'each hour spent viewing is associated with less social trust and less group membership'. Television privatizes leisure time, and therefore erodes social capital. He finds, surprisingly, that although participation is usually associated with higher levels of education, and educational levels have increased, the decline in social capital has affected all levels:

> The mysterious disengagement of the last quarter century seems to have afflicted all educational strata in our society, whether they have graduate education or did not finish high school.
>
> (Putnam 1996: 67)

On this he concludes that the rise in education has mitigated what would otherwise have been an even steeper decline, but it has not succeeded in reversing it.

Putnam's approach is overtly normative. His indicators of active engagement are selective (he excludes environmentalist movements, and other types of engagement which European investigators show to appeal to younger adults). But his deployment of empirical data is substantial and compelling as an identification of a significant trend. The failure of rising educational levels to halt the decline in social capital is a powerful indication of a rather different form of instrumentalism than that which is usually pointed to. Moreover, the differentiation, crude as it is, between different types of mass media – some as positively informative, and encouraging participation, others as sapping social energies – opens up important avenues for exploration in relation to the information society.

Although he draws on earlier uses of the term, James Coleman can probably claim to be the real originator of the concept of social capital, so we can turn to him with some expectation of a starting definition. He acknowledges the diversity, if not the diffuseness, of the concept.

Social capital is defined by its function. It is not a single entity but a variety of different entities, with two elements in common: they all consist of some aspect of social structures, and they facilitate certain actions of actors – whether persons or corporate actors – within the structure.

(Coleman 1988: S98)

Coleman goes on to specify three forms of social capital. The first deals with the level of trust which exists in the social environment and the actual extent of obligations held. Social capital is high where people trust each other, and where this trust is exercised by the mutual acceptance of obligations. Coleman gives the example of Egyptian markets where neighbouring traders help each other by bringing commissions or providing finance without entering into legal or financial contracts. The second form concerns information channels; here Coleman cites a university as a place where social capital is maintained by colleagues supplying each other with ideas and information. Third, norms and sanctions constitute social capital where they encourage or constrain people to work for a common good, forgoing immediate self-interest.

Coleman then turns to examining the effect of social capital in creating human capital, in the family and in the community. Family background plays a large part in educational achievement; first through financial capital – the wealth which provides school materials, a place to study at home and so on; and second through human capital, measured approximately by parental levels of education and influencing the child's cognitive environment. To this Coleman adds social capital, defined in terms of the relationship between parents and children. By this he means not so much the emotional relationship as the amount of effort parents put directly into their children's learning. At the community level, social capital involves the extent to which parents reinforce each other's norms, and the closeness of parents' relations with community institutions. Where households move frequently, and little social-interchange occurs between the adult members of the community, social capital is likely to be low. This may occur even where financial and human capital levels are high. Coleman uses this to explain why Catholic and Baptist schools in poor but relatively stable neighbourhoods often outperform many private schools: 'the choice of private school for many of these parents is an individualistic one, and, although they back their children with extensive human capital, they send their children to school denuded of social capital' (Coleman 1988: S114).

Both authors are quite explicit about the normative content of their conceptualizations. The emphases are different, with Putnam seeking to regenerate political health and Coleman to explain the effects of social relationships, but both give primacy to the role of norms. Second, there is a clear commitment to collective values. Coleman, for example, does not pause to consider whether the imposition of norms by the Catholic church, aligning itself with parents to achieve educational success, might through its authoritarianism undermine nonconforming forms of social capital.

Third, and crucially for the purposes of this paper, both call into question the value of human capital when it is divorced from wider social relations. They challenge the individualism and the assumed rationality of orthodox human capital approaches. Coleman draws on economistic notions of utility-maximization as well as on sociological models of socialized behaviour, but he concludes by identifying social capital as a public good, and pointing out that the social structural conditions that overcome the problems of supplying it as a public good – strong families and strong communities – are less in evidence than in the past, and we can therefore expect a decline in human capital as a consequence. Finally, both offer rather different sets of specific measures by which the accumulation or erosion of social capital can be assessed. These certainly have their weaknesses, but they make a striking contrast with the narrowness of the assumptions made in most human capital computations.

Twins, siblings or enemies?

Now for a brief exploration of the relationship(s) between human and social capital. This means pointing to differences; however, the purpose is not to substitute social capital for human capital, as some kind of friendlier, more collective form of investment. To argue along these lines would be to fall into the trap of counterproductive dichotomizing. Nor, incidentally, does the whole argument in favour of bringing social capital into the equation avoid issues about power and conflict; these remain to be worked through.

Here is an initial summary of the differences from the discussion thus far:

- Human capital focuses on the individual agent, social capital on networks and relationships.
- Human capital assumes economic rationality, and transparency of information; social capital assumes that most things are seen through lenses of values and norms which are socially shaped.
- Human capital measures inputs by reference to duration of education or numbers of qualification; social capital by the strength of mutual obligation and civic engagement.
- Human capital measures output in terms of individual income or productivity levels; social capital in terms of quality of life.

The relationship between human and social capital is not necessarily an antagonistic one, conceptually or practically. But in what ways is it conceivable that we might have an expansion of human capital, as conventionally measured, and a decline in social capital? Coleman's example is one of highly educated parents failing to convert their human capital into social capital by not building it into their parental relationships. This is a matter of neglect, rather than active erosion of social capital. Another example, closer to the current theme, might be called the Walkman nightmare version of the learning society (Schuller 1997). This is the dystopia of whole series of individuals permanently plugged into their personal training programmes, but with no sense of the value of learning as something shared with others, including friends, colleagues, families or their wider social milieu. Human capital rises, as they are guided to higher and higher qualifications, but at the expense of the means of personal communication and relationships. To some extent this is satire, but if human capital accumulation does occur independently of such social contexts it will be, at best, of very limited social and economic value, and it may well be actively erosive.

In this case, the relationships are personal ones. But it would be wrong to conceive of social capital as only about maintaining these kind of relationships, crucial though they are to many forms of effective learning. A second type of relationship is the institutional, the way in which different institutions (educational and non-educational) communicate, collaborate or compete with each other (healthy competition being as much of a valid relationship as fruitful collaboration). There is much food for thought here, analytically and politically: how do we construct or maintain institutional relationships which support rather than impede learning? But there is a third form of relationship, which illustrates well the difference and the complementarity of human and social capital.

This in turn brings us to the long-running debate about specialized versus general knowledge. In one form it runs parallel with the history of human capital theory, since one of the early theoretical distinctions was between general and specific skills, and who should be expected to invest in these. But it can have a wider sense. There have been many arguments, notably in relation to English higher education, about undue specialization. The critique is powerful, but has often taken the form of a rather unreflecting condemnation of specialization *per se*, leading to another counterproductive dichotomy. Of course specialized skills and knowledge are needed; the issue is the balance between them and wider forms of knowledge. The point, though, is not just that a balance is needed. It is that the claim of more generalist knowledge must be not just that it covers more areas, for this would leave it open to the jibe that a generalist is someone who knows less and less about more and more. Its essential value depends on the ability it confers to see the relationships between these different areas. Without that relational knowledge, generalism loses its cutting edge.

How does this fit with the point that human capital theory has already made a distinction between general and specific skills? The short answer is that 'general' in this sense is equivalent to transferable; they are the skills which are usable in several contexts, but may still be highly specialized. But social capital cannot be characterized as the meta-knowledge which enables an individual awareness of the relationships between other skills and knowledges to emerge. It refers rather to the ways in which diverse areas of knowledge, or skills, are pieced together by more than one person, not necessarily operating at the same level but complementing each other at least to the extent which makes forms of learning possible which would not otherwise have been so. For this to work, it requires norms to operate, implicitly or explicitly.

An operational typology

We now turn to the specific ways in which social capital may influence life-long learning. Coleman's chief interest has been in the effects of social relationships upon young people's attainment in schools, and as we have seen his argument is essentially that high social capital tends to favour high levels of attainment among the young. Our typology is concerned with aspects of lifelong learning, and not solely with learning among school pupils: this is expressed in the three grids, which try to relate levels of social capital as defined by Coleman to levels of achievement in the schools system: to levels of participation in continuing education (defined as any formal adult education and training programmes); and levels of participation in non-formal education (defined as learning which takes place during social interaction which is primarily undertaken for non-educational purposes).

In the case of schoolchildren, Coleman's findings are that high levels of social capital are normally associated with high levels of educational attainment; conversely, low levels of social capital usually lead to low levels of educational attainment. The virtuous circle in this relationship is therefore found in quadrant B of our grid, while the vicious circle is located in the outer reaches of quadrant C (figure 1). Among the UK regions, Northern Ireland appears to provide a strong empirical demonstration of Coleman's thesis: levels of social capital are high (as indicated by family structures, church and other voluntary society membership, or levels of charitable giving) and so are levels of schools attainment (as expressed in GCSE and GCE results [Field and Schuller 1995]), so that this small and reasonably compact UK region seems to sit in quadrant B.

Things become more complicated when we come to consider lifelong learning as a whole, and not simply the initial school cycle. Coleman's thesis may hold good for school attainment, where family, church and other social networks function to reinforce the message given by teachers to young people. Is it likely that similar processes will operate in the case of continuing education, as measured by levels of participation in adult education and training (figure 2)? Taking Northern Ireland once more as

High social capital

A   B

Low   High
school   school
attainment   achievement

C   D

Low social capital

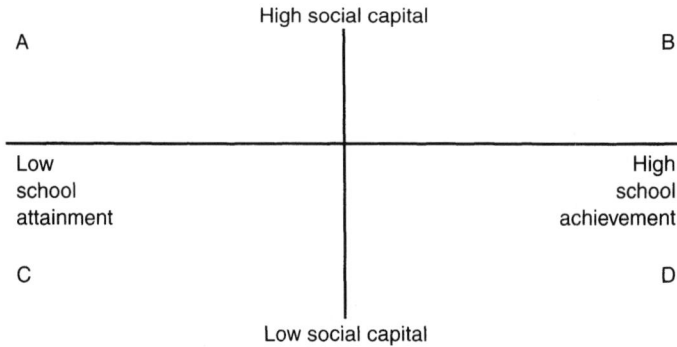

Figure 1 Social capital and human capital – initial education.

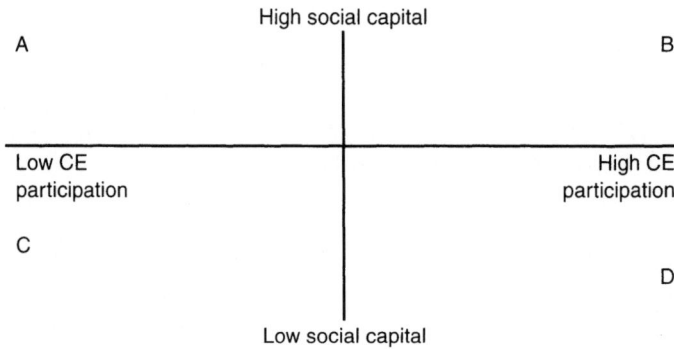

High social capital

A   B

Low CE   High CE
participation   participation

C

                                                     D

Low social capital

Figure 2 Social capital and human capital – continuing education and training.

an illustrative empirical example, we find that a compact UK region with comparatively high levels of social capital is also characterized by very low rates of participation in continuing education (Field and Schuller 1995, Sargant 1997); it therefore falls into quadrant A. What appears to happen in this case is that formal adult education and training – particularly in their certificated forms – are comparatively unimportant to actors who can draw on other resources to gain access to employment or promotion or any other benefits associated with lifelong learning.

If access to social capital appears to discourage adults from participating in formal education and training, its relationship to informal learning is likely to be different again. While membership of close social networks may be expected to produce high volume flows of information, and foster mutual approaches to problem solving, they may also restrict the range of actors (and hence expertise) from whom information is sought. Thus, the owners of family businesses will typically seek advice and final information within personal networks, but may have poor networking with such external and unknown (personally) actors as bank managers. Moreover, close networks can sometimes also lead to the screening and even hoarding of information (and including information about valuable sources of expertise) in an attempt to gain or maintain competitive advantage; as Baldacchino puts it, 'face-to-face relations are complemented by back-to-back relations' (Baldacchino 1995: 271). More recently, in the context of globalizing tendencies, the link between space and social capital is being further uncoupled, so that one may share few relations of reciprocity and trust with neighbours and kin, yet engage in and construct close social networks and institutions which are remote and perhaps even short-lived (Beck 1997). As the example of the Walkman dystopia shows, though, this is by no means a unilinear process. Furthermore, measuring non-formal learning is – by definition – an awkward business. Nevertheless, it seems plausible to suggest that high levels of social capital lead, in general, to higher-than-average levels of informal and non-formal learning (figure 3). Whereas formal learning is associated with the development of routinized systems for transmitting and recognizing knowledge and skills, less formal types of learning are promoted by the pooling of information and sharing of capacities which arise when levels of trust, reciprocity and common norms are high. To pursue the example of Northern Ireland once more, the evidence available to us at present is consistent with this view (see also Moreland 1993); provisionally, we would place this compact UK region somewhere within quadrant B.

This typology remains somewhat hesitant and incomplete, but it does appear to be suggestive. More work certainly needs to be done to identify empirical examples of communities (spatial, occupational or values-oriented) which have comparatively low social capital in relation to life-long learning, quadrants C and D are as yet underexplored. We are as yet unclear about the impact of scale (cf. Baldacchino 1995): while it may be possible to generalize about social capital in Northern Ireland, it is more difficult to extend this approach to larger social systems. We are also aware of the risks of implying a simple dichotomy between low and high levels of social capital: rather than smuggling notions of *Gemeinschaft* and

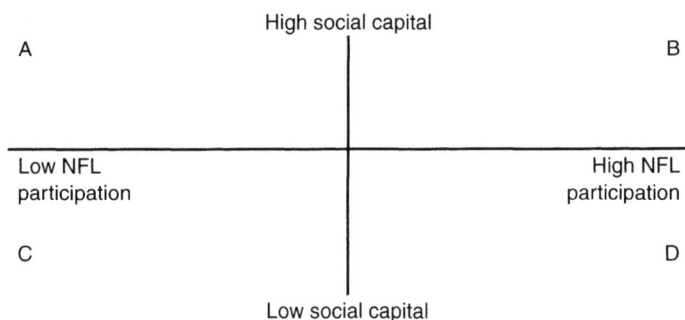

High social capital

A   B

Low NFL   High NFL
participation   participation

C   D

Low social capital

Figure 3 Social capital and human capital – non-formal learning.

Gesellschaft back into sociological respectability, we prefer to see social capital as both internally differentiated and constantly changing. This in turn generates further difficulties of analysis and coherence, which are easily overlooked in creating – largely for heuristic purposes – the provisional typology outlined above.

Conclusion: some further questions

Some of the social capital terminology is distinctly woolly, especially the last two measures listed above: mutual obligation and quality of life. The task is to develop measures – and policies – which will stand up. This is the challenge which the human capital approach has met forcefully and head-on, with its calculations of rates of return to education at all levels and in all countries, best known in the corporate work of the World Bank.

The first set of questions is therefore about measurement. What kind of constructive critique can be mounted of the measures used in respect of human capital? And how do we pursue the development of adequate measures for assessing the accumulation or erosion of social capital? It might be helpful here to think not of alternative and competing sets of measures, but of nested sets, from the narrowest qualification-focused to the broadest set of social indicators, each fulfilling different roles. There may be tradeoffs between specificity and focus on the one hand, and contextualization and scope on the other. Building such a nested structure should help to avoid the quantitative spuriousness of the human capital approach on the one hand, and the overinclusive vagueness of social capital on the other.

The second set of questions concern the nature of the relationships which form the essence of the social capital concept, and have more of a practical or policy-related character. Attention here might concentrate on three areas. The first is the personal: what are the kinds of context and culture which promote communication and mutual learning as part of the fabric of everyday life? This is surely at the heart of a learning society. Second, what kinds of institutional relationship are most supportive of learning? These will definitely be plural; in some instances, collaboration may be the appropriate mode of coexistence, but in others competitive relationships will be the ones which most actively foster learning. The need is to sort out which is which, and what are the most fruitful forms of competition and collaboration. Finally, relationships between different knowledge areas merit further reflection. Rather than accumulating certificates as individual pieces of evidence of human capital, we need to ask what the balance is across the portfolios held by individuals and by groups, so that the awards are related to the social units which are to deploy the knowledge and skills.

Note

1 *John Field* is Professor of Lifelong Learning at the University of Warwick (England) and *Tom Schuller* is Director of Continuing Education and Professor of Continuing Education at the University of Edinburgh (Scotland). They contributed the chapters on Northern Ireland and Scotland to the recent large-scale study of participation in adult education in the UK, published by NIACE as *The Learning Divide* (edited by Naomi Sargant). The present paper arose from a study of relations between initial education and lifelong learning, which the authors are undertaking within the Economic and Social Research Council's Learning Society Programme.

References

Baldacchino, G. (1995) Labour formation in small developing states: a conceptual review. *Compare*, 25(3), 263–278.

Beck, U. (ed.) (1997) *Kinder der Freiheit* (Frankfurt: Suhrkamp Verlag).

Becker, G. (1964) *Human Capital, a Theoretical and Empirical Analysis, with Special Reference to Education* (New York: Columbia University Press).

Carnoy, M. (1995) *Encyclopedia of Economics of Education*, 2nd edn (Oxford: Pergamon Press).

Coleman, J. (1988) Social capital in the creation of human capital. *American Journal of Sociology*, 94 (Suppl.), S95–120.

Coleman, J. (1994) *Foundations of Social Theory* (Cambridge, MA: Belknap).

European Commission (1995) *Teaching and Learning: Towards the Learning Society* (Luxembourg: Office for Official Publications).

Field, J. and Schuller, T. (1995) Is there less adult learning in Scotland and Northern Ireland? A quantitative analysis, *Scottish Journal of Adult and Continuing Education*, 2(2), 71–80.

Moreland, R. (1993) Towards a learning society: a study of formal, non-formal and informal adult learning opportunities. DPhil. thesis, University of Ulster at Jordanstown.

Mulligan, C. and Sala-i-Martin, I. (1995) *Measuring Human Capital*, Centre for Economic Policy Research, Discussion Paper 1149 (London: CEPR).

Putnam, R. (1995) Tuning in, tuning out: the strange disappearance of social capital in America. *PS: Political Science & Politics*, 28(4), 664–683.

Putnam, R. (1996) Who killed civic America, *Prospect*, March, 66–72.

Ranson, S. (1994) *Towards a Learning Society* (London: Cassell).

Sargant, N. (ed.) (1997) *The Learning Divide* (Leicester: National Institute for Adult Continuing Education).

Schuller, T. (1997) Building social capital: steps towards a learning society, *Scottish Affairs*, 18, 77–91.

Schultz, T. (1963) *The Economic Value of Education* (New York: Columbia University Press).

22 Lifelong learning and welfare reform

Colin Griffin[1]
University of Surrey

This is the second of two papers which explore the scope and limitations of lifelong learning as an object of policy. In the first (see Griffin 1999) the evolution of the social democratic perspective was described. According to this perspective, it was suggested, the attempt to render lifelong learning as an object of policy entailed a reductionist concept of learning, so that it stood for little more than the expansion of education and training provision. In the following paper, an alternative perspective on lifelong learning, also emerging from the policy literature, removes it from the possibility of traditional policy analysis, relocating it in culture, civil society and patterns of lifestyle, leisure and consumption. Analytic distinctions between education and learning, function and provision, policy and strategy, and markets and quasi-markets are employed to explore various policy models. It is suggested that this perspective on lifelong learning needs to be understood in relation to policies for welfare reform and the crisis of the welfare state. In effect, it amounts to the integration of education policy into wider policies for welfare reform.

Introduction

It has long been recognized that lifelong education can be thought of as either concept or policy, at least in terms of analytic philosophy (Lawson 1982). Whether or not we accept this kind of either/or logic, there is no doubt that the shifting emphasis away from education to learning in the lifelong context *does* signify some kind of substantive development away from a conceptual to a policy-oriented approach.

Lifelong learning has been incorporated into the policy discourse at the national and international level and the transition from principle to practice, or from policy formulation to policy implementation, is already underway. In his opening address to a recent conference of the European Commission, Allan Larsson summarized the current situation in these terms:

> The fact is that 1999 is a crucial year for life long learning. 1999 is the year when the principle of life long learning will move from being

merely a popular conference theme, a matter of good intentions, to becoming a matter of firm commitments by governments, in all the Member States, across the European Union.

(Larsson 1999)

In fact, the principle of lifelong learning, as far as the European Commission is concerned, is one of employment policies and 'continuous reskilling of the workforce', with associated tax and other incentives, the objective of this being the 'common economic health' of member states. As was the case with the Commission's general approach to lifelong learning and the learning society, the focus is strongly on training, so that it is no longer *education*, but *learning* itself, which is being incorporated into economic and employment policy.

This shift away from education towards learning really must be construed in policy terms and this too is coming to be recognized, albeit rather slowly. Thus, in a recent exploration of the politics of the new learning environment, Geoffrey Elliott begins to unravel the policy significance of the abandonment of education as social *policy* in favour of individual learning as government *strategy*:

> My suspicion is that there is a growing movement in education which purports to privilege empowerment of the individual learner, alongside large-scale policy initiatives on the part of multi-national industries and governments, thereby clouding the real impact of government policies of the Right throughout Europe and else-where which are anti-educational in that they are in effect disempowering learners through resource starvation, market-driven policies and sycophantic campaigns which offer the illusion that action is being taken to promote learning.
>
> (Elliott 1999: 26)

This somewhat convoluted suspicion can readily be translated into terms of policy analysis: what has driven 'education' out and 'learning' in, is not only the forces of technology and globalization, together with the changing role of the state, as identified in the first of these papers. What fuels Elliott's suspicion is that education policy is something that the government is no longer prepared to fund as it used to be under the social democratic conditions of the welfare state. Individual learning, however, whereby the costs are borne largely by learners themselves, is the 'illusion' represented by the retreat from policy to strategy. This was implicit in the first of these papers, but it was also noted that the association of lifelong learning with the reform of the welfare state was sometimes quite explicitly made: 'learning ... will be at the heart of the government's welfare reform programme' (DfEE 1998a: 6).

If it is indeed the case that lifelong learning is part of the government's strategy to reform the welfare state, then it could be argued that learning to do without welfare is what lifelong learning is really about. And in this sense, lifelong learning policies really *are* anti-educational in the sense that they are intended as a kind of smokescreen to disguise the systematic dismantling of the welfare state and the social democratic basis of state education systems.

In the first of these two papers, it was suggested that two approaches to lifelong learning have emerged in the policy literature. Whereas international organizations such as UNESCO (1996), the OECD (1996) and the EC (1996) project what was called a *social democratic* approach to lifelong learning and the learning society, national governments and bodies in Britain at least (NAGCELL 1997, DfEE 1998a) project an idea of lifelong learning which reflects a *neo-liberal welfare reform* policy approach, which can be contexted in the so-called crisis of the welfare state in Britain and other countries.

The distinction lies between an approach to lifelong learning which reflects the continuing and redistributive role of the state, and one which envisages a minimal role for the state and a view of lifelong learning which has more to do with lifestyle, culture, consumption and civil society. In short, the social democratic version continues to project lifelong learning in the form of educational and training provision as a welfare function of the state. On the other hand, the welfare reform version sees lifelong learning as a strategy for replacing a provision model of education by one reflecting the centrality of learning in the lives of individuals and in the culture of society itself. Such a model is therefore consistent with a policy of withdrawing state support from a whole range of social benefits and other social welfare services, which is what Elliott's suspicions amount to.

Why there should be this kind of distinction to make between the policy approaches of international organizations and those of national governments (and there is no reason to suppose that Britain is alone in this respect) is interesting in itself, but will not be pursued in detail here. Suffice it to say that international organizations are not accountable to taxpayers in the way that national governments are in democratic societies. This second paper is concerned with identifying the elements of the second of these approaches and therefore with the proposition that, in policy terms, lifelong learning and the learning society may be construed as strategies for the reform of the welfare state.

Education and learning

It has also been recognized that the distinction between education and learning is crucial to any understanding of lifelong learning as education policy and the failure to make it has brought about the confusion between various perspectives on lifelong learning:

> Let us put aside the familiar confusion and sometimes calculated obfuscation between education, provided by increasingly various

forms of teaching and study support, and the learning that education is intended to foster but which can and often does also occur without deliberate educational intent. We need an operational understanding of 'lifelong learning' in the context of 'the learning society' and reinforced by 'learning organizations' to be able to see how postgraduate and postexperience education relate to lifelong learning. 1996, the European Year of Lifelong Learning, saw something of a climax to the rhetorical debate on these matters. To some extent, the old European debate of the early 1970s on recurrent and permanent education is coming together with and being reinvigorated by new interest in the learning organization and learning society.

(Duke 1997: 83)

The two approaches to lifelong learning being distinguished here do, to some extent, represent alternative 'operational understandings' of the distinction between learning and education: the argument here is that we need to see this in terms of *policy* and *strategy* on the part of governments and international agencies, rather than as simply a 'rhetorical debate'.

Terms such as 'lifelong learning' or the 'learning society' have, in effect, been hijacked by advocates of an education model in order to make the case for particular sectors of provision, such as higher education (Burgess 1997, DfEE 1997, Watson 1998) or community development (Moreland and Lovett 1997). These are representative examples of the social democratic policy of lifelong learning, seeking to achieve redistributive educational provision through increased educational opportunity, be it formal, informal or non-formal. They are recognizable social welfare ideologies of education. Adult education, for example, will be seen as a fundamental strategy for lifelong learning by its practitioners and, for many, there will be little to choose between two names for the same thing. Indeed, the confusion of education and learning has sometimes led to the supposition that *either* could be an object of policy. This is said to have been the case in the USA, for example, during the development of the post-industrial period:

With the changing social conditions of the 1960s, new ways of thinking about adult education began to appear under labels such as lifelong education, lifelong learning, and recurrent education. Each of these in some way reflected an attempt to make adult education an object of public policy.

(Stubblefield and Keane 1990: 35)

It is evident, however, that the *learning* focus of lifelong learning could never have been an object of public policy in the same way that the *provision* one could. It is being argued here, on the contrary, that this way of thinking about lifelong learning should be understood more in terms of the *withdrawal* of the state from public policy-making as part of a strategy to reform the welfare state.

Distinguishing between learning and education is crucial to the analysis of the two approaches to lifelong learning which are being identified here. The social democratic one can always be reduced to the case for securing more educational opportunity by way of structural provision along the lines of traditional *educational* divisions. It is, above everything else, a *provision* approach, lending itself therefore to traditional welfare policy analysis, as described in the first of these papers. However, as has been suggested, there is a sense in which learning, as distinct from education, could not be an object of social policy at all. The conceptual distinction between learning and education must be maintained if we are to make any sense of the issues raised by the learning society and lifelong learning. For one thing, learning is something we *attribute* to people without being able to *mandate* it or secure it in the way that social policy must presume, to some degree at least: learning eludes social policy because it cannot, like educational provision, be directly controlled. At the level of government strategy, people may be variously persuaded, cajoled, bribed, threatened or shamed into becoming active individual learners: their learning cannot be mandated.

Education itself has been represented as an archetypal project of modernity, expressed as a form of social welfare policy. But in conditions of *reflexive* modernity, it has been suggested that:

> ...human learning cannot be objectively 'controlled', as many expert professionals tend to assume. Human learning is a very complex activity which is in the first place 'meaningful' to the actors involved. This implies that learning activities are always affected by the way learners define the situation in which they find themselves. Definitions of the situation are rooted in biographical trajectories which are both unique and common. They are unique because every single individual processes her experiences in a unique way. They are common, because single individuals process their experiences with the help of interpretations provided by others.
>
> (Wildemeersch 1998: 8)

If this reflexive view of learning is taken, it is beyond the reach of policy. It becomes, in a way, de-politicized and re-positioned away from social welfare provision into lifestyle, culture, organizations and civil society itself. According to such a view, the attribution of learning to a learner, traditionally the role of the professional educator, is an act of *interpretation* rather than of measurement (Bauman 1987), and to confuse measurement with interpretation is a form of reductionism. The social democratic approach is reductionist in this sense, in that it reduces learning to what can be measured (because 'controlled') in terms of the outcomes of policy.

This can be illustrated by, for example, the view of CEDEFOP, an education and training body of the EU. In a recent policy statement (Cresson 1996) the traditional ('modernist') view of the connection between education and training on the one hand and social democracy and progress on the other is restated. Anticipating the recommendations of the EC White Paper (EC 1996), the context of policy is seen as one of increasing competitiveness and growth, individualized learning, accessible training, updated knowledge and combating social exclusion. The focus is upon social problems of employment and labour market skills, and upon the European dimension. The recommendations of the White Paper were in terms of the acquisition of knowledge, links between schools and business, the need to combat social exclusion, community languages and tax breaks for training. Lifelong learning itself is approached as a *style* of learning, as well as a 'seamless web' of organization, in which the worlds of education, training and work are more closely linked. Indeed, links and 'bridges' constitute a major element of lifelong learning policy rhetoric.

The *policy objective* of lifelong learning remains, for Europe at least, that of economic growth and increased productivity and competitiveness. However, the need for flexibility in employment, together with the new instability of work, is linked with that for increased training in order to limit social exclusion, and advance social mobility and cohesion. In summary, this is a reductionist model of lifelong learning as a form of progressive and redistributive *education* policy, in global market conditions, and from the perspective of the industrialized countries of the world as they move through the post-industrial era.

Another reductionist model of lifelong learning policy is the one that is often associated with the study of adult participation in learning activities.

The adult participation model

Studies of the degree to which adults participate in learning activities are one of the most characteristic examples of the redistributive social democratic approach to lifelong learning policy, focusing as they do upon *barriers* to participation. Such barriers are usually of a social structural nature, but there is often reference to issues of the unequal distribution of cultural capital too. It is usually taken for granted that the level of adult participation in learning is a measure of the degree to which a 'learning society' is becoming a reality. There has been, in fact, a 'silent explosion' of adult learning, according to a recent six-country comparative study of adult learning (Belanger and Tuijnman 1997: ch. 1). This is brought out in other such participation studies, both comparative (Belanger and Valdivielso 1997) and national (DfEE 1998b). The question remains, however, whether policies for lifelong learning, or the identification of a learning society, could follow from any such survey.

These studies represent a reductionist model in that they deal with measurement rather than interpretation, and although sometimes presented within a multi-disciplinary framework, the key discipline of policy analysis is not adequately represented, if at all, even where policy contexts or implications are suggested. They also represent a particular, if somewhat heterogeneous sector, that of adult education and adult learning. Thus, although they add considerably to our knowledge about adults' participation and non-participation in education, they do little more than make a case for removing barriers to participation and expanding provision. They are also generally lacking in any analytical or critical perspective with regard to policy issues, particularly in the industrialized countries, which are precisely those in which welfare policies have often collapsed:

> Although some progress has been made in the preceding two decades, since the term 'lifelong learning' became popular in the industrialized countries, much remains to be done. A major gap in the provision of lifelong learning concerns the adults. If the lifelong learning target is defined as reaching at least secondary level education for all, some 76 million adults in the OECD countries need to be reached. Adult learning targets are defined more modestly in developing countries, but still represent a huge task. The question is not only one of resources but also concerns appropriate policies and practices.
>
> (Belanger and Tuijnman 1997: 245)

It seems to follow from this that there is no distinction to be made between a 'learning society' and one that is simply better educated and trained.

This kind of conception of lifelong learning and the learning society is very problematic, not only because it is reductionist, but because from a policy analysis perspective, many issues remain unaddressed:

- The nature of the connection between education, training and economic development is by no means straightforward or thoroughly understood.
- The widespread failure of welfare policies and the worldwide crisis of the welfare state have led to a general retreat from policy-making on the part of governments.
- On the other hand, it would be a mistake to suppose that globalization and market economics have resulted in a complete loss of control on the part of the state.

These are the kinds of issue that generations of social welfare policy analysts have posed, and which need to be addressed as a condition of any analysis of lifelong learning *as* policy. What we learn from such analysis is that there is no straightforward connection between, for instance, the identification of need and the formulation of policies to address it: this is precisely the reason why so many welfare policies have been abandoned or have failed.

There is, then, a general problem involved in attempting to derive conclusions about policy from participation studies, or indeed from any basis in the study of post-industrial society, technological determinism, or the global economy. The only conclusions which could be derived from such studies are those concerning the expansion of educational provision along the lines of the kind of social democratic approach identified in the first of these papers.

There also exists a good deal of conceptual confusion over the idea of a learning society, not least in that it is associated with lifelong learning itself. The former, however, is a *collective* concept, whereas lifelong learning is something usually attributed to *individuals*. As a result, it is possible to analyse these ideas from any number of positions, and over the last few years, they have been. The learning society and lifelong learning have been analysed as concept (*Journal of Education Policy* 1997), myth and ideology (Hughes and Tight 1995, Strain and Field 1997), rhetoric (Griffin 1998), economy (Strain 1998), and so on. All of these analyses reflect a social democratic approach to educational provision: as with the adult participation model, the main problem is said to be that the learning society doesn't exist. They all rather beg the question of whether it *could* exist, and if so, what are the political dynamics around its existence: these are critical analyses, but they tend to focus upon 'learning' and 'society' in a reductionist way from the perspective of policy analysis. The challenge is from post-industrial society or even from postmodernism itself (Usher *et al.* 1997), and it is a challenge to educational provision and practice.

In a model of lifelong learning which is not only post-industrial or postmodern but *post-welfare*, we have another kind of account of the new 'grand narrative' of learning which is apparently displacing the modernist project of education. Policy analysis provides another perspective, and a more critical one with respect to globalism, technology and the market, and the other taken-for-granted elements of the social democratic approach. For example, from this perspective, lifelong learning could be conceived as a function of the grand narrative of social welfare reform. Perhaps lifelong learning is little more than a relatively cheaper and more effective means of solving the kinds of social problem which the welfare state was intended to address but has failed to solve, such as poverty, exclusion, disaffection, and their social and economic effects?

In order to explore the neo-liberal welfare reform approach to lifelong learning, however, it is necessary to look again at the distinction between education and learning upon which it rests.

Function and provision

The social democratic approach to lifelong learning was described as reductionist because it reduced statements about learning to statements about education, substituted measurement for meaning, and generally confused the concept of the 'learning society' with that of a better educated and trained one. The welfare reform approach, however, maintains a clear separation between education provision and the function of learning in individual and social life.

This distinction may be used to locate a whole range of models of lifelong learning and the learning society. It has already been suggested that a reflexive concept of learning both distances it from education and puts it beyond the reach of social policy, at least in the sense in which social policy is conventionally understood. Nevertheless, any concept of learning has a social dimension, and the role of learning in the welfare reform approach to lifelong learning can perhaps be best understood by thinking of learning as a *function* of individual and social life. At present, evolutionary theories of learning are much to the fore (they mirror the technological determinism also to be found in the policy literature), seeing learning as a function of survival or growth in both individual and social terms. 'There is no alternative' is the phrase often used in the rhetoric of lifelong learning policy discourse, precisely as it is in the discourse of welfare state reform: globalism, technology and the market having apparently narrowed our scope for individual choice. As will be suggested, however, individual lifestyle choice is fundamental to our life in postmodern times and this is where learning is increasingly coming to be positioned: this is what our models now suggest.

So there are two dimensions to reflect in locating the two broad models of lifelong learning in relation to each other: along one lies education and learning, and along the other social policy and social function.

Figure 1 locates the neo-liberal welfare reform models of lifelong learning in the bottom left-hand corner, signifying that they are concerned with learning rather than education and with learning as a *function* of individual and social life, rather than as an object of public policy. Our other models, which are really education policy models of lifelong learning, appears at the top right-hand corner of the diagram, being concerned with the *provision* of education and training opportunities.

Thus, reference to a 'learning society' or a 'learning culture', or to any of the discourses which emphasise the need for a change in peoples' attitudes, values, beliefs and lifestyles towards the place of learning in their individual and social lives, can be located here. It refers more, therefore, to learning as 'a way of life' rather than to the provision of opportunities for education and training, and it could therefore be identified as a feature of postmodern society. This is not only because it reflects the knowledge base of production and economy, and therefore peoples'

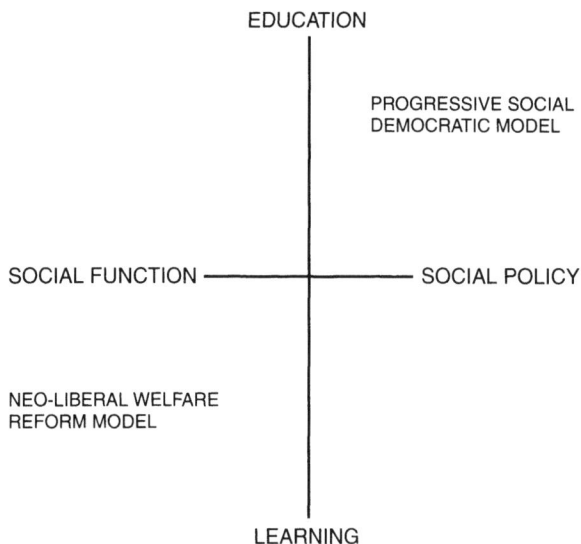

EDUCATION

PROGRESSIVE SOCIAL
DEMOCRATIC MODEL

SOCIAL FUNCTION ——————+—————— SOCIAL POLICY

NEO-LIBERAL WELFARE
REFORM MODEL

LEARNING

Figure 1

working lives, but also because of the significance of learning for new patterns of lifestyle, consumption and culture. As will be seen, theorists have already begun to take account of this in the literature of adult education, if not of lifelong learning itself.

As for the other two sectors of figure 1, the top left-hand one might be occupied by a sociological account of the function of education systems in society. It could therefore be filled by the study of education as socialization, control, selection, or mobility and so on, either from a functionalist or a more phenomenological perspective. In the bottom right hand corner of the figure, lies the issue with which these papers are primarily concerned, that of the sense in which learning *could* be an object of policy, with its objectives as attainable as any other object of policy. If this *is* the case, then lifelong learning is just another name for the provision of education and training opportunity, and the learning society just another name for a better-educated and trained one. If not, then lifelong learning refers to learning as a *function* of individual, social and cultural life, and in this sense it could not be an object of policy as such.

Policy and strategy

Failure to distinguish between policy and strategy is another source of confusion about lifelong learning. But these concepts need to be separated and distinguished in exactly the same way as those of education and learning themselves. For while it is impossible for lifelong learning to be an object of public policy in the conventional sense, it does not follow that governments and other agencies are powerless to promote opportunities for *learning* as a function of individual and social life.

The role of states and governments in the face of globalism, the market and the new technologies has changed. And even though they will no doubt continue to retain national control over significant aspects of policy, nevertheless it has become apparent that their role with regard to many social and economic functions has become much more *strategic* and less oriented towards old-style *policy* making. Embracing the market and the global economy entails that the role of the state is much more one of enabling or making possible certain economic conditions, rather than rigidly controlling and mandating the outcomes of policy. The retreat from command to free-market economies is not only an economic but a social revolution, so that the role of the state with regard to individuals is better described as one of managing autonomy and permitting the widest possible scope for lifestyle choices. At least, this is the typical situation of those states, such as Britain, where reform of the welfare state reflects quite a wide political consensus.

The difference between policy and strategy can be illustrated by the difference between educational policies for schooling and strategies for the learning society. Schooling is an object of national policy because it is subject to compulsion and regulation in every possible way: with regard to participation, curriculum, professional and administrative control of every aspect of the process. School education is a classic instance of policy formulation, and lifelong learning a classic instance of governmental strategy. Since learning *as such* cannot be mandated or controlled, the strategic role of governments can only be one of creating the conditions in which as many people as possible have opportunities to learn. The welfare reform model by no means implies that governments are impotent in respect of learning, or that there is not much that they can do to encourage it.

In fact, since the 1970s and 1980s there has been a tradition of regarding such initiatives as recurrent education, paid educational leave, work-based learning and so on, as *strategies* to achieve the learning society or lifelong learning itself (Houghton and Richardson 1974, Flude and Parrott 1979, Himmelstrup *et al.* 1981, Titmus 1981). Adult education has, in fact, often been thought of in strategic rather than in policy terms, certainly by governments themselves. This has never been true of schooling, which is much less often thought of in relation to lifelong learning, and continues to be neglected in this respect by national policy, at least in Britain. Again, there is somewhat of a contrast here with the work of international agencies such as the UNESCO Institute of Education, which has maintained a tradition of including school education systems in the conceptualization of lifelong *education* at least (Dave 1976, Skager and Dave 1977, Cropley 1977, Ingram 1979). This tradition is, however, as the stress on lifelong education suggests, a social democratic model of education provision. This point might also be suggestive in terms of the alternative approaches to lifelong learning policy which are being explored here: as has been suggested, there is a detectable difference between policies of national states and international organizations with respect to the *scope* of policy in relation to strategy. Such organizations are not, in the way that national governments are, subject to political pressures to reduce the role of the state in respect of welfare provision generally.

Thus, the strategic role of post-welfare states is one of managing markets, choice and autonomy, and they do not formulate *policies* in relation to lifelong learning in the way some of the adult participation models, and many other lifelong learning discourses, seem to suggest. The reason why they do not is not only because of the impossibility of formulating learning as an object of public policy, but because the political choice is *not to do so*. The strategy of governments is to create the conditions in which people, families, communities and organizations are most *likely* to learn for themselves, thus obviating the need for education policy in the traditional sense. This is a characteristic function of governments in post-welfare conditions.

The failure to make conceptual distinctions between learning and education or between policy and strategy has characterized much of the debate about lifelong learning. It is also important not to confuse *theorizing* education policy and *analysing* it from original documentation. For example, Ranson (1995) has argued that policy analysis perspectives need to be supplemented by political theory and sociology, in his overview of the debates between the Marxists and the pluralists in education. He further suggests that 'the idea of policy itself, especially policy-as-public-policy, remains under-conceptualised' (Ranson 1995: 439). In fact, there is a vast conceptual literature on policy as such, to the extent that it constitutes an academic discipline in its own right and historically linked to the fate of social welfare, as was outlined in the first of these papers. Ranson goes on to assert that 'the literature on policy analysis, however, has lost a sense of the "strong values" which provide the meaning and purpose for public policy. These values ... are the need to regenerate a democratic domain for the learning society' (Ranson 1995: 443). This merely reinforces the need to distinguish *normative* theory of education from policy *analysis* of education, which is where the conceptual distinctions between learning and education, and policy and strategy, are made possible. So long as these distinctions are obscured, public policy will remain, as Ranson says, under-conceptualized. However, one of the most important distinction of all is that between normative theory of the kind Ranson himself espouses, and public policy analysis itself: critical policy analysis has always been informed by 'strong values' of a Marxist or social democratic kind. This is not so very far away from Ranson's own vision of the learning society as a learning democracy (Ranson 1998: 23–24). Nevertheless, the visions of normative theory need to be distinguished from the processes of public policy analysis if we are to unravel the political rhetoric of lifelong learning (Griffin 1998).

Another familiar mistake to be found in the literature of lifelong learning policy is the assumption that in such political conditions, there exists a market in education. This is, from a policy analysis perspective, a somewhat superficial assumption, and, from this perspective, it is suggested that the concept of the *quasi-market* is much more productive for analysis and much nearer to the reality of things.

Markets and quasi-markets

One of the most characteristic features of the classical market in goods and services, is the principle of *caveat emptor* ('buyer beware'). This means simply that market choices are assumed to be made on the most rational possible basis, on the fullest possible information. Market rationality entails that mistakes made in market choices cannot be retrieved. In the case of education and welfare services, however, this has rarely been the case: consumer protection, in the form of quality assurance, public standards, transparency, and a host of other publicly-funded mechanisms to curb the free operations of the market, are taken for granted as essential conditions for its role in post-welfare society. Thus in the case of health, housing, pensions, insurance and so on, governments curb markets with consumer protection which is an object of *policy*, that is, it is not on the voluntary basis of consumer protection in the rest of the market for goods and services. The policy literature of lifelong learning in the welfare reform model reflects this *quasi-market*, and not that of an economic market in the *laissez-faire* or classical sense.

The social democratic, or reductionist, approach thus continues to make traditional, but rather simplistic, assumptions about a 'market' in adult education on the basis of post-welfare conditions such as vocationalism, deregulation and competition in industrialized societies: 'The notion of the adult education market ... is central to an understanding of the new policy context of adult education in many industrialized countries' (Tuijnman and van der Kamp 1992: 210). This is a version of the adult participation model of lifelong learning, with policy conclusions derived from assumptions about policy which have long been challenged in the policy discourse itself. In so far as lifelong learning is conceived as a welfare function of society, which it clearly is in these kinds of models, it has proved more appropriate to think in terms of quasi-markets, rather than markets *as such*.

The characteristics of quasi-markets have been described in a classic source as follows:

> They are 'markets' because they replace monopolistic state providers with competitive independent ones. They are 'quasi' because they differ from conventional markets in a number of key ways. The differ-

ences are on both the supply and the demand side. On the supply side, as with conventional markets, there is competition between productive enterprises or service suppliers. Thus ... there are independent institutions (schools, universities, residential homes, housing associations, private landlords) competing for customers. However, in contrast to conventional markets, all these organisations are not necessarily out to maximise their profits; nor are they necessarily privately owned.

(Le Grand and Bartlett 1993: 10)

This is a supply-side analysis of quasi-markets, which undoubtedly better fits the situation of lifelong learning suppliers more accurately than a conventional market analysis. We shall see that the demand-side perspective also offers more to our understanding of lifelong learning as policy later.

The need for an alternative to conventional market analysis in education has also been usefully formulated in terms of an 'administered market', an idea which reflects the point made above about consumer protection and like the 'quasi-market', more accurately expresses the situation in lifelong learning policy than the conventional market idea:

The market is a political creation, designed for political purposes, in this case to redistribute power in order to redirect society away from social democracy and towards a neoliberal order. The market in education is not the classical market of perfect competition but an administered market. Exchange is carefully regulated, with, for example, stringent controls placed upon professional powers to redistribute resources and admissions. The market is thus an institution which is constituted by government and underwritten by legislation to define the relative powers and contractual responsibilities of participants.

(Ranson 1994: 97)

Thus, the concept of the 'administered' market expresses the changing role of the state in a way that the classical model of the market does not: it represents the government's *strategic* role in ensuring the transition from a command to a market economy, and from a welfare state to a neo-liberal order. In so far as lifelong learning strategies are analysed in this way, then lifelong learning itself is implicated in the reform of welfare, and the retreat from policy-making to strategic role can be understood in terms which both reflect the essentially *political* nature of the process, and the *reality* of it. These policy analysis perspectives, derived from welfare and educational policy contexts, are a fundamental element in the various neo-liberal welfare reform models of lifelong learning with which this paper is concerned.

This point may be illustrated by returning to the demand-side perspective of quasi-markets mentioned above, in the form of an important example from the social democratic or reductionist model of lifelong learning policy, that of vouchers and similar consumer-oriented participation schemes:

> On the demand side, consumer purchasing power is not expressed in money terms in a quasi-market. Instead either it takes the form of an earmarked budget or 'voucher' confined to the purchase of a specific service allocated to users, or it is centralised in a single state purchasing agency.
>
> (Le Grand and Bartlett 1993: 10)

Voucher schemes for education and other kinds of welfare provision are highly characteristic of the neo-liberal welfare reform policies of states such as Britain, and have certainly been attempted with varying degrees of success, not least in adult education (Jarvis *et al.* 1998) They are an example of the strategic approach to lifelong learning, which incorporate significant aspects of quasi-market and administered market policy models.

The consumer credit model

A recent study of lifelong learning accounts embodies both the strategic and 'culture change' elements of the neo-liberal welfare reform approach, arguing that a shift towards a new 'mass culture' of learning can be achieved through consumer credit models of participation and provision. The role of Individual Lifelong Learning Accounts [ILLAs] has been described in relation to policies for economic and social welfare policy reform:

> As ILLAs come on stream, there will be major opportunities for using them in tandem with other areas of Government policy: savings policy, regional and national devolution; the whole set of learning policies – those which come under the heading of the University for Industry, those relating to records of achievement, and training time off for 16+ school leavers in employment, to name but a few.
>
> (Smith and Spurling 1997: 78)

There could not be a clearer example of the integration of lifelong learning strategy into neo-liberal welfare reform policy. It is essentially a 'banking' model of education, bringing to full fruition the idea of Freire (1972) in that it does not shift the concept of education away from provision towards the learning function, but suggests at the same time that some kind of 'cultural' shift is necessary. This can be interpreted as the need to shift peoples' dependency upon the welfare state to provide educational and other services, towards a consumer credit system whereby individuals take responsibility for their own lives in every possible context.

The ILLA is 'held by individuals at banks or other financial institutions as a lifelong store of value; is dedicated to the purchase of learning, whether of services or materials; is owned only by individuals. Only they have the say on withdrawals; can be used to buy learning at any stage in a person's life; is separate from any other current or deposit accounts the individual may hold' (op cit: 16). The basic financial functions of ILLAs are saving, borrowing and credit. This clearly reduces learning to a commodity in classical quasi-market conditions. It is therefore a social democratic model in respect of its reductionism. But it also lays stress upon the key elements of the neo-liberal welfare reform approach: culture, lifestyle and consumption.

Policy conclusions are based on the need to move from the current culture of learning (based upon a participation model) towards 'a mass culture for lifelong learning', and it is this element which identifies the consumer credit model with welfare reform policies of the state. However, it remains basically a participation and provision model of learning culture, in which learning itself can be thought of as an object of social and public policy. Not only that, but culture change itself is conceptualized as subject to policy, so that if peoples' attitudes to learning do not spontaneously change, they must be made to, for reasons that are by now familiar in the analysis of the neo-liberal model: competition, globalization, technology and the social threats these bring with them:

> The task of changing to a mass culture of lifelong learning is a huge challenge. It is tempting to hope that it could happen naturally, but we believe it will not – certainly not on any acceptable time scale. So the change has to be *made,* and the reasons for it are compelling ... Two factors come together to make the case for change: the threat to the UK economy from globalisation; and the ever-growing threat of social exclusion for a large minority of UK citizens.
>
> (Smith and Spurling 1997: 7)

Thus, the consumer credit model of lifelong learning policy reflects the reductionism and provision-based social democratic model, on a typically nationalistic basis. But its political rhetoric is that of neo-liberalism, in so far that it invokes elements of culture, lifestyle and consumerism in its analysis of the need for culture change, attempting to reconcile the extreme individualism of learning accounts with a concept of mass culture, by way of quasi-market strategies urged upon the government. It is this kind of position that might be located in the bottom right-hand corner of figure 1. On the one hand, it sees a major role for social policy in changing attitudes and values, and on the other it sees learning in highly individualistic terms and in terms of peoples' attitudes towards it. In other words, in terms of the figure, it is a hybrid, and represents above all the view that learning can (and must be 'made') an object of public policy. But this is the sector of the diagram which is where, above all, the hypothesis of lifelong learning as policy is tested, both for rhetoric and substance.

The neo-liberal welfare reform approach, as has been seen, lays stress upon aspects of culture, lifestyle and consumption, and the need for changing these, in the way that social democratic or wholly reductionist models tend not to. This is the case even though the same policy/strategy objectives may be envisaged: globalization, markets, risk, social disorder, competition, technology. These can be summarized as the ills and consequences of post-industrialism. But if we assume, on the contrary, that learning cannot be an object of policy in the same way that educational provision can, and if we assume that *political* changes are also underway, then a model of policy to reflect these elements can be identified. The fact is, that much of the policy discourse of lifelong learning is both apolitical and deterministic at the same time: it is the language of inevitability in the face of technological and global change. Paradoxically, at the same time, the discourse is one of individual choice, lifestyle and consumption, and these elements of the neo-liberal model will now be examined.

The cultural/lifestyle model

If learning is a complex activity, associated with meaning and interpretation, then it is difficult to conceive it in policy terms. If it is a matter of attribution, and if it is a function of human life and social existence then it must be a central attribute of culture and lifestyle. Social democratic approaches to lifelong learning policy reduce learning to education and make learning a commodity, to be secured in market or quasi-market conditions. But, as has been seen in the consumer credit model described above, such an approach is constantly infiltrated by cultural elements in the course of the rhetoric around it, so that changing culture itself becomes an object of public policy. The 'life events' and 'barriers' of participation studies (DfEE 1998b) become transformed into lifestyle and consumption patterns for a quite different approach to lifelong learning.

In postmodern analysis, the significance of lifestyle for adult education has been recognized, and the relation between learning and consumption begun to be conceptualized. Culture as the practice of learning may be contrasted with culture as an object of policy, and this is an important element in any neo-liberal welfare reform model:

> In the postmodern, the educational is recast as the cultivation of desire through experience, both conditional upon and responsive to contemporary socio-economic and cultural fragmentation. Learning does not simplistically derive from experience, rather, experience and learning are mutually positioned in an interactive dynamic. Learning becomes the experience gained through consumption and novelty,

which then produces new experience. Consequently, the boundaries defining 'acceptable' learning break down – in lifestyle practices learning can be found anywhere in a multiplicity of sites of learning.

(Usher *et al.* 1997: 107)

This kind of non-reductionist model of lifelong learning clearly removes it from the realms of social policy and into the world of strategy, markets and individual lifestyle practices. This has implications for the role of the reflective educational practitioner, as Wildemeersch (1998) has observed, and for the social status of authority figures such as educationists themselves, as Bauman (1987) suggests. This is a significant development of postmodern society:

> Educational practitioners rather than being the source/producers of knowledge/taste become facilitators helping to interpret everybody's knowledge and helping to open up possibilities for further experience. They become part of the 'culture' industry, vendors in the educational hypermarket. In a reversal of modernist education, the consumer (the learner) rather than the producer (educator) is articulated as having greater significance and power.
>
> (Usher *et al.* 1997: 107–108)

Although we need to bear in mind the differences between markets, quasi-markets and hypermarkets amidst all these analogies, it is apparent that this is a model of learning far removed from the social democratic approach, and as much in tune with the consequences of postwelfarism as postmodernism. It is a culture and lifestyle practice made possible by the socio-economic and technological conditions of society and *not* one that could be produced by social policy.

However, as soon as we begin to think of lifestyle we begin to think of class, which remains a completely unexamined idea on the part of advocates of a 'mass' learning culture 'for all'. There are major divisions in any way that 'culture' could be conceived and they need to be taken into account in an analysis of lifelong learning policy. The 'culture industry' is a targeted rather than an undifferentiated field, and lifestyle practices reflect the divisions of class and culture:

> ...knowledge becomes important: knowledge of new goods, their social and cultural value, and how to use them appropriately. This is particularly the case with aspiring groups who adopt a learning mode towards consumption and the cultivation of a lifestyle. It is for groups such as the new middle class, the new working class and the new rich or upper class, that the consumer-culture magazines, newspapers, books, television and radio programmes which stress self-improvement, self-development, personal transformation, how to manage property,

relationships and ambitions, how to construct a fulfilling lifestyle, are most relevant.

(Featherstone 1991: 19)

So there are links between learning, culture and class which are central to our understanding of learning in this kind of analysis. As Featherstone goes on to put it: 'The new petit bourgeois therefore adopts a learning mode to life: he is constantly educating himself in the field of taste, style, lifestyle' (op. cit: 91).

The idea of the 'learning mode', associated with culture, class and lifestyle, is another major element in the neo-liberal welfare reform approach to lifelong learning policy. It removes the idea of the 'learning society' a long way from that of the better educated and trained society which is characteristic of the social democratic approach to lifelong learning. Such analyses of consumer culture and postmodernism therefore lay great stress upon patterns of consumption and leisure, and it is not difficult to reconceptualize the strategic role of the state in relation to such social and economic changes as these. They owe much to the reconceptualization of commodities and consumption away from the economic to the social and symbolic level of analysis associated, for example, with Baudrillard (1998). Patterns of leisure (play stations as much as work stations) are amongst the most important of cultural significations, and no attempt to change the culture of learning is likely to succeed without a much deeper analysis of the meaning of leisure than could usually be derived from the policy literature. In particular, it is necessary to context learning in what Baudrillard called 'The Drama of Leisure or the Impossibility of Wasting One's Time' (Baudrillard 1998: ch. 9).

The leisure/consumption model

Field (1996) has argued that adult education and training can be regarded as a form of consumption in four respects: affluence and increasing exercise of choice on the part of most adults; a more consumer-oriented public policy; the market nature of adult education provision; the dominance of human capital theory in educational thinking (Field 1996: 137–138). Field is critical of the approach taken by writers such as Featherstone, at least as far as adult education is concerned, arguing that it neglects the degree to which patterns of consumption indicate *individual* practices of individuation and differentiation, in favour of an analysis based upon the identities of groups. Writing from within a provision and participation perspective, Field provides a critique of the neo-liberal perspective, reflecting therefore much more of a social democratic viewpoint:

Consumption is, I believe, to some extent a useful perspective from which we can examine aspects of the education of adults. It is only one among a number of perspectives, and its value is bound to vary between different sectors, levels and styles of provision. Yet compared with production, reproduction and citizenship, consumption's place in the study of adult education is consistently downplayed by both scholars and practitioners.

(Field 1996: 146)

Field is here primarily concerned with open learning in adult education, rather than with lifelong learning policy analysis, but he argues that adult education and training provide a 'test case' for the consumer culture hypothesis, and that there may be a 'loose fit' between consumer culture theory and adult learning.

Clearly, what would be needed in order to take such a hypothesis further would be to broaden out the scope of the analysis from adult education provision, together with its own economy and problematic orientation to the market. This is what is at least implied in the policy discourse of lifelong learning at many points: the consumer credit model, for example, itself problematizes culture, economy and the market and is suggestive, it has been argued, of alternative policy models. The problem with the traditional analysis, from educational sectors such as adult education or elsewhere, is that they focus narrowly upon post-industrial, post-Fordist, or post-modern effects. There is rarely sufficient reference to the ways in which *learning*, as distinguished from education and training, is implicated in the crisis of the welfare state, or with the attempt to analyse the changing role of the state in favour of *strategic* orientations to, for example, human capital development. The presentation of learning as a kind of 'lifestyle drug', as a way of *integrating* the whole range of government policies which constitute welfare state reform, perhaps offers better scope to test hypotheses based on culture, lifestyle, leisure and consumption. It also raises the question whether learning, or any other 'lifestyle drug', should be paid for out of taxation?

Patterns of leisure, as well as of working life, have changed, as has what *counts*, not only as leisure but work and learning itself. This needs to be reflected in the analysis. The crisis of the welfare state not only affects the economy of adult education and training, as Field says, but it goes much deeper. This paper will therefore conclude with a brief review of responses to the crisis of welfare in so far as these might have a bearing upon policy models of lifelong learning.

The crisis of welfare

It has been observed that even in those cases where a 'postmodern' awareness of issues for lifelong learning are concerned, these are rarely contexted in the general crisis of the welfare state. And yet, of all the projects of modernity, it is the welfare state that is the most identifying and characteristic.

So, how is what has been called a neo-liberal welfare reform approach to lifelong learning policy related to the kinds of developments which are usually taken to constitute the postmodern condition? We are now in a position to identify and distinguish the elements of the approach as follows:

- A stress upon *learning* as distinct from and not reducible to *educational provision*.
- A stress upon learning as an attribute or function of peoples' *lifestyles* rather than as a function of *educational provision*.
- A stress upon learning as an aspect of *culture*, rather than upon education as a function of the social *structure*.
- A stress upon learning in the *lifeworld* of meaning and action, rather than upon learning in the education *system*.
- A stress upon the *strategic* role of the *state*, rather than upon the role of the state in educational *policy-making*.
- A stress upon learning as a form of *consumption* on the part of individuals, rather than upon the *institutional* framework of educational provision.
- A stress upon the policy-derived formulation of *quasi-markets* in which learning is contexted, rather than in the *market* of classical economics.
- A stress upon the *management* of learning-related activities, rather than upon the *direction* and *control* of such activities, such as continues to be the case with the state in relation to schooling.
- A stress upon the *integration* of individuals' lives, in terms of their social, economic and recreative and *leisure* activities, rather than upon the *division* of lives into *private* and *public roles*.

These then, are the elements of the neo-liberal approach to lifelong learning policy, in contrast with those of the social democratic approach usually associated with the international agencies, which promote such policy. Ideas such as the 'learning society', the 'learning culture', the 'learning revolution' or whatever, could only be operationalized in these terms. Whether such cultures, or such societies could be 'made' to exist is problematic, since so many of the elements of the model refer to what are essentially *spontaneous* aspects of life and learning. To construct them as objects of public policy in any meaningful sense would be contradictory and self-defeating. This is why, from a cultural perspective on learning, the social democratic approach is reductionist: because it reduces the individual and social *function* of learning to the measurable outcomes of educational *provision*.

The policy literature of lifelong learning contains elements of both approaches, in greater or lesser proportions. But what identifies the neo-liberal welfare reform approach most clearly is the integration and implication of lifelong learning into the welfare reform policies of the state.

Those nation states which, under the pressure of globalization, markets, technology and the pervading ideology of neo-liberalism, move away from policy interventions to strategic roles in relation to lifelong learning (if not in relation to schooling, education and training) are projecting it as the only alternative to a social welfare provision which can no longer be afforded and which, in any case, many believed to have failed. However, lifelong learning continues to be strategically positioned in relation to traditional welfare state concerns: the development of human capital, the need for social inclusion and common cultures or social consensus.

From a critical point of view, the near monopoly of social welfare functions on the part of the state is a relatively recent development in history (Barry 1990). But it is the alleged failure of the welfare state, and of traditional education systems, to achieve the purposes for which they existed, that has often been an identifying characteristic of the 'post-modern'. The 'crisis of welfare', in which some models of lifelong learning policy have been contexted, has attracted some attention from policy analysis, so this paper concludes with a brief account of one or two positions on the welfare state. These pose the question whether or not traditional forms of policy analysis are any longer relevant to our understanding of this particular project of modernity, or whether new analytic concepts are needed for this purpose. In a recent book, for example, O'Brien and Penna (1998) have suggested that:

> Recent interest in questions of modernity and postmodernity designates a series of intellectual disputes about the adequacy and legitimacy of theoretical and analytic traditions in the social sciences.
>
> (p. 206)

They have argued that the contribution of postmodernism to welfare state analysis has, in fact, been to expose it as a failed project, and that such states (and the social democratic politics that brought them into existence) have 'exclusions, discriminations and iniquities' in their foundations:

> ...postmodernism has questioned critically the integrative ideology of social policy, indicating that the problem of social and political inclusion is not equivalent to the extent to which a public sphere bestows rights or entitlements on citizens as a means of mitigating their socioeconomic disadvantage.
>
> (O'Brien and Penna 1998: 207)

If this view of the impact of postmodern analysis upon social welfare policy is taken, then it follows that there is little possibility that a social democratic or education provision model of lifelong learning would achieve any more in combating social exclusion than did the welfare state itself. In other words, the expansion of educational provision and opportunity will be just as likely to promote social *exclusion* as was to be found under any welfare system. In traditional policy analysis terms, social exclusion might be an *unintended consequence* of the implementation of a social democratic policy of lifelong learning, of the kind described in the first of these papers.

On the other hand, we can, from a postmodernist perspective, begin to think of the 'learning society' or the 'learning culture' as themselves 'integrative ideologies' of social policy. Following his theme of the permanent need people have to reconstruct community life on whatever basis, Bauman has said that:

> Postmodernity does not necessarily mean the end, the discreditation or the rejection of modernity. Postmodernity is no more (but no less either) than the modern mind taking a long, attentive and sober look at itself, at its condition and its past works, not fully liking what it sees and sensing the urge to change.
>
> (Bauman 1991: 272)

According to Bauman, the 'postmodern political agenda' can be thought of in terms of the need to form social solidarities along new lines, after the collapse of the promise of social democracy, whether these are described as forms of 'neo-tribalism' or 'aesthetic communities', in the face of the fragmentation and social indifference of the market. The 'learning society' and the 'learning culture' are often represented, in the policy literature, as integrative strategies against social exclusion, and the consequences of the failure of social democratic policies to achieve their communal purposes. However, social democratic policy models, as we have seen, continue to reflect faith in redistributive institutional provision, despite the failures of welfare. In Bauman's words: 'Modernity is still with us. It lives as the pressure of unfulfilled hopes and interests ossified in self-reproducing institutions' (Bauman 1991: 270–271). It is in this spirit that so many post-compulsory education sector institutions have hijacked lifelong learning, namely, to better secure their own self-reproductive functions in a changing world.

It is possible to express the direction of policy models from education to learning and from provision to culture, in relation to the theorization of postmodern society.

The progression from left to right in figure 2 represents the movement from faith in the social welfare project through criticism of its effectiveness to its final 'crisis'. The critical social policy perspective has always, as O'Brien and Penna imply, reflected a view of the welfare state as being founded in social inequality. In educational terms, this has generally meant seeing education as social control. Obviously, lifelong learning lends itself to this analysis in its social democratic construction as the expansion of education and training systems: there is no more effective

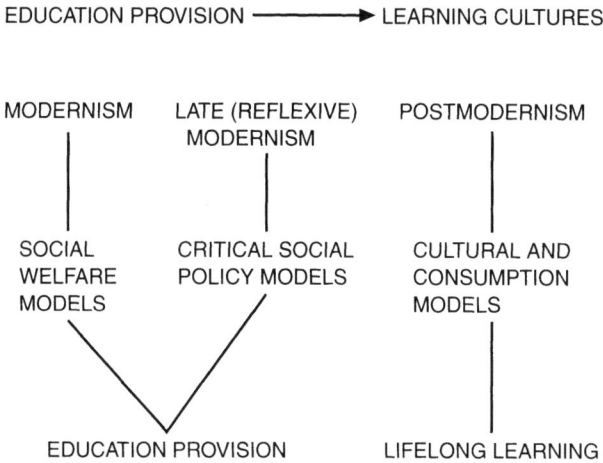

EDUCATION PROVISION ──────▶ LEARNING CULTURES

MODERNISM   LATE (REFLEXIVE)   POSTMODERNISM
                       MODERNISM

SOCIAL   CRITICAL SOCIAL   CULTURAL AND
WELFARE   POLICY MODELS   CONSUMPTION
MODELS   MODELS

EDUCATION PROVISION   LIFELONG LEARNING

Figure 2

form of hegemonic social control than that achieved by way of learning that is self-motivated, self-regulated and self-policed.

Peters and Marshall (1996) have attempted to outline the possibility of 'critical social policy in the postmodern condition'. They base this upon a range of theoretical considerations, such as the cultural studies perspective, Foucault's discourse analysis, reflexivity, modes of signification, new social movement analysis, modes of production and information, new forms of state surveillance, and so on (Peters and Marshall 1996: 208–209). Nevertheless, the possibilities of framing critical policy analysis in postmodern conditions remains problematic, especially if 'totalizing perspectives' are ruled out in such conditions:

> If critical social policy is not to remain mired in critique it must develop an offensive potential which means it must be able to go beyond the task of contesting meanings to provide alternative comprehensive policy frameworks. How it can perform this necessary service without invoking the dangers and risks of a totalizing perspective is still a critical question.
>
> (Peters and Marshall 1996: 214)

What all this illustrates as far as policy models of lifelong learning are concerned, is that those who would criticize the social democratic approach, of the kind described in the first of these papers, must themselves have some kind of alternative to put forward which does not fall into the same traps. For example, if the social democratic model is reductionist, as far as learning is concerned, then what *is* a 'learning culture', and how would we recognise it if it existed? Answers to this question, except those that prove

in the end to be themselves more or less reductionist, are far to seek in
the policy literature of lifelong learning.

Whatever the consequences of the attempt at postmodern critical
policy analysis, it seems clear that the role of the state in respect of education continues to be a central issue. Until this changes virtually beyond
recognition, then postmodern perspectives can only have a rather limited
purchase. So far, there is little evidence that the control and surveillance
functions of the state are diminishing, and probably for this reason the
relevance of such perspectives remains small:

> There is clearly no such thing yet as a postmodern theory of educa-
> tion. However, there has been an increasing tendency for writers on
> education, both from the Left and the Right, to question many of
> those core values and organizing concepts which have underpinned
> social democratic systems of state education in the postwar era and
> which postmodernists have identified as typical products of moder-
> nity.
>
> (Green 1997: 8)

This can clearly be related to the kind of analysis of policy models of lifelong learning which have been identified here, in which the *possibilities* for
analysis are determined by such factors as the policy role of the state in
particular, stressed by the social democrats, but largely ignored (or relegated to strategy) by the alternative, cultural model. This may be represented in terms of figure 3, in which the centrality of the role of the state can
only be expressed in *educational* rather than *learning* terms.

The role of the state, which is crucial in identifying possibilities for
policy analysis, is changing, and this does suggest that new analytic frameworks are appropriate in understanding it. The shift away from old-style
policy-making towards strategy-formation has been identified as one key to
understanding lifelong learning in policy terms. This, in turn, creates the
tension between the two policy approaches identified in this paper. On
the one hand, the social democratic approach associated with international agencies continues to project a redistributive welfare policy role
for the state. On the other, in the case of a national government such as
that of Britain, where the reform of the welfare state is a primary political
objective, lifelong learning, and other ways of achieving a 'learning
society' or a 'learning culture', are to be discovered in the policy literature. These, in turn, project lifelong learning as a strategy of welfare
reform, implicating it in the process and integrating it with other reform
strategies which have the effect of making individuals less dependent
upon the state. It follows that the stress moves away from unaffordable
institutional provision, and towards a concept of learning more embedded
in culture, lifestyle and consumption.

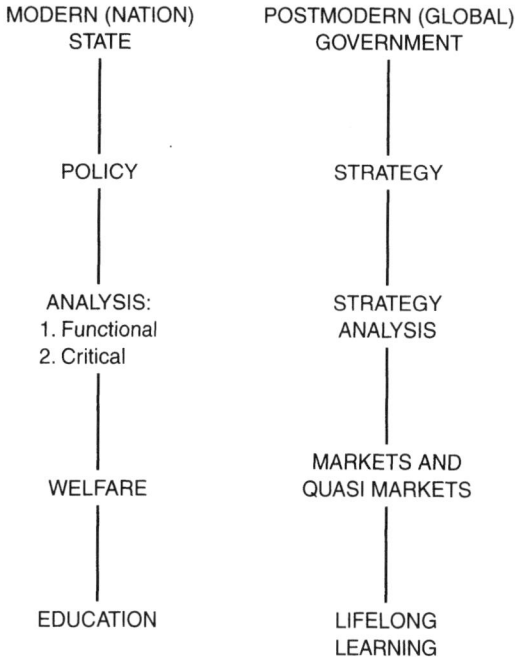

```
    MODERN (NATION)              POSTMODERN (GLOBAL)
         STATE                        GOVERNMENT

           |                              |
           |                              |
           |                              |

         POLICY                        STRATEGY

           |                              |
           |                              |
           |                              |

       ANALYSIS:                       STRATEGY
      1. Functional                    ANALYSIS
      2. Critical
                                          |
           |                              |
           |                              |
           |                           MARKETS AND
        WELFARE                       QUASI MARKETS

           |                              |
           |                              |
           |                              |

       EDUCATION                       LIFELONG
                                        LEARNING
```

Figure 3

Conclusion

What these alternative approaches do, therefore, is to bring out the fundamentally different assumptions it is possible to make about learning and education when the policy literature is analysed. Lifelong learning and the learning society are often simply ways of integrating education policy into wider policies for the reform of the welfare state. As has often been observed, it is possible to position lifelong learning at several points along a continuum running between utopian rhetoric to some fairly traditional arguments for the expansion of education and training provision. Policy analysis of lifelong learning and the learning society needs to be based upon clear distinctions between learning and education and between policy and strategy on the part of the state. Above all, analysis is needed in terms of post-welfare, as well as post-industrial or post-modern society.

Note

1 *Colin Griffin* is an Associate Lecturer in the School of Education Studies at the University of Surrey, where he works in the Centre for Research in Lifelong Learning.

References

Barry, N. P. (1990) *Welfare* (Milton Keynes: Open University Press).

Baudrillard, J. (1998) *The Consumer Society: myths and structures* (London: Sage Publications).

Bauman Z. (1987) *Legislators and Interpreters: on modernity and intellectuals* (Cambridge: Polity Press).

Bauman, Z. (1991) *Modernity and Ambivalence* (Cambridge: Polity Press).

Belanger, P. and Tuijnman A. (eds) (1997) *New Patterns of Adult Learning: a six-country comparative study* (Oxford: Pergamon Press and UNESCO Institute for Education).

Belanger, P. and Valdivielso, S. (eds) (1997) *The Emergence of Learning Societies: who participates in adult learning?* (Oxford: Pergamon Press and UNESCO Institute for Education).

Burgess, R. G. (ed.), (1997) *Beyond the First Degree: graduate education, lifelong learning and careers.* (Buckingham: SRHE and Open University Press).

Cresson, E. (1996) Towards a policy of lifelong learning. *Vocational Training 8/9 European Journal*, Dec. 1996 II/III CEDEFOP: 9–12.

Cropley, A. J. (1977) *Lifelong Education: a psychological analysis* (Oxford: Pergamon Press for UNESCO Institute for Education).

Dave, R. H. (ed.), (1976) *Foundations of Lifelong Education* (Oxford: Pergamon Press for UNESCO Institute for Education).

Department for Education and Employment (DfEE) (1997) *Higher Education in the Learning Society* (The Dearing Report) (London: The Stationery Office).

Department for Educationand Employment (DfEE) (1998a) *The Learning Age: a renaissance for a new Britain* (Green Paper CM 3790) (London: The Stationery Office).

Department for Educationand Employment (DfEE) (1998b) *National Adult Learning Survey 1997* (London: The Stationery Office).

Duke, C. (1997) Lifelong, postexperience, postgraduate – symphony or dichotomy? In R. G. Burgess (ed.), (1997) *Beyond the First Degree; graduate education, lifelong learning and careers* (Buckingham: SRHE and Open University Press).

Elliott, G. (1999) *Lifelong Learning: the politics of the new learning environment* (London: Jessica Kingsley).

European Commission (EC) (1996) *Teaching and Learning: towards the learning society* (White Paper on Education and Training) (Brussels: EC).

Featherstone, M. (1991) *Consumer Culture and Postmodernism* (London: Sage Publications).

Field, J. (1996) Open learning and consumer culture. In P. Raggatt, R. Edwards and N. Small (eds), (1996) *The Learning Society: challenges and trends* (London: Routledge in association with The Open University).

Flude, R. and Parrott, A. (1979) *Education and the Challenge of Change: a recurrent education strategy for Britain* (Milton Keynes: Open University Press).

Freire, P. (1972) *Pedagogy of the Oppressed* (Harmondsworth: Penguin Books).

Green, A. (1997) *Education, Globalisation and the Nation State* (London: Macmillan).

Griffin, C. (1998) Public rhetoric and public policy: analysing the difference for lifelong learning. In J. Holford, P. Jarvis and C. Griffin (eds), (1998) *International Perspectives on Lifelong Learning* (London: Kogan Page).

Griffin, C. (1999) Lifelong learning and social democracy. *International Journal of Lifelong Education*, 18, 329–342.

Himmelstrup, P. *et al.* (eds), (1981) *Strategies for Lifelong Learning 1: a symposium of views from Europe and the USA* (Esbjerg: University Centre of South Jutland with Association for Recurrent Education).

Houghton V. and Richardson, K. (eds), (1974) *Recurrent Education: a plea for lifelong learning* (London: Ward Lock Educational).

Hughes, C. and Tight, M. (1995) The myth of the learning society. *British Journal of Educational Studies*, 43 (3), 290–304.

Ingram, J. B. (1979) *Curriculum Integration and Lifelong Education* (Oxford: Pergamon Press for UNESCO Institute for Education).

Jarvis, P., Holford, J. and Griffin, C. (1998) A market for lifelong learning?: the voucher experience in the City of London. In J. Holford, P. Jarvis and C. Griffin (eds), *International Perspectives on Lifelong Learning* (London: Kogan Page).

Journal of Education Policy (1997) The Concept of the Learning Society Explored, 12 (6).

Larsson, A. (1999) Continuous learning for continuous change. Opening Address of the Competence for Europe Conference. Federal Ministries for Labour and Social Affairs, and for Education and Research, and the European Commission. 21 April 1999. (Berlin: European Commission).

Lawson, K. (1982) Lifelong education: concept or policy? *International Journal of Lifelong Education*, 1 (2), 97–108.

Le Grand, J. and Bartlett, W. (eds), (1993) *Quasi-Markets and Social Policy* (London: Macmillan).

Moreland, R. and Lovett, T. (1997) Lifelong learning and community development. *International Journal of Lifelong Education*, 16 (3), 201–216.

National Advisory Group For Continuing Education And Lifelong Learning (NAGCELL) (1997) *Learning for the Twenty-First Century* (The Fryer Report) (London: NAGCELL).

O'Brien, M. and Penna, S. (1998) *Theorising Welfare: enlightenment and modern society* (London: Sage Publications).

Organisation For Economic Co-Operation And Development (OECD) (1996) *Lifelong Learning for All* (Paris: OECD).

Peters, M. and Marshall, J. (1996) *Individualism and Community: education and social policy in the postmodern condition* (London: Falmer Press).

Ranson S. (1994) *Towards the Learning Society* (London: Cassell).

Ranson S. (1995) Theorising education policy. *Journal of Education Policy*, 10 (4), 427–448.

Ranson S. (ed.), (1998) *Inside the Learning Society* (London: Cassell).

Skager, R. and Dave, R. H. (eds), (1977) *Curriculum Evaluation for Lifelong Education* (Oxford: Pergamon Press for UNESCO Institute for Education).

Smith, J. and Spurling, A. (1997) *Individual Lifelong Learning Accounts: towards a learning revolution* (Leicester: National Institute of Adult Continuing Education) (NIACE).

Strain, M. (1998) Towards an economy of lifelong learning: reconceptualising relations between learning and life. *British Journal of Educational Studies*, 40 (3), 264–277.

Strain, M. and Field, J. (1997) On the myth of the learning society. *British Journal of Educational Studies*, 45 (2), 141–155.

Stubblefield, H. W. and Keane, P. (1990) The history of adult and continuing education, in S. B. Merriam and P. Cunningham (eds), (1990) *Handbook of Adult and Continuing Education* (San Francisco: Jossey-Bass).

Titmus C. (1981) *Strategies for Adult Education: practices in Western Europe* (Milton Keynes: Open University Press).

Tuijnman A. and vander Kamp, M. (eds), (1992) *Learning Across the Lifespan: theories, research, policies* (Oxford : Pergamon Press).

United Nations Educational, Scientific and Cultural Organisation (UNESCO) (1996) *Learning: the treasure within* (The Delors Report) (Paris: UNESCO).

Usher, R., Bryant, I and Johnston R. (1997) *Adult Education and the Postmodern Challenge: learning beyond the limits* (London: Routledge).

Watson, D. (1998) *Lifelong Learning and the University: a past-Dearing agenda* (London: Falmer Press).

Wildemeersch, D. (1998) Lifelong learning and the significance of the interpretive professional [unpublished].

23 The concept and problem of public enlightenment

Bo Jacobsen

Outline of the problem

A new problem seems to be emerging in the Western industrialized countries concerning the relationship between the ordinary person and the information he or she receives from the surrounding world. I shall argue that the problem is serious, that it ought to attract more attention from scholars as well as from the informed public, and that it is a problem for educationalists to face, not least those concerned with adult education and communication.

The problem is, in short, that there is a vast and increasing number of important things which the average person ought to know about in order to live as an informed and responsible citizen in a democracy. On the other hand, much of this information does not seem to come over when attempts are made to transmit it through books, television programmes, teaching etc. I call this problem the problem of public enlightenment. (The term 'public enlightenment' is closely related to the Scandinavian term 'people's enlightenment', compare Nordhaug (1986: 48).)

An important part of this concerns global problems. There is at present a growing discrepancy between, on one hand, the serious global problems (such as arms race, rich and poor countries, ecological balance) and on the other, the fact that most European adults (with 9–12 years of schooling behind them) tend to fill their minds with unimportant trivialities or tend to turn away from the problems of the world scene and choose to focus on idyllic home situations or other aspects of private life. In order to build a bridge across this gap, i.e., to mediate between the 'big world' of global problems and the 'little world' of privacy, there ought to be a system of proper public enlightenment. Instead, there exists a system of one-way mass communication with very questionable effects as far as active understanding of world events is concerned (Simonds 1982). In short, then, there is a cleavage between the serious problems of the world and the not-so-informed lack of commitment of the individual citizen. If the world is to reach the 21st century with a minimum of human dignity, this structure will probably have to be changed (Morin 1981). Educationalists have an important role to play here.

Although most of the examples in this article are concerned with global matters, the problem does not stop here. It also concerns other political issues, existential and religious questions, technical developments such as space research, fifth generation computers, and biotechnology, as well as other things. It is a problem about a variety of new, copious and complex information, on the one hand, and an average consciousness which is not at all geared to this, on the other.

What makes this situation a new one from an educational point of view is not only that I am recommending that teaching and mass communication should be analyzed together because they have come to interact very strongly: it is also a specific assumption about information today. I assume that the reason why so much information does not come over to pupils, listeners and viewers is that people have become saturated with information. In some cases there seems to be psychological blockages against more information (Jacobsen 1984). Some later recommendations in this article are to be seen in the light of this assumption.

The idea that adult education should serve a purpose of enlightenment, emancipation and democratic citizenship is in itself not a new one. The writings of C. Wright Mills (1959) in the USA, and the Frankfurt school in Europe, together with a number of practical experiments in workers' education, folk high schools, etc., are among many developments and elaborations of this idea. What is wholly new, however, is that where some years ago the idea was a possibility, it has today become a necessity. It is a necessity if we want to secure the world as a place for democratic, autonomous human life. The background for the change from possibility to necessity is:

1   the internationalization of the national economies so that the fate of every nation is today knit together with that of the rest of the world
2   the corresponding internationalization of political decisions
3   the development of mass communication and telecommunication into an international system of information exchange (Gelpi 1985).

These developments have for the first time in history turned the world into one world with one common fate (Morin 1981). In the exposition that follows, I have tried to bring together the idea of enlightenment and the facts of this new world situation.

Is the public enlightenment problem a legitimate educational problem?

I can think of three objections to dealing with this problem at all and to seeing it as an educational problem. I call these the complexity argument, the individual chooser argument and the historical argument. Let us discuss them separately.

According to the complexity argument, most world problems are very complex and therefore not suitable for ordinary people to deal with. Complex problems should be left to experts and delegates. The problem of the arms race and the nuclear threat is a good example. Understanding arms technology, Soviet foreign policy and the like requires a lot of knowledge and insight, according to this argument, and should be left to experts.

But the fact, first of all, that ordinary people gain a certain amount of insight into a problem does not prevent the expert from still being an expert in his or her field. I am not saying that the expert shall not have the final word. (He shall, unless there is a moral opposition between him and the ordinary people.) What I am saying is that it is desirable that ordinary people gain as much insight as possible into expert fields. And should somebody, through this, be able to trounce the experts, then the question arises whether there was any real expertise to begin with. Second, the complexity objection seems to express a peculiar and irrational fear of complexity. Modern man has to deal with many complex matters. Why should it be a virtue to avoid and to fear complexity? On the contrary, to encourage people to be able to face complexity and to develop a taste and capacity for dealing with complexity must be a virtue in a civilized world. (Morin 1980: 434 ff). Avoiding complexity is to be associated, rather, with a traditional peasant society. Third, even complex world problems often require one's taking a rather fundamental moral stance, such as choosing between showing confidence and goodwill, or relying on means of control and power. To let the citizen refrain from making his or her position clear on basic moral matters and leave it to scientific and administrative experts and politicians is dangerous in a democracy.

But what if the ordinary man simply does not want to deal with world problems? He may prefer to watch sports on TV, work in the garden, or go to the pub. Should people be forced to do something they do not want? This is the individual chooser argument.

Here one must ask: What does it mean to say that people want something? People in our society pursue their wishes or wants in a given space and time structure, which contains objects to attract their attention. Today, for instance, most men and women live in a space structure with centrally located colour television. Somebody in the house will often put on the TV to watch a programme (produced, by the way, on the basis of highly developed, research-based techniques of attracting people's attention). It is difficult to read, think or discuss problems when a programme is on. The same men and women live in a time structure where it is extremely difficult to make any provision for uninterrupted reflection. And in our towns it is difficult to enjoy unpolluted air, beautiful flowers, birds flying over the forests, and the sunset over the sea. So people want what they want – beyond any doubt – but their wants and wishes are shaped by their immediate surroundings.

Although information about global issues is around in our society, it is not immediately around. To assert that it would be good if people had other preferences – even to work or fight for it – is not to go against peoples' wishes. It is to say, I want there to be other opportunities for these people in their daily life. (Among many other things, there might be common rooms in all local communities, where people could meet and discuss current problems.) Given these opportunities, I still want to leave it to peoples' wishes what they shall do. This is not to impose upon them. It is to add to their possibilities for pursuing their wishes.

Even so, there is still a problem concerning the individual chooser. Assume that a group of people in a local community have become committed to a social problem; for instance, the nuclear threat or racial tension in the area or a local traffic problem. They contact their neighbours and invite them to a meeting, stressing that they consider the problem utterly urgent and important. The question is now whether A has any duties if they ring his or her door bell. Does A have any moral obligation to attend their meeting or does A at least have a moral obligation to consider their cause seriously? To both these questions I would answer firmly, No. Let A be a flute teacher and flute player whose only interest in life is music. As long as he abides by the law, the highest moral claim that can be made upon him is that he should politely say, 'No thanks' when he opens the door.

The example touches on an important problem concerning participatory democracy. In a participatory democracy (and in an emerging one), what moral obligations does the individual have, if any? In her book on the subject, Patricia White argues that there are such moral obligations. She writes: 'In general, then, there is a duty to participate in the exercise, or control, of power in relevant institutions' (White 1983: 19).

Although I am much in favour of the general line of thought in the book, I find it necessary to object at this point. First, because it is a highly risky affair to attribute moral duties to one's contemporaries with the consequence that one makes a certain proportion of people into moral inferior creatures. The basis of such attributions will always be questionable and open to charges of subjectivity and self promotion. Second, there is much to be said for the thesis that all attempts at collective social change, from the beginning and without exception, should be combined with the most rigorous respect for individual liberties, with special reference to minority groups. This principle is of great importance for two reasons. Strategically, it will make the social change in question much more acceptable to its opponents. And basically, it is a *sine qua non* because history is so full of examples of revolutions and other social changes which have defeated freedom of thought and expression and have later gone astray.

Turning back to the previous example of the community group and the perspective of public enlightenment, the point of view here, then, is this. Nobody has any moral obligation to be interested in peace, the Third World, local traffic, and what not. What this article asserts is that the many people who are concerned have a right (and maybe a duty) to attract attention to their cause. They have a right to do and they ought to do a lot more than they presently do, and to do so in much more unconventional ways than are now common, in terms of ringing door bells, putting posters up in the street, etc. So it is the concerned people who have duties, not the unconcerned.

The historical objection to the project on public enlightenment consists in the assertion that constitutional democracy (parliamentary democracy) has so far worked reasonably well. Informed leaders tell the people what has to be done, and these leaders may be replaced by others if they go wrong. So, according to this argument, there is no reason to work towards an enormous release of activity and commitment which may appear very artificial and ultimately pointless.

But relying on past historical experiences is always problematic in that it presupposes an unchanged society. And in our case changes certainly are under way. Our society, it may well be said, now requires a new working relationship between political problems and the citizen. There are two components in the present situation: international trade and international interdependence have drastically increased – this 'internationalization' of the world has had the effect that everybody today is totally dependent on what happens in the USA, in the USSR, in the OPEC countries, etc. – and through the new communication technology (TV satellites, etc.) every citizen has instant access to international development.

So our life today is vastly influenced by international events. A crucial aspect is the increased distance between ordinary people and the power centres. The distance to the leader of one's own country is much smaller than the distance to the world leaders and, today, the last distance is the important one. This change is the reason why we, today, have to work out a new relationship between international events and individual lives. The conceptual understanding of the nature of this relationship has been forcefully worked out by Wright Mills (1959: Ch. 1). One could argue that this new relationship has become a necessity for the solution of world problems as well for the individual, if he or she is to lead a decent, responsible life with a minimum of mastery over his or her own life.

The concept of public enlightenment

It is time to try to map out important concepts which will have to form part of a project of public enlightenment.

'Public information' is a neutral term that covers information irrespective of its use for good or evil purposes. By 'public information' is here understood any message which any agent in society communicates to others in public. So this broad category will contain TV programmes, newspapers, school textbooks, advertisements, demonstration banners, pamphlets, public lectures, and a variety of other messages.

However, this broad concept of public information is unsatisfactory from an educational or any other normative point of view, in that it does not point to any aim, except that of sending information out into the world. Since much of the information in question seemingly does not get through, or gets through in peculiar ways or with peculiar results, we must find another concept which says more about the aim of public communication. For this purpose I want to introduce the concept of public enlightenment. By this term is to be understood all public information, which is collected together and communicated under the guidance of one principle; namely, that by receiving it people will acquire a coherent understanding of and an active commitment to the issues which the information is about in their social and cultural context.

This definition requires that, as far as technical information is concerned, there is an attempt to place the information in a social or cultural context. There is, however, no requirement about what this context shall be or how much time and space is to be allotted to it. The requirement is based on the assumption (developed in the next section) that at this moment, in our society, we have too much isolated technical information and that this fact is, to a certain extent, responsible for our problems within the field of public information.

The notion of enlightenment may need a commentary. The term refers to a mental process, which has an intellectual/rational component as well as an emotional/commitment component. The first component is to do with getting a cognitive grasp of and mastery over a situation. The second component is a matter of attaching importance to the acquired insight.

The commitment is not primarily to be thought of as commitment to a specific solution of a problem. The intention is rather an open-ended commitment; i.e., a commitment to the problem being studied and possibly to certain broad principles for its solution. Also the commitment is not laid down beforehand. It develops out of the educational situation so that the relationship between understanding and commitment is of an internal (dialectical) character.

Some people, on first inspection, might find the concept of public enlightenment too close to a kind of massive ideological indoctrination. But there is an important difference. In some countries, ideology is by definition the truth, and the task of educators is to get the truth into the heads of people by any means available. In contrast to this, the concept of public enlightenment does not imply that you require people to accept your message or your world view, if you have one. What you require is only that they listen to it, understand it, and make their position clear in relation to it. They are, however, completely free to reject it. The relationship between sender and receiver does not presuppose that the sender has a solution. It is rather a relationship between two searching people.

What is it, then, to be enlightened? It is to have received an insight into the real, social world, an insight which contains the double quality of profound, coherent intellectual understanding and emotional and moral commitment to that world.

The problem in a historical and social context

Having mapped out the concept in a preliminary way, let us now turn to an analysis of how the concept has developed in its contemporary social and historical manifestations. Where is the need for public enlightenment today? On what aspects of life in contemporary society and culture should it focus? And what are the chances of constructive social change through public enlightenment?

In an exhilarating and at times enigmatic survey of almost three thousand years of European history, the Frankfurt philosophers Horkheimer & Adorno (1969) try to trace the origin, the rise, and the decay of enlightenment. Deeply depressed by their experience of the barbarism of fascism and totalitarianism, they ask the question: Why has not man been able to use enlightenment to make the world more truly human?

Horkheimer & Adorno use the word enlightenment in a broader sense than the one I have used in this article. By the word enlightenment they understand, basically, the collection of knowledge and insight which man has at his disposal, at a given stage in history, to throw light on and become master of what is happening in society at that moment. In this broad sense, enlightenment encompasses critical thinking and theoretical depth, together with the ideal of being a free person. Enlightenment is, one could say, that element in society which tells society about itself. Understood as progressing thinking or insight-evolving-through-history, say Horkheimer & Adorno (1969: 7), enlightenment has since early times pursued one definite goal: to take fear away from human beings, and transform them into masters.

The vision of enlightenment (at its height late in the 18th century) was a society characterized by freedom, equity and humanity. But before these ideas (of the 18th century) were able to be universally realized, there began, say Horkheimer & Adorno, a process of liquidation and self-destruction. Enlightenment went into decay.

Many contemporary readers may not immediately understand what is meant by the decay of enlightenment. Have we not more knowledge and enlightenment than ever before?

In order to understand what Horkheimer & Adorno may mean, one can, I suggest, look at their thesis from the perspective of the sociology of knowledge (Berger & Luckman 1967).

In any society you will find, at different historical times, a given amount of knowledge or enlightenment which, seen from the outside, may be characterized and classified in certain ways, given certain names, etc. If, like Horkheimer & Adorno, you try to step outside our own society, you can then ask, What kind of knowledge and enlightenment do we have in our own, contemporary society?

The answer, following Horkheimer & Adorno (1969: 26), is that we have a kind of knowledge characterized by abstraction, distance, accountability, impartiality, and a neutral language, a kind of knowledge where thought has become 'an autonomously running automatic process, which resembles a machine'. In our society, you have to focus your attention on facts, and you pay the price of obediently submitting reason to this world of facts. In this way, you have to renounce vast amounts of insight, accumulated through the history of European thought, i.e., insights connected with the relationships between singular facts on one hand and their location on the other, in a context of societal, historical and human development.

Horkheimer & Adorno suggest an explanation of this trait. Knowledge has become intimately interwoven with domination (Herrschaft). Our thought forms reflect the domination of the capitalist division of labour (Horkheimer & Adorno 1969: 23).

It is not fully clear whether the authors see the relationship between capitalism and a fact-orientated knowledge structure as a necessary or a contingent one. Their language points to a necessary relationship. But although becoming aware of this relationship may often have a powerful impact on one's mind, it is probably a contingent relationship. This recognition might lead to greater optimism than Horkheimer & Adorno have with regard to the possibilities of social change. And for those who see the fact orientation as an important progress, it should be pointed out that it is possible to preserve fact-orientation without preserving capitalism.

Another point which is not fully clear is whether the authors see the change that has taken place in our knowledge structure as undesirable. The most fruitful move here, in the view of the present author, would be to describe neutrally the situation in our knowledge structure as it is today and then formulate the types of changes that would be desirable, together with plans for moving in that direction.

An attempt to sketch a desirable development in our knowledge structure (or knowledge and belief structures) of this type might look like this (I still keep very close to the categories of Horkheimer & Adorno): It would be desirable if our knowledge and belief systems developed these characteristics:

1   Art products and utopian beliefs, which have been dissociated from knowledge, should be reintegrated with it.
2   The value domain (especially ethical and political discourse), which has been dissociated from knowledge, should become reintegrated.

3   Subjective life experiences, which have also been dissociated, should become reintegrated.
4   Theoretical depth and insight, including attempts at holistic explanations, should be given higher priority.
5   The stylistic and intellectually autonomous character of the above-mentioned four areas, should be maintained in this integration.
6   The integration should be non-dogmatic and always open to criticism. This implies that more than one universe of thought should be developed, so that it becomes a human right to choose between different forms of explanation of the phenomena in the world.

The term 'reintegration' in the above sketch does not imply 'strong' integration of a type that annihilates its components. If, for instance, scientific and artistic discourse were to be blended together in one book, they would be in separate sections so that each discourse preserved its own character. What is intended with this rather 'weak' integration is that if you write a book (or article or TV programme) on subject X, you should incorporate in your product some of the above-mentioned discourses and, hopefully, in such a way that they comment upon and illuminate each other. In that way, you would contribute to giving low-priority domains the higher priority they deserve and you would help to bring about both a more coherent knowledge and belief system in our culture and, hopefully, also more enlightened citizens. With this, I am not saying that the separations which have brought us so many advantages should be abolished and everything mixed together again. I do say, however, that it is time to carefully consider the costs of the separations and to make some reintegration and some new priorities. I do say, also, that the total picture should be rather different.

In order to make this more clear, it might be of interest to compare this sociology of knowledge view with an epistemological view on domains or forms of knowledge. These two perspectives have never been reconciled and a weak integration of the two is a major task ahead.

Let us take, for instance, Paul Hirst's forms of knowledge thesis (Hirst 1974) as an example of the epistemological perspective, and try to reformulate the Adorno/Horkheimer position in that kind of language.

1   There are such things as distinctive forms of knowledge.
2   They have a universal character in the sense that they reflect nature, the human species, etc.
3   The forms are differentiated through social evolution.
4   Two societies having comparable degree of differentiation may have widely differing development of knowledge forms. Society A may, for instance, place most weight on scientific-technical knowledge, whereas in society B, religious and artistic knowledge is highly developed. That a form of knowledge is 'highly developed' or has

'weight' refers both to its internal differentiation and to the amount of space it occupies in that society (e.g., in libraries or in school lessons).

5   In our society, a technical-scientific knowledge (i.e., mathematical knowledge and science) is overdeveloped in comparison with the aesthetic, moral, and the religious domains.

6   In our society there are deep gulfs between domains, especially between the mathematical and scientific domains on one side and the other ones on the other side.

7   It is desirable that the underdeveloped domains become radically strengthened. It is desirable that a moderate reintegration (bringing together) of the forms take place.

Although the above sketch is extremely provisional (and contains a number of unsolved problems), it indicates quite clearly, I think, that there are gains in clarity and precision when transfer is made to the epistemological perspective.

Principles of public enlightenment as an educational enterprise

What can now be said about writing a good newspaper article or lecture, producing a good radio or television programme, writing a good pamphlet for an organization, etc? ('Good' is here understood as 'good for enlightenment'.)

I shall suggest four guiding principles, which can at the same time function as criteria for the evaluation of public information material. The four principles are derived from the previous analysis, but the general influence of the works of Jürgen Habermas should also be mentioned. For the public enlightenment project, reference should be made to Habermas' theories on the structural changes of public life (Habermas 1962), especially his analysis of manipulative versus critical publicity in the industrialized democracies (Habermas 1962: 287–294).

First, coherence. According to this principle, information material is good when characterized by attempts to emphasize contexts, interrelationships, connections between events. It is bad in so far as it consists solely of non-related entities such as isolated news items, events, or disjointed dictionary information.

The justification of this principle is that understanding (as opposed to perception or memorization) presupposes relations between phenomena. The principle is important because people nowadays are heavily overloaded by discrete facts and isolated bits of knowledge.

Second comes the principle of relevance. It could also be termed a principle of centrality, or of giving priority to what is essential or important as opposed to peripheral. This is a very difficult principle to approach, but an attempt has to be made. Actually, the term 'relevance' points in two directions, each with its own meaning. First, the information must be important for the pupil or the receiver in the context of his or her life. (This is not identical with appealing to the person's spontaneous interests or whims.) Second, what it says must be important in order to understand or explain the phenomenon in question. On the nuclear arms situation, for example, just another bit of information on various missile types or the number of missiles in East and West (such as often fills the newspapers) would usually be less relevant than, say, information on assumed causes of the nuclear situation, or on the interplay between technical and social forces in the arms race.

The criterion of relevance is founded on the assumption that we are currently in a situation where minds are being filled with or exposed to far too many irrelevancies, at the same time as many people feel quite hopeless about the future. This, again, is founded on the more basic value that people should be given the opportunity to take personal responsibility for their own fate.

Next comes the principle of truth. This states that public information should come as close as possible to what is true, and in that way avoid being false and ideological. The problem here is not about agreeing that information should not be incorrect. The problem is that much public information is partly true, but does not tell the whole truth. It is selective. Therefore the truth criterion is connected with the principles of coherence and of relevance (in the second sense).

I hold the value of truth to be self-evident. But for those who do not, one can also point to the instrumental value of maintaining the credibility of the whole system.

Fourth and last is the principle of active mastery. It holds that public information should be structured and designed in such a way that individuals' propensity for action is stimulated. This means also that one should seek not to generate mental states such as hopelessness, misery or lack of belief in one's own power. How this is to be done is another story, which is largely a matter of practical experimentation. It is, however, easy to show that different types of article or TV programme have different effects on this dimension; compare for instance typical interviews, documentaries, fact-laden lectures, etc.

The justification for this last principle is twofold. First, most people would prefer a human life characterized by strength and confidence to one characterized by weakness and hopelessness. Second, to follow this principle is to strength the democratic society. It is dangerous for a democracy if people get too hopeless in relation to the society they live in.

If these principles are followed, our information material will look very different and function very differently from that to which we are now accustomed.

A note on political machinery

The public enlightenment project visualizes and strives towards a social life which is changed in important respects. Citizens will tend to be considerably more active and committed than today. It should be stressed that this does not necessarily mean that everybody will devote a lot of time to new activities and meetings, and it certainly does not imply that anybody shall be forced to do things they dislike.

The public enlightenment project is envisaged as taking place within the framework of a parliamentary democracy. It is also envisaged, however, that there will be a vast increase of grassroots activity and that this will in turn give rise to a number of more permanent committees, associations, organizations and the like, which will make the total picture rather different from that of today.

It is unwise to try to sketch in detail the structure or form of these changes, it will be up to future generations to devise what kind of structures and forms they want. They will form the groups and organizations they need (the power of which will, of course, in turn be felt in parliament). If a sketch had been attempted it would have faced the objection that this is not going to work because people are often lazy, ignorant, selfish, narrow-minded. One must, however, envisage that social life – and individuals along with it – will tend to change. This change can be followed by modifications in the social and political structure.

Summary and conclusion

A new problem has emerged in the world, a problem which has to be taken very seriously and which is also a problem for educators. The problem lies in the relationship between the Western adult and the information they receive from the surrounding world. An acute aspect of the problem is the growing discrepancy between global problems and the uninformed lack of commitment of the ordinary citizen.

As a solution, I recommend a new kind of mass communication under the concept of public enlightenment. What is new is the role in public enlightenment played by active understanding and moral commitment. Public enlightenment on a vast scale will arouse a significantly increased level of responsible activity in the population as a whole. It is difficult to find rational arguments against this. But there are arguments for it. It means a revitalization and making safe of democracy. It accords with the ideal of individual autonomy and responsibility. And it may have an effect upon the problems of this globe.

Acknowledgements

I want to thank Professor Paul H. Hirst, University of Cambridge, and reader John White, University of London Institute of Education, for their constructive criticism and many valuable hints.

References

Berger, P. L. & Luckman, T. (1967) *The Social Construction of Reality*, Allan Lane.

Gelpi, E. (1985) *Lifelong Education and International Relations*, London, Croom Helm.

Habermas, J. (1962) *Strukturwandel der Öffentlichkeit*, Neuwied, Luchterhand.

Hirst, P. H. (1974) Liberal education and the nature of knowledge, in P.H. Hirst, *Knowledge and the Curriculum: a collection of philosophical papers*, London, RKP.

Horkheimer, M. & Adorno, T. W. (1969) *Dialektik der Aufklärung. Philosophische Fragmente*, Frankfurt a.M., Fischer.

Jacobsen, B. (1984) The Negation of Apathy: On how to educate the public in nuclear matters, in: Bishop of Salisbury *et al. Lessons Before Midnight: Educating for Reason in Nuclear Matters*, Bedford Way Papers 19, University of London Institute of Education.

Morin, E. (1980) La Méthode II. *La Vie de la Vie*, Paris, Seuil.

Morin, E. (1981) *Pour Sortir du Vingtiéme Siécle*, Paris, Fernand Nathan.

Nordhaug, O. (1986) Adult education in the welfare state: Institutionalization of social commitment, *International Journal of Lifelong Education*, Vol. 5, No. 1, pp. 45–57.

Simonds, A. P. (1982) On Being Informed. *Theory and Society*, Vol. 11, No. 5, pp. 587–616.

White, P. (1983) *Beyond Domination. An Essay in the Political Philosophy of Education*, London, RKP.

Wright Mills, C. (1959) *The Sociological Imagination*, NY, Oxford.

24 Adult learning for citizenship

Towards a reconstruction of the social purpose tradition

Rennie Johnston[1]
Southampton, UK

This paper seeks to review and re-frame the idea of social purpose adult education in the context of a contemporary Risk Society and the interface between modernist and postmodernist influences on learning. After interrogating and critiquing the social purpose tradition in adult education, it relates this to the changing nature and widening scope of adult learning within a developing Learning Society. The paper puts forward the idea of Adult Learning for Citizenship as a way of maintaining and reconstructing social purpose learning within a Risk Society and as a necessary challenge and counter-focus to the dominant discourse of Lifelong Learning shaped by the economic imperative and framed very much in terms of human capital. In developing this argument, the paper proposes a new framework for Adult Learning for Citizenship which consists of four different but overlapping dimensions of social purpose learning: learning for inclusive citizenship, for pluralistic citizenship, for reflexive citizenship and for active citizenship. Within this framework, it develops new rationales for social purpose adult learning linked to instructive examples of practice from a range of international contexts. In conclusion, it examines the implications of such a framework for the praxis of adult educators.

'If you don't stand for something, you'll fall for anything'.

(Marx)

Maybe Groucho Marx got it right. The above quotation has a particular resonance for adult educators working within a rapidly-changing world of adult learning. This paper is looking to 'stand for something', to identify key values and purposes which can shape the work of adult educators in the contemporary world so that they don't 'fall for anything' in the confusing interface between the modern and the postmodern.

It has its origins in my own struggles to maintain and develop a social purpose as an adult educator. On the one hand, I feel rooted in the modernist social purpose tradition arising out of both my personal egalitarian beliefs and my past experience of participatory action research with unwaged adults, collaborative work with a wide range of community groups and access initiatives with adults from under-represented groups. On the other hand, I am increasingly conscious of the rapid societal changes and unpredictability of a late modern or postmodern world which call into question many of the modernist certainties of the social purpose tradition and raise new questions for adult educators, for example, how to work within an increasingly consumer-oriented and marketized world, how to engage meaningfully with the politics of difference and identity.

Lifelong Learning is now centre-stage and adult educators should welcome it for the emphasis it places on adult learning. However we also need to look at it critically and attempt to engage in the debate about what Lifelong Learning means and how it develops. It is a site for struggle. In this paper I will argue that a focus on adult learning for citizenship is an appropriate, necessary and productive counter-focus to the dominant discourse of Lifelong Learning shaped by the economic imperative, framed very much in terms of human capital and concerned with the 'economic individual'. I will put forward a new framework for developing and supporting Adult Learning which takes account of the traditional values of social purpose adult education but tries to locate and review them in the contemporary context of what is variously known as late modernity, postmodernity or the 'risk society.'[2]

Social purpose adult education has a long and rich tradition extending over many years and a wide variety of contexts. According to Fieldhouse, it aims at:

> ...providing individuals with knowledge which they can use collectively to change society if they so wish, and particularly equipping members of the working class with the intellectual tools to play a full role in a democratic society or to challenge the inequalities and injustices of society in order to bring about radical social change.
>
> (Fieldhouse 1992: 11)

As such it has significant overlaps with the different understandings and traditions of popular education, community education, radical adult education, Freirian adult education, social action education and critical pedagogy. Its key values can be identified as social justice, greater social and economic equality, the promotion of a critical democracy, a vision of a better, fairer world where education has a key role to play. In its purposes it foregrounds 'praxis', an intention to act appropriately, truly and justly in a socio-political situation where both ends and means are seen as problematic and a matter of choice about the right action to take (Carr and Kemmis 1986: 17), or put more succinctly by Freire as '... reflection and action upon the world in order to transform it' (1972: 28). Perhaps equally important are the ways of working associated with these values and purposes: a concern for informality and autonomy; working through networks rather than hierarchies; developing problem-posing, issue-based, critical learning; building dialogue and trust; ensuring respect for different cultures.

Interrogating the social purpose tradition

In trying to make sense of contemporary society, Anthony Giddens identifies the key theme of 'detraditionalization'. By this he does not necessarily mean moving away from traditions, but rather: 'In a context of global cosmopolitanism, traditions are today called upon to defend themselves: they are routinely subject to interrogation' (Beck, Giddens and Lash 1994: viii). With this in mind, the first part of this paper will try to review and problematize some aspects of the social purpose adult education tradition identified above.

Traditions are always changing. In past years, there has been a growing recognition by many social purpose adult educators that:

> ...the working-class has never been a single unitary subject but has been simultaneously fractured by skill, gender, ethnicity, region and the cultures engendered by these divisions.
>
> (Westwood 1992: 234)

Thus, for example, Taylor and Ward, in revising their conception of social purpose adult education in the context of the mid 80s, have explicitly recognized five aspects of social structure which reproduce inequality, namely education, gender, race, age and geography. In responding to these factors, they advocate two guiding principles: the necessity for in-depth, preliminary groundwork and dialogue to co-investigate the real felt needs of target groups in local communities; allied to educational approaches centred on local manifestations of structural issues rather than conventional academic 'subjects' (Taylor and Ward 1986: 172).

Alongside this trend has been a parallel move away from once prevailing modernist patriarchal assumptions and attitudes, a development which has been prompted at least partly by powerful feminist and postmodern critiques (Luke and Gore 1992, Weiler 1993). A recent example of this has been demonstrated in the way Paulo Freire has reviewed and up-dated his own historical position to stress that:

> ...we must not lose sight of the need to recognize multiple constructions of power and authority in a society driven by inequalities of power and exclusionary divisions of privilege and how these are implicated in the constitution of subjectivity differentiated by race, class and sexual preference.
>
> (Freire 1993: x–xi)

Such a perspective emphasizes the need to bear in mind the distinction – and sometimes the connections – between exploitation, arising out of structural position, and oppression, linked more to cultural identity or interest, an inter-relationship which is central to the modernist/post-modernist debate (Martin 1998a).

Beside this more pluralistic notion of oppression, there is also a more sophisticated understanding of the different contexts of analysis and action. While the analytical distinction that no education is neutral is still seen as valid, it is also becoming understood that, in the complex world of practice, choices for educational action are rarely so starkly outlined as 'education for liberation' or 'education for domestication'. Certainly in my own experience of working with unwaged adults (Johnston 1992) and female colleagues' experience of work with women in very different international contexts (Ismail 1997, Clarke 1998) it is clear that within an increasingly flexible and fragmented labour market and an economically and socially polarized world, one person's domestication can easily be another's liberation. The postmodern notion of the 'de-centred subject' helps us here in understanding how one can be both oppressor and oppressed in different contexts and relationships simultaneously. Indeed, postmodern and other critics have helped us to understand that education is perhaps less a matter of domestication or liberation rather than of negotiating the terms of participation in a society where subjection and autonomy co-exist (Gilbert 1992).

Notwithstanding the above progressive developments, some old, as yet unresolved, problems remain in relation to the social purpose tradition. In terms of practice, there is still a tension between individual learning and group/collective involvement which is difficult to resolve satisfactorily. This has been long evident in trade union and community education but more recently exacerbated by the global growth of credentialism and accreditation systems centred on the idea of individual progression. In addition, there are still attendant dangers of marginalization in that 'target groups' can be (often inadvertently) stigmatized as part of a social pathologization which sees difference as deficit and can amount to a naive understanding of the compound nature of inequality and disadvantage.

In terms of rhetoric too, there can still be detected a residual arch modernist tendency towards high flown statements of moral purpose, pious expressions of hope, grand visions of an alternative, fairer, more equal society where Adult Education plays a central role, as exhibited most recently in some of the literature associated with the 1997 UNESCO conference (DVV 1997). The role of rhetoric is, of course, an important one in developing a social purpose. However, there is another danger here that in our vision of a better society and the role that adult education can play, we begin to establish within our discourse what feminist/postmodernist commentators, following Foucault, have dubbed 'regimes of truth', that are 'teleological and totalizing'. For example in our concerns about empowerment, we adopt '... an overly optimistic view of agency, a tendency to overlook context, an overly simplistic conception of power as property, the theoretical pronouncement of discourses as liberatory, a lack of reflexivity' (Gore 1992: 63) If we are not careful we end up kidding ourselves.

In addition to the above unresolved problems linked to the traditions of social purpose adult education, are new factors arising from the specific contemporary context of the 'Risk Society'. Ulrich Beck identifies the 'Risk Society' as being typified by increased risk and uncertainty: 'new areas of unpredictability are created quite often by the very attempts that seek to control them' (Beck, Giddens and Lash 1994: vii), which, in turn, requires an increased reflexivity on the part of the general population about risks in society. Within the context of the Risk Society, Beck and Giddens both identify the key process of 'individualization', described by Beck as the '... disembedding and re-embedding of ways of life by new ones in which individuals must produce, stage and cobble together their biographies themselves (Beck 1994: 13). Of course, individualization is not the same as individualism and not necessarily emancipatory. Of particular note for the social purpose tradition is Giddens' observation that: 'the more the demand to make one's own life becomes acute, the more material poverty becomes a double discrimination', that is through lack of material rewards and lack of capacity for autonomy (Giddens 1994: 188).

The idea of a 'Risk Society' and of 'individualization' clearly throw up new areas of problematization which have implications for adult educators. One of the most immediate ironies is that while we live in an increasingly unequal world, oppression has also become more diffuse. For example, we all suffer from the growing pressures of 'employability', from the unemployed person on a government training scheme to the high flying executive, forced to work too long hours and update knowledge frantically in order to 'stay ahead of the game'. Here there may be emerging a link between individual interests and common interests in that greater inequality appears to be in no one's personal interests and social cohesion in everyone's interests – this might provide a potentially productive focus for adult education.

In addition, a growing focus on 'life politics', the politics of life decisions about identity and lifestyle (Giddens 1991: 214) related to the family, caring, health, food, sexuality, the body, previously kept very much in the private domain, may require a rethinking of the role and scope of an adult education which seeks to understand and engage with the interface between the public and the private. Lastly, in another linking of the public and the private, the place of 'desire' demands serious engagement by adult educators. It is no longer possible or indeed advisable for adult educators to ignore or 'wish-away' a situation where educational activities are increasingly being seen as consumer (and positional) goods within a market-place which emphasises educational choice as part of consumption (Field 1996: 137–138). Indeed, in a specific UK context, Bob Bell takes this point much further when he asserts that the radical, rationalist focus of professional and academic adult education has served to marginalize the interests of the majority of adult learners who, he believes, are more concerned with issues of consumer choice than emancipation (Bell 1996).

So what do all these changes mean for the adult educator working within the 'Risk Society'? In shaping their response, Jansen and van der Veen believe that we need to be more modest about our contribution to resolving social problems and more cautious in offering alternatives for the 'existing society' (1996: 134). Certainly we may need to combine a necessary ambition and vision with a degree of modesty, to be less 'teleological and totalizing' in our approach to adult education, more circumspect in the claims we make regarding our 'social purpose' and clearer about the key areas for intervention and leverage in relation to adult learning.

Adult education, adult learning and lifelong learning

Some postmodern commentators identify a move from the 'bounded field' of adult education to the more open 'moorland' of Adult Learning (Edwards 1997, Usher, Bryant and Johnston 1997). This involves, amongst other things, a greater diversity of learners and sites of learning, closer links with consumer culture, development of new more flexible modes of learning, and a questioning of traditional forms of knowledge. Such a development has clear implications for adult educators. As Usher, Bryant and Johnston put it:

> ...More and more adults are engaged in learning programmes. The dream of adult educators that lifelong learning should become a universal condition is now closer to realisation than ever before. This, however, makes problematic the institutionalised forms that adult education should take.
>
> (Usher, Bryant and Johnston 1997: xv)

If this is a predominant and inexorable trend, then it would appear, at first sight, to be a major problem for adult educators, threatening our very *raison d'etre*. However, this is not necessarily the case. On the contrary, such a transition opens up new possibilities in adult learning and new roles for adult educators. In the first place, it allows some creative and freer space outside the growing restrictions of the more formal system. For example, in seeking to develop 'A European and UK Perspective on Education for Citizenship', Leni Oglesby draws out a clear tension in the UK between the democratic and collaborative traditions of adult education and the effects of centralised funding models (Oglesby 1997). In its move towards mainstream status, adult education can be seen to have become increasingly 'colonized' within the top-down, bureaucratic and managerial paraphernalia of performance indicators, (prescribed) learning outcomes, league tables, and assessment and accreditation regimes which cramp the autonomy, trust and respect of educator and learner alike. Indeed, such direct controlling measures are now supported by other, more subtle forms of governmentality where the growth of 'confessional practices', like educational advice and guidance, creates new forms of 'expert' upon whom learners are increasingly dependent to help them find their way through the maze of provision (Usher Bryant and Johnston 1997).

In similar ways, the Access movement, so long a source of inspiration for adult learners and a focus for progressive educators, has been colonized too. Thus innovative efforts to improve 'accessibility', particularly for non-traditional students, can often be frustrated or off-set by the centralizing and standardizing counter-tendencies of quality measures primarily intended to defend traditional academic territory. The effect of this is that Access is very often reduced to access to relatively conventional traditional courses, underpinned by a competitive financial regime that is based on a reductionist understanding that 'a student is a student is a student is a unit cost' (Johnston and Croft 1998). As a number of commentators have noted, such an approach doesn't deal with the issues of culture and power which underpin institutional practices (Dadzie 1993, Edwards 1997: 123), is in danger of constructing non-participation as cultural deficit, and achieves outcomes which, at best amount to a 'second skimming' process, integrating predominantly middle-class women into Higher Education and, at worst, can leave some learners alienated and 'Imprisoned in the Global Classroom' (Illich and Verne 1976, Weil 1986, Rosen 1993).

With the above in mind, it may be instructive to make a brief expedition into the 'moorland' of adult learning. Adult learning is flourishing and evidence of this continues to accumulate. For example, the 1996 European Year of Lifelong Learning has been documented as involving a proliferation of forms of adult learning in the work-place, the home, the wider community, in relation to leisure, often amongst adults previously untouched by more conventional forms of adult education (Sargent *et al.* 1997, Tuckett 1997). Such developments have been fostered and supported by recent initiatives like the growth of a European network of Learning Cities with a clear focus on the learner rather than the educational provider and grassroots learning developments arising out of the successful creation of Adult Learners' weeks in the UK and, more recently, Australia.

There is little doubt that a lot of this has been directly or indirectly influenced by the economic imperative and very much in the economic domain, encouraged by national and local governments so completely sold on the value of human capital that they see it as some kind of modern-day economic panacea. This trend is well-illustrated in Edwards' astute and slightly cynical observation that:

> While the economy produced sufficient surplus through taxation, the field of education and training and its relationships with the economy could be left to employers, trade unions and individuals. However, as the economic competitiveness of certain countries deteriorated, it

became important for consideration and action to be taken to provide learning opportunities to more satisfactorily meet the perceived needs of the economy – even if the policy is directed at encouraging employers and individuals to take greater responsibility for lifelong learning.

(Edwards 1997: 93)

However, in addition to this trend, there has been a wider dimension to what Edwards calls the de-differentiation of adult learning (Edwards 1997), with a growth of adult learning related to the private dimension of life: the consumer society, leisure, information technology, the Internet. This is a less controlled and controllable learning environment but still closely affected by available economic and cultural capital, a good example of the uneven effects of individualization. Still further, there has also been a perceptible growth of adult learning within 'civil society', '… that public space that is independent of the state' (Krygier 1996: 14). For example, Elsdon (1995) has recent evidence that the voluntary sector in the UK is much bigger than anyone realised with 25 voluntary organisations in existence per 1000 of population, mostly personal-interest-based (c80%), which can be extrapolated into 1.4 million throughout the country involving up to 30 million adult members – and according to Elsdon, they are all involved in learning! This in some ways mirrors longstanding developments in relatively autonomous study circles in Sweden where 75% of the adult population are estimated to have been involved at some time or other in their lives (Larrson 1997: 1). Indeed, on the other side of the world, similar developments, albeit on a smaller scale, are also taking place with the Australian Association of Adult and Community Education establishing Learning Circles on issues like aboriginal reconciliation, environmental dangers and the nature of citizenship itself (AAACE 1997). When these examples are seen alongside the learning activities of community groups and a growing variety of social movements, the incidence of adult learning activity in civil society would appear to be widespread.

So adult learning is flourishing. As it proliferates, we need to link this somehow to the wider concept and discourse of Lifelong Learning which is gaining increasing global recognition. While there is little doubt that the dominant emphasis is on Lifelong Learning in the service of the needs of the economy (and with it, the economic individual), it also offers new opportunities for a different adult learning focus which embodies the values of the social purpose tradition, albeit up-dated and re-focused to take account of contemporary aspects of the 'Risk Society'.

Thus, a move from Adult Education to Adult Learning may not be just a reluctant acknowledgement of an unwanted societal trend, not only a postmodern indulgence. It may also offer new opportunities for social purpose adult educators. In this context, Michael Welton acknowledges a major shift in discourse in Western Countries from education to learning but adds to it a warning that:

Unless civil societarian adult educators claim 'learning' for themselves, giving it a socially anchored, contextual meaning, the neo-
conservatives will run away with it. And for them it will most assuredly
mean an adaptation of isolated individual learners to the corporate-
determined status quo.

(Welton 1997b: 33)

Perhaps a key question for adult educators committed to developing a
contemporary social purpose is: how can we link the values of social
purpose adult education to the world of Adult Learning without falling
into the trap of unreflexive arch-modernism, 'kidding ourselves', or value-
free postmodernism, 'falling for anything'?

Adult learning for citizenship – developing a framework for a new social purpose

The main theme of this paper is that a focus on adult learning for citizenship will enable adult educators to operationalize a new social
purpose that is clear about its underpinning values yet avoids the arch-
modernist dangers of adopting totalizing imperatives; that engages with
the uncertainties and reflexivities of the Risk Society without succumbing
to the paralysis-inducing moral relativism of the worst kind of postmodernism. In the specific context of the Risk Society and the associated
processes of 'detraditionalization' and 'individualization', it is possible to
identify four different social purposes for adult learning: for inclusive citizenship, for pluralistic citizenship, for reflexive citizenship and for active
citizenship. These different dimensions of social purpose are not discrete
but clearly overlap considerably. Indeed, in relation to adult learning, they
could be seen as consisting of a continuum where the role of adult learning becomes increasingly important and evident as we progress along it.

Adult learning for inclusive citizenship

Within the Risk Society, learning needs to be inclusive in the face of economic and social exclusion. Evidence from across the world highlights an
increasingly unequal contemporary world (Joseph Rowntree Foundation
1995, Commission of the European Communities 1993 and 1995,
UNESCO 1997, Korsgaard 1997: 10–15). Social commentators are increasingly concerned with the associated decline in social cohesion as
demonstrated in burgeoning crime rates, the exclusionary, disenfranchis-
ing and alienating effects of the privatization of previously public services,
the dangers of increasing welfare dependence seen within an overall questioning of the funding basis and role of the welfare state (Jackson 1997).
In this context, we need to look closely at the role played by education
and training. In many instances, it can be seen as acting as a form of

regressive taxation, being readily available to educational 'haves' and being both expensive and in short supply to the 'have nots' (Johnston 1994: 38–40). As UNESCO puts it:

> While there is a growing demand for adult education and an explosion of information, the disparities between those who have access and those who do not are also growing. There is therefore a need to counter this polarity, which reinforces existing inequalities by creating learning structures and lifelong learning environments that can help to counter the prevalent trend.
>
> (UNESCO 1997: 2)

International organizations have a role to play here, as do state governments. For example, the European Social Fund has already made valuable contributions to the education and training of under-represented groups throughout Europe, notwithstanding its over-bureaucratic and reductionist tendencies. At a national level, a notable example of a recent governmental attempt to redress the educational balance and move towards more inclusive citizenship through learning has been offered by the UK Blair government's advocacy of 'Individual Learning Accounts' which afford the potential for the poorest section of the British population to be actively subsidized in taking up new learning opportunities (DfEE 1998). Of course, it remains to be seen to what extent such a market-based approach will actually be used by adults with limited or little positive experience of learning and to what extent this entitlement will be directed, circumscribed or vocationally-driven. Nevertheless, if it is targeted at those on the lower levels of the 'Learning Divide', it may offer a new focus on learning in the cause of greater equality.

Learning for inclusive citizenship also implies learning for all, exploring values and purposes across society as a whole, flagging up issues like social cohesion and trying to move away from an inward-looking 'culture of contentment' (Galbraith 1991). It can focus on learning in the common interest, for example in critically analysing labour market developments in a way that stresses the inter-connections and enhances the solidarity between employed and unemployed, between workers at all levels. In another context, it can also pick up and build on a phenomenon that Beck cryptically and rather cynically identifies: 'poverty divides, smog unites' (quoted in Jansen and Van der Veen 1996: 123) Certainly, environmental issues have brought together a wide variety of different interest groups prepared to co-operate, learn together and act in defence of environmental and human rights.

An effective example of adult learning for all can be seen in the development of Study Circles on Aboriginal Reconciliation by the Australian Council for Aboriginal Reconciliation and the AAACE (Australian Association of Adult and Community Education) (Council for Aboriginal

Reconciliation 1993). As result of this initiative, key groups and individuals amongst the white majority within Australia have raised their awareness and understanding of aboriginal perspectives on the fundamental national issues of land rights, racial equality and social justice with a consequent impact on the overall national profile and consciousness of aboriginal rights.

A learning focus on inclusive citizenship can encompass both individual and group learning, through engaging with '... people's rights as individuals and their life as social beings (Hill 1994: 9). It has the potential to open the way to a different and positive learning identity for some disadvantaged groups of learners as well as serving to remind everyone of their role as stakeholders in society, their responsibility for that society and the learning and action this can involve in the interests of social justice and social cohesion. This is a key contribution to learning for citizenship, in many ways still within the broad tradition of liberal adult education. However, in a contemporary Risk Society, this may not be sufficient in itself to take full account of new forms and understandings of citizenship.

Adult learning for pluralistic citizenship

A learning focus on pluralistic citizenship can build on but extend beyond inclusive citizenship. As such it can incorporate aspects of both the modern and the postmodern. Pluralistic citizenship recognises the existence of basic universal human rights but also leaves room for negotiation and variability, so taking account of the postmodern emphasis on heterogeneity, fragmentation and de-centring. It is a citizenship that is no longer based on sameness, that, on the contrary, embraces diversity and cultural pluralism.

At a relatively simple level, adult learning for pluralistic citizenship can help to transcend traditional understandings of and divisions between left and right and contribute to the exploration of the idea of active citizenship, a concept common, albeit in different forms, to both the civic-communitarian and liberal-individualist traditions of citizenship (Hill 1994: 10–28). With more specific relation to the contemporary Risk Society, learning for pluralistic citizenship can take account of globalization, the decline of the nation-state and concerns for ecological endangerment through encouraging a focus on world citizenship or regional citizenship that acknowledges but moves beyond primarily parochial issues. In educational terms this can translate into 'thinking globally and acting locally' where local learning, community initiatives and citizenship rights are developed within an informed context of the continuing worldwide struggle for equality of gender and race, for conservation and the more equitable distribution of the earth's resources (Hill 1994: 25)

Adult learning for pluralistic citizenship also has the potential to respond to the effects of individualization, the concerns of life politics and the growing inter-connection of the public and the private. Here an educational dimension can be developed to Chantal Mouffe's argument that:

> ...a democratic idea of citizenship must find a way of constructing the public and the private that does not relegate all differences, diversity and plurality to the private ... Democratic politics has to make room for particularity and difference.
>
> (Mouffe 1988: 30)

Certainly, in the areas of adult literacy work (Shore *et al.* 1993, Brady 1994), experiential learning (Brah and Hoy 1989, Fraser 1995) and the rapidly-developing field of autobiographical learning (Stuart 1993, Thompson 1995) there is a wide range of examples of good educational practice in engagement with and respect for identity and difference while at the same time exploring common ground and common interests. Learning approaches like these are very important in engaging meaningfully and seriously with postmodern identity politics whilst also avoiding the modernist dangers of the marginalization, silencing and exclusion of certain groups. Indeed a focus on and a dialogue about difference and identity appear more necessary than ever within the Risk Society and growing tendencies, in the light of global uncertainty and the decline of the nation-state, to revert to what Barry Hake calls 'pre-modern' sources of identity such as nationalism, localism, racism, ethnicity, xenophobia and fundamentalism (Hake 1997: 150).

In relation to pluralistic citizenship, there may be another important role within adult learning in trying to link explorations of common interests and a common culture to the politics of identity and difference. In a contemporary context, this involves a recognition that within multicultural societies, different cultures are not completely 'bounded' but can overlap, explore together differing understandings and meanings, identify common interests and interact for mutual and collective benefit. The prospect may exist here for a re-conceptualization and re-operationalization of 'community' that goes beyond the uncritical, cosy romanticism 'Gemeinschaft' yet is something more grounded and meaningful than the impersonal contractuality and bureaucracy of 'Gesellschaft', an idea of community that actively embraces and explores heterogeneity. Within this context, there may be the potential for an adult learning contribution towards closer cross-cultural dialogue and an understanding that the existence of common interests and common actions does not necessarily involve convergence to the same culture: we can begin to explore, encourage and develop the idea of 'solidarity in diversity' (Martin 1998b).

Adult learning for reflexive citizenship

Reflexive learning is reflective, self-critical and dynamic. It has a key role to play in making sense of the complexities, uncertainties and diversity of the Risk Society. In the context of citizenship it involves unpacking and exploring citizens' rights and responsibilities as well as their inter-connectedness. Much of the traditional literature of citizenship has concentrated on citizen's rights. In his classic work on 'Citizenship and Social Class', Marshall identified three different sorts of citizen's rights: the civil, the political and the social. The civil incorporates individual legal rights, for example to a fair trial, to hold property; the political includes the right to vote, to participate in democratic processes; and the social is linked to social entitlements, for example to health, education and unemployment benefits within the context of the welfare state (Marshall 1950). Although much has changed since 1950, these categories are still useful in identifying differing democratic deficits across the world where adult learning may have a role to play, for example in relation to social rights in the light of growing evidence of an impending retreat from the traditional welfare state in a number of advanced countries.

Rights are clearly important within citizenship and adult learning can help people to be in a position to know about and exercise them. However, in the context of the Risk Society and the greater reflexivity this can require of the public, there may be a need for adult learners to engage more actively and critically with the idea of both citizens' rights and their responsibilities. For example, in the crucial context of work and employment, adult learning has been identified as having a key role for citizens in a move towards more active employment policies. This is another contentious issue involving fears of increasing social authoritarianism and social control on the part of central governments and it is a real danger. However, having worked with unemployed and unwaged adults, I welcome moves to explore and develop active employment initiatives within a more active welfare state in that it affords unwaged adults opportunities for developing and practising their skills and knowledge as well as the chance to have the new and more positive identity of 'learner' within a developing Learning Society. The problem of course comes when 'active' is confused or conflated with both compulsory and cheaper. Here again, a broader emphasis on adult learning for the different rights and responsibilities of citizenship may afford a productive and necessary counter-focus to the economic imperatives of reducing the costs of the welfare state.

Furthermore, in the context of endemic unemployment, it also raises the more alternative and idealistic idea of a citizen's income – payment for participation in society whether in full-time or part-time paid employment; voluntary, community, environmental, caring or house work; or different forms of learning or citizens' service (Johnston 1994). It offers the prospect of new learning approaches for a new social order and has already attracted considerable interest in some parts of mainland Europe. For example, in examining an alternative to the current limitations and stigmatization within a growing and increasingly separate 'second labour market' in Germany, Peter Alheit raises the issue of a citizen's service for all, allied to a citizen's wage which would involve payment for diverse options and forms of participation in society. Thus, at a stroke, unemployment could be reduced whilst also fostering every citizen's involvement and responsibility for society as a whole (Alheit 1996).

Another important dimension to reflexive citizenship can come with a recognition that in an adult learning environment there can be sufficient space to involve a focus on everyone's potential for both learning and teaching, so incorporating a more open-ended and egalitarian epistemology. This approach has already been used successfully with the development of learning and skill exchanges amongst unwaged and other disadvantaged groups in the UK (Groombridge 1987, Johnston 1987, 1992) as well as in a wide variety of community development approaches world-wide where the recognition and fostering of indigenous knowledge is central to both the empowerment of indigenous and womens' groups as well as to the development of human and environmentally sustainable values (Walters 1997). Indeed, such a reflexive learning approach needs to move well beyond conventional ideas of knowledge to embrace a focus on skills, values and attitudes. This offers the possibilities of playing to individual strengths, starting points, interests and abilities amongst a wide variety of social groups, without falling into the old traps of an unduly hierarchical and conservative view of different forms of learning for different social roles (Rogers 1992).

Adult learning for active citizenship

Learning for active citizenship can incorporate inclusive, pluralistic and reflexive approaches and, at the same time, provide the most recognisable and distinctive context for adult learning for citizenship concerned with social purpose. As such, learning for active citizenship has the potential to be an important counter-point to the more individualistic, economistic and controlled aspects of Lifelong Learning. A lot of active citizenship takes place in 'civil society', which offers the prospect of alternative forms of political representation and involvement at some distance from the direct influence of the state or the economy. In the past, Gramsci has identified civil society as ethical or moral society within which the dominant hegemony can be challenged: 'it is precisely in civil society in which intellectuals operate especially' (Gramsci 1986: 56). In this vein, Michael Welton (Welton 1997a: 71) sees learning in civil society as the key to understanding 'deliberative approaches' to democracy within a contemporary Risk Society. Active citizenship involves learning by doing across a wide spectrum. Here we can perhaps trace a soft–hard continuum in civil society from local adult education classes or groups, to study-circles, to voluntary organizations, to different types of community groups to social movements. Common to all these groups, is that they are involved in learning and in different ways they promote and develop their individual and collective 'voice'. In this context, Robert Putnam makes the point that the more citizens are civically engaged, the more understanding they are likely to be, the more willing to make sacrifices for the public good and the better prepared to respect and defend the rights of others (Putnam 1996).

This argument can be supported and developed by examining some brief examples of groups learning in civil society. Firstly, in his empirical work on voluntary organizations in the UK, Elsdon has identified a clear 'adult education dividend' where active membership of voluntary organisations has translated into significant learning process and outcomes for those involved. His research identifies that over 50% of his respondents report that they have become more politically conscious as a result of their involvement in voluntary organisations, 25% have become more politically active and 53% have been able to produce evidence of constructive transfers of learning and change to their jobs, careers etc (Elsdon 1997: 23).

Another instructive example of active learning in civil society has emerged from the earlier-mentioned Australian Study Circles on Aboriginal Reconciliation. Evidence from South Australia in particular shows that an increasing proportion of the Study Circle work is being translated into community action on the part of participating members or groups and, this in turn has impacted on non Study Circle members to the effect that a growing number of people are beginning to see Aboriginal Reconciliation not just as a discrete learning project but as part of a wider social movement where they have a role to play (Morgan 1997).

An aspect of civil society which has attracted much attention from adult educators is the rise of social movements and the learning that takes place within and through them (see Finger 1989, Welton 1993, Holford 1996, Newman 1995). Commentators have tended to make a distinction between 'old' and 'new' social movements. The former, for example trade unions and the churches, are seen to be more rooted in tradition, more centrally organized with a defined membership and specific aims. Indeed, there is a long history of adult educators engaging actively with these social movements in both formal and informal learning situations. The latter, for example, environmental groups, consumer groups, groups coalescing around issues of gender, race, sexuality, disability, age, are seen to be more knowledge-based, issue-orientated, to be acting in the defence of the public realm, concerned with the autonomy of the people (Newman 1995, Jarvis 1997: 163) It is perhaps more difficult for adult educators to engage directly with such movements as an important part of their *raison d'etre* is that they take responsibility for their own learning activities.

The divisions between these two categories is clearly far from hard and fast. Indeed, in the contemporary Risk Society it could be seen that old social movements are gradually becoming more reflexive and less totalizing in their stances, while new social movements are becoming increasingly influential and powerful within a re-invigorated, diverse civil society. What is readily apparent in relation to both is the centrality to their development of the power-knowledge nexus which affords strength to their collective voice and shapes their strategies of resistance. In fact, in the specific context of the Risk Society, yet another category of social movement is beginning to be identified, dubbed by Newman as a 'postmodern social movement'. Such movements are seen to be more flexible and permeable, have no universalistic cause but share a general dislike of injustice, are involved in cultural and community action, and place an emphasis on making people think through performance (Newman 1995, Johnston and Usher 1997).

A possible example of this emerging category of social movement and its attitude to learning can be identified in the work of a so-called Bürgerinitiative (Citizen's Action Group) in Hamburg with whom I recently became briefly involved. This was a community group in St Pauli Süd, the poorest area of the City, near the Reeperbahn, Hamburg's well-known red-light district, an area where over 50% of the population were of non-German origin. The Bürgerinitiative's immediate cause was to oppose the construction of multi-storey flats on the last piece of open land in that neighbourhood overlooking the River Elbe. In its place they set out to develop a community garden, a kind of small-scale people's park.

What was particularly interesting and instructive about the approach of this particular Bürgerinitiative in the context of adult learning within social movements was: the involvement of a mix of environmentalists and ex-political activists; its ironic, ludic approach, for example, with the motto 'more green for the red light', and adopting the name of 'Park Fiction'; its emphasis on fun and performance involving a close link between art and environment, the local and the global, participation and community decision-making; a long-term learning emphasis involving high quality and artistic information, open lectures on environmental issues, participatory/performance methods, the fostering of democratic planning structures at local and city level; and developing learning links with other community and social movements, both in Hamburg, Germany and the wider world (Park Fiction 1997). This specific case study of learning and action within a new type of social movement is perhaps indicative of a world-wide trend towards 'red-green' alliances, a linking of the local and the global where adult learning has a key role in developing active citizenship (Mayo 1997: 170–1)

Learning is central to the development of social movements, whether 'old', 'new' or 'postmodern'. While there may be considerable potential for adult educators to help develop learning links with social movements in the exploration of connections between advocacy of their particular interests and the broader interests of active citizenship, it would appear to require a new role and attitude on the part of educators, making the idea of a negotiated curriculum and of learning partnerships more appropriate then ever.

Indeed, this conclusion can be extended to all learning for active citizenship. It is clear that within civil society a diverse range of adult learning is already taking place; that there is the considerable potential for building on and developing active learning for citizenship as a counter-focus to Lifelong Learning dominated by the economic imperative; and that adult educators need to review critically their traditional roles, purposes and working contexts if they want to make a meaningful (and acceptable) contribution to learning for active citizenship within our contemporary Risk Society. One of the key issues to be resolved here is the tension that exists between adopting a technical/functional role that is essentially non-directive, for example, becoming involved when asked in an agency role, designing and developing leadership training, management and information skills and so on; and a more interventionist and political role in active support and partnership with social movements, perhaps around productive links with other groups and social movements and the exploration of common citizenship and social purpose aims.

Purposes, partners and processes

Within our contemporary Risk Society, I believe that the underlying values of social purpose adult education are still valid. However, in the context of an increasing proliferation and diversity of forms and sites of adult learning, as adult educators we need to be more modest in our aims, more flexible in our partnerships and more reflexive in our praxis if we are to play a meaningful role in maintaining and developing social purpose learning. As a key part of this, a framework of learning for citizenship, as outlined above, may provide an attractive, productive and necessary challenge and counter-focus to the dominant discourse of Lifelong Learning shaped by the economic imperative. In this way, we can perhaps maintain and develop a contemporary social purpose: we can continue to 'stand for something' and avoid 'falling for anything'.

Notes

1 *Rennie Johnston* is Lecturer in Adult and Community Education at the University of Southampton New College where he is currently Director of the Widening Provision Project. He was co-author of *Adult Education and the Postmodern Challenge: learning beyond the limits*, (London: Routledge, 1997) and has written widely in the areas of community adult education and experiential learning.
2 From now on, I will use the term 'Risk Society' to refer to this broad context.

References

AAACE (Australian Association of Adult Community Education) (1997) Learning Circles Australia in *AAACE Newsletter*, 5, 23–24.

Alheit, P. (1996) A provocative proposal: from Labour Society to Learning Society in *Lifelong Learning in Europe*, 2, 13–15.

Beck, U. (1994) The re-invention of politics: Towards a theory of reflexive modernization in U. Beck, A. Giddens and S. Lash *Reflexive Modernization*, (Cambridge: Polity), 1–56.

Beck, U. Giddens, A. and Lash, S. (1994) *Reflexive Modernization*, (Cambridge: Polity).

Bell, B. (1996) The British adult education tradition: a re-examination in R. Edwards, A. Hanson and P. Raggatt (eds) *Boundaries of Adult Learning*, (London: Routledge), 152–169.

Brady, J. (1994) Critical literacy, feminism and a politics of representation in P. McLaren and C. Lankshear (eds) *Politics of Liberation: Paths from Freire*, (New York: Routledge), 142–153.

Brah, A. and Hoy, J. (1989) in Weil SW and McGill (eds) *Making sense of Experiential Learning: diversity in theory and practice*, (Buckingham: SRHE and Open University Press), 70–80.

Carr, W. and Kemmis, S. (1986) *Becoming critical: education, knowledge and action-research*, (Lewes: Falmer).

Clarke, J. (1998) Deconstructing domestication: women's experience and the goals of critical pedagogy, Unpublished PhD thesis, University of Southampton.

Commission of the European Communities (1993) *Growth, competitiveness, employment: the* challenges *and ways forward in the 21st century*, (Luxembourg: Office for Official Publications of the European Communities).

Commission of the European Communities (1995) *Teaching and learning: towards a learning society*, (Luxembourg: Office for Official Publications of the European Communities).

Council for Aboriginal Reconciliation (1993) *Australians for Reconciliation study circle kit*, (Canberra: Council for Aboriginal Reconciliation).

Dadzie, S. (1993) *Working with black adult learners*, (Leicester: NIACE).

DfEE (1998) *The Learning Age: a renaissance for a new Britain*, (London: DfEE Publications).

DVV (Deutsche Volkshochschule Verband) (1997) *Confintea V: Adult learning: a key for the 21st century*, (Bonn: DVV).

Edwards, R. (1997) *Changing places? flexibility, lifelong learning and a learning society*, (London: Routledge).

Elsdon, K. (1995) with Reynolds J and Steward S *Voluntary organisations: citizenship, learning and change*, (Leicester: NIACE).

Elsdon, K. (1997) Voluntary Organisations and Communities: a critique and suggestions in *The role of adult learning in building local and regional communities*, Proceedings ESREA Conference, 1, Strobl, 22–32.

Field, J. (1996) Open learning and consumer culture in P. Raggatt, R. Edwards and N. Small (eds) *The Learning Society: challenges and trends*, (London: Routledge), 136–150.

Fieldhouse, R. (1992) Tradition in British university adult education and the WEA in C Duke (ed.) *Liberal Adult Education: Perspectives and Projects*, (Warwick: Continuing Education Research Centre, University of Warwick), 11–14.

Finger, M. (1989) New social movements and their implications for adult education in *Adult Education Quarterly*, 40 (I), 15–21.

Fraser, W. (1995) *Learning from Experience: empowerment or incorporation*, (Leicester: NIACE).

Freire, P. (1972) *Pedagogy of the oppressed*, (Middlesex: Penguin).

Freire, P. (1993) Foreword in McLaren and Leonard (eds) *Paulo Freire: a Critical Encounter*, (New York: Routledge), ix–xii.

Galbraith, (1991) *The Culture of Contentment*, (New York: Sinclair-Stevenson).

Giddens, A. (1991) *Modernity and self-identity: self and society in the late modern age*, (Cambridge: Polity).

Giddens, A. (1994) Risk, trust, reflexivity in Beck U, Giddens A and Lash S *Reflexive Modernization*, (Cambridge: Polity), 184–197.

Gilbert, R. (1992) Citizenship, education, post-modernity in *British Journal of Sociology of Education* 13 (1) 51–69.

Gore, J. (1992) What we can do for you! What can "we" do for "you"?: struggling over empowerment in critical and feminist pedagogy, in C. Luke and J. Gore (eds) *Feminisms and Critical Pedagogy*, (New York: Routledge), 54–73.

Gramsci, A. (1986) *Selections from prison notebooks*, edited and translated by Q Hoare and G Nowell Smith, (London: Lawrence and Wishart).

Groombridge, J. (ed.) (1987) *Learning for a change*, (Leicester: NIACE).

Hake, B. (1997) Lifelong learning and the European Union: a critique from a "Risk Society" perspective in J. Holford, C. Griffin and P. Jarvis (eds) *Lifelong Learning: reality, rhetoric and public policy*, Conference Proceedings, (Guildford: Department of Educational Studies) University of Surrey, 147–153.

Hill, D. M. (1994) *Citizens and cities*, (London: Harvester Wheatsheaf).

Holford, J. (1996) Why social movements matter: adult education theory, cognitive praxis and the creation of knowledge in *Adult Education Quarterly* 45 (2), 95–111.

Illich, I. and Verne, E. (1976) *Imprisoned in the global classroom*, (London: Writers and Readers Cooperative).

Ismail, S. (1997) "When People Take Control" – innovative experiences of homeless women in South Africa in *The Role of Adult Learning in Building Local and Regional Communities*, Proceedings from ESREA Conference, 1, Strobl, 94–108.

Jackson, K. (1997) The state, civil society and the economy: adult education in Britain in S Walters (ed.) *Globalisation, adult education and training: impacts and issues*, (Leicester: NIACE), 47–56.

Jansen, T. and van der Veen, R. (1996) Adult education in the light of the Risk Society in P. Raggatt, R. Edwards and N. Small (eds) *The Learning Society: challenges and trends*, (London: Routledge), 122–135.

Jarvis, P. (1997) *Ethics and education for adults*, (Leicester: NIACE).

Johnston, R. (1987) *Exploring the educational needs of unwaged adults*, (Leicester: NIACE Replan).

Johnston, R. (1992) Education and unwaged adults: relevance, social control and empowerment in G. Allen and I. Martin (eds) *Education and Community: the Politics of Practice*, (London: Cassell).

Johnston, R. (1994) Unemployment and education for work in *Studies in Continuing Education* 16(1), 37–52.

Johnston R. and Croft, F. (1998) Mind the Gap – Widening Provision, guidance and cultural change in Higher Education in J. Preece (ed.) *Beyond the boundaries*, (Leicester: NIACE), 11–19.

Johnston, R. and Usher, R. (1997) Re-theorising experience: adult learning in contemporary social practices in *Studies in the Education of Adults*, 29(2) 137–153.

Joseph Rowntree Foundation (1995) *Inquiry into income and wealth, vols 1 and 2*, (York: Joseph Rowntree Foundation).

Korsgaard, O. (1997) Internationalisation and globalisation in Korsgaard O (ed.) *Adult learning and the challenges of the 21st century*, (Odense: Association for World Education), 10–15.

Krygier, M. (1996) The sources of civil society in *Quadrant* (November 1996) 12–32.

Larrson, S. (1997) The significance of study circle tradition: past, present, future in *The Role of Adult Learning in Building Local and Regional Communities*, Proceedings from ESREA Conference, Strobl, 1, 1–21.

Luke, C. and Gore, J. (eds) (1992) *Feminism and Critical Pedagogy*, (New York: Routledge).

Marshall, T. H. (1950) *Citizenship and social class*, (Cambridge: Cambridge University Press).

Martin, I. (1998a) Personal Communication.

Martin, I. (1998b) Introduction in Crowther J, Martin I and Shaw M (eds) *Popular education and social movements in Scotland today*, (Leicester: NIACE).

Mayo, M. (1997) *Imagining tomorrow: adult education for transformation*, (Leicester: NIACE).

Morgan, C. (1997) Interview 14.12.97, Silver Sands, South Australia.

Mouffe, C. (1988) The civics lesson in *New Statesman and Society*, 7th October.

Newman, M. (1995) Locating learning in social action in *Social action and emancipatory learning*, (Sydney: School of Adult Education, UTS).

Oglesby, L. (1997) A European and UK perspective on education for citizenship in *Centreline, the Journal of The Education Centres Association* May 1997, 17–22.

Park Fiction, (1997) *100% Park für St Pauli-Sued*, (Hamburg: Arbeitsgruppe Park Fiction).

Putnam D. (1996) Who killed civic America? quoted in Benn R and Fieldhouse R The role of adult learning in promoting active citizenship in Britain in the twentieth century in *The role of adult learning in building local and regional communities*, Proceedings from ESREA Conference, (2), Strobl, 54–65.

Rogers, A. (1992) *Adult learning and development*, (London: Cassell).

Rosen, V. (1993) Black students in Higher Education in M. Thorpe, R. Edwards and A. Hanson (eds) *Culture and processes of adult learning*, (London: Routledge), 178–193.

Sargent, N. with Field, J. Francis, H. Schuller, T. and Tuckett, A. (1997) *The Learning Divide: a study of participation in adult learning in the United Kingdom*, (Leicester: NIACE).

Shore, S., Black, A., Simpson, A., and Coomde, M. (1993) *Positively different: guidance for developing inclusive adult literacy language, and numeracy curricula*, (Canberra: DEET).

Stuart, M. (1993) 'Speaking Personally'; the self in educational oral history work in N. Miller and D. Jones (eds) *Research: reflecting practice* (Manchester: SCUTREA Conference Proceedings), 95–97.

Taylor, R. and Ward, K. (1986) Adult education and the working class: policies, practice and future priorities for community adult education in K. Ward and R. Taylor (eds) *Adult education and the working class: education for the missing millions*, (London: Croom Helm), 169–191.

Thompson, A. (1995) Starting with self: life history approaches to training adult educators in I. Bryant (ed.) *Vision, intervention, intervention,* (Southampton: SCUTREA Conference Proceedings), 171–177.

Tuckett, A. (1997) *Lifelong learning in England and Wales,* (Leicester: NIACE).

UNESCO (1997) *Confintea V: agenda for the future of adult learning,* (Hamburg: UNESCO Institute).

Usher, R. Bryant, I. and Johnston R. (1997) *Adult education and the postmodern challenge: learning beyond the limits,* (London: Routledge).

Walters, S. (ed.), (1997) *Globalization, adult education and training: impacts and issues,* (Leicester: NIACE).

Weil, S. (1986) Non-traditional learners within traditional higher education institutions discovery and disappointment in *Studies in Higher Education,* 11 (3), 219–235.

Weiler, K. (1993) Freire and a feminist pedagogy of difference in P. McLaren and C. Lankshear (eds) *Politics of liberation: paths from Freire,* (New York: Routledge), 12–40.

Welton, M. (1993) Social revolutionary learning: the new social movements as learning sites in *Adult Education Quarterly,* 43 (3), 152–164.

Welton, M. (1997a) Repair, defend, invent: civil societarian adult education faces the twenty-first century in O. Korsgaard (ed.) *Adult learning and the challenges of the 21st century,* (Odense: Association for World Education), 67–75.

Welton, M. (1997b) In defence of civil society: Canadian adult education in neo-conservative times in S. Walters (ed.) (1997) *Globalization, adult education and training: impacts and issues,* (Leicester: NIACE), 27–38.

Westwood, S. (1992) When Class became Community in Adult Education in A Rattansi and D. Reeder (eds) *Rethinking radical education,* (London: Lawrence and Wishart), 222–248.

25 Beyond lifelong learning

A call to civically responsible change

Ian Baptiste

Pennsylvania State University, USA

The discourses of lifelong learning and the learning society are taking pride of place on the education agenda, but the question needs to be raised as to whether there are other matters that should assume an even more significant place. This paper seeks to refocus the debate on some of the major ethical issues confronting education.

Introduction

At a time when our world is growing more and more unequal, many adult educators are embracing practices (such as lifelong learning) which divert their attention away from serious human plights to narrow personal and technical considerations. In this paper, I attempt to refocus our attention. First, I give a brief sketch of the state of our world to establish the need for civically responsible change. Then I show how discourse about lifelong learning and such like, detracts us from serious ethical pursuits. Next, I define civically responsible change and discuss how it might be promoted. Finally, I critically analyse dominant practices of adult education, assessing the degree to which they are likely to foster civically responsible change.

Setting the stage: the unequal state of our world

Our world is socially unequal and probably getting worse. Inequality exists at global, regional, national, and local levels. Poverty, underemployment and income inequality are on the rise in most countries. Health, housing and social services are declining for the majority of earth's population, while the very rich enjoy an exponential increase in those services. Within any given country, children seem to be the hardest hit, followed by minorities and women. Looking at it internationally, most of sub-Saharan Africa seems to be plunging deeper and deeper into a socio-economic abyss.

This view is corroborated by major international agencies such as the United Nations Development Program (UNDP), the World Bank, and the World Health Organization (WHO). Take income inequality, on a global scale, for instance. Thirty years ago the poorest 20% of the world's people earned 2.3% of the world's income, in 1996 they earned 1.4%. In that same period, the richest 20% have increased their share from 70% to 85% (The Economist 1996: 34). In 1984, the ratio of GNP per capita between the richest and the poorest nation was 149: 1. The ratio was almost 500: 1 in 1994. The World Bank classifies countries as either low-income, middle-income, upper-income, or high-income. Over the 11 year period (1984–1995) the only category to experience an increase in its ranks was low-income economies. In 1984, 39 countries were classified as low-income economies, that number was up by 12 in 1995, to 51.

The widening economic gap is also experienced at regional and national levels. For instance, the World Bank notes a marked increase in income inequality among countries making up the so called transitional economies – i.e. those Eastern European countries, and former Soviet Union republics, moving from non-market-driven to market-driven economies (World Bank 1996: 67). And the problem is the same for well established market economies like the United States. Despite substantial increase in employment (the US Department of Labor announced an unemployment rate of 4.9% in April 1997), underemployment, poverty and income inequality continue to rise in America. In 1995, more American family members were holding multiple jobs and working longer hours (including more overtime), for less pay, less benefits, and less job security than their 1970 counterparts. The situation is significantly worse for poor, inner-city families, especially blacks. During the same period, the richest 1% of American families has experienced an almost steady rise in income share (Mishel and Bernstein 1994, Yates 1994, Wilson 1995, World Bank 1986–1996).

Regarding health and human services, the situation is no better. In its Executive summary: the world health report 1996, and fifty facts from the world health report 1996, WHO paints the following picture: half of the world's population (2860 million) is without needed essential drugs, and at risk of many endemic (treatable) diseases; 1000 million people live in extreme poverty; the gaps between the richest and poorest nations, are widening with regards to, infant mortality, general child health, and life expectancy (WHO 1996a, 1996b). According to the Social Work Almanac (Ginsberg 1995), similar conditions exists within countries such as the United States. Contrasting the social health of Americans in 1995 to their 1970 counterpart, the Almanac concluded that there has been: a decline in the social health of the lower two-thirds of Americans families; a decline in the social health of children, youth, minorities, and the elderly; and a marked decrease in affordable (low-income) housing. This downward trend persists in the face of soaring health costs. Americans spent a whopping $721 billion on health care in 1991–13.2% of GDP (Mishel and Bernstein 1994: 9).

Lifelong learning: a most excellent ethical decoy

In the midst of such inequalities, why has lifelong learning emerged as a dominant discourse in the field of adult education? Learning is as integral an aspect of living as breathing. People are lifelong learners whether they wish to or not. Why then do we need a movement (lifelong learning) to promote something so natural and inevitable? Discourse about lifelong learning, it seems to me, is a decoy – a distraction from the ethical responsibility of the adult educator. Like its predecessors, andragogy and self-directed learning, discourse on lifelong learning shifts the focus from broader considerations of public good, to narrow personal and/or technical ones. Most of the discourse on lifelong learning centres around the 'human capital requirements' of the 'new economic order'. Lifelong learning is really manpower planning with an added twist, the requirement of continuous retraining brought on, apparently, by the 'imperatives' of the new order technology, the information revolution, globalization and demographic shifts (Candy 1991, Carnevale 1991, Apps 1992). Advocates of lifelong learning do not stop to ask: Is the so called new order really inevitable? Why is the new order billed as technologically inevitable? Is the new economic order enhancing the quality of human life? If so, for whom? At what social and environmental cost are we achieving this new world order? And where is the place of justice and equality in this new world order? This paper attempts to refocus the discourse by placing emphasis squarely on these broader and deeper ethical questions. I begin by outlining my ethical commitment.

Educating for civically responsible change

Lifelong learning advocates and I share a common belief that change is constant and inevitable. But we disagree on what are the nature and sources of desirable change. Proponents of lifelong learning assume (by default) that desirable changes are market/technologically-driven changes. I disagree. The Great European Enslavement, European Colonialism, Industralization, and Urbanization are all, arguably, examples of 'market-driven' changes. But they have all benefited some at the expense of others (Williams 1966, Beckford 1972, Rodney 1972, UNESCO 1974, Appelbaum *et al.* 1976, Williamson 1997). Important considerations then for adult educators are therefore: What is the net effect of changes we promote? Who benefits most and least? And who is seriously harmed?

Civically responsible change strives to address all of these questions. Some changes are responsible but not civically so. For example, a change might be responsive to the concerns of owners of a company but not to workers. Some changes are economically responsible but medically irresponsible as is the case with some managed health care provisions (Kraus *et al.* 1991). Civically responsible change is balanced change – change that makes concerted efforts to address (justly and fairly) the concerns of all potentially affected parties and domains over time and space (Barber 1984). It is also change which takes very seriously the universal impact of localized action.

For civically responsible change to occur, two important conditions must obtain. We must equalize power distributions in social transactions, and promote public accountability. We live in a world of scarce resources, limited amounts of valuable goods and services, and a limited number of high status positions. We also live in a world populated by self-interested persons, individuals concerned with promoting their personal well-being. Power is the means by which we secure our self interests. It follows there-fore, that in a situation of unequal power, some will be better able to secure their interests than others. Civically responsible changes (because it must consider, equally, the interests of all affected parties) is more likely to occur in situations where power is equally distributed. But equalization of power will not guarantee civically responsible behaviour. Equal power without public accountability is a recipe for what Hobbes (1961/1968) called a State of War – a state of perpetual aggression in which 'every man is against every man' – where society is reduced to a human menagerie, and avarice is tempered only by fear and economic rationality. Educators who are interested in civically responsible change must therefore seriously attempt, not only to equalize power but, also, to curb greed and selfish-ness.

Civically responsible change involves three interrelated moments: trans-forming institutions into public agencies, forging a civic agenda, and facil-itating consensual action (Baptiste 1994). The first and third moments (developing public agencies and consensual action) are concerned largely with equalizing power. The second moment (forging a civic agenda) is primarily intended to foster public accountability. I will now discuss each moment in turn.

Transforming institutions into public agencies

The word public as used here does not refer to state or governmental control, dejure or titular ownership. Public is determined by *de facto* influ-ence. A public agency seeks to be optimally influenced by all of its con-stituencies (individuals, groups, organizations, communities, societies, nations, globe, etc.). It strives assiduously to involve all interested parties. Membership is open to all who are potentially affected by its decisions. In some instances this could mean a few individuals or a small village. At other times it could mean the entire globe. The size of the public is deter-mined by the scope of the change. Institutions and programs are trans-formed into public agencies to the degree that they address questions such as:

1   What constituencies ought we to be serving?
2   Is every constituency adequately represented?
3   Which constituencies are under-, or over-, represented?
4   What can we do to optimize representation?
5   How can we best neutralize the forces of greed and evil?

Forging a civic agenda

A civic act or agenda aims to fulfil some public good. Benefits accrue to groups, communities and/or societies as a whole, not merely to private actors. Civic actions transform private interests into common goods. Civic actions are here distinguished from philanthropy. Firstly, unlike philanthropists, the interests of civic actors are integrated into the interests of the public they purport to serve. A civic actor's interests are fulfilled, when (and only when) the public's interests are satisfied. A philanthropist's interests need not be integrated with the interests of the public he purports to serve. Secondly, when someone is acting civically, she holds herself publicly accountable. She consciously subjects her goals and actions to the scrutiny of the public she purports to serve (whether that be a few individuals or the entire globe). For example, philanthropists do not usually seek public advice when making decisions regarding which charity to support, how much to give, and for how long. Their commitments are usually initiated and terminate privately, as their pleasure demands. By contrast, a civic actor's commitments are initiated and terminated in dialogue with the public he or she purports to serve. Programs promote civic actions to the degree that they address questions such as:

1   What are the various interests represented in this situation?
2   What are the competing interests, and how do they compete?
3   How can a common good be forged from our separate and/or competing interests?
4   How can we best neutralize the forces of greed and evil?

Encouraging consensual action

A consensual act is any interaction in which everything is equally negotiable to, and by, all interacting parties. What public agencies achieve at the macro level, consensual action accomplishes at the micro/balanced representation. There is no point in having everyone present if a few will dominate. It's one thing to get everyone at the table (public agency), but quite another to achieve an 'ideal speech situation' – a situation where everyone's views and interests are equally considered (Habermas 1984: 86ff, cf Collins 1990: 11ff). Programs might foster consensual action to the degree that they address questions such as:

1   How are day-to-day decisions made in this program, class, organizations, etc.?
2   Which decisions are sacrosanct, and why?
3   Who benefits most (and least) from sacrosanct decisions?
4   Whose voices dominate and whose voices are not heard?
5   How can we increase the likelihood that all voices are equally heard?
6   How can we best neutralize the forces of greed and evil?

The question: 'How can we best neutralize the forces of greed and evil?', appears in each moment. It underscores the fact that inequalities and injustices are not merely due to unenlightenment and ignorance, but also to greed and evil. This issue will be discussed at greater lengths below, when I critique proponents of critical consciousness.

The three moments discussed above are highly interactive and inter-related. We cannot forge a civic agenda without balanced representation and consensual action. Likewise, it is our desire for the common good (civic agenda) which obligates us to foster balanced representation and consensual action. Space does not permit an elaboration here, but elsewhere, I have outlined some of the factors that enable and impede achievement of these three moments (see Baptiste 1994: ch. 5).

A critical assessment of adult education practices

As pointed out above, civically responsible change demands that we equalize power distributions in society, and foster greater public accountability among social interactants. How likely is this to occur in our practice of adult education? My analysis suggests that those of us who wish to promote civically responsible change, respond, generally, in one of four interrelated ways; through theories and programs which emphasize: 1) individual and/or group access to valued information, 2) self-improvement, and 3) critical theory/pedagogy, and 4) critical consciousness. I will examine each response in turn, showing its ethical commitments and shortcomings.

Access theories and programs

Access theories include lifelong learning, andragogy, and self-directed learning. There are individual-, as well as group-, access programs. Individual-access programs include graduate adult education, workforce education, adult literacy, human resource development, continuing professional education and so on. Group-access programs include multicultural education and affirmative action programs. Educators who emphasize information access differ in many respects. Among them are liberals, conservatives, marxists, feminists, afrocentrists, and so on (Ravitch 1990, Asante 1991, Banks and Banks 1993, Tisdell 1993). But despite their differences, they are united in the primary commitment to make valued information and skills accessible to individuals and/or groups.

Access programs, by themselves, will not foster civically responsible change. They make little or no attempt to promote public accountability, and feeble, and/or misguided attempts to equalize power distribution. Public accountability is not a serious concern of individual-access theorists and practitioners. After taking into consideration resource and institutional constraints, their only other concern (see lifelong learning or workforce education programs for instance) is to satisfy the private desires of individual learners. Learners, treated as clients or customers, bring their privately formulated needs to the educational market-place to be met. Then, within resource and organizational constraints, the workforce educator or lifelong learning facilitator strives to meet them. Educational success spells customer satisfaction.

What is absent from this approach, is an acknowledgement of conflict of interests between and among learners and institutions. Individual-access theorists and practitioners give little or no consideration to the fact that one learner's or organization's interests might be met precisely at the expense of another. Operating under a consensus view of the world, the spurious assumptions of human capital theory (Schultz 1961, cf Maglen 1990), and the misguided dictum that knowledge (meaning information) is power, individual-access theorists and practitioners act as if social maladies are due largely to 'illiteracy.' Presumably, people are poor, homeless, disenfranchised, and without adequate health and human services because they lack adequate human capital. Discounting human conflicts (of race/ethnicity, class, gender, nationality, etc.), and scarcity, individual-access theorists and practitioners operate as if we would alleviate social maladies simply by equalizing the distribution of valued information and skills.

Group-access theorists and practitioners (eg. proponents of affirmative action and multicultural education) focus on groups not individuals. Some group-access practitioners do not question the information and skills produced by the dominant society. Accepting them as legitimate and prized, they simply concentrate on making them more readily accessible to disenfranchised groups (Ravitch 1990). Others, especially feminist and afrocentric scholars, seek not only to gain access to information and skills produced by the dominant culture, but more importantly, to augment and in some cases, produce information which stands in opposition to those of the dominant culture (Asante 1991, Tisdell 1993). Clearly, this approach is more likely (than the individual-access approach) to equalizing power. But it runs the risk of ghettoization – the situation in which each group is only interested in increasing the value (power and influence) of its members. Group interests are elevated above the common good, and we're back again to the Hobbesean State of War where groups, instead of individuals, now fight to devour each other.

Theories and programs emphasizing self-improvement

These theories and programs seek to alter some state of the individual. This is not necessarily true of access programs where the emphasis is on providing access to information and skills. It's possible to provide information without changing a person's state of being. Important differences exist among self-improvement theorists and practitioners. For instances, they differ on what aspect of the person they chose to alter physical, cognitive, psycho-social, emotional, spiritual, and so on. Self-improvement programs might improve the personal power of individuals. But because of their individualistic moorings, public accountability is not stressed. Perspective transformation typifies self-improvement theories in the field of adult education (Mezirow 1978). Following this theory, a group of women could be considered to have undergone a perspective transformation if they shifted from hero worshipping their husbands to wishing that all men were dead. Such a shift in perspective fulfils all of Mezirow's criteria for perspective transformation, but in no way improves the human condition. This is because perspective transformation, like most self-improvement theories, lacks a theory of, and commitment to, public accountability (Mezirow 1978, 1991, cf Collard and Laws 1989).

Critical theory/pedagogy

Critical theorists and pedagogists add to self-improvement theories the requirement of public accountability (Brookfield 1995, Shor 1996). But, by and large, accountability is narrowly confined within the boundaries of the classroom, or institution. Critical pedagogists admit that the school is not a closed system, shut off from the rest of society. However, it seems to me that such admission is lip service only. Most critical pedagogy classrooms focus largely on the behavior of, and consequences to, students, teachers, and staff within that classroom or institution. As a university teacher, I find myself guilty of this practice. When discussing a particular societal concern, for instance, I make little attempt to have students collaborate with other affected groups in the wider society. By restricting wider societal involvement, this sort of micro socio-political orientation seduces me to draw self-congratulatory, but false, conclusions about my educational prowess. For instance, we (students and myself) often revel in the knowledge that, because of our efforts, students now have a greater voice in determining course content, methods of evaluation, and so on. What we do not seriously consider are questions such as: which students are receiving access to this valued information and which students are not? How is such access benefiting and/or hurting the society at large, and so on? We let the localized benefits of our actions obscure their wider potentially harmful effects.

Critical consciousness theories and programs

Critical consciousness programs incorporate all of the positive elements of the first three approaches. They promote educational access, self-improvement and require public accountability. However, critical consciousness practitioners also make concerted efforts to collaborate with the wider society. The works of Paulo Freire epitomize this practice (Freire 1973). Freire attempts to link both learners and community in collective social action. But though firmly rooted in local contexts, Freire understands and takes into account the reciprocal impact of local, regional, national and global forces.

Freire's short comings lay in his humanist orientation. He accords free humans (especially the oppressed) absolute goodness. Evil, it would seem, is either the product of ignorance, or coercion. Freire recognizes that oppressed people do commit oppressive acts, as in the case of massification. But he attributes such oppressive actions, not to enlightened thought, but to naive transitivity – meaning uncriticality or relative ignorance (Freire 1973:19). For Freire then, it seems that those who really know the good will always do the good. If someone is not doing the good, it can be presumed that they do not really know it. On the basis of such reasoning, the ethical responsibility of the educator is to enlighten individuals. People, it is assumed, will act right once they learn to think right. Because, to know, critically, is to act responsibility. Vice is recast as ignorance and mistakes, and the ethical responsibility of educators recast in epistemic terms, i.e. the development of critical consciousness.

I believe that, like goodness, evil is inherently human. It seems to me that free, critically conscious, persons can, and do, act in socially irresponsible ways. In other words, I will not reduce vice to ignorance or mistakes. Consequently, in my quest to promote civically responsible change I must do more than enlighten. Civically responsible change often requires political action to neutralize oppressive forces. Freire (by his actions) recognizes this. But because of his humanist leanings, I believe that this aspect of his theory remains underdeveloped. A theory that would adequately guide the actions of civic-minded educators must treat seriously evil and greed. It would involve, at the very least, uncoupling our epistemic task (developing critical consciousness) from our ethical responsibility (promoting a common good). Fostering a common good sometimes requires not just enlightened discourse, but also political action to neutralize the forces of greed and evil.

Conclusion

While our world continues to be plagued by gross injustices and inequalities, adult educators embrace theories and practices (such as lifelong learning) which divert our attention away from grave human plights. In this paper, I have attempted to refocus the discourse, pointing out the ethical failings of our practices, and proposing a corrective civically responsible change.

References

Appelbaum, R. P., Bigelow, J., Kramer, H. P., Molotch, H. L., and Relis, P. M. (1976) *The effects of urban growth: a population impact analysis* (New York: Praeger Publishers).

Apps, J. (1992) *Adult education: the way to lifelong learning* (Bloomington, ID: Phi Delta Kappa Educational Foundation).

Asante, M. K. (1991) Multiculturalism: an exchange. *American Scholar*, Spring 267–272.

Banks, J. A. and Banks, C. A. M. (1993) *Multicultural education: issues and perspectives* 2nd edn, (Needham Heights, MA: Allyn & Bacon).

Baptiste, I. (1994) Educating politically: in pursuit of social equality. Unpublished Doctoral Dissertation, Northern Illinois University, DeKalb.

Barber, B. R. (1984) *Strong democracy: participatory politics for a new age* (Berkeley, CA: University of California Press).

Beckford, G. (1972) *Persistent poverty: underdevelopment in plantation economies of the third world* (New York: Oxford University Press).

Brookfield, S. (1995) *Becoming a critically reflective teacher* (San Francisco, CA: Jossey-Bass).

Candy, P. C. (1991) *Self-direction for lifelong learning: a comprehensive guide to theory and practice* (San Francisco: Jossey-Bass).

Carnevale, A. P. (1991) *American and the new economy* (Alexandria, VA: American Society for Training and Development, and the U.S. Department of Labor).

Collard, S. and Law, M. (1989) The limits of perspective transformation: a critique of Mezirow's theory. *Adult Education Quarterly*, 39(2), 99–107.

Collins, M. (1991) *Adult education as vocation: a critical role for the adult educator* (New York: Routledge).

The Economist (1996, July 20) 'The global poverty trap'.

Freire, P. (1973) *Education for critical consciousness* (New York: Continuum).

Ginsberg, L. (1995) *Social Work Almanac*, 2nd edn, (Washington DC: NASW Press).

Habermas, J. (1984) *The theory of communicative action: reason and the rationalization of society* (Vol. 1). (Boston, MA: Beacon).

Hobbes, T. (1651/1968) *Thomas Hobbes: Leviathan* (New York: Penguin).

Kraus, N., Porter, M. and Ball, P. (1991) *Managed care, a decade in review 1980–1990*, special edn (Excelsior, MN: InterStudy).

Maglen, L. R. (1990) Challenging the human capital orthodoxy: the education-productivity link re-examined. *The Economic Record*, 66(195), 281–294.

Mishel, L. and Bernstein, J (1994) *The state of working America, 1994–95* (New York: M. E. Sharpe).

Mezirow, J. (1991) *Transformative dimensions of adult learning* (San Francisco, CA: Jossey-Bass).

Mezirow, J. (1978) Perspective Transformation. *Adult Education*, 27(2), 100–110.

Ravitch, D. (1990) Multiculturalism: E. Pluribus Plures. *American Scholar*, 337–354.

Rodney, W. (1972) *How Europe underdeveloped Africa* (Washington, DC: Howard University Press).

Schultz, T. W. (1961) Investment in human capital. *American Economic Review,* 51(1), 1–17.

Shor, I. (1996) *When students have power: negotiating authority in a critical pedagogy* (Chicago: University of Chicago Press).

Tisdell, E. (1993) *Feminism and adult learning: power, pedagogy, and praxis.* New Directions for Adult and Continuing Education, 57, 91–103.

UNESCO (1974) *Hydrological effects of urbanisation: report of the sub-group on the effects of urbanisation on the hydrological environment* (Paris: UNESCO Press).

WHO (1996a) *Executive summary: the world health report 1996,* Http://www.who.ch/whr/1996/exsume.htm.

WHO (1996b) *Fifty facts from the world health report 1996,* Http://www.who.ch/whr/1996/50facts.htm#Birth.

Williams, E. E. (1966) *Capitalism and slavery* (New York: Capricorn).

Williamson, J. G. (1997) *Industrialisation, inequality and economic growth* (Brookfield, VT: Edward Elgar Publishing Company).

Wilson, J. W. (1995) *When work disappears: the world of the new urban poor* (New York: Knopf).

World Bank (1986 through 1996) *World development report* (New York: Oxford University Press).

Yates, M. D. (1994) *Longer hours, fewer jobs: Employment and Unemployment in the United States* (New York: Monthly Review Press).

Index

References to notes are prefixed by 'n'.